MENNINGER

MENNINGER

The Family and the Clinic

Lawrence J. Friedman

ALFRED A. KNOPF NEW YORK 1990

THIS IS A BORZOI BOOK
PUBLISHED BY ALFRED A. KNOPF, INC.

Copyright © 1990 by Lawrence J. Friedman

All rights reserved under International and Pan-American Copyright
Conventions. Published in the United States by Alfred A. Knopf, Inc., New
York, and simultaneously in Canada by Random House of Canada Limited,
Toronto. Distributed by Random House, Inc., New York.

Library of Congress Cataloging-in-Publication Data
Friedman, Lawrence Jacob
Menninger : the family and the clinic / Lawrence J. Friedman.—1st ed.
p. cm.
Bibliography: p.
Includes index.
ISBN 0-394-53569-3
1. Menninger Foundation—History. I. Title.
RC445.K3T626 1990
362.2'1'0978163—dc20   89-15498 CIP

Manufactured in the United States of America
First Edition

For Sharon, Beth, Lena, B.,
Gerry, and Irv

Contents

Illustrations

Preface

Menninger—both the family and the medical institution—have received widespread attention. Charismatic and articulate, the Menningers have sometimes been characterized as the Kennedys of psychiatry and regarded with faddish devotion. Walter Cronkite accompanied a CBS television crew to Topeka in 1962 to develop a special program on the psychiatric success of the family and its treatment center. When a new stained-glass window was installed in the Washington Cathedral in 1979, two Menninger brothers, Karl and Will, together with their father, were depicted in a vignette on the healing arts in the lower-right-hand corner. Popular films such as *The Exorcist* and television soap operas like *General Hospital* have included passing references to the Menninger Clinic as a center for psychiatric expertise. By the mid-1980s, *Family Circle* magazine had designated Menninger as the nation's top psychiatric hospital, and a wealthy widow had bequeathed $40 million to the institution.

The Menningers did not always enjoy such wide recognition and support. In the 1920s and 1930s, organizational profits were meager, and treatment of very disturbed patients often yielded unsatisfactory outcomes. By 1935, to be sure, *Fortune* magazine included the Menninger Clinic in a small cluster of private "new psychiatry" centers—well-managed facilities on beautiful grounds where America's celebrated families paid handsome fees so that their loved ones could benefit from active milieu therapy treatment programs. But the Menningers remained ambivalent on the value of their enterprise until 1946, when the Veterans Administration allowed them to transform a local army hospital into a pilot psychiatric training facility for the entire VA system. Next, Kansas officials let them turn the custodial Topeka State Hospital into an active teaching center, and by 1951, Menninger was recognized as the major facility for mental health professional education in the nation. "Here on the midwestern plains of Kansas are trained 15 percent of all psychiatrists now being schooled in the United States," a Chicago *Tribune* article emphasized. In 1954, the Congress of Industrial Organizations presented the Menningers with its Philip Murray Award for leadership in mental health.

Within the past thirty years, however, mental health specialists have lost much of their enthusiasm for the activities of the "psychiatric capital of the nation" as they moved away from the psychoanalytic traditions that were almost synonymous with Menninger therapeutic approaches. As other, more biologically oriented psychiatric training programs arose in major university settings, Harvard clinician-researcher Philip Holzman recalled, "Topeka ceased to be the unique place that it was." Yet Menninger's popular image as a center of excellence outdistanced its ebbing professional fortunes. It continued to receive large private philanthropic donations, and the nation's affluent households persisted in regarding it as an optimal facility for their disturbed relatives.

If the varying external perceptions of Menninger have been consequential, they have not always comported with the internal dynamics of the place. Through 1945, when the organization was small, referred to as a clinic, and comparatively obscure, social-emotional patterns of behavior within the Menninger family had great impact upon workplace operations. But the influence of family dynamics upon institutional activities receded in the face of postwar expansion and formal status as a nonprofit foundation. Day-to-day staff life came increasingly to depend upon the leadership and structure of the specific departments to which staff were assigned and upon the rapport among the professional specialty groups within each department. Yet, unlike the Mayo Clinic/Foundation and many other rapidly developing professional institutions, familial aspects of the Menninger Clinic/Foundation workplace never entirely dissipated.

This connection between the family and the organization lies at the heart of my book. Journalist Walker Winslow helped me to understand it in *The Menninger Story* (1956). With access to but a small fraction of the primary documents, Winslow felt that he had to exclude "material that was very loaded with danger to the Menningers." He also treated the organization from an uncritical perspective—as an institution evolving toward greater and greater psychiatric excellence. Nonetheless, Winslow developed a strikingly sensitive picture of the emotional life of the Menninger family, and that allowed me to discover social and emotional connections between family life and organizational activities. Above all, *The Menninger Story* revealed how emotional life within the family assumed a cyclical pattern, with its members experiencing periods of intense missionary fervor that were cut short by times of emotional embattlement (Menninger against Menninger). As I became attentive to this family cycle, I saw how it often helped to explain the specific course of workplace history. Therefore, my book picks up conceptually where Winslow's left off.

I I

It is not entirely clear why the Menningers permitted me access to the detailed documentation that Walker Winslow lacked. When I arrived in Topeka in August 1981, I had no intention of writing this book. I had taken a sabbatical leave to satisfy a long-standing curiosity. I wanted to study diverse psychoanalytically oriented theories of personality within a clinical setting, and the Menninger Interdisciplinary Studies Program made that possible.

By December, as my sabbatical was about to expire, I had become quite curious about the evolution of this family institution. I requested full and unrestricted access to the organizational archives in order to write a comprehensive history. Knowing of the futile attempts of several predecessors, I anticipated a rebuff. But after three months of negotiations, my request was accepted. Good timing contributed to this outcome. The Menningers and their senior staff had become apprehensive, by the late 1970s, that if they continued to discourage researchers from writing Menninger histories, they would not live to read any. When I stated my conditions, a senior scholar on the Menninger campus who had read my prior books joined forces with the archivist and pleaded the case convincingly before the "first family."

In March of 1982, the Menningers formally agreed to let me see all. Legal requirements put most patient medical records off bounds. Reliable internal data listing or enumerating the initial diagnoses of the patients were also lacking. Although the medical records officer provided aggregate in-house data on the condition of adult patients at discharge, information on released children was fragmentary. With these deficiencies, I found it impossible to reconstruct a typical day in the life of a mental patient, and that was disappointing. But save for this dearth of patient materials, I had access to virtually all surviving documents on the Menninger campus. In addition to the substantial organizational archives and those of every other campus facility that housed historical material, the Menningers opened their extensive personal files. I was especially fortunate that Karl provided me with many letters and other documents unavailable to the editors of *The Selected Correspondence of Karl A. Menninger* (1988). Despite the extensive censorship he imposed on these editors (even over sentences and paragraphs within the letters that he allowed them to print), Karl honored my request to reveal everything that was relevant to my narrative.

The openness of the Menningers to my investigation was courageous. They knew that serious scandals and other shortcomings in their history would be presented and that public awareness of these details might affect patient referrals, staff recruitment, and private donations.

But if the openness of the family represented a scholar's dream, it also presented a major methodological dilemma. There were hazards in assessing the strengths and failings of Menninger as a treatment center unless it could be compared to similar reform-oriented "new psychiatry" institutions, such as Austen Riggs in Massachusetts, Sheppard and Enoch Pratt in Baltimore, and Bloomingdale in New York. Yet the historical accounts of these rival centers had not been built on the kind of comprehensive in-house detail that the Menningers made available to me. How, then, was I to evaluate my rather negative internal data on treatment outcomes for adult patients during the 1930s, for example, in the context of more upbeat accounts of treatment results at rival institutions? At certain points, it proved judicious simply to avoid comparing Menninger with its rivals. At other times, comparison had to be qualified. If rival "new psychiatry" centers become more open with their documents, researchers may well discover that their histories involve comparable shortcomings.

In addition to the considerable Menninger archival record, it was necessary to seek out more materials through visits to or correspondence with several other institutions. The Archives of the History of American Psychology, the Manuscript Division of the Library of Congress, and the library of the New York Psychoanalytic Institute were particularly useful. But the value of these proved to be less important than information obtained from dozens of people who had been connected with the Menninger family or organization at various times. I traveled throughout the country, from San Francisco, California, to Lillington, North Carolina, to meet with these people, tape recorder in hand. They told me stories ranging from the social and psychological dynamics of the Menninger household at the turn of the century to the first strike by psychoanalysts in American history. Although not all of these stories proved to be entirely true, the direct personal contact offered valuable clues for ways to access contemporary written documents. Indeed, after formal interviews or informal conversations, a surprising number of people opened sealed boxes and safe-deposit vaults for crucial documents that might have perished with their deaths. Once they began to open these materials, many never stopped. I have yet to experience a week in the past five years when an interviewee has not mailed vital new documents or telephoned to urge me to visit soon to see new data.

The abundance and significance of much of this documentation in private hands modified my perspective on historical research. I came to see great value in extensive interviewing, even though much of the data that I tape-recorded or noted were tangled with the interviewees' current concerns. Through open-ended interviews, crucial "buried" documents were often uncovered as individuals struggled to recall and relive key moments in their past. By being sympathetic and candid about his own interests and concerns, I discovered, the historian can be more than a collector of imperfect oral recollections. He may become an archivist and accumulate crucial documents. This is hardly a contestable proposition. But it goes against the pervasive division of labor in the processing of historical information through which the archivist and the research scholar are regarded as participants in different callings.

III

In Diderot's commentary on a journey taken by Bougainville, he explained how an explorer had to "put on the costume of the country you visit, but keep the suit of clothes you will need to go home in." Since the early 1980s, I had grown accustomed to a Topeka "costume." I spent long intervals on the Menninger campus and developed many close friendships among family and staff. "Welcome home" represented a typical greeting each time I arrived for a period of research. By the mid-1980s, it was sometimes difficult to conclude a research trip and return to my home in northwest Ohio.

Nevertheless, it was necessary to find a "suit of clothes . . . to go home in" if this volume was to go to press. My first draft focused on in-house details (many of which have been shifted to the endnotes). But I failed to delineate the broad stages of organizational development or to place the Menninger enterprise within a national context. It became necessary to stay "home"—to distance myself (somewhat, at least) from the sights and sounds of Topeka in order to write from a broader perspective. This hardly meant complete detachment. Memories of conversations and emotions experienced there helped immeasurably during the writing process. On many occasions, memories allowed me to fill gaps between historical documents more accurately than would otherwise have been the case. In the end, it was therefore essential both to wear "the costume of the country" and to take it off.

As I approached the completion of this volume, I wondered what life would be like "after Menninger." Days, evenings, weekends, and vacations have been consumed with the topic for so many years that the shape of a future "without Menninger" was difficult to imagine. During subsequent visits to Topeka, I will be traveling in my northwest Ohio "suit of clothes," and it will feel strange.

Acknowledgments

This was a very difficult book to research and to write. It could not have been completed without a great deal of assistance, and I can only partially acknowledge those who helped.

Access to the Menninger archives might not have been possible without the intervention of Verne B. Horne and the late Paul Pruyser. Subsequently, B taught me how to work within that large but understaffed facility. Other Menninger employees, particularly Laura Fisher, Alice Brand, John Fitzpatrick, Mark West, Lillabelle Stahl, Peter Novotny, Kelly Burket, Ray Thompson, Emlin North, Kathleen Bryan, and Ann Minihan, helped me to retrieve data from all parts of the campus. Irving Sheffel was remarkable at locating less than accessible information. Telephone calls to Irv always led to crucial missing data and to helpful suggestions for placing that data within a historical context.

I am also grateful to members of the Menninger family for opening their personal as well as their organizational files to me, for allowing me to select an unlimited number of photographs for this volume, and for willingly sharing their memories. Catharine, Jeanetta, Roy, Philip, Walter, Edwin, Jr., and Robert Menninger, and Josephine Boam, were always helpful and encouraging. But if not for the hundreds of hours I was able to spend with Karl—talking, walking, eating, driving, and rummaging through books and letters—this would have been a very different volume. Although Karl never saw a page of this manuscript before publication, virtually every important point was discussed with him.

Dozens of Menninger staff and former staff were interviewed over the past eight years. But it was necessary to call upon some repeatedly. Lou and Harlan Crank, Ruth and Irving Kartus, Joan and the late Edward Greenwood, Lester Luborsky, Merton Gill, Milton Wexler, Martin Mayman, Margaret Brenman Gibson, Harry Levinson, and James Pratt were especially obliging. When he learned that his days were numbered, the late Lewis Robbins opened to me his home, his memories, and the many documents he had collected in researching Karl's life. Although I fumbled through the first interview of this project with Philip Holzman, he became a wise counselor in the years that followed.

The massive amount of information I accumulated over the years needed to be integrated, and that was difficult. Each chapter was rewritten at least four times. Drafts of some chapters were sent to Ronald and Janet Numbers, Anne and Bertram Wyatt-Brown, Gary Hess, Ryan Tweney, Bernard Sternsher, Judith and Thomas Knox, Mark West, Nathan Hale, and Ronald Dole. All of them sprinkled words of encouragement between analyses of important deficiencies. My daughter, Beth, demonstrated that my criticisms of some of her school papers had not been in vain. She rarely let an awkward or imprecise sentence survive.

Thirteen friends patiently worked through the entire manuscript (some did so several times). Verne and James Horne and James Carney verified details and assured me that the interpretive structure accorded with the Menninger family and organization they knew. Edmund Danziger, Richard King, Paul Henggeler, Ronald Takaki, Sheldon Silverman, Charles Strozier, and Donald Nelson forced me to explain how the Menninger experience exemplified larger historical, political, and intellectual forces. My editor, Ashbel Green, underscored the importance of a closely crafted narrative and helped me to achieve it. His associate, Jenny McPhee, was also quite helpful and understanding. With remarkable insight, Ellen Joseph showed me how an essay designed for the meticulous scholar could also appeal to wider reading publics. From start to finish, Gerald Grob displayed the teaching, research, and writing skills that make him one of America's leading historians. Only when Gerry told me that chapter drafts were assuming polished form was I confident that this book might be completed satisfactorily.

The expense of a project like this, involving frequent travel and heavy telephone usage, far exceeded professorial salary scales. Knopf provided the level of advance that was necessary to launch the project. The National Endowment for the Humanities funded a year away from teaching duties so that I could prepare a rough draft of the manuscript. Above all, I must thank administrators and others at Bowling Green State University for assisting with the financial requirements of this project from start to finish—usually on short notice. Michael Ferrari and John Eriksen provided backing when I gained access to the Menninger archives. Kenneth Baker was ready with follow-up support. Nan Edgerton and Christopher Dunn taught me much about successful grant preparation. Dwight Burlingame, Eloise Clark, and Louis Katzner covered large if unexpected last-minute completion costs. Ann Bowers and Paul Yon of the Center for Archival Collections absorbed the expenses of their services. So did Jeff Hogue and Christine Eberle, two very creative contributors to the dust jacket design, and Joseph Arpad, who facilitated photographic efforts.

There were other forms of assistance. My agent, Gerard McCauley, built my confidence in the importance of this study. My attorney, Jeffrey Twyman, demonstrated that legal problems are easier to avoid than to resolve. Although Walling Mariea offered encouragement and counsel from the start, her wise words were particularly important when I needed to return, emotionally, from Topeka and bring this study to a close. In ways that I do not entirely understand, my seventy-seven-year-old mother was also important during that emotional return home. It is even more difficult to describe the full impact that my wife, Sharon, had upon this project. But it was there from the start and was always very substantial. I am especially grateful to Sharon for helping me to see that there was "life after Menninger."

PART ONE

"A Family Spirit"
1919–1945

A family spirit grew up in the Sanitarium and the doctors were like fathers and big brothers with the patients as our children.

KARL A. MENNINGER

CHAPTER ONE

The Menningers of Topeka

The most intriguing histories of Kansas have rarely been calm, balanced, or detached. With a climate marked by tornadoes, blizzards, prairie fires, and droughts, plus the border wars of "bleeding Kansas" in the 1850s, the Indian raids that followed, the notorious horse thieves and outlaws, and the demagogic politicians, it has been easy for some to characterize the state in unflattering terms. H. L. Mencken spoke of Kansas's "moronic" intellectual development. Carl Becker characterized much of Kansas history as "a series of disasters," while William Allen White called the state "a plague spot" in a "garden" nation. But Kansas has also promoted railroad regulation, the eight-hour workday, serious state involvement in public health and compulsory education, limitations on child labor, and a juvenile court system. Even Becker and White appreciated these accomplishments. For Becker, Kansas became "an experiment station in the field of social science." White agreed: "When anything is going to happen in this country, it happens first in Kansas."[1]

Many of the progressive innovations occurred during the reform climate of the last years of the nineteenth century and the first two decades of the twentieth. These were years when Kansas instituted the direct primary election, significant measures for public utilities and railroad regulation, and depoliticization of her welfare institutions. The reform ventures of the period often involved medical care. Several physicians learned the new findings concerning the germ theory of disease by studying in Berlin and Vienna; they returned to teach their Kansas medical colleagues about the revolutionary implications of that scientific discovery. Samuel Crumbine used this knowledge to reform the state public health system and reduced significantly the spread of infectious diseases. The spirit of close consultation and camaraderie carried into neurology and psychiatry. Two Kansas doctors, Clarence Goddard and Samuel Glascock, studied the newest theories of mental abnormality in Vienna and returned to instruct their colleagues. The *Journal of the Kansas Medical Society* eagerly published articles on mental disease. Reform-minded superintendents were recruited for two of the state's mental hospitals, while a Lawrence physician established a small private hospital for mental disorders.[2]

In 1919, Karl Menninger of Topeka founded one of the most significant and innovative psychiatric institutions in America. One is tempted to characterize the origin and early development of the Menninger Clinic as a product of the Kansas reform era. Karl himself has often made that connection. And he paid homage to Kansas physicians who "came to my rescue" when he began his rather unorthodox psychiatric practice. They encouraged him in his scientific investigations and "had confidence in me and sent me some patients. Then they sent me some more. And they've been sending 'em ever since."[3]

Yet, in a more reflective mood, Karl has singled out his family—his parents and his youngest brother, Will—for the clinic's success. In 1971, Frederick Hacker, a protégé of Karl's who had established his own clinic in southern California, posed the traditional question concerning the origins of the Menninger Clinic and Karl's long-standing commitment to reform. Karl retorted that it was insufficient to cite simply the progressive traditions of his state, for there were also retrogressive traditions. At a deeper level, he told Hacker, it would be necessary to understand the development of the Menninger family, particularly the rapport of the Menninger sons with their parents. But he would go no further.[4]

It is important to probe where Karl left off, with his parents, Charles Frederick Menninger and Flo Vesta Knisely Menninger, and their lives with their children. For a "family spirit" quickly moved to the center of organizational life, just as the organization moved to the center of early-twentieth-century Kansas reform tradition.

I I

Karl's grandfather August Valentine Menninger was born in Frankfurt am Main in 1826. When August's father, Andrew, lost his wife to typhoid in 1843, he migrated with three sons and two daughters to Baltimore. In 1847, Andrew Menninger took August and the others to Cincinnati. But Andrew drowned in that river city by falling (apparently accidentally) off a dock. Thereafter, the Menninger family dispersed. August remained in the large German community of Cincinnati, where he became a blacksmith. He met Katarina Schmidberger, who had migrated from Boenstadt, Germany, in 1848. Although August was a Roman Catholic and Katarina was a Lutheran, he married her in 1850 and agreed to raise their children in the Protestant church.[5]

Like many nineteenth-century German-Americans, August and Katarina Menninger were determined to put considerable distance between their past and their future. They rarely spoke to their children of their European origins and maintained little contact with their relatives in other parts of America. In 1860, the couple moved with their children downriver to Tell City, Indiana. The town had been settled only two years earlier by German migrants. August became a partner in a local sawmill and owned it within seven years. The family was comfortable financially though by no means wealthy. Charles Frederick, the sixth child, was born in 1862. Two sisters came after him; he remained the youngest son.[6]

Katarina and August reared their children within the Tell City German community. Katarina never learned English, while August spoke it only sparingly. The oldest son, Gus, was mechanically inclined and attracted to his father's sawmill. Charles, considerably more studious and curious, sought stimulation beyond the town. After going through the local public schools, he served for five or six years as deputy to a brother-in-law clerking in the Perry County district court and attended night school. In 1879, he entered Central Normal College in nearby Danville. By 1882, Charles had completed his bachelor's degree. His parents urged him to return to Tell City and support himself in a local law office. Because they had younger children who required their resources, they would not continue to fund his educational aspirations. But Charles received an offer from Campbell College—a new institution in distant Holton, Kansas—to teach with several of his former Central College classmates. August and Katarina opposed Charles's leaving Indiana. Charles, however, saw teaching as an opportunity to continue learning, defied his parents, and accepted the Kansas position. Thereafter, his trips to Tell City were infrequent.[7]

Not long after he arrived in Holton, Charles met, courted, and married Flo Vesta Knisely. Early Knisely genealogy is skeletal. Legend had it that two Knisely brothers were Hessians who fought for the British during the American Revolution. They settled in Pennsylvania, married, and raised families. Flo's mother, Amanda, was a Heikes. The Heikeses traced their lineage from Württemberg, Germany, to Pennsylvania Dutch farmers in the vicinity of York County. Flo was born in 1863, the first of eight children. When she was ten, her father died after a grueling battle with cancer and left his family impoverished. Mother and children moved to the nearby farm of Flo's Heikes grandparents. There, Amanda took on odd jobs and required Flo to care for her youngest siblings. She had to parent before she was an adolescent, in a very precarious family economy. To add to the strain, grandfather Heikes informed Amanda early in 1878 that he could no longer afford to keep Flo and her siblings. He proposed that they be taken in by friends, but Amanda refused. She had heard that life might yield greater economic security in central Kansas and migrated there with her children. In the small town of Industry, near Abilene, Amanda established a modest farm, worked in the fields, marketed her produce, and maintained her financial accounts. The example of a strong, assertive, and independent woman who did not require a husband to get on in the world was not lost on her eldest daughter.[8]

As it happened, Charles and Flo arrived in the same part of Kansas within a few years of each other. Willing to teach so that he could learn, Charles felt that it was necessary to distance himself from the more pragmatic, acquisitive milieu of his parents. In contrast, Flo came with her mother and her siblings to find economic security. Having experienced the stability of a German middle-class home, Charles sought to carve out an independent personal identity that centered upon education and the life of the mind. Flo had lived through acute hardship and was seared with an overpowering fear of returning to poverty and losing her family; she continued to cling to her mother and her siblings and to count material possessions zealously. Charles had been a successful law clerk and was offered a teaching post at a new college in the West. With these achievements, he had acquired social poise and self-confidence. Self-educated and forced to mother her siblings before she could grow into womanhood, Flo felt awkward in social situations and watched uneasily for impending crises. These differences between Charles and Flo would have profound effects on their children.[9]

When she arrived in Kansas, a scared and withdrawn sixteen-year-old, Flo took a teaching job in Clay Center to supplement the income of her mother's farm. She also took up reform. Amanda became a leading Kansas prohibitionist who wrecked Industry's lone saloon with a hammer. Flo, using her resourceful mother as her principal role model, quickly took up the cause against liquor. While teaching at Clay Center, however, Flo roomed with a woman who provided still another model. Kansas had led the nation in 1872 by admitting women to the state medical society; Flo's roommate was one of the first women who had trained in a Kansas medical school and joined the state society. This contact seemed to have given Flo a taste for advanced training despite her mother's Mennonite deemphasis upon formal education. At the close of her second year of teaching, she decided to attend the summer term at Campbell College.[10]

The college had recently opened its doors and was short on staff. When Charles arrived from Tell City, he was assigned to teach physics, chemistry, botany, physiology, and German. "My dream was for a husband who would be tall and slender, intelligent, and interesting—and I hoped we would like the same things," Flo subsequently noted. She met the young professor and was pleased when he began to call on her.[11]

In Holton, Flo rented rooms with her brother Elmer, who was also enrolled in the college. Desperately poor and uninterested in the traditional recreations of dancing and cards, they spent their spare time studying. Charles soon joined them several evenings each week. He read various scientific materials, while Flo studied art and music. "The three of us lived in a dream of delight," Flo recalled. Collectively, they found an alternative to the less than stimulating environments of Tell City, Indiana, and York County, Pennsylvania. It had shades of what Erik Erikson has characterized as a youthful quest for identity distinct from the parental generation. Flo noted that she felt most comfortable with Charles when another or others were present; the proximity of Elmer seemed to have provided linkage for two very different people. Even with Elmer present, however, several Campbell faculty considered it improper for Charles to be spending so many evenings in Flo's rooms. But "Charlie would not agree to limit his calls." Consequently, although her mother had warned that "a girl's chances for doing things were often handicapped by marriage," Flo accepted Charles's marriage proposal, with the condition that "I would continue going to school."[12]

After the couple married, in January 1885, Flo pursued her courses in the college. Advanced education for unmarried women was permitted within certain limits in nineteenth-century Kansas. But it was a very different matter for a married woman to stay in school. After the marriage ceremony, Charles moved into the rooms that Flo shared with Elmer, and the three went on with their daily schedules almost as if nothing significant had happened. Evening studies persisted as the common social bond.[13]

During the first seven years of their marriage, Flo and Charles lived together amicably. When Elmer died of typhoid fever late in 1886, Flo was distressed. Like her father, another man in her immediate family appeared to have deserted her. Moreover, the death left her alone, for the first time, with Charles, and this felt awkward. Yet Charles continued to support Flo's values. He, too, became a prohibitionist. When Flo voiced displeasure over his Lutheran church affiliation and proposed that they both join the Presbyterian church, he agreed. In this rather unusual nineteenth-century marriage, Flo established family values and practices while insisting on the right "to go everywhere my husband went and do everything he did."[14]

During the late 1880s, Charles decided to become a physician, despite the sparse income and low status of the profession in Kansas. Much of a doctor's work then was essentially charitable, because of depressionary farm income levels. But Flo recognized that a physician's income exceeded a professor's and acquiesced in her husband's plans; medical training would allow him to make sufficient salary "to earn a home for both of us." Charles entered Chicago's homeopathic Hahnemann Medical College in 1887, and Flo supported him by teaching school in Holton.[15]

Charles concluded that Topeka would offer the best opportunities for a medical practice when he graduated. While he continued to study in Chicago, Flo moved to the state capital in September 1888 and taught at a school in the city's low-income district. He would join her the following year after completing his medical training. Even with its surrounding communities, Topeka had a population of only 48,000, primarily unpaved and muddy streets, and a water supply that bred typhoid when the late-summer rains were scarce. Nevertheless, the city supported various urban cultural amenities, including two orchestras, three opera houses, and some music halls. Unlike most small western cities, it housed libraries with respectable collections. There were also several dozen churches, representing practically every denomination. Moreover, the Topeka economy was strong and growing. Flour, sugar, cotton cloth, iron castings, artificial limbs, wagons and carriages, and farm implements were the major manufactured items. Commerce was facilitated because Topeka was also a major railroad center, which included the Atchison, Topeka and Santa Fe Railroad and three other important lines. With manufacturing and transportation in abundant supply, thirteen banks prospered in the city.[16]

Charles was particularly impressed with the Topeka medical community. Local physicians had developed a tradition of cooperation and trust. They operated a small medical school in a ramshackle building affiliated with Washburn College. They also used Christ's Hospital, particularly after 1889, when Christ's established a nurses training program. The construction of at least two other local hospitals were distinct possibilities. There was, in addition, the decade-old Topeka Insane Asylum, headed by a young and reform-minded superintendent who was determined to run it as a topflight medical institution. Local doctors got together in the city's Academy of Medicine and Surgery, the Mental Science Club, the Homeopathic Medical Society, and even the Society of Natural Science. They were particularly proud of publishing the state medical journal.[17]

Not long after he joined Flo in Topeka, in 1889, Charles became a well-regarded practitioner. His services were in demand among the city's four thousand German-speaking immigrants. He also had the good fortune of becoming a close friend of Henry Roby, a leading Kansas homeopath, who took him in as junior partner. Much of Roby's time was spent trying to breach the long-standing quarrel between homeopathic and allopathic (i.e., "regular") practitioners. He convinced his young partner and a goodly number of other Kansas homeopaths that because of their essentially eclectic approaches to treatment, and especially in view of the new discoveries coming out of Germany in bacteriology and anesthetic surgery, the traditionally monistic homeopathic theory of cure had ceased to be tenable. The homeopathic perspective—that what seemed to bring on an illness in a healthy person would cure that illness in a sick person— was far too vague. Pathologies were localized, and cures needed to be specific. To learn the new ideas of Koch, Pasteur, and others who were revolutionizing medical practice, Charles took postgraduate courses in the allopathic Kansas Medical College and read prodigiously. This investment of his time was well placed. Over the years, he became the first Topeka physician to use a microscope in his office, the first to develop systematic laboratory procedures, the first to study Charcot's new methods of hypnosis for treatment, and the first to inject insulin in treating diabetes. Although all Kansas physicians at the turn of the century were general practitioners, Charles demonstrated particular competence in internal medicine, especially metabolic disorders.[18]

The time that Charles and Flo had together decreased during the early 1890s, as Charles's reputation spread and his practice increased. Even when they were together, they rarely discussed their work. A pattern of separation, emotional as well as spatial, had emerged. "She pursued her line and I pursued mine," even though Charles "felt the need of talking with somebody" about his work. The custom of studying together in the evenings ended after Flo's brother died. Every night she had Charles empty his pockets of money that he earned visiting patients during the day. If there was too little, she fretted that she could not cover the family's expenses—sometimes there were tears in her eyes. But if the money was considerable, she feared that his practice was too active, that his health would break down, and that she would be left without funds. Flo's childhood memories of poverty and desperation were intruding upon her marriage.[19]

Flo had worked since she was a child and taught school since 1879. Late in 1892, she became pregnant, and custom made it necessary for her to quit her teaching job. Family income was reduced as expenses were about to increase. Consequently, the tensions inherent in the evening ritual were bound to mount. Unemployed and uncomfortable in the role of a middle-class urban housewife, Flo felt at loose ends: "It was hard to think the schools could go on without me." To fill her day, she took up sewing and occasionally traveled with Charles as he made house calls.[20]

Karl was born in July 1893. Judging from her autobiography and her diaries, this neither eased Flo's despair nor drew her closer to her husband. Rather, it may have rekindled the insecurities she had felt as a child at having to rear her younger siblings. Edwin arrived in 1896 and William Claire, the last child, came in 1899, but neither her autobiography nor her diaries suggest that Flo grew any more at ease with her mothering. Further, her marriage to Charles became more difficult. For example, telephone calls from Charles's patients had always been frequent. But in her new role as mother, Flo began to complain: the telephone awakened her babies. Similarly, she worked diligently to prepare formal dinners as a diversion from child-rearing duties. But too often, she insisted, the invited couples came, dined, and left before Charles returned from emergency house calls.[21]

As Flo's anxiety became chronic, Charles began to wonder whether he should stay married. Accustomed to striving to satisfy his wife's wishes, he sensed that he was not good enough for her, that he was the cause of her deepening agitation and unhappiness. But he decided to persist. In 1898, Charles bought a large new house and hoped that it would augment Flo's contentment. The beneficial effect was temporary.[22]

Because she was more comfortable studying and working outside the home, Flo's domesticity placed considerable strain on her marriage. Her subsequent immersion in a Bible studies program enhanced her spirits and significantly transformed the marriage over the long term into a more tolerable relationship. Throughout the 1890s, Flo had attended a Bible study class conducted by her pastor's wife. When she was informed in 1898 that the class would be restricted to unmarried women, she set out to organize a Bible class for all Topeka women.

Flo found this task deeply gratifying and began to prepare an extensive outline for her classes. She designed a chapter-by-chapter, book-by-book study outline of the Bible for a four-year term. As she drafted and revised her outline, Flo seemed to be articulating for herself what she considered to be her personal philosophy of "practical Christianity." She sought "to make the Book itself understandable" so that "those who want to find God in their daily lives" could do so. That is, Christianity was not valuable primarily for the formal theology that it revealed in Scripture. Rather, the inspiring stories in basic morality contained in the Bible, when made interesting, would encourage people to practice morality in their everyday lives. The Topeka YWCA supported Flo's Bible study, even when she took the unprecedented step of inviting black women to participate. As the years passed, preparation for and administration of the classes consumed more and more of her time. Classes outside Topeka were organized around her outline. By 1938, she may have directly instructed over six thousand Topeka women in Bible study and thousands more through their subscriptions to her outline.[23]

Friends and relatives noted that Flo turned her Bible classes into a full-time vocation. The classes seemed to give her a sense of purpose and importance that she did not feel as a mother. She was participating in Kansas's women's club movement. Female Bible classes, prohibition chapters, and similar groups represented extensions of domestic feminism. They allowed many middle-class women to break from their otherwise undifferentiated days at tedious domestic chores. Although their ventures rarely competed with the activities of fathers, brothers, or husbands, women often returned home with new feelings of validity and self-confidence. This happened to Flo. Bible classes launched her upon a proud and active career as a missionary reformer.[24]

Although the Bible study classes drew Flo out of her depression, her marriage was never more than tolerable again. Husband and wife walked in distinctly separate spheres. Charles was very busy with his medical practice and filled his spare time with new hobbies—rock, mineral, and shell collecting, plus flower gardening. In the evening, the two rarely discussed the events of the day. "She is sitting here by me but don't [sic] seem to be able to get away from them [Bible lessons]," Charles wrote. "So here I am all alone in a way and yet not, for mother is right here with me." Only one of their many surviving photographs after 1902 reveals the couple embracing; few of their friends recalled this ever occurring.[25]

Charles's willingness to continue with the marriage, to submit passively to the wishes of his strong-willed wife, suggested a certain readiness to accept the station that the Cult of the Lady—the nineteenth-century code for gender propriety—prescribed for wives. Passive acquiescence helped him avert major arguments with Flo. Edwin, the second son, noted: "Father believes in peace at any price." But disputes were not always averted. When Charles was in the hospital for a gallstone operation, for example, Flo was informed by a Topeka bank that the family checking account was overdrawn. Horrified, she berated Charles for bringing the family to the "brink of poverty and humiliation." On another occasion, Charles faced a fifty-thousand-dollar malpractice suit by a patient who had violated his instructions. A two-hundred-dollar out-of-court settlement arranged by his lawyer humiliated Charles, but Flo required him to accept it. She "smiled complacently at her bankbooks" and felt relieved at losing so little. Every year as Memorial Day approached, Flo insisted that she could not stand Charles's many peonies (midwestern flowers of remembrance) going to waste. Charles retorted that they beautified the landscape. But like the commercially prudent husband of Cult of the Lady advice manuals, Flo regularly ordered the peonies to be harvested and sold. The old pattern of bickering over finances persisted.[26]

Still, the richness each found in work seemed to ease marital strains. When conflicts came, Charles usually (if sometimes angrily) backed down. Flo continued to refer to him affectionately as "Charlie," and he rarely returned from a trip without special silk handkerchiefs for her. Indeed, they often traveled together. If their marriage was no paradise, neither was it persistent misery.[27]

III

The worst decade of Flo's marriage was the 1890s, when she gave birth to her three sons. Confined to domestic burdens, she enjoyed few outlets, and her spirits were low. In this atmosphere, the Menninger family defined itself.

Flo was a firstborn herself, and her experiences with Karl were the most fundamental in shaping her self-image as a mother. Karl's birth seemed to kindle memories of her own father, who had died when she was young. "Her father died when she was a little girl, and she always had a tendency to cling to me, therefore, so she wouldn't lose me," Karl reminisced. But though Flo channeled enormous energy into her relationship with her first infant, her diaries for the period reveal much dissatisfaction. At times, Karl refused to eat, "much to the annoyance of his mother." When Flo accidentally broke a parlor lamp, Karl "deliberately" broke another. She fed him a can of food with an unusual taste and fretted for weeks about the consequences.[28]

Control was crucial to Flo. But despite her experience rearing her siblings, it was "a great puzzle to know how to manage sometimes" when it came to her firstborn. "I scarcely know how to plan for or manage my boy," she noted. "I think he often feels just the opposite of what I would have him." What "I want most to know is how to raise him just right," she acknowledged. Because Flo felt inadequate to the task, she encouraged Karl to nap.[29]

Flo's relationship with Karl was complex. He seemed to appeal to her warmth and her fear at the same time. Flo noted how she loved it when "he put his arms about my neck & thanked me" for reading. But "I almost fear my baby too." Her fear and her difficulty in controlling Karl seemed most acute when she realized that the unusually bright child was a separate entity: "Our baby has such a mind of his own that some times it is hard to know how to manage him." It was hard because Flo identified closely with Karl and found it unsettling whenever she and the child were out of step. She realized that Karl "is like me in many ways," especially in his constant mood swings from warmth and thoughtfulness to depression and crossness. Therefore, it often seemed strange to punish him for unpleasant conduct; it was like punishing herself.[30]

Flo found that in her relationship with Karl she was examining aspects of herself. As such, she seemed unwilling to allow him to satisfy fully what therapist Alice Miller has characterized as the legitimate narcissistic needs of a baby to gain a firm sense of inner worth by projecting himself outward on the world—by looking initially to his mother and other objects as mirrors of himself. Owing to Flo's apprehensive self-preoccupation and her determination to find herself in her child, she inhibited him from developing a strong self-imaging "mirror" of his own and a concomitant set of self-values and self-images. Because Karl grew up without a strong sense of self-worth, he would spend much time and experience considerable sadness in trying to find it as an adult.[31]

As he matured, Karl became conscious of his close identity with Flo: "I was the oldest. Like my mother, I was given a feeling of responsibility for my brothers, which she had for her brothers and sisters in large numbers." When Flo died, he identified himself as "her oldest problem child." Karl felt that he had been a "problem child" largely because he could not always measure up to Flo's persistently high demands for the two of them. Her highest standard had been her insistence upon total candor: "I think the main thing I inherited from my mother, temperamentally or characterologically—almost [an] allergy to any kind of faking." If less than totally truthful, the son (like the mother) felt deep guilt and anxiety. When Karl was a student at the University of Wisconsin, his roommate accused him of being insincere in the love he professed for others. Karl wrote an urgent letter to his mother to erase all doubt: "please mamma, tell me what you think. I am convinced that you know me better than I." In most matters concerning integrity, Flo tended to reassure her son: "You have always been fine in revealing your real self no matter how much to your own disadvantage it was." The mother had a stake in affirming the son's candor, for he was "like your mother in so many ways that I know you better than any one else."[32]

Karl understood Flo's changing feelings toward him and characterized them as "undoubtedly the most determining influence" in his life. He often remembered his mother trying to please him—reading aloud, playing music, staying with him when he was ill—just as he had tried to please her. But he also recalled distressing things Flo had done to him, including painful enemas and tying bells to his body at Christmas. Her frequent bouts with depression were even more distressing. When he tried to cheer her up, she would often burst into tears and then describe his father's "wasteful" spending or insufficient drive. Karl sometimes felt relieved when his mother left the house. "Where or why she is going I do not know nor do I care," he would note in his adolescent diary. He did care, of course, and emulated the mood swings of the parent who meant so much to him.[33]

In his first book, *The Human Mind* (1930), Karl described "an over-anxious, fear-ridden mother who robbed her son of his self-confidence." Although referring to the case of a student who had difficulty taking chemistry examinations, he was also talking about himself. Because he could never develop a sturdy self or mirror image separate from his mother, he found that he could never quite satisfy all of Flo's persistent demands for both her son and herself. Consequently, Karl sometimes sought to create distance or emotional space between them.[34]

The process through which Karl expanded that emotional space was gradual, difficult, and transpired over many decades. Flo always wanted him to become a prosperous businessman, for example; it was not until 1913 that he decided instead to go into medicine. But he deeply regretted that "I hurt you [Flo]" by thus trying "to go my own way." Two decades later, Karl began a personal analysis, in which he struggled to diminish her hold upon him: "Mother, I must confess to you; I said bad words about you." Similarly, Flo found it difficult to allow her son to separate from her. On his thirty-seventh birthday, she handed Karl the "Baby Book" diary in which she had made observations of his earliest years, acknowledging that "it *may be* you have had 'too much mother,' but 'weaning time' has no absolute date."[35]

Edwin was born in March 1896, and Flo regarded him with mixed feelings: "We were looking for a girl, but were happy to have this chubby, strong, ten-pound boy." Given the constant strains and worries over Karl, Flo was relieved that Edwin was "good-natured" and "made us very little trouble." She could go on focusing upon her firstborn. Flo was pleased, for example, that Edwin's digestive system seemed so durable that she did not have to fret over what he ate the way she concerned herself with Karl's dietary habits.[36]

Flo often found herself thinking of Edwin not so much as a child with qualities and needs in his own right but in comparison to his older brother. Edwin was "a beautiful little sunbeam and I pray God to grant that he may bring into his brother's serious, selfish life, some sunshine." "Dear little Edwin was born with a disposition that makes him and all his friends rich," Flo noted, while "poor Karl may struggle and fight, but he will never be happy." When her husband offered to take the two boys for a ride, Flo observed, Edwin worried that " 'Mama will be alone.' Karl never hesitates."[37]

By holding Edwin up to Karl, Flo was not easing household strain. Edwin realized that Karl was his mother's primary concern. At times, he even sensed that Flo and Karl were so closely bonded because they were very much alike. Karl was always "very close to mother," he recalled. But while Edwin felt that he was secondary, Karl was resentful when his mother compared him to Edwin. Sometimes Karl struck his brother. At other times, Flo noted, Karl "wishes Edwin and Mama were both dead," and felt that they were "no good and always in the way!" There was a special intensity to the sibling rivalry of the firstborn who had trouble separating himself from his mother.[38]

If Flo was modestly disappointed that her second child was not a girl, she was acutely distressed when the third, whom she named Clara Louise in advance, was born, in October 1899. The baby had to be renamed William Claire, and Karl would look upon him as another rival for his mother's attentions. Flo, who insisted on calling him Claire rather than Will until he turned forty, determined never to have another child. Once when a minister consoled Flo because she had no daughters, he put his hand on the young child by her feet and declared: "This one should have been a girl." Will clung to his mother's skirt and yelled: "No. I don't want to be a girl." Like Edwin, he had gotten the message—that he was less than central to his mother.[39]

Flo was especially displeased by the male qualities that came with Will's adolescence. She forbade his dating girls. By the time Will went away to school in New York, he had probably internalized Flo's reticence concerning his maturation. He felt compelled to ask her approval for his Sunday walks and mailed clothes for her to repair as she had done when he was younger. At twenty-two, he referred to himself half-jokingly as the "baby" but noted that he was slowly learning to stand on his "own legs."[40]

As Will learned to be more independent, Flo's attentions drew more markedly to other concerns—her Bible study classes and, of course, the unending troubles of her oldest son. These other obligations may explain why Flo seemed to give Will more emotional space and to be less controlling. When, for example, Flo discovered that Will had been stealing money from her coin box, she did not fly into a rage and thrash him as she would have done with Karl or even Edwin. Rather, she simply told Will that she knew what he had been doing and hoped he would not do it anymore. While he was pleased that Flo let him off lightly, Will also sensed that she seemed indifferent. He perceived this, again, when she prodded him dogmatically yet unfeelingly to attend Sunday school and to practice his musical instrument, and it cooled him toward both church life and music. Karl clearly led in their rivalry for her affections.[41]

Although Flo's practice of holding up Edwin's deportment as a model for Karl promoted family tensions, it conveyed to Edwin the sense that his mother thought well of him. Flo occasionally upheld Will in the same way, asking Karl: "Why can't you be like your brother?" But this was a much less frequent occurrence. More, even, than Edwin, Flo tended to leave Will to his own resources. Identifying with the more passive and less expressive personality of his third son, Charles correspondingly drew closer to him as Will grew older. The result was an informal alliance between the father and the youngest son.[42]

This alliance was not formed until the Menninger sons were well into adolescence. Until then, Charles busied himself with a growing medical practice and was rarely at home. When he was home, he took his meals after the boys finished and studied medical books in the interval between dinner and their bedtimes. Only after his sons matured did he begin to take pleasure in being with them. And only at that point did the boys feel that family life involved more than contact with their mother and her preoccupation with Karl. Charles began inviting his children to travel with him as he made house calls and to tend to his horse and buggy when he was home. As they went on to high school and college, he became quite attentive to what they were studying and to their vocational preferences. The three boys discovered a significant new parental presence in their lives. However, they found that he focused on one of them considerably more than the other two, just as their mother had.[43]

It was predictable that Charles would eventually come to identify with the youngest male in the household, Will. But he did so without Flo's frenzy or her overt efforts at control. Will recalled fondly how Charles's influence was more subtle and sensitive, as when he persuaded him and then his brothers to practice their musical instruments by inquiring if they were ready to perform in a "family orchestra." Charles playfully advised Will to have fun during his medical education and noted how he was "looking forward with no small amount of real sincere joy" to the day when Will might join him in medical practice. "I love you very dearly" typically ended a letter from Charles to his youngest son.[44]

Despite this blend of nurturing with a certain amount of emotional space for growth, Charles's alliance with Will included certain tensions. At times, Will found Charles stubborn and somewhat irritable. But what sometimes distressed him keenly was what he also regarded as his father's greatest strength—being "so sweet and so adjustable and so magnanimous" that he avoided disciplinary measures and other difficult tasks of child rearing and assumed that Flo would attend to them. He never "hit me or slapped me—perhaps leaving that for mother." In essence, Will loved Charles for his mild, flexible, loving manner. But he was upset at Charles's unwillingness to play the part of the stern and forceful Victorian father, for leaving displays of paternal discipline and power to his wife. In some measure, Will felt this ambivalence because he found Charles's primary strength and weakness in himself as he grew older.[45]

Nevertheless, Charles's increasing attentiveness to Will was salutary, enhancing Will's sense of belonging within the Menninger family. Edwin needed Charles's support as well, for he lived in the shadows of the intense Flo-Karl alliance. Initially, Charles did pay attention to his middle son. Charles saw in Edwin's disposition to accept and to work with life's limitations (not to war against them) a bit of the outlook that differentiated Charles from Flo. But ultimately, Charles's attentions shifted decidedly toward Will. Increasingly, Edwin found himself outside both alliances.[46]

If Will was generally comforted by Charles's kindness, Karl was not. Like Edwin, he respected his father's learnedness and his even temper. And he never forgot the night he told his father of his decision to become a doctor. Charles gave him a tearful embrace: "I'm glad, Karl."[47]

Nevertheless, there were diverse feelings that complicated the Charles-Karl relationship. Karl was jealous of Charles's preference for his siblings, particularly for Will. He feared that "my brother will replace me with my father." Deeply troubled by sibling rivalry, Karl felt that he could not compete with Will for his father's affections or head off that emerging Charles-Will alliance. In addition, Charles did not relate as well as Flo to Karl's unusual temperament and intellectual capability. He could not understand, for example, how Karl could complete an algebra lesson properly if hastily while whistling loudly, or outline a sermon that he had not listened to attentively.[48]

More important, father and son had strikingly different and rather incompatible personalities. Karl learned to identify with and to behave like his mother. Strong and assertive, both approximated the traditional male role within Victorian prescriptive literature. Consonant with that role, both mother and son needed constantly to innovate, to expand the realm of their activities external to the home. Flo created a national Bible study network, while Karl built an internationally recognized mental health center. In contrast, Charles and his favored son appeared passive and restrained; both displayed some of the "mildness" and "kindness" prescribed for the Victorian Lady. Although both were skillful organization builders, like Flo and Karl, they covered their Prussian-like managerial styles with compassion and a willingness to accommodate others.[49]

A characterization of the family from the standpoint of neatly contrasting Victorian gender roles should not be pushed too far. The Victorian code acknowledged though it did not sanction mood swings for women; emotionality was a trait of the "weaker" sex. The code expected men to maintain even tempers and sobriety in order to lead successful lives. Yet Karl and his mother—the assertive, "male" part of the Menninger family—experienced constant emotional swings and pained "sensitivities," testifying to insecurities within. On the other hand, Charles and his youngest son—the more passive, "female" participants in family life—were fairly even-tempered. Far more skillful in dealing with people than Flo and Karl, Charles became a respected member of Topeka's medical and business communities, while Will eventually became the leading spokesman for American psychiatry.

I V
_____

In a family structured by two alliances, it was difficult for the three boys to get along. Their only effort at collective action came when they formed the KAWCEAM Stamp Company [*K*arl *A*ugustus, *W*illiam *C*laire, *E*dwin *A*rnold *M*enninger] to sell jointly the surplus from each of their separate stamp collections. To establish safeguards against anticipated quarrels, they drew up incorporation papers and formal company rules. Notwithstanding, each boy remained apprehensive over his share in the proceeds of their sales. They made their mother arbitrator, but this did not forestall quarrels over assets when the company liquidated.[50]

The KAWCEAM undertaking concluded cooperative ventures among the three boys. Between 1914 and 1935, they were never together in the same place at the same time. Yet Karl and Will were always concerned about each other. Will's attentiveness to Karl was predictable, and it cannot be ascribed entirely to sibling rivalry. Other, if related, issues of family structure were also relevant. In *Family Constellation,* a classic study of sibling orders, social psychologist Walter Toman noted how the youngest of several brothers has tended to be impressed by the dominance of the oldest brother. He has often been willing to subordinate himself to the oldest and even to tolerate the oldest's abuses. This was particularly true in a family where the oldest was aligned with a mother who was the most powerful and assertive figure in the family. Will struggled constantly to emulate Karl and to please him. Because Karl took a "mental bath" on Sunday from his studies, Will followed suit. When Karl began to write professionally, Will thought he might too. When Karl left for the University of Wisconsin, Will felt directionless and "had a very good cry."[51]

Karl expressed pleasure that Will "imitated me," was loyal, and was usually "attached to me like a son." This was more than the typical older brother expecting deference from the younger. Karl was viewing matters from the perspective of the dominant family alliance expecting acquiescence from the subordinate alliance. Just as Flo commanded compliance from her husband, Karl expected Will's obedience. This was why he was particularly disturbed by a certain "very independent, very stubborn" quality in Will. When Will decided to attend a different medical school, Karl was dismayed. Karl often felt inadequate in meeting his mother's expectations; when his "little brother" charted another course, Karl took it as added confirmation that he was lacking.[52]

Karl struggled constantly to keep Will under his control. He would conduct himself toward Will like a powerful parent trying to keep a firm thumb on a potentially defiant child. When the brothers spent their summers at grandmother Knisely's farm, Karl insisted on standing in for his mother and maintaining her standards. Practically echoing Flo's words, Karl typically told Will: "I am glad you did so well in your school work. Don't run yourself down—be proud of having done good work and keep it up." He offered to support Will financially if Will became a missionary, and he advised him continuously on career choices. When Will married, Karl even gave instructions on the proper activities for a wife.[53]

As the bond between Karl and Will became apparent, Edwin found himself in a less than optimal position. He lacked strong emotional ties with either parent and was not crucial to either of his brothers. Liked by all the Menningers for his kind and considerate manner and his good cheer, Edwin was vital to none.

On the evening of March 2, 1915, Edwin and his friend Marshall Sanders mixed phosphorus, a reducing agent, with potassium chlorate, an oxidizing agent, in a test tube in their chemistry laboratory at Washburn College. Knowing that they had created a potentially explosive compound, the boys walked outside toward an isolated part of the campus to test its explosive force. Edwin carried the test tube. A junior with three years of experience in chemistry classes, he knew that chlorate was quite sensitive even to slight shocks. Yet in shifting the tube from his right hand to his left as he walked toward the test site, Edwin caused movement. A massive explosion resulted. Sanders was not hurt, but Edwin lost most of the flesh from his left hand, and glass splattered into his right eye. His life was in jeopardy, and attending physicians considered amputating his arm. But Charles worked feverishly over his son's hand and arm wounds with injections of peroxide. Gangrene was averted, and the arm was saved, but Edwin ended up with a finger amputated and with no vision in his right eye. He was also left with permanent facial disfigurement. Considering the extent of his injuries, Charles and Flo acknowledged that he would have difficulty practicing medicine and advised him to drop his premedical courses. Since he liked journalism—he was associate editor of the *Washburn Review* and would be chief editor in his senior year—they urged him to pursue journalism as his major and promised to send him to Columbia University's prestigious Pulitzer School for graduate training.[54]

Edwin edited the *Washburn Review* his senior year and left for Columbia. He never returned home for any significant length of time. After he took a degree at Columbia, he served as cable editor of the New York *Herald Tribune,* married Ella Waldron, and had two children. In 1922, he took his family to West Palm Beach, Florida. He bought his own newspaper there and moved it to Stuart, a nearby town. Edwin took up permanent residence in Stuart as a colorful editor and later as a national expert on flowering trees. But his life was troubled. His wife ran off with a lover in 1926 and took the children with her. In 1928, he married Patricia Underhill, a devout Christian Scientist. The couple experienced serious difficulties raising Patricia's children from a prior marriage. Despite these and other problems, however, Edwin tried to avoid asking his parents for even minimal assistance. Flo and Charles worried about him constantly but acknowledged that they simply did not know what they could do for him.[55]

Even before the chemical explosion, Edwin had been prone to erratic behavior and had run away from home repeatedly. On one occasion as a young child, he had rested his hand on a red-hot stove and burned it severely. Another time, he cut off the end of his thumb, and Charles rushed home to sew it on. In the months before the test tube incident, he often carried powerful chemicals and performed tricks with them. Accident prone, Edwin seemed to be sending signals to his parents and his brothers in advance of the 1915 mishap.[56]

Some of these advance signals are probably common to middle children. Lacking a first or last spot in the sibling order, they often tend to feel that they lack a unique place in the family, that they are not special. According to some sociological research, many try to call attention to themselves in odd ways and eventually move away or opt for a career different from those of others in the family. This research does not explain fully Edwin's despair. Beyond the usual social difficulties of the middle child, Edwin belonged neither to the Flo-Karl connection nor to Charles's league with Will.[57]

V

The desperateness of Edwin's situation should not promote an exaggerated view of Menninger family tensions. Just as Charles had learned to defer to Flo, the alliance he established with Will usually deferred to the alliance of the mother with Karl. Consequently, the Menningers were not a particularly disunited family. Indeed, before Edwin's departure, all five members felt strong commonalities that gave family life, in Karl's words, "a certain belonging quality to it." There was a regular family routine: rising and chores at 5:30, breakfast at 7:00, dinner at 12:30, supper at 6:30, and a Sunday afternoon family outing. Reflecting Flo's "practical Christianity," a religious schedule also drew the Menningers together. There were Sunday morning church services and recitations of Biblical passages at the start of every meal. The family often sang "Jesus Wants Me for a Sunbeam" and shared a sense of special election to shoulder God's duties.[58]

According to Walker Winslow, another sign of family cohesion was in mood swings that the Menningers experienced in common. At certain points—often *but not always* when home life was particularly troubled— the family would turn inward and focus on private matters. The difficult childbirth years of the 1890s, the period of Edwin's chemistry accident and departure, and the 1939–41 years, when Karl turned against Flo by deciding to divorce his wife, were among those intervals. At other times, the family's mood was expansive, reaching out to the community, as when Charles became a prominent Topeka citizen while Flo developed a reputation for Bible studies. The half decade following Flo's death in 1945 represented another enthusiastic, outward-reaching period of missionary fervor: the family turned the clinic into an international educational center.[59]

However, it is hazardous to consider these family cycles as polarities. Quite the contrary, the family's preoccupations with private and external issues were only matters of degree. In almost every situation, the private, intrafamilial issue conditioned the public, missionary venture, while the public venture influenced private concerns. This was particularly evident in the family's habit of reaching out to somewhat troubled or disoriented people and bringing them home as boarders.

Will Kercher, the first boarder, came in 1895. Others followed until the early 1940s, often as many as four or five at one time. The most striking quality these boarders shared was their need for medical or economic assistance and, especially, emotional support. This reflected Charles's and Flo's childhood experiences. Charles's father was accustomed to visiting the Tell City, Indiana, courthouse whenever a hearing for a homeless child was scheduled. The judge would appoint him as temporary guardian, and the Menninger family would care for the child until August could arrange for a permanent home. The Menninger dwelling was, in a sense, a public orphanage. Flo's memories of her grandfather Heikes were analogous: "it was his lifelong habit to help anyone he thought needed it if they asked him to do so." It was predictable that he would take in Amanda and her children when her husband died. But grandfather Heikes was also disposed to offering food and shelter to any needy passerby. Flo also recalled that when Amanda moved her family to central Kansas, they were taken in as boarders at the small prairie house of Jackson and Jane Coulson. Once the family established itself on a farm near Abilene, Amanda always boarded the local schoolteacher.[60]

In large measure, Charles and Flo were influenced by the nineteenth-century boardinghouse tradition. By living closely with a pious family, sharing meals and lodgings, the boarders were to benefit from salutary examples of morality and social propriety. By the end of the century, however, this tradition was disappearing. In a number of cities, the boardinghouse was gradually supplanted by the lodging house, which simply rented out sleeping rooms; the roomer obtained his meals and social life outside the dwelling. In parts of Kansas, the boarder without much money might even have to seek lodging in a dirty and ill-run "hospital." Despite these general changes, Charles and Flo were committed to the boardinghouse tradition. Three months after they wed, the couple jumped at the opportunity to help Flo's mother operate a boardinghouse in Holton, Kansas. They ran it like a family dormitory for financially disadvantaged students in the vicinity. Flo cooked, while Charles made beds and attended to the laundry. The boarders were charged so little, Flo recalled, that "it was impossible to realize any profit."[61]

As she and Charles began to take in boarders in the 1890s, Flo felt that the practice was inseparable from general service to the unfortunate.

Indeed, when she had taught low-income children at Topeka's Branner School, while planning with Charles to open their home to boarders, Flo persuaded a local missionary society to provide clothing for her school-children's families and helped their mothers with household chores.[62]

As the person principally in charge of the boarders, Flo regarded the practice as part of her general commitment to missionary benevolence, which grew stronger as the early warmth and enthusiasm in her marriage began to ebb. Charles supported her in this and in all her benevolent ventures. He approved of the reforms and recognized that his wife's activities eased family tensions. His sons also supported their mother in these ventures. But boarding differed from Flo's other missionary activities in one respect: the beneficiaries lived with her family.

One advantage of this was to remedy a certain sense of inadequacy the Menningers felt at being cut off from their extended families. To be sure, Flo and Charles had chosen to make this break. And they sensed how it actually helped to unify the five of them. But the decision to very nearly sever links with parents and relatives was also the source of considerable distress. This helps to explain why a number of the boarders were relatives in need. When Flo's brother Dave and his wife and child became ill with typhoid fever, for instance, the Menningers opened up beds in their front room for them. Learning that Will Kercher, the fourteen-year-old son of one of Charles's sisters, had dropped out of school and was suffering from emotional problems, the Menningers took him in and attended to his education. Later, they did the same for Charlie Menninger, the distressed adolescent son of Charles's older brother. Psychiatrist Murray Bowen and his colleagues at the Georgetown Family Center have observed that people who feel cut off in this way from their families of origin are often deeply desirous of mending the "damage," but not by reestablishing fully extended family bonds. Rather, repair comes by forging substitute families. The stream of relatives as boarders in the Menninger home helped accomplish this.[63]

A second benefit from the boarders was financial. In nineteenth-century American cities, there were economic incentives for boarding. The host secured physical labor and sometimes even limited boarding fees in exchange for food and lodging. Certainly, the opportunity of making money was not lost on Flo, for she was always apprehensive about the economic survival of her family. But as Charles's medical practice developed and Flo devoted most of her time to her Bible study program, her more pressing need was for boarders who could care for her three children and attend to household chores. Will Kercher was taken in to milk the cow, fire the furnace, cook, attend to the washing, and keep "track of the children when we went to a lecture" or other activity. Two local Negro boys, Frank Delancey and Frank Preer, were invited to live with the family almost exclusively to do errands, to help Flo with housework, and to attend to her sons. Foy Ernest, a disoriented Spanish-American War volunteer, met the Menningers when he was stationed in Topeka. He had no parents, and after his discharge, the family took him in and provided him with emotional support. He performed many household chores and milked the cow.[64]

The third benefit of boarders was educational. Flo and Charles had been teachers. They always loved study for self-improvement and sought to imbue this orientation in their children. Quite consciously, they recruited several boarders who might "elevate" the family. A few were Biblical authorities, who would set a good example for the boys and help Flo improve her Bible classes. Some, like Annie Bundy and Myrtie Radcliffe, were musicians, and Charles always considered it a great honor to have them in his home. Periodically, the Menningers put on "An Evening of Music and Art" for their friends, and these always featured the musician or artist who happened to be boarding with them.[65]

Boarders made domestic life considerably more pleasant than it might have been. When sundry pressures seemed to turn the Menningers in upon themselves, the presence of outsiders made the interval less difficult than it would have been with the two family alliances confronting each other. At the same time, boarding proved to be an excellent outlet for the family's benevolent missionary impulse. Flo's autobiography also cites subtler contributions the boarders made to family life. When she acknowledged, for example, that Clara Louise was an inappropriate name for her third son, Will Kercher offered a solution. "Cut out the Louise and call him Will, after me." Flo agreed.

On May 30, 1903, heavy rains swelled the Kaw River to seventeen feet above flood stage, and 23,000 Topekans were driven from their homes. As he rushed about town on medical emergencies, Charles recognized that efforts to aid the victims were neither systematic nor effective. Seeing thousands of people with neither food nor shelter, Charles telephoned home. He told his wife that seventeen victims were on their way to their house: "we'll have to take care of them." Over thirty arrived, and the Menninger family fed and housed them for a week. The children among these victims came down with measles, and the Menningers ran a "hospital" for them for several more weeks. Their household relief effort was very well organized. Charles took charge of the medical care. Flo administered a regular meal schedule and called upon members of her Bible classes for labor plus donations, clothes, and bedding. The three young boys were impressed by the way their parents conducted this relief effort. They played with the children and went on errands for their mother to find additional clothing and food. Edwin noted that the relief venture resembled the family practice of taking in unfortunate boarders, if on a larger scale.[66]

Grace Lonegram Tanner was a five- or six-year-old orphan who had come to the Menninger house as a flood victim. Flo saw in her the daughter she wanted. Consistent with nineteenth-century gender attitudes, Flo assumed that Grace would provide "the refining influence of a sister" for her sons. As well, she may have hoped that Grace might propagate her values more fully than her eldest son did. But Flo was not to have her daughter. The three boys quarreled constantly with Grace and accused her of telling lies. They ganged up against her and made family life exceedingly unpleasant. Karl and Edwin told their parents that they did not want Grace as a permanent family member. Flo herself had a difficult time tolerating Grace's apparent dishonesty and was appalled by her squabbles with her sons. After a year, adoption proceedings were halted, and Grace was placed elsewhere.[67]

Pearl May Boam was the last boarder to enter the Menninger home before Charles and Karl launched their clinic. She had been a member of one of Flo's Bible classes. Her mother was long dead. She had been quite dependent on her father, a local physician, and dropped out of school at the end of eighth grade to take care of him. When he died, she felt adrift. In 1917, Flo and Charles spotted Pearl in a local hospital, recovering from an appendix operation. She was acutely depressed and lacked the will to recover. They took her for a ride and then home for the night. Both sensed that familial support might enhance her spirits and aid her recovery; they urged her to stay. She took well to the household, recovered quickly, and, according to Flo, "has been a comfort and a good daughter to both of us ever since." Charles agreed; for decades, he referred to her as "Pearl May Boam, my daughter."[68]

Although Pearl, twenty-nine or thirty in 1917, was never adopted, she stayed with the Menningers considerably longer than any other boarder. The family was willing to open itself to her in ways it would not to Grace Tanner. Several factors explain why. The Menningers needed Pearl for labor considerably more than they had their earlier boarders. Flo had temporarily lost the use of her hands, owing to undiagnosed causes. Pearl attended to Flo's chores and even dressed and cared for her until she recovered. A warm, courteous, and intensely devout doctor's daughter, experienced in household management, Pearl performed so well that Flo felt no need to resume many of her domestic duties when she regained full use of her hands. As well, Pearl arrived just as the Menninger sons were departing to pursue their education. Her presence as a "daughter" of an aging couple, who would always remain home to manage their household (as their sons had not), may have helped to compensate for the departure of the boys.[69]

Over the years, the Menninger house welcomed others. Flo's Bible classes had initially been conducted there. So had Will's Boy Scout meetings, Edwin's boys' group, and the Washburn Alpha Delta fraternity. Charles hosted medical society gatherings there, and Flo showed art reproductions to members of the community. Years before the Menningers opened their clinic, the family was taking in needy and sometimes disoriented people and was staging diverse "outpatient" gatherings for the benefit of the local citizenry. It was as if this family were a small community center that refused to close its doors despite internal disturbances.[70]

VI

It did not follow that a Topeka-based neuropsychiatric clinic would inevitably evolve from this family tradition of social services. During the first decade of the century, Charles made two trips, one to Rochester, Minnesota, and the other to Boston. Experiences there left him with an intense desire to establish a group medical practice of some sort in Topeka. In Rochester, a town scarcely one fifth the size of his own, he was impressed by the collective surgical and diagnostic innovations of the Mayos, a father and two sons. In Boston, he was even more impressed by the group practice of Elliott Proctor Joslin. Charles had been particularly interested in diet control and other means of keeping diabetic patients alive, and Joslin was a pioneer in the pre-insulin treatment of the disease. He had taken some young physicians into his Bay State Road home to assist him with his practice. Charles was disturbed to learn that one of the most promising of them had broken away from Joslin. The Mayo visit seemed to suggest that sons were more likely than junior physicians to be loyal. Still, the importance of group practice in explaining Joslin's progress was not lost on Charles. After insulin treatment became available, he "went back to Josselyn [*sic*] and studied again with him for several weeks to learn how to use it" in a group treatment setting. Charles became increasingly certain after his trips to Rochester and Boston that "the responsibility and the loneliness of my work seemed almost too much to bear. . . . Over and over again I thought, 'I wish I could talk

to some other doctor about this. I wish I knew where to go for help.' "
By the outbreak of World War I, Charles had decided to try to establish
"a group like a family." If Karl and Will would join him, as the Mayo sons
had joined their father, and other young doctors came into his group
practice, as they had with Joslin, then camaraderie and more diversified
medical knowledge would be assured.[71]

Because of his rapport with Will, Charles had some hope of eventually recruiting him for his group practice. But just as Charles deferred
regularly to Flo, Will had become accustomed to following Karl. If Karl
refused to pursue medicine and return home to practice with him,
Charles knew that he might lose Will as well.[72]

This pointed to a subtle but significant change within the family as
Charles's plan took hold. Up to then, Karl had been only a junior partner
in the family's dominant alliance. But as Flo became preoccupied with her
Bible studies, Karl seemed to operate less explicitly within her shadow or
from her strength. With the relaxation of his mother's overbearing guidance and restraint, Karl tried his own wings. Slowly replacing Flo as the
center of family attention, he looked to his father and brothers for an
image of himself that he had craved since early childhood—one of virtue,
competency, and capability. As Karl was to discover in his first extended
psychoanalysis, he had come, more and more, to "seek for myself world
adulation . . . everyone must praise me and tell me I'm alright and fine
etc. when I secretly know better." As Charles drew closer to his sons, he,
too, sensed that despite his fondness for Will, he would have to acknowledge in Karl a certain crucial hegemony of the sort that he had long
accorded his wife.[73]

Because Karl was becoming central to family life, Charles hoped his
eldest son would pursue a medical career. Flo, on the other hand, had
urged him to study business and become a prosperous banker. While he
studied at the University of Wisconsin, however, Karl often conducted
Sunday church services in nearby rural communities. That, plus participation in the Student Volunteer Movement of idealistic Christian youth,
had disposed him to consider a ministerial and missionary career. He felt
that such a course might exemplify his mother's brand of "practical
Christianity." Flo argued that the ministry was insufficiently practical. She
was supported by Grace Gaines, a bright and attractive Washburn student
and Karl's fiancée. A Topeka dentist and family friend, Fred Koester,
made the same point when Karl visited him late in the summer of 1913.
Koester noted that a medical practice like Karl's father's represented a
more promising career. As he left Koester's office, Karl agreed: "I am
going to become a doctor." Although Charles was overjoyed, he realized

that Karl would not necessarily join him in a medical partnership. After all, they had never been close.[74]

According to a widely accepted account of events, Karl finished Harvard Medical School and went to Boston Psychopathic Hospital in 1918 to study neuropsychiatry under the renowned Elmer Ernest Southard. Southard took to the bright young resident, and Karl came to venerate his mentor. Consequently (the story goes), he took Southard's advice in November 1918 to return home and establish a mental health facility with his father: "Go home and establish the Clinic that your father has dreamed of. . . . Teach people what psychiatry can and should do." However, this account of the formation of the Menninger family practice overlooks an obvious detail: Southard could not have assumed that Charles wanted to form a neuropsychiatric group practice. He had met Charles and knew of his preference for internal medicine generally or perhaps a group diabetes specialty. But if Southard did not tell Karl to satisfy his father's dreams for a neuropsychiatric clinic, Charles was not opposed to such a facility. He wanted to have his oldest son as his partner and was not going to let Karl's interest in neuropsychiatry stand in the way of this larger goal. More fundamentally, the accepted account of the origin of the partnership makes little of the complex factors developing over many years that were moving Karl toward a mental health specialty and toward a working relationship with his father.[75]

Publicly, Karl propagated the accepted explanation for the origins of his partnership with his father. In private, however, he admitted that he repeated that story because people liked to hear it, and, in fact, the explanation only skimmed the surface. Karl acknowledged that his interest in the mentally unbalanced really began when his mother taught him and his brothers to sing "Rescue the Perishing." He recalled how his family, oriented strongly toward pious missionary ventures, had "rescued" a number of outsiders—like Will Kercher, Charlie Menninger, and Grace Tanner—who had been mentally unbalanced or at least very troubled when the family took them in. Karl even remembered how one of the earliest boarders, Foy Ernest, introduced him to psychiatry. While the rest of the family was upstairs under a scarlet fever quarantine, he and Ernest had tried to make sense of materials downstairs on the multiple personality and on hypnotic techniques.[76]

Despite Karl's early fascination with psychiatric processes, however, when he enrolled in Washburn College as a freshman in 1910, he heeded his mother's admonitions about the practical side of "practical Christianity" and majored in business. He was extremely studious and rather unsocial. A good friend belonged to the Phi Delta fraternity, and Karl expected to be asked to rush, but no invitation came. Karl learned that the friend had voted against him on the ground that he was feebleminded; the friend had convinced other members to oppose Karl. Phi Delta had rejected this bright freshman, and Karl was devastated: "I never got over the hurt." It seemed to rekindle his sense of inadequacy. It also reawakened another long-standing concern—"the sense of rejection" that the mentally unbalanced feel. In addition, the fraternity turndown made him more power conscious and political. He determined to organize and control groups so that he might less often feel victimized by them: "I not only organized a fraternity but I organized several other societies, and as I grew older I began to feel the necessity of them."[77]

Karl transferred to the University of Wisconsin to complete his college course, and he decided to go to medical school. Charles was happy that his son wanted to become a doctor. Recalling his own inadequate homeopathic training, Charles claimed that he "chose Harvard for Karl. . . . I saw my own deficiencies and wanted him to get the best." Given family dynamics, it is more likely that Charles suggested Harvard and Karl found merit in the proposal. The son was particularly pleased at his father's pledge of financial support.[78]

Karl did not excel at Harvard Medical School. He averaged a low B and received six B's and six C's during his fourth year. On a 100-point scale, he scored 64 and 84 on his two general examinations. Moreover, he took a C in psychiatry and considered joining a foreign missionary society as a medical practitioner. One day in 1915, however, he attended a lecture by Louisville Emerson at the nearby Massachusetts General Hospital. Emerson, one of the staff psychologists and a founding member of the Boston Psychoanalytic Society, expounded Freud's ideas. Like a great many Americans in their initial reactions to psychoanalysis, Karl found Freud's emphasis on sexual aspects of early childhood "fishy." Nonetheless, he was fascinated as Emerson expounded Freud's general theories on the importance of subconscious factors in the maladies of lost souls. He approached Emerson after the lecture, and the two talked freely about unconscious psychological symptoms of physical abnormalities. Emerson also told the young medical student that he was not the only American hospital practitioner sympathetic to Freud. Though Karl found psychoanalysis a vast improvement over the rigid categorization of mental diseases that passed as psychiatry at Harvard, he was not yet won over to a neuropsychiatric specialty as the best way to promote the family commitment to helping the needy.[79]

When Karl graduated from medical school, Charles felt that the next task was to bring his son closer to home for his internship. Their relationship was better than it had been in some time. Charles realized that Karl had some interest in surgery and learned that Kansas City General Hospital, only seventy miles away, had a good surgery program. Consequently, he urged the hospital superintendent to facilitate admission procedures. Perhaps because Charles never pressured his son to accept the Kansas City internship, Karl acquiesced. He arrived at Kansas City General in 1917, disposed to specializing in surgery somewhat more than in psychiatry.[80]

Within a matter of weeks, however, Karl found himself fascinated by patients with neurological ills (particularly neurosyphilis) and other brain-related problems. Many of these patients were derelicts that the police brought to the hospital simply to keep them off the streets. Karl found that despite ineffective medical techniques, some of them "did improve a little." The physician's attitude of caring and concern seemed more crucial than his scientific learning. "This impressed me a great deal," said Karl, who remembered how his family had cared for distressed boarders. In 1918, Karl decided to accept the advice of Lawson Lowrey, a close friend, and applied for a residency at Boston Psychopathic Hospital. There he met its well-known director, Elmer Ernest Southard.[81]

Southard taught Karl how to diagnose a mental malady by exclusion of less than plausible diagnostic possibilities. In the process, he taught Karl to photograph diverse brains and to compare the structures in the photographs in order to locate pathology in a specific brain. Southard also taught Karl how to preside over an interdisciplinary staff conference, where, beyond the psychiatrist's medical report, a psychologist presented his test results and a social worker reported on the patient's family and community life. Southard even sold Karl on the merits of the mental hygiene movement in its crusade against custodial psychiatry. Finally, Southard encouraged Karl to write up his most instructive cases for publication, out of a sense of professional obligation.[82]

Karl studied with Southard for little more than six months. Even before that, he had been less than enchanted with the descriptive nineteenth-century approach to psychiatry, which characterized visible abnormalities and correlated them to standard diagnostic labels. Consequently, he detected a shortcoming in Southard early in his residency, which became increasingly disturbing. The man was a "superficialist," who "felt that the nature of things was patently apparent even on the surface if one but looked carefully." Karl knew that he himself was moving from "superficialism" to "deep subsurface" disturbances that had been triggered by "surface" abnormalities. When Southard died unexpectedly in 1920, Karl never considered working with another "superficialist." He turned to Smith Ely Jelliffe, an American psychoanalytic pioneer, who "took me under his wing." As he conversed with Jelliffe, Karl acknowledged the truth in the new mentor's claim that Southard "never got into the other fellow's skin."[83]

What impressed Karl with Southard were his personal qualities more than his psychiatric lessons. Southard allowed a perennially insecure young man whose quick wit had sometimes been regarded as insolence to feel that his ideas were "brilliant and important." Southard was "the first man of any note who took a serious interest" in Karl and gave him the sense that he could "come up with new combinations to apply to old problems." Karl knew that Southard, much like his mother, regarded him as his "favorite child"; he took special joy in the fact that Southard "was more intimate with me than with any of them" (the other residents). Feeling in his mentor's presence reassured as rarely before, Karl "spent every available moment with him."[84]

Evenings off the hospital grounds were often crucial to the relationship. Southard was less than content with his wife and was not eager to return home at the close of the workday. After two years of marriage to Grace Gaines, Karl was able to empathize with Southard. An imaginative mathematics major at Washburn, Grace had reverted to entirely domestic interests. But she had no children, and even the most diligent maintenance of their small lodgings could not fill her day. Karl recognized that Grace was discontent but found it easier to stay away. Indeed, he discovered that whereas his appetite lagged when he was with Grace, he could consume hearty dinners with Southard at restaurants near the hospital. After dinner, the two often enjoyed a contest at a local chess club or simply walked through the streets of Boston. Because of the strongly reassuring quality of these hours together, in which the young doctor could feel his own worth reflected in his mentor's warmth and respect, he was shattered by Southard's premature death at forty-three. "When Southard died," Karl reminisced, "a light went out of me."[85]

Clearly, the familiar narrative line in medical biography, where the prominent and dispassionate mentor advises the promising young resident on his future professional course, is inappropriate here. Southard's emotional tone was more important than the professional content of his advice when he told Karl in November 1918 to return to Topeka to establish a medical partnership with his father. Southard was essentially suggesting to Karl that Charles would be able to reassure and sustain him as the mentor had done.[86]

Karl measured Southard's advice. Although his father was still closest to Will, Charles had been coming to regard Karl as an equal in the alliance with his mother. Just as Charles had supported Flo's Bible studies career, he had committed himself to Karl's professional future. When the twenty-one-year-old son told him of the decision to be a physician, he had responded in an emotionally supportive way that Karl found moving.[87]

As he pondered Southard's advice, Karl remembered, too, that Charles had gone on vacation the previous summer and let him take over his medical practice. Karl regarded this as an important demonstration of trust and support. On his last day of filling in for his father, he wrote Charles a letter that amounted to a long list of recommendations. Pleased that Karl's letter praised him for his "self-education" and "ultra-progressive" receptivity to innovation, Charles assured Karl that he regarded all the recommendations as cogent; he planned on implementing as many as possible. At this point (months before Southard advised him to return), Karl realized that he had been so pleased with the respect, understanding, and support from his father that he had very nearly committed himself to a medical partnership. He wrote to Charles that "nowhere in the world will I get the help and pleasure from medical co-operation that I will from working with [my] father."[88]

Thus, as Karl reflected on Southard's suggestion that he return to Topeka, he found the emotional content of the proposal altogether satisfying. But would the father let the son specialize in the field of the mentor? More important, in view of Charles's interest in internal medicine and his two models for group practice (Mayo and Joslin), would he be receptive to a partnership that specialized in emotional cases? Would "probably the leading man in the specialty of internal medicine and diagnosis in this state" allow the new family firm to focus on the primary interest of the novice son?[89]

Although he would have preferred a group practice in internal medicine, Charles promptly and convincingly assured Karl that his neuropsychiatric practice would become the specialty of their group. Although Karl did not quite know it at the time, Charles would have given a great deal more for his oldest and youngest sons to return to Topeka. He had a sure sense, now, of a family medical calling; there was a pious meliorative mission that he and his sons had very nearly been elected to perform. The specific kind of work was less than crucial. Moreover, Charles had some interest in mental abnormalities. Besides his attention to his boarders, he had written a paper (in 1890) on "The Insanity of Hamlet," in which he sought to delineate Hamlet's precise mental state. He had studied Charcot on hypnosis as a treatment and had visited regularly with his friend B. D. Eastman, the superintendent of Topeka State (Mental) Hospital. From this background and from everyday horse-and-buggy doctoring, he realized that a good many of his patients with no detectable physical ills suffered from emotional distress. And though he had never called attention to it, he had even attempted to treat a few obvious mental cases. Thus, Charles could sincerely respond to Karl that he found neuropsychiatry both a "most interesting field" and a developing one. Moreover, he recognized that his "practice had grown large enough to enable us to make a good living while we pioneered in this new specialty."[90]

"I concluded that I must gradually relinquish my work and help him in every way to rise," Charles reminisced. "I was responsible for his birth and I felt that I ought to be responsible for his development in medicine." Charles's choice of words was instructive. In some measure, he had invoked the language of Victorian literature that designated the wife's proper sphere supportive of her menfolk. He would "relinquish" a career to help the son for whose "birth" he was "responsible" to "develop" and to "rise," just as the Victorian wife and mother was expected to "relinquish" career opportunities to help her sons to "develop" and her husband to "rise" in his career. But Charles was not only describing his role as the supportive wife and mother. It is significant that he also used language prescribed for the Victorian husband and father who supervised his son's career: "I ought to be responsible for his development in medicine."[91]

A family alliance system that accorded the oldest son senior status, plus Charles's emotional support, were crucial, then, in enticing Karl back to Topeka. He arrived from Boston Psychopathic Hospital in June 1919, moved into his father's office, and claimed that he was ready to commence a lifelong partnership. But between then and Southard's death, he took trips back to Boston to "visit." Only when his mentor died, in February 1920, was he irrevocably committed to Topeka.[92]

Family patterns seemed to be repeating themselves. Late in 1892, Flo had quit her teaching job to bear and raise her first son. Twenty-six years later, Charles was relinquishing his medical practice to help in the development of that same son. A Karl-centered family was to become a Karl-centered family business. Soon it came to be called the Menninger Clinic.

CHAPTER TWO

Family Configurations

At the time Karl Menninger established a partnership with his father, in June of 1919, American psychiatrists were in the midst of a crisis concerning their place in society. The crisis had taken root late in the nineteenth century, when psychiatrists began to view themselves as representatives of a backward medical specialty, one that was out of touch with the more advanced scientific directions of the medical profession. Most psychiatrists had worked in the increasingly crowded state mental hospitals, where the preponderance of patients' illnesses—senility, paresis, mental retardation, brain tumors, and the like—could not be cured or palliated by existing medical therapeutics. The majority of patients simply needed custodial care—food, shelter, friendship, and some chores so they would feel useful—and staff psychiatrists struggled with variable success at providing these basics. The problem was that, with the discovery of the germ theory of disease and related breakthroughs of the scientific revolution, the key figures in many other medical specialties were thinking of cures rather than custodial comforts.

Excited by the knowledge that they could finally fight certain infectious diseases and make surgery a safer and less painful procedure, medical and surgical specialists came to chide their psychiatric colleagues for mere patient management. Neurologists criticized psychiatrists for deficient knowledge of anatomy and pathology. Other specialists claimed that psychiatrists had no theories of mental disease, conducted little scientific research, and enjoyed only minimal contacts with medical schools and general hospitals. Reflecting this near-outcast status, psychiatrists were among the lowest-paid specialists. When medical schools redesigned their curricula to reflect the scientific revolution, few of them bothered to incorporate psychiatric courses.[1]

During the early years of the twentieth century, psychiatrists struggled in diverse ways to resolve this crisis within their profession. As leaders of a "new psychiatry" intent on meeting the challenge, men like Adolf Meyer, William Alanson White, Lewellys F. Barker, and Karl's mentor, Elmer Ernest Southard, urged their colleagues to focus more on disease and less on patients, more on medical therapeutics and less on custodial care. Following these suggestions, a number of the more ambitious and scientific psychiatrists moved from the state asylums to new research institutes, to innovative general hospitals, to medical schools, to new child guidance clinics, and even to private offices. They hoped to work more actively with a smaller (often wealthier) patient population, which suffered from more curable illnesses than those found in the state hospitals—illnesses such as neuroses and the early or more treatable stages of psychoses, depressions, and alcoholism. They also hoped to find time for research and perhaps some teaching.

With this more active and cure-oriented attitude, the "new psychiatrists" and their followers slowly won for their profession during the first three decades of the century a more conspicuous place within medical school curricula, in research centers, and on the wards of general hospitals. Many also became active in the mental hygiene movement, where they sought to spread the most advanced knowledge on the prevention and cure of mental abnormalities to schools, courts, prisons, and other community agencies. If their therapies and research impressed many prison wardens, judges, social workers, and medical colleagues, a few of the "new psychiatrists" acknowledged privately that the state of actual psychiatric knowledge was not terribly different in 1920 from what it had been in 1880. Even the theories of Freud and Jung had yet to register a major impact. In a paper directed to his psychiatric colleagues and published in the *Journal of the American Medical Association,* I. S. Wechsler maintained that despite these and other new theories advanced and new evidence accumulated, "the ultimate cause or causes of nervous and mental diseases is [still] unknown." Consequently, "it ill benefits us to play the role of high priests."[2]

But Meyer, Southard, and other "new psychiatrists" were more optimistic than Wechsler about their therapies and especially about the knowledge their research would yield. They also knew that they had to play the part of high priests if they were to gain legitimacy within the increasingly scientific medical profession. Although they were encouraged by their success with medical school curricula and community agencies and at initiating research projects, several of the "new psychiatrists" envisioned a hospital specializing in research, teaching, and the cure of mental illness as the most promising avenue for professional revitalization. As the church had been the symbolic center of Western society in

the medieval world and the legislative hall may have been in the nineteenth century, so, they perceived, the hospital would eventually be in the
twentieth century. Psychiatric specialty wards in general hospitals were
important to that vision, and "new psychiatrists" campaigned for them.
On these wards, mental illness could be treated just as seriously and
urgently as were acute diseases of the lungs or the stomach in other
wards. The well-known Pavilion F of the Albany (New York) Hospital,
established in 1899, and the psychopathic ward at the University of Michi-
gan Hospital, inaugurated two years later, were early examples of the
specialty wards. But for the most prominent and influential "new psychiatrists," the big prize was a whole new type of psychiatric hospital. It would
admit a small and rather exclusive clientele in the early or acute stages
of mental disease. These patients could be treated intensively and then
released. With custodial requirements thus eliminated, staff efforts could
center on research and teaching. Once this sort of facility was established,
the psychiatric profession could occupy a high place in medicine.[3]

Not all of the psychiatric specialty hospitals developed between
roughly 1900 and 1925 were actually new. Several were simply older
institutions that redefined their missions and abandoned their custodial
care. Although a disproportionate number were private institutions,
some of the more prominent were not. St. Elizabeths Hospital in Washington, D.C., was a 4,800-bed federal facility, which William Alanson
White took charge of in 1903. White secured adequate federal funding,
hired a large and competent medical staff, and encouraged psychoanalytically oriented research and teaching. Even though it was much larger
than most of the other hospitals promoted by the "new psychiatry," St.
Elizabeths gained recognition within the medical profession as a proficient research and treatment facility.[4]

Boston Psychopathic Hospital was another of the few facilities in the
public sector that exemplified the new psychiatric spirit. It opened in
1912 as a department of Boston State Hospital, to provide intensive care
for patients in the early but acute stages of their illnesses. Its director,
Southard, drew upon its close relationship with Harvard Medical School
to exclude most chronic patients and to limit the number of beds. By the
time Karl Menninger arrived as a resident in 1918, it was regarded as a
model for what the new psychiatric hospital should be—a facility for
comprehensive diagnosis and quick but intensive treatment. If the patient
improved, he was discharged. If he remained the same or regressed, he
was retained only if he could provide the staff with significant instructional or research opportunities. Most unimproved patients were transferred to a regular state hospital for long-term care.[5]

For the most part, however, the psychiatric specialty hospitals were private undertakings. Reliable and comprehensive historical data on most of these facilities are quite scarce. According to Bureau of the Census records, between 1911 and 1923 the private institutions proliferated significantly—from 118 to 213. Yet the proportion of the total number of institutionalized mental patients that they cared for decreased—from nearly 4 percent to less than 3.5 percent. Public (primarily state) hospitals had not only increased in numbers (from 248 in 1910 to 313 in 1923); by 1923, they were caring for over 96 percent of the patient population. Compared to the public hospitals, almost all of the private institutions were quite elitist. Because they did not have the stigma of the public hospitals, voluntary admission of patients was considerably greater. However, as psychiatrist Walter Bromberg recalled from his visits to many of these facilities, the modes of treatment for the overwhelming majority "functioned in a way similar to the state hospitals." Still, patients came to them and their reputations grew, owing to "the attention and comfort they provided patients and in the appurtenances they offered." In a 1935 article on America's private mental hospitals, Dwight Macdonald agreed with Bromberg. Despite their public proclamations, he noted, only a small proportion of these facilities were actually intent on rendering cures through active programs for therapy, teaching, and research. Concentrated almost entirely within the northeastern and middle Atlantic states, the cure-oriented private hospitals therefore represented the elite within an assuredly elite cluster of institutions. Committed like Southard to intensive, cure-directed psychiatry within an institutional setting, Karl made special visits to several of these facilities shortly after he returned to Topeka in 1919. More than the state-supported Boston Psychopathic Hospital, they would serve as models for the type of facility he would proceed to develop.[6]

Karl was especially impressed with the Henry Phipps Psychiatric Clinic. Phipps was affiliated with Johns Hopkins in Baltimore, the most prestigious medical school in the country. Since it opened in 1913, it had been regarded as a model institution for the elite private hospitals. Adolf Meyer provided leadership and insisted that Phipps was dedicated to curing mental patients regardless of financial costs or the seriousness of their problems. With this perspective, he was less than pleased at certain financial constraints within which he had to operate as the result of "inadequate feeding" from the Johns Hopkins medical complex. In administering therapy, Meyer relied on his principles of "psychobiology." These placed the patient's specific psychological and physical disorders within the context of his general life style. Subordinating neither the

physical to the emotional nor the emotional to the physical, Meyer
stressed diagnosis and treatment within a holistic perspective. Finally, he
embraced the tradition of European mental health clinics, in which teaching, research, and patient care were complementary objectives—as they
were in many American internal medical clinics. Meyer encouraged all
three at the Phipps Clinic. Staff received education by administering
therapy under supervision, engaging in case conferences, using conference reports as a basis for research and publication, and participating in
seminars based on specific reading and writing assignments. This practical combination of therapy, teaching, and research yielded visible results—nearly one hundred staff papers and books during the clinic's first
six years. Meyer's holistic approach and the productivity of the Phipps
staff were not lost on Karl.[7]

If private "new psychiatry" hospitals all operated from pleasant campuses and practiced activist approaches to therapy designed to render
cures, they differed from one another in certain respects. Phipps was the
only one associated with a medical school. Whereas the Bloomingdale
Hospital in White Plains, New York, and the Hartford Retreat could both
admit over 250 patients—the capacity of some state facilities—most of
the private hospitals were considerably smaller. The Austen Riggs Center
in prosperous Stockbridge, Massachusetts, took in only forty. Chestnut
Lodge in Rockville, Maryland, admitted twenty-two, while the Harding
Hospital (formerly the Indianola Rest Home) in Columbus, Ohio, began
with only eight beds. Bloomingdale openly acknowledged a preference
that all but the Sheppard and Enoch Pratt Hospital in Towson, Maryland,
and the McLean Hospital near Boston shared. They wanted patients who
were "persons of education and social refinement." Indeed, Austen
Riggs accepted only mildly neurotic, cultured patients, who walked po-
litely through the small Berkshire town, attended the cultural events, and
frequented the local tennis courts. At Craig House in the hills above
Beacon, New York, the fifty patients were transported in chauffeur-driven
limousines, enjoyed their own golf course, and drank wine from the
hospital's private vineyards. At the Hartford Retreat, there were techni-
cally no patients, only "guests," who were free to enjoy the city's culture
and its gourmet restaurants. By 1915, Bloomingdale, too, had cultivated
the appearance of a private estate, with well-manicured trees and shrubs.
Eschewing the country club atmosphere of Craig House and the Hartford
Retreat, Chestnut Lodge resembled a rural farm. A substantial and attractive hospital building was surrounded by a grove of oak trees, where farm
animals wandered freely.[8]

Whether sizable or small, refined or rustic, the milieu of most of these elite facilities was designed to suit the tastes of a decidedly upper-class clientele. In Craig House a patient paid $150 a week. At Austen Riggs it was $70, well beyond middle-class means in the postwar years. Sheppard-Pratt stood out as the exception, owing to heavy subsidization of patient fees. In 1911, 37 percent of the patients paid an average of only $2.55 a week. By 1939, the average Sheppard patient was charged $38, still well below other private hospitals.[9]

As with Meyer at Phipps Clinic, the personality and values of the director usually determined the professional activities at the facility. Despite Meyer's renown, only Sheppard-Pratt and the McLean Hospital (under Frederick Packard) embraced his emphasis on research. At Sheppard-Pratt, both Edward Brush, who ran the institution from 1891 to 1920, and Ross McClure Chapman, superintendent in the decades that followed, were enthusiastic about Meyer's holistic "psychobiology." Brush emphasized "re-education" to teach the patient self-awareness, self-control, and the capacity to live with his own limitations. While Chapman was not averse to "re-education," he stressed a pleasing environment and emphasized the uniqueness of each patient. Austen Riggs also emphasized "re-education," with stress on books, assignments, and formal lectures to teach the patients to improve their ability to adjust to circumstances. C. Jonathan Slocum's "practical psychotherapy" at Craig House was also a form of "re-education." Slocum instructed his staff to advise patients in an encouraging and friendly manner. Occupational therapy and hydrotherapy could be useful as supplements to this advice. George Harding, Jr., emphasized Christ's teachings as the key to healthy living at his Seventh-Day Adventist Ohio facility and coupled this with approaches much like those at Craig House. At Bloomingdale, superintendent William Russell saw some value in formally instructing the patients in mental hygiene, but even more value in systematic programs in occupational and recreational therapy. At the Hartford Retreat, Whitefield N. Thompson and then his successor, C. C. Burleigh, stressed a supportive environment that the patient would find more relaxing than in the outside world. Burleigh encouraged each patient to find some area of creative expression—to write a novel, sculpt, paint, or perhaps prepare written commentaries concerning current events, with the help of supervisory staff.[10]

All of the superintendents entertained definite opinions about psychoanalysis as a relatively new and controversial treatment. Riggs and Slocum detested it, Brush, Harding, and Russell were fairly noncommittal, while Thompson and Burleigh relied on psychoanalytic insights somewhat sparingly. Frederick Packard brought it into McLean by the mid-1920s, if on a very modest level. When Chapman became director of Sheppard-Pratt in 1920, he emphasized Freud's "science" for the theoretical orientation of his treatment staff. In 1922, Chapman recruited Harry Stack Sullivan, who pressed for a sociological and interpersonal rather than a biological and biography-centered psychoanalytic perspective (in a marked departure from Freudian orthodoxy). On the other hand, Ernest Luther Bullard and especially his son Dexter were committed to a rather orthodox and comprehensive version of psychoanalysis at Chestnut Lodge.[11]

As Karl visited the small group of private facilities with active, cure-oriented treatment programs, he was exposed to a wide variety of therapeutic approaches. However, all stressed interpersonal relationships within pleasant environments. None did a great deal with potential somatic elements in mental disturbance, even though the scientific revolution had promoted greater attention to biology and chemistry in medical exploration. Professed dedication to scientific medicine and cures may have been sufficient, however. After all, criticism of psychiatry by other medical specialists receded as the new elite hospitals became known. In 1924, Owen Copp, a distinguished physician from the Pennsylvania Hospital, told the leaders of these private facilities that they were rendering an altruistic service by helping to align psychiatry with the medical profession in status, scientific spirit, and contributions to education and research. Even though they were serving a very small, affluent, and potentially curable segment of the population, few directors of these elite facilities were distressed about turning their backs on the state hospitals, where most psychiatric patients resided. As the Bloomingdale annual report for 1914 suggested, the private facility cared for "the more productive classes, and their restoration to usefulness is a distinct contribution to the public good." Two years earlier, Bloomingdale's annual report had characterized the state-hospital alternative as catering to "mere numbers" by allowing inept governmental regulation to retard therapy. Chapman and Sullivan of Sheppard-Pratt disagreed with such justifications for ignoring most of the mentally ill. But they stood almost entirely alone within private-hospital circles.[12]

Karl was impressed with his investigation of these private "new psychiatry" facilities. Their patient programs seemed to be the best in the country, the staffs were strong, and the institutions were winning the respect of the medical profession. Yet he was uneasy about the money that was lavished on buildings and grounds, often at the expense of treatment, staff upgrading, or research. He realized that a mansion-like physical plant was expected by the wealthy clientele; this worried him further. If he was going to do something significant with his career—to be a medical missionary much as his mother was a missionary in Biblical instruction—he would somehow have to reach the masses. By 1935, he boasted that his own hospital lacked the expensive physical facilities of his private competitors but that his staff development and treatment programs were better. Still, the problem of reaching beyond a few wealthy patients remained troublesome for Karl, much as it had been for Chapman and Sullivan.[13]

Since the overwhelming number of the elite hospitals were situated along the Atlantic coast, Karl anticipated little competition as he began to establish his own facilities in Topeka. Though there were no such hospitals in Kansas or any bordering state when he left Boston Psychopathic Hospital to join his father, he still had to confront a number of very serious problems.

I I

On his return to Kansas, the major problem Karl faced was how to avoid the fate of his predecessor, Topeka physician-neurologist W. S. Lindsay. A former assistant superintendent at Topeka State Hospital, Lindsay had resigned and entered private practice because that facility had become increasingly custodial. In 1910, he had had a two-story, eight-room building constructed on the grounds of Christ's Hospital, the city's most prominent general medical facility, to house those of his mental patients who required inpatient treatment. But townspeople protested against Lindsay's new building. A family living across from the hospital won a lawsuit against him on the ground that his patients disturbed and endangered the neighborhood. Then the city passed an ordinance prohibiting any structure from being used as a mental institution within five hundred feet of a residence. But earnings had been too sparse for Lindsay to afford to build again, outside the city. Consequently, he abandoned his hospital and moved his patients into the private home of a former state hospital attendant, who boarded them. This was an unsatisfactory setting for active therapy, and Lindsay soon abandoned his psychiatric practice. When Karl arrived from Boston to begin a partnership with his father, Lindsay told him that it was pointless to crusade for the "new psychiatry" in a town like Topeka.[14]

There were other serious problems. Karl knew that there were mentally disturbed people all over Kansas who needed help (the appalling number of rejections for military service on mental grounds suggested this). A private mental facility—a Kansas equivalent of the Phipps Clinic—was not necessarily the answer, for private hospitals of all sorts were experiencing financial difficulties throughout the state. Many owners had been forced to sell their interests to religious organizations or municipal authorities.[15]

Nor was the morale of the Kansas medical profession cause for encouragement in the immediate postwar years. Samuel Crumbine, who had almost single-handedly led a vigorous and effective public health crusade throughout the state and had given Kansas doctors pride in their profession, was gone. In the postwar years, the best-known physician was John Brinkley, a demagogue who announced over the radio that he could transplant goat glands to humans, rejuvenating their bodies while reducing enlarged prostates. The trend that made a folk hero of Brinkley fueled tremendous public opposition to Kansas doctors who sought to take up medical specialties. Public and press bemoaned the passing of the old family doctor in favor of the specialist who abandoned his community for the urban medical center. Popular opposition to psychiatric specialization was particularly keen. Kansans tended to assume that all mental illness was hereditary; some considered sterilization a more plausible remedy than psychiatric intervention.[16]

Thus, Karl was hardly encouraged to launch a private psychiatric hospital in Topeka. There were a number of private general sanitariums in Kansas City; some accepted mental patients. Over weekly lunches, Karl made friends with half a dozen Kansas City physicians, and they warned him of possible competition from these facilities in the years ahead. More important, they told him of serious talk in Kansas City medical circles of establishing a university-linked or private psychiatric hospital like some eastern institutions. They urged him to limit himself to a few hours with mental patients, in conjunction with a larger general practice.[17]

These obstacles to a Topeka-based neuropsychiatric specialty vexed young Menninger, for he had a family to support. Grace Gaines, whom he had married in 1916 while he was in medical school, was, like Karl's mother, an intelligent, well-organized, hard-working, and emotional woman. She was also practical and explained to her husband that neither a minister nor a doctor-missionary earned sufficient wages. As Flo became apprehensive that her influence over Karl was declining, she seemed pleased that in Grace she had an ally who might keep her son in line. Although Karl did not realize it at first, Grace differed from Flo in her affinity for domestic duties. She was exceedingly pleased by the birth of her first baby, Julia, shortly after she and Karl returned to Topeka. The child seemed to legitimate the importance Grace attached to home life.

An infant also caused her to press her husband, all the more, to be practical and attentive to domestic responsibilities, just as he was preparing to establish a risky medical enterprise.[18]

Karl proceeded slowly with his plans for a specialty clinic. After nearly a year in Charles's cramped quarters, father and son rented a downtown suite. Consistent with the pattern of the early household, where the passive alliance submitted to the dominant one, Charles quickly made it clear that his son was in charge. He insisted that Karl take the largest of the new offices and the larger salary, and did not protest when his son dismissed his longtime secretary. When Charles's Topeka medical colleagues chided him because Karl had ordered Wassermann tests run on patients to detect syphilis, he deferred to his son.[19]

As Charles was an internist, the Menningers' initial practice could not have been wholly psychiatric. Influenced by Flo's values, Karl's first goal was not to specialize but to make money. Charles continued to earn significant fees with his general practice and his work in internal medicine. Putting aside his interest in diabetes, the senior Menninger read the books and articles Karl recommended on neurology and new psychiatric concepts. Slowly, he began to apply what he learned. When Karl took on several local patients with apparent mental abnormalities that other doctors did not know how to treat, Charles had to work with them when his son was out of town. Otherwise, income would be lost, and his son would be angry with him at work, much as his wife would be at home.[20]

Karl realized that if the partnership was to evolve into the intended neuropsychiatric specialty, he himself would have to attract a larger clientele. In fact, after a few years, Charles started "feeling like I wanted to·retire." He bought Oakwood, a small farm on the outskirts of town, where he could immerse himself in horticulture. Flo, who felt that Charles was "falling down and not keeping up with what Karl expects," told Karl to encourage his father to spend more time at Oakwood, which afforded him greater pleasure. Karl did, but he recognized that he would have to earn sufficient income to support his father as well as himself. This meant that he could not afford to turn down any general cases until that point when income from neurological and psychiatric patients became considerable.[21]

Despite all these obstacles in the way of a specialty clinic, Karl traveled all over Kansas on neuropsychiatric referrals, making diagnoses and instructing local physicians on treatment. He also established small branch offices in a few of the larger cities of the region. Guiltily, Charles urged his son not to press so hard in pursuit of patients. But Karl's arduous efforts yielded recognition. By 1924, he reported: "I do most of the running around of this firm," and physicians already knew him better "over the state" than they knew his father. At the age of thirty, he was surpassing his father's reputation. The nineteenth-century American view of success almost required the ambitious son to exceed his father; Karl had done that after only a few years.[22]

Nonetheless, the young man was discontented. By the early 1920s, he was earning enough to keep the partnership afloat. Yet he was not satisfying his idealistic goal of ameliorating human suffering. His old interest in foreign missions remained alive: "Personally I am not altogether relinquishing the hope that I may sometime develop neuropsychiatric work in China," he wrote in 1921. Three years later, he told his youngest brother: "sometimes I think I should like to go there [New York City] to practice." The growing Topeka practice and its income may have satisfied his parents and his wife, but Karl felt that money, however important, was not enough. He had to "get away occasionally" to rekindle his dreams of a life of missionary reform.[23]

Some of Karl's uneasiness over the limitations of the hometown practice abated as he started to hire additional staff and to shift toward a comprehensive diagnostic clinic. He took on a young physician to handle general practice and dermatology, and retained the part-time services of another to diagnose x-ray films. At this point, Karl began to refer to the firm as the Menninger Diagnostic Clinic. He went on to hire a psychiatric nurse, a general nurse, a physiotherapist, and two stenographers. In July 1921, Mildred Law, a bacteriologist from McPherson County, who had been a laboratory technician for the State Board of Health, found herself unemployed. Karl persuaded her to direct the clinic's laboratory. Seeing that she was assertive, moralistic, independent, and eminently competent, Karl felt that she was like "family" and gave her considerable authority.[24]

Even more than Law, a young man from Barnes, Kansas, John Stone, was to be Karl's closest associate in these first years. As an undergraduate at Washburn, he was a devoted student in a pioneer abnormal psychology course Karl offered at the college. For the first time in his life, Karl felt like a mentor. Thus, despite his father's distrust of Stone and his own misgivings over Stone's socialist leanings, Karl hired him in 1923 to do psychological testing and perhaps some psychotherapy. To improve Stone's therapeutic skills and acquaint the Menningers with the psychoanalytic process, Karl then persuaded him to take a personal analysis with Lionel Blitzsten in Chicago. In the midst of the analysis, Karl became anxious about the costs and insisted that his protégé return immediately to Topeka. The aborted therapy affected Stone decidedly. Thereafter, he tried desperately to control extreme mood swings and find emotional stability by striving to be cold, objective, and dispassionate. Karl found him to be "a changed boy," no longer capable of working effectively with disturbed patients. Consequently, he encouraged Stone to assume direction of clinic finances and general institutional management. Reflecting, perhaps, his distress over his role in breaking off Stone's analysis prematurely, Karl allowed him to join the partnership as the owner of a 10 percent financial interest. No other non-Menninger was ever permitted to become a partner.[25]

The hiring of Law and Stone suggests that Karl was disposed to recruit people he liked and trusted rather than to seek out psychiatric specialists. A radiologist friend of his father's became a staff physician, and his sister-in-law was retained as a medical secretary. Personal and familial considerations seemed at least as important as professional concerns.

Indeed, the Menninger Diagnostic Clinic was hardly a psychiatric facility at all. It admitted patients with certain neurological symptoms that various doctors in northeastern Kansas could not diagnose. Each patient was given a thorough physical and neurological examination and some laboratory tests. These diagnostic workups, unusually comprehensive for their time and place, revealed a diversity of maladies. A few patients turned out to be diabetic. Reflecting his work with Elliott Joslin, Charles prescribed insulin well before the new drug had been marketed. A few patients had infantile paralysis. Instead of the standard immobilization treatment, Karl treated them with heat therapy plus muscle development programs. Some patients were epileptics; a few suffered the consequences of a thirteenth rib, and some were World War I veterans with neurological injuries. Though word spread that Karl was interested in "mental cases," the transition from general practice to psychiatry was slow and uncertain.[26]

During the early 1920s, Karl took personal charge of all the "mental cases." They fell into three general categories. One category consisted of victims of syphilis. During the last half of the nineteenth century, researchers discovered that syphilis was caused by the *Treponema pallidum* organism, which eventually inflicted massive damage upon the brain or the central nervous system. Bizarre behaviors, dramatic neurological symptoms, paralysis, and even death sometimes resulted. The Wassermann test offered a fairly reliable means of determining whether *Treponema pallidum* was present. This was why Karl instructed his staff that all symptomatic patients were to be given Wassermanns, despite the substantial twenty-five-dollar cost. Up to 25 percent of males in mental hospitals were afflicted with the organism, and Karl calculated that roughly 10 percent of the general population was infected. At Boston Psychopathic Hospital, he had learned about the newly discovered arsenical compound alternatively referred to as Salvarsan and 606. Although the administration of 606 was an expensive and prolonged process, Karl gave it to all his syphilitic patients, and with considerable success.[27]

A second group of "mental cases" comprised victims of the national influenza epidemic of 1918. Karl noted that a number of the clinic's patients displayed mental abnormalities that would have been diagnosed as dementia praecox (schizophrenia) in almost all state hospitals and even most private institutions. However, a significant proportion of them had manifested mental disturbance only after they succumbed to influenza. Karl launched a detailed exploration of mental repercussions of influenza. As early as 1921, he began to suspect that the disease could trigger delirium and depression as well as schizophrenia and other so-called psychoses. Because of their organic origin, a number of these maladies were reversible; as the influenza ran its course, the mental disturbances ceased. Contradicting Emil Kraepelin, Eugen Bleuler, and other psychiatric theorists who had advanced very unfavorable prognoses for dementia praecox, Karl suggested "reversible schizophrenia" for serious (usually influenza-induced) inflammatory disease of the central nervous system. Although Karl did not delineate systematically the precise meaning of his observations, he had begun to break from the therapeutic nihilism and the sense of hopelessness that had shackled much of institutional psychiatry at the end of the nineteenth century. Like Philippe Pinel and Dorothea Dix of earlier reformist eras, Karl radiated hope for victims of serious mental illness, much as his mother had spoken of hope for victims of moral ignorance by spreading Biblical truths. "Diagnosis is chiefly useful for prognosis," he proclaimed. "Prognosis depends upon reversibility. It remains then to determine the conditions of reversibility. They are the touchstones of treatment." As his clinic staff replicated his optimism in their treatments, Karl found that most influenza victims with serious mental disorders recovered. In retrospect, he was a pioneer in the viral hypothesis for certain schizophrenic illnesses. Even contemporary exponents of the "new psychiatry," such as Adolf Meyer and William Alanson White, started to take note of Elmer Southard's student as an important new voice for hope in the treatment of difficult mental disorders.[28]

The third category of "mental cases" treated at the clinic comprised patients with no detectable organic disorders. The external symptoms varied enormously, from sexual impotence to constipation to sleepwalking. Reading Freud and the Freudians prodigiously, talking with John Stone about his psychoanalytic sessions, and even allowing psychoanalytic pioneer Smith Ely Jelliffe to analyze him for a session or two, Karl felt that this new "science" might help certain of these patients. He attempted to give several of them short personal analyses. He claimed, for example, that ninety-two of his therapeutic hours in August 1924 "were devoted to psychoanalysis." By the mid-1920s, he concluded that he was dealing with two very different types of patients in his analytic sessions. With rich language indicating that he was, indeed, a psychoanalytic pioneer, Karl described the "neurotics," who suffered deeply within themselves, and the "psychotics," who did not feel as much inner torment but made others suffer. Initially, he had difficulty understanding how he was helping his patients simply by listening to them talk. Freudian primers provided few answers, for they focused on theory and not on analytic technique. But Jelliffe counseled him to keep his patients talking. In time, as various patients recovered, Karl became a more confident analyst. But he never forgot the effect of the technique on John Stone; under certain circumstances, it could be more crippling than curative.[29]

Early in the 1920s, then, with his clinic scarcely known within the psychiatric profession, Karl was building a national reputation for his attentiveness to the potential effects of syphilis and influenza on the brain and to psychoanalytic therapy. At this time, John Stone, Mildred Law, and even his father began to refer to him as "the founder." They did this out of the sense that if their clinic was to become famous, it would happen because of Karl's reputation. Thus, there could be no dispute as to who decided clinic policy, despite reference in the partners' formal "Articles of Agreement" to decisionmaking through "equal suffrage and majority rule." Karl ran the organization unrivaled, with Charles distinctly second in command, John Stone third, and Mildred Law fourth.[30]

Stone justifiably claimed: "We operated more like a family than a business group." Indeed, the smallness of the staff and the sense of family (with Karl as the patriarch) were such that it was difficult to institute the professional values of occupational specialization and formal division of labor, even when Karl appeared to encourage them. For example, he was unable to establish psychiatric teams as Southard had at Boston Psychopathic Hospital, with a psychiatrist, a psychologist, and a social worker cooperating as a specialty unit evaluating a given patient. Because of the sparseness of the staff, the physiotherapist often performed other functions. Stone frequently doubled as both a social worker and a psychiatrist, while both Charles and Law served in even more varied capacities. Moreover, regardless of who participated on the patient's treatment unit, the highest-ranking member of the clinic hierarchy on the unit made all vital decisions. This was not the way a professional medical organization was supposed to function.[31]

The power of family and hierarchy over medical division of labor was hardly the clinic's most pressing problem. As Karl's reputation grew and the number of difficult "mental cases" referred to his clinic increased, the inadequacy of the facility became apparent. It was particularly important to establish some sort of place for patients too disturbed to be treated on an outpatient basis. Initially, Karl followed the practice of W. S. Lindsay and boarded his very disturbed patients with the former Topeka State Hospital attendant with whom Lindsay had placed several of his patients. Like Lindsay, he soon found this less than adequate. Patients were confined to their rooms all day, and the ex-attendant tied them to their beds at night. Next, Karl tried to place disturbed cases requiring inpatient care in a wing of Christ's Hospital, as Lindsay had. Somehow circumventing a restrictive city ordinance that had been drafted to remove Lindsay's patients, Karl was able to install five or six patients on a dilapidated floor, where they were supervised by a psychiatric nurse from his clinic. He also ordered his physical therapist to administer daily massages to each of his patients at Christ's and to combine them with assortments of cold sheet packs, showers, and prolonged bath treatments. Although this arrangement was less custodial than the home of the ex-attendant, it left much to be desired. More patients needed to be hospitalized, but the Christ's administration allowed Karl only half a dozen beds. The wing he used was a firetrap. More important, the surgical concentration of the hospital and the hostility of Christ's regular staff nurses provided an inappropriate milieu for mentally disturbed patients.[32]

By the spring of 1923, it was obvious that Christ's could not continue as the inpatient facility for the Menninger Diagnostic Clinic. Karl felt that he needed his own sanitarium, a place such as Meyer ran in Baltimore. By establishing an inpatient facility of his own, he would finally be creating the psychiatric specialty operation that Southard had encouraged him to establish. When he did, the broader Menninger organization would shift from a diagnostic focus toward a general therapeutic emphasis. The Diagnostic Clinic (renamed the Menninger Neuropsychiatric Clinic) would continue in its downtown offices as an outpatient facility. But organizational energies would concentrate upon an inpatient sanitarium (the Menninger Psychiatric Hospital) on the outskirts of town.

Sometime in mid-1923, Karl was conversing with Tim N. Neese, one of the more proficient and ambitious attendants at Topeka State Hospital. A large, ruddy Irishman with a pleasant smile and a quick wit, Neese made an impression on him. When Karl told him of the woes of his inpatient practice at Christ's Hospital and spoke of the desirability of a facility of his own, Neese made him an offer. Together with his wife, Daisy, also an attendant, Neese proposed to locate a facility for the Menningers that could serve as a psychiatric sanitarium. The couple would invest their savings of five thousand dollars in the facility, manage it for the Menningers, and profit from room and board charges. They would take care of the patients' living needs and their daily routines, leaving the Menningers to administer psychotherapy. (This was hardly an innovative proposal. Throughout the nineteenth century, married couples had traditionally occupied rooms in Kansas lunatic asylums. The husband usually served as guard and superintendent, while the wife was cook and caretaker.) Karl jumped at Neese's proposal. Charles cautioned his son, however, that if it was to be their sanitarium, they would have at least to match the Neese investment; Menninger control was no less imperative in the new facility than it had been in the clinic. John Stone supported Charles's concerns.[33]

To secure financial backing, the Menningers planned a dinner and invited fifty prominent professional and business people from the community. During the evening, Karl announced that the family wanted to establish a psychiatric sanitarium and would issue stock far in excess of the five thousand dollars the Neeses planned on investing. After a moment of silence, Sam E. Cobb, an influential banker and former Kansas state treasurer, pledged to buy a large number of shares. This gave the investment an aura of safety and respectability, and several of the other guests made financial commitments. One was David Neiswanger, a local realtor, who had gone to high school with Karl. He volunteered to take a leadership role in the newly formed Menninger Sanitarium Corporation. Neiswanger was intensely loyal to the Menningers—"like another brother," Karl once declared. He pledged himself to see that the corporation deferred to the family's wishes, much as Stone and Law had learned to do. Cobb agreed with Neiswanger. With this backing, Karl could write confidently to his youngest brother: "We have drawn up the articles of incorporation for a sanitarium which we [the Menningers] will practically control." A month after the first meeting, corporation officers were elected. Charles was president, Neiswanger became secretary, and Cobb served as treasurer. The Neeses had been outflanked.[34]

Tim and Daisy Neese had no choice but to accept their minority position as stockholders. They spent nearly two years searching for appropriate property for the Sanitarium Corporation to purchase. Early in the spring of 1925, they located a twenty-acre farmsite on the western edge of town. The Menningers liked it, and the Sanitarium Corporation authorized the purchase for forty thousand dollars. The family farmhouse was transformed into a twelve-bed sanitarium. Patients were assigned to the upstairs rooms. Downstairs were offices, a reception room, a reading room, a library, a dining room and a kitchen, and the Neeses' bedroom.[35]

During its first five years, the Menninger Sanitarium was not even as big as smaller "new psychiatry" hospitals like Austen Riggs. It resembled the eight-bed Harding Hospital in Columbus, Ohio. During its first six months of operation, thirty-six patients came and went, the average staying five to six weeks. Whereas the earliest sanitarium patients were from Topeka and outlying areas, the pattern changed quickly. Within a year, the majority were being referred from other parts of the western Middle West, particularly from the Mayo Clinic in Minnesota. The Menningers realized that their facility, as one of the few cure-oriented private psychiatric hospitals in that part of the country, soon would need more bed capacity than the farm could accommodate.[36]

Early in 1926, an old garage near the main farmhouse was remodeled to provide six separate rooms, and bars were fitted on the windows. It was to house the more disruptive patients from the main building. In January 1928, construction of East Lodge—a twenty-six-bed Tudor-style building—was completed. It was intended to be homelike in appearance. Calming interior colors—greens, browns, and grays—were used. Instead of the traditional mental-hospital bars, like those on the converted garage, sturdy steel strips seemed to blend inconspicuously into the horizontal and perpendicular support lines of the windows. The window screens were made of stainless steel, which could not be cut. Because all patients from the farmhouse building were transferred to East Lodge, the Neuropsychiatric Clinic staff was able to move out of its downtown suite of offices into the farmhouse, now designated as the clinic building. Provisions had already been made to rent the former American Hospital building, across from the sanitarium grounds, for nurses and other employees who needed sleeping quarters. By midsummer of 1928, the clinic and sanitarium occupied a single, unified campus on the outskirts of Topeka. Collectively, the two were designated as the Menninger Clinic.[37]

Although the grounds were beautiful and were distant from most of the sounds and disruptions of urban life, problems remained. The county constructed a public road that crossed the grounds within a few feet of the clinic building. This created noise and dust from passing cars. A combination roller-skating rink and dance hall a block away produced noise too; patrons walked across the Menninger grounds as they came and went. After much haggling, the Menningers persuaded local officials to eliminate the road and close the rink. As they lobbied for relief, they realized that beyond their small group of corporate stockholders, there was little sympathy for the clinic in Topeka and in Shawnee County.[38]

As managers of the sanitarium during its first five years, the Neeses recruited a staff that was inexpensive and compatible with the custodial tradition they knew. A local handyman, Jerry Levett, helped Tim work with patients at gardening and livestock maintenance. A recent German immigrant with no hospital experience, Sophia Schweers, assisted Daisy with cooking.[39]

This is not to suggest that the Neeses were uninterested in their patients and motivated entirely by profit. Like a good many state hospital directors and supervisors, they were also committed to making ample provision for the physical needs of their patients. Tim kept the buildings and grounds in sound repair and went to great lengths to secure "the best food at the lowest prices." Daisy, in charge of all meal preparation and housekeeping, was adept at these tasks. She also supervised nurses. True to her custodial background, she occasionally handcuffed a few very disorderly patients to their beds. Like staff at a good many private hospitals, she was so busy attending to the patients' physical well-being that she rarely thought about formal therapy. However, Daisy was a kind woman and demanded that her nursing staff treat the patients with warmth, courtesy, and understanding. Indeed, she seemed to embody the very qualities that Karl underscored for the effective psychotherapist: "One must really be interested in the sufferer—one must, in a way, really love his patients."[40]

The role of the Menningers during these years was in transition. Until July 1928, when they moved the clinic to the sanitarium grounds, they continued to render outpatient services in their downtown Topeka offices. From these offices, they drove to the hospital grounds to spend an hour or two in the morning and returned late in the afternoon for another hour. When the Menningers were on the grounds, they made rounds, conducted therapeutic sessions, and supervised the staff in the use of hydrotherapy, actinotherapy (ultraviolet radiation), and other common treatments of the day. Karl also ran special classes for the sanitarium staff and taught them the lessons in modern perspectives on mental illness that he was imparting to an undergraduate class at Washburn College. Above all, he sought to break the Neeses and their staff of their custodial attitudes. The insane could improve; with staff empathy and understanding as well as clean rooms and good food, almost all mental patients could recover.[41]

Although the Neeses were empathetic, they did not share Karl's vision, and conflict was inevitable. When the Menningers took up permanent residence on the hospital grounds in the middle of 1928, the conflict intensified. They insisted on a routine of morning temperatures and meticulous chartings of all patients, instituted an occupational therapy program, and began to replace the Neeses' nursing staff with nurses who had graduated from medical training programs. The Neeses were distressed by the expense of graduate nurses. More important, they were upset because the medically trained nurses took their orders from the Menningers, who required them to render "unnecessary" services for the patients. Consequently, when the Neeses heard of the Menningers' plans for an accredited school of nursing on the sanitarium grounds, they feared that their authority was being entirely undermined. "Educated" nurses would soon constitute a majority on the sanitarium staff under the Menningers. Tim and Daisy read the situation accurately, as Karl and Charles intended.[42]

Late in January 1930, Karl called a meeting of the corporation's board of directors, consisting of the Menningers and John Stone, the corporation officers, and other large stockholders. On paper, at least, it was the governing body of the hospital. At the beginning of the meeting, Karl informed the board that the Neeses "have worried us" increasingly. The implication was obvious: the Neeses were to be fired. The board gave the couple notice in February and bought out their shares. Late in April, the Neeses packed their bags and left the grounds. Soon afterward, the Menningers dismissed most of the nurses still on staff who had been hired by the Neeses and replaced them with graduate nurses. They also took on a steward and a kitchen supervisor to assume Daisy's duties. Thus, the family assumed control over all aspects of the hospital as well as the clinic.[43]

Karl had felt that the controversy over graduate nurses was the "final straw" in a deteriorating relationship. This was probably true. The Neeses felt out of place and threatened by the medical orientation of the graduate nurses. But it is also true that the Neeses—unlike Stone and Law—sought to be independent of the family. They had tried to buy a controlling financial interest in the hospital and to command staff loyalties. The Menningers would not tolerate this sort of autonomy within their organization any more than they had tolerated boarders who did not defer to the family.[44]

Following the departure of the Neeses, Will Menninger was designated the new sanitarium-hospital director. The appointment suggests
that the family ousted the Neeses for yet another reason—to provide a
secure place for Charles's youngest son. Will quickly proclaimed a new
spirit of loyalty and love in patient-staff relationships.[45]

Charles had not been certain that Will would join the Menninger
Clinic. When he graduated from Washburn in 1919, Will thought about
pursuing Boy Scout work. But he began at Cornell Medical School in the
fall of 1920, "chiefly because that was the place where Father had wanted
to go and, in part, because it was a different school from which Karl had
attended." Charles made it clear that he expected Will to join the partnership after he completed his schooling, and Will was "tentatively planning" to do so. However, in the course of his medical studies, he specialized in internal medicine and cardiology rather than neuropsychiatry.
Like Karl, he considered becoming a medical missionary abroad (he had
a special interest in China). During his medical studies, he had fallen in
love with Catharine Wright, who was herself intent on missionary work
in China. The couple dreamed of going to the Far East together. They
spoke of it openly on December 11, 1925—the day of their marriage.[46]

Even as the couple pledged themselves to China, Will realized that
he was not willing to abandon Topeka and the family organization. He
had just completed internships in surgery and medicine in Bellevue Hospital and was facing heavy pressure to return home. As always, Charles
was restrained. His letters indicated that he could survive if his son
elected to take a fellowship at the University of Pennsylvania or to go to
China. But Flo insisted that her youngest son had a family obligation to
return to Topeka. She dismissed his "impractical" missionary dreams as
she earlier had dismissed Karl's. Karl was more emphatic, noting that
their father "really needs some rest and relief. He can't keep it up forever
and it will be a pleasure to both of us if you could be with us soon."
Charles was no longer a fully active colleague, and though John Stone
helped considerably, blood relatives "are the only people you can be
frank with when you have points of difference."[47]

Will returned to Topeka late in 1925, eleven days after his wedding.
Charles and Flo were in Florida, spending the holidays with Edwin, when
Will arrived. On Christmas Day, Karl departed for a meeting in New
York, leaving his brother to run the downtown clinic and to supervise
medical matters at the new sanitarium. The implication of this arrangement was obvious. With an aging father moving toward semiretirement
and an ambitious older brother whose professional obligations were
often drawing him out of town or toward his writing desk, someone in

the family was needed to take charge of day-to-day affairs. Will could understand this. He was disturbed, however, because he had been brought in as a salaried employee. Karl and Charles delayed three months before they made him a legal partner.[48]

Between December 1925 and the departure of the Neeses, in April 1930, Will's principal assignment was to oversee medical and therapeutic work with sanitarium patients. But he felt out of place there, and the custodial orientation of the Neeses was only partly responsible. An internal medicine specialist, Will had no training in psychiatry. At Karl's urging, he spent four months in 1927 as a resident at St. Elizabeths Hospital. Its director, William Alanson White, was perhaps better equipped than any other American physician to teach psychoanalytically informed psychiatry. But Will did not seek a training analysis from White and had little contact with him. Instead, he spent most of his time conducting extensive research on juvenile paresis. When he returned to Topeka, he blamed Karl for having "coerced" him into psychiatry. Moreover, whenever he could break away from his sanitarium duties, he studied diabetes and other maladies with clear "physical-psychical relationships," even though few of his patients provided clinical data for such investigations. His medical preferences resembled his father's.[49]

Will was less than satisfied in the Menninger organization. His dissatisfaction disturbed Karl and Charles, especially because Catharine was urging her husband to reconsider a medical mission abroad. The two senior partners realized that they had to do something to make Will happier. So when they fired the Neeses, they made him sanitarium director. Originally, Karl had wanted the director to be a man like Adolf Meyer or Ross McClure Chapman, an assertive exponent of the "new psychiatry" who would transform the sanitarium into one of the leading private psychiatric hospitals in the nation. But family came first, even though Will's heart had never been in psychiatry and he was hardly aggressive.[50]

I V

In April 1930, the Menninger directors named Will Medical Director of the sanitarium. In August 1931, the board broadened the title to Clinical Director of all patient-related operations. From 1930–31 until November 1942, when he went into the army, Will became the most influential authority over daily organizational life. The hospital he supervised quickly became the most crucial part of the organization. West Lodge— the second regular hospital building—was completed the year he took over. East Lodge had usually been filled to capacity despite the (then) rather steep minimum price of seventy-five dollars a week, and a new building had been needed to accommodate more patients. Architecturally, West Lodge closely matched the Tudor style and interior of East Lodge; it added eighteen beds to total hospital operations. In all, Will administered a moderate-sized private facility (forty-four beds, plus a few more in the converted garage). If patient demand remained strong despite the onset of the Depression, he hoped to separate acute cases (East Lodge) from the nonacute (West Lodge). Karl accurately acknowledged that "Dr. Will's hospital" was the "main thing" in the organization.[51]

Will, in running the "main thing," found that he could conduct his wide-ranging duties with a certain freedom from his brother, quite unlike his situation in the early Menninger household. Will had earned a reputation for medical competence through his work on the hospital grounds during the Neese period, and he assumed his new position with strong staff support. Most of the patients liked him too. As well, he had been achieving recognition in medical circles and was outpublishing his brother. Between 1923 and 1926, for example, he wrote twenty-three scientific articles. Through them, he acquired a reputation among American physicians as an expert on paretic neurosyphilis, cerebrospinal fluid, epilepsy, thyroid gland dysfunctions, and chronic appendicitis. Less than enthusiastic about dynamic psychiatry, he nonetheless hoped that he had some of the qualities needed to make the hospital "the best of its kind" and even superior to some of the leading centers of the "new psychiatry."[52]

This is not to say that Will was unimpeded as he established a therapy program. For one, John Stone made it clear that the old clinic hierarchy of Karl, Charles, himself, and Mildred Law could not be dispensed with in the hospital. Irrespective of formal titles, it was up to the four of them to decide "things by protracted counselling back and forth," much as a "family" made decisions. What Stone was insisting upon was recognition for himself and Mildred Law, as very nearly members of the Menninger family, under any new sanitarium arrangements that Will developed.[53]

Within months of becoming director, Will also discovered that he had to deal sensitively with a maintenance man, an assistant treasurer, and the head nurse. Pearl Boam's brother Ben had been brought in to replace Tim Neese. Ben worked eighteen-hour days and weekends; he attended to building repairs, landscaping, and even the control of disorderly patients when a skeletal medical staff was on duty. Will was able to secure these tremendously useful services simply by treating him as "family," in the Menninger tradition. In contrast, assistant treasurer Merle

Hoover was not interested in being "family." A financial adviser for International Harvester, he was hired to bring order to the organization's books. Hoover established an advanced accounting system for the various components of the firm. By bypassing Stone (Hoover's supervisor) and sometimes even Law, and approaching Hoover directly, Will had access to detailed and reliable financial information on almost any aspect of hospital management. Finally, Will established a close rapport with Isabel Erickson, the superintendent of nursing. An intensely ambitious woman and a skillful administrator, she took charge of all staff who stood between the hospital doctor and the patient.[54]

Late in 1932, a formal residency program in neuropsychiatry was launched. By July 1933, six doctors were in residence and serving as hospital physicians. Combined with graduate nurses on staff, this gave Menninger one of the best ratios of professional staff to patients among the elite psychiatric hospitals. As Erickson became the dominant figure among the nurses, Robert P. Knight, one of the initial residents, emerged as the premier therapist. Will liked Knight a great deal and turned to him for information on the feelings and conduct of other staff doctors. Over time, Knight, like Stone and Neiswanger, sometimes came to be regarded by the family as a "Menninger brother," though Isabel Erickson was never quite thought of as a "sister." Through close contact with Knight and Erickson, Will was able to exert strong control over his staff.[55]

Despite his skill in establishing bonds, Will would never have been able to consolidate authority in the hospital if Karl had wished to block him. However, the early 1930s was an interval when the older brother wanted fewer organizational responsibilities. Principally, this was because of his experience with *The Human Mind* (1930), his first book, a Literary Guild selection on the way to becoming the best-selling mental health volume in American history. The popularity of the book resulted in many speaking invitations, a vast increase in Karl's professional correspondence, and plans to write other books and articles. The revenues from the book also made it possible for him to go to Chicago for a full training analysis. Karl explained that he simply had to relinquish responsibility to Will and give his younger brother a greater stake in the organization.[56]

Although there was a certain plausibility in Karl's explanation, it ran contrary to his need for authority and control in both the family and the organization. There had to be a more fundamental reason. It began to press upon him even before he finished writing *The Human Mind.*

The book grew out of his lectures for his freshman mental hygiene course at Washburn, one of the first such instructional ventures in American higher education. Because there was no appropriate textbook for his students, Karl collected material on unusual human behavior from newspapers, magazines, and the Bible, and from records he kept of his patients. When the course became a college-wide requirement, in 1923, he saw the importance of formalizing and elaborating his lectures so that they might eventually come together as the first comprehensive textbook for mental hygiene classes in the country. With an undergraduate audience in mind—not a group of medical specialists or even general practitioners—Karl drafted portions of what became *The Human Mind* in a popular style. The book lacked scholarly rigor or analytic mastery of complex clinical materials. The overall structure followed Karl's course syllabus, with the opening chapter defining mental health and mental illness, followed by chapters on aberrant personalities. A chapter on motives illustrated the dynamics of the unconscious. Another concerned treatments. The last dealt with applications of psychoanalytic theory to wider community and philosophic issues. The college freshman or the uninformed reader might put down *The Human Mind* feeling that he or she had learned about all phases of mental and emotional life.[57]

This was not the case. The book contained many interesting comments on a number of important points. However, none of them was supported convincingly or with attention to nuance. Karl defined mental health, for example, as "the ability to maintain an even temper, an alert intelligence, socially considerate behavior, and a happy disposition." But he failed to explain what mental and emotional factors were at work when a person exhibited these qualities. It was insufficient to say that they operated during "the adjustment of human beings to the world and to each other with a maximum of effectiveness and happiness." Nowhere did Karl define "alert intelligence," "a happy disposition," "adjustment," or "effectiveness." Presumably, the many stories he quoted were somehow to perform that function. Similarly, Karl insisted that "psychiatry must sooner or later totally displace existing legal methods" in criminal law proceedings. The justification for this far-reaching proposal was the unsubstantiated claim that psychiatrists had a "scientific attitude," while police, courts, and lawyers did not. With no explanatory justification, Karl reversed Freud's priorities by noting that "psychoanalysis as a research technique . . . is secondary to psychoanalysis as a method of treatment." He explained "growing up emotionally" as "the increasing capacity to take from this self-directed love [of the young child] and invest wisely in externally directed love." But he did not indicate why he (or for that matter Freud) had arrived at that important observation.[58]

The major deficiency of *The Human Mind* was in Karl's basic approach to psychiatric cure. Throughout the book, he showed an optimism that was unprecedented, even among "new psychiatrists" like Meyer and

Chapman, for the cure of the most serious mental illness. But though he had demonstrated in his earlier articles, through close explication of case studies, just how a "reversibility" from illness to health might take place, *The Human Mind* housed only optimistic general assertions. Karl maintained, for example, that a hopeful therapist who was strongly "interested in the sufferer" could render cures. But he never characterized the dynamic process that this therapist facilitated, which transported the patient from "illness" to "health." Consequently, whereas his earlier articles had focused closely on patterns of change and "reversibility" through which people moved from degrees of "illness" to degrees of "health" and from "health" to "illness," in *The Human Mind* Karl invoked a simplistic and commonplace dichotomy between "illness" and "health."[59]

Clearly, Karl had come up with a great many insights about human personality and society. The problem was that in his book they were advanced hastily between lengthy quotations that did not quite sustain the insights. Still, he opened *The Human Mind* with one of the richest descriptions of mental illness in the history of American psychiatry:

> When a trout rising to a fly gets hooked on a line and finds itself unable to swim about freely, it begins a fight which results in struggles and splashes and sometimes an escape. Often, of course, the situation is too tough for him.
>
> In the same way the human being struggles with his environment and with the hooks that catch him. Sometimes he masters his difficulties; sometimes they are too much for him. His struggles are all that the world sees and it usually misunderstands them. It is hard for a free fish to understand what is happening to a hooked one.
>
> Sooner or later, however, most of us get hooked. How much of a fight we have on our hands then depends on the hook, and, of course, on us. If the struggle gets too violent, if it throws us out of the water, if we run afoul of other struggles, we become "cases" in need of help and understanding.[60]

But by the second page, the loose presentation of massive amounts of unanalyzed examples commences. An author of considerable intelligence and literary capacity had produced a popular but superficial first book.

As he was writing *The Human Mind,* Karl recognized it had little conceptual strength or analytic development. He became even more convinced of this when his editor at Knopf told him to "go home and reorganize" the manuscript he had submitted, because "it won't do in this shape." Two weeks before it was published, he acknowledged privately that "there will be better things written all the time" and wished that he "had never written it at all." Within the book itself, he offered two excuses for the shallowness. First, he simply lacked the time to write a profound volume because of his other responsibilities: "I've had to put together this manuscript under difficulties. I have rolled off pages of it in the cabooses of freight trains. . . . Parts of it were conceived in railroad depots and in the wards of the hospital." By turning over supervisory responsibility to his brother and having his mornings free, he would certainly be able to write a deeper book. Indeed, in his preface to the second edition of *The Human Mind,* in 1937, Karl acknowledged that he had finally had the time to patch up some of the most glaring superficialities for which his medical colleagues had criticized him.[61]

Another excuse Karl offered was that he had never been analyzed. The session or two of trial analysis with Smith Ely Jelliffe in the early 1920s had meant little to him. Karl felt that though he had some sense of the language and theory behind Freud's "science," he lacked an emotional level of understanding. This was a sensitive self-appraisal. *The Human Mind* contained one example after another of his uneasiness about the psychoanalytic process, beginning with his dedication: "To My Father and Mother, An invincible Laius and a discerning Jocasta" (the names of Oedipus' parents and awkward notice that Karl had an Oedipus complex). With Will as hospital director, Karl could spend the winter of 1931 and intervals until February 1932 in analysis with Franz Alexander at the Chicago Institute for Psychoanalysis.[62]

The 1930 understanding between the brothers giving Will authority over the hospital had hardly gone into effect before John Stone admonished Karl for "criticisms and suggestions [in the clinical realm] that are so tinged with the emotion of disappointment & exasperation that Bill instinctively resents them." Stone failed to understand an essential point: Karl never felt the accord precluded his pressing Will on hospital affairs. Rather, Karl thought that he had agreed to a life style that would allow him to be the scholar, the thinker, and the innovator in all aspects of the Menninger organization, while Will would implement his ideas and stabilize daily operations. After all, he had customarily behaved in this unfettered manner in the Menninger household, where Will had learned from Charles to be supportive.[63]

CHAPTER THREE

A Hospital Treatment Program

At the 1932 annual meeting of the American Medical Association, Will Menninger read a paper entitled "Therapeutic Methods in a Psychiatric Hospital." It outlined, for the first time, the essential principles of what was emerging as the Menninger hospital's pioneering milieu therapy program—its principal contribution to the "new psychiatry." The hospital environment, Will argued, should above all be "adapted to the individual patient's needs." Specifically, the hospital staff should build a relatively consistent set of "scientific" relationships with each patient "in the course of a daily schedule of therapeutic activities." Through these relationships within the context of activities, the patient's "energies" would be moved "into more productive channels," so that he could return safely to his "home environment."[1]

As director of a hospital with more than forty beds, one hundred twenty annual admissions, and an average stay of three to four months, Will successfully instituted this type of "scientific" medical program. Retrospectively, he would feel that it provided the essential structure governing the conduct of everybody on the grounds—staff as well as patients—between 1930 and 1942, when he ran the facility. However, Karl thought otherwise. Looking back upon the years of the Neeses, and even of Will's directorship, Karl reflected that "a family spirit" on the grounds was far more vital than the "scientific"-medical program of milieu therapy. Utilizing that "spirit," Karl recalled, "the doctors were like fathers and big brothers with the patients as our children."[2]

Actually, the hospital was considerably more complex. Will was right in asserting that his "scientific" program had been central to hospital life. But that program by no means undermined a strong "family spirit" within the institution, which Karl emphasized. Moreover, both brothers failed to acknowledge two other important aspects of hospital life.

All these aspects can be described as the different "faces" of the hospital's day-to-day existence. "Face" is not used pejoratively or to suggest duplicity ("two-faced") in the Menninger hospital. The word is taken from the social-interactionist tradition within American sociology. Typical of the interactionists, Erving Goffman uses "face" to delineate "the positive social value" that a person asserts in his own behalf when he presents himself to others in social situations. Although interactionists focus on individuals, most acknowledge that face-to-face contact is often more than interpersonal. People also present themselves in group or in organizational representational faces (e.g., Richard Smith, a physician, from a particular community, working in a certain part of a specific organization).[3]

Menninger hospital life presented four faces when Will served as director. There was a professional or what he preferred to characterize as a "scientific" face—a well-coordinated and up-to-date medical treatment center. A family face also existed—what Karl referred to as a "family spirit," where the hospital constituted an extended family. The hospital also had a pluralist face; staff presented themselves as members of competing interest groups rather than as cooperative professionals. Doctors, nurses, activities therapists, and attendants vied for hospital resources and recognition. Finally, Will's facility had a community face, wherein staff represented themselves and their patients within a self-sustaining utopian community in miniature.

I I

When Will became hospital director, he was essentially an internist and enjoyed those aspects of medical practice that involved precision and certitude. Consequently, he was far more impressed with the prime fruits of the scientific revolution—bacteriology and aseptic surgery—than with the less specific treatment methods of the "new psychiatry." Indeed, Will spent considerable time during the late 1920s searching for a scientifically reputable drug treatment for mental illness. The effort represented his first significant failure as a medical researcher, and he refused to publish any part of his investigation. This experience made him exceedingly suspicious, for the rest of his life, of organically based research projects that held out claims of discovering *the* drug or *the* operation that could cure mental illness. Owing to his own failure in that realm, he was disposed to seek out scientific cures from various psychiatric programs that focused instead upon the social milieu and interpersonal relationships between patients and staff. Retrospectively, of course, even the most rigorous social programs scarcely represented science. But Will was intent on fashioning a "scientific" social regime for treatment, and his determination differentiated him from Adolf Meyer, Elmer Southard, and most other leaders of the "new psychiatry." Will agreed with them that mental illness had to be linked (at least partially) to organic factors. But he outdid them in stressing the social environment as the primary area for psychiatric innovation.[4]

It is small wonder that nineteenth-century "moral [psychological] therapy," as practiced by mental health reformers like Dorothea Dix, Thomas Kirkbride, Luther Bell, and Samuel Woodward, strongly appealed to Will. If staff manipulated the hospital environment in specific ways, the "moral therapists" had charged, the patient could learn to cope with the past associations contributing to his mental illness. This environmental control was possible in a relatively small hospital, Dix, Bell, and others had noted; only in such a facility were specific bonds of trust between the patient and the staff truly possible. With occupational therapy, religious programs, and recreation specifically designed for individual patients, each of them would be reeducated in a proper moral atmosphere, which eschewed violence and mechanical restraints. The patient would learn to master his emotions in this protected, instructional setting.

A second important source for Will's hospital therapy regime was the program of Adolf Meyer. At Worcester State Hospital and the Phipps Clinic, Meyer had broken from the prevalent postbellum psychiatric practice of basing diagnoses upon cerebral lesions and hereditary defects. He urged the practitioner to focus instead upon the total patient and to analyze the patient's unique "trends" and "cravings" in conjunction with his specific environment. Meyer referred to this as "psychobiology"—the study of interactions between the individual biological-psychological organism and the surrounding social environment. Will was especially taken by Meyer's elaborate record keeping and the precise and comprehensive case conference report on each patient that he required of physicians. It satisfied Will's preference for scientific exactitude; he adopted it.[5]

Even more than "moral therapy" and Meyer's hospital program, Will was influenced by his father's medical practice. Specifically, he was impressed with Charles's compulsive attention to detail in the treatment of his patients. Will was also taken by the importance Charles attached to the physician's medical assistants. Indeed, Charles had offered a pioneering class for the nurses of Christ's Hospital in the mid-1890s. When Will joined the family firm, he noted how his father carefully instructed the adjunctive staff of the Diagnostic Clinic concerning appropriate approaches to patients and activities beneficial to patients suffering from particular maladies. Will ascribed what was to be one of the most important types of patient activities in his milieu therapy program—work and recreation in the out-of-doors—to the love of plants and animals "which you [Charles] instilled in my being."[6]

Practical problems confronting most "new psychiatrists" during the 1920s and 1930s also influenced Will's "scientific" milieu therapy program. For one thing, there were no satisfactory drugs to sedate deeply disturbed patients. With his inclination against imprecise drugs and his preference for cure through interpersonal contacts, Will quickly recognized that neither opium nor the bromides that several practitioners used did much good. He was also suspicious of new treatments like Metrazol, insulin therapy, electroshock, and prefrontal lobotomies, all of which promised to link psychiatry with the general medical sciences, as active therapies. Suspicious of organic approaches, Will never embraced any of these enthusiastically or extensively. Perhaps more than any other pioneer in the "new psychiatry," however, Will was impressed with the hydrotherapy and patient work programs that various nurses and activities therapists were instituting. He made it a point to hire the most innovative of these auxiliary staff he could find and to ignore the long-standing hostility between professional organizations of psychiatrists and nurses. Will also championed the development of the Menninger School of Nursing and the organization of special recreation and therapy departments within the hospital. Nurses, activities therapists, and other auxiliary staff would soon become vital to his milieu therapy program.[7]

Will was also influenced by Schloss Tegel, a psychoanalytic sanitarium on the outskirts of Berlin, established by Ernst Simmel. Firmly committed to Freudian psychoanalysis, Simmel had enrolled as inpatients several neurotic clients with serious physical handicaps. To enhance the daily psychoanalytic hour—the main component of each patient's therapy—Simmel encouraged patients to build transference relationships with nurses and other hospital personnel. Detailed communication between the analyst and the auxiliary staff concerning each patient would help to sustain these transference relationships and thereby enhance the progress of the daily analytic session.[8]

Freud had added to the reputation of Schloss Tegel by staying there as a guest while undergoing treatment for cancer of the jaw. Impressed by Simmel's contribution to psychoanalysis, he sought to raise funds for the hospital, until right-wing political pressure caused it to be closed in 1931. Simmel's importance was recognized in psychiatric circles by 1933, when Will visited European medical facilities in search of ideas for his hospital treatment program. In Berlin, Will and Simmel talked enthusiastically about the nature of a psychoanalytic hospital and about reconciling the inpatient setting with traditional outpatient and individual-centered psychoanalytic technique. They also discussed specific hospital procedures that had existed at Schloss Tegel, particularly the scheduling of therapeutic activities supervised by auxiliary staff. Following this meeting, Will described Schloss Tegel as a model for the therapeutic program he wanted to build. A few years later, when Simmel visited Topeka, he claimed that the Menninger hospital was "working according to the principle which I had tried to realize during my own work at clinical psychotherapy on a psychoanalytic basis." This Menninger facility, he said, "would have been a particular satisfaction to Freud."[9]

Even though Simmel characterized Will's hospital as a second Schloss Tegel, the German institute was only theoretically a model for the one in Topeka. Differences between the two institutions were obvious. First, Schloss Tegel admitted only analytic patients, whereas a minority of Menninger hospital patients were in analysis. All of Simmel's patients were neurotics; but many Menninger patients were so sick that analysis was inappropriate: they lacked the inner psychological strength necessary to cultivate transference relationships with their analysts. Another difference between the institutions concerned the place of the analyst in the general treatment structure. At Schloss Tegel, Simmel advised his auxiliary staff on how they could enhance his own analytic sessions with each specific patient. In Topeka, the analyst could influence auxiliary staff only indirectly, by persuading the physicians to instruct nurses, activities therapists, and attendants to support his analysis. Nevertheless, Simmel gave Will both a vocabulary and a comprehensive theory with which to package "scientifically" the various hospital procedures he had already begun to implement.[10]

I I I

Will drew upon a diverse variety of sources, then, to develop the "scientific" face of his hospital. Once it was developed, he presented it as a facility that followed a clear and efficient format for medical treatment. Exalting the stability of his hospital, Will also characterized it as a pioneering institution. More than Sheppard-Pratt and Chestnut Lodge, the Menninger hospital was integrating Freud's new science of emotional life with Pasteur's and Koch's revolutionary scientific discoveries that promoted medical specificity.

The aura of stability and competence came from a sense of time-tested medical precision that Will tried to convey in his programmatic outline. The therapeutic program he was developing centered on "The Specificity of Psychiatric Hospital Management." "As medications are prescribed for specific results," he noted, psychiatric therapy could be prescribed for specific results as well, if that therapy was administered in "exact doses." Through the prescription of therapies and staff attitudes in administering these therapies—all in precise "doses" to meet the particular needs of the "specific" patient—the underlying and largely subconscious problems of the mentally ill could be remedied. Thus, "scientifically controlled" staff-patient relationships and therapies were the key to his therapy program.[11]

Drawing heavily upon the language of treatment "specificity" and orderly management, Will used Freudian drive theory to explain his hospital practices. He borrowed heavily from Freud's *Beyond the Pleasure Principle* (1920). Like Freud's earlier formulations on the concept of drives or instincts, this essay bore the stamp of nineteenth-century mechanistic scientific thought. Only in subtle ways had he pointed to more complex formulations. Freud noted in the 1920 essay that there were two conflicting drives in people. For the first time, he explained how one of them was not only aggressive but self-destructive. The second was libidinal and life-sustaining. Citing this, Will maintained that "all the symptoms and the behavior of the neurotic and psychotic patient represent disturbances in the proper fusion and expression of these [two] instincts." All mental illness represented "either a mismanagement of the erotic drive, i.e., misdirected love relationships, or of the hostile drive, i.e., misdirected destructive energy, or both." Therefore, mental health could be restored when specific therapeutic interventions "correct disturbances in the Aggressive Drive" or "correct disturbances in the Erotic Drive," or remedied disturbances in both. The disturbances were corrected when therapeutic intervention encouraged the patient to avoid directing a drive toward the socially unacceptable target that was prompting his disturbances and instead to shift toward a socially acceptable object. In this way, the patient could govern his behavior. By managing his inner drives, the patient would feel pleasure untainted by the guilt that came from socially unacceptable conduct.[12]

Like William Alanson White before him, Will was stressing the building of drive displacement skills. The more adept the patient became in displacing the objects of his drives, the better he had adapted to his environment. By the late 1930s, psychoanalytic literature would refer to adaptational skills, beginning to categorize them as mature and immature ego defenses. Despite his language of Freudian drive theory, Will's therapy program was in the forefront of this shift toward a psychoanalytic ego psychology.[13]

The capacity to discover and correct misdirected drives was therefore crucial in the format of his hospital therapy program. Will maintained that the hospital physician would make the discovery and devise the correctives for the disturbed patient. The physician was to remain dispassionate—"unaffected by these emotional attitudes of [the] patient"—as he conducted a careful evaluation of the unconscious conflicts that plagued the patient and prescribed very specific procedures for the auxiliary staff to carry out. Initially, Will required the physician to consult a short hospital document called the Abbreviated Guide to Therapeutic Aims. He was to note on it underlying drive disturbances that he had diagnosed. Next, the physician was to direct auxiliary staff by designating on his order sheet the corrective procedures they would use to help the patient with his drive disturbances. By the late 1930s, the guide had evolved into a long and detailed document to assist the doctor in the use of his order sheet. After consulting this guide to the order sheet, the physician was to write his general diagnosis (schizophrenia, alcoholism, etc.) and his general therapeutic aim ("to give patient love unrequested," "to afford relief of introjected hostility," etc.) at the beginning of his order sheet in conformity to instructions and choices in the guide. Then he was to complete sections of the order sheet as the guide required, in order to communicate two essentials to the auxiliary staff. Obviously, he had to inform them of the specific medicines and therapeutic activities the patient would receive. But he was also to instruct nurses, attendants, and others in specific attitudes they were to maintain as they gave medication and administered activities programs. Listed in the guide, these attitudes could range from "active friendliness" and "praise" to "firmness" and "minimal attention." Clearly, the guide ensured precise and comprehensive communication from the physician to auxiliary staff.[14]

By designing and revising the guide to the order sheet in consultation with his hospital staff, Will exerted subtle influence over his physicians. Control over them was also inherent in the preparatory format for the physicians' case conference. Although the doctor was to complete a preliminary order sheet shortly after a patient arrived at the Menninger hospital, the final order sheet was to be filled out only after the supervising physician submitted detailed written and oral reports on his patient at the case conference. The written report was to conform to yet another guide that Will drafted.[15]

The Menninger brothers sought to structure the daily physicians' case conference along hierarchic lines. Will and Karl (when he was available) sat at each end of the conference table and asked Robert Knight, their premier psychotherapist, to sit next to either of them. The Menningers assigned remaining seating on the basis of seniority, with the most junior resident sitting as far away as possible from either brother. After the physician presented his case report, the most junior-level doctors commented on the case, followed by senior physicians. A senior physician (usually Knight) then provided a synthesis of the discussion, after which Karl and Will presented their views.[16]

According to case conference procedure, exchanges and debates among the physicians could follow. A senior physician like Knight would state a posture acceptable to the conferees. It needed to be worded so that all of the disputing parties could agree. But the Menningers had the option of modifying this final conference position. If the brothers differed, the custom of the early household obtained. Karl had the last word. The presenting physician was then to complete the order sheet in line with this final position.[17]

Clearly, a rather circumscribed role for the doctor was one unique feature in the format of the milieu therapy program. Both the guide to the order sheet and the brothers' hegemony in the case conference were instrumental in a doctor's diagnosis and therapy regime. The doctor was not even to write a letter to a patient's family unless it was cleared with Will.[18]

The role Will delineated for the lower staff was also unusual. He insisted that nurses, activities therapists, and attendants understand not only the supervising physician's orders for the patient's hospital routine but "the rationale for the orders in each instance." By understanding the unconscious sources of patient maladies, they would be in a position to implement the order sheet and to suggest appropriate revisions to the physician. In fact, Will required hospital nurses to write detailed and specific notes on each patient, in the form of daily reports. The patient's doctor was to treat these reports seriously; they were to provide the basis for a give-and-take between doctor and nurse.[19]

It is striking that Will assigned a role to the auxiliary staff, particularly his nurses, that far exceeded the influence of auxiliary workers at most "new psychiatry" facilities of the 1930s. Whereas the physician would see his patient for only thirty minutes or an hour every day, Will was struck by the fact that nurses, attendants, and activities therapists would be in contact with the patient for the remaining hours of the day. Their supervision would determine, to a large extent, whether the drive disturbances of sick patients were successfully corrected. It is noteworthy that Will also gave unprecedented responsibilities to janitors, barbers, and other workers on the hospital grounds. All staff contact with patients had serious therapeutic consequences. The labor of every person who worked in the hospital was potentially important; the lowest employee could be the one most responsible for a patient's recovery. Hence, despite his decree that the doctor was to give orders to the auxiliary staff, Will had hardly designed a traditional doctor-centered facility. Physicians could find their influence circumscribed on the one side by the Menningers and on the other side by the auxiliary staff.[20]

Will maintained that his auxiliary staff would be particularly useful "medicine" if they properly supervised patient activities programs. If the central factor behind mental illness was a distortion in the patient's unconscious drive mechanism, activities therapy routines geared toward the specific problems of each patient represented the most fruitful way of eliminating the distortion. Will explained how the mentally ill person usually suffered from "pent-up hatred" toward people closest to him, especially family members. Through planned recreational, educational, and occupational activities, he could learn to refocus or displace his hatred and the hostile and erotic drives behind the hatred onto socially acceptable targets. Rather than feel agitated because he craved to kill a parent or a sibling, for example, a patient might learn, through his occupational therapist, to channel his aggressions toward a pile of wood and to make something from that wood. Similarly, a recreation therapist could shift the target of the patient's hatred or envy from a loved one to an opposing team.[21]

Even if the physician made a proper diagnosis and prescribed the right medicine, nursing, and activities regime, Will insisted that recovery would be limited unless the staff went about their tasks with the proper attitudes. The "atmosphere created through our attitudes is actually more important than what we say and what we do. Many patients react to our feelings and manners much more than they do to our words." This was why Will attached extreme importance to the long list of possible staff attitudes detailed within his guide to the order sheet. Collectively, they were equivalent to the drug to cure mental illness that he had sought to discover. In the guide, Will was able to summarize his approach to cure quite clearly:

> if we are to accomplish the therapeutic aim, it is essential that all persons who come into contact with the patient should maintain a uniform attitude insofar as possible; in other words, one nurse must not be indulgent and another severe, one therapist must not be solicitous and another indifferent.

The whole point of the physician's checking appropriate attitudes on his order sheet was to ensure that the entire staff displayed the same attitudes toward a particular patient. "Uniform direction toward a specific goal in treatment" was vital if the patient was to be cured; a disparity in staff attitudes could throw the patient into hopeless confusion.[22]

More than anything else, a sentence from Will's paper at the 1932 annual meeting of the AMA summarized the nature of the "scientific" psychiatric hospital he was struggling to build: "Above all, it must be a highly organized, efficient institution—and at the same time conceal the organized efficiency and the impersonal institutional air."[23] The formal design for his treatment program seemed to meet these aims. Although staff efficiency was a very high priority, patients were not to be instructed in this aspect of the program. Rather, Will wanted patients to regard staff behavior toward them as spontaneous but consistent.

IV

Both the terms of a 1930 agreement between the Menninger brothers and "scientific" hospital guidelines placed Will, as director, at the top of the command structure. Karl was to restrict himself to writing, to a limited number of analyses, and to supervision of psychotherapists stationed in the clinic building. But by the mid-1930s, if not earlier, the older brother was exerting substantial influence over the various hospital-based physicians. Referring to himself as a senior consultant to the facility, Karl came increasingly to order hospital residents and to perform control work (i.e., supervision of analytic technique) with doctors undergoing training analyses. This increasing authority Karl wielded over hospital physicians may have had some bearing upon Will's decision to give his auxiliary staff unprecedented responsibility and to confine the authority of the doctors. Certainly, it was decisive in Will's attempts to limit Karl to hospital rounds on Sundays. This pointed to a significant disparity between the formal guidelines that Will developed to structure hospital practice and the social reality of daily hospital life. But there were other disparities.[24]

The guide to the order sheet was vital to the social structure of the hospital, for it linked doctors, auxiliary staff, and patients. The guide was also crucial to the highest medical council in the hospital—the physicians' case conference. The case report that a physician wrote for this conference and the issues that were discussed were influenced heavily by the fact that the physician's order sheet had to be completed as soon as the conference ended. In determining how Will's formal "scientific" plans for the hospital were instituted, it is useful to examine how the guide to the order sheet was constructed and implemented.

Even though the formal language of the guide had physicians giving orders to auxiliary staff in the traditional hierarchic fashion of the medical profession, the document was formulated—and revised—in the course of the 1930s along very democratic lines. As Will recalled:

> We would meet with a big blackboard—we had all these squares marked off on the blackboard, and we would argue about them and fill them in, the committee from the nurses or the committee from the recreational people or the occupational people. . . . We had lots of fun. We used to go on picnics and social things together.

By "we," Will obviously meant himself and nurses, recreational therapists, and occupational therapists. It was essentially an auxiliary-staff undertaking, with members of each of the staff occupations present to represent the interests of fellow specialists. This fostered pluralistic specialty divisions within the staff.[25]

Perhaps because hospital attendants were supervised by the nursing staff and performed random support services for doctors, nurses, and activities therapists, they did not participate in sessions to draft and revise the guide. A few doctors came to certain meetings, but nurses and activities therapists attended all the sessions—sometimes even in full force rather than through their representatives. At these meetings, Will assumed full command as hospital director. He came with drafts of portions of the guide and conducted himself like the instructor in a seminar, "spending a lot of time explaining the rationale of milieu therapy and the meaning of the Guide."[26]

Clearly, Will's sessions to draft and revise the guide to the order sheet showed realities of hospital life that were not indicated in his formal outline. Hospital formalities never revealed that the director was bypassing his attendants (who, in the 1930s, were entirely males) and to a somewhat lesser degree his physicians (mostly men) in establishing the primary governance document for his staff. He was favoring his nurses (almost all females) and his activities therapists (primarily women). By 1938, Will had institutionalized this rapport. He had drawn together the director of nursing, several occupational therapists, the director of recreational therapy, and one physician in his own informal executive cabinet, to administer the hospital treatment program. By underrepresenting the physicians, who were often tied to Karl, this arrangement helped to limit the power of his older brother over hospital life.[27]

This is not to say that Will entirely violated a premise of his milieu therapy outline—that the daily physician case conference was to be the chief agency in hospital therapy. What if the prescribing physician, supported by a case conference consensus but not the auxiliary staff, completed his order sheet and refused to change it? In that event, were those on the auxiliary staff to treat the patient along prescribed lines although they disagreed with the physician? The possibility that under Will's regime, lower staff could not always "be themselves"—that they sometimes had to repress their basic feelings and become passive agents—is one of the most serious charges against the Menninger hospital of the 1930s and the guide-to-the-order-sheet tradition. According to critics like Ezra Stotland and Arthur Kobler, the repression felt by auxiliary staff was surely communicated to patients, producing an antitherapeutic atmosphere.[28]

This charge ignores another important departure from Will's formal outline—one that he stressed in random conversations. The nurse, activities therapist, or attendant was expected to execute the prescribed attitudes only within the limits of his or her own personality structure. Hence, although "nearly uniform" staff execution of designated attitudes was most desirable for the patient from a medical standpoint, "variation" was inevitable, given "the differences in the personalities of those attempting to apply them." Will had "no illusions that people can change their personality" or simply adhere to a prescribed attitude "if patient, John Dokes, took a slug at you."[29]

This is not to say that auxiliary staff could subvert a physician's prescribed attitudes for treatment. Will was a strict if reasonable disciplinarian and heralded "scientific specificity" as one of the cardinal innovations of his program. When he learned that several night nurses were ignoring order sheet prescriptions, he had no reservations about firing them.[30]

Although most auxiliary staff did not directly and regularly violate prescribed attitudes, several found it difficult always to be diligent. With eleven potential "management devices" from which to direct patients and seven possible "attitudes" to follow, one activities therapist recalled, the physician's order sheet was overprecise and therefore laborious for an auxiliary staff member to follow. Nurses seemed to have a particularly trying time, especially those who came to the hospital with training and experience elsewhere. They tended to compare attitudes prescribed on the order sheet to alternative modes they had learned in other hospitals and sometimes found the alternatives more plausible. Owing to such difficulties, auxiliary staff tended to implement their orders somewhat loosely. By the late 1930s, for example, recreation therapists divided their labors so that they could avoid working with patients whom they found especially disagreeable and avoid using therapies that felt "uncomfortable."[31]

Nurse Mildred Pratt found herself deemphasizing her order sheet prescriptions during certain emergencies; she followed intuitive responses instead. Once, for example, she departed from the prescribed attitude by yelling at a patient who had upset a rack of cafeteria trays. But after every breach, Pratt experienced guilt, feeling that she "could have done better" or that her response "could have been more appropriate." She was happier when she adhered to the order sheet as closely as possible. Activities therapist Peggy Ralston, on the other hand, never departed significantly from order sheet prescriptions. She had a profound loyalty to Will and felt good about herself when she pleased him.[32]

When a variety of factors are considered—Will's rivalry with Karl, the language and detail of the guide to the order sheet, divisions within the hospital staff, contacts between physicians and nurses, differences in staff personalities—it is understandable that there was a lack of uniformity in treating patients. There were simply too many variables for appreciable consistency in the way physicians, auxiliary staff, or for that matter the Menninger brothers behaved. The formalities of Will's "scientific" program sometimes contrasted sharply with the social realities.

V

Will's most distinctive contribution to the "new psychiatry" was to delineate a clear and precise "scientific"-medical therapy program in describing his hospital operation. However, there were major departures from the medical chain of command in that hospital and disparate competing power centers among the staff. That is, alongside the hospital's "scientific" face there was a pluralistic face or mode of operation, characterized by competing specialty groups. More than any other factor, the unusually important role Will assigned to his auxiliary staff enhanced their power against that of the physicians and essentially promoted pluralism. He also contributed to two other faces within his hospital—a community face and, even more significant, a family face.

At times, Will openly acknowledged that he was out to build a "model" albeit "miniature community." Indeed, he strongly promoted the appearance and feeling of a community because it would facilitate "a major reeducation of the individual [patient] in a protected environment." In addition to the hospital buildings, he proposed a row of shops to house the barber and beautician, plus a snack center and craft pavilions, an art center, a club room, and a small theater. To be sure, C. Jonathan Slocum at Craig House, William Russell at Bloomingdale, and C. C. Burleigh at the Hartford Retreat had somewhat similar visions. But in the name of a community-centered existence, Will went further. He promoted the tradition of unmarried staff, particularly nurses and activities therapists, dwelling on or adjacent to the hospital grounds. He expected all who worked in the hospital to take at least one meal a day in the hospital dining room. To be on the director's good side, and for convenience as well, many staff took two of their meals at the facility. Will also tried to build a sense of community through collective staff-patient celebrations of holidays. But in a characteristic intrusion upon Will's plans, Karl insisted that regular parties, picnics, and birthday celebrations were preferable occasions to cement community feeling.[33]

Both brothers were committed, then, to the vision of the hospital grounds as an intimate and friendly community. It meshed well with their missionary vision of leading an organization in the forefront of the "new psychiatry." Other measures were forthcoming. A library was established; amateur theatrical productions by patients and staff for the hospital community were encouraged. Provision was made for a patient newspaper and for two staff publications—a newsletter and the *Bulletin of the Menninger Clinic* (for staff professional papers). Although bias against minorities may have been somewhat less conspicuous at Menninger than at Sheppard-Pratt or other centers, a craving for community harmony through homogeneity was particularly responsible for the exclusion of black patients, a quota on Jewish physicians, and a separate dining room for black staff.[34]

If the third face of Will's hospital was that of an intimate community, the fourth was of the hospital as a large and cohesive family. The familial quality of the facility was stressed frequently, elaborately, and movingly.

Staff often referred to "the homelike atmosphere" of the place, where people lived as "a small intimate family group." Belonging to "the same family," they "worked, studied, and played together." The Menninger blood family was characterized as the basis for this larger "family spirit." All others—staff and patients—were somehow to be assimilated or absorbed into the blood family and become an "extended family," so that everybody in the community felt "part of the family." During business slumps in this Depression decade, when the patient census was low, most staff cited "family loyalty" as the reason for taking voluntary leaves without pay. Will proudly noted that everybody—patients and staff—belonged to "our family."[35]

In August 1932, as Will's milieu therapy program was being initiated,

Karl claimed that despite his brother's "scientific" format, the hospital was organizing itself along familial lines: "employers, for example, represent parents, and employees represent children or offspring, and again in the hospital doctors represent parents, the nurses sometimes children, sometimes teachers, sometimes siblings." As the decade progressed, Karl changed his mind several times on which segment of the hospital community played particular family roles. But he remained adamant that one got a profound sense of personal relationships in the hospital by thinking in familial terms.[36]

In characterizing hospital life as familial, most staff (and some patients) noted that Will was more than a thorough hospital director. Leaving to John Stone, Merle Hoover, and Mildred Law the financial aspects of hospital affairs, he ran all other phases with considerable administrative efficiency. Will made rounds daily. He knew all the patients and staff members by name and something about their backgrounds. Despite his good cheer, he was a stickler for rules and insisted that hospital procedures always be observed. It was equally clear that Will stayed at the hospital long beyond his scheduled hours and often on weekends, to be available to patients and staff.[37]

Naturally, Will's competence and availability won him considerable support within the hospital. So did his calm, unflustered manner. He could walk through a hospital unit that was experiencing momentary disarray and restore order merely by voicing a few suggestions. Will also had the capacity to criticize a staff member or to inquire about his professional or personal problems in a way that was "always warm, gracious and supportive," so that "everyone tried not to disappoint him or to let him down." Will exemplified so well the attitude of "firm kindness" specified in his guide to the order sheet that the majority of the staff and many of the patients regarded him as the "good father" of the hospital. Although some objected to his tight management, he usually cultivated the loyalty of every person on the hospital grounds. "That's what kept you here," one activities therapist recalled. He "made you feel appreciated and part of the place." In essence, he represented an ideal father.[38]

If traditional medical hierarchy and the guide to the order sheet placed physicians atop the chain of command, doctors deferred to Will almost instinctively. Their loyalty to him kept some of them at the hospital longer than they thought was in their professional interest. Others felt they betrayed him when they resigned. More even than with physicians, Will cultivated a sense of obligation in the auxiliary staff. He was their warm yet strong teacher and leader, encouraging them to develop professionally (several made significant contributions to professional journals) and explaining how to deal with particularly difficult patients. Nurse Garland Lewis recalled what was hardly an unusual encounter. She had violated hospital procedure by taking a violent patient to the bathroom without an accompanying nurse. When the patient attacked her, she had no backup staff support. The incident left Lewis fearful that in breaching hospital procedure she had betrayed Will. But he put her at ease the next morning, asking if she had been hurt. Avoiding formal admonitions or a lecture on procedures, he then questioned Lewis softly, as his father had questioned him: "What did you learn from the experience?"[39]

If Will was the paterfamilias, what familial role did the other physicians play? Although there were twelve to eighteen doctors at any one time during Will's directorship, their functions varied tremendously. Some, like Ralph Fellows and Norman Reider, were also considered father-like. Others, such as Robert Knight and Douglass Orr, spent most of their time conducting individual psychotherapy sessions; they lacked extensive roles or representations within the hospital "family spirit." As a rule, female physicians were not regarded as equals among the doctors, despite their medical credentials. A few, like Sylvia Allen, were not always taken seriously by the Menningers or other senior doctors because of their "wild [psychoanalytic] interpretations" and their habits of using a "jumble of words" instead of precisely phrased comments in case conferences. Others, like Anne Benjamin, distressed them with "feminine perversity" and strong-mindedness. Clearly, the perception of the staff physician in the hospital's family face varied considerably, and gender was important in the differentiation.[40]

If female doctors were not always "trustworthy," female nurses were highly regarded. Will clung to the familial vision of the nurse as a mother who served as "hostess of the ward" and "carries out the orders of the physician." This was hardly unusual for hospital psychiatry at the time. But his elaboration of the vision was striking. Will maintained that women entered nursing to "sublimate their maternal desires" and to "outclass" their mothers. Because male nurses lacked "maternal instincts," they would probably never "be able to compete with female nurses in usefulness." Consequently, Will hired an almost entirely female nursing staff. Olga Weiss recalled how Will taught her that the nurse was the hospital mother and "her primary duties are seeing to the comfort of those persons within her unit." Through this role, she exercised much power. In her presence, "the patient will unconsciously put himself into the role of a small child," susceptible to considerable influence.[41]

Isabel Erickson, Will's influential superintendent of nursing, elaborated his perspective of the nurse as a comforting and nurturing mother.

Even more than the hospital director, Erickson stressed the significance of the nurse as crucial to the patient's eventual recovery. She was "the doctor's chief observer of the patient's behavior" and overcame patient resistance to his treatment measures. Will idealized Erickson and insisted that the nurse was to spend her time helping the doctor just as Erickson helped him. He added that the greatest evil in psychiatric nursing was for nurses to become enmeshed as a "family of sisters." "Sisterhood" constricted support for the physician.[42]

It can hardly be doubted that Will was thinking of his mother as he sketched out his role for the hospital nurse. Flo had been more than "the physician's hand"; her role had been crucial to family life, and Charles had hardly been able to get along without her direction. Yet Will also felt that Flo had sometimes been lacking as a nurturer during his early years, as she became involved with her Bible studies classes. In some measure, Will's ideal nurse for his hospital family seemed to merge his mother's strength and competence with the more nurturing and acquiescent "kinner, kich, korrich" (children, kitchen, church) traditions of her Pennsylvania Dutch heritage.

The position of the activities therapists was closely linked to that of the nurses. Most nurses and activities therapists lived together in the nurses' residential house. They socialized and attended the same training classes. Both groups met regularly with Will to draft and revise the guide. It was predictable that a number of female activities therapists came to be regarded, alongside nurses, as hospital mothers, while several male therapists (particularly activities department heads) shared with some doctors the image of fathers. But Will tended to lump less skillful activities therapists with attendants. Both the ineffective activities therapists and almost all attendants required firm supervision.[43]

Clearly, attendants were held in low regard: "many of our attendants came to us because they cannot obtain other employment." Will felt that attendants had to be closely regulated because of their lower class status, their "low" intelligence, and their irresponsibility. Otherwise, they might mistreat a patient and contribute to his misconduct or even a suicide. More than any other group on the treatment staff, attendants—if unregulated—could bring unfortunate litigation against the hospital, destroying its reputation. Nurses, doctors, and several activities therapists shared Will's perspective on the poor character of attendants. Attendants assumed a station in the familial hospital as "younger" and considerably less adept than their "older sister and brother" activities therapists. William Roberts recalled that it was a difficult position to occupy. When he joined the hospital in 1938 as an attendant, he was never sure whether he was "part of the Menninger family."[44]

Within the "family spirit," the patients were characterized almost universally by the staff as "very like children." They had returned, through "infantile regression," to a "childhood situation," where they could make "childish demands" and find "delusions of childish power and satisfaction." Because they were so childlike, it was incumbent upon all members of the hospital family to take care of them, to see that their daily needs were met, to ensure that they did not hurt themselves, and even to censor their mail home so that they "did not distort facts."[45]

Anywhere from 95 to 158 patients were admitted in a given year. Most were about thirty-five or forty years old and very bright. Their intelligence test scores ranged from high average to brilliant, and they had especially strong verbal abilities. "They represent for the most part the upper strata of society," Will noted, "people with broad cultural background and many of them very prominent in their communities." In this sense, they resembled the patients at elite eastern private hospitals. However, most came from the western Middle West; few were from the Atlantic seaboard. Unlike many of the patients in the eastern hospitals, few at Menninger were from established, aristocratic families. Rather, their parents had moved from middle-class to moderately wealthy status, or they had made the shift themselves. Menninger's male patients were usually successful professionals or businessmen. There were even a few prominent movie stars. Yet many felt that they were not keeping up with their fathers in entrepreneurial pursuits. In most cases, the stock market crash and the Depression had only marginally affected their earning power. Most female patients were married and homemakers. Despite the Depression, they had been able to entertain lavishly. Some worked with their husbands, while a few had successful careers in entertainment and the professions. Surprisingly, religion was not important to very many patients; few had much contact with a local minister or priest. Before coming to Menninger, most patients had undergone some outpatient treatment from psychiatrists; a few had tried other private hospitals. More than many of the "new psychiatry" facilities, Will's hospital tended to be a place of last resort.[46]

The wealth and intelligence of most patients were obvious to the hospital staff. The auxiliary staff had been very hard pressed by the Depression. Even physicians belonged to the struggling middle class. Case records suggest that both physicians and auxiliary staff whose own real incomes were declining were sometimes irked by patients who could continue to pay high fees and wear expensive clothes. *Roundabout,* the patient newspaper, was wholly inattentive to the Depression. It printed several clever and sometimes cruel exposés of the frugal habits of various staff members.[47]

Relational problems, particularly marital discord, were common-place among Menninger patients. Roughly 40 percent of them were clas-sified as psychotic and the remainder as psychoneurotic. In a revealing comparison of Will's facility to eastern hospitals of the mid-1930s, Dwight Macdonald found that Menninger had a far more varied clientele: "It treats people suffering from every type of nervous and mental disease, from epilepsy to neurasthenia, from pernicious anemia to alcoholism." Diagnoses in monthly hospital reports listed three preponderant mala-dies—schizophrenia (paranoid and catatonic), "neurotic character," and alcoholism. Combined with these, patients also suffered from various drug addictions, depressions, hysterias, and eating disorders. Most suf-fered from learning disabilities brought on by poor memory, senility, and anxieties. Arrested sexual development and inappropriate emotional out-bursts were commonplace. The staff propensity to characterize patients as children may have been a hopeful label to signify growth, spirit, and a future for a group of people who needed to believe in all three.[48]

During Will's directorship, the daily patient census ranged from twenty-three to forty-four. It was not unusual for a patient to stay only two months—considerably less than the discharge period at state hospi-tals and even at a number of private facilities. Given the hospital's psycho-analytic orientation, staff preferred a significant level of patient improve-ment—for the patient to "develop insight" and to learn to "work through" fundamental emotional problems. Neither stabilization nor the relief of symptoms was regarded as an important improvement. Measured against this demanding standard, the statistical results at the time of discharge were less than optimal. Only 5 to 10 percent of the patients were classified as having "recovered" fully from their afflic-tions. About 25 percent were listed as "unimproved." The majority— anywhere from 55 to 75 percent—had "improved" somewhat. The Men-ningers and their doctors acknowledged that few patients had "enough depth" psychologically to withstand the extensive psychoanalysis essen-tial for full "recovery." Rather, they felt that many patients clung des-perately to various compulsive rituals and rigid thoughts in an effort to fend off deep psychotic outbreaks. Analysis might free them of compul-sions, but it could open them to full-scale schizophrenia. Therefore, it was best to "improve" the patient somewhat through a directed but not excessively probing therapeutic regimen of psychoanalytically informed procedures, even if many on staff did not regard this as a momentous accomplishment.[49]

Given the social and psychiatric characteristics of these patients, and the fact that most made only modest recoveries, the staff characterization of them as children is troubling. Staff attitudes toward patients were regulated, and everything the patient did conformed to a tight schedule. Like children, patients were taught not only "to play" but what to eat and when to sleep. Will defended this protective atmosphere as essential for schizophrenic and other highly regressed patients. Like immature children, he insisted, they had lost the capacity to organize their lives. The hospital had temporarily to provide external structure while patients rebuilt their internal regulatory mechanisms.[50]

Will's analogy of patients to children was problematic when applied to regressive psychotics, but no less questionable as a characterization of alcoholics and neurotics. A few Menninger doctors and nurses, who had worked at or visited other "new psychiatry" facilities, where the environment was less protective, maintained that the child image prompted hospital controls that made it difficult for some of the patients to mature and leave. After a few years at Chestnut Lodge, where the treatment program was less regimented, physician Robert Morse returned and severely criticized Will's program. Too many Menninger patients were slow to learn to fend for themselves, he warned; they were reluctant to return to their families and their jobs.[51]

Will might have replied to Morse and to other staff critics that if Chestnut Lodge and other "new psychiatry" centers were less rigid, their treatment outcomes were not demonstrably better, while their patient suicide and self-mutilation rates probably exceeded rates at Menninger. And he could have defended his image of the patient as child with Simmel's observation that hospitalizations often prompted regressive longings to be cared for like a youngster. But he decided against these rebuttals and chose instead to answer critics by stressing the "family spirit" as a face of hospital life. He explained how the family face, with doctors and nurses as parental figures and patients as children, promoted a sense of warmth and cohesion among the staff that nicely complemented his "scientific" program for precise regulation of all phases of the treatment program. By emphasizing a "family spirit," Will derived three significant benefits: he justified the kind of institution he was struggling to develop; he did not weaken his promising career as an innovator within the "new psychiatry" by casting aspersions upon other prominent psychiatrists and their programs; finally, he averted explicit debate on whether his milieu therapy program was too protective of his patients.[52]

It is important to recognize that Will's program regulated the attitudes and actions of staff almost as much as it regulated patients. Only the Menningers were exempt. In some measure, this seemed to parallel the family household, where the boarders' activities had been more closely supervised than those of family members. In that household, the boarders had been both patients and staff in some rough sense. Like patients, many had suffered from varied emotional distresses; like staff, they had performed chores for the family. This suggests a fourth benefit—by carefully distinguishing most staff (the adults) from patients (the children), the family face seemed to distinguish the hospital from the family household. That distinction may have provided staff at least some vague assurance that despite regulation, they were in fact mature, free, and fully autonomous adults. Only the patients—the children—might be said to live within a paternalistic and protective environment.

VI

Will's therapy program was demanding. Before World War II, to be sure, American hospital staff generally were not expected to have much time for themselves. At Menninger, it was even more difficult to enjoy much of a life off the hospital grounds. When combined with pluralistic divisions of power and competition for authority, Will's "scientific" face required an intense staff presence no less than six days a week. The community and familial faces drew him and his colleagues even more fully into their hospital activities. At times, it appeared as if the hospital could cut off staff from their private lives and personal concerns. The family face especially had this capacity.

One of the sanitarium's earliest policies contributed to just such a gap between private life and hospital life. At some point in the late 1920s, the brothers decided to exclude staff spouses from all buildings and grounds. The policy amounted to the exclusion of wives, for most married staff were men. The precipitating event that led to this decree was the admission of a Topeka resident who was well known to several staff wives. The fear was that because the wives had no psychiatric training, they would not know how to respond properly to the patient within a hospital setting.[53]

There were other advantages to the policy. John Stone stated the first: it assured medical confidentiality. Because of the specialized nature of hospital psychiatry and the stigma attached to being a mental patient, strict exclusion of all outsiders was imperative. The Menningers and a few of their doctors advanced the second justification: spouses complicated patient transference relationships with the medical staff. Patients were prone to transfer images of their own parents, siblings, and spouses to their physicians, their analysts, and even their nurses and activities therapists. In "working through" those images, the patients discovered crucial but repressed information about their lives. However, when the patient saw his doctor's wife in the flesh, the transference relationship to that doctor could be impeded if not destroyed.[54]

These two justifications for spouse exclusion were sanctioned by the "scientific" face of hospital life, under which confidentiality was important and therapeutic effectiveness could hardly be ignored. The problem was that Will's hospital was more than a medical facility. It was rooted in a family household, and a strong "family spirit" was encouraged. With family feelings so prevalent, it is easy to understand why staff wives resented the policy. Catharine Menninger was particularly disturbed that she could no longer take her child to the hospital grounds on Sundays to join Will for dinner. Physician Douglass Orr recalled that he was as upset over the policy as his wife. When the Orrs adopted a son, hospital staff threw a baby shower on the grounds, "but my wife was not invited." Florence Knight complained that the hospital was like a "jealous mistress" who drew her husband away from her home.[55]

In the early 1940s, the spouse policy was modified. Psychiatrist Milton Erickson visited Topeka and, in the course of his stay, hypnotized a physician's wife as part of a demonstration. Under hypnosis, the wife bitterly criticized Karl for excluding wives. Taken by the outburst, Karl sent her roses. Then he announced—over his brother's objection—that the exclusion policy was modified. He intruded upon Will's hospital domain by declaring that wives would be invited to certain general meetings and various staff social events. But they were to be kept out of sight of patients.[56]

Florence Knight's recourse to the term "jealous mistress" was hardly fortuitous. The separation of the hospital family from the personal family carried obvious sexual implications. "I suppose most of us made passes at the secretaries or nurses at clinic parties with wives excluded and bourbon very much included," Douglass Orr acknowledged. Catharine Menninger and Margaret Stone felt the parties were scheduled so that doctors could dance with female staff instead of their wives. Charles was known by staff secretaries as a "fanny pincher." Nurses, activities therapists, and doctors frequently conducted surreptitious liaisons in defiance of hospital policy that precluded staff dating. Senior female staff, like administrator Mildred Law, were encouraged to stay unwed. In fact, Law felt pressured to break off her engagement. She feared that she would disappoint men on staff if she wed an off-campus man, and she might even feel compelled to resign. It was somewhat veiled, but there was an erotic side to hospital community life. The separation of the "family spirit" of the workplace from the family at home contributed to this quality.[57]

Karl was probably referring to this sexual aspect of hospital existence when he recalled: "We deliberately did not involve our wives in [hospital] details, but they *knew.*" Grace was aware that her husband had taken up with several women during a marriage that never seemed to work. Lillian Johnson, the wife of a Topeka judge, had been one of these women. At the time, Karl was in analysis with Franz Alexander, who encouraged him to have a mistress. When the Johnson affair ceased in the early 1930s, Karl became involved with his secretary, Jeanetta Lyle. The relationship persisted for several years, and finally he divorced Grace and married Jeanetta. Karl maintained discretion in these liaisons; only a few staff associates knew. He was away from the hospital so frequently that his private life was not a conspicuous topic for discussion.[58]

Will, of course, was another matter. When word spread that he was having an affair with the nursing superintendent, Isabel Erickson, every member of the hospital staff was concerned.

Will's marriage had begun under less than happy circumstances, for Catharine had not wanted to become part of his Topeka family. According to Will's diary, she suffered from "a temporary but recurring depression on the shortcomings of marital life" during their first year of marriage. He suspected this was related to "the amount of time I spent away from home." In part, he was right. Throughout his first months at the clinic and for several years to come, Catharine was fretting "over my humdrum existence, and envying the exciting, worthwhile lives of the (to me) glamorous nurses who worked with Dr. Will." This underscored her concern over his interest in "pretty girls" while she stayed at home to raise three sons. Will valued her domesticity, but she remained less than sanguine.[59]

To alleviate Catharine's resentment, Will tried to separate work life from home life. He almost never mentioned the hospital at home. He seemed particularly intent on maintaining this separation during the twelve years when he built the hospital's milieu therapy program. "I'm sure my own home life runs smoothest when divorced from business," he stressed. And though he certainly cared for his three sons, Sunday was the only time he did much with them. All three wanted him around to inspire them, as he inspired his hospital staff, but he rarely obliged. Will "had problems communicating with his own children," his middle son recalled. He was so zealous in executing the spouse exclusion policy that no member of his family felt welcome on the hospital grounds, even after Karl made the policy more flexible. Indeed, Catharine recalled sulking in a car in the hospital parking lot during a marriage ceremony in which her husband gave away the bride.[60]

Clearly, Will lived in two distinct worlds and devoted most of his energies to the hospital. As this became an obvious pattern, he began to take an interest in Isabel Erickson. Born on the outskirts of Topeka, Erickson graduated with high honors from the Christ's Hospital nursing school. She arrived on the Menninger grounds in 1932 for a six-month course in psychiatric nursing, performed brilliantly, and was hired as a staff nurse. In 1934, Will had no hesitation about naming her superintendent despite her junior status. Will supported Erickson's enhanced authority because he respected her deeply; he was impressed by her organizational skills and her mastery of detail when she accompanied him on his hospital rounds. But when she began to put a flower in his lapel in the morning and to polish his white shoes in the summer, Will started to take a deep emotional interest in the woman who, more than any other, was regarded as his counterpart—the kind but firm and efficient hospital mother.[61]

The affair followed as a matter of course. It lasted until Will reported for army duty in 1942. Much of the time they spent with each other was at Erickson's house, where she lived alone. They also attended many professional meetings together, usually rooming in the same hotel. Periodically they traveled by train to view a new hospital procedure or technique. Once Will asked Erickson to drive with him to attend a friend's funeral in Nebraska. Erickson had even visited Will in Chicago when he was in analysis with Franz Alexander. During one of her visits, he wrote to his wife of Erickson's stay with him: "I hope she had a good time—said she did. . . . I had a good time with her, but I wished many times it was my own girl!" Catharine did not need this letter to realize what was happening. She already knew that Alexander had encouraged her husband to continue his affair with the head nurse and that Will was doing just that. Indeed, when she met with Alexander in 1934, he had even urged her to take a lover. "I wished wildly that I could be his [Will's] mistress instead of his wife," she recalled.[62]

In a 1937 article on psychiatric hospital nursing, Erickson wrote: "As Dr. William Menninger has stated, 'the psychiatrist expects the nurse to be a confidential friend, a companion in recreational and occupational activities.' " Erickson and Menninger maintained such a relationship for many years. It symbolized the merger of chief physician and head nurse in both the "scientific" and the familial faces of the hospital.[63]

Almost all hospital staff knew about Will's affair, but few chose to discuss it. "I didn't want it to be there," nurse Mildred Pratt remarked. "I wanted everything perfect." She hoped nothing would tarnish her ideal hospital community, "so I shut my eyes." So did recreation therapist Lou Davie. Will seemed far happier and better adjusted than Karl, Davie recalled; he had no cause for an illicit relationship. Will's second in command, Dr. Norman Reider, wondered why the head of the hospital required a mistress if he had completed successful training analysis under Alexander. Other staff shared in this puzzlement. Should they be operating a hospital built upon psychoanalytic principles if psychoanalysis had not given Will a satisfactory home life? Even Karl was distressed by the affair, because of the effect it might have upon the hospital community. Unlike the others, however, he could testify that an analysis with Alexander hardly promoted marital fidelity.[64]

Only one member of the staff—junior physician Harlan Crank—was willing to confront Will directly. To verify in his own mind what he assumed was taking place, Crank drove by Erickson's house several evenings and spotted Will's parked car. Sometime in 1941, he called Will aside and told him that the affair was eroding staff confidence in the director's leadership. Crank even underscored the hypocrisy of a hospital director who officially prohibited staff from dating while having a relationship with the head nurse. But Will would not listen. Repeating what Alexander had told him, he owned up to the affair as one of life's more common occurrences; kind and caring husbands often had mistresses. He added that the affair was a private matter and had no bearing upon the management of the hospital community. The hospital was one thing, he told Crank, and personal matters were another.[65]

VII

On November 10, 1942, Will received a commission as army lieutenant colonel, with orders to report to Washington by November 24. The issues of concern to hospital staff were obvious. Who would direct operations in Will's absence? When the war ended, would he return and run the hospital as he had over the past decade? Could the complex and unique hospital social world and treatment program that he had developed maintain themselves during his absence?

Will made his intentions clear: "when I return I would much prefer to run the hospital—doing the job as I did before." He designated himself medical director on leave and appointed Karl acting medical director. Believing that a Menninger must head the central institution in a family organization, Will nonetheless tried to impress upon Karl that he was to be only nominally in charge: "I do not believe your best talents are in the direction of actively managing the hospital." Instead, Will designated a young hospital doctor, Robert Worthington, to administer the facility and to supervise day-to-day operations. Worthington was to be de facto director. Merton Gill, another newcomer to the physician staff, was to head the new outpatient department and to help Worthington with hospital problems. Robert Knight would remain head of psychotherapy operations. Charles Menninger was asked to come out of semiretirement and make rounds with Worthington two or three days a week. With this physician staff assigned primary responsibilities, Will sought to insulate hospital policy and operations from Karl. His brother might be consulted concerning specific patients in difficult situations and on broad legal and financial matters, but these were to be the limits of his duties. However, Karl had time on his hands. Despite the publication of two more books, *Man Against Himself* (1938) and *Love Against Hate* (1942), lectures, travel, study, and a second analysis, with Ruth Mack Brunswick, he was not fully occupied.[66]

Indeed, Karl had distressed Will by gradually assuming a larger role in hospital affairs in the late 1930s. He attended physician case conferences regularly. Transcripts of those meetings reveal that he came more and more to dominate both the questioning of the patient under review and the psychiatric evaluation of the patient's condition. As well, he supervised the analysts in the clinic building with increasing rigor, demanding a say whenever hospital staff required the services of "his" analysts. By the early 1940s, Karl was so involved with hospital affairs that he sometimes changed policies over Will's opposition. In certain circumstances, he had nearly become hospital director. If he had made such incursions upon his brother's responsibilities while Will was running the facility, complete takeover seemed certain in the brother's absence. Consequently, Will made detailed preparations for others to govern the hospital.

Will felt that although Robert Worthington was only a resident, he had more detailed knowledge of internal hospital operations than others on the physician staff. Consequently, he was the logical figure to administer hospital affairs. But Karl was Worthington's analyst and was not above using an analytic relation for political gain.

Karl's troubled analysis with Franz Alexander promoted a sense that it was sometimes permissible to breach accepted professional standards in the analytic process. Alexander had often cut short his full analytic hour with Karl and had mocked his patient's religious devotedness. Although analysts of the period tended to give priority to sexual satisfaction, Karl felt that Alexander had violated analytic neutrality by urging him to maintain both a wife and a mistress. All in all, "my analysis with Alexander had left me with a certain insincerity." It had also left Karl with the image of an analyst who imposed his own values on his analysand and seemed in some vague way to elevate his own interests over those of the analysand. This was why Karl ended up, even in his final session with Alexander, protecting himself by "concealing some memories from Alex." Karl's analysis with Ruth Mack Brunswick, seven years later, provided still another model of an analyst who seemed somehow to regard her own values and interests over those of her analysand. Brunswick was addicted to morphine and sleeping pills in the period when she worked with him. Karl had some sense of these addictions but was even more disturbed because she complained constantly of her physical ills. Because of Brunswick's own difficulties, as well as her tendency to fall asleep and even to receive telephone calls during his analytic hour, he felt she was sometimes less than concerned with his problems.[67]

If Karl had not been entirely respectful of the analytic process before he experienced it firsthand, analyses under Alexander and Brunswick deepened that tendency. When Will left in 1942, Karl had no compunction about using his analysis of Worthington to advance his own ends. Worthington dropped out of that analysis prematurely and suffered enormously for it. He was depressed and withdrawn for the remainder of the war years, offering no opposition as Karl consolidated authority over hospital operations.[68]

Yet Karl was less aggressive with most of Will's staff loyalists. To be sure, he criticized them severely and sometimes refused to speak to them for prolonged periods. He was particularly irked when the staff complained about working an extra hour or two. Although these loyalists executed guide-to-the-order-sheet activities and therapy routines better than most new staff that he hired, Karl rarely complimented them. After a difficult first few months, however, most of Will's staff came to realize that Karl was not really rebuking them or pressuring them to leave; he was simply his usual erratic self and lacked his brother's warmth and tact.[69]

Perhaps Karl might have been tougher with Will's loyalists if he had not been faced with the war's manpower drain. Severe employee shortages also affected most other centers of the "new psychiatry." As male staff was recruited into the military, Karl's work force became increasingly female. However, with job opportunities for female doctors and nurses considerably better than they had been before the war, and with other "new psychiatry" facilities bidding for their services, it was difficult to retain the best of them. The persistence of the patient count in the face of decreasing staff made hospital work particularly burdensome for those who remained, and this created additional pressures for a wholesale staff exodus. To ease the situation, Karl reduced the supervision over inexperienced employees and lowered requirements for staff reports, but these measures did not solve his fundamental problem. He had to retain as many staff as he could, find new employees, and determine how to modify significantly his brother's milieu therapy program to lessen the work load.[70]

Karl was simply unable to replace most of his departing employees. Thus, he had to modify the "scientific"-professional face of the hospital—the heart of Will's staff-intensive milieu therapy program. Despite Karl's seemingly insensitive manner, most of his changes were quite sensible. With psychiatric nurses in short supply, Karl had no choice but to assign more patient care responsibilities to attendants. He regarded this as a temporary and undesirable practice. The doctor shortage was a more serious problem. Karl responded to it in a way that Will might not have considered. Decades earlier, Karl's mentor, Elmer Southard, had created a pioneering social work program at Boston Psychopathic Hospital, with an eye to creating a new class of professionals who would assist the physician. Now Karl brought social workers into the hospital to assist his few remaining physicians. Most were only second-year graduate students specializing in psychiatric social work. Initially, they did little more than take social case histories from the patient's family. But some of the more promising were allowed to try their hand at inpatient psychotherapy. Their case write-ups were taken very seriously in case conferences. Influenced by a suggestion from his friend the anthropologist Margaret Mead, Karl even urged some of his social workers to present in staff discussions their investigations into the general place of the patient in American society. With these innovations, he was keeping pace with the sudden interest in the psychiatric social worker that was occurring in the military to meet massive demands for mental health services.[71]

By drawing more upon attendants and social workers (and even some clinical psychologists), Karl was able to arrest a potential drift toward custodial care that threatened all "new psychiatry" hospitals during World War II. But he still lacked a sufficient number of staff to conduct the specific patient-centered therapy basic to his brother's treatment program. Also, many of his new staff had difficulty working within the guide-to-the-order-sheet tradition. The "scientific" face of hospital life appeared to be somewhat in disarray.

However, Karl again followed the innovative lead of the military. He pioneered in the use of group therapy in a "new psychiatry" inpatient setting. He maintained that it was senseless for staff to be "walking around with individual patients while they let a dozen other patients sit around quarreling and criticizing and having no organized reaction." Karl recognized that group therapy ran against the grain of many of the older staff, who had helped Will to construct his "whole program of individual therapy and meeting unconscious needs, etc." Yet there was no choice but to forge ahead. To ensure that new group ventures were therapeutically effective, Karl sought to make the patients in each group relatively compatible and to exclude the more disturbed patients who disrupted group activity.[72]

By no means did Karl eliminate the hospital's traditional focus on the individual patient. To be sure, he increased the patient population to balance the hospital budget when he assumed control of the facility. In less than a year, though, he recognized that with staff shortages, a larger patient population reduced the quality of patient care regardless of changes in the therapy program. Thus, in 1944, Karl discharged many chronic patients and increased the number of staff capable of doing psychotherapy, compensating financially through increased patient fees and philanthropic donations. Consequently, whereas only a quarter of the hospital patients had daily individual psychotherapeutic sessions at the beginning of 1944, almost half had by December.[73]

Other changes Karl instituted in the hospital routine were less directly responsive to the wartime crisis. He fostered psychoanalysis with a greater experimental spirit than his brother. Departing from a central tenet of Freudian orthodoxy and ongoing practice in Will's hospital, he tried out full-scale psychoanalytic sessions on certain patients with only average intelligence, little "psychological mindedness," and severe ego weaknesses. At the same time, he instituted the practice of bringing innovative and exciting thinkers into the hospital for brief periods. S. I. Hayakawa was recruited to conduct staff seminars on semantics and psychiatry and to work with patients on creative writing and linguistics. Margaret Mead came to teach cultural anthropology. J. L. Moreno, who introduced the concept of group therapy, conducted workshops on his newest techniques. Finally, Karl persistently reminded those in the clinic building as well as the hospital staff that as Southard, Meyer, and the other pioneers in the "new psychiatry" had initially conceived, research and professional education were at least as important as treatment. They had to become more active in these neglected areas if the Menninger organization was to persist with its mission.[74]

Milieu therapy therefore changed dramatically during the war years. There was less emphasis on clearly defined social relationships or precise treatment procedures, more stress on innovation within the broadly psychoanalytic perspective Karl shared with Will. Interestingly, Karl chose no drastic departures from that perspective in the face of a drain on staff that Will never had to deal with. Unlike McLean Hospital, for example, he did not try to increase less staff-intensive techniques, like electroshock and lobotomies.

Aggregate data on the results of hospital treatment did not differ significantly under Karl from what had been reported under Will. Nevertheless, at the end of the war, Will chided Karl about what had been done to "his" hospital. He underscored the need to return to "former treatment standards" in the "scientific"-professional face of hospital life. With thinly veiled anger, Will charged that "our milieu therapy, including the enforcement of attitudes, the rigid prescription of schedules has broken down somewhat." Freer with their criticisms, Will's loyalists indicated that more was involved than the formal changes in various medical procedures. A new staff had come aboard, physician Edward Greenwood charged, that did not understand "our basic philosophies."[75]

Between 1943 and 1945, the director of the hospital had gone and Isabel Erickson had resigned. Influential doctors and nurses—other parental figures in the "family spirit"—had also left. Though the new figures in the hospital—Worthington, diverse social workers, several new attendants, and especially Karl—tried desperately to retain a fully supervised patient day and as much of the milieu therapy program as possible, they did not carry the same familial representations. Graduate-student social workers were not the same mature father figures as certain prewar physicians. Attendants were too young to seem maternal. Most important, Karl was too erratic and temperamental to convey the same familial representation as Will. Although he succeeded in maintaining many of the "scientific"-professional dimensions of the hospital program, Karl simply could not perpetuate the deep loyalties and devotions of the prewar "family spirit."

Indeed, a different though still decidedly familial dynamic was developing within the hospital, which neither brother could quite understand. Instead, Will attacked Karl for lowering treatment standards. Karl fired back that it had been "quite unpsychiatric" for Will to have fostered personal loyalty to himself and an emotional interdependence of the staff rather than professional rapport. World War II ended with the familial face of the hospital having undergone fundamental alteration and the tension between the brothers at an unprecedented high. This was unfortunate, for despite their different styles of leadership, Karl and Will shared two fundamental qualities, which they had woven into the fabric of their organization.[76]

First, the brothers felt compelled to make Menninger a missionary outpost within the "new psychiatry." They had established a reputable inpatient diagnostic clinic in the 1920s and had transformed their hospital into a leading center for psychoanalytically informed milieu therapy in the 1930s. Yet both felt that success was no reason to slacken the pace of missionary innovation.

However, the brothers shared a second quality that was not always compatible with this missionary thrust outward. Their involvement with psychoanalysis was periodically shifting their attentions toward intramural organizational affairs. Rather than being freed of inner conflict, as they had been led to expect, their energy doubled for missionary ventures in behalf of the "new psychiatry," Karl and Will completed their analyses with Franz Alexander with very mixed emotions. Although they seemed to possess more self-knowledge, they fought more with each other over hospital affairs. Will boasted as his analysis was about to conclude, for example, that he had "as big a penis as Father and big brother," and that he would return to Topeka "considerably more aggressive" and intent on making the hospital " 'my group' and not Karl's."[77]

To be sure, both brothers realized that there was much more to the psychoanalytic process than intramural struggle. Will used psychoanalysis in the 1930s to build a milieu therapy program that was unique even among "new psychiatry" centers. During the war, Karl was able to merge the process with his missionary spirit and to attempt highly innovative experimental uses of Freud's "science"—in group therapy and with patients traditionally unqualified for analysis. Never quite the antithesis of their missionary spirit, the brothers' formative experience with psychoanalysis had not freed either from the tensions and preoccupations of the early Menninger household.

CHAPTER FOUR

Southard School

Will's hospital was the largest and most important center for psychiatric practice at Menninger during the 1920s and 1930s. A year and a half after the hospital opened, a second inpatient facility began. Named Southard School in honor of Karl's mentor, it was a treatment and educational institution for a mix of mentally retarded and emotionally disturbed youngsters. Whereas the hospital had a stable and secure existence, the school did not. Karl's second wife, Jeanetta, recalled in 1943 that it "has always existed in a state of emergency." Karl concurred, characterizing the school in terms of its high deficits and other serious difficulties. From the beginning, Southard was seen as a "problem," an anomaly of sorts within the larger organization.[1]

This was not Kansas's first pioneering venture in child care. Forty-five years earlier, the State Asylum for Idiotic and Imbecile Youth was established. In the progressive period, the legislature authorized a special Child Hygiene Division to promote baby clinics and infant welfare stations, pure milk for children, and special instruction to young girls. And the Kansas Board of Health sought out children suffering from physical defects. Charles had supported certain of these early efforts to aid disadvantaged children, and some of his first patients had been youngsters. He had been especially interested in assisting diabetic children.[2]

But Charles had never suggested establishing a facility for mentally retarded and emotionally disturbed children. Karl proposed it to him after Elmer Southard recommended it to Karl: "Don't forget the children." The mentor based his advice on his own work at Boston Psychopathic—the first American mental hospital to study and treat children in any number, through a special program within its outpatient department. Southard encouraged his doctors and nurses to work with children because he considered their maladies crucial in understanding the sources for adult mental illness. He also used social workers to assist parents, teachers, and others important to the child within his community. But Southard refrained from endorsing a community social psychiatry approach to child care; it departed too drastically from the hospital- and doctor-centered traditions that he judged essential.[3]

William Healy was a pioneer in the community-centered approach who made Karl's mentor uneasy. Under the auspices of the Cook County Juvenile Court, Healy developed a model facility to study and assist juvenile offenders. He went on to establish the Judge Baker Foundation clinic in 1917 and promoted it as a model for the various demonstration clinics that the Commonwealth Fund and the National Committee for Mental Hygiene soon came to sponsor. Unlike Southard, Healy eschewed medical prescription or didactic instruction. And he made the well-being of the child the center of clinic endeavors. Child psychiatry was no mere training ground to enhance adult treatment techniques; for Healy, the child guidance clinic had to involve an interdisciplinary team of psychiatrists, psychologists, and social workers who assisted the child, his parents, his teachers, and others in his neighborhood. To underscore his difference with Southard, Healy acknowledged that he dealt with children first as social beings and then as organic entities.[4]

Karl was fascinated by Healy's approach, but he was more comfortable with Southard's. Although he knew and liked Healy, he shared Southard's misgivings over major departures from a hospital-centered medical practice. Karl wondered whether there was a third approach, better suited to his and Charles's values and their Topeka setting, as he tried to make sense of the fluid and developing field of child psychiatry.[5]

Lawson Lowrey, Southard's chief medical officer at Boston Psychopathic Hospital, offered Karl an attractive alternative. When Lowrey left Boston in 1922 to become director of the new Iowa State Psychopathic Hospital, he sent small hospital-clinic interdisciplinary teams around the state to examine potential patients. The venture convinced Lowrey that community-centered child guidance clinics were necessary. Unlike Healy, however, he wanted the clinics connected to his hospital. He established three such guidance clinics, welcomed children regardless of intelligence and deficiencies, and invited Karl to see them. Karl liked what he saw, especially Lowrey's open admissions policy. He admired the community-based aspect of the clinics but felt Lowrey gave them too much autonomy. Despite the visit, Karl remained committed to Southard's emphasis on adult patients, and he left Iowa bent on establishing a children's clinic linked to a hospital in order to facilitate adult treatment.[6]

Karl was leaning toward the more conservative, medically oriented side of the early child guidance movement. Influenced heavily by Southard and Lowrey (and to a lesser extent by Healy), he rejected one of their shared premises, the efficacy of an outpatient setting in treating both retarded and emotionally disturbed children. Karl assumed that a children's center in Topeka would involve a much larger proportion of mentally retarded patients than Southard, Healy, or Lowrey treated. Because most treatment centers for retarded children were inpatient schools, Karl felt that his would have to be. Had he consulted Walter Fernald, O. J. Cobb, or others working with mentally retarded youngsters, they would have told him that the reformist direction in their field, too, was toward outpatient treatment. New studies were indicating that most mentally deficient patients exhibited better behavior while living with their families in normal communities and attending special outpatient clinics.[7]

The field of child psychiatry was in flux during the interwar period, and there was no protracted national debate over outpatient status. State hospital directors and heads of schools for the mentally retarded never felt compelled to justify their inpatient facilities as reformers established diverse outpatient programs. Neither Karl nor Charles perceived a controversy over the outpatient question as they made plans for Southard School. Nor did they contest the premise of the advocates of outpatient treatment that the child's parents, teachers, playmates, and others were a significant part of his malady and therefore important to his cure. Rather, they simply announced that Southard would admit inpatients who would benefit from constant supervision. Some children had made good progress in the Diagnostic Clinic but regressed markedly when they returned home. Most of those children lived in Topeka. The Menningers assumed that once their school became known, children would come from wealthy out-of-state-families; they could not return home each day. But whether their prospective patients were retarded or of normal intelligence, Topekans or out-of-staters, Karl and Charles wanted to treat them as inpatients because troubled children required time to cultivate resistance against the emotional imbalances of the neighborhood setting.[8]

The Menningers had invoked this same justification when they established their hospital. Adult patients had to be separated from the sources of their maladies until they could gain strength to return home. Why were they extending this rationale to youngsters when the psychiatric reformers they respected felt that troubled children were different?

Neither Karl nor Charles ever considered an outpatient facility very seriously. They even dismissed combining an outpatient clinic with boarding homes for out-of-state children. Remembering the disturbed children, abandoned or abused by their parents, who had been taken into the Menninger household and there developed resilience, they were ready to allow disturbed children to be separated from their parents and their communities and to reside in their school. Consequently, when John Stone returned from a brief study of child treatment in Chicago to tell Karl and Charles what they already knew—that the most innovative facilities were for outpatients—they dismissed his observation without discussion. A successful family practice was to contour the workplace.[9]

Memories of the early Menninger household also contributed to their dismissing the restrictive admissions policies of the more prominent child guidance clinics of the East and the urban Midwest. The aim of many of these clinics was to admit minimally disturbed children with normal or superior intelligence whose parents could afford fairly steep fees. At Boston Psychopathic Hospital, Southard had instituted somewhat less discriminatory admissions criteria. The Menningers went further. Like the children they had taken into their home, they admitted patients regardless of intelligence or malady and sometimes of income. To be sure, their average fee of $112.50 a month exceeded the wages of middle-class families in the 1920s. But they were ready to lower it and sometimes to waive it when the parents lacked financial resources. Southard School opened in 1926 with children of widely diverse income levels and classes. Although most were "feebleminded," they suffered from a diversity of maladies.[10]

I I

Much as the Menningers· had depended on the Neeses to organize their sanitarium program, they turned to Stella Pearson, a native of Muskogee, Oklahoma, to set up Southard School. Trained in the educational care of physically handicapped children, she and her sister, Lulu Holcombe, had established a school for mentally retarded youngsters in their hometown. An inpatient institution, it embraced modestly the postwar shift away from custodial values. Pearson brought one of her students to Topeka for a consultation early in 1926. Her cheerful disposition, her faith in the capacities of feebleminded children, and her years of experience appealed to the Menningers. Soon after the visit, Karl invited Pearson to move her school from Muskogee to Topeka and to affiliate it with his organization. She accepted.[11]

In the fall of 1926, John Stone rented a house a mile from the hospital grounds as the site for the school. The Menningers entered a formal agreement with Pearson: she and they were to own the school "in equal partnership." She was to be educational director and to manage school finances. They were to provide referrals from their clinic and to conduct psychiatric examinations of the children. "We have helped her," Karl noted, "without any financial recompense whatsoever directly." Entirely a residential facility, it was equipped initially to handle no more than ten children. When the school opened, five mentally retarded youngsters were enrolled.[12]

The Menningers assumed that they were to have a "supervisory interest" in the school. Through Stone and especially through Charles, they hoped to make this interest clear. Stone was to serve as school psychologist. More important, he was to control the institution's financial affairs, just as he was doing at the hospital. Charles was to become school physician and gradually to increase the family presence over the facility. At first, he met these expectations. He was a constant presence at Southard and devoted at least an hour each week to every child there. He talked and played with the youngsters long after he completed their physical examinations. In turn, the children were awed by his kind, grandfatherly bearing.[13]

However, neither Charles nor Stone was able to exercise substantial authority. In her "equal partnership" with the Menningers, Stella Pearson held on to the account books, paid the bills, and collected the revenues. She, and not Charles, established basic policy. He rarely challenged her.

Attentive to monetary matters and zealous of her power, Pearson was a caring director. So was Lulu Holcombe, who moved from Muskogee to assist her. Neither understood the therapeutic techniques at the more prominent child guidance clinics, but Karl acknowledged that "intuitively she [Pearson] knows how to handle children." And unlike many therapists at the guidance clinics, who worked only with children of normal intelligence, Pearson "has helped us to learn . . . that the hopelessness that we ordinarily associate with feeble-mindedness is a mistake." Through the sisters' high expectations, "We have actually sent back into the public schools several children for whom a few years ago I should have recommended permanent state institutional care." But there was another side to the Pearson reign. With their livelihood tied to financial success, the sisters were intent on impressing parents of potential patients and other visitors. Before they allowed any adults into the school, they locked unruly children in their rooms; some hyperactive patients were tied to chairs and hidden away. Holcombe sometimes used "the old methods of punishment." Both sisters felt that the children should be prepared for eventual return to their home environment through contact with Sunday school classes and public school groups.

Pressured in this way, a number of the children became quite anxious, reacted in socially unacceptable ways, incurred staff disapproval, and regressed emotionally.[14]

If the sisters subscribed to some less than desirable practices, the Menningers were grateful for the one thousand dollars in profits they turned over each month. And they were pleased that the sisters provided some youngsters with learning skills and self-discipline to function in the public schools. All in all, the Menningers did not feel that they could do much better themselves. They were disposed to defer to the sisters, despite their hopes of bringing the school into the family fold.[15]

In the fall of 1929, however, Pearson fell ill with tuberculosis and left for a sanitarium in Oklahoma City. During her absence, Holcombe ran the school with Stella Coffman, a teacher Pearson had hired. When Karl, to reflect the interim arrangement, proposed listing Holcombe on South-ard stationery as educational director and Pearson as educational coun-selor, Pearson protested, insisting she was still in charge.[16]

In June 1930, Pearson returned with a letter from her physician: though she continued to suffer from sundry lung complications, she was not contagious. She insisted she had completely recovered and would be taking charge again. But the Menningers discounted both the letter and her claim of full recovery. In view of her medical history (this was her third or fourth bout with TB), Karl insisted that her illness might merely be in remission; she might infect the children and provoke damaging lawsuits from their parents. Pearson should resign her position; her origi-nal arrangement with the Menningers was terminated. Accordingly, Karl transferred the lease on the school building from Southard School to the Menninger Clinic and offered the sisters two conditions if they wanted to remain. First, the school was to be owned by a special corporation in which the clinic would possess 51 percent of the stock; the sisters could have an option to acquire the balance. Second, the sisters were to be salaried employees; Holcombe could work at the school, but Pearson was to perform administrative tasks from a distance.[17]

Pearson rejected Karl's conditions. She charged that the facility was properly the Pearson School and offered to buy out the Menninger inter-est in the partnership. Karl turned down her proposal and demanded that she accept his. At this point, the sisters met secretly with several parents. They had decided to move the school to Muskogee and wanted to take the children with them. A handful of parents assented. The sisters then incorporated under Kansas law as the Southard School Association to secure a legal monopoly on the name. Returning to Muskogee, they advertised as the reconstituted Southard School.[18]

The Menningers fought back. They hired a replacement for Holcombe, augmented Stella Coffman's responsibilities by making her interim manager, and drafted legal documents establishing Menninger Clinic ownership over the facility. They also hired lawyers to challenge Pearson's use of the Southard name and won favorable rulings from the Special School Association of New York and the Federal Post Office Department. They advertised too, proclaiming that they owned and managed Southard School. Despite these efforts, they knew that they had an enormous task of rebuilding ahead. By September 1930, the school had one youngster left. Pearson had proved a match for Karl.[19]

I I I

As Pearson and Holcombe left for Muskogee, Karl wrote a note to Stone. The Southard School venture had gotten off to a bad start, he confided. The task at hand was not simply to find new leadership and more students but to transform Southard into a scientific and professional operation. He wanted the school to follow the guidelines for treatment Will was developing as he reconstructed the hospital. Karl called for special assignment charts that registered staff doctors' prescribed activities for each patient at the school. He also sought staff with significant medical training, plus new facilities for comprehensive recreational and occupational therapy programs. A new Southard School was to match the standards of Will's hospital, treating child patients much as the hospital treated adults.[20]

With the sisters' departure, Karl wanted Charles to become more influential—to exert at the school a family presence such as Will exerted at the hospital. The children loved Charles, and he enjoyed working with them. Although he knew less than Karl about children's programs in "new psychiatry" hospitals and child guidance clinics, he could travel and learn. Consequently, Karl asked him to administer the educational and therapeutic programs of the school in addition to the weekly medical examinations.[21]

Karl's broader vision was clear. As Will and Charles brought both adult and children's facilities more fully into the family fold, he would complete his training analysis, continue to run the clinic, travel, lecture, and drop by the hospital and school periodically to oversee developments.

Unfortunately, Charles at sixty-seven lacked Will's energy and ambition. Still, he increased his hours at Southard, spending most of every morning there, and successfully encouraged the staff to supplant some of the old-fashioned methods of the Pearson sisters with progressive educational techniques. He launched a research project on the emotional re-education of children. Preliminary findings of the project revealed that some children categorized as mentally retarded were actually emotionally disturbed. Charles admonished the staff to cease thinking of the facility as a haven for imbeciles. He invited Ruth Shaw to work with Southard children on her finger-painting techniques for "a graphic record of a child's feelings, phantasies, and thoughts," and offered her a permanent position. In the interests of research and cures, Charles also insisted that any child who made measurable progress at the school would continue "at our expense" if his parents could no longer afford the fees. He resolved a number of staff grievances. When Ernst Simmel visited Southard School in 1936, he characterized Charles as "the serious, benign father that those children need who have been frustrated in their first strivings for love and understanding."[22]

Yet Charles did not implant the Menninger "family spirit" in the school to the extent that Will did at the hospital. Instead, an alternative family constellation, with different values, secured hegemony. During the dispute between the Pearsons and the Menningers, Stella Coffman had supported the Menningers. When she agreed to serve as the next education director, Karl heralded her as the woman who "literally saved our School's life." But rather than defer to Charles, as Karl had hoped, Coffman hired a nonmedical staff of five relatives and several intimate friends. Behaving much like a family, they ate together and often went off on swimming or skating parties. And their squabbles were much more familial than professional.[23]

Coffman's group was conscientious in running the educational program and other facets of school life. Like Charles, they discounted the rote drilling exercises of Pearson and Holcombe in favor of games and other indirect routes of instruction compatible with John Dewey's teaching methods. Moreover, they kept the children neat, clean, happy, and relaxed. But the Menningers grew increasingly determined to outflank Coffman. Karl charged that she and her associates lacked managerial skills and financial responsibility. Though their approach to children was humane, they undermined his scientific, professional, and administrative goals for the school.[24]

The more basic objection to the Coffman group was obvious. Karl saw that Charles "didn't have the energy or the power to develop" the school; he was distressed that Charles had not been able to establish family hegemony. Just as Pearson had thwarted his father during Southard's first years, Coffman and her staff now stood in his way.[25]

Karl lost hope that his father could ever represent a strong Menninger presence at the school. In 1933, he had tried to augment the Menninger presence by hiring psychiatrist Margarethe Ribble, who he assumed would be loyal. She left within six months, and Karl turned to Leona Chidester, who had a psychology doctorate from the University of Kansas (the Menninger Clinic's first professionally trained psychologist). Chidester conducted psychotherapy with the children but could not wrest control of the educational program from Coffman. Early in 1935, Karl appointed Nathan Ackerman, a young, energetic, and ambitious psychiatric resident, as assistant medical director. He persuaded his editorial assistant, mistress, and wife-to-be, Jeanetta Lyle, to help Ackerman.[26]

By mid-1935, a coalition of Ackerman and Lyle, joined by Charles, was in command. Gradually, they rid the school of the Coffman group. Lyle—bright and energetic, secure in Karl's support, and familiar with finances and budgeting—emerged as a major Southard leader. But Karl was also pleased with Ackerman's managerial skills and his ideas on pediatric treatment. His theory of therapy for children was strikingly similar to Will's for adults. Like Will, he focused on confining the aggressive instinct "within the necessary [social] limits" by conveying to the patient "a feeling of security" through appropriate management of the treatment environment. In this environment, Ackerman underscored consistent staff attitudes toward each patient.[27]

With Ackerman and Lyle assuming authority under Charles's titular leadership, the entire character of the school was transformed. Mentally retarded children still typified the patient population. But the number of emotionally disturbed children with normal and superior intelligence was increased, and they received regular if eclectic analyses. Individual, broadly psychoanalytic sessions were arranged for retarded children too, so as to restore their "capacities for learning which were apparently lost." Each child, normal or retarded, was visited daily for an hour by a school psychologist, for testing and therapy. The psychologist would draft a case report on the child, which was to be reviewed weekly by a senior physician-psychoanalyst from elsewhere in the organization. This case review method was intended to shift child psychotherapy closer to the professional, doctor-centered therapy of the adult hospital. Educational specialty departments were established, each headed by a teacher trained in progressive education and specializing in a particular skill within the school program. The child was to spend the hours of his day when he was not in therapy going from one specialty activity to another, just as the adult patient moved from recreational to occupational to educational programs.[28]

The shifts in leadership, policy, and therapeutic procedure appeared to make Southard more scientific and professional. (Unfortunately, fragmentary medical records, and very limited access to the few that exist, make it impossible to determine treatment effectiveness.) Financial problems—not present under Pearson and Holcombe, who had tried to maximize fees while reducing fee waivers and maintaining a skeletal nonmedical staff—emerged. Under Ackerman and Lyle, patient fees were often adjusted or suspended, especially when waivers brought in working-class children with normal or superior intelligence. Furthermore, expenses increased substantially as more staff, with higher professional credentials, were added to the payroll. Southard's balance sheet shifted from black ink to red. Evaluating the school through an adult-hospital perspective, Will shared Karl's anxiety over this growing "financial liability." Although Will recognized that professional therapy rarely yielded great profits, he had averted persistent hospital deficits and felt Southard leaders had failed on this count. Both brothers characterized the school as a major "problem."[29]

They forced Southard to run on an increasingly limited budget despite protests from Ackerman and Lyle. Discouraged, Ackerman left Topeka in 1937, and Lyle spent less time at the school. Though Charles was Southard's titular chief of staff, he provided no firm leadership, and the unified treatment program and close management of the facility eroded. Staff pursued diverse treatments, ranging from custodial care to eclectic psychoanalysis. In 1939, Earl Saxe replaced Charles, as temporary head of the school. "We worked day by day not knowing what the hell we were doing," he recalled. "There was no organized system to it."[30]

A mounting deficit during the Depression decade encouraged the Menningers to resist the costly Ackerman-Lyle program. But there was a complementary reason. Because Will's modestly profitable, familial hospital was the yardstick for success in the larger organization, a school with a mounting deficit and a decreasing family presence had to be regarded as a failure. Charles acknowledged the washout of the Southard experiment by spending a minimum amount of time at the school. Karl voiced no objection when Charles's name was withdrawn from the Southard staff roster in 1939.[31]

IV

When a new spirit of reform erupted at Southard in the early 1940s, it came without even token family presence. In 1940, three psychiatrists—

Elizabeth Geleerd, Mary O'Neil Hawkins, and Anne Benjamin—joined the staff. Geleerd had worked at the Poetzl Clinic in Vienna and had taken her training analysis with Anna Freud. Hawkins, who had also worked at Poetzl, took her training analysis from Grete Bibring. Benjamin had her training analysis with Lucia Tower and Thomas French. Because Geleerd and Hawkins were Southard's first employees with medical specialties in child psychiatry and were regarded as pioneer child analysts, the family and all senior staff were deferential. By 1944, the Menninger executive committee took the unprecedented step of thanking Geleerd and Hawkins for developing a distinctively professional atmosphere at the facility: "For a long time the School was operated without the benefit of intelligent psychotherapeutic guidance, but now that we have had Hawkins & Geleerd there we cannot conceive of any other way of handling problems." Benjamin also rose quickly. Possessing unusual administrative capacities, she emerged in a managerial role and turned the school into a smoothly running facility.[32]

Psychoanalysis and psychoanalytically informed psychotherapy were crucial to treatment in the hospital. Consequently, the brothers were encouraged when Geleerd and Hawkins began to use both extensively. By 1942, most of Southard's children received some form of psychoanalytic therapy. Benjamin donated six hundred dollars in personal funds for the purchase of special instructional equipment. Hawkins and Geleerd offered many extra hours for psychotherapy without demanding compensation. Clearly, the three doctors were committed to Southard's success.[33]

Together, they made some striking innovations. They replaced all feebleminded and epileptic children—still dominating the facility's enrollment—with emotionally disturbed neurotic youths of average and superior intelligence. It was only possible to shift to advanced child therapy techniques when children of at least average intelligence were involved. Indeed, the three hoped to turn Southard into an advanced therapy, teaching, and research facility. In time, it might even handle troubled youngsters from the public schools. By 1942, the admissions policy became more selective. Feeling their analytic efforts were most effective on children with superior intelligence, the three concentrated their recruitment efforts on the unusually bright. Simultaneously, they replaced all employees disposed toward custodial care with staff of better professional training. And as in Will's hospital, they worked to maximize the transference effect of analytic or semianalytic therapy sessions; they assigned particular staff to specific patient activities, to promote relationships that roughly approximated the patient-staff relationship in therapy sessions.[34]

Their select admissions policy threatened to limit revenues. But
Benjamin, Geleerd, and Hawkins counted on the prestige of their program to attract about twenty children paying full fees. They expected
their analytic approach to be recognized as superior to both Healy's child
guidance clinic tradition and Elmer Southard's hospital-centered medical
approach. They also anticipated substantial contributions from the Commonwealth Fund and other donors. These assumptions proved erro-
neous. By February 1942, the school had only ten children and was
running a monthly deficit of one thousand to fifteen hundred dollars. By
May, the Menninger executive committee resolved that "the school will
be given up completely" if nonsubsidized enrollment did not increase
one third by fall. Jeanetta Menninger made a fund-raising trip to Chicago.
Karl, however, demanded tough financial accountability without assistance from external sources: "it just seems absurd to go on spending
money so extravagantly."[35]

At this crucial point, another reform—the placement of children in
foster boarding homes with select Topeka families—became the subject
of heated debate. Hawkins had earlier suggested this measure, coincident
with the new admissions policy. She had argued that the Menninger
organization must recognize that emotionally disturbed children were
not treated optimally within an inpatient facility. Life completely away
from their homes and families subjected children to "severe trauma."
Moreover, inpatient children generally had "a deleterious effect upon
each other." Nevertheless, Hawkins realized that the school could not
instantly transform itself into an outpatient facility, for the families of
most Southard children were hundreds of miles away. As an alternative,
she had recommended placement of Southard children with families in
the community, where they could attend public schools. The Menningers
had summarily dismissed her idea.[36]

However, they accepted it in modified form during the school's
growing financial crisis. Those children who had progressed to the point
where they no longer required the protective environment of a residence
facility were permitted to board at night in foster homes. But they were
not to attend public schools or partake in many activities with their foster
families. The plan promised to reduce the cost of around-the-clock child
supervision and to increase Southard's sleeping space. Since a full treatment program would continue, the fee structure would not have to be
reduced substantially for those who boarded. Stone supported the proposal as a way to reduce the deficit. Financial considerations were important to Karl too, but so was benevolence, and he insisted that the boarding home be regarded as a vital bridge between Southard and the

eventual discharge of the child to his own home. Will agreed. After the brothers endorsed the proposal, the executive committee implemented it.[37]

The effects of the measure were noteworthy. Although it did not eliminate the deficit, losses declined. Enrollment increased substantially. By October 1943, eleven of Southard's twenty children resided in boarding homes. The modest fee reduction for boarding contributed to the increased enrollment. To make the boarding program work, Southard hired its first social workers. They were charged with finding foster families for the children, with arranging payment schedules to those families, and with instructing the families on how they were to relate to their young boarders.[38]

Opinion divided on the therapeutic benefits of the boarding out program. The dearth of patient data makes it impossible to evaluate competing claims. The new social workers claimed that the foster home gave the child a sense of family that he could not find in a traditional inpatient situation. Jeanetta agreed, characterizing the boarding program as "one of the most progressive things that the School has attempted." But the school directors were less sanguine. Anne Benjamin had strong reservations. She noted that Karl and the executive committee had required three children to move into boarding homes against her recommendation. All three had been ill and required twenty-four-hour care. To further reduce the deficit, Benjamin claimed, the committee discharged some scholarship children who could not afford boarding out. Geleerd and Hawkins supported Benjamin. Feeling that their views were not being considered, and resentful that social workers ran the boarding program, the directors realized they were losing control of Southard operations.[39]

Karl was central to their discontent. Since the demise of the Charles-Ackerman-Lyle coalition, he felt Southard had "not had a steady constant male head." The facility lacked "masculine assertiveness" to soothe the preponderantly female staff, as Will had soothed, comforted, and directed women at the hospital. The wartime manpower shortage had required Karl to settle for female "forcefulness," but by 1943, he had come to believe that Benjamin, Hawkins, and Geleerd had not been sufficiently "forceful." He attributed the school's continued deficit to their select admissions policy. And their persistent lobbying for conversion to a full outpatient operation threatened the profits, however scant, of an inpatient facility and contradicted his conviction of how children should be treated. Karl concluded that continued bickering with the three women was pointless; the school could do without their leadership. Moreover, his suspicion that Geleerd was homosexual made him uncomfortable about her cooperation with Benjamin and Hawkins.[40]

With social workers on their staff who did not entirely share their aims for a boarding out policy, with the executive committee under Karl's control, and with Karl often opposing them, the three psychiatrists felt they had to leave. Early in 1943, Benjamin accepted an offer from the Institute for Juvenile Research, a prestigious Chicago children's center in the Healy tradition. Hawkins left at the end of the year, and Geleerd departed somewhat later, both for private analytic practice in New York.[41]

By early 1944, the new school director, Eunice Leitch, found that despite twelve- and fourteen-hour days, she could not restore Southard to the efficient operation her predecessors had achieved. Southard's small departments began to seek greater autonomy. Teachers in the educational department went one way, psychotherapy department members another, and recreational therapists still another. Because of an eight-hundred-dollar deficit, Leitch secured no new funds for salaries or even to paint the school building.[42]

Nonetheless, the staff Leitch had inherited was psychoanalytically oriented and committed to working with emotionally disturbed children. Psychoanalytically informed treatment remained the dominant therapeutic approach. And though Karl urged Leitch to augment revenues by admitting a feebleminded child or two, the commitment to treat nonretarded youngsters of normal and superior intelligence remained.[43]

Moreover, efforts to offer outpatient treatment similar to that at other "new psychiatry" centers were not entirely in vain. By 1944, roughly half of the school's children resided with foster families, and Southard leaders boasted that "home life had contributed to the [children's] improvement to a greater or lesser extent." This seemed to calm the Menningers regarding children as outpatients; they listened more closely to Leitch's request to have the few outpatient children customarily treated in the clinic building placed under Southard's jurisdiction. At the same time, several social workers called for a regular outpatient treatment service within the school. In making their case, they underscored Southard's outpatient community activities since the late 1930s—participation in a free clinic plus consultations with the Kansas Children's Home Service League, the Shawnee County Welfare Board, and the local juvenile court. More and more, school staff had assumed tasks that resembled those at community-based child guidance clinics. The accumulation of these developments demonstrated to the brothers that there was at least a modest local market for children's outpatient services.[44]

By 1946, Karl was reconciled to a formal outpatient children's service, so long as inpatient work remained the mainstay of the program. Few were surprised when the Southard School Corporation was legally dissolved and replaced by a two-branch Children's Division: Southard School would handle all inpatient operations, and an outpatient department would assume jurisdiction over children formerly treated in the clinic building. The new department was also to take jurisdiction over every other children's outpatient service. Although he had resisted such outpatient ventures for twenty years, Karl now seemed interested in innovative fusion of inpatient and outpatient operations of the sort developing at Langley Porter and other reformist psychiatric centers during the immediate postwar years. He even suggested cottages on the Menninger campus, so that Southard children might live with their parents. Child psychiatry in Topeka appeared to be moving in exciting directions.[45]

V

Despite the slow drift toward professional standards during its first two decades, the school never ceased to be characterized as Menninger's primary "problem." Family and staff used the term frequently and vehemently to describe the Southard deficit. Early in 1942, for example, Will was so distressed over the size of the shortfall that he characterized the school as an unresolvable "problem"; it "has lost us so much money and it seems practical to disband it." Karl and Charles agreed that finances represented the heart of the "problem." Their apprehensions were well grounded. There was always the prospect that Southard's monetary losses might bankrupt the entire organization. Nevertheless, the Menningers knew what they had become involved in; they acknowledged that proficient services for children cost at least as much as services to adults but commanded slightly more than one third the fees. A shortfall was almost inherent in the undertaking.[46]

The family and many staff were also disposed to characterize Southard as Menninger's major "problem" because they evaluated its activities with an adult-hospital yardstick and found it wanting. School employees were derided for failing to institute Will's treatment procedures and for eschewing the physician–nurse–activities therapist hierarchy of the adult facility. Apprehensions were voiced over the many teachers, social workers, and psychologists at the school—mostly women—with decidedly nonmedical backgrounds. And it was difficult to understand why some

Southard leaders wanted to operate as an outpatient facility. One assumption underlay these reservations. Neither the Menningers nor the majority of their staff believed in a distinctive treatment approach to children. They assumed that psychotherapy for disturbed youngsters could not differ substantially from adult treatment. This perspective was understandable, for child psychiatry was in its infancy. Psychologist Sibylle Escalona discerned the attitude when she arrived in 1943. Trained to emphasize nonverbal communication in work with emotionally disturbed children, she stressed play and interpreted body language. But hospital staff chided her for this approach, for they were accustomed to verbally based treatment. Karl was among them.[47]

Indeed, emotions deep within Karl also contributed to the Southard "problem." It was "hard" for him to "get along with children to whom one must always be giving, giving, giving." Although he always felt free to criticize and pressure school staff, he rarely visited the facility more than once a year. When he came, he arrived unannounced and never stayed more than a few minutes. Early one Saturday morning, he discovered that the children were eating breakfast in their pajamas. Furious at the apparent impropriety, he stormed out. Sometimes he wondered why Southard children could not be counted upon to honor and respect him. He occasionally felt that the children wanted him to stay away. At other times, he felt guilty over his absences and invited them to his farm. "I feel that I should let them have the privilege of the place," he once noted, while he worried that they might "tear up everything" and "do plenty of damage." He seldom agreed to work with a child patient—"the most depressing, futile work I've ever done."[48]

Karl's distress with Southard's disturbed children was rooted in memories of his own childhood. When his mother died, in 1945, he characterized himself as "her oldest problem child." "I was an invalid in my childhood," he acknowledged. Flo had empathized with Karl's deep sense of insecurity and inadequacy. She realized that her neighbors, friends, and even Charles considered Karl odder than some of the other youngsters who boarded in her house, and she knew that this was behind much of his anguish and self-doubt. As he matured, Karl continued to fret because many considered his manifest intelligence, mood shifts, and peculiar habits as covers for a deeper mental imbalance.[49]

If he sometimes felt more disturbed than insightful, Karl hardly needed to be reminded that this condition was rooted in his childhood. The more he thought about children with mental problems, the more he fretted about his own early years. "Don't forget the children," Elmer Southard had told him as he returned to Topeka to establish a partnership with his father. He created a school and named it after his mentor. However, the affairs of that facility, and particularly the children in it, provoked such unrest within him that he minimized his contact with the school. Every now and then, however, he delivered a diatribe about the Southard deficit, its director, or its treatment procedures, shifting onto other people and practices the fact that the Southard "problem" was very much Karl's problem.[50]

CHAPTER FIVE

Karl Menninger and the Émigrés

In September 1933, Will arrived in Vienna. He had come to Europe to gather ideas for his milieu therapy program and had expected to be able to meet and to converse with Sigmund Freud. But after a few of Freud's customary rebuffs, Will became discouraged and concluded that the founder of psychoanalysis was unapproachable. He settled for conversation with Heinz Hartmann, an analysand of Freud's, and left with no burning desire to return. Because Will was confident that American psychiatry was already "more advanced than European," he did not regard it as an irreparable loss to have missed Freud.[1]

Karl's first trip to Vienna, in August 1934, was more consequential. He had been traveling with Franz Alexander to the International Congress of Psychoanalysis in Lucerne. Rather impulsively, they decided to take a side trip to Vienna, to visit with Freud. Alexander had been an exceptionally brilliant student at the Berlin Psychoanalytic Institute, whom Freud had held in high regard. He telephoned when they got to Vienna and told Freud that he would be coming by to present his own analysand, Karl Menninger. When the two arrived, Alexander entered the house alone, maintaining that it was appropriate to give Freud background on Karl. An hour went by before he summoned Karl. Apparently, Freud had chided Alexander for having migrated to America, for his close ties with American physicians, and especially for his growing discomfort with the psychoanalytic movement. Karl, who sat in the garden with Anna Freud and Ernest Jones, was an afterthought to both men. As they concluded their conversation, Alexander hastily told Freud that Karl was very narcissistic; he cautioned Freud not to praise his analysand very much.[2]

After listening to Ernest Jones "slicing me to ribbons" for deficiencies in psychoanalytic theory, Karl found the "utterly impersonal" Freud disappointing. "I don't believe he had the slightest idea to whom he was talking," Karl recalled; "my narcissism received a terrific blow." He sensed that Alexander had betrayed him by neglecting to tell Freud about his accomplishments. Consequently, Karl tried to tell Freud "that I was a doctor from the hinterlands of America running a small hospital with my father and my brother, trying to use some psychoanalytic principles in a psychiatric hospital." Freud replied that he "never had success with psychoanalysis on severely mentally ill [and usually hospitalized] patients." The implication was that Menninger hospital cases were too severe for Freud's therapy. Just as Karl sensed that "we were getting well started," that Freud may have been warming to him, Alexander entered the room, to disappoint Karl once more. Announcing that Freud was tired, he suggested that they should be leaving. Karl had brought a paper he had drafted two years earlier, to prove that he endorsed Freud's much maligned theory of the death instinct. But with Alexander escorting him from the house, he "never got the chance" even to raise that topic with Freud.[3]

The importance of Karl's visit with Freud was incalculable. There had been little rapport between them, but Karl held Alexander responsible. Although Freud had not invited him back, Karl was determined to communicate with and learn from this pioneer. Indeed, he seemed intent on proving to Freud—despite new self-doubts that the visit promoted—that he could understand and implement the psychoanalytic lessons Freud imparted to his top European students, such as Alexander. He would learn from Freud, comprehend Freud's nuances, and make him realize that Karl was one of the few Americans Freud could trust for thoroughly understanding the full range and breadth of his contributions. However, Karl knew that time was of the essence: Freud was engaged in his long bout with jaw cancer.

Unlike Will, Karl wanted desperately to be invited back to Vienna. Freud subsequently met with Menninger staff psychiatrist Robert Knight and invited him to return. Karl felt that he hardly merited less. He counted upon Alexander and others close to Freud to secure the invitation, but none was forthcoming. Finally, in December 1936, Karl wrote to Freud. He recounted his "deep pleasure" at his "short visit" in 1934 and thanked Freud for autographing a personal photograph for him and sending it back with Knight. He alluded to Ernst Simmel, who had been impressed favorably with the Menninger grounds during a recent visit, and suggested obliquely that Freud might allow Karl "inspiring opportunities" to talk of that and other matters in Vienna as he had in the past. Freud's true "spirit" visibly "hovers over this place and inspires all of us," Karl concluded.[4]

Freud never replied to the letter. In March 1938, Karl learned that

Freud was preparing to depart from Nazi-occupied Austria. He sent the founder a cable inviting him to Topeka. Freud could work in the Menninger organization in any capacity he chose, and Karl would attend to all his needs. Once again, Freud did not reply; he moved to London. When Freud died, in the fall of 1939, Karl wrote a rather impersonal eulogy for *The Nation,* in which he acknowledged that Freud felt Americans shared "an unthinking optimism and a shallow activity. . . . It is an ironic paradox that America should today be the country in which his theories are best known and most widely accepted." Several months later, Karl wrote to Alexander: "Freud did not treat me very nicely, as you know, but none the less, I think his ideas, his grasp, his formulations are so infinitely ahead of anything else that has been proposed, that I have nailed my banner on his mast, and I'll defend it against assault for the rest of my life."[5]

Many factors had prompted Karl's interest in psychoanalysis years before his visit to Vienna. But that 1934 meeting launched him on a personal crusade to prove that he could thoroughly master and explicate what he regarded as the most important collection of ideas in modern times. He determined that he would change and grow so that Jones would never again be able to criticize him and Freud's successors would never question his clinical use of psychoanalytic theory. Karl assumed that profound understanding of Freud's thought could come only if he comprehended the full European intellectual culture from which it had been developed. But if Freud would not give him a personal tour of that culture, Karl assumed that there was an alternative. He would seek out those European analysts who had been schooled in the culture and make them his teachers.

Karl pursued therapists who had been victimized by the rise of fascism. Shortly after the Nazis seized power in Germany, they declared psychoanalysis a Jewish invention designed to corrupt Aryans. Freud's works were burned ceremonially, while Jews and other undesirables were removed from the Berlin Psychoanalytic Institute. The death sentence for psychoanalysis was extended to other European countries as fascism spread. Many Central European analysts and their students were forced to participate in the migration of intellectuals between 1933 and 1945, first to Britain and then to America. Before 1942, approximately forty analysts or analysts in training had landed in New York. Perhaps as many as one hundred fifty more arrived over the next four years. Some remained in New York or moved to nearby urban centers along the Atlantic seaboard. Others went farther west. During the journey westward, several stopped in Topeka to lecture and to meet the Menningers. Fifteen stayed, for differing lengths of time—from a few months to a number of years. After peace returned to Europe, even more émigré analysts arrived to work at Menninger. Although Karl expected them to serve as senior clinicians and training analysts, his primary motivation for recruitment was always to secure personal instruction.[6]

Menninger was not the only "new psychiatry" center to recruit émigré analysts. Three other facilities—Chestnut Lodge, Sheppard-Pratt, and St. Elizabeths Hospital—welcomed them. Even the Judge Baker Foundation and Harvard Medical School opened their doors. However, none of these institutions hired as many émigrés as Menninger did. And at Menninger, unlike several other mental facilities during the 1930s and early 1940s, the émigrés became important to the social and intellectual life of the organization.

Much of their importance derived from the fact that they represented a major staff constituency which could not be coaxed to work within the "family spirit" of the Menninger workplace. Their primary allegiance was to Freud and to their European mentors from Freud's "family group" of devout psychoanalytic followers. Consequently, none was willing to acknowledge the tutelage of the Menningers. They were astonished by Karl's assumption of a sort of fatherly eminence over the entire organization and even by Will's paternal role within the hospital. The émigrés rejected this patriarchy as unearned and meritless. This distressed Will, Charles, and associates like John Stone and Robert Knight. They wondered whether the organization would be better off without the Europeans. Karl was also upset because the émigrés would neither defer nor assimilate to the customs of the Menninger Clinic. Nonetheless, he was determined to keep them and to recruit others, for they were indispensable to his quest to gain acceptance from Freud and from those within Freud's inner circle. Despite their "arrogance," he told his associates, they had the capacity "to instruct."[7]

II

The very initiation of an immigration to Topeka, then, was largely an outgrowth of Karl's 1934 visit to Vienna and the personal mission it had fostered. Will, in Europe the year before, had learned that "Jewish writings" such as Freud's had been burned publicly and that "fine Jewish scientists," including several psychoanalysts, were scrambling for visas and entry permits. He showed little empathy, however, for the victims and no sense of the crisis that was emerging. "The Germans seem very happy and remarkably optimistic," Will wrote from Wiesbaden. "Hitler seems to have done a great deal for the country, of which every one seems agreed." Of course, Freud and other Jewish analysts did not agree, but Will never made contact with most of them and gave no thought to recruiting any for the Menninger Clinic.[8]

In the months after his visit with Freud, Karl wrote letters and made telephone calls to draw anybody remotely connected with Freud's "family group" of analysts to Topeka. Late in 1935, he succeeded in recruiting Gertrude Jacob, a German physician with a training analysis under Frieda Fromm-Reichmann at the Frankfurt Psychoanalytic Institute. Shortly afterward, he persuaded Austrian psychologist Wally Reichenberg (analyzed by Wilhelm Stekel) to come to Topeka. Both took issue with Will's account of events in Europe and charged that a tragedy of enormous proportions had begun. To Karl's distress, Jacob and Reichenberg stayed in Topeka very briefly and contributed minimally to his intellectual quest.[9]

Systematic and energetic recruitment of émigré analysts did not begin until Ernst Simmel—the first of the prominent Berlin analysts to escape from Germany—visited Topeka early in 1936. He was one of the few analysts with whom Will had spoken at any length during his 1933 trip. The brothers admired Simmel for his experimental psychoanalytic hospital at Schloss Tegel and listened intently when he told them that several highly innovative analysts would soon be following him into exile. Specifically, Simmel urged the Menningers to reach Martin Grotjahn and Bernard Kamm. Karl, excited, proposed that Robert Knight be sent immediately to Berlin to interview both physicians.[10]

Grotjahn had taken his medical training at the University of Berlin and his training analysis with Simmel. He specialized in neurology but had a limited psychoanalytic practice. Grotjahn's wife, Etalka, had concealed from German authorities her partially Jewish heritage, but the couple realized that it was only a matter of time before it was discovered; they were desperate to escape. One of Grotjahn's neurology professors had warned him that "the Menningers are gangsters and they will abuse you." He evidently considered that a better fate than living in uncertainty in the Third Reich. Kamm, a Czechoslovakian, was also a Christian. He had studied medicine in Kiel and Basel before matriculating at the University of Frankfurt am Main. Kamm's two analysts, Karl Landauer and Jenö Harnick, had been persecuted by right-wing authorities in Germany. In time, Landauer committed suicide, Harnick succumbed to psychosis, and Kamm became a confirmed antagonist of the German right. He practiced neurology in Berlin between 1932 and 1936, took on a few analytic cases, but realized that his well-known hostility to the Nazis' anti-Semitic policies made it essential that he leave Europe. Unlike Grotjahn, he knew nothing about the Menningers. However, he realized that the Europe he loved was in shambles, and he was ready to accept the first American offer.[11]

Clearly, Knight did not have to persuade Grotjahn or Kamm. Both found him warm and cordial. But they were perturbed by his naive and insensitive response to political events in Germany. Indeed, he even ignored Karl's advice and attended the Berlin Olympic Games. Knight interviewed Grotjahn at the Berlin airport. Hitler happened to arrive, and Knight climbed on a bench to photograph him, while Grotjahn nervously prodded the nearly seven-foot-tall American to get down: he could be shot. Knight could not understand why Grotjahn was apprehensive.[12]

When Knight returned to Topeka, he recommended hiring both Grotjahn and Kamm. Questioned by the Menningers on the two Europeans' English, Knight conveyed positive assurances about Kamm and reported that Grotjahn "will learn. They all learn." With direct orders from Karl and acquiescence from Will, their Topeka associates spent considerable time and energy getting travel funds to the émigrés and overcoming the resistance of immigration authorities. As they approached New York harbor, Grotjahn told his wife and son that the Menningers "had saved our lives." Kamm arrived in New York a short while after Grotjahn. John Stone was there to greet him and put him on the train. When the two émigrés finally arrived in Kansas, Karl and his colleagues found them homes, explained to them how to get about in Topeka, and kept inquisitive FBI agents at bay. All the while, Karl claimed, he and his staff felt awkward: "We did not know whether we were extending a helpful hand or taking advantage of a situation." Grotjahn and Kamm were reluctant to talk about events in Europe, and this distressed Karl. But he refrained from pressing them for details during their first weeks in Topeka.[13]

Next, Karl ordered his associates to recruit several of the émigrés who had already arrived in America. For the most part, these refugees were more prominent than Kamm and Grotjahn. Edoardo Weiss, an old member of the Vienna Psychoanalytic Society, had been a leading organizer of the Italian psychoanalytic movement, and Freud regarded him highly. Elizabeth Geleerd, who had received her analytic training in Vienna under Anna Freud, also worked closely with Sigmund Freud after he fled to London. Fritz Moellenhoff, a member of the German aristocracy, was a prominent intellectual. He took his training analysis with Hanns Sachs, from Freud's inner circle, and was an archfoe of Hitler.

David Rapaport was a brilliant Budapest psychologist, analyst, and poet, whom Karl discovered on the staff of a nearby Kansas state mental hospital. Ernst Lewy had studied at the University of Munich and been analyzed by Felix Boehm, director of the Berlin Psychoanalytic Institute. Treated as a "white," or privileged, Jew in Germany, Lewy watched conditions deteriorate and left for New York in 1936.[14]

Moellenhoff and Lewy, comparatively pleasant and convivial, were the best liked. Weiss, the most reclusive, was less popular. By 1939, it was clear that the Menninger associates had lost their initial enthusiasm for émigré recruitment. They charged that most of the Europeans were too solemn and disagreeable, had strange habits, and simply did not fit within the "family spirit" of the place. Karl, who had sparked the recruitment effort, was the most disappointed. "Will and I agree with you fully about the difficulties of absorbing the foreign doctors," he wrote Charles. "I am trying hard to get hold of some men, some Americans, but it is very difficult." The relatively few Americans who had received training analyses tended to prefer lucrative private practice in large eastern urban centers to a middle-class salary in isolated Topeka. Apparently, the more marketable émigrés showed the same disposition. Stone recommended that until they attracted Americans and a "better class" of Europeans, they either establish a moratorium or be less energetic about signing up émigrés. It was better to lose "income from three or four patients within the next year because we are short an analyst," Stone maintained, "if that means that by waiting we shall be able to take on a good American analyst that may be available at the time." Karl felt ambivalent and a bit distressed with Stone's proposal, for he still sought émigrés who might "instruct" him. But he agreed to go along on a trial basis.[15]

By 1943, however, Karl ordered full-scale resumption of émigré recruitment. Owing to wartime staff shortages, Menninger needed psychiatrists. Within the small pool of psychiatrists available, few were willing to work at the hospital if they could not be assured of on-the-job training analyses. To recruit these psychiatrists, Karl argued (and Stone agreed) that émigré analysts had to be hired. Unlike Stone, however, Karl hoped that recruitment could promote educational as well as staffing benefits.[16]

Karl asked David Rapaport to act as a talent scout and locate refugee analysts who might come to Topeka. Rapaport found only one analyst, Frederick Hacker. Hacker had graduated from the University of Vienna and obtained his medical degree from the University of Basel. He took specialty training at the Vienna Neurological and Psychiatric Clinic, and secured analysis under Edouard Hitschmann, of Freud's early Vienna circle, and from Ludwig Jekels. After interning at St. Francis Hospital in Jersey City, Hacker completed a residency at New York State Psychiatric Institute but had not yet taken on analytic cases. Like Hacker, Rapaport's other recruits were young and inexperienced. By 1945, most had departed. Because of the brevity of their stay and their willingness to placate Karl while they sought jobs in more favorable locations, association with these émigrés was neither disagreeable nor memorable.[17]

<hr>

III

Psychiatrist Douglass Orr worked at Menninger between 1937 and 1941. He spent most of his time in the clinic building, analyzing patients. Several of the émigrés conducted analyses there in nearby offices. Karl, too, maintained an office there, where he conducted some analyses. Orr got to know the émigrés well and was able to see how they got along with Karl. What impressed Orr was the differences among the émigrés. Some were "urbane, sophisticated and witty," some "wise-cracking and intense," while others were "serious, sober and ramrod stiff." He also observed that none seemed very comfortable. It was difficult to adapt well to Topeka. Moreover, there were salary disputes with Karl. The émigrés wondered why Karl had recruited them if he was unwilling to pay them adequately.[18]

Discomfort with Topeka is easiest to explain. There were no more than a dozen émigrés in the city at any one time. Given their small numbers and sharp differences, conditions were not ripe for the comforting enclaves of several dozen refugee families that developed in more cosmopolitan cities, such as New York, Boston, and Los Angeles. Still, there were subtle ties in Topeka based on the émigrés' common hobbies and cultural interests, shared snubs from the local citizenry, specific kinds of prior allegiance to the Freudian "family group," or even a shared sense of estrangement from the Menninger "family spirit." Bonding through estrangement was particularly conspicuous when they discussed common difficulties in dealing with Karl.[19]

But the comforts of bonding rarely overcame the difficulties of residing in Topeka. Though Karl sentimentally regarded Topeka as his hometown, the contrast between the Kansas capital and the great European cities can hardly be exaggerated. The newcomers characterized Topeka as a cow town. Deprived of classical music, art, and theater, they were bored. Even the routine social services of European cities were missing. Yet they acknowledged their good fortune at being in America and sometimes cried at the sight of markets filled with food. As Grotjahn told Charles, "Our butter was better, but we didn't have any."[20]

If the contrast between cosmopolitan European cities and a provincial midwestern town was unsettling for the émigré analysts, it was doubly so for their wives. After all, the men had the benefits of association with the Menningers' efforts in hospital therapy and with the prominent and intellectually stimulating if difficult Karl. Though impressed by the well-stocked markets, the absence of troops in the streets, and a secure existence, the wives tended to feel that these material benefits were outweighed by cultural poverty and by the icy stares of neighbors suspicious of foreigners.[21]

Financial controversies contributed at least as much as culture shock to the émigrés' sense of separateness and their feelings of transience. When Karl revealed to Ernest Jones a disappointment at his inability to keep and assimilate émigrés, he claimed that they left for larger urban centers because they preferred to "hobnob with a lot of other foreigners" and to "make more money than they ever made before in their lives." They were unhappy with his seemingly fair and adequate salary scales.[22]

The first argument between Karl and the émigrés over salary came in 1937, a year after Martin Grotjahn and Bernard Kamm had arrived; it set the stage for many bitter confrontations. Kamm had been hired at $250 a month. Because his analyses brought in substantial revenues, Kamm had been assigned a full schedule. Aware of the sharp disparity between the several thousand dollars of income that he generated every month and his salary, and cognizant of what analysts made in cities like New York and Chicago, he asked for a raise. Karl became agitated and claimed that no employee had ever asked for a raise, that one did not speak of salary issues in a professional American medical organization. Kamm had always negotiated his salary in Europe. Moreover, he could not understand why the leader of an institution with a psychoanalytic orientation, one that prided itself on the utmost candor, would place such a topic off limits to discussion.[23]

After several such bitter confrontations over salary, Karl asked John Stone to assume some of the burden. But he left Stone with strict guidelines: émigré salaries were to remain substantially unchanged. Consequently, if Stone appeared somewhat more reasonable and less outraged, the results were the same. When Ernst Lewy, the most gentle and conciliatory of the refugees, asked Stone for more money, he was rejected with specifics rather than Karl's angry outbursts. Stone told Lewy that he was not helping the organization enough with earnings or public relations work in the community to justify a raise.[24]

The émigrés believed that they had sound reasons for salary increases. Their life styles were unnecessarily austere, yet they felt that they could command considerably higher salaries elsewhere in the country. Moreover, they assumed that because European psychoanalysis was gaining prestige within American psychiatric and psychoanalytic circles, many private practitioners as well as psychiatric organizations outside Topeka would welcome them. The émigrés also objected to a situation unlike Europe where patients did not pay them directly. They firmly believed that the therapeutic success of the analyst-analysand relationship was partially determined by the money patients sacrificed to them in order to be analyzed. At Menninger, patients paid a business office rather than the analyst, and at a rate much below the European rate.[25]

What distressed the émigrés most was the realization that Karl or Stone treated all their salary arguments as equally frivolous, regardless of the services performed. In patronizing tones, Karl warned them repeatedly that in a facility such as his, with heavy staff costs and maintenance bills, overhead was substantial. High overhead dictated relatively low salaries. But this was the price of working for a benevolent organization, in which the Menningers, too, made great financial sacrifices. They earned considerably less than they might have in private practice, they frequently went without pay increases, and they sometimes returned their monthly wages to keep the organization solvent. If the family and the American staff continued making "terrific sacrifices" but the émigrés refused, Karl insisted, the latter would be paid "disproportionally as compared to what we pay ourselves." Finally, Karl maintained that all those privileged to serve on his staff were healers first; medical personnel should not be corrupted by the quest for money. The more Karl argued, the more distressed the refugees became.[26]

Late in the 1930s, Etalka Grotjahn confided to Catharine Menninger that she, Martin, and the others were unyielding in their salary demands despite Karl's intransigence because money represented a form of security to people who had fled from Hitler's armies. After the Nazis had extracted the gold from her teeth and confiscated all the worldly possessions that her family and even her father's family had owned, money became crucial in determining whether any of them escaped from Europe. With money, she, her husband, and her son had managed to flee. With funds, they had then been able to restore their worldly goods, a home, and feelings of worth and dignity that went with those acquisitions. If another tragedy faced the Grotjahns in the New World, she maintained, money was the only asset that she could depend upon to keep her family together. For this reason, she insisted that Karl had to pay her husband properly or he would leave.[27]

Similarly, when Karl offered Ernst Simmel a job in Topeka after

German authorities closed down his sanitarium, Simmel declined because his money demands could not be met. He needed funds to pay off the debts caused by the forced closing of his facility. Money could also provide safety for his family in the New World as it had in the old.[28]

Will, Charles, Knight, and Stone backed Karl on salary policy but had no sense of what refugees like Grotjahn and Simmel were actually demanding. Karl came close when he suggested that the émigrés pursued high salaries because "they have had terrible insecurity in their lives in the past few years" and were "rather suspicious" that they might be "hurt" in America as they had been in Europe.[29]

It is important to know why Karl, possessing this insight as well as a desire to learn from the émigrés what Freud had never conveyed personally to him, was so unyielding in salary discussions. In fact, he harbored certain resentments against Freud and his European followers, which hampered his rapport with them. These resentments were rooted in the way Freud, Jones, and Alexander had treated him when he visited Vienna, but they were also deeply rooted in his small-town Protestant missionary upbringing. Much more than Stone, Will, or Charles, however, Karl was driven by his cosmopolitanism, his sense of professionalism, and especially his commitment to the life of the mind, which led him to resist and often even to deny his provincialism.

One gets some sense of Karl's inner struggle and the tensions and contradictions it engendered from an incident that occurred in April 1939. Ernst Lewy, on staff less than half a year, asked Karl for a paid vacation. Karl was indignant. "Why should we alter our rules that we have always used with regard to Americans just because these Europeans have the audacity to ask us to do so," he wrote to Stone. "They are not in Europe now, and ought to be damned thankful." He strongly opposed "giving Lewy any vacation on pay." Karl then went on to connect Lewy's salary request to his Jewish background: "and while I am talking about this, I want to say I don't think this is Jewish—it is refugee. Look at Kamm and Moellenhoff. They are just as bad as any of them [the Jewish émigrés]." Soon after, Karl complained to his father about refugees' financial demands and added that he was "not at all adverse to Jews, but I think we must not get too many Jews in the Clinic or it will be bad for them as well as for us."[30]

On still other occasions, Karl mixed provincialism and cosmopolitanism by associating Jews with émigrés who demanded money while denying that very connection. Ambivalent, his pride mixed with resentment, Karl noted that Jewish physicians gave something to his organization that others could not: that "us Christian boys don't seem to be

sensitive enough or smart enough to make good psychiatrists and analysts." He denied bias because "my oldest daughter is married to a Jewish
physician." He acknowledged having become a better doctor since he
mastered Freud's "Jewish science," yet castigated Otto Fenichel and
other émigrés in California who championed the rights of lay analysts for
displaying an almost inherent Jewish propensity toward bonding. He
wrote to Lionel Blitzsten, the eminent analyst who had trained several of
his staff associates, that "I am not in sympathy with Zionism" because "I
am opposed to separatism," a form of "prejudice." Because of this Jewish
separatist or "ghetto" mentality, Karl had instituted a rule in the Menninger residency program "not to accept more than one Jew at each
appointment date" (January and June).[31]

I V

In reproving refugees for their salary demands while pressing to recruit
others, Karl at once opposed and promoted a Menninger workplace that
was provincially American and "essentially Christian and Protestant."
His associates were far less ambivalent. With Will in the lead, they stood
firmly for the "family spirit" within the larger organization and invoked
the established clinical techniques and practices of the hospital as a mea-
suring stick to evaluate the émigrés. Almost inevitably, the émigrés came
up short. Consequently, they pressed Karl to halt recruitment efforts.[32]

One can understand why. Like Freud and his inner circle, most of the
Topeka émigrés had maintained small private outpatient practices in
Europe; they had worked primarily with neurotic clients, who had usually
been able to function on their own. In the Menninger hospital or even
in the clinic building, conducting analyses, the Europeans had to contend
with considerably more disturbed patients and to use more elaborate
treatments. Some failure was predictable, and Will and his colleagues
made this known. But rather than master milieu therapy procedures to
enhance their treatment and silence their critics, the émigrés tended to
mock those procedures. Several criticized the guide to the order sheet as
unworkable. Others derided the physicians' case conference for dealing
superficially with maladies and for obscuring patient behaviors with imprecise language. The émigrés also charged that Menninger's American
staff understood only those aspects of Freud's "science" consistent with
their melioristic, upbeat outlook. This especially rankled Will and his
colleagues and made them hope, all the more, that Karl would conclude
his experiment with émigré labor.[33]

Karl agreed that the émigrés were troublesome and often rather "unscientific," but he was never quite willing to abort his experiment. Moreover, he was deeply concerned with the émigrés' claim that Menninger clinical operations were only superficially psychoanalytic. A 1940 controversy was illustrative. Several American staff within the Topeka Psychoanalytic Institute had accused Edoardo Weiss of treating his analytic patients in sitting postures and seeing them only three times a week "in conformity to his wife's thinly disguised Jungian approach." Whereas Will stood ready to reprimand Weiss for departing from five-day-a-week sessions in the supine posture, as Freudian orthodoxy required, Karl suggested that his American colleagues scarcely knew what Freud's orientation was. Weiss had been a colleague of Freud in the Vienna Psychoanalytic Society, Karl reminded them, and Freud had strongly supported Weiss's efforts to organize a psychoanalytic movement in Italy. It seemed inappropriate to berate one of Freud's most eminent colleagues for alleged heresies. At the very least, they should learn from Weiss and other European analysts essential aspects of Freudian psychoanalysis.[34]

The Weiss episode underscored Karl's bind after half a decade of émigré recruitment. He alone among Menninger's American staff was determined to continue the experiment. But he also had misgivings, for refugees like Weiss provoked internal problems. Indeed, it seemed as if unfortunate disputes over working conditions occupied far too much of his time with the émigrés and instruction from them in psychoanalytic culture far too little.

For Karl, the ultimate test of the utility of that instruction was his capacity to write important books that elaborated Freud's insights. Even before he visited Vienna, he had written "Psychoanalytic Aspects of Suicide," which he felt had book-length potential; it was this paper he had wished to show Freud as proof that at least one American embraced Freud's theory of an all-powerful death instinct. Back in America, Karl began to revise and to flesh out the paper, in anticipation of sending Freud a copy for evaluation. As the first émigrés arrived in Topeka, he showed them drafts and discussed related ideas with them. Two books came of his efforts: *Man Against Himself* (1938) and *Love Against Hate* (1942). By developing Freud's concept of a deep, powerful force of thanatos (the death instinct) emerging and contesting eros (the life instinct) within a person, Karl sought to outline in these volumes what he regarded as Freud's most important message—man's tragic intrapsychic struggle. If he succeeded in capturing this struggle with accuracy and depth, the émigrés' instruction would have accomplished its purpose, justifying the difficulties of having them as colleagues.

Karl's writing effort misfired. To be sure, *Man Against Himself* was a rich and creative book. It represents one of the classic studies of suicide in modern Western culture. Grounded in citations from *Man Against Himself*, *Love Against Hate* had multiple printings; the volume resembled Freud's *Civilization and Its Discontents* in the author's masterful shifts between clinical phenomena and the broad functions of civilization. Yet these two texts yielded an exposition of psychoanalysis closer to the writings of Will, Knight, and other American therapists on Karl's staff than to those of Freud and his European "family group." Like most Americans interested in Freud's new "science," Karl was never quite able to deal comprehensively with the dark, archaic quality of Freud's dual instinct theory—to acknowledge that the theory concerned a closed system for channeling intrapsychic energy. Reflecting the optimistic, reformist, environmentalist thrust of early American psychoanalysis, Karl became preoccupied with what was very nearly a cognitive and transactional approach to psychoneurosis.

In both volumes, Karl treated the death instinct as a less ominous force than Freud had given his followers to believe. He claimed that its manifestations were detectable in a clinical examination, and he characterized it as an eminently manageable phenomenon. Every illness, from impotence to organic disorder, was attributed to the death instinct or its derivations. In all cases, the remedy was to cultivate the life or erotic instinct. Whereas Freud had become exceedingly skeptical of the capacity of eros to conquer the death instinct, Karl was very optimistic. He did acknowledge that death was the "ultimate conqueror." However, there was a remarkable human capacity for "prolonging the game [of life] with a zest not born of illusion." Indeed, "the logical inference of Freud's theory is that hate means death and that love is stronger than hate, and therefore stronger than death." He preferred to call these two primary instincts "constructive and destructive tendencies of the personality." The essential task of the therapist was to "encourage love and diminish hate," through hobbies, education, play, and other activities that "make it possible for us to live and to love, because they help to absorb the aggressive energy which would otherwise overwhelm us." Thus, Freud's bleakest and most disturbing concept became an exercise in optimism through therapeutic manipulation.[35]

This is not to classify *Man Against Himself* and *Love Against Hate* as distortions or popularizations of Freud's dual instinct theory—as the struggle between eros and thanatos filtered through the ethos of progressive period reform and the American self-help ethic. Rather, in certain areas, Karl openly and thoughtfully departed from key Freudian tenets.

On the basis of twenty years of clinical observation, he insisted that it was during the oral rather than the genital stage of psychological development that the death instinct turned at once inward on the self and outward against elements of the outside world: "Persons of this undeveloped infantile or 'oral' type of character organization are, therefore, prone to react with this splitting and rebounding of the instinctual trends when exposed to certain—for them unendurable—disappointments." Karl also disagreed with Freud's emphasis on sexuality as the strongest and highest form of the life instinct. Coming from a family with strong evangelical Protestant values, he could hardly have reacted differently. While he defended the legitimacy of Freud's focus on sexuality, Karl argued that sexuality usually represented a mixture of death and life instincts—hate and love. It was not sexuality per se, then, but the death instinct within sexual expression that was a concern. The death instinct had to be modified or rendered less destructive in any of its manifestations, including sexual expression. By the time Karl was preparing *Love Against Hate,* he was willing to propose that discussions of the life instinct should concentrate on "love" rather than libidinal sexuality. He insisted that love was no mere sentimental idea. Nor was it reducible to an erotic force. It was love and not sexuality that had the capacity to control aggression. Checked by the power of love, elements of the aggressive or death impulse were transposed into less aggressive forms. "It is better to love than to sublimate," Karl argued, for sublimation involved no more than a mode of neutralizing the aggressive impulse. But it was "better to sublimate than to hate."[36]

Karl felt that by stressing sublimation—of sexual urges and other phenomena containing elements of aggression—he was simply elaborating on the compromises of life that Freud had emphasized most pointedly in *Civilization and Its Discontents.* A passage within *Love Against Hate* underscored the essential theme of *Civilization and Its Discontents:*

> In order to achieve what we hope to be the greater ultimate satisfactions of civilization, we have increasingly held back the immediate gratification of some of our instinctual needs, with the result that the civilization we achieved has kept making greater and greater demands for renunciation until it has reached a point that we can now scarcely afford.

The pessimistic tone of this passage was consistent with the general tone of gloom in Freud's book, but it was at odds with the more upbeat tone of *Man Against Himself* and, especially, *Love Against Hate.* Particularly in the latter, Karl insisted that sublimation of aggressive instincts could be taught and mastered. This could lead to a relatively happy existence; it was a viable alternative to instinctual "renunciation" to a "point that we can now scarcely afford."[37]

Although many factors explain why the foregoing passage seemed rather anomalous in Karl's two books but consistent with *Civilization and Its Discontents*, perhaps most important were the differences between Menninger and Freud on the value of religious experience. Quite unlike his cautious, indirect way of articulating other differences with Freud, Karl did not mince words on the psychological value of religious experience. "Freud's skepticism [on religion] hinged on his lack of conviction that religion could in any realistic way mitigate the sufferings inflicted by the outside world upon the helpless individual," Karl noted. However, the founder of psychoanalysis had "disregarded the fact" that religion could be just as helpful as psychoanalysis—perhaps more so—in "controlling and directing aggressions" toward love and away from the hateful death wish. Religion was "no illusion and not a neurosis," as Freud had characterized it. Rather, religion enhanced the life instinct by sublimating and thereby weakening and redirecting the death instinct. Consequently, religious experience represented "a very real defense against the threat of internal danger." This was why psychoanalytically oriented psychiatrists would do well to look upon religious leaders as colleagues in the healing art:

> Essentially, both are trying to do the same thing: to make people more comfortable and to save them from evil. . . . They both use verbal techniques and employ their own personalities to accomplish their results. They both recognize the value of confessional catharsis. . . . For both [psychoanalytically oriented] psychiatrist and priest, love is the greatest thing in the world, whether one calls it God or an instinct.

With this perspective, Karl found it necessary to take issue with Freud on the isolated quality of the psychoanalytic movement. Although few realized it, psychoanalytic psychiatrists were actually associates of the clergy. Thus, there was much cause for optimism in the battle of "love against hate." Karl came close to saying that the evangelical missionary tradition of his family was compatible with the values and approaches of Freud's psychoanalytic "family group."[38]

In discussing Freud's death impulse and dual instinct theory, Karl departed clearly and cogently from the founder in three particulars: the

developmental stage where the death instinct turned outward, the importance of sexuality, and the value of religious experience. There was a
fourth difference, which, from the standpoint of personality theory, was
considerably more important than the others. In his 1920s articles on
influenza and schizophrenia, Karl had broken with his predecessors by
suggesting that mental "illness" and mental "health" were not distinct
and separate entities. Rather, there were dynamic patterns of change
from "health" to "illness" and from "illness" to "health" through "reversibility." In *The Human Mind,* Karl had retreated from that bold perspective; he characterized mental "health" and "illness" in the more rigid
and traditional sense. But over the next several years, as he committed
himself to Freud's perspective on the struggle between the death and life
instincts, he revived and amplified the suggestion of his provocative
articles. *Man Against Himself* contained an important elaboration of the
viewpoint, and *Love Against Hate* invoked it too.

The principal task of *Man Against Himself* was to explain why some
individuals committed suicide while others did not. Karl addressed the
question by postulating a "sort of equilibrium, often very unstable,"
within a person between eros and thanatos. The equilibrium was destroyed, eros capitulated to thanatos, and a person ultimately committed
suicide when the confluence of three wishes occurred: the wish to kill, the
wish to be killed, and the wish to die. But Karl illustrated through rich
case studies, newspaper articles, and sundry other sources how a great
many near suicides, slow suicides, and assaults on specific parts of the
body occurred where eros had not fully succumbed to thanatos. These
cases were evidenced by self-mutilations, purposive accidents, toxin addictions, neurotic invalidism, and other self-destructive behaviors. Sometimes these patterns represented efforts to *resist* self-annihilation: partial
punishments that neutralized self-destructive tendencies. But there were
healthier, more effective ways to repudiate the death instinct, such as the
outlets of play, humor, work, and the arts. Whatever might encourage the
flow of love and joy, release repressed emotion, and enhance erotic
pleasure, while mollifying the harshness of the superego, could help.[39]

Karl thus essentially examined Freud's dual instinct theory in a
unique way. Rather than absolute qualities, eros and thanatos represented the polar extremities between which most people shifted. Freud's
clash between the two instincts was reformulated so that the focus was
no longer on either of the polar extremities but on how and why a person
moved from one pole to another. Process on a continuum became the
crucial element of concern for the skillful diagnostician. It was unfortunate that this innovative and important framework in *Man Against Himself*

tended to be obscured by hundreds of examples of suicides or near suicides, to the point where only a small number of readers were able to extract it from the illustrative detail. Although Karl retained the framework in *Love Against Hate,* his theme was even less conspicuous, because his primary focus had shifted from self-destructive behavior to the role of love and sublimation in reducing and redirecting hate. Indeed, it was not until 1963, with *The Vital Balance,* that he stated with ample clarity and precision his concept of shifts on a continuum between eros and thanatos.

In some measure, Karl did not clarify this new and important use of dual instinct theory because he was preoccupied with cultivating an emotional and quasi-spiritual relationship with Freud and his European associates. In the opening pages of *Man Against Himself,* he went out of his way to characterize his effort as no more than an attempt to use the theory as Freud and colleagues like Sándor Ferenczi and Franz Alexander had elaborated it. Rather than state explicitly that his continuum concept represented much more than an application of the clash between eros and thanatos, Karl simply noted that it was the "compromises between life- and death-instincts as we observe them in human beings that form the subject matter of this book."[40]

Karl was hardly unaware that *Man Against Himself* and *Love Against Hate* departed from Freud's dual instinct theory at least as significantly as they embraced it. Chronically insecure, he tended to regard the departures as personal failings more often than he considered them important contributions to an evolving dialogue. Unfortunately, Freud was no longer alive to read and react to the two books in order to facilitate improved future volumes. This left for guidance those who had studied with the founder or with his closest associates. Karl would seek them out more actively in the early 1940s and listen to them more closely than he had in the past. When Frederick Hacker arrived in Topeka in 1943, for example, he detected in Karl a "feeling of mild inferiority . . . that he was just an American doctor, and here we are all those European intellectuals." Resenting the haughty, arrogant qualities of certain of these émigrés, yet feeling that he needed them, Karl related to them with "respect and hostility at the same time," Hacker found.[41]

Karl's relationships during the early 1940s with Otto Fenichel and Ernst Lewy illustrated this "respect and hostility." Fenichel had long been regarded as one of the most brilliant and creative members of Freud's "family group" and was a major contributor to the discussions of the Berlin Psychoanalytic Society. In 1938, he had stopped in Topeka on his way from Europe to California, where he intended to establish a practice. Although Karl was distressed by Fenichel's poor English and "foreign" eating habits, he was taken by the brilliance of his lecture to the Menninger staff. Karl was sure that his European guest could teach him much about the deeper intellectual and spiritual lessons of Freud's "science." Four years later, he sent Fenichel one of the first copies of *Love Against Hate*. Expecting that the refugee would find it a deficient and superficial rendering of psychoanalytic thought, Karl accompanied the book with a letter claiming that it represented "a faithful adherence to Freudian principles." If Fenichel took exception to the conceptual foundation of *Love Against Hate*, Karl suggested, perhaps Fenichel himself was departing from Freud's ideas. He was baiting Fenichel, to encourage an instructive reply and perhaps a sustained intellectual exchange.[42]

Karl's rapport with Ernst Lewy revealed more "respect" and less "hostility." After their stormy dispute in 1939 over finances, the two became close as they discovered that they were both intrigued with the theologian Paul Tillich. When the discussion shifted to psychoanalysis, Lewy's concurrence in many of Karl's observations gave Menninger confidence that he was moving beyond the rather practical, reformist, and generally cure-oriented perspectives on psychoanalysis that typified much of the American response to Freud. Karl even construed Lewy's occasional periods of depression-related silence and detachment as spiritual communication of an element in the mind and mood of European psychoanalytic culture. Consequently, he was exceedingly distressed when Lewy announced, late in 1944, that he was leaving Topeka for a private analytic practice in New York. Not even this kind and cordial friend would remain in town for very long.[43]

V

Clearly, Karl's quest for European psychoanalytic truth was a personal but also deeply intellectual pursuit. By the late 1930s, his efforts were pertinent to an institutional dilemma of crisis-like proportions, which also tested his managerial and political skills.

More even than at Will's hospital, émigrés and Americans had come together in the Topeka Psychoanalytic Society and Institute. This Menninger Clinic–affiliated structure had its beginnings in 1932 as a special study seminar for staff who wanted to discuss psychoanalytic issues with Karl. By October 1936, a second, more exclusive, and more formal body, the Psychoanalytic Study Group of Topeka, was formed. Run by Karl and to a lesser extent by Robert Knight, it was restricted to the six analysts (émigrés among them) on the Menninger staff. At the time, the Chicago

Psychoanalytic Society was the only midwestern organization recognized by the American Psychoanalytic Association (APA). It was therefore designated to assume jurisdiction over the Topeka study group and over all formal Menninger psychoanalytic enterprises. Consequently, Chicago leaders were responsible for new Topeka training analyses. Between 1936 and 1938, the Topeka study group met monthly, sometimes with Karl's psychoanalytic seminar but usually apart, to discuss case histories and technical problems and to hear guest speakers.[44]

By the beginning of 1938, the Topeka group had expanded to thirteen members, the majority Menninger analysts. However, a few were from Kansas City, Oklahoma City, Los Angeles, and San Francisco; they had wanted membership affiliations closer than Chicago. In spring 1938, the group renamed itself the Topeka Psychoanalytic Society, absorbed Karl's old psychoanalytic seminar, and had its constitution approved by the APA. Under the auspices of Chicago, Topeka now assumed responsibility for the training and supervision of analytic candidates in Kansas and more western locations. If it performed to the satisfaction of the APA, it would gain full recognition as an independent psychoanalytic institute (the Topeka Institute for Psychoanalysis) and would exercise formal jurisdiction over all psychoanalytic training in the western states.[45]

Because the stakes were high, Karl insisted on dominating the affairs of the Topeka society. He was willing to share certain responsibilities with Knight only, and the two established "a sort of unofficial protectorate" over policy and management. This upset many of the émigrés who joined the Topeka society. It especially upset those, like Otto Fenichel and Siegfried Bernfeld in California, who had grown accustomed to managing their own professional affairs. Fenichel and Bernfeld knew, too, that in other American psychoanalytic societies, émigrés with firsthand experience in European psychoanalytic practices were often treated as elders; they dictated procedures for training analysis and analytic supervision, and they even determined local society membership policies. Consequently, these émigrés within Topeka jurisdiction insisted upon continued autonomy and elder status precisely at the time when Karl was being watched and measured by the APA.[46]

The conflict over authority took place within the context of the controversial issue of lay analysis. In *The Question of Lay Analysis* (1926), Freud had defended the rights of nonphysicians to practice psychoanalysis. By 1938, he supported those rights "even more intensely than before, in the face of the obvious American tendency to turn psychoanalysis into a mere housemaid of psychiatry." Freud attacked the willingness of American doctors with psychoanalytic specialties to monopolize psychoanalytic practice—not through the force of their ideas but by controlling training procedures. Specifically, he castigated them for excluding non-physicians from training privileges. In periodic remarks, he alluded to American physician-psychiatrists as rather narrowly educated. At times, he suggested that they embraced too few lay colleagues, had insufficient ties with the humanities or the social sciences, and clung dogmatically to the premise that psychotherapy of any sort was their exclusive province. For Freud, these were not the kind of people who could ponder, discuss, and elaborate the complexities of his psychoanalytic formulations. He feared that American doctors might simplify those formulations and subordinate them to their pragmatic psychiatric activities. Among the many factors behind his advocacy of lay analysis was the hope that it might ensure more psychoanalytic practitioners in both Europe and America who had wide-ranging intellectual interests.[47]

A man with diverse intellectual interests and friendships, Karl was sympathetic with Freud's hopes for psychoanalysis. Moreover, Alexander had impressed on him the dangers of dogmatic thought control within the field. However, like Smith Ely Jelliffe, Abraham Brill, and most other early-twentieth-century physician-psychiatrists committed to Freud's "science" of the psyche, Karl also felt compelled to win for it a respectable place within the American medical profession. He supported a 1938 rule change within the APA to achieve that end. Lay analysts were to be denied membership and accreditation within any APA constituent society.[48]

Because this assault on lay analysis directly contradicted Freud, and since several European analysts were not physicians, those émigrés under the jurisdiction of the Topeka Psychoanalytic Society were outraged. Several in California were determined to defy the rule change. Led by Mme Francis Deri and Hanns Sachs, with strong support from Simmel, Bernfeld, and Fenichel, they had created agencies like the Los Angeles Psychoanalytic Study Group before the rule change, and the groups continued to admit lay members as well as doctors after the change. As leaders of the Topeka society, Knight and especially Karl recognized a primary consequence of this defiance of APA policy. If the rule change was not accepted, the APA would almost certainly deny Topeka full recognition as an entity independent of Chicago. In 1939, therefore, Karl and Knight exposed publicly the embryo form of what was soon to become the Los Angeles Psychoanalytic Institute for defying their jurisdiction by permitting lay analysis. Then they encouraged ten California physician-analysts supportive of the rule change to form the San Francisco Psychoanalytic Society. They insisted that San Francisco could better enforce the ban on lay analysis than Topeka, fifteen hundred miles away. The APA agreed and recognized the San Francisco society. This relieved Karl and the Topeka society of responsibility for the conduct of the California rebels. In the eyes of APA officials, he had acquitted himself well. Permanent recognition of his Topeka society would come as a matter of course. In 1942, the APA recognized the society by approving its decision to establish and lodge itself under the Topeka Institute for Psychoanalysis. The authority and power of the Menninger organization grew for its defiance of a position that had been important to Freud and his "family group."[49]

Although Knight, Will, and other senior associates had no qualms about putting down the rebellion, Karl was troubled. He went to considerable pains to explain to émigrés in Topeka as well as in California why it was in their interest to uphold the APA ban. Unlike Knight and Will, who insisted that only physicians were properly qualified to conduct analyses, Karl acknowledged that some "European lay analysts are regarded as competent individuals," and he admitted "a certain sympathy" with those lay analysts among the California rebels who had been close to Freud in Europe. They were "leaders and initiators" of the Freudian movement, and "it was a decided gain to our country" that they had come to impart their wisdom to himself, his colleagues, and other Americans. But though most émigré analysts could enlighten Americans to the deeper truths in Freud's teachings, they had to understand the difficult political situation in which the California rebellion had placed his organization. Moreover, how could he and his associates create a secure place for psychoanalysis "in organized science and organized medicine" in the United States when émigrés like Fenichel, in defending lay analysis, incurred the wrath of American physicians? By making American physician-psychiatrists apprehensive of their control over analytic practice, these émigrés simply promoted "the risk of having psychoanalysis condemned as being an illegal form of medical practice." Worse yet, they ran the risk of fostering "an organized front of Americanism against foreign dominance." Thus, Karl begged each émigré analyst under Topeka's jurisdiction to "adjust himself to our [American] rules and ideals" in his own interests and as a favor to his Menninger associates.[50]

There was an element of expediency and a consideration of power in Karl's plea. He knew that the rebellion would hardly promote American nativism; but it could curb the authority of his Topeka society. However, he was far too agitated to be operating entirely from the power motive. He deeply empathized with émigrés who were properly leaders and teachers within the analytic movement, and he craved to be instructed by them. Karl was also asking the émigrés to understand his political dilemma as one of the few American physicians who genuinely sympathized with and needed them. If they could put down their banners in behalf of lay analysis, he could help them advance their interests within the structure of the APA and the medical profession.

Though several of the California rebels accused Karl of insensitivity to psychoanalytic culture and values, it is noteworthy that in the course of the 1940s he became increasingly supportive of their position on lay analysis. Privately, he conceded that a European lay analyst with the capacity to elaborate the intricacies of psychoanalytic text would probably be as effective therapeutically as a narrowly trained American psychiatrist and perhaps more effective. Therefore, while continuing to defend the ban on lay analysis (especially before APA officials), Karl recruited several émigrés who were not physician-psychiatrists and allowed them to conduct training analyses. As Frederick Hacker recalled, Karl seemed to be defending the APA ban "in order to break it, because he constantly acted against it." Bolstered by Karl's support for lay analysts and their increasing presence at Menninger, the new Topeka Institute for Psychoanalysis gradually eliminated formal limitations upon the activity of nonphysicians within its membership. When APA officials learned of this and considered expelling Topeka, Karl told them that nothing had changed, that his associates were simply making "exceptions" to the 1938 ban for a few "teachers and research men." Clearly, he was trying to reconcile the values of Freud's "family group" with his own needs and those of his family organization.[51]

V I

It is noteworthy that Karl was far less concerned with the psychoanalytic émigrés who arrived after World War II than with those of the prewar period. But while he came increasingly to believe that the postwar refugees had few insights to convey, Will and key administrative staff thought they had become essential to the growth and financial health of the organization. By the early 1950s, therefore, the economic calculation of the younger Menninger was replacing the intellectual and spiritual quest of the older as the principal factor assuring a continued émigré presence.

More than any other event, Karl's trip to the Buchenwald concentration camp on April 23, 1945—twelve days after it was liberated—undermined his quest to master European psychoanalytic truths. "It was an experience that probably will take me the rest of my life to digest," he wrote to Erik Erikson after his return to Topeka. Not even Freud's "science" of the psyche—the most profound personality theory he had ever encountered—could explain what he had seen.[52]

In the late winter of 1944–45, Will, chief of army psychiatry during the last years of the war, appointed a small commission of American psychiatrists to visit the European Theater of Operations and report on Allied troop morale and psychiatric practice. Karl was appointed, along with four of his good friends—John Romano, John Whitehorn, Lawrence Kubie, and Leo Bartemeier. In the main, they visited military hospitals and medical relief stations in Britain, Belgium, France, Luxembourg, Czechoslovakia, Austria, and Germany. Quite unlike his colleagues, Karl was intent on seeing actual combat situations; he endangered his life on several occasions to reach the front lines. His mother's death, shortly before the commission departed for Europe, had pained him deeply and may have contributed to his less than cautious conduct. On what would have been her birthday, Karl recalled, a former prisoner took him and his colleagues to Buchenwald. Apparently, he saw only the main facility and not the adjacent "little camp," where the worst atrocities had occurred. Karl would never forget that day.[53]

He reported on boxes of human ashes from the crematoriums and on inmates dying of disease. He discovered that eighty thousand prisoners had been crowded into a facility designed for twenty thousand and that most had died from a combination of starvation, overwork, illness, and Nazi brutality. Some of the victims had sought revenge; Karl saw the remains of camp guards who had been killed when the prison was liberated. The commission learned about prisoner-doctors who made an x-ray machine out of smuggled parts to help patients, attended secretly to the ills of other inmates, and sometimes held medical meetings at night after sixteen hours of hard labor. Karl praised them for staying "alive by hope."[54]

When Karl wrote home about Buchenwald, however, he did not convey the full extent of his feelings. There was a superficiality to his reports. He sent a letter to *TPR*, the Menninger staff newsletter, noting that though Buchenwald was "a truly terrible and depressing place," it "has been cleaned up and the nationalities—Czech, Luxembourg, Polish, Russian, etc.—classified and fed and hospitalized where necessary." In a letter to his wife and his father, he noted that it was "terrible and depressing" that "hundreds of thousands were worked and starved to death in a matter of 2–3 months each." He concluded the letter: "Everything is fine with me—an incomparably wonderful experience!"[55]

Karl was responding on different levels to what he saw. His "an

incomparably wonderful experience" suggests massive denial of the hor-
rors before his eyes. His discussion of the particulars of the postliberation
cleanup seemed to represent an effort to brush aside the most atrocious
vestiges of the carnage. His vision of a "terrible and depressing place"
of death and horror underscored his struggle to fathom the deeper meaning of the Holocaust and a realization that it could "take the rest of my
life to find out."

At Buchenwald, Karl discovered an underside of European life more
frightening (in some measure because it was more hopeless) than the
unconscious or even the Freudian vision of a death instinct. He was so
disturbed that he simultaneously embraced and backed away from the
deeper meanings of what he saw. It is instructive that in several of his
accounts of Buchenwald, Karl focused on a Jewish guard who had es-
corted the commission through the camp. To stay alive, the guard had
cooperated with the Nazi caretakers and thereby suffered enormous inner
torment. But to survive in the postwar world, the guard tried desperately
to distance himself from his complicity and from the Holocaust generally.
Despite his own commitment as a psychoanalyst to fathom the repressed,
Karl seemed to understand why it was necessary for that scared little man
to deny certain memories of the past. Buchenwald taught Karl that he
could go too far in trying to understand "the sterner, sadder tradition of
Europe." To a degree, at least, it had shifted him toward a surface melio-
rism. He never entirely regained his earlier enthusiasm for exploring
psychoanalytic insights at their deeper levels of meaning.[56]

This consequence of Buchenwald was reinforced by his contacts with
refugees who arrived in Topeka in the immediate postwar years. Postwar
émigrés like Hellmuth Kaiser, Robert Jokl, Michalina Fabian, and Alfred
Gross had initially migrated from Central Europe to western parts of the
continent unoccupied by Hitler's armies. When occupation came, they
moved to safer locations, particularly Britain. Ultimately, they landed in
the eastern United States, where they worked for several years before
arriving in Topeka. Owing to the substantial interval between their escape from Europe and their employment in Topeka, these émigrés had
time to become familiar with the social customs, the language, and the
medical community. Whereas earlier émigrés had regarded themselves as
representatives of an avant-garde Freudian intellectual and cultural
movement, those of the postwar years tended to be more conventional.
Reflecting the "normalization" of psychoanalysis generally, they regarded themselves as skilled specialists who could cooperate with practitioners of other medical specialties. Most avoided far-ranging theoretical
discussions. They lacked Freud's concern with the war between id and

superego and concentrated on ways in which the patient's ego facilitated adaptation to society. Privately, most of these émigrés dismissed exciting and innovative Menninger research projects in perception and diagnostic testing as mere American scientism. Conducting seminars in the Topeka Institute for Psychoanalysis, they required their students to examine the text of Freud's writings as a devotional exercise rather than a stimulus to critical reflection. Bright young psychiatrists in those seminars, such as Gerald Aronson and Maimon Leavitt, learned that, quite unlike the earlier group of refugees, one did not seek out the postwar émigrés for "new thinking."[57]

Karl found these new émigrés less than compelling. He revealed some of his reservations to Menninger psychologist Robert Holt, in words that tended to idealize his rapport with their predecessors. The early refugees had been "drawn into psychoanalysis because of this very breadth of outlook and interest" in the triumphs and tragedies of mankind—the concerns that had preoccupied Freud's inner circle. If some of them were "feverish, even erratic," their "minds were not closed to something new and challenging." Karl had been attracted to them because of their openness. In contrast, he explained, the postwar émigrés were dull, "cold-blooded," and conventional. They resembled many of their American analytic colleagues, sitting all day with a few analysands, earning high salaries, and closing their minds to new and challenging ideas. Karl was castigating postwar psychoanalysis for becoming a "narrowing," conservative, establishment medical discipline.[58]

During the early decades of the century, Freud had voiced certain fears that his "science" would not develop properly in the United States. By the late 1940s and early 1950s, Karl Menninger agreed with him. For Karl, Freud's "science" had lost its bold, pioneering, exploratory spirit in the New World and hence its capacity to fathom the deepest, darkest layers of human motivation. Even if it could penetrate these layers, Karl, after the Buchenwald experience, was reticent in utilizing psychoanalysis to that end.

Though Karl was not impressed with the postwar émigrés, their skills were needed within his organization. Robert Wallerstein, a young resident of the late 1940s, accurately observed that they "were all over the place . . . they were the supervisors; they taught psychotherapy throughout all the training programs . . . they had major administrative positions." The émigrés exerted their greatest influence as training analysts. Owing to the newfound respectability for psychoanalytic therapy, a great many residents and junior-level psychiatrists sought out training analyses—the major requirement for entry into that specialty. However, only two or three Americans on staff could conduct these analyses. Thus, most émigrés had a competency that was very much in demand. Dozens of young staff physicians requested their services as one of the primary benefits for taking residencies in Topeka. This development was not lost on Will and his associates.[59]

Because the new émigrés provided such valued services, they could exert a leverage over salary issues that their predecessors lacked. By early 1951, they chose to push this advantage. George Klein, a staff associate, explained sensitively that they pressed for higher wages to turn Topeka into "more than a beneficent prison" for their families. Higher salaries would allow them to travel and to turn their homes into "as reasonable a facsimile of Vienna as possible" amid Topeka's "cultural poverty." With money, Klein noted, the émigrés might thus restore something of the milieu of their lives before the right-wing persecutions in Europe.[60]

The émigrés discovered that while most of them were training analysts, their annual salaries (roughly ten thousand dollars) were much lower than those of senior hospital psychiatrists, several of whom had been their analysands. They knew that analysts in big-city private practice were also outearning them. Led by Rudolf Ekstein—a former activist in Austrian socialist politics, a prominent child psychologist, and a lay analyst—they began to band together. Ekstein explained that collective action was required if they were to secure wages proportionate to their skills.[61]

One Sunday late in March 1951, the émigré training analysts gathered at Robert Jokl's house. One of them telephoned Karl and Will to announce that they were on strike. They would not return to work unless a fourteen-thousand-dollar minimum salary for training analysts was instituted. Irving Sheffel, a young Menninger administrator, tried to resolve the crisis. He spent the day driving back and forth between three houses—Jokl's, Karl's, and Will's—carrying demands and counterdemands. Sheffel felt that the émigrés were justified in calling for rough economic equality with senior hospital psychiatrists and Will agreed. However, both realized that no settlement was possible without Karl's approval, for issues concerning émigrés continued to be considered part of his jurisdiction.[62]

Karl told Sheffel that he would not accept the fourteen-thousand-dollar base; his response echoed that to the money demands of the earlier refugees. He was quite angry and insisted that the Europeans were being disloyal to him and to the spirit of his organization; it was "dirty" that they requested more money. As the day progressed, however, Sheffel convinced Karl that the émigrés had more bargaining power in 1951 than before the war. If their demand was not met, they could all obtain high-paying jobs elsewhere in the country. If they quit, over forty doctors and psychologists on staff would be without training analysts. Many of these promising young staff might leave, and it would be difficult to recruit replacements. By Sunday evening, Karl's anger finally subsided. Just as his mother's mood had changed so often in the course of financial squabbles, he became morose. But like Flo, the gloom did not yield to inactivity. He agreed calmly to the fourteen-thousand-dollar salary base effective April 1 and told Sheffel that he had spent enough time on the matter; other tasks required his attention. News of the émigré victory filtered quickly through the organization.[63]

The Menninger brothers had hardly come to regard the émigrés as part of the "family spirit" of their workplace. Rather, both recognized that their organization needed the European analysts. This did not mean that Will fully shared Karl's perspective. The brothers had changed in different ways since their visits to Vienna. In 1933, Will had not been attracted deeply to Freud or to many of his associates. (Simmel was an obvious exception.) By 1951, however, he knew that whatever their ideas, émigré analysts at Menninger had assumed indispensable functions. Moreover, Will had developed a personal affinity with the postwar émigrés; he enjoyed their "housebroken" and rather conventional social and professional qualities. They seemed to comprehend the imperatives of a complex professional workplace.[64]

Karl's grudging acceptance of the émigré strike demands pointed to a more discouraged outlook—a near reversal of the intense intellectual pursuit that commenced after his visit to Freud. Through his own analyses, he had come to associate elements of abuse, betrayal, and political manipulation with the therapeutic dimension of Freud's "science." His visit to Buchenwald and his contact with the "normalized" qualities of the postwar émigrés disillusioned him further. By the time of the 1951 strike, he had also come to question psychoanalysis as "a great educational experience." Indeed, he had very nearly abandoned his effort to fathom the European intellectual roots of Freudian doctrine. It was a sign of that abandonment that he shouted angrily to Sheffel, on the day of the strike, that it would suit him fine if the émigrés returned to Europe.[65]

PART TWO

The Making of a National Institution 1941–1953

The Menninger Clinic now belongs to the world. It no longer belongs to my brother and myself.

KARL A. MENNINGER, 1949

CHAPTER SIX
The Cobweb Effect

The writer William Gibson, who moved to Topeka in 1940, captured the interlocking worlds of the Menninger family and the Menninger organization—the "family spirit"—perhaps better than any other observer. Married to Menninger psychologist Margaret Brenman, Gibson—who would later write *Two for the Seesaw, The Miracle Worker,* and other extraordinary plays—became intrigued by the workings of the organization. Although he left with Brenman for the Austen Riggs Center in Massachusetts eight years later, Gibson's interest in Menninger persisted. In 1954, he published *The Cobweb,* a novel about the inner workings of the fictional Castle House Clinic in Platte City, Nebraska, which was based on Menninger and on Austen Riggs.[1]

The theme of *The Cobweb* is that all inhabitants of Castle House—founding family, staff, and patients—"were inextricably caught in the tangle and weaving of each other like a giant cobweb, each strung to each other, hand and foot." Castle House was plagued by two fundamental, interrelated problems. One revolved around the decision to change from a private enterprise, still dominated by the founding family, to a foundation, where power could potentially.shift to the large donors. The second problem was the gradual unraveling of the marriage of the guiding spirit of the clinic, plus his decision to divorce his wife and then, in all likelihood, marry a staff associate. In the course of the novel, Gibson showed how these two seemingly disparate developments were "inextricably" related, because the clinic was "like a giant cobweb."[2]

During the late 1930s and early 1940s, Karl called repeatedly upon Maurice Finkelstein, an attorney, and Ruth Mack Brunswick, a psychoanalyst, to help him with what he regarded as the two most important decisions of his life. One was "the conversion of our [Menninger family] possessions into the Foundation." The other was to buck "terrific obstacles in the nature of inertia, tradition, convention, misunderstanding, and, I may even say, malicious gossip," by divorcing his wife and marrying an associate. When he began to evaluate these two decisions in earnest, Karl felt that they had little in common. But in the course of discussions with Finkelstein and Brunswick, he discovered connections.[3]

The divorce and the move toward foundation status were related, Karl realized, because both touched fundamentally upon issues of power and control. The marriage breakup threatened to weaken the Menninger family because it sparked squabbling and divisiveness. Foundation status undermined family power as well, for it placed trustees rather than Menningers in legal charge of the organization. Clearly, the two developments had extraordinary significance for both the family and the workplace.

I I

Pearl Boam had moved into the Menninger household just as the three sons were leaving. The last of a long chain of boarders, she soon took charge of household management. Flo, who suffered from arthritis and had her Bible studies program to coordinate, relied on Pearl for cleaning and marketing and for help with meal preparation. With part of the inheritance from her father's estate, Pearl purchased land adjacent to the Menninger's Oakwood home so that Charles would have sufficient space to grow flowers. And she took charge of a new member of the household, Edwin's son, who came to Oakwood after inept surgery on a broken leg and the separation of his parents had left the boy distressed and disoriented.[4]

By the late 1920s, Pearl had become more than the manager of Oakwood. She had emerged as the binding spirit of the family. She sent Christmas and birthday greetings to all the Menningers. She arranged regular family visits and urged the family to keep in touch with one another. Under Pearl, the Oakwood household was the hub that bound together three distinctive groups or subfamilies—Karl's, Will's, and Ben Boam's. (Pearl's brother was the devoted hospital maintenance man. After his wife died, Ben lived with his niece Josephine and his three children, a block from the campus.) Almost every Sunday, Pearl invited Ben's group or Karl's or Will's for dinner. On holidays, birthdays, and other occasions, she invited all three groups. During the summer months, she had them meet regularly in a large outdoor screen house. The grandchildren grew up with fond memories of these dinners in the screen house—the symbol of family cohesion.[5]

Pearl, in enhancing the Menningers' sense of kinship, was competing with an earlier and more powerful family focus—Karl. In the course of the 1930s, the family became deeply concerned with Karl's marital problems. Flo from the start had recognized that his marriage to Grace was troubled, that the relationship was probably "conceived in hell," but she was thankful that it had endured. Karl had apparently been distressed to the point where he could not eat at home for prolonged periods during the first two years of the marriage. Grace had hardly been less upset and looked elsewhere for relief. An excellent cook, a gracious hostess, and a conscientious mother, she became preoccupied with children and household. Consequently, she became less than attentive to her husband's long-standing personal insecurity in the face of his outward success—his apprehension that he was not meeting the expectations of his mother and the family. To secure reassurances that he did not receive at home, Karl befriended another woman who could not comprehend his inner doubts. But unlike his wife, she was ready to flatter him.[6]

Lillian Johnson, the wife of a local judge and sanitarium corporation board member, was warm and cheerful. If she lacked introspection, she could still provide for Karl a "grand beautiful night" that he never enjoyed at home. Less than discreet, Lillian boasted publicly that she had been more supportive of Karl than his wife in his efforts to complete *The Human Mind*. Grace, meanwhile, turned periodically to Judge Beryl Johnson for understanding and assurances of her sexual attractiveness. These extramarital relationships were hazardous in a small midwestern city in the 1930s. After a few years, the two couples decided that it was too risky to continue. Public scandal could erupt, and prominent careers could be destroyed. But termination of what Karl characterized as a "foursome" did not improve his marriage. In 1935, Grace wrote to Karl that his many psychiatric activities and the long hours spent on his farm "are merely substitutes for Lillian—so nothing more is given to me than you did before."[7]

What Grace did not know was that Karl had commenced a new liaison. Jeanetta Lyle, a reporter for the Utica *Daily Press* and a secretary at the Kansas City, Missouri, board of education, came to work as Karl's secretary in 1931. Karl began to rely on her judgment regarding literary matters and even pressing organizational issues. She assisted him in all his writing and became founding editor of the *Bulletin of the Menninger Clinic*. Much less mercurial than Grace, she accepted his constant ups and downs without becoming disturbed. "As to your being married," Lyle told him in 1939, "I knew from the first day I worked for you that you did not love your wife. You were attracted to me the first time you saw me and I to you." This was why she had no qualms about "letting you make love to me." The liaison continued for almost a decade. Grace observed that "the entire clinic is aware of the affair." So were members of the family. Adoring Grace, the other Menningers urged Karl to end the association. When Grace pressed him to choose between herself and Jeanetta, he refused, blaming his indecision on his analysis with Franz Alexander. He claimed that the analysis had not helped him to come to grips with his relationship with his mother; consequently, he could make no decision on his future with Grace or Jeanetta. His associates worried that if Karl was not able to keep his own house in order, it was less than clear if his organization had much of a future. One well-placed leak to the national press could terminate patient referrals.[8]

Consistent with Gibson's cobweb effect, Karl was also apprehensive about the future of the organization, but not because of adverse publicity. Rather, he wondered for the first time since joining his father whether it was worth preserving despite a letter now and then from a prominent physician like David M. Levy of New York on how "you boys are fast becoming the Mayos of psychiatry." The firm usually ran an annual deficit of about eight thousand dollars, which Karl, together with his brother, his father, "and one or two of our personal friends," made up out of their own pockets. Holders of sanitarium stock received no more than 2 or 3 percent dividends; some years they got none. Staff in all quarters "received salaries less than the prevailing standards." Worse yet, only by charging very high fees and thereby limiting themselves to a wealthy clientele could the Menningers secure sufficient income to pay salaries, service the physical plant, and maintain liability insurance. Consequently, it was very nearly impossible, Karl complained, for the Menningers to undertake the many missionary ventures in mental health they envisioned. In 1932, he told William Alanson White that "we are not in a position to take charity cases, not even . . . fine research cases." Notwithstanding financial constraints, by 1935 he had established a free clinic on the Menninger grounds to treat financially needy referrals from Topeka city agencies. But the time Menninger doctors spent at the facility jeopardized the income from profit-making segments of the organization and had to be minimized. Thus, rather than expand the free clinic beyond one day a week, Karl felt compelled to turn it over to the Shawnee County Medical Society. It was moved off the Menninger grounds and into a new city building. By the end of the decade, he complained to his associates that "in our actual work we labor with a few rich individuals . . . whose personal salvation or lack of salvation will not make very much difference to the world."[9]

In the course of the 1930s, Karl therefore regarded his organization as he considered his marriage. He had launched both institutions with great hope, but both appeared to have lost their drive and perhaps their reason for being. For Karl, static, self-perpetuating institutions were wholly insufficient. Periodically, he tended to blame Topeka for both his problems. Grace and her parents were eminent members of the city's upper class. As the rumor spread that Karl had lured Grace into a distasteful exchange with the Johnsons, members of the Topeka Country Club considered revoking his affiliation. When he dropped the Johnsons and took up with a "nobody"—Jeanetta Lyle—his standing in Topeka social circles tumbled further. If Karl resented the snubs of the city's elite, he was more distraught that Topeka would not support his mental health ventures. By 1938, he complained to a Topeka *Daily Capital* staff writer that Menninger spent about one thousand dollars a day in the city but received less than twenty dollars in return. "I think we suffer considerably in Topeka—I mean the Menninger Clinic, from the lack of respectability of psychiatry," Karl explained to John Stone, and "I think perhaps we have been mistaken all these years in assuming that we could make psychiatry respectable." From time to time, he therefore proposed that they move the organization to greener pastures—to San Francisco, Seattle, Chicago, or Asheville, North Carolina. He was particularly impressed with Santa Barbara, having discovered a beautiful old hotel there that might make an ideal campus. But his partners, especially Stone, persuaded him not to move. They insisted that he was running not only from his hometown but from his marriage and his organization as well.[10]

III

The web was tightening. By the late 1930s, Karl felt that he had to think much harder about his marriage and his organization. He knew that his analysis with Alexander had not provided him with the self-understanding to extricate himself from this crisis. So he left for New York in October 1938 to enter what he hoped would be a more effective analysis. As he became clearer about himself, Karl hoped, he would be able to discover appropriate remedies for his dying marriage and his seemingly static organization.

Ruth Mack Brunswick, an American who was one of Freud's closest Vienna confidantes and analysands, had formerly specialized in Americans who sought out analysis in the Austrian capital. Elegant, well read, and with a flexible and daring intellect that eschewed dogma, Brunswick was one of the few Americans whom Freud trusted. Karl knew that she had gone through a complex divorce and remarriage, and he was aware that she stressed the role of the mother in personality development. He had some inkling of her addiction to drugs, but this seemed minor compared to the opportunity to learn the mysteries of European psychoanalytic culture through the tutelage of an American who had experienced personal upheaval similar to his own.[11]

Karl lived in New York from October 1938 to May 1940—the entire period of his analysis with Brunswick. By April 1939, he wrote home that he had finally decided against leaving the Menninger organization: "Topeka is my home and it always will be." He still did not know how the organization was to be rescued from its static existence or what to do with his marriage. To make these decisions, he was examining in his analytic sessions "certain problems which began many years ago, and not only in certain recent complications." He was discovering and evaluating the whole basis of his life and work.[12]

During his nineteen months in New York, Karl wrote often to his father, his wife, and his mother. His letters to and from Charles were the least revealing. Karl assured Charles that he would not abandon their partnership but asked him how to explain his stay in New York to his mother. He recognized his father's long-standing apprehensions about presenting Flo with unpleasant news and noted that "I have been under the impression that the less I tell her, the less she will be disturbed. Let me know what you think, and I will try to write her something." Charles replied that both he and Flo were quite upset over Karl's "continued absence." Sleeplessness, depression, and occasional palpitations accompanied their worry about the potential effects of their son's conduct upon the "blood of your blood"—his children and his wife, his partners and staff doctors. Charles suggested rather obliquely that his son's torment over whether to divorce Grace had reawakened his own feeling that he and Flo might be better off apart. Nevertheless, he assured Karl that "What ever you decide, remember that Mother['s] and my attachment will always be to our eldest and first born one of love and devotion of your highest best self."[13]

Correspondence between Karl and Grace was more revealing. Half a continent apart, they seemed able to probe more deeply. Early in his analysis, Karl defined the issue as one of wanting to be married to both Grace and Jeanetta: "I can't marry you both, or be married to you both. I wish I could." Grace retorted that the wife-mistress pattern was not the crux of what plagued her husband. The more basic issue was his inability to break away from his mother's control: "I guess it would have been

better far if I had walked out the night you told me you'd written home
to your mother and asked her if *we* could have a baby now." Ever since
then, Grace wrote, she realized that Karl considered her "to be your
mother." He hated his wife "underneath that endearing exterior," because he confused her emotionally with his mother and hated the controlling influence Flo had always exerted over him. She and Karl had never
been able to live together happily as husband and wife, Grace concluded,
because he could not free himself from the domination of his mother. His
hatred for his wife masked his more fundamental distress over his continuing dependence upon his mother.[14]

Grace understood the most vital issue her husband was wrestling
with in his analysis with Brunswick. She could now see more clearly why
he had dismissed the possibility of an analysis in Europe a decade earlier:
"I don't think that I have the courage to stay away from my mama that
long," he had said. Karl acknowledged the validity of Grace's observation. But though he loved and respected her as "a wonderful wife and a
wonderful mother," he could never "feel entirely satisfied and happy
living with you exclusively." This was because "I married you with my
mother too much in my mind, and that part of my mother which terrified
me as much as it comforted me." "Knowing my childhood," he told
Grace, she would understand that he had to separate from his wife to
become independent of his mother. Only then would he "get at the root
of my dependent attitude, my inability to act definitely and firmly in
the direction of my real needs and desires without subterfuge and
pretenses."[15]

Karl was able, then, to explain to Grace why he would have to leave
her. It was quite another matter to communicate with his mother. When
Flo learned, through unguarded family chatter, that Karl was in New York
to decide whether to divorce his wife, she telephoned and demanded that
he return immediately to talk with her. Karl rushed back to Topeka. Flo
spoke to him as a moral missionary apprehensive of social degeneration
more than as a mother worried about her son. She charged that Karl was
considering the most sinful of acts, severing the marital bond. She continued to barrage him with letters after he returned to New York: "My
world is getting black before me . . . for you to take this angle on life is
certainly a travesty on every thing I have ever thought or done." He
would be casting "the Menninger name into nothingness and believe me
my Dear Boy you will take us all with you." Her "boy" had to reject
divorce, return home, take "more faith in God and yourself," and shift
his primary allegiance from himself to the well-being of the family—to
"those who love you and come to you for help and depend on you for

support." "People have gone too far away from the *Home* in which father loved mother and mother loved father." Karl must resist this current of modern life.[16]

A month before concluding his analysis with Brunswick, Karl wrote a long letter to his mother announcing his decision to divorce. In essence, he told her that he would not give her what she had prayed for and what she had told her family and friends that she had expected. On one level, Karl was proclaiming his independence. He was telling Flo that "my MOTIVES are the important thing, and not my conformity to a plan that you or anyone else has in mind for me." He would feel "dishonest" and would "diminish my effectiveness in my work and life immensely" if he continued to "live with her [Grace] for the sake of appearances." The force of this declaration of selfhood by a forty-six-year-old man was diminished by his simultaneous plea that his mother continue to support him: "Mother dear, I'll tell you what you can do that will help me most. You can believe in me. Believe that I will work out my problem honestly . . . be convinced that whatever I do was the best thing to do, because I will be convinced of it." By urging Flo to believe in him and in his judgments, Karl continued to confer upon her at least a certain authority over him.[17]

When Karl returned home in May 1940, he resumed his duties in the family organization and initiated divorce proceedings. He found Will relatively supportive and lived temporarily at his house. But he sensed that his three children, without quite realizing it, were pressuring him to reconsider his decision. By December, he wrote to Brunswick: "I am a little disturbed by the fact that my son is failing in two of his subjects at college" despite his "superior intelligence." He was also distressed that Julia, his older daughter, had to go through a second surgery to correct acute mastoiditis and that his youngest child, Martha, seemed to have lost her characteristic fervor and enthusiasm. Most of all, he was upset when he learned that his mother was blaming herself because her son had "failed"; she had become acutely depressed. Karl had finally made a decision on his marital future, but neither his children nor his mother seemed able to accept it.[18]

IV

Consistent with the web effect, Karl, during his hiatus in New York, had considered the future of the Menninger organization as well as that of his marriage.

Early in 1935, Jeanetta Lyle had called upon a number of consulting firms and private foundations in New York to figure out how to raise money for the financially troubled Menninger organization. With better funding, Karl told her, it might perform a greater research and service function to the ation. Jeanetta received a mix of negative responses and evasions until she met with George O. Tamblyn. Tamblyn had pioneered during World War I in systematic mass solicitation for the Red Cross and the Community Chest and had conducted successful fund-raising campaigns for several eastern psychiatric hospitals. He told Jeanetta that no granting agencies would donate to a private midwestern enterprise unless it became a nonprofit corporation. Tamblyn was echoed by John Price Jones, whose successful campaigns of the 1920s for the National Unitarian Association had underscored the value of high-powered professional fund-raising.[19]

Tamblyn had offered to visit Topeka to explain his position to the Menninger partners. Jones had promised to send a representative from his consulting firm if they required additional guidance. Arriving in July 1935, Tamblyn encouraged the partners to convert the entire organization into a nonprofit foundation. Will urged his associates to reject the suggestion, because "we might lose control of the organization that we had spent so much time and labor and energy upon building up." Though Tamblyn countered that there were legal safeguards they could adopt to ensure control of the organization while Charles, Will, and Karl were alive, strong doubts remained. Will had invested most of his savings in the enterprise and feared that they could be lost if it was dissolved in favor of a nonprofit foundation. John Stone worried that the tax-free status of a nonprofit institution might force the partners to accept all patients sent by state and county agencies; the sanitarium might become another dreary state hospital. Karl wondered how the partners might continue running the corporation once legal authority shifted to a foundation board of trustees. Only Charles felt that the venture was worth the risks. When Karl voiced his apprehensions about retaining control, Charles retorted that control usually rested where it properly belonged. He reminded his partners that a nonprofit venture represented "applied Christianity."[20]

In their skeptical discussions of the Tamblyn proposal, the partners were hardly aware of the significance of nonprofit foundations. Like most other "new psychiatrists," they were not very familiar with the development of some of the largest and most influential of these institutions at the turn of the century as the millionaire's answer to his "wealth problems." John D. Rockefeller and Andrew Carnegie were the pioneers, followed by Russell Sage, Julius Rosenwald, James B. Duke, John Simon Guggenheim, Andrew W. Mellon, and others. Few of these wealthy donors held precise and detailed perspectives on why they were transforming and expanding their various small-scale charitable enterprises into substantial and complex foundation structures. Mrs. Stephen V. Harkness said she provided the money that established the Commonwealth Fund simply "to do something for the welfare of mankind." An expert class of managers was retained to formulate more precise goals and to create particular nonprofit structures oriented toward those goals. These managers also assumed public relations functions to allay general suspicion of the new institutions.[21]

More than public relations efforts, however, the $154 million that nine of these early donor foundations gave to medical research and education (half of their total grants between 1902 and 1934) generated goodwill. Through these funds, the nonprofit foundations would link their benevolence with dramatic successes in eliminating pellagra, hookworm, typhoid, yellow fever, and malaria. Yet despite the favor the foundations earned when these medical breakthroughs occurred, most "new psychiatry" facilities seemed uninterested in the nonprofit status that would make them eligible for donations. To be sure, the Phipps Clinic had been established and sustained by Henry Phipps's bequests and a solid Johns Hopkins Hospital endowment. And the Austen Riggs Center had transformed itself to a nonprofit recipient foundation. But their colleagues balked.[22]

By the 1930s, however, it was increasingly difficult for the Menningers and the heads of other "new psychiatry" facilities to remain oblivious to Phipps and Austen Riggs. Consultants like Tamblyn and Jones had advised most of them on the advantages of nonprofit status to entice large donations. More money would be available in the years ahead because tax rates were starting to increase and deductions for charitable contributions would become more compelling for large corporations. This was especially so after the Federal Revenue Act was amended in 1935 to allow corporations to deduct up to 5 percent of their taxable income for charitable donations. Moreover, the capital gains tax and even the personal inheritance tax stood to be reduced through donations of appreciated stock and other assets to philanthropic causes. Legally, it was easiest for the corporate rich to secure these tax advantages by establishing foundations that directed their money to select nonprofit ventures. Consequently, despite the Depression, significant new foundations like Henry Ford and Eli Lilly emerged. Nevertheless, even though the Rockefeller Foundation established a medical science division to upgrade the proficiency and the status of psychiatric practice (awarding substantial funding to Franz Alexander at the Chicago Psychoanalytic Institute) and although other donor foundations contemplated similar ventures, Phipps and Austen Riggs remained the only "new psychiatry" facilities that were nonprofit institutions.[23]

The Menningers were not unmindful of increasing resentment throughout the country, and especially in Kansas, toward physicians who earned sizable incomes during the Depression decade. Pressure for state regulation of excess profits and even for state insurance programs to lower the consumer's medical bills was widespread. Eager to combat the view of many Topekans that the Menningers made money through dubious professional efforts, the partners could not entirely dismiss the Tamblyn proposal. Although hardly unconcerned about their personal profits, they wondered whether the public might better appreciate the missionary aspect of their venture if they became a nonprofit enterprise.[24]

Jeanetta Lyle noticed this ambivalence as the Menninger partners discussed Tamblyn's recommendation. Unwilling to become a full nonprofit foundation for fear of losing their savings and the control of their organization, they also knew that the status quo was untenable. Jeanetta suspected that they would accept a more modest proposal. Since 1934, there had been casual talk about alleviating the Southard School deficit by tapping the funds of foundations. Knowing that the Menninger partners had regarded Southard as a dispensable facility, Jeanetta proposed that it become nonprofit. If a nonprofit Southard Corporation commanded funds from Rockefeller and other foundations, she suggested, its perennial financial crisis would be alleviated and other Menninger institutions might proceed with confidence toward nonprofit status. Failure could hardly harm the larger organization; Southard would remain the "problem" institution it had always been.[25]

Initially, both the Menningers and the Southard directors rejected Jeanetta's modest proposal. But after Karl came to support it, the other partners followed. Legal conversion of Southard into a nonprofit Menninger School Corporation came in mid-1937. A small board of trustees was appointed, and several members made personal donations to the facility. The Rockefeller Foundation awarded a four-thousand-dollar grant, and Southard leaders hurried off applications to other foundations. John Stone felt encouraged; the economic advantages were obvious. In addition to grant moneys, Menninger would be relieved of paying state and federal income and Social Security taxes for the school. Stone proposed carrying the nonprofit experiment further.[26]

If Stone was willing to accept the Tamblyn proposal, Karl was not.

He remained skeptical even after John Price Jones sent a consultant to Topeka. However, in July 1938, not long before he departed for New York for his analysis with Brunswick, Karl wrote to Ernst Simmel that "the private psychiatric hospital and, for that matter, the private general hospital, is doomed." Just as he was almost ready to abandon his marriage for Jeanetta Lyle, he seemed increasingly willing to abandon a "doomed" private organization for the nonprofit foundation she favored.[27]

In New York, Karl sought out Maurice Finkelstein, general counsel to the New York State Mortgage Commission and a specialist in family and corporate law. Aware that he might eventually be talking to this brilliant and compassionate rabbi's son about divorce matters, Karl broached the topic of transforming the entire Menninger organization into a nonprofit foundation. Finkelstein was enthusiastic. He claimed that with the donations that would accrue, Menninger could become a great institution. When Karl voiced his fear about loss of control, Finkelstein dismissed it as nonsense; he could draft legal documents to "give us a reasonable assurance that this would not occur." Next, Karl visited Alan Gregg, director of the Rockefeller Medical Science Division, which dispensed funds for psychiatric projects. Gregg firmly supported the Finkelstein recommendation. He added that by appointing as chairman of a foundation board of trustees someone who was loyal to the Menningers—"a sort of absolutely trusted older brother as it were"—they could retain full authority over decisionmaking. "Like myself, he [Gregg] feels that the private sanitarium is doomed," Karl informed his partners. There was no point in being "on the losing side when one might as well be on the winning side without sacrifice of principle." Foundation status would enable the partners to get out of their current rut, where they were dependent on "a few rich individuals" to make a living and to enlarge their practice, which now did not "make very much difference to the world." With the funds that nonprofit status would generate, Karl reported, the organization could care for less prosperous patients, conduct extensive research, and "stress psychiatric education." At the promptings of Finkelstein and Gregg, Karl plunged ahead.[28]

In January 1940, he instructed Stone to "devote your energies to formulating a plan" for foundation status. Karl urged his business manager to visit the Mayo Clinic, which had established a Mayo Foundation for Medical Education and Research a quarter century earlier. To develop that nonprofit entity, separate from the rest of the organization, Will and Charles Mayo had transferred $1.5 million worth of personal securities to the new foundation board of trustees, and Karl wanted to know if they had also relinquished much of their power. He urged Stone to talk specifically with Harry Harwick, Mayo's nationally prominent secretary-treasurer.[29]

Harwick understood Karl's apprehension. He explained to Stone that the Menningers should "take a pretty paternalistic attitude toward the rest of the medical staff." The partners had to guard against shifting "some of the vital aspects of their responsibilities to others." Specifically, Harwick urged them to create a separate nonprofit foundation through a direct cash donation or a gift of sanitarium corporation stock. In the first several years of its existence, this foundation might lend financial support to certain clinic and sanitarium projects, but it was to assume no governing authority over either. The Menningers could control the foundation, Harwick advised, through a seven-member board of trustees, consisting of the four partners plus three prominent Kansans who "aren't hard to handle" but would give the foundation the appearance that "the public is being properly represented." Next, the partners should follow the Mayo example and wait four or five years, while the foundation accumulated private donations and government grants. Once this separate nonprofit Menninger Foundation was on solid financial footing and firmly under the control of the partners, they could work out plans incorporating the clinic and the sanitarium under the foundation's banner. During the transition period, the Menninger partners would retain ownership of all clinic and sanitarium property and capital.[30]

Stone drafted a detailed report of the Harwick proposal and circulated it to the other partners. Charles was as enthusiastic as ever. However, he had deeded over his $34,642 interest in the partnership to his two sons and Stone in exchange for a guaranteed salary of $450 a month until his death (to go to Flo, should she survive him). Though Charles remained a legal partner, he retained only symbolic ownership in the organization. Karl and Will each owned 42.5 percent, while Stone held 15 percent. One assumption behind this arrangement was obvious: Charles was stepping down, while Stone was to continue as a somewhat minor partner. As the dominant partners, the brothers would decide whether to adopt the Harwick proposal.[31]

A few months after his visit to the Mayo Clinic, Stone wrote Harwick that the Menninger brothers were receptive to his proposal, but they needed more information on how the partners could "have fairly good assurance of maintaining control. We have been our bosses up to now and I don't know how well we should be able to function if too much of that authority is passed on to others." Harwick reiterated how the Mayos had retained control by creating a Mayo Foundation separate from their Mayo Clinic. Indirectly, they had been able to dominate the foundation and even to exert hegemony over the clinic after conveying clinic facilities and capital to the Mayo Properties Association (a self-perpetuating charity). But these nonprofit structures had promoted the image of a democratic benevolent organization, and this appealed to donors.[32]

The Menninger partners carefully evaluated Harwick's response. Then, at a medical society meeting in Wichita in May 1940, Will sought further assurances from Harwick. Harwick explained that according to his proposal to Stone, the partners could back off if, after creating a foundation, they were unable to retain control of its trustees. They could return to their original legal structures. The low risk appealed to Will, who found wisdom in retaining a private family enterprise and devising ways of increasing its profits, while he perceived the concrete advantages of a separate nonprofit institution. One of his former patients had pledged ten thousand dollars for a badly needed manual arts building if the money could be donated to a nonprofit institution. With this and other potential donations in mind, Will would accept a separate foundation so long as it excluded from its jurisdiction all profit-making Menninger facilities. He could consider, at a later date, whether to make this new foundation the governing agency of all Menninger enterprises. Ready to authorize this separate foundation, Will left the final decision to his brother.[33]

Karl delayed. He was impressed by Harwick's proposal, which outlined a way to reverse the current course of organizational stagnation: "People are not interested in hearing about our Clinic as such, but the idea of a Midwestern institution holding up its head high as a place for scientific research, with the implication of a certain amount of charity work included, etc. interests people immediately." In April 1940, he advised his partners: "It seems perfectly logical to put this in a practical form by converting ourselves into a foundation" in the way Harwick had suggested. But Karl did not give the ultimate word to proceed. He wanted his executive committee to study the Harwick plan and give him a final recommendation. Meanwhile, he talked with both Finkelstein and Brunswick about the state of his marriage and the wisdom of launching the foundation. His executive committee issued a carefully worded recommendation: the Menninger Foundation should be established formally on February 1, 1941, as a separate institution. Beyond this immediate goal, nothing further was to be done unless ways were devised to assure the perpetuation of control by the Menningers over all their institutions. After telephone calls to Finkelstein and Brunswick over the committee report, Karl considered potential foundation trustees. It was imperative that they do as he asked. Buoyed by the feeling that he was independent of his mother and on the way out of a troubled marriage, and confident of a plan that would revitalize his organization while he retained his authority, Karl finally assented to the recommendation. In February 1941—the very month Karl divorced his wife—the Menninger Foundation for Psychiatric Education and Research was established.[34]

V

Most of Karl's emotional energies during his time in New York were concentrated on his analysis with Brunswick. For the second time in a decade, he was struggling through the analytic process to discover and achieve mastery of his personal history. At the same time, he prodded his parents to undertake historical endeavors of their own. He assisted his mother in finishing her autobiography, which was largely a family history. As soon as he delivered her manuscript to a publishing house, Karl urged his father to prepare a history of the Menninger organization. It was as if he needed to establish a record of his past as he moved toward decisions that would alter the family and the organization in very fundamental ways.

Flo had begun to write her autobiography in 1899, just before Will was born. After reading a few pages of her text to a friend, Ella Brown, she placed the manuscript in an unlabeled envelope and put it aside. Twenty-two years later, Brown wrote to her and suggested that a magazine like the *Atlantic Monthly* might want to consider it. Karl and his brothers urged her to find the manuscript. Flo rescued it from a barn loft and read it to her sons. They asked her to update the story for their benefit, and she carried it to Will's birth. In September 1939, she brought it up to date so that Karl could have it published. This, at least, is what she claimed in a brief foreword to the first edition.[35]

Although the foreword indicated that she was the sole author of her autobiography, this was not quite the case. She wrote the first sixteen chapters (the years up to 1899) entirely on her own. But more was involved with the last five chapters (1899–1939). Karl had prodded her to recount the four decades after Will's birth, and she wrote rather unsatisfactory drafts. "I know it is terribly disappointing to you," she told him, "and I would disappoint most any other rather than you." Karl sent Flo's chapters for the 1899–1920 period to Edwin "to revise," while he himself spent "quite a lot of time" working on the final chapters. When Karl showed the revised manuscript to his mother, she raised two objections. Condensation of the description of her Bible classes was "depressing mother a good deal." More important, she would not let the book go

to press if it contained any reference to the first Menninger divorce—
Edwin's from Ella Waldron. Flo would not allow Karl to cite family precedent for the path to personal happiness that he was contemplating.[36]

Karl worked during the fall of 1939 to get a draft of *Days of My Life*
acceptable to his mother into print. "I hope you won't think I am pre-
sumptuous in having gone ahead with this thing," he told Edwin. "I feel
that I am the chief loafer in the family at present, and have the time to
do it, and I know that you and Will don't." Though he did almost all the
negotiating with the Richard Smith publishing house and attended to
page proofs and other particulars, Karl cautioned Edwin not to tell Flo
"exactly the circumstances under which it is being published." She was
to know only "that we three boys are managing it someway," not that he
was principal architect of the project. Above all, she was not to learn that
Richard Smith was demanding $1,200 to $1,400 from Karl as a hedge
against financial loss or she would cancel publication plans. The book
came out at the end of 1939. Karl selected a number of favorable reviews
and letters that he received on the volume and forwarded them to his
mother. For a while, this seemed to divert Flo's attention from the "sinful" transgression her son was about to commit: "I enjoy Karl's notes and
apparent pleasure over the whole situation." But the publisher's suspicion that the book would have limited appeal proved accurate. Within a
few months, it was clear that *Days of My Life* was a financial liability. Karl
and Edwin were ready with an explanation. The Topeka YWCA had failed
to provide a roster of former students in their mother's Bible classes,
thousands of whom would have bought the volume had they learned it
was available.[37]

Although Karl wanted *Days of My Life* to sell well, completion of the
volume served his purposes sufficiently. He had a full and up-to-date
family history that concentrated on his remarkable mother. The process
of completing what he considered to be a satisfactory book seemed to
augment his efforts to reckon with her more fully in his analysis with
Brunswick. In addition, *Days of My Life* provided the last account of the
Menninger family before it was confronted with what Flo warned would
be a major catastrophe—Karl's divorce.

Shortly after he sent *Days of My Life* to the publisher, Karl turned to
the Menninger organization and his father's book. He wrote Charles a
letter filled with optimism because Charles had accepted his suggestion
of preparing "the firm history." "This is going to be your book," he told
his father, "and it is a very important book to us, and no one can do it
as well as you." He urged Charles to work with a historical file that his
secretary, Alice Dangerfield, had prepared. Charles was to collect addi-

tional documents, arrange them chronologically, and synthesize them through a comprehensive narrative.[38]

For Karl's sake, Charles started out conscientiously and pasted historic materials in loose-leaf scrapbooks. But he was never excited by the venture, and his efforts soon began to lag. The project was dropped.[39]

Karl's failure to achieve a portrait of his organization—on the verge of what appeared to be the most drastic change in its history—as he had achieved a family portrait, was due to the dramatic difference between his parents. Flo focused her interests rather narrowly and forcefully but usually accomplished her goals. In contrast, Charles was much more diffuse in his interests. He engaged in many projects and hobbies simultaneously and was usually more intrigued by the pursuit than by the end result. Moreover, whereas Karl had assisted Flo, he made no effort to help his father. Her story was more important to his self-understanding and to the two decisions he needed to make.

VI

At the end of 1941, Karl told Smith Ely Jelliffe about a momentous change in his personal life: "Grace and I were divorced last February and in September I married to a girl I have loved for a long time." He also complained bitterly about the cost of supporting his ex-wife plus three college-age children. Karl showed this same awkwardness—relief mixed with distress—in other situations. During the month of the divorce, for example, he called in a group of forty Menninger staff to assure them that he planned to remain in Topeka despite the rumors of his imminent departure. "It was as if he was telling his family and explaining," one recalled. Yet a few months after his remarriage, he asked his friend John Whitehorn to advise him on his job prospects elsewhere.[40]

During these months of divorce and remarriage, Karl relied heavily on Finkelstein and Brunswick. Finkelstein would defend him against Glen Hamilton, a tough and aggressive Topeka attorney retained by Grace. At first, Hamilton demanded that Karl pay out $100,000 as a divorce settlement and threatened adverse publicity if he did not comply. Finkelstein whittled the financial settlement to more reasonable proportions. In the course of the negotiations, Finkelstein's mix of strength and sagacity gave Karl a sense that he was being well protected. He began to relax and even to entertain Finkelstein with off-color jokes.[41]

Karl's communications with Brunswick at this time revealed greater anguish. The "preposterously high" financial demands of Grace's attorney had "reduced my ambivalence" concerning his first wife, he confided. And he disliked Grace's "general air of suffering womanhood and pitiful martyrdom." But he wondered if he still loved her—as he continued to love his mother. "I have a very beautiful relationship with my children," he boasted, although he was "a little disturbed" that his son was doing poorly in college and that Grace had made "nasty cracks" about him to the boy. His analysis drew him closer to his son, he told Brunswick, but he was apprehensive of the effect of the divorce upon his daughters. The two girls seemed distant. Two weeks before marrying Jeanetta, he confided to Brunswick: "I have been a little jittery and ambivalent about the wedding," but "perhaps everyone is at such times."[42]

The immediate effects of the divorce and remarriage were readily discernible. The first publicity appeared in Topeka newspapers on the sixteenth birthday of Karl's younger daughter, Martha. Menninger staff quickly cut it from the papers they purchased for patients, but of course the patients heard the news. The wives of some Menninger physicians voiced apprehensions that they, too, could lose their spouses to staff. Local physicians kept their distance. Some influential figures in the American Psychoanalytic Association suggested that Karl ought to be denied the right to hold an official position in the APA despite his skillful handling of the California lay analysis crisis.[43]

Grace continued to live in Topeka, and when they were not away in college, the three children resided with her. Although Karl did not visit his ex-wife, he often dropped by Oakwood when he learned that Pearl Boam had invited Grace over. His children were visibly upset during this whole period. Julia, the oldest, tended to sympathize with her father. However, Karl felt that she was somewhat hostile, owing to "that subtle pernicious influence which her mother exerts and which it took me such a long time to recognize." Though Karl felt he was drawing closer to Robert, the boy sided with his mother. So did Martha, particularly after Karl told her not to come home from college during spring break in 1942 so that he could conserve his financial resources.[44]

Another immediate consequence of the divorce and remarriage was that ties within the larger family began to erode despite Pearl's efforts to maintain them. While the family adored Grace, Karl was blood and the traditional center of family affairs. Most felt compelled to side with one or the other. Although Will idolized Grace, he felt that Jeanetta had restored his brother's happiness. Will welcomed her and Karl as houseguests when he learned that his mother was uneasy about putting up the new bride. Karl was grateful for this show of "affection" and "loyalty." Ben Boam's family was outwardly friendly with both Karl and Grace.

While instructing his niece and his children to be neutral, Ben grew fearful that Karl might fire him, as he had "fired" Grace. To protect against this possibility, he began a file concerning any of the brothers' improper personal involvements that he could learn about. Although Pearl embraced both Karl and Grace, Edwin junior shed his adoration and esteem for Karl. Flo and Charles continued to see Grace, but neither even contemplated repudiating Karl.[45]

The Menninger family became fragmented. Social gatherings among the three groups ceased. We "can't get them all together," Flo complained. "One of the family always breaks the chain." An even clearer sign that the traditional family structure was in shambles was the behavior of the matriarch herself during her final years.[46]

Flo was traumatized by the action of her eldest. Karl's divorce represented a repudiation of her wishes, her values, and even her identity. Flo felt weak and depressed, seeing that she could not control the affairs of her family as she had in the past. She thought that the family was adrift. Her children and grandchildren visited less. Edwin junior had left for college, and Will had departed for the army. Charles helped Karl more at the sanitarium in Will's absence; when he came home, he seemed to spend much of his time talking with Pearl. In an effort to fill the void in her life, Flo worked incessantly on her Bible classes and other projects. But compulsive activity did not seem to provide the sense of fulfillment and consequence that it had in the past: "There is nothing definite that I seem to accomplish, but keep busy, and the days hurry by," she wrote in 1944. She told Karl of "my foolish dreams of filling the days." The day before she died, she complained in her diary that she no longer seemed able to do enough.[47]

Flo arose at six, her usual time, on the morning of February 9, 1945. She had not felt well the previous day and had some difficulty catching her breath, but she began to work at her desk. Letters to twenty-four Bible classes in three states had to be completed and mailed. Ben Boam, who was in the house at the time, heard Flo call for her mother and father. He helped her to bed. Although she was not in pain, he realized that she was dying and knew that he had to reach Karl. He drove out to Karl's farm in the country. When the two returned, she was dead.[48]

The family mourned Flo's death at eighty-one in unusual ways. Although Charles had come home from work on the day of her passing, he returned to the sanitarium the next morning. "In a little while I'll be able to do my spring planting," he told Karl. "But I wonder who we'll get to take care of the harvest." Will had been in town for a short visit when Flo died. He appeared pale but said little, busied himself with his stamp collections, and became more serene. Karl wrote Brunswick about the "anxiety and depression" he initially felt. But after a few days he was "glad that her poor troubled spirit is resting." "There is a certain kind of freedom which it implies," he informed his New York analyst. Indeed, the whole family felt somewhat freer. After they buried Flo, family members returned to Charles's house, where they uncorked liquor and lit cigarettes. This contrasted markedly with the continuous prayers and solemn meals that had followed the burial of Flo's father and prior generations of Heikeses and Kniselys.[49]

VII

From the time of Karl's divorce and the beginning of the Menninger Foundation, the family felt a sense of fragmentation but also the possibility of renewal and restructuring. So did the Menninger partners. They created a separate nonprofit foundation to accept a limited number of donations that might be funneled to needy divisions of the larger organization. A legally independent board of trustees governed this separate foundation, but the partners retained legal authority and power over the neuropsychiatric clinic and the sanitarium, and they held claims to the $250,000 they had invested in the two institutions.

Nonetheless, Harry Harwick had recommended in no uncertain terms that eventually all Menninger institutions be absorbed by the foundation. Large-scale donors would provide the organization with substantial funding only if Menninger became a full-scale nonprofit entity. They would be deterred, Harwick warned, so long as all profit-making Menninger enterprises remained protected for the partners.

The creation of the initial Menninger Foundation had not been an eventful development. The foundation deferred in all matters to the partners, and the partners themselves were trustees. So were Mildred Law and Merle Hoover. Other trustees, like John Whitehorn, head of the Johns Hopkins Psychiatry Department, Winfred Overholser, superintendent of St. Elizabeths Hospital, and J. Roscoe Miller, dean of Northwestern Medical School, were close friends of the Menningers. This essentially left the partners with freedom to use donations to the foundation as they saw fit. But only a limited number of donations had been made, and they ranged from a few hundred dollars to a few thousand. Because foundation income was so skimpy, the Menninger partners could do little more than channel small dollar amounts to the *Bulletin of the Menninger Clinic,* to a few select research projects, and to two or three psychiatric residents to help defray their expenses.[50]

The partners, particularly Karl, were not entirely displeased with this arrangement. So long as the level of foundation operations was small, they could be fairly certain that the independent trustees would leave them to do as they wished. An upturn in sanitarium profits during the war years also militated against further change. Therefore, Karl felt free to report at the October 1943 annual meeting of the board of trustees that though the sanitarium "should perhaps some day be taken over as a property of the Foundation," that day had not yet come. Such a level of "absorption is unfeasible due to the capital involved." Neither he nor his brother was eager to relinquish several hundred thousand dollars they had invested, primarily in the old sanitarium corporation. Nor were they particularly desirous of going on fixed foundation salaries, in view of increased wartime profits.[51]

Stone reminded the brothers that they had created the foundation as the first step in Harwick's long-term proposal. They should not have taken that step if they were not committed to the foundation's absorbing all other Menninger institutions. In the long run, absorption would promote greater organizational efficiency, Stone argued, and would render all Menninger institutions tax exempt. He conceded that the partners would have to turn over the physical plant and other assets to the foundation. And they would constitute a minority within an enlarged fifteen-member board of trustees. But this did not mean that the partners would lose their traditional controls. Indeed, "the best assurance that the present leadership may retain control comes from the dynamic fact of their leadership and their functions rather than from the static fact of an arrangement in which authority is frozen to certain individuals." If they continued to exert effective leadership, Stone told the brothers, they would control the organization in the future as in the past.[52]

Will was not entirely convinced. "Outside of my interest in the Clinic and my life insurance I don't have a cent," he told his partners. Therefore, "it isn't going to be without some reluctance that I agree to give up any large percentage of our meager life savings." And despite Stone's optimism, Will remained skeptical about the retention of partner control over the trustees. At the very least, he recommended that the partners delay foundation takeover of the clinic and sanitarium until they knew how "to insure its control for at least a generation."[53]

In the fall of 1944, Karl announced that he favored absorption of all other Menninger agencies by the foundation. He acknowledged that the move did not serve the immediate financial interests of the partners. They would have to turn over perhaps as much as $300,000 of personal assets to the foundation; roughly one third of those assets belonged to him. By relinquishing them and going on salary, they would lose all "opportunity for big money and [have] no opportunity for ever going away." But they would not lose control. Through "sufficiently stringent stipulations in making the transfer" that Finkelstein recommended, it would be possible for the partners to "retain life control, so that the essential thing will be just as it is now." The organization would remain an "autocratic, oligarchical setup." But the major reason Karl insisted upon full nonprofit status was that it would provide funds to pioneer in significant areas of the mental health field—to regain the innovative spirit that he felt had once characterized his organization:

> We should be training larger numbers of psychologists, therapists and nurses. We should be providing resident instruction in the management of difficult children for teachers. . . . We should be undertaking combined research, teaching and public service projects in cooperation with the schools, universities, industrial organizations, courts, reformatories and prisons. We should make psychiatric consultation available to every person in the community regardless of his financial status.

Concerned with issues of profit and control, Karl was also imbued with his mother's missionary spirit and with a temperament that was intolerant of staid arrangements. So he plunged ahead.[54]

On October 27, 1944, Stone and the brothers deeded over all stock and other assets in the various Menninger institutions to the Menninger Foundation. According to Karl, they were "renouncing all ownership and special privilege in connection with the development of this work." Documents were to be executed, he asserted, through which all Menninger programs would be unified under the foundation. A few days before the partners signed the deed, however, Karl wavered. He still wondered whether "the Foundation should be permitted to remold all our other organizations or whether it should be fitted in as one department of the whole." Retaining the foundation as a separate, distinct unit "would be by far the more convenient, but it is probably already impossible." Karl delayed execution of certain final technical documents for an unduly long period of time. The clinic and the sanitarium were not legally incorporated until December 31, 1945, fourteen months after the partners relinquished their assets. Southard School did not dissolve as a separate nonprofit corporation, to become part of the Menninger Foundation, until the middle of 1946.[55]

It is not easy to explain why Karl took so long to execute the final legal documents. He was ambivalent about absorption in October 1944, but that cannot account for a fourteen-month delay. Other factors came into play. It took several months for holders of sanitarium corporation stock to transfer their assets to the foundation. Roughly one third of the stock was simply donated to the foundation, another 20 percent was purchased for cash, and the balance was acquired for 3 percent unsecured notes, payable in December 1945. The process of contacting all stockholders and negotiating with them in the face of income tax variables and contractual requirements took time. Karl noted that hour after hour was consumed negotiating with certain stockholders, who "held out for every penny" of their investment. However, considerably less than fourteen months were required to buy out even the most recalcitrant stockholders.[56]

The added time can be attributed to Karl, for he controlled much of the negotiating pace. He required assurance that the new full-fledged foundation was not dramatically unlike the old organization. If its board of trustees was to be enlarged, he needed to be certain that the new members showed deference and support. Some sanitarium corporation board members were drafted. So were various friends of the family. Karl allowed only a few of the fifteen trustee seats to be filled by people whose allegiance to the Menningers was at all in doubt. He began the practice of setting basic policies in his own staff executive committee and convening the board of trustees only once a year, for ceremonial purposes; it was a figurehead body from the start. At executive committee meetings and in larger staff gatherings, Karl made it abundantly clear that he was "to remain as the 'boss' and that the Fdn By-laws could not be changed to permit any kind of real democracy."[57]

Karl therefore spent a great deal of time trying to reconcile staff and trustees to the fact that neither was to assume significant governing functions. Power was to reside where it had always been—with the original partners and especially with him. Karl may also have needed this interval to be sure that he was still able to wield power as he had in the past. He may have required time to assure himself that Flo's death had not usurped his energies. In the weeks after her passing, he noted "a certain kind of freedom" in the knowledge that her "troubled spirit" was "resting." But he also felt like a "child" again and was unsure whether he could fully assume adult responsibility now that his lifelong dialogue with his mother had ceased. She had always expressed herself "in a white hot intensity of purpose, profound sincerity, and keen alertness of mind within a restricted range of interest." Automatically, it had caused him to summon considerable force and power on his own—often to resist her. When he had gone against her by becoming a doctor, Karl recognized that he had power of his own. When he divorced his wife, he realized again that his inner reservoir of strength remained—if bound neurotically to Flo. She had opposed turning over the family's wealth to a nonprofit foundation even though she "did not understand the details of our work here." With her death, Karl seemed to wait to gather the strength and the "freedom" to go against her one last time.[58]

VIII

By the end of 1945, a full-scale Menninger Foundation had been established. But neither trustees nor staff anticipated far-reaching changes. Rather, there was a sense that the organization might exist in the future much as it had in the past, heavily influenced by the "family spirit," over which Karl retained hegemony. But consistent with the web effect, the family was changing just as the organization altered itself.

One sign of family change was that the brothers terminated their extramarital affairs and enjoyed stronger marriages. Karl's marriage to Jeanetta—who had a calming effect upon him—brought him the domestic tranquillity his first marriage had lacked. Jeanetta made it clear that she was to continue as his writing partner and professional colleague. In *Love Against Hate,* he proudly acknowledged her as his "collaborating author." Because of Jeanetta, private and public phases of Karl's life merged in greater harmony. Catharine, observing Jeanetta's involvement in Karl's work, calculated that she could head off Will's liaison with Isabel Erickson and improve their future together by following suit. She assumed diverse tasks to promote the new foundation and joined Will in his travels. He was enormously pleased.[59]

Karl's children, unhappy and insecure, had all rushed into marriage—Julia to a physician, Martha to her latest boyfriend, and Robert to a woman from Ottawa, Kansas. Karl told Jeanetta that they needed a child to cement their marriage. Because she was beyond safe childbearing age, they decided to adopt. They learned of a prospective situation early in 1948. An unmarried Englishwoman had arrived in New York to deliver an illegitimate child and put her up for adoption. The child was born on February 2. Before legal procedures for the adoption were finalized, Karl arranged a glimpse of the biological mother from a distant table in a New York restaurant. Jeanetta had the baby undergo a variety of medical tests. They named the child Rosemary. Karl would tell Bee Jelliffe that their daughter was "the joy of our hearts. She is beautiful and loving, and precocious, and happy." It was a pleasure to come home at the end of a workday.[60]

Despite improvements in their marital lives, the relationship between Karl and Will remained difficult. Separated from the family during the war, Will pursued army psychiatry with vast energy. Beginning as a lieutenant colonel and neuropsychiatric consultant for the Fourth Service Command, he rose rapidly to the directorship of the Neuropsychiatric Consultants Division in the Office of the Surgeon General. By 1944 Will headed the army's psychiatric effort. He was promoted to colonel and then to brigadier general. At the end of the war, Will continued to focus on issues outside the family and its organization. He became founding chairman of the Group for the Advancement of Psychiatry in a successful revolt against the staid policies of the American Psychiatric Association. By the conclusion of his army service, Will was touted as a future APA president. He received several important job offers, including the deanship of the University of Pittsburgh Medical School and the chair of the Yale Medical School Psychiatry Department.[61]

Karl was acutely aware of his brother's prominence. Indeed, he boasted publicly that Will had thoroughly transformed the army's psychiatric service. He also realized that Will had many good job offers. Catharine made it clear to Karl that if he expected the most prominent psychiatrist in the nation to return to Topeka, he would have to treat Will as an equal and stop denigrating him.[62]

Karl realized that the organization needed Will more than Will needed the organization. He wrote to his brother stressing that the two of them were the heart of the enterprise: "everybody around here could leave, including John Stone, Isabel Erickson, Mildred Law, etc. and you would still be my partner and it would still be up to you and me to make the place go." He wrote again, acknowledging that "You will never be just 'Karl's brother' again; I will often be 'Bill's brother' or we will be brothers, but you have a prestige and an honor and a fame that is far beyond mine." Karl admitted that for decades he had made Will feel "that you were in a position of 'second fiddle.'" But he assured Will of a more flexible relationship: "We can divide the authority and responsibility for the work in any way that seems expedient—you can write your own ticket." For the first time in their lives, Karl assured Will that if he returned home, he "will have every opportunity and obligation to be 'top hat' around here."[63]

Will felt that there was sincerity in Karl's offer. As they conversed over long-distance telephone, Karl assured him again and again that their old paternalistic relationship was at an end. This pleased Will, for he genuinely wanted to return. Despite years of resentment at the conduct of his brother, he found it difficult to conceive of permanent employment away from Topeka.[64]

At first, Karl seemed true to his word. He turned over the administration of all Menninger institutions to Will as he launched new ventures in psychiatric education. But in a short time, tensions were detectable. It was apparent that Karl was jealous of his prominent brother. He loved Will deeply and had come to regard him as an equal. But early family patterns continued. Given Will's fame and achievements during the war, Karl feared him as a competitor. He found it awkward and distressing to have more than one boss in the organization. To make matters worse, Karl began to badger his brother as he had formerly badgered Grace. He complained to Will about his every act, mixing jealousy with hostility. For self-protection and peace of mind, Will tried to stay away from his brother. Never once during his first three years back from the service did he accept an invitation to dine at Karl's home. He tried to delineate rigid distinctions between his and Karl's duties and came more and more to communicate with his brother through administrative aides. Moreover, Will pursued other interests in psychiatry, outside Topeka.[65]

By the late 1940s, the animosity between Karl and Will began to affect their sons. Just as Charles had appealed to them to join in a family medical practice, the brothers began to think of their boys. Both Karl and Will realized that their sons would have to become psychiatrists and return to Topeka if there was to be any hope of keeping organizational power within the family under precarious new foundation rules. Aware that he had a strategic advantage in the future leadership of the foundation because he had three sons while his brother had only one, Will urged all four boys to "someday return." We "are planning for them," he said. Indeed, he even tried to help Karl's son, Robert, to gain admission to a prestigious medical school so "that he will come back here to Topeka with us." While not opposing the return of Will's sons, Karl focused on the medical education and eventual return of his own boy. Robert was not the best of undergraduate students and was in fact more interested in veterinary medicine than in psychiatry, but Karl pressured him to complete medical school so that he could eventually take over from his father.[66]

Clearly, the Menninger family had changed significantly. Strong conflicts persisted, but they were rooted in tensions between the brothers more than between husband and wife or workplace and home. Moreover, without Flo's presence as a visible symbol of nineteenth-century morality and austere self-restraint, family members appeared less intent on mastering their social situations, both at work and at home. More than any other event, eighty-six-year-old Charles's marriage in 1948 to sixty-year-old Pearl Boam underscored these changes.

After Karl's divorce, as Flo became bitter, reclusive, and feeble, Pearl had felt obligated to quit her job in a local school to take care of her and attend to the house. In the evening, Charles would chat with Pearl over a bottle of alcoholic "grape juice," while Flo withdrew. More and more, he and Pearl found themselves cooperating to circumvent Flo's tight controls over the household purse strings. In time, the two began periodically to travel together; Flo usually remained at home.[67]

After Flo died, the bonds between Charles and Pearl became stronger. Pearl was far more solicitous than Flo had ever been. She inquired about Charles's activities at Menninger, visited the campus, and tried to make life at home comfortable for him.[68]

Charles pondered a long time about marrying Pearl. He decided it was the best way to protect her financial interests. He was apprehensive of the increasing combativeness between his sons; both had rejected some of his attempts at conciliation. He also felt pressed financially when he discovered that he could not pay Flo's funeral expenses. Karl and Will took care of those bills, but the monthly allocation they gave their father limited the range of his activities. Moreover, Edwin wanted a share of Flo's inheritance. What would become of Pearl when Charles died? Would Karl and Will be less generous with her? Would Edwin come up from Florida to seek out his meager estate and leave Pearl entirely to her own resources?[69]

Charles sought legal counsel. A local attorney advised him to marry Pearl and to give her power of attorney for him. This would ensure that his estate and the payments he received from the foundation would go to her when he died. This legal advice was not the best; it neglected various protective measures short of marriage. But it appealed to Charles. Marriage would also eliminate Pearl's qualms about living with him.[70]

For a variety of motives, late in 1947 Charles asked Pearl to become his wife. She refused because his sons would not approve. Six months later, Charles approached Will and Karl, asking them their opinion of his marrying Pearl. Both were surprised yet reacted favorably. Will told Charles: "If I had such young ideas at 86 I would certainly want backing in them." He noted in his diary that the marriage "would simplify a lot of things and in fact change nothing in the actual setup as it has existed since mother died." Indeed, his father and Pearl would feel less embarrassed sharing rooms when they traveled together. Armed with favorable responses from his sons, Charles asked Pearl again. She consented.[71]

The day after Pearl accepted Charles's proposal, Catharine took charge of wedding preparations. For the next few weeks, Karl and Will

would be in town at the same time, and Catharine recognized the importance of having them both at the wedding. Jeanetta extended Karl's offer
to put on the wedding at their house. But Pearl had been closer to
Catharine and Will, and she accepted Catharine's offer of their home.[72]

Pearl invited thirty-five guests to the June 15 ceremony. The family
at the wedding differed markedly from the early Menninger household.
This time, women—Jeanetta and Catharine, in particular—were making
their presence felt in their husbands' professional worlds. Moreover,
unlike Flo, Pearl had no qualms about being on the hospital grounds. If
the three Menninger husbands were happy with their spouses, they knew
that the relationship between Karl and Will had become more troubled
than ever before. Charles feared that tensions between his sons were
becoming so acute that they might one day throw both family and foundation affairs out of control.

Still, on the wedding day the Menningers could gather together
assured that they had all survived several difficult years in reasonable
condition. Their new foundation was receiving significant private donations, cooperating with the federal government on an exciting experiment in psychiatric education, and gaining national recognition, even as
the family ran it with perhaps somewhat less concerted authority. From
the self-possession and joy of an old man as he kissed his bride and
rushed off with her to honeymoon in Kansas City, the other Menningers
drew a certain confidence that they, too, could face their future with hope
and assurance.[73]

CHAPTER SEVEN

Education and Pluralism

In a letter of August 1945 to George A. Elliott of the Brattleboro Retreat in Vermont, Karl explained how he planned to concentrate the activities of his organization on psychiatric education:

> The instruction of residents—not only physicians, but psychologists, nurses and therapists—is the thing that is closest to my heart. We have felt so strongly about it that we have converted our whole institution into a non-profit Foundation with its primary aim as education.[1]

Karl was exaggerating the educational goals behind the conversion of Menninger into a nonprofit foundation, but he had become quite interested in educational reform. He knew that agencies like the National Committee for Mental Hygiene had been critical of the psychiatric training that most medical personnel received. And he realized that the Rockefeller Foundation's Medical Science Division was providing substantial grants to universities for innovative programs in psychiatric education. Early in World War II, moreover, Karl had calculated that the need for thoroughly trained mental health workers would soon be enormous. He reasoned that the large number of military rejections on neuropsychiatric grounds, plus the emotional instability caused by combat, would create a vast patient population. By expanding significantly the pool of resident physicians, nurses, and activities therapists trained at Menninger, he might help to satisfy the national demand for psychiatric personnel. At the same time, Karl hoped that this redirection of priorities might rekindle the Menninger tradition of innovation. These twin goals—national service and organizational revitalization through education and training—were "closest to my heart."[2]

Education had always been a family objective. Charles started out as a college instructor; Flo established Bible study classes; Will's hospital programs trained Menninger and army staffs. Karl lectured widely and wrote his first three books to teach students and the general public about mental illness and the cures promised by Freud's new "science." "I am essentially a teacher, not a healer," he claimed in assessing his professional contributions.[3]

This family tradition of educational instruction—a tradition sustained by considerable missionary fervor—might possibly turn the new foundation into a national center for psychiatric education. For that to happen, the Menningers would have to resist allowing implosive family developments to detract from their commitment to reform. With Karl happily remarried and concerns of retaining family control over the foundation largely satisfied, the Menningers appeared ready for a dedicated reform effort. Only the problems inherent in the Karl-Will relationship stood in the way.

I I

In January 1939, Karl proposed a modest increase in the number of psychiatric residents (to eight or ten) and a second year of psychiatric residency for special psychoanalytic training, to provide "something that is nowhere available in the United States." Nothing came of these suggestions, because his partners were not enthusiastic.[4]

After America entered the war, Karl's proposals were taken more seriously. Selective Service screening underscored the need to train thousands of new psychiatrists and other mental health workers. At least 1,100,000 and perhaps as many as 1,875,000 men were rejected for military training on the basis of mental and neurological disorders. Policymakers failed to understand how new psychiatric definitions and classifications had contributed to this apparent doubling in the rejection rate since World War I. Some psychiatric leaders, particularly Harry Stack Sullivan and Winfred Overholser, claimed that the rate would have been higher still if screening techniques were better able to detect men predisposed to mental disorders. It was apparent that the nation's three thousand psychiatrists could not be expected to serve both civilian and military needs.[5]

By early 1943, military health care workers were preoccupied with the treatment of neuropsychiatric casualties. Between January 1942 and December 1945, a million patients with such disorders were admitted to military hospitals. Of army inductees discharged on medical grounds, about 40 percent had been dismissed for psychiatric reasons. In addition to these discharges, army hospitals had admitted approximately fifty thousand neuropsychiatric patients by April 1945. The experiences of the Guadalcanal and North African campaigns (the earliest offensive operations involving U.S. forces) had convinced the army that environmental stress played a crucial role in emotional maladjustments. To reduce "combat exhaustion," military psychiatrists successfully recommended fixed tours of duty with limits on combat exposure, regular rest periods, and measures to promote group cohesion. Some even undertook brief preventive psychotherapy. But they recognized that these steps only modestly reduced the number of discharges for reasons of mental health. Many more trained mental health workers were required, both to augment the military's efforts and to care for those being released daily. As Jeanetta Menninger wrote early in 1944 to justify Karl's proposals for new training programs, "the shortage of personnel in psychiatry is the bottleneck. . . . When at least 1/3 of the War casualties are psychiatric and approximately 1/50 of the doctors are psychiatrists, what happens to the psychiatric patient in the War?"[6]

As the war continued, both Karl and Will realized that a wholly new perspective on the nature of mental illness would have to be taught if educational efforts were to be effective. This perspective, rooted in the writings of both Freud and Adolf Meyer, required the dismissal of the traditional psychiatric demarcation between normal and abnormal mental conditions. In *Man Against Himself,* the most penetrating of his early books, Karl had focused not upon Freud's concept of a life instinct at war with a death instinct but upon the process through which people moved along a continuum between eros and thanatos. Neither of the two opposites was as relevant to effective diagnosis and therapy as the patient's shifts toward and away from the poles. As Karl studied combat exhaustion and other mental problems during the war, he came to understand that if specific situations caused people to become confused, disorientation (a point on a continuum) was usually temporary. Will readily accepted Karl's perspective of mental illness and health as processes along a continuum. As his authority increased in the Office of the Surgeon General, he disagreed with Chief of Staff General George Marshall's opinion that combat troops diagnosed as mentally disturbed were often cowards and malingerers. Will thought that quick and appropriate psychiatric intervention could facilitate the reorientation of these troops and shift them away from self-destructive behavior. By August 1945, he had laid the basis for an army system of psychiatric classification that reflected his perspective. More important, he had done much to improve the military's psychiatric care system, with treatment stations near the front lines, rear echelon camps practicing group therapy, and the conventional hospitals with psychiatric wards. Different treatment agencies and techniques were to be used for different degrees of disorientation.[7]

The wartime experience convinced the Menninger brothers that they could contribute significantly to the need for well-trained mental health workers. It disposed them to look to the federal government to support their ventures in education and training. Karl had also established close rapport with Alan Gregg, director of the Rockefeller Foundation's Medical Science Division, and counted upon Gregg to be liberal with grant money. He had heard that the Commonwealth Fund was considering support for short courses to update the psychiatric skills of general practitioners. Karl felt that it was necessary to explore such private options, for the government had played a limited role in mental health ventures despite the creation in 1930 of a Mental Hygiene Division in the United States Public Health Service. But the crises provoked by massive Selective Service rejections led to a shift of federal policy that interested Karl. Congress, through its military support appropriations, sustained various wartime efforts at psychiatric reform. In some measure, the 1946 National Mental Health Act provision of direct federal aid for professional training represented an extension of this wartime change in mental health policy.[8]

Although Karl had made contact with federal agencies as early as 1928 in the hope that they might support various Menninger functions, he did not mount a sustained appeal for funding of psychiatric training until 1941. At that time, he indicated to Surgeon General James Magee that his organization was willing to expand its psychiatric training program with "special application to military problems." Within a year, he converted that program from a one- to a three-year psychiatric residency and was pressing the surgeon general's office even more aggressively to fund and support it. He urged the army to invest in Menninger as a place to train not only psychiatric residents but also psychologists, nurses, and occupational therapists for the wartime emergency.[9]

Two years later, Karl focused his proposal for expansion upon the 2,300-bed Winter General Army Hospital in Topeka. It opened in 1941 as a temporary wartime facility in which three miles of corridors and ramps awkwardly connected various buildings. Although it had been designed to deal only with physically ill patients, Karl urged the surgeon general, the War Manpower Commission, and the Veterans Administration to allow his institution to play an important role there. Initially, he requested permission to send Menninger consultants to Winter Hospital. Late in 1943, he suggested that Menninger establish "a School for medical officers not previously trained in psychiatry." The school would be run by Menninger professionals; in a four- to six-month crash course, they would offer lectures, case conferences, and supervised clinical work at Winter to train army medical staff in the care of psychiatric patients. Although Karl hoped that the army would compensate his organization for establishing the school, he was so eager to establish a firm tie between his organization and Winter Hospital that he offered to "get the faculty compensated through the Menninger Foundation from one of our donors who wants to see psychiatric education pushed."[10]

As he campaigned for Winter Hospital, Karl evolved into a crusader for new training centers in the service of a nation at war. "The War has shown us that some 30 to 40 percent of military casualties are psychiatric in nature; yet less than 2 percent of the physicians in our country are psychiatrists," he reported toward the end of 1943. The ninety-five or so psychiatrists being trained in university hospitals throughout the country were insufficient. Consequently, the Menninger organization felt obligated to launch a massive new program in psychiatric residency. A year later, Karl suggested that Menninger alone could not meet the demand for new psychiatrists; he urged the American Psychoanalytic Association to encourage large-scale training of psychiatrists and psychoanalysts. By March 1945, according to Karl's research, the armed services were daily discharging one thousand people suffering from mental problems. Many more psychiatrists had to be trained, and his organization was determined to do its part. Karl's long-standing missionary disposition was merging with his growing sense of obligation to the nation.[11]

When he traveled in the spring of 1945 to the European Theater of Operations, Karl witnessed firsthand the toll of combat. His commitment deepened to help the troubled soldiers, "who have done so much for us." He was determined to convince the reluctant Veterans Administration to permit him to establish a special training school at Winter Hospital.[12]

Under Brigadier General Frank Hines, the VA had become a lackluster and insular bureaucracy that presided over mediocre hospitals. Muckraking journalists like Albert Q. Maisel and Albert Deutsch published exposés that documented ineffective treatments and penalties for staff who attempted reforms. The Hines administration was unmoved. It was not about to let Karl Menninger establish an innovative training center in one of its largest hospitals.[13]

The exposé of the VA system appeared in popular journals like *Cosmopolitan* and *Reader's Digest* and prompted a congressional investigation, which resulted in Hines's removal. Officials close to President Roosevelt were determined to give the new VA leadership wide latitude in instituting far-reaching reforms. When General Omar Bradley was appointed Veterans Administrator in April 1945, he was ordered to make significant changes quickly. Seeking a chief medical director for the system, Bradley turned to General Paul Hawley, who had earned praise for establishing effective medical services for American invasion forces. Hawley called upon Lieutenant Colonel Arthur Marshall, a Legion of Merit winner for his management of army hospitalization in Europe, to take charge of VA hospital programs. Under the leadership of Bradley, Hawley, and Marshall, the Veterans Administration undertook the largest hospital-building program in American history. Sixty-nine general veterans' hospitals were constructed, each with a psychiatric unit. Sixteen psychiatric hospitals were also built. Hawley relied on Public Law 346, a mid-1944 congressional enactment, for authorization to create a VA residency program. He and Bradley felt that the best way to assure topflight hospitals was to make them major teaching facilities and to locate them near large medical centers that could provide instructional staff.[14]

Karl described to Hawley his idea of establishing a residential psychiatric training center for departing medical officers at Winter Hospital. Hawley was impressed by Karl's willingness to establish a pilot hospital training program. What worried him was the dilapidated condition of the hospital and its expensive operation because of the distances between buildings. If Winter became a mental facility, more staff would be required, escalating expenses further. Therefore, Hawley concluded that despite Karl's encouraging offer, it was probably best to shut down Winter. But he asked Arthur Marshall to visit the hospital in October and give him a report. While Marshall was in Topeka, Hawley said as an aside, he might want to chat with Brigadier General William Menninger's older brother.[15]

Marshall was unimpressed with Winter Hospital. While in Topeka, he visited a cousin who had recently married Maimon Leavitt, a Menninger resident. Leavitt persuaded Marshall to delay a final decision on Winter until he had spoken with Karl. Watching the two men shake hands, Leavitt sensed that something important was about to emerge: "They came together like tinder. I came back an hour-and-a-half later and the two of them were on cloud nine . . . they fed each other's most grandiose fantasies."[16]

Marshall spoke to Karl about his cutting through red tape to establish army base hospitals in Europe during the war. Karl chortled over stories of how Marshall defied army regulations and felt a certain camaraderie with this VA official. When Marshall told him that Winter Hospital was "deadwood," Karl suggested that despite its poor condition, he could immediately send instructors to establish a school there. In a period when no American medical center was training more than fifteen psychiatric residents a year, he could train twenty-five at Winter. The VA could not afford to spurn this offer, Karl emphasized, if it was concerned about the vast number of veterans requiring psychiatric treatment. Though not a specialist on psychiatric training, Marshall warmed to Karl's vision of transforming a dismal hospital into an innovative institution. He was also taken by Karl's determination to aid soldiers in need. Marshall wondered aloud whether Menninger would be willing to try to turn Winter Hospital into a major psychiatric training center—a pilot program and model for the entire VA hospital system. Karl would recall the moment: "It was something like a little hydrogen and oxygen getting together with a bang and producing some real water." Marshall shared this recollection: "Something happened and we were walking on air and this was [to be] the very best and biggest place for training and treatment and research." The notion of a Menninger School of Psychiatry emerged from the meeting. With the support of the VA and all the medical operations of Winter Hospital under VA control, the newly consolidated Menninger Foundation would establish the MSP—the largest and best psychiatric training, treatment, and educational center in the world. Karl was to manage Winter Hospital and to turn it into a first-rate psychiatric specialty facility. He would have enough doctors, psychologists, social workers, nurses, and attendants on his staff "to give every patient continuous individual attention and treatment" and every resident physician lessons in quality psychiatric care. Marshall promised to persuade his superiors to make a large and long-range commitment of VA resources. He even guaranteed the resources before checking with them.[17]

Marshall reported his ambitious plan to Hawley and Bradley. He stressed (indeed, exaggerated) the training capacities of the Menninger operation and the availability of Winter Hospital to serve as a VA neuropsychiatric facility. In the course of their discussions, the problems of Wadsworth Hospital—a VA psychiatric facility about forty miles east of Topeka, in Leavenworth, Kansas—became a relevant consideration. The VA had not been able to secure enough consultants for that facility. By transferring the patients and some staff to Winter Hospital, Wadsworth might appear to be less of a white elephant to Congress. Hawley and Bradley were persuaded to accept the general outlines of the Marshall-Menninger proposal.[18]

Hawley asked Karl how many psychiatric residents he could begin to train at Winter Hospital by early 1946. Mindful that his institution had worked with only thirty-six resident physicians since 1931, Karl retreated from his pledges to Marshall. He offered to train a dozen for the first class of the Menninger School of Psychiatry. Hawley countered that thousands of former military doctors were pressuring the VA to provide them with psychiatric training. He requested that Karl take no less than one hundred in the 1946 class. While apprehensive that one hundred would be too many too soon, Karl let his missionary fervor and sense of national obligation get the better of him. He agreed to that number, hoping that the challenge would turn the Menninger organization into an internationally known psychiatric center. Although Hawley touched base informally with Bradley after reaching an accord with Karl, he felt too pressed for time to go to other officials for proper authorization. Like other harried federal planners plagued by insufficient lead time (owing to the unexpectedly early conclusion of the war), Hawley never completed mandatory paperwork before allocating VA resources to Winter Hospital and the Menninger Foundation. It took four years for an official in the inspector general's office to detect his impropriety. In the interval, Winter Hospital came to exceed in reputation the successful VA hospital in New Bedford, Massachusetts, and the agency's prize Los Angeles Mental Hygiene Clinic. Topeka became the nation's premier psychiatric training center.[19]

It is difficult to discern Will's precise role in the discussions that led to the agreement. Because he was director of the Neuropsychiatric Consultants Division in the Office of the Surgeon General, it was common knowledge that he essentially constructed and supervised the army's psychiatry program during the last two years of the war. In that capacity, he sometimes informed Karl of army concepts about postwar psychiatric education. Not unmindful of the potential of Winter Hospital, he had even urged a special Menninger education committee to consider whether it wished to utilize Winter as one of various training centers for medical officers after the war. He also told Colonel James Duckworth, director of the hospital during much of 1945, how pleased he was that Duckworth was calling upon Karl for consultant services. An important behind-the-scenes role for Will in the Menninger-VA accord is probable, in view of his close rapport with Bradley and Hawley. It is significant that they asked him to head the entire VA psychiatric program only five weeks before Marshall's first visit to Topeka. Moreover, Will was probably the first to inform Hawley of the capacity of the Menninger organization to train psychiatrists for the VA system. Yet his role in the negotiations was circumscribed; Will was too astute politically to ignore possible conflict-of-interest charges. Although he probably applied subtle pressure upon Hawley and Bradley, he was nevertheless shocked on learning the extent of Karl's commitment of Menninger resources to the Winter Hospital program.[20]

If Will was reluctant to take on a group of residents at Winter within a few months of the VA accord, many at Menninger considered the agreement absurd. The pace was frantic enough within the hospital, owing to wartime staff shortages; an increased work load to train residents seemed impossible. David Rapaport, who was trying to organize a research department, opposed the plan, believing that the new responsibility would seriously dilute the organization's other efforts. The strongest opposition came from Robert Knight. Plans for the Menninger School of Psychiatry "are an illusion and a fool's Paradise," he told Karl. "We haven't got the time or the offices or the teachers or the spare energy to do it." When Knight reported that senior staff were reluctant to help with the school, Karl countered that although the VA insisted that he manage Winter and run the school, he would teach the courses too if nobody else was willing.[21]

Karl's tenure as manager of Winter began on December 1, 1945. He resigned temporarily as Menninger chief of staff and president of the foundation. Knight replaced him as chief of staff and Will was to become foundation president when he returned from the army.[22]

The problem of insufficient time to establish the MSP was compounded by the absence of models for large psychiatric training centers. Previously, residents had secured three-year board certificates through combinations of clinical and tutorial instruction in a variety of medical facilities. Training in clinical psychology had been equally unstructured. At the Phipps Clinic some years earlier, Adolf Meyer had tried to devise a graduated curriculum for psychiatric residents. But though Meyer's treatment program at Phipps had considerable impact upon "new psychiatry" institutions, his curricular innovations were neither well known nor wholly appreciated. The Menninger staff knew of no curriculum, teaching facility, or educational center that accepted scores of residents and taught them to work as a team. In January 1946, the MSP would change all that.[23]

Throughout December, Karl worked at a frantic pace with VA associates and advisers. Winter Hospital's capacity was reduced from nearly 2,300 to 1,400, of which 900 would be psychiatric beds. Karl had decided to establish a general hospital with a psychiatric specialty. Buildings were hastily repaired and remodeled. Special indestructible screens and similar protective devices were installed in rooms to be occupied by mental patients. By mid-January, 1,700 employees had been hired. To oversee the first psychiatric residency classroom instructional program with a graduated curriculum, Karl established a Menninger Educational Department. Through that agency, he called upon analysts from the Topeka Institute for Psychoanalysis, Menninger staff psychiatrists and psychologists, several senior Menninger nurses, and even a few second- and third-

year Menninger residents to organize and teach courses and to supervise
the incoming residents. This task was so formidable that Karl had to delay
bringing in clinical psychologists for similar training for several months.
He also moved slowly on plans for the training of psychiatric nurses and
put off his psychiatric social work program until the fall of 1947.[24]

On a day-to-day basis, however, Karl was operating at the same
frantic pace of other innovators making the transition into the postwar
world. All were responding to enormously high public expectations of
what promised to be an "American century." The United States was
emerging as the world's strongest military power, with vast industrial and
agricultural potential. There were markets to develop for American ex-
ports. The magical remedies penicillin and streptomycin had been discovered. It was incumbent on American planners to achieve full employment and reduced work weeks and to facilitate the conquest of
tuberculosis, infantile paralysis, cancer, and mental illness. Karl, like
other important planners, felt obligated to respond to these expectations
within months. He was inspired by an evangelical vision: "The Foundation will become the mother of everything."[25]

III

In January 1946, twenty-seven psychiatric residents arrived at Winter
Hospital. A group of twenty-one came in April, forty-four in July, and
sixteen in October. With over seven hundred applicants to choose from,
the task of selecting more than half of all the psychiatric residents to be
trained in the VA system that year was enormous. Errors in selection were
inevitable. Several enrollees who appeared capable at the interviews were
in fact unstable. At least two and perhaps as many as eleven of these
doctors committed suicide the first year of MSP operations (like other
Menninger officials, Robert Knight veiled this fact). Midway through the
year, Knight boasted that the MSP had become the major training agency
for the nation's psychiatrists. The following year, the school continued
to train roughly half the psychiatrists in the VA system—one third of all
psychiatric residents in the United States. Chestnut Lodge, Austen Riggs,
and Boston Psychopathic Hospital could not come near this figure.[26]

Almost overnight, the MSP became the focus of American psychiatric
education and the center of psychiatric care for all veterans in Kansas,
Missouri, southern Nebraska, and northern Oklahoma. By the middle of
1946, the VA was holding up the program as a model for all psychiatric
training and treatment. In addition, Menninger was assured significant

federal funding. Congress in 1946 made substantial appropriations for psychotherapy training through the National Institute of Mental Health; the MSP expected the lion's share. It appeared as if the Menninger tradition of shoestring budgets was about to end.[27]

Karl and Arthur Marshall had anticipated more than psychiatric residential training for Topeka. In 1946 and 1947, various smaller programs were implemented for social work, nursing, and neurological and internal medicine residencies under the MSP umbrella. Although each of these programs had separate directors, Karl essentially ran them.[28]

In fall 1946, the Menninger School of Clinical Psychology began as a major training program operating out of Winter Hospital, but Karl was not its central figure. The school emerged as a historically unique cooperative venture between a private agency, a state body (the University of Kansas Psychology Department), and the federal government through the VA and the Public Health Service. A four-year curriculum led to a doctorate in clinical psychology at the University of Kansas. The VA and the Public Health Service put considerable money behind the school, so that it could operate as a model for fifteen other federally sponsored clinical psychology training programs. Although Karl wanted to run the school, the University of Kansas and the other funding agencies demanded a prominent clinical psychologist. Karl felt he had little choice and named David Rapaport, who had headed the wartime effort to bring émigré analysts to Topeka and conducted major investigations into diagnostic testing for the armed forces. The courses he taught for the school were sometimes more probing and always more scholarly than Karl's at the MSP. Rapaport also occupied incoming psychologists with the diagnostic testing of Winter Hospital patients and with research projects. Fifteen students initially entered Rapaport's program, and though the VA pressed for forty, Rapaport held to a ceiling of twenty. Unlike Karl's admissions policy at the MSP, Rapaport underscored the dangers of expansion until there were more supervisory personnel at Winter and the buildings were renovated. Although the school came, in time, to be recognized as a semiautonomous component of the MSP, Rapaport was jealous of Karl's authority. He was convinced that he managed the smaller program more prudently than Karl ran the umbrella program. There is no evidence of student suicides during the first year of training, and that may have testified to Rapaport's more cautious management. This, coupled with his brilliance as a teacher, signaled to Karl that he had a serious rival.[29]

Hawley and Marshall had been willing to finalize the VA contract with Menninger only if Karl officially managed all activities within Winter

Hospital. But he was not up to the task. He throve on innovation but was uncomfortable with daily routine. Knowing that Will had to manage the Menninger home campus and unwilling to give Rapaport authority beyond the psychology school, Karl enlisted three key assistants to help him administer the large and complex VA facility. Although none of them rivaled him in authority, they assumed control over day-to-day MSP operations to the point where little changed when Karl officially stepped down as administrator after two and a half years.

It had been assumed that Karl would appoint a nationally recognized psychiatrist as dean of instruction and registrar for the MSP. Instead, he hired Bert E. Boothe, a professor of English who had taught at several colleges before serving in the Office of War Information and Education. Karl was particularly impressed with Boothe's capacities in educational administration and his work on the editorial board of a professional journal, *College English.* The Boothe appointment underscored Karl's hope that solid teaching and emphasis upon clear, precise prose would become salient qualities in his school. Moderately successful in advancing these goals, Boothe created a three-year curriculum within a few months. He also instituted writing requirements for graduation, though they had been deemphasized in traditional medical education.[30]

Early in 1946, Arthur Marshall joined Boothe at Winter Hospital. He had been so taken with the potential of psychiatric education that he asked Hawley for permission to enroll as an MSP resident. But Marshall quickly assumed administrative duties. He headed a large Winter Hospital treatment section, advised other section chiefs, and instituted sundry clinical innovations through his skills at cutting red tape and circumventing professional jurisdictional wars. Perhaps his most significant reform was to insist on the near equality of psychiatrists and psychologists on treatment teams. As psychiatry and psychology residents worked closely together and even attended several of the same courses, the distinction between the schools of psychiatry and clinical psychology became blurred. By late 1947, all Winter fellows considered themselves part of the MSP.[31]

The psychiatrist J. Frank Casey was selected by Karl as Winter's first chief of professional services. After a few weeks on the job, Casey realized that his task entailed more than professional staff supervision. He gradually assumed control of hospital management. In July 1948, Karl resigned as hospital manager, but no one in Topeka or Washington voiced apprehension about the future of the experiment. Indeed, Casey's administrative abilities sent the Menninger brothers in search of an equally effective manager for their own facility.[32]

The impact of Boothe, Marshall, and Casey upon curriculum, clinical leadership, and management of Winter Hospital was invaluable. They kept the facility operating efficiently despite the rapid growth and complexity of its activities, hundreds of new staff and patients, highly technical budgets, and numerous federal regulations. This did not mean that Karl was less than vital to operations. He constituted a powerful presence. Sitting at an oversized desk with four telephones in a former Winter dayroom, Karl worked frantically to turn the facility into a premier psychiatric center. Former army barracks had to be converted into staff apartments. Old patient wards were modernized and new ones constructed. A recreation center was erected, and a park area in the middle of the campus was developed. Moreover, supplies of all sorts were required, from medications to chairs and blackboards. Feeling he had no time for VA requisition procedures, Karl often disregarded the advice of Casey and Boothe, ordering his staff to act first and justify later. When he heard that an army hospital in Oklahoma was being vacated, he dispatched every available Winter truck and instructed the therapists he recruited as drivers to fool federal officials. Inform them that "you're authorized and take anything you see that we can use," Karl ordered. When federal bureaucrats tried to counteract some of Karl's irregular methods by citing the VA *Rules and Procedures* manual, he retorted that such procedures were irrelevant at Winter Hospital. He seemed to take special delight in circumventing VA requirements by making direct calls to Washington or asking Marshall to provide post hoc justifications for his breaches. Angry civil service functionaries determined to "get" Winter for bypassing the rules.[33]

A VA Administrator in Washington, Thomas Dolgoff, recalled that Winter Hospital's "costs were outrageous." The money the VA sent to Topeka was "absolutely out of line" with its disbursements to other hospitals. Though Karl operated on an "extravagant" level, he was always demanding more: "He upset the apple cart all the time," Dolgoff noted. VA officials were not excessively distressed by the cost of Winter Hospital so long as their congressional appropriations remained constant. But during the early months of 1947, Omar Bradley felt that a new Republican congressional majority was intent on instituting substantial budget cuts. As a protective measure, he ordered a freeze in spending for all VA hospitals. Hiring and promotions were barred, major staff reductions were mandated, overtime pay was eliminated, and new construction projects were halted. Karl was asked to stop all hiring and to terminate eight hundred fifty Winter employees. He refused, telling Bradley and Hawley that they were reversing the commitment made to him, destroying the hospital all three had envisioned, and turning Winter into a custodial facility. Bradley denied that this was his intention, and Hawley claimed that Winter was overstaffed by any standards. In the end, Washington scaled down its termination figure to forty or fifty—a much smaller staff reduction than was required of other VA hospitals. Still, Karl's sense of command was challenged. He characterized the cuts as a moral outrage. By the fall of 1947, his rapport with Bradley and Hawley had diminished, despite their continued commitment to Winter Hospital.[34]

Under continuing threats of congressional budget cutbacks, Bradley and Hawley resigned in the winter of 1948. Carl Gray became Veterans Administrator and Paul Magnuson replaced Hawley. Gray and Magnuson were more willing to accommodate Congress than their predecessors. Moreover, Gray had little tolerance for Karl's budgetary extravagances. When Congress slashed the VA budget on several occasions, Gray's protests were muted, and he was reluctant to single out Winter Hospital as an exception in his staff reduction directives. Karl recognized that with leadership in the hands of "mediocrities," the VA was becoming "a lifeless bureaucracy, which just tried to stay out of trouble and save money." He appealed to Kansas congressmen to shield Winter Hospital from cuts, and he made direct contact with President Truman. These efforts yielded mixed results. Between 1946 and 1953, Winter lost nearly two hundred fifty employees; but the proportion was small compared to other VA hospitals. It remained the premier psychiatric facility in the system, though its success came increasingly to be measured by its maintenance of the status quo and not by improvements. This was antithetical to Karl's disposition.[35]

It is well to note that Karl was not entirely intransigent in his dealings with the VA bureaucracy. Above all, he was intent on having the Winter experiment succeed. So he was willing to acquiesce in two policy areas that he considered dispensable.

In a period when civil rights was becoming a national concern, Karl balked at making a firm commitment to racial equality at Winter—this despite the fact that two blacks had boarded in the early Menninger household, Flo had admitted black women into her Bible studies program, and Charles had retained a black receptionist as his principal medical assistant during his early practice. The VA was willing to hire blacks as nurses and attendants, but though it had no regulations barring blacks as physicians, it refused to issue them contracts. In 1946, both the MSP Education Committee and Robert Knight wanted to challenge this informal policy by hiring a qualified black physician who applied for Winter residency. Karl prohibited such a direct challenge to the policy. To be sure, he opposed racial discrimination in principle and had quietly persuaded the Grey Ladies volunteer group at Winter to allow blacks to join their ranks. Yet he told his colleagues that an open breach with Washington over black physicians "would be a great distraction from the teaching of psychiatry." Only after private discussions revealed that the VA would not bar the black resident from Winter did he give his colleagues the go-ahead.[36]

Similarly, Karl balked at involving Winter or Menninger staff in Linda Brown's challenge to the long-standing *Plessy* v. *Ferguson* ruling upholding racial segregation as public policy. When Brown sued the Topeka Board of Education for promulgating public school segregation, her attorneys asked Karl (a donor to the NAACP) if he and his staff representatives might testify in the federal district court on the psychological effects of segregation. Privately, Karl made clear that he "did not wish to involve" Menninger or its affiliated institutions in what was becoming a landmark case. Only one member of his staff testified. Once again, Karl had demonstrated little passion for racial equality and calculated that involvement in civil rights might jeopardize his more primary professional and economic goals. He had long believed that because psychiatrists were treaters, they compromised themselves and violated their professional obligations when they testified as expert witnesses or became otherwise involved in court proceedings. None of his staff should engage in this professional breach, especially when the reputation of the MSP and the funding for other vital programs might be at risk, as by participation in so controversial a case.[37]

In this vein, Karl tolerated the anti-Communist hysteria of the postwar decade, especially from Washington and within the VA system. Late in 1947, he withdrew his nominee for a high position in the psychology school when he learned that the candidate was suspected of Communist affiliation. He confided to Will that if he defended the nomination, his own favor with the federal government might be endangered. Karl justified the termination of another Winter employee on these same grounds, even though he privately characterized pressure from Washington to fire the man as "gestapoing" and spoiling "a beautiful word, namely, loyalty." When a psychology intern at Winter Hospital faced dismissal on charges of being a Communist and asked for help, Karl expressed sympathy but refused to get involved. He claimed ignorance of procedures for "clearing it up." Nor would he intervene with the government to recruit a European doctor suspected of Communist leanings: "We do not want to convey the impression to the authorities that we are trying to import communists to Topeka." Here, too, the Menninger partnership with the federal government was not to be endangered for peripheral causes. Karl proved much less willing than his brother, Knight, or other key associates to resist what became the most dangerous Red Scare in American history. With narrowed visions on race and civil liberties, he had some attributes of a conservative reformer.[38]

I V

Most of the MSP fellows were not entirely aware of Karl's dealings with Washington over appropriations, bureaucratic regulations, racial policies, or early McCarthyite pressures. They trusted him to keep federal dollars flowing and focused on more immediate concerns.

The priority was to return to postwar normalcy—to get on with their careers and their families. Most fellows had served as armed forces physicians. Already in their thirties, with career plans delayed and separations from spouses sometimes exacerbating marital problems, they felt they had to make up for lost time. As a committee representing them proclaimed early in 1946: "A great many of the Fellows have . . . a great sense of urgency. Their War experience—while by no means wasted, has been time lost from undergoing proper training or getting properly situated in a permanent way. The responsibilities of families impels them so that they have something of an impatience." Not surprisingly, a number of fellows were troubled. But the suicides that occurred in 1946 suggested that too few measures had been instituted to protect them in the rush to establish the MSP. The shock of student deaths prompted thoughts of closing the entire Winter-MSP operation, but instead, Karl established a comprehensive staff psychotherapy service. At the same time, a research project was launched to study the way residents were selected and to recommend improvements.[39]

The fellows had further difficulties. Most of them were from urban centers of the East and Midwest. Over 40 percent had at least one parent born abroad. One third were Jews who had grown up in large ethnic neighborhoods where they could take their religious identities for granted. Several fellows, their parents and relatives factory laborers, sympathized with trade unions and socialism. Backgrounds akin to those of the European émigrés who preceded them ("Yidlack like ourselves") caused the fellows a comparable distress with the town of Topeka. Some referred to it as "the sinkhole of the United States," a hick town that lacked foreign films, classical music, even a delicatessen. Topekans tended to be suspicious of the newcomers. Rumor spread among them "that Karl Menninger had imported lots of foreigners, Jews and Reds from New York." As it became clear that the Winter Hospital operation was contributing substantially to the Topeka economy, however, there was greater acceptance of MSP fellows and their families. And the fellows began to import music and film. Arthur Marshall and his wife even persuaded a local grocer to stock lox and bagels. But there was always the hunch that local merchants looked at fellows as "Hebrews" and "Reds" and charged them higher prices for lesser products. As long as they were in Topeka, most fellows assumed, they would have to create their own miniature community.[40]

In constructing this community, the fellows found they had several assets. One was the former army barracks at Winter Hospital, where they were permitted to live with their families, owing to the postwar housing shortage. Families shared sitting rooms and bathrooms; bedroom walls were almost paper thin. Given these living arrangements, one could hardly retreat from close contact with other families. Friendships lasted long after the fellows left Topeka. With children playing together and wives on intimate terms, most fellows found it senseless to emphasize professional distinctions. Psychiatric residents became close with psychologists in training.[41]

The Winter Wives represented another asset for the MSP community. The organization grew out of a social gathering that Jeanetta hosted to greet the wives of new fellows. The women complained of the loneliness of living in Topeka and about their husbands being away so much of the time. They also noted how desirable it would be to have a nursery school for their children. It quickly became clear that an organization was needed to institute the nursery, to combat loneliness, and to deal with other practical problems.[42]

Common political loyalties also drew a number of MSP fellows together. Several from eastern urban centers, with Jewish immigrant parents and trade union sympathies, were leftist. Some founded the Topeka chapter of the American Veterans Committee, a liberal-left alternative to the American Legion and the Veterans of Foreign Wars. They championed racial equality, worked to integrate a city pool, and opposed universal military service.[43]

The MSP location on the Winter grounds, several miles from the Menninger campus, separated fellows from the Topeka citizenry and drew them away from the "family spirit." There was limited student contact with the teaching staff, who spent much of their time working on the home campus. And if Karl was often present at Winter Hospital, the other Menningers and longtime associates like John Stone and Mildred Law were rarely there.

The sense among Winter fellows of belonging to a student community that was no mere extension of the "family spirit" was reinforced by their educational experience, which they characterized as the intellectual high point of their careers. Scores of bright and excited residents and psychologists had come together in an educational facility that was not limited by traditions and bureaucratic imperatives, and intellectual excitement and a free flow of ideas pervaded the atmosphere. Through the success of figures like Will in shaping army psychiatry during the war, most of these returning veterans assumed that psychoanalytically informed psychotherapy was the wave of the future. Now, mastering and elaborating its essentials, they imagined themselves as pioneers who would move Freud into grass-roots medical practice in America. So they talked among themselves far into the night about the seventh chapter of Freud's *Interpretation of Dreams,* about the meanings of their own dreams, and on transference and drive theory.[44]

Perhaps owing to the unprecedented nature of large-scale classroom instruction for psychiatric residency and insufficient time for curricular design, the formal MSP curriculum left much to be desired. Menninger psychiatrists and psychologists were often asked to put together courses at two weeks' notice, and many tended to improvise. Most instructors provided neither a review of relevant theoretical literature nor clear and comprehensive links between theory and specific case material. By 1949, the fellows pressed successfully to remedy the inadequacy by shifting from a traditional classroom format to a seminar mode of instruction. The seminar would eliminate the typically disorganized faculty lecture, allow for freer and fuller participation from fellows, and reduce the distinction between teacher and student.[45]

The fellows also exercised considerable influence on the subject matter of course offerings. For example, they noted that despite the Freudian orientation of the school, the theory of psychosexual development was not taught. An instructor was quickly recruited to make it a regular course offering. In response to critical student evaluations of existing courses and demands for alternative courses, a fuller and more stable curriculum appeared by the late 1940s.[46]

With the deficiencies of several of their courses apparent, fellows opposed formal assignments, examinations, and grades. As mature professionals, they resented these as childish devices. In large measure, their demands were met. It was not until 1949 that any fellow was dismissed for inadequate academic performance. Even then, the primary emphasis was upon clinical work and not on classroom success. Formal examinations were not instituted until 1952.[47]

Through the force of their protests and demands, residents and psychologists therefore bore much of the responsibility for the persisting softness in structure and coverage of courses. Boothe and Karl generally acquiesced, if reluctantly.

The fellows' quest for independence also affected patient management. The senior neuropsychiatric staff at Winter was too small, during 1946 and 1947, to administer an entire fourteen-hundred-bed facility specializing in mental cases. Consequently, a number of residents were asked to serve as ward and section chiefs and in secondary administrative posts. Former army colonels or majors often got these assignments, as did certain of the more respected second- and third-year residents. Just as a tradition developed in curricular matters for residents to contribute much to their own education, the custom arose on the hospital wards that they work with only minimal supervision. By the late 1940s and early 1950s, Winter officials like Frank Casey and Herbert Modlin acknowledged that "the residents have been left too much to their own devices" and knew too little about schizophrenia and even about basic organic abnormalities like multiple sclerosis and paresis to be allowed such independence. A modest increase in senior supervisory staff was sought, to reclaim the authority over hospital management. But the residents balked at relinquishing their freedom on the wards. Most were willing to be taught new techniques of patient management by senior staff, but they were reluctant to be heavily supervised. Owing to congressional unwillingness to appropriate at a level where Winter Hospital could substantially increase its supervisory personnel, the tradition of considerable ward autonomy persisted.[48]

V

The fact that the fellows were essential to the expanding Menninger community gave them leverage to achieve considerable freedom. There was a risk in slighting their requests. If word spread of widespread student discontent, the applicant pool and the flow of federal dollars might decline. However, two factors did much to limit the fellows' independence. One involved training analysis. The second was the broader relationship between the fellows and Karl.

Psychoanalytic topics not only dominated the formal school curriculum; they were central to almost all the informal discussion groups. Changing the signs on the male and female rest rooms in their housing units to "with" and "without," the fellows jokingly alluded to the Freudian concept of penis envy. Supervisors complained that some of the fellows were so enamored of Freudian theory that they were inattentive to organic problems and traditional techniques for patient management. By the fall of 1950, Karl tried to steer them along these more practical lines. He emphasized that the school's stress upon psychoanalytic psychiatry did not mean that residents were to conduct full-scale analyses of their patients or anyone else. His warning did not stop them from using analytic techniques on their wives or on one another.[49]

As advocates of Freudian theory, most fellows demanded training analyses. Through formal analysis conducted by a senior analyst at the Topeka Institute for Psychoanalysis, plus other requirements, they hoped to secure approval from the American Psychoanalytic Association to practice analysis on their own. Psychoanalysis was prized as the key to career success and fulfillment.[50]

Because most of the early residents and a number of psychologists wanted training analyses, the demand on TIP personnel was excessive. Seventy-four percent of the MSP residential class of 1946 applied. In April, there were two training analysts to take them on; each could carry no more than five or six students. By 1948, the situation had hardly improved. Although a few more analysts had been hired, only twenty-four MSP students were undergoing training analyses; eighty were on waiting lists.[51]

Despite their desire for training analyses, fellows commonly referred to the Topeka Institute as "the pimp and whore" among Menninger-dominated institutions. The lure of analytic training (the pimp) caused them to seek out the institute. To qualify for training analyses, they had to pledge nearly one third of their paltry salaries (the whore function) and to distinguish themselves from their classmates with the institute admissions committee for their analyzable qualities or "psychological mindedness." Analysts like the Menninger brothers and Robert Knight held the applicants' futures in their hands. If, during admissions interviews, the analysts got on well with certain students, they were disposed to judge them as "psychologically minded" and appropriate for advanced positions on the admissions list. Student rebels who prized neither cooperation nor rapport with senior analysts tended to have less favorable interviews and were less likely to be approved. Several were disqualified for being "closed" emotionally and having primitive ego defenses.[52]

The "pimp and whore" characterization of the Topeka Institute extended further. To finish analysis and secure TIP endorsement before the appropriate American Psychoanalytic Association committees, a fellow had to satisfy his analyst of sufficient progress in disclosing his deepest personal thoughts and understanding those thoughts. This was accomplished principally through his transference relationship with his analyst. Thus, he exposed his interior life to his training analyst in a relationship not unlike that of confessor and priest. Only when the fellow convinced his analyst that he had revealed what troubled him and had incorporated the insights from his revelation into his personality ("working through") could he hope for successful termination of the analysis.

In this context, it is relevant that Freud regarded mental health or normality as an illusion that had to be perpetuated. He never assumed that analysis could remove all major pathologies. Thus, termination was essentially a fiction; analysis was truly interminable. Freud's perspective placed enormous power in the analyst to proclaim a certain arbitrary point as the end of the therapeutic process. Both the MSP resident and the TIP training analyst, with their relatively orthodox Freudian perspectives, recognized that termination could be very nearly at the whim of the latter.[53]

The psychoanalytic process in general, then, gave the analyst great discretion as to whether he kept the analysand in the subservient position or terminated the analysis. Two factors made this a particularly hazardous process for fellows as analysands. The Menningers usually paid them junior-level wages during the period of the training analysis; a fellow could not leave for a better salary elsewhere until his analysis was concluded successfully. There was thus a financial incentive for the organization—by means of the training analysis—to keep him on for a considerable period. As well, not only the training analyst but other senior TIP officials knew intimate details of the fellow's life. Consequently, he felt vulnerable and powerless not only before his own analyst but before Karl and other foundation analysts. "Soon all of that delicious poison will be out of my system and water substituted," one of them noted, "leaving me a jellyfish." Theoretically, this weak "jellyfish" state lasted only until analysis was terminated. But in contrast to most analytic institutes, the fellow might stay on in Topeka, working in the same facilities as his training analyst (who was often a senior administrator). If so, and if some residue of the transference phenomenon remained, the fellow would continue to invest extraordinary powers in his analyst. To militate against this possibility, efforts were made to keep analyst and analysand apart socially and professionally. Still, quite a few trainees continued to side with their former analysts on professional issues long after their analyses had been completed. Thus, the Topeka Institute was more than "the pimp and whore" for MSP fellows. "Seducing" and "gratifying" many of them through training analysis, it limited the strength and autonomy of student culture.[54]

All training analysts obtained significant leverage over fellows through this analytic process. But Karl went further than most. He was so intent on resisting student incursions upon his authority that he sometimes abused the training process. In his dealings with a number of fellows, he did not heed Franz Alexander's warning that the analyst restrict his potentially totalitarian controls, holding himself to a strict accountability. When he could not persuade one student to reject employment at the Public Health Service, for example, Karl threatened to bring the matter before TIP and have the career choice "analyzed out of him." Possessing a great deal of personal information about all fellows in analysis, he freely volunteered data concerning many of them. From time to time, a fellow discovered that Karl had passed on personal information to his hospital supervisor. When Karl volunteered data on several fellows in analysis for a Menninger research project on TIP candidate selection, the project director rebuked him for violating the privilege of confidentiality.[55]

Clearly, Karl offered a dangerous example in his conduct as a TIP official. Abused and exploited in his own analyses under Alexander and Brunswick, he had no full sense of the ethical proprieties of the process. He also bore significant responsibility for another serious challenge to MSP student culture. As the fellows' principal teacher, he regarded himself as the essential spark for gentlemanly intellectual exchanges at every level of the school. He sought to institutionalize this role by developing a Saturday morning colloquium for all fellows. Presiding over each colloquium, Karl eschewed formal structure and logical sequence but emphasized the importance of broad-based knowledge and a spirit of intellectual inquiry. He would talk randomly but authoritatively about whatever topic came to mind, from the earthworm to an important historical personality he had known. Occasionally he would bring in a prominent guest lecturer. But he would never allow the guest to outshine him. Sometimes he would even read a book or a case report while the guest was talking. At other sessions, he might interrupt the lecture or summarize it with insightful commentary. When Karl had a good morning, one early MSP resident recalled, it was like "steel against a wheel, and the sparks came out."[56]

Partially to enhance his role as the prominent teacher at the largest mental health education center in the country, Karl published his fourth book in 1952. Unlike his earlier work, *A Manual for Psychiatric Case Study* was not written for the general reader. It was a textbook for mental health students (primarily psychiatric residents). The volume had been a long time in coming. It started as rough revisions of Boston Psychopathic

Hospital instructional forms from his days as a resident. He had revised the forms slightly when he opened the Menninger Diagnostic Clinic; reworked these revisions to guide clinic and sanitarium staff during the 1930s; and revised them again in 1946 to accommodate the MSP program. But he recognized that the new fellows needed a well-organized and comprehensive text that would integrate their entire educational experience in Topeka. Only that would adequately supply "a blueprint for a standard procedure of studying psychiatric patients, recording and organizing clinical data in a purposeful way, and presenting the conclusions and recommendations to which these data have led." Karl labored between 1950 and 1952 to prepare a book principally for residents, to show them how to become psychiatrists.[57]

An instructional tone underlined the entire *Manual.* Chapters informed the resident how to approach his patient, how to conduct physical and psychological examinations, how to collect and record data, how to analyze the data and prescribe efficacious treatment, how to maintain records on the patient's progress, and how to write case reports and other professional communications. A final, extensive chapter provided examples of properly written case records. The very organization of the *Manual* conveyed a tone of certitude. In this, it differed markedly from August Hoch and George Amsden's *Guide to the Descriptive Study of Personality* (1913), which simply listed broad questions for the psychiatrist to ask his patient and set the tone for psychiatric manuals of the 1920s and 1930s.[58]

Specific passages throughout Karl's *Manual* reinforced this positivist answer-oriented tone of the mentor. The resident was warned "to counteract . . . the unfortunate specialization and isolation of function among personnel which has been taking place in our large psychiatric hospitals." The psychiatrist was to organize the reports of psychologists, social workers, and attendants into "a single framework" for understanding and treating the patient. All diagnostic labels had to be accompanied by precise descriptive material about the particular patient, or they lacked scientific legitimacy.[59]

Both the organization and the tone of the *Manual* conveyed the essential message of the Saturday morning colloquium. Karl was to be regarded as the supreme authority on matters psychiatric. There was another, less developed and rather random, message within the *Manual.* It contradicted the dominant tone of the book by suggesting that psychiatric practice was essentially a subjective, humanistic art rather than a positivist science. The truly effective psychiatrist could draw qualities from his inner self to assure the patient of his empathy and optimism: "The physician himself in all his wisdom may not know exactly why he believes he can help the patient . . . but if he does believe it and shares that belief with the patient he has already taken a step toward realizing it." At one point in the *Manual,* Karl openly acknowledged that psychiatry was "to a certain extent an art," because "the boundaries between observation and inference" were "not so distinct as in other fields of medicine." He noted elsewhere that an effective psychiatrist had almost a mystical "reverence for the mystery of pain, of impaired life and growth." Karl acknowledged, as well, that the "dignity, sympathy, earnestness, courtesy, respect for suffering, alertness to unspoken needs and fears," and other subjective qualities that defined the effective psychiatrist "are not things that can be taught to a student from a book." In essence, he was telling his readers to look beyond textbooks and formal instruction to their own resources.[60]

This conception of psychiatric practice as an art was compatible with several of Karl's earlier writings. But by suggesting to his students that they trust themselves, he did not augment his role as the all-knowing chief instructor at the MSP. Instead, he tried to elevate himself by drawing upon familial and paternalistic language and manners. It was no mere manipulative effort, for he had spent his entire psychiatric career mixing familial with medical-professional terms and visions. When Karl stepped down as manager of Winter Hospital, he wrote to the journalist Albert Deutsch about his future role in the MSP: "I wouldn't desert this baby once I had fathered it and brought it up to the age of 2 years and a half, you know that." During the first decade of MSP operations, Karl found comfort in conceiving of himself as "father," the school as his "baby," and the fellows as his "growing boys." Thirty years after MSP resident Murray Bowen, who became a leader in the family therapy movement, had left Topeka, Karl wrote to him: "You are still a boy to me, one of my young boys who seemed wise enough to advise me and help me in trying to marshall 100 other boys into learning how to help people."[61]

Karl invoked a paternalistic bearing to cultivate a dependence and perhaps even to infantilize the fellows. However, he was not entirely successful as a father figure. Most fellows found him too moody and unpredictable to resemble the ideal, nurturing father. "One minute he's the nicest, most gracious man in the world," James Hodge noted, "and the next thing he's so haughty and supercilious and he puts you down . . . you never knew what to expect." William Robinson was never sure whether Karl remained silent during case conferences to rebuke him for making a mistake or simply because he was in a bad mood. Other fellows underscored various erratic qualities that made them uneasy with Karl as "father."[62]

Indeed, whatever his influence upon MSP fellows, Karl never destroyed the semiautonomous aspect of student culture. The fellows continued to push for curricular revisions, to participate in the American Veterans Committee and in community organizations of their own choosing, and to work with minimal clinical supervision on the wards of Winter Hospital. At times, this disturbed Karl and provoked verbal assaults. He chastised some fellows for violating federal regulations by eating with their wives in the Winter dining room and others for spending evenings in study groups rather than with their wives. Periodically, he criticized Jewish fellows who neglected synagogue; but he also chided those who went to services—the few "enthusiastic Zionists around here," who "want to teach their babies to speak Hebrew and generally make themselves as different as possible." Sometimes he voiced distress with certain fellows' leftist politics: "I don't want a witchhunt around here." When a leader of the Fellows Association suggested that the group become a collective bargaining agent, Karl characterized him as "a querulous disturbed embittered troublemaker."[63]

Most of the fellows were anguished when Karl spoke out against their activities. If he could not exert fatherly jurisdiction and shape student culture in many particulars, he did engender tremendous apprehension. In order to neutralize Karl's assaults, the fellows sometimes invoked clever and skillfully measured retorts that reminded him that he was in an educational center that prized crafted language. The retorts tended to calm him. He became less aggressive and abusive, and the fellows were able to go on with the activities he had attacked. But they did not do so with complete equanimity, for psychoanalysis had taught them to express inner feelings rather than resort to defensive verbalization.[64]

V I

Clearly, the degree of autonomy the fellows enjoyed should not be exaggerated. Better than any other phenomenon, the "Freudian Follies" captured a certain tension in student culture at Winter Hospital—a culture under modest siege.

The "Follies" began as a skit about "Dr. Newcomer," an incoming MSP fellow. Winter Hospital students produced it in 1946 for a Veterans Round Table session at the Chicago meeting of the American Psychiatric Association. At the 1947 American Psychoanalytic Association convention, seven Menninger fellows staged a longer "Freudian Follies" production. They modified a few currently popular songs for humorous skits satirizing life at Winter.[65]

The full-scale "Follies" of 1948 was performed at Winter and underscored the students' ambivalence toward Karl and the politics of training analysis. To the tune of "Carefully Stealing" from *H.M.S. Pinafore,* one skit began:

> I am Karl Menninger,
> I'm the manager, the boss—
> I'm the ideal father figure,
> With a little dash of Santa Claus.

Another skit, adapting the "Lord Chancellor's Song" from *Iolanthe,* focused humorously on the politics of the Topeka Psychoanalytic Institute's selection of fellows for training analysis and concluded: "No one can seem to understand/How we select an analysand." The final skit in the 1948 "Follies" was set to the tune of "Winter Wonderland" and alluded humorously to "the zeal" of Winter Hospital residents attempting to construct the "team" with a "scheme" for a vibrant student culture.[66]

Skits in other years concerned "Foreign Analysts in Topeka," "The Rorschach," and sundry developments important to student life. But the preponderance of "Follies" material continued both to mirror and to afford a certain release from the tensions at Winter. The tensions continued to concern the clash between a viable MSP student culture on the one hand and, on the other, Karl and the politics of training analysis.

Not surprisingly, Karl and other Menningers often found "Freudian Follies" performances disturbing. For the first time in the history of the organization, there was a large facility and scores of personnel that could not be absorbed within the traditional "family spirit." The psychiatry school operated at Winter Hospital within a semiautonomous culture, and the "Follies" were a conspicuous manifestation of that culture. The MSP brought in too many federal dollars and too much national recognition to be dealt with summarily, however. Heterogeneity had therefore to be allowed as an indispensable element within Menninger operations. Fortunately, the family, having survived its own internal crisis earlier in the decade, had become somewhat more flexible and less intent on imposing controls in the face of this change. Just as the development of significant organizational heterogeneity tested the flexibility of the "new," post-divorce Menninger family, greater openness within the family and its "spirit" made it less antagonistic to workplace diversification.

Actually, by the late 1940s and early 1950s, Winter Hospital was becoming separate structurally as well as culturally from the Menninger Foundation. As the early fellows completed their training program, a

number of them joined the Winter staff. Gradually, they replaced foundation consultants as Winter's primary supervisors and teachers. According
to a comprehensive contract between the foundation and the hospital,
signed in July 1948, experienced Winter staff were to be principally
responsible for the hospital's training programs. Menninger consultants
were to make only supplemental contributions. A year later, Will observed that the demands on the foundation for services at Winter had
tapered off. With R. C. Anderson replacing Frank Casey in June 1952 as
manager of the hospital, this transition toward Winter autonomy was
accelerated. A proficient administrator who followed the VA *Rules and
Procedures* manual, Anderson was intent on independence for his hospital.
Although he continued the Menninger traditions of active treatment and
the avoidance of chronic patients, Will noted how "he leans over backward to maintain the separateness of Winter from the Foundation" and
resented foundation interventions. Once Anderson became so angry with
Karl's efforts at interference that a special security guard was engaged for
two weeks to protect Karl.[67]

The overwhelming majority of Winter fellows left Topeka when their
training analyses concluded or after a few years as regular staff. Just as
he had often been unhappy as a boy when boarders left the household,
Karl was upset by the departures of most of the fellows. In December
1950, he announced that though far too many spurned his job offers, he
was proud that the overwhelming majority had gone into public medical
institutions and universities, "rather than into straight private practice for
personal profit." Articulating the family missionary tradition, he was
pleased that his "boys" had "assumed the [public] responsibility that is
the mark of educated men."[68]

Although Karl could not possibly have employed half the fellows to
whom he offered long-term positions, the rate of acceptance was so low
that he was undeterred. It is not difficult to understand why most fellows
rejected his offers. Leaving Topeka represented a logical outgrowth of
the cultural autonomy that had been developing among them since 1946.
Away from Topeka, a fellow knew that he would be less likely either to
regard himself or to be regarded as one of Karl's "boys."[69]

VII

In the fall of 1945, Karl approached his father's longtime friend Middle-
ton L. Perry, superintendent of Topeka State Hospital, about training
MSP residents at his facility. Perry was uninterested. He told Karl that the

proposed collaboration would turn Topeka State into "a sideshow to the Menninger Clinic."[70]

When Perry ended his thirty-year tenure in 1948, however, the national political climate was different. Exposés of the dehumanizing environment of state mental hospitals in various parts of the country were receiving widespread attention. An array of books, articles, and news reports underscored the rapid deterioration of medical care and even living necessities in many of these facilities. They called for significant new funding for buildings and personnel to remedy the conditions.[71]

Kansas was a suitable target for these revelations. Before World War II, the state's mental hospitals had compared well with facilities elsewhere. They operated only 7.1 percent over capacity, staff-patient ratios were better than in most states, and the voluntary admission rate of 25.7 percent was three times higher than the national average. However, expenditures per patient had been somewhat below the national norm. In the course of the 1940s, the appropriation level fell to one third below the U.S. average. When Perry retired, Kansas spent only seventy-five cents a day per patient. Moreover, staff-patient ratios had slipped markedly since 1939. Kansas hired fewer professional employees proportionate to the number of patients in its facilities than any other state. Consequently, it was not possible for any Kansas mental hospital to offer humane medical care.[72]

As conditions in all Kansas public mental facilities deteriorated during the 1940s, Topeka State Hospital came under attack. In prior decades, Perry had done an exemplary job with limited state appropriations. He kept wards clean, required staff to treat patients without brutality or cruelty, and had hopes of one day transforming the hospital into something more than a custodial facility. By 1948, however, his hopes were dashed. Niggardly state appropriations over recent years had reduced Perry to five doctors, two nurses, one psychologist, and one hundred twenty aides to care for nearly two thousand patients. Many rooms lacked lighting and heat, electrical wiring had become obsolete and hazardous, wooden staircases were turning into firetraps, and the wards were dark and gloomy. Perry retired discouraged. He was replaced by a superintendent who abandoned efforts to keep the patients clean and properly fed.[73]

Pressed by the situation at Topeka State and the much publicized death of a patient there, Governor Frank Carlson appointed a commission to investigate the state's mental hospital system. The commission consisted of some legislators, the president of the Kansas Medical Society, and two medical reformers—Franklin Murphy, dean of the University of Kansas Medical School, and Karl Menninger. Supported by Murphy, who admired the Winter-MSP program, Karl quickly took charge of the commission. More than anybody else, he was responsible for its report to the governor. In view of the Menninger brothers' opposition to the American Psychiatric Association old guard (who rejected most reform efforts beyond the upgrading of state hospital facilities to the standards of general hospitals), Karl's partial defense of the old-guard position in his report was ironic. Because conditions in state hospitals had become "extremely bad," he called for substantial increases in appropriations. To secure competent personnel at every hospital at double the present number, his report recommended that Topeka State become a teaching hospital. It was to train large numbers of staff for the entire state system, with new moneys for the training program made available by the legislature. Karl's intentions were not quite those of APA conservatives. Winter Hospital, and not the general teaching hospital, was his model for reform. He was intent on extending his Winter achievements to Topeka State and from there to other Kansas mental hospitals. Karl was essentially seeking to have Kansas fund the MSP so that it could extend its Winter-based training program to Topeka State.[74]

Governor Carlson accepted the commission recommendations. In 1949, the legislature appropriated $21 million over a two-year period for state hospitals and other welfare institutions. This represented a 60 percent increase over the prior biennium. At Karl's urging, the money was earmarked for staff and programs rather than buildings. More than a million dollars went to Topeka State Hospital for a special teaching program. Topeka State was to use most of that money to enable Karl and the MSP to institute the teaching program, though Murphy would assist through staff and facilities from the University of Kansas Medical School.[75]

Preoccupied with other duties, Karl never attempted to manage the Topeka State–MSP program as he oversaw Winter. Leonard P. Ristine, who had earned a good reputation administering a state hospital in Iowa, was appointed Topeka State superindendent and prepared to work out the details of the MSP program with the Menninger Foundation. Karl designated Harry Levinson, a young graduate student in psychology at the University of Kansas and a Menninger intern, to represent the MSP in these negotiations. Levinson had been active in the campaign to secure significant legislative assistance for the state hospitals, and Karl looked upon him as a favorite son—a "very lively and effective agent for me." After Ristine and Levinson developed and implemented the program, Karl assigned Levinson to Topeka State on a full-time basis as director of professional education. He chose a former MSP resident and junior-level foundation psychiatrist, William Rottersman, to help Levinson. Finally, he persuaded a capable MSP resident and Winter Hospital psychiatrist, John A. Anderson, to become clinical director of Topeka State. Anderson joined Levinson and Ristine as Topeka State representatives on the MSP executive committee. Quickly showing himself to be a better general administrator than Ristine, he replaced him as superintendent in 1951.[76]

The work of Levinson, Rottersman, and Anderson on the Topeka State campus during the early 1950s was substantial. They reduced the patient population from nearly two thousand to roughly fourteen hundred. That plus the presence of numerous well-supervised residents, clinical psychology graduate students, registered social workers, and psychiatric nursing students on the grounds altered the patient-staff ratio to the point where more than custodial care was possible.[77]

This "revolution" at Topeka State would not have been possible without Winter Hospital. To some degree, Topeka State represented an extension of Winter-MSP culture. Fellows at Topeka State drove to the Winter grounds for classes, study sessions, and Karl's Saturday morning colloquiums. Like Winter fellows, they were expected to study preliminary drafts and the published edition of the *Manual for Psychiatric Case Study*. Several Winter-MSP graduates assumed positions at Topeka State as regular staff psychiatrists. They tried to establish as much of a hospital training program based upon the Winter model as conditions would allow. Owing to this transfer of Winter-MSP graduates to the Topeka staff, several state hospital section chiefs operated from a psychoanalytic orientation—a first for the nation's state hospital system. Winter Hospital led the VA system in nondiscriminatory hiring, and Topeka State pioneered with that policy in the state hospital system.[78]

However, the "revolution" at Topeka State differed in important respects from that at Winter half a decade earlier. When Robert Holt and Lester Luborsky (authors of the classic study of the selection of MSP fellows) characterized Topeka State in the early 1950s as the new "frontier, the focus of greatest excitement and enthusiasm in the MSP,"[79] they referred principally to the difficulties that State had to face because its material resources were far more circumscribed and its traditions more custodial than Winter's had ever been. Indeed, a major experiment was taking place at Topeka State to determine how an elite private "new psychiatry" facility like Menninger, through its MSP program, might service a large middle- and lower-class clientele in its immediate vicinity. Nothing quite like this had ever occurred in American psychiatric history—not even at the few intensive-treatment, cure-oriented state facilities of the early 1950s, like Warren in Pennsylvania and Medfield in Massachusetts.

Although Levinson, Rottersman, and Anderson had launched the "revolution" at Topeka State by vastly improving the quality of staff, staff-to-patient ratios, and the treatment program, they had not quite adjusted their reforms to the fact that even with unprecedented funding levels, the Kansas legislature would never support them the way the federal government backed Winter. Their successors, Alfred Bay and Paul Feldman, more fully grasped this limitation when they took over early in 1954. Bay and Feldman recognized that a staff of fifteen psychiatrists, thirty psychiatric residents, six psychologists, thirty-five nurses, thirty-three social workers, thirty-nine occupational and recreational therapists, and three hundred thirty-five aides was the best the facility would ever be able to hire for fourteen hundred patients. Such a staff was far too light at the top of the psychiatric hierarchy and far too heavy at the bottom to even approximate Winter Hospital. Bay and Feldman understood that the psychoanalytic orientation and the principles of both Will's milieu therapy program and Karl's *Manual for Psychiatric Case Study* were strongly grounded in a rapport between a physician and his patient, which could never be established under the doctor-patient ratios at Topeka State. Consequently, while not phasing out either psychoanalytic perspectives or Menninger treatment concepts, they focused more heavily upon biological factors in mental illness. Thorazine and other new psychotropic drugs came to be relied upon as the principal vehicles for patient management. Indeed, Topeka State became one of several hospitals to lead the way in the use of these medications.[80]

Bay and Feldman also recognized that their staff had to focus far more on the material conditions of their patients than had been necessary at Winter Hospital. A patient could hardly respond well to even the most sophisticated therapeutic approaches from Menninger and Winter if his feet hurt for lack of shoes or his entire body sweltered in the summer because his room lacked adequate ventilation. The two therefore ordered section chiefs, senior psychiatrists, and residents, as well as nurses and aides, to spend much of their time attending to the basic physical wants of their patients.[81]

The priorities of Bay and Feldman indicated that by the mid-1950s, Topeka State Hospital was starting to break away from Menninger influence, much as Winter had half a decade earlier. As a Topeka State psychologist, Wilfred Miller, recalled, high-level staff at the facility wanted increasingly "to avoid being swallowed up by TMF [The Menninger

Foundation] control and the TMF image" as they recognized that their hospital approaches differed from those at Menninger. When Karl and other Menninger officials were insensitive to this position, conflicts erupted.[82]

VIII

Despite the growing autonomy of Winter and Topeka State, the bold series of decisions the Menningers had made—to sign an unprecedented contract with the VA in 1945, to establish the Winter-MSP connection, and to extend that connection to a custodial state facility—testified to the missionary evangelism that had been a conspicuous family trait for over half a century. It was no accident that Karl chose the twenty-fifth-anniversary celebration of the MSP to recall how the missionary teaching spirit that his parents had conveyed to him came alive in 1946 with his "small intrepid band" of teachers and fellows as they worked for "a new future, a new world, a new kind of medical practice, a new way of helping suffering people in an old, much beat-up world."[83]

The success of the MSP experiment involved the Menningers in a long-term reform venture that tended to channel family energies away from internal preoccupations. The entire MSP structure represented an unusual historical partnership. "Never before in history," Karl boasted, "have the federal government, a state government, and a private institution combined to set up a teaching machine." In order to maintain this level of cooperation, the Menningers and their senior staff had to negotiate with federal and state officials almost daily. This was especially true as Winter and Topeka State became increasingly autonomous and the family had to come to terms with officials on each campus as well as with those in Washington and the statehouse. As federal and state governmental developments commanded their attention, the Menningers found that they sometimes lacked the time for familial conflicts.[84]

Perhaps the clearest sign that the MSP experiment encouraged and enhanced the public-spirited missionary quality of the family was in the students it graduated. More than trainees elsewhere, MSP fellows left Topeka committed to public service over personal gain. By August 1953, Will reported that of all psychiatrists who had trained in the program, 152 worked for the VA and other governmental facilities, 40 were at private hospitals and clinics, and 47 were in military service. Only 121 had established their own practices—and most of them served also as consultants and visiting professors at public service institutions. Max Levin, director of the Foundation's Fund for Research in Psychiatry, proclaimed that the MSP was leading the nation in a public-spirited group approach to psychiatric treatment.[85]

The Menningers were exceedingly proud of the public commitment of the fellows. It had the effect of confirming their own decision to abandon private practice for nonprofit philanthropy. Both Karl and Will could claim some credit for the career choices of the fellows, for both brothers urged them to extend psychiatry into the public sphere to better mankind. As the principal instructor, Karl insisted that he was chiefly responsible for the fact that "more than 80% of the graduates have gone to public hospitals, public clinics, medical schools and universities rather than into straight private practice for personal profit." But if the role of the Menningers, especially Karl, was very important in explaining this outcome, the strength and focus of the fellows must not be discounted. In MSP classrooms and informal discussion groups and on the wards of Winter and Topeka State, little value was attached to remuneration. The life of the mind, the reform of backward hospitals, and the recovery of incurable patients were crucial to a mental health career.[86]

By 1951, 15 percent of all psychiatrists being trained in the United States were enrolled in the Menninger School of Psychiatry. Fellows drawn from nineteen states and five foreign countries studied in Topeka. When they graduated, most went on to spread the "Menninger way" and the students' values. By 1954, over 350 alumni practiced in thirty-eight states and abroad. Franklin Murphy proclaimed: "Topeka today is probably the greatest psychiatric teaching center in the world." With these numbers and that billing, there were strong incentives to move even further from the family-centered institution of old. According to one astute staff psychologist, the Menninger brothers sometimes seemed "more involved . . . with practical economic and public service problems" than with family politics. But old traditions proved resilient. Especially on the Menninger home campus, the past had ways of coexisting with the present and the future.[87]

CHAPTER EIGHT

The Home Campus

In October 1949, Karl proclaimed to the Menninger board of trustees that the "teaching program must be the primary function of the Foundation." Because of the new teaching mission, "the actual treatment of private patients, originally the main thing we did, now is secondary." "The chief need" of the home campus and its central institution, the hospital, "is income producing"—to help sustain the MSP programs at Winter Hospital and those programs being prepared for Topeka State Hospital.[1]

Will, as head of home campus operations, agreed with his older brother that the MSP represented the public "essence of the Foundation." But he also recognized the tremendous strain the programs placed on home campus operations and resources. Three years earlier, he had noted how everybody on the staff "sort of hangs on, doing much more than they should be doing, with the hope that some place there's going to be a break and we'll get back to some sort of normal living again." Will had warned the foundation executive committee that no further expansion of Menninger operations should take place without significant expansion of staff. Knowing full well that the home campus and its hospital provided not only revenue but teachers, consultants, and auxiliary services for the two MSP campuses, Will resented Karl's limited perspective and publicly rebutted his older brother for the first time. Before the trustees, Will charged that Karl was wrong to characterize the home campus as merely "income producing": "I think that's very fallacious. The reputation of this place was made on what we did in that hospital, and if that goes down, the whole place goes down."[2]

This confrontation reflected the tensions that had been mounting between the brothers during the postwar years. Will felt that Karl had defaulted on a promise to treat him as an equal. Although Karl had announced that he belonged "first and foremost to the Clinic," Will felt that his brother had come to identify with the two MSP campuses. The only use Karl had for him at the home campus, Will believed, was for revenue production and auxiliary support.[3]

Will was never entirely able to ease the work pressures on his staff or to improve the tattered appearance of facilities. But he increased some internal resources significantly and put into place an administrative team that managed existing resources more efficiently. Despite these improvements, postwar expansion triggered nostalgia in some key staff for the simpler days of smallness, closeness, a less frantic pace, and familial warmth and predictability. Several resigned and left Topeka. Will officially stayed, but he gradually separated himself from the home campus. By the early 1950s, he spent most of his time traveling as the chief foundation fund-raiser and as an activist in national psychiatric reform. Almost by default, the home campus as well as MSP became the responsibility of the new administrative team and a new chief of staff—Karl.

II

The tasks and responsibilities of staff on the home campus grew dramatically by the early 1950s. While much of the increase was in their support of MSP operations at Winter and Topeka State hospitals, some was due to a large and growing patient population. The rather skeletal staff of the war period could not possibly meet these needs, and new employees were added. Between the start of the MSP operation at Winter in 1946 and full-scale activities at Topeka State in 1952, the staff on the home campus increased from 266 to 395. Because of the need for consultant services at Winter and Topeka State, this growth concentrated in the professional staff. In 1946, for example, five new psychiatrists were hired, along with two clinical psychologists and three psychiatric social workers. Between fall 1945 and spring 1949, the number of foundation psychiatrists, psychologists, and social workers more than doubled. In 1947, 46 percent of the staff was classified as professional and 54 percent as nonprofessional, but by 1952, the proportions were 56 and 44 percent.[4]

In addition to the enlarged staff, home campus revenues rose significantly between 1946 and 1952, partly as the result of increased federal and state subsidies for MSP operations, partly owing to a 63 percent growth in patient population. Enlarged staff and enhanced revenues led, in turn, to more internal operations. For example, the *Bulletin of the Menninger Clinic* expanded its coverage and became one of the most widely read psychiatric journals in the country. The research department

grew significantly and commenced independent fund-raising. The Institute of Psychological Medicine expanded its administrative offices, while
internal training programs in clinical psychology, graduate psychiatric
nursing, and social work were increased.[5]

This expansion strained the physical plant. Doctors doubled up in
modest offices and often moved about among three buildings to treat
patients. To provide space for new personnel and patients, a filling station, a garage, a hamburger stand, and two barns were remodeled. Still,
Will considered instituting two full-staff work shifts to double the work
space. The maintenance crew could not keep up with servicing demands. It took sixteen months for a stage to be renovated and seven
months for a night light to be installed outside the craft shop. Some
problems went unattended, even a serious acoustical problem in the
clinic building that enabled patients to overhear staff dictation concerning their progress.[6]

Despite the cramped quarters and the increased work load, the net
worth of the foundation tripled between 1947 and 1953. It had become
a much larger and more complex operation than most other "new psychiatry" hospitals. But as Lewis Robbins, a senior psychiatrist, pointed out,
this had created internal problems as well as opportunities:

> In a very brief period of time, almost overnight, The Menninger
> Foundation was transformed from a family, small group situation,
> which sociologists call a "face-to-face group," to a factory . . . no
> longer are the various workers able to relate themselves by day-
> to-day contact and communication to one another and to all as-
> pects of our program. We have however tried to continue to
> function on the basis of a face-to-face group.[7]

Efforts to operate like a "face-to-face group" were attributable to
Will, the man who had developed the hospital's family face and the milieu
therapy program, with its sensitive, one-on-one structure of personal
relationships. But the campus had become too large for Will to meet each
member of the staff daily or even weekly. He considered it important to
convene every week with two or three staff members, until he had seen
all employees, "so that I can learn to know them and they learn to know
me." Because of the proliferation of foundation services and personnel,
Will divided the organization into four sections or services: clinical, administrative, educational, and research. Service directors were appointed, and Will met each of them regularly. With every Menninger
staffer he encountered, regardless of rank, Will demonstrated his charac-

TOP: *Karl Menninger at four, 1897*
RIGHT: *Flo Menninger, 1909*

Karl and Flo, 1912

Will, Edwin, Karl, and Charles Menninger, ca. 1919

TOP: *Will and Karl after a day fishing, 1912*

ABOVE: *Karl, Grace, Edwin, Catharine, and Will Menninger, 1920*

The Menninger Clinic building, 1925

Charles Menninger visits the Southard School, 1927

Advertisement for the sanatarium, 1929

RIGHT: *Mildred Law, ca. 1939*
BELOW: *Staff softball game, 1934*

LEFT: *Franz Alexander visits the clinic in the company of Charles and Karl, 1934*

BELOW: *Jeanetta Lyle with Karl and Will, 1937*

TOP: *Isabel Erickson with the Menninger brothers, 1937*

RIGHT: *John Stone, 1939*

Robert P. Knight, ca. 1941

Karl and David Rapaport, 1942

Karl's colloquium at the Winter Hospital, 1952

Irving Sheffel, 1952

Lester Roach, 1954

Arthur Marshall and Karl, 1964

Peter Fleming on the hospital patio, 1963

Robert Switzer in front of the Children's Division complex, 1964

Gardner Murphy and Robert Wallerstein, 1964

Two generations of Menningers—foreground: Will and Karl
background: Robert, Philip, and Roy, 1964

OPPOSITE: *Karl riding on the West Campus, 1965*

TOP: *Karl and Roy viewing
bust of Will, 1967*

RIGHT: *Otto Kernberg, 1969*

teristic warmth and interest. He was especially adept at empathizing with the misgivings of older staff about the pace of change.[8]

Nevertheless, Will was intent upon keeping power centralized. It was neither professional nor efficient to be "entirely democratic," he noted. He insisted that the office of general secretary be the only direct link between specific service divisions and the executive committee. His office alone was to communicate between the committee and the board of trustees. In essence, he was trying to become the locus of authority for all operations in the postwar organization, much as he had dominated the hospital in the 1930s.[9]

If Will had been able to concentrate all his time on the home campus, he might have accomplished this goal. However, his dramatic rise to the top of army mental health services carried other implications. He became exceedingly active in the American Psychiatric Association and continued as an army consultant. These professional commitments meant a lot of travel for Will—ninety-five days out of town in 1947 and increased absences in the years that followed. By the middle of 1947, he noted in his diary that there were "many, many things to be done within our organization," but nobody had "time enough to think and plan. . . . I have the feeling I'm not doing my job here at all adequately."[10]

Up to this point, Will had depended upon the assistance of John Stone and Mildred Law. When the organization had been small, with limited staff and simple budgets, administrators had only to learn from experience and to be loyal to the family. But with complex federal and state contracts to implement, with hundreds of new students and staff, and with a significant increase in the patient population, professionally trained administrators became essential. Realizing that he did not have the time to hire and direct an administrative team, and with no stomach to fire loyal administrators, Will engaged Lester T. Roach in October 1948 and gave him the title of executive secretary. He told Roach to acquire an administrative staff that would manage foundation functions, especially those on the home campus.[11]

Roach, with a master's degree in public administration from the University of North Dakota, had taught political science at the University of Minnesota. During the war, he met Will in Washington where he worked for the Office of the Surgeon General. When the Veterans Administration was organized, Roach became the chief of administrative management for the Medicine and Surgery Department. It was there that he learned of the bold education experiment in Topeka. Respecting Will enormously and recognizing the national significance of the MSP, Roach undertook his new job enthusiastically.[12]

John Stone, quite ill at the time, willingly ceded most of his administrative responsibilities to Roach. Mildred Law was another matter, but
Roach had no qualms about curbing her discretionary authority; he limited her duties to planning an addition for the hospital. Roach considered
comptroller Maurice Nuss inadequate for the foundation's increasingly
complex budgets and replaced him with Irving Sheffel, a Harvard M.A.
in public administration who had worked in the army's Finance Department during the war and then in the Bureau of the Budget.[13]

As strong New Deal–Fair Deal liberals in Washington, Roach and
Sheffel both had regarded the VA-sponsored school in Topeka as a logical extension of federal responsibility. By the middle of 1949, they hired
a like-minded Washington associate, VA administrator Abel D. Swirsky.
Swirsky conducted a number of useful studies of internal procedures, but
his moodiness antagonized staff. In 1952, Roach replaced him with
Thomas Dolgoff. At City College of New York, Dolgoff had taken a B.S.
degree in social science and an M.S. in education. He served in army
military intelligence in France and then became an organization and
methods examiner for the VA Department of Medicine and Surgery,
where he met Roach. Basil Cole, personnel director in the pre-Roach
period, was the sole old-line administrator upon whom Roach conferred
significant administrative powers.[14]

For the most part, the members of Roach's team were broadly educated and experienced public administrators. Roach expected each to
master the others' jobs, in case it was necessary to fill in on short notice.
But Roach and Sheffel jointly assumed the most sensitive task—coordinating the efforts of the increasingly antagonistic Menninger brothers.
Karl quickly recognized that Roach's loyalties were with Will and demanded Sheffel as his own administrator. Sheffel served in that capacity
but continued to cooperate very closely with Roach. Consequently, the
Roach team did not become absorbed by Menninger family conflicts to
the extent that earlier administrators had.[15]

Roach worked assiduously to build an administrative structure that
would support the overworked professional staff. He assigned administrators to clarify and improve divisions of labor between various departments and other units. Procedural simplifications were instituted. To
minimize overlapping work functions, Cole compiled updated descriptions of all jobs in the foundation. After an analysis of hospital revenues
and expenditures, Roach concluded that deficient fees for hospital patients were jeopardizing the foundation's financial structure. When he
raised the fees an average of $150 a month, the organizational books went
into the black. Sheffel reorganized the procedure through which the

foundation negotiated its contracts with the Veterans Administration, outlining the types of services Menninger staff rendered to the VA, the time involved, and the financial value of each service.[16]

Generally helpful and considerate, the Roach administrative team got on well with most of the staff, as well as with the Menninger brothers. As financial statements improved and organizational procedures became clearer, more consistent, and more efficient, there was a somewhat less frantic and distressed air about the home campus. By the early 1950s, the organization was working smoothly, and Will felt less guilty for spending so much time away. Karl, too, had fewer qualms about concentrating on the MSP programs, lecturing and traveling widely, and writing. Indeed, for the first time since the organization began in 1919, the Menningers themselves did not visibly dominate home campus affairs. Roach and his associates, free from extensive family control, though still loyal to the Menningers, continued to institute changes that reduced the pull of the "family spirit." In this, they were unintended allies of the MSP fellows.[17]

III

If Roach's administrators eased the burdens of home campus staff, the prospects for patients appeared less hopeful. Most of them had been shifted about from one mental hospital to another well into midlife, and Menninger was often a place of last resort.

The number of patients far exceeded that of the prewar facility, where a low census had sometimes placed the entire organization on the verge of bankruptcy. Buildings were usually filled to the hospital's maximum capacity of 67. (With the completion of a major addition in 1954, maximum capacity increased to 113.) To take on more patients and enlarge revenues, a day-hospital program was established in 1949. Patients were admitted who had the emotional capability to room in specially selected homes within the community. By the early 1950s, roughly one third of all hospital patients were on the less costly day program.[18]

Despite the enlargement of the patient roster, the hospital remained a facility for the rich and nearly rich. The small outpatient service represented an exception, for patients with annual incomes below four thousand dollars sometimes met with a psychotherapist for an hour or two each week. As in the prewar years, the typically affluent patients continued to come from nearby western and midwestern states, though some arrived from as far away as California and New York. The proportion from Kansas declined.[19]

The postwar patients differed in two respects from their predecessors in employment characteristics. First, although most males continued to be professionals and successful businessmen, far more females had departed from the unemployed daughter-homemaker role. Many females had gone on to college and sought employment as secretaries, laboratory technicians, and social service workers, among other professions.[20]

Second, as a consequence of the high national profile of the postwar organization, the hospital became a facility of choice for entertainers with serious difficulties. Actor Robert Walker had a drinking problem, engaged in periodic brawls, and could not keep a wife (he was divorced from Jennifer Jones and had a "kissless marriage" with director John Ford's daughter). To help stabilize his life and enhance his career, Metro-Goldwyn-Mayer sent him to Topeka for treatment. He returned to the studio half a year later, praising the Menninger hospital for his newfound happiness. Jane Froman had struggled through twenty-five failed operations for leg injuries sustained in an air crash. She lauded Menninger for enabling her to understand her emotions and thereby walk again. Dan Dailey checked into the hospital after his wife divorced him and he had difficulty completing his films. He stayed for five months and returned to Hollywood ready to star in *Mabel and Me.* Akim Tamiroff's experience was similar. Gene Tierney had been in the process of finishing *The Left Hand of God,* with Humphrey Bogart, when she experienced an acute disorientation that evolved into a prolonged depression. Treated at the Hartford Retreat and discharged, she attempted suicide and was rushed to Menninger, where she underwent several months of therapy. Other movie stars came and went. When Karl visited Los Angeles in 1953, over twenty Hollywood celebrities who had been treated at the hospital threw a party at Romanoff's to honor him and his organization.[21]

Celebrities or not, most postwar patients at Menninger suffered from very serious maladies. Many were diagnosed as schizophrenics with schizoid personalities. Several were severely depressed, some were alcoholic, and a few more catatonic. There were those who talked in silly, childish ways or painted their faces. One ate her feces, while another was orgasmic near churches. Most lived isolated, restricted lives; several abandoned their spouses and their children. Employment histories were usually irregular, and sexual activities often unorthodox. In 1951–52, members of Menninger's Psychotherapy Research Project created a Health-Sickness Rating Scale and asked the hospital staff to rate all their psychotherapy patients. (A "1" rating revealed extreme personality disorganization, no contact with reality, and total inability to function on one's own; "100" indicated normality, with "happiness and social effectiveness.") Sixty-three percent of the hospital's patients at the time of initial diagnosis had an average rating of 37. The least disturbed 8 percent of the patients rated only an average of 55. Patients with scores approximating these did not ease the burdens of the hospital staff. Although there was no scale to yield comparable data for prior decades, it would be difficult to characterize these patients as less disturbed than earlier Menninger patients.[22]

Will's generation of psychiatrists returned to civilian life convinced they could cure most serious mental maladies, but their optimism was misplaced. Scientific and demonstrably effective treatments were simply unavailable. As in the prewar era, knowledge of brain structures and functions was rudimentary. Whether organic or psychodynamic in their orientation, therapies were empirical and nonspecific. Although electric and insulin shock were widespread as components of psychiatric treatment, they were used only sparingly at the Menninger hospital. Early in the 1950s, new psychotropic drugs (particularly reserpine and chlorpromazine) began to be used in many mental facilities. But it was not until the end of the decade that psychotropic drugs were employed even modestly at Menninger.[23]

Cautious with certain widely used treatments and reluctant to perform lobotomies, Menninger staff clung to Will's milieu treatment program of the 1930s. Most patients were put through a highly individualized treatment program that corresponded to the guide to the order sheet, with its meticulously prescribed attitudes toward patients. To be sure, the guide had been abbreviated substantially. Moreover, it came to be understood increasingly from the perspective of ego psychology, with a stress on successful social adaptation, rather than prewar drive theory. Then, too, new hospital physicians tended to draw upon preliminary drafts of Karl's *Manual for Psychiatric Case Study* as a primary reference. Yet, like Will's hospital of the 1930s, inpatient therapy focused on sympathetic staff who talked frequently with their patients and put them through rigorously scheduled activities.[24]

It is exceedingly difficult to assess the impact of hospital treatment on the patients. The typical patient stay far exceeded the two-month average of the pre-1946 era; half of the patients remained for more than a year. Far fewer were discharged within an ambiguous "somewhat improved" middle category. Most were released as either "improved" or "unchanged" (unimproved). The hospital report for July 1946 to June 1947 was typical. It listed 55 percent of discharged patients as "improved," 41 percent as "unchanged," and nearly 4 percent as "worse" than when they arrived. Although the Psychotherapy Research Project did not evaluate all hospital patients at the time they were released, it attempted to measure the annual "improvement" of 1952 patients with the 100-point rating scale. "Improvement" ranged from a rather negligible 5 points to a more significant 13, with most patients "improving" roughly 9 points. The most optimistic figures derived from a December 1950 analysis of patients in treatment. It predicted that 31 percent would make "marked improvement or recover," 37 percent would achieve "moderate improvement," while 32 percent had "very limited prognoses." Clearly, different hospital documents carried somewhat different implications about the condition of patients after treatment.[25]

However variable the results, all reports were influenced by changes in patient admissions criteria. Early in 1949, those criteria were modified significantly. For the first time, admissions preferences were given to emergency cases involving temporary acute conditions. This pointed to a willingness of the staff to deal with external symptoms for disturbance as well as with more basic psychic conditions. But the admissions office was also to give preference to patients more likely to benefit from intensive psychoanalytically oriented expressive therapy. Obviously, these policy changes enhanced the shift evident since 1946 away from mixed or middle categories for evaluating improvement. The patient experiencing the acute crisis was almost certain to change; his problems would either cease or be regarded as a serious, long-term malady. Similarly, the patient deemed likely to benefit from intensive expressive therapy was also likely to change significantly. According to the Psychotherapy Research Project, such a patient made the greatest improvement.[26]

Contrasting with earlier practice, many postwar patients were released even when staff anticipated future hospitalization. In fact, the readmission rate mounted steadily, from 18 percent in 1946 to 40 percent in both 1953 and 1954, before it began to subside. It may be (as the 1949 admissions priority for acute conditions suggests) that the postwar staff was willing to settle for work with some patients over a long haul. The patient may have been allowed to test himself in society, returning to the hospital eventually to improve further.[27]

Despite the crudeness and inconsistency of many of the statistics on postwar treatment, it is noteworthy that they sometimes compared favorably with prewar and wartime results. Especially after the changes in admissions criteria, postwar staff felt they could classify more patients as clearly "improved." The December 1950 report of hospital patients currently in treatment predicted, for example, that nearly a third would make "marked improvement or recover." Similarly, the Psychotherapy Research Project claimed that all 1952 hospital patients had "improved" to at least a small degree. During the earlier era, one simply could not find these indications of at least guarded optimism in hospital documents.

I V

The care of a troubled and increasing patient population exerted a tremendous drain on staff energies. The consultant, teaching, and other MSP support functions that home campus workers had to perform added enormously to their burdens. By the middle of 1947, John Stone warned Will that "a continuation of its [MSP's] expansion can bust us organizationally," owing to an overworked staff. Will did not have to be reminded, for he had detailed the extraordinary work pressures in his diary. Even Karl had to concede to Omar Bradley that "Members of our teaching and professional staffs have worked 12, 14, and 16 hours a day" and that nonprofessional staff was following their example. Despite these long hours, overtime pay was rarely budgeted for staff, even though wages were somewhat below those the federal government paid to the more junior Winter Hospital medical staff. Moreover, clerical personnel could earn more money for less work in various private enterprises in the Topeka community.[28]

Overwork for insufficient pay on a shabby campus had also been evident during World War II, when there was a severe labor shortage. Will's intensely loyal staff had been distressed because he had gone off to the army and had been replaced by a less empathic brother, bent on modifying his routines. But most of these loyalists remained, evoking the "family spirit." With the launching of the MSP in 1946, however, the attractions of that "spirit" had been diluted. Will never fully resumed his dominant role in the hospital. Veteran staff saw his milieu treatment program compromised by a greatly abbreviated guide to the order sheet and a patient population enlarged to the point where the individualized prescription of attitudes became cumbersome. And Karl seemed to be slighting staff for the more exciting training programs at Winter (and soon at Topeka State), which were bringing in so many new faces. As Lewis Robbins, who had taken his residency before the war, complained, the old workplace seemed to have evolved from a family atmosphere to an impersonal factory.[29]

Like other staff veterans, Robbins recognized that intellectual excitement was to be found at the two new teaching hospitals. Aside from a small group of psychologists who gathered about David Rapaport, there was no equivalent to Karl's Saturday morning Winter colloquiums or the informal student discussion groups. Postwar hospital director Robert Worthington complained that the home campus was becoming a sideline to the stimulating MSP teaching programs. John Stone agreed; daily work pressures and administrative concerns were reducing the import of intellectual endeavor: "Ideas don't rate so high."[30]

Rather than lament the passing of intimacy, intellectual life, and a spirit of inquiry, older leaders like Robbins, Worthington, and Stone might have looked for new opportunities. They might have pressed for a firm university affiliation, such as the Mayo brothers had established in 1915 between their clinic and the University of Minnesota or as the Phipps Clinic enjoyed for decades with Johns Hopkins University. Leaders of both facilities had recognized that a meaningful university affiliation offered considerably more than financial support, for the center of gravity in American intellectual life was shifting to institutions of higher education. Yet in 1949, the Menninger brothers declined an offer to merge with the University of Pittsburgh, which would have provided an unprecedented $1 million discretionary budget and access to major philanthropic donors in the vicinity. It would also have established their presence on a major urban campus and ensured extensive exchanges between campus academics and Menninger clinicians. Instead, the family allowed donations raised by trustees to dissuade them from accepting the Pittsburgh offer. "My interest in Pittsburgh is extremely weak and I think Karl feels that same way," Will confided. Both brothers acknowledged that they simply were afraid that the Menninger workplace would be absorbed and altered beyond recognition on the Pittsburgh campus. Shortly after they rejected the merger, the brothers decided to reduce their only other academic connection. They discontinued a very successful cooperative program with the University of Kansas to train doctoral students in clinical psychology. In its place, programs were established for predoctoral psychology internships and postdoctoral supervision, which greatly reduced the university role.[31]

Karl and Will were backing away from what historian Daniel M. Fox has characterized as "hierarchical regionalism"—a system for medical services that became conspicuous after World War II. Within this system, the university, particularly its medical school and its affiliated teaching hospital, came to be regarded as the apex of medical activity for a particular region in the country. At this apex, highly specialized research projects yielded new medical knowledge, which was imparted to all trainees. In turn, most of the trainees moved to community hospitals in the region. The assumption was that community hospitals and local practitioners would attend to routine cases, referring all difficult or unique patients to the region's university medical complex. By rejecting the Pittsburgh offer and then reducing rather than extending their contacts with the University of Kansas, the Menningers were excluding the foundation from the two developing regional medical summits. The fact that the foundation continued to be linked to Winter Hospital compensated somewhat for the Menningers' refusal to cultivate a significant university affiliation. But resources from the VA might have been greater still if the foundation's university connections had been strong. After all, key officials from the Washington office had often recommended such ties. Moreover, as Winter came to rely upon its own staff more and Menninger consultants less, the foundation's claim of belonging to the major VA medical center for the region became less credible.[32]

As the home campus grew without the excitement and professional benefits of a university affiliation, staff veterans dwelt increasingly upon the intimacy of earlier years. For example, senior psychologists circulated a petition in 1951 and presented it to Will. "The rapid growth of the Menninger Foundation during recent years," the petition read, "has all but put an end to the former intimate participation of the staff in the life of the organization." Certain key figures from the earlier period resigned and moved away. Robert Worthington left for the Northwest Clinic in Seattle on the assurance of Douglass Orr that staff life there was intimate and cordial, as earlier at Menninger. With similar hopes, Harlan Crank departed to become one of the first practicing analysts in Texas. But two losses during these years loomed above all others—John Stone and Robert Knight.[33]

Stone was extremely distressed with the postwar programs and especially with their effects on home campus staff. Indeed, he attributed the overwork and loss of familial feeling almost entirely to the emergence of the MSP. Stone characterized Karl as "like a bull let out to pasture," intent on establishing one new program after another, regardless of whether the foundation had the funds or the staff to cover them. Karl had somehow to be stopped, he felt, or the cohesiveness and direction of the prewar family organization could never be restored.[34]

Stone turned in 1948 to Will, who he felt saw the "devastation" expansion had produced. He told Will that the foundation, especially its home campus, would be ruined if Karl was not stripped of his powers. He urged Will to recommend with him that the trustees force Karl to resign his MSP directorship plus his chief consultant functions at Winter Hospital. Despite Will's mounting self-confidence, he was not ready to challenge Karl. Moreover, such a move might create a precedent that could diminish the authority of the Menningers over the trustees. So Will backed Karl and turned angrily on Stone: "I feel you have threatened the organization. . . . I wonder if you fully realize that the VA wouldn't stay [in Topeka] without him." Karl soon discovered that Stone had gone not only to his brother but to Charles and to MSP consultant Leo Bartemeier, an old family friend, in an attempt to strip him of authority. He was furious and accused Stone of disloyalty; partner or no partner, he had no authority to speak out as he had.[35]

Following repudiations from both brothers, Stone recognized that he had never been more than a junior partner in the organization—and precisely because he was not a Menninger. For a man in midlife who had long assumed that "the support & patience & forbearance" of the Menningers was responsible for "the happiness I've found or the sense that my life after all & finally did come to have some significance," that was an upsetting discovery.[36]

At this point, a malignant tumor was detected in Stone's abdomen. After what appeared to be successful treatment at New York Memorial Hospital, Memorial offered him the job of hospital manager for considerably more than his Menninger salary. Karl urged Stone to take the offer; it was "too good a job for him to pass up." Never having worked outside the Menninger organization, Stone wavered. But he knew he had no future in Topeka. Before he formally accepted the offer, he fell ill again. This time, Topeka surgeons found a large and inoperable sarcoma attached to his aorta. Before Stone died, early in 1949, he watched Lester Roach dismantle his management procedures. Stone's wife attributed his untimely death to the Menningers' forcing him out.[37]

Robert Knight departed before Stone died. When Will went into the army, Knight had assumed full authority over psychotherapy services. He was officially designated chief of staff in April 1945 and named director of the Topeka Institute for Psychoanalysis in 1947. Thus, his departure was quite significant.[38]

Knight felt victimized by the postwar changes. He had to divide up a small salary budget among members of an overworked home campus professional staff. He and not the Menningers heard their complaints. At TIP, he was charged with satisfying the demands of MSP fellows for training analyses, with only a fraction of the senior analysts necessary to accomplish the task. Not long into 1947, Knight told Will of his strong feelings of "oppression and distress," owing to the tasks he had to accomplish and the pace of his professional life. He also informed Will he had been offered the directorship of the Austen Riggs Center. Though Riggs was small and rather isolated—hardly a psychoanalytically oriented and residency-centered institution on the Menninger scale—Knight warned

Will that he considered it a viable option if he was not relieved of some of his more onerous duties. Will was surprised that the responsibilities had "oppressed Bob terribly." But he knew that Knight was the premier Menninger therapist and analyst, as well as the most popular MSP instructor. To keep him, Will agreed to assume his chief of staff duties while continuing as general secretary. Knight appeared satisfied, and the crisis passed. But three weeks later, when Will was attending a National Research Council meeting in Washington, he learned that Knight had just accepted the Austen Riggs offer.[39]

Many factors contributed to the decision. First, Knight never ceased to view the 1930s as the Camelot years. Because Riggs was not large and was receptive to psychoanalytic therapy, Knight hoped that he would be moving to a place such as Menninger once had been. When he compared Menninger to Riggs shortly after his move, he announced to his new staff only half jokingly, playing on a current advertising slogan, that "L.S.M.F.T." (Little Stockbridge Means Fine Therapy).[40]

Like the spouses of many staff, Florence Knight had had difficulty adjusting to Topeka when the couple moved there in 1933. This was exacerbated by her husband's long hours and his emotional absorption into the "family spirit" of the organization. His work hours grew longer in the course of the postwar expansion. Her social life revolved around the Topeka Country Club, and that relationship ended in 1946, for when the black singer Paul Robeson was denied accommodations at Topeka hotels, Knight brought him home, and Florence's country club crowd was outraged. Florence rarely returned to the club after the Robeson incident and felt increasingly isolated and depressed. The marriage deteriorated. To rescue Florence from her doldrums and revitalize their relationship, Knight saw benefits in a community where his work hours might be shorter and his reputation was less scandalous. (The Knights divorced shortly after they arrived.)[41]

It was also relevant that as his influence at Menninger increased, Knight had fancied that he was becoming another "Menninger brother." However, when Will returned from the army, he was unwilling to tolerate Knight or anyone else on staff getting ahead of him, and Knight became disillusioned. Roughly a week after Knight accepted the Austen Riggs offer, Will wrote in his diary that "Bob Knight's decision to leave has brought us [himself and Karl] even closer together." Karl had delivered on a promise to place the younger brother above Knight and all others when he returned from army duties.[42]

Finally, Knight left because of his role in MSP operations. He enjoyed teaching and supervising the bright young fellows, and they loved him, finding him consistently supportive, unlike Karl, as well as intellectually stimulating. The problem was that the MSP was at the heart of the expansionist thrust that made Knight's clinical duties exhausting. Although he loved "this new School project," he felt it "will drain us further, both financially and temporally and emotionally." Indeed, he was so exhausted that he felt he did not have sufficient time or energy to prepare good lectures for the fellows, and "I can't be happy dishing out warmed over hash."[43]

The departure of perhaps the most gifted teacher-clinician in Menninger history underscored the gravity of the conflict between the old traditions and emerging realities. The small workplace with its focus on treatment did not mix well with a vastly enlarged multicampus setting where training was at least as important as treatment and where powerful groups like the MSP fellows and Roach's administrators often operated outside the "family spirit."

V

To a significant degree, then, key figures like Stone and Knight left because they could not let go of the traditions and the feelings that had existed before the war. In the 1930s, Will had promoted many of those traditions in the hospital. Like Stone and Knight, he voiced nostalgia during the late 1940s and called for a return to "normal living." At staff meetings, he spoke openly about his misgivings concerning MSP operations at Winter and Topeka State and the erosion of former Menninger hospital standards and routines.[44]

During his wartime years away from Topeka, however, Will changed, as Stone and Knight had not. He discovered new energy and creativity in himself and succeeded in selling an activist psychoanalytic psychiatry to a recalcitrant Army Medical Corps. Through his *War Department Technical Bulletin No. 203*, even army diagnostic nomenclature came to reflect the psychoanalytic concept of personality development. In recognition of this achievement, Will became the first American psychiatrist in the twentieth century to be promoted to general.[45]

Will's success in reforming the army's psychiatric program led young psychiatrists to turn to him for leadership after the war in their struggle against the staid traditions of the American Psychiatric Association. These Young Turks wanted an association that took stands on pressing social issues and campaigned for preventive mental health measures. They chose Will as founding chairman of the insurgent Group for the

Advancement of Psychiatry. He relished that leadership role, particularly as the group assumed control over the association and transformed it to a broadly reformist orientation. His election in 1948 as association president was the most conspicuous signal of that triumph, though he was also chosen president of the American Psychoanalytic Association and the Central Neuropsychiatric Association.[46]

Will even found energy to write several books. *Psychiatry in a Troubled World* (1948) summarized the problems that military psychiatry faced during World War II, then sought to apply the lessons learned from the war to the mental health of postwar civilian society. Although the work lacked the insights and the creative style of Karl's books, it provided a cogent case for enlarging the general concept of mental illness to address what soon came to be the principal concerns of community psychiatry. *You and Psychiatry* (1948) and *Psychiatry: Its Evolution and Present Status* (1948) were less substantial books, designed to acquaint the lay public with the evolution of psychiatric techniques and the essentials of modern psychoanalytically informed treatment.

Will's demanding activities outside Topeka were so significant and rewarding that he could only periodically (and sometimes halfheartedly) bemoan the loss of the old "family spirit." And with the press of new national responsibilities, he never actually returned to the Menninger campus on a full-time basis after the war.[47]

By the early 1950s, Will was spending almost all his time away. His Menninger job assignment had changed. The foundation required fresh funds to establish preventive psychiatry programs and research projects that the brothers strongly supported. Professional fund-raisers had not secured enough money, and Roach urged Will to take on that responsibility. The trustees and governors felt that either he or Karl would have to assume it on a full-time basis. Both initially declined, and Will was the most adamant: "I just cannot and will not do [it]." However, when it became "more likely" that Karl would have to assume the job, Will recognized that his brother would probably be even less effective than the professional fund-raisers. Moreover, tensions between him and Karl had reached the point where it was more pleasant to stay away or to talk with Karl only when others were present. In the end, Will realized that he enjoyed life most when he was away from his brother. By combining the fund-raising role with his professional obligations, he would be able to distance himself from Karl just as he had during the war. So he allowed himself to be recruited for the position.[48]

For the most part, the change was a good one for Will. By 1953, he and Catharine were spending most of their time on long train trips to solicit funds. "From the original point where I refused to have anything to do with fund raising to my present point of view—an enthusiastic keen interest in doing so—is an amazing change," he wrote in his diary.[49]

Will was remarkably effective at raising money for the foundation. Calling on his many contacts from the American Psychiatric Association, from fellow leaders of the Boy Scouts of America, and from Menninger trustees and governors, for introductions to the corporate elite, he attracted large donations. Contributors ranged from the Rockefeller Brothers Fund to the Schlitz Brewing Company and the Reader's Digest Foundation. By the mid-1950s, when the expanding Menninger Foundation required about $500,000 a year beyond revenues and grant moneys to balance its budget, he was raising approximately double that amount. Some potential donors were reluctant. They recognized the strong family role within the organization and feared that unlike a university, with a permanent institutional life, the foundation would not necessarily survive the Menninger brothers. But Will's considerable charm did much to overcome this obstacle. By the 1957–58 fiscal year, Will was responsible for over $2,000,000 of the foundation's $5,385,000 income. He was keeping most of the non-income-producing operations afloat, and he was the major source of revenue for new programs.[50]

Despite Will's crucial contribution, he was away so often that he participated minimally in home campus management. Over time, he knew fewer and fewer staff (once, he failed to recognize the hospital director). He did return with Catharine to Topeka a few months every summer, when Karl would be leaving for an extended vacation. But aside from occasional conversations with Roach on the Menninger grounds, Will would remain at home, where he and Catharine occupied themselves with stamp albums and other hobbies. They enjoyed life together and found "more satisfaction out of sitting at home and puttering" than in "stirring ourselves to go over and see friends."[51]

Will's accomplishments as a fund-raiser and a psychiatric statesman plus his newfound enjoyment in being with Catharine gave him much peace of mind. "I have a thoroughly rich life and [am] enjoying it a great deal," he wrote to Edwin. The "Freudian Follies" of 1955 captured Will's spiritual independence from his organization, to the tune of "Where Have You Been, Billy Boy":

> I'm glad that I'm back,
> But I'd better not unpack.
> Yes, I'm real glad to be back in Topeka.[52]

V I

As Will separated from the home campus, Charles spent several hours a day at the hospital, trying to find ways for a very old man to be useful. And he tried to moderate the hostility between his sons. He urged Karl to be more cordial and less aggressive toward Will and Will to be more trusting of Karl's good intentions. Charles's promptings had little direct effect, but the knowledge that their wrangling distressed him had a restraining influence upon both.[53]

In November 1953, Charles was stricken with a vascular lesion in the brain. Ninety-one years old, he deteriorated rapidly and died at the end of the month. The local Presbyterian minister, who had married Charles to Pearl, conducted the funeral service and praised him as "a great teacher, a helpful physician." Karl and Will (Edwin remained in Florida) followed the pallbearers to Charles's cemetery plot, adjacent to Flo's. Karl found it difficult to put his feelings into words: "I'm sixty now. I'll soon be old." Asked by the editors of the staff newsletter for a personal statement on his father, he quoted from a memorandum Will had prepared for the occasion: "The greatest honor we could do him is to carry on. His spirit will remain all around the place." But Will acknowledged in his diary that he felt isolated and alone without Charles, and that "there wasn't any senior partner now—or senior generation."[54]

Karl had been chief of staff since earlier in the year and had assumed other functions that limited both the time and the attention he could channel into this primary position. He was responsible for MSP activities at Winter Hospital and Topeka State. He also supervised the directors of four MSP support programs (clinical psychology, psychiatric social work, psychiatric nursing, and occupational therapy) plus the staff of the *Bulletin of the Menninger Clinic* and the Menninger Research Monographs series. In addition, he had separate if overlapping responsibilities as chief federal consultant for the Winter VA program. Although his *Manual for Psychiatric Case Study* had been published in 1952, he was considering the preparation of another book on psychoanalytic technique. His Saturday morning colloquium consumed additional time, and he taught classes in both the MSP and the Topeka Institute for Psychoanalysis. On top of these responsibilities, he remained one of the few TIP training analysts and stayed active in the institute's governance.

But Karl had an almost unlimited supply of energy and could direct an enormous array of activities when he wanted to do so. He might have been a vigorous chief of staff and provided a more viable Menninger presence on the home campus. Yet he lacked a zest for his new duties; he was preoccupied with philosophic and ethical concerns.

Two of Karl's published essays for the period reveal what these concerns were. One, "A Psychiatric Fable," dealt with "John Smith," a psychiatric resident in Karl's MSP program. Smith was neither excessively intelligent nor articulate. His staff presentations and case conference reports "were rather dull," and he "rarely got any praise from the service chiefs." Smith did not seem to grasp all the subtleties of psychoanalytic theory or to pursue a research specialty. Moreover, he never pushed like the other residents to secure a training analysis. He displayed neither great promise nor brilliance and "wasn't made chairman of anything or secretary of anything, or even sergeant-at-arms." Having accumulated this less than impressive record, Smith wondered toward the end of his third year of residency whether he had much of a future as a psychiatrist— whether any "good positions" would be open to him.[55]

Despite the apparent mediocrity of his record, however, Smith's "patients loved him," while the hospital nurses and aides "thought he was a man they could trust." He enjoyed being with his patients, to whom he devoted a great deal of time (including Sunday afternoons and holidays). Even though he received a low mark in his psychotherapy course, Smith's patients "all seemed to improve." If he never mastered any specialized body of psychiatric knowledge, Smith was "the best all-round psychiatrist in the hospital."[56]

Only a few years before he wrote "A Psychiatric Fable," Karl and Knight had made intellectuality, articulateness, and scholarship important criteria in the selection of residents. Doctors like John Smith, who would probably not publish in psychiatric specialty journals or assume leadership roles in professional organizations, had often been rejected for the MSP program. Now, in 1950, Karl was questioning the very selection standards he had instituted. More fundamentally, he was questioning what historian Burton J. Bledstein has called the "culture of professionalism." This was a generalized "social faith in [individual] merit, competence, discipline, and control," which had taken firm root in American universities and spread to other institutions as the basis for conceptions of achievement and success. What mattered most in this culture were the professional qualities an individual developed; it mattered less how students, patients, and other recipients benefited from the professional's actions. Because articulateness, publication, mastery of highly specialized bodies of knowledge, and peer recognition were more basic to the evaluation process in psychiatry than the improvement of patients, Karl realized that doctors like John Smith would be found wanting even though they were among the few psychiatrists whose patients always "seemed to improve." This suggested that though the MSP had made Menninger an international center, its values might be misplaced. Karl questioned whether the foundation actually represented an improvement over the prewar center of the "family spirit."[57]

Karl subsequently acknowledged that the resemblance between "John Smith" and Charles Menninger was hardly happenstance. Like Smith, Charles's medical interests had never been limited to psychiatry, and he demonstrated talents beyond his medical duties. Like Smith, Charles could fix "the radiator in the men's toilet" and repair "a patient's cigarette lighter." Charles, like Smith, was deeply committed to people of all classes and callings; he had always been willing to lend a helping hand irrespective of professional or pecuniary benefits. Smith "went on picnics with the patients and played cards with the aides . . . and helped the nurses to get up a dance. . . . He relieved an aide . . . and listened sympathetically to a social worker." For decades, Charles had been esteemed for precisely these qualities. As Karl questioned the advancement of his renowned organization, he was asking whether it had bypassed the values of a generalist and humanist like his father.[58]

If John Smith very closely approximated Charles in his strengths, he resembled Karl in his deficiencies. Smith was "no social lion" (Karl frequently felt awkward in social situations). More fundamentally, Smith had strong self-doubts despite his diligent efforts to do good: "he wondered if he was any good at all as a psychiatrist." Karl, too, had deeply questioned his adequacy for as long as he could remember.[59]

It was more than coincidence that Karl gave John Smith both Charles's warm and caring qualities and his own self-doubts. "A Psychiatric Fable" ended with the residents at large rejecting Smith as "the most brilliant and the most likely to become [professionally] successful" among them. But then senior residents and faculty selected him as "the best all-round psychiatrist." Karl would have outpolled Charles as the more brilliant and successful Dr. Menninger. But in the end, Charles may have been "the best all-round," owing to the breadth of his interests and his caring, compassionate qualities. Karl seemed to be wondering whether, despite the professional recognition he had achieved for the foundation, it would have been a more compassionate and better "all-round" workplace if Charles's qualities had dominated his own.[60]

Questioning the professionalism and progress of his organization, Karl could hardly have been enthusiastic about his new chief of staff duties. But more than doubts about the nature of professionalism nagged at him in these years to limit his interest in home campus leadership responsibilities. Late in 1953, he published a second essay, "What the Girls Told," which revealed as much of what troubled him as had "A Psychiatric Fable." It was an extended commentary, for the *Saturday Review,* on Alfred Kinsey's new book, *Sexual Behavior in the Human Female.* [61]

Just as Karl had embraced pervasive professional criteria for selecting residents, he had praised Kinsey's historic 1948 volume, *Sexual Behavior in the Human Male.* More than Freud or Havelock Ellis, he felt, Kinsey's first volume crushed "the iron curtain of social hypocrisy." Kinsey's mastery of new and highly specialized quantitative and other scientific research techniques had enabled him to present systematic data that documented the many varieties of human sexual experience. The first book, Karl had maintained, properly showed "that individual variation [in sexual activity] deserves respect, and not intolerant condemnation." But though Kinsey's 1953 volume was not methodologically and thematically much different from the first, Karl no longer praised the innovative specialty research. He attacked Kinsey for a "compulsion to force human behavior into a zoological frame of reference." In the process, Karl angrily condemned "hard" quantitative social research, highly specialized research generally, and a pervasive relativism underlying all such endeavors. [62]

Karl's critique of Kinsey was two-pronged. First, he charged that by simply counting varieties of human sexual activity and suggesting that those sexual ventures that "let out" the most chemical energy (i.e., orgasm) were "the better," Kinsey had typified much of modern social and even biological science. He had left "the impression that it is possible to describe the mechanics of human behavior in purely physical and chemical terms." But unlike more primitive life forms, Karl insisted, a human being could not be understood without "mystic vagaries" that could hardly be measured, such as love and hate. Without considering love and its opposite, one ended up equating the orgasm "of a loving husband in the arms of his wife" with the orgasm "of a violent and sadistic brute raping a child." Kinsey and his systematic statistics had failed to distinguish true love from the brute sexuality of the rapist, which "represents an abnormal state of affairs in the human being." This led to Karl's second and more passionate criticism of the book. He scored Kinsey for belittling morality and assuming that all sexual release was useful. There were morally appropriate norms in society and inappropriate norms. Those that were based on sound "religious training" were to be followed, even if they invoked guilt feelings that prompted sexual restraints. Karl noted that in *Civilization and Its Discontents,* Freud had shown how restraints on sexuality were inevitable in modern society. But he went one step further than Freud in his assault on Kinsey. Morally based social restraints were proper and useful, Karl insisted, even if they induced guilt. He concluded that there were higher if more subjective values in life than "the achievement of frequent orgasm."[63]

Karl's tone of moral indignation toward Kinsey resembled Flo's assaults on social improprieties. Like his mother, Karl was playing the part of the pious missionary battling against the sins of modern relativism. The frequency with which people engaged in sinful acts did not make those acts proper. Yet Kinsey's writing was apparently lifting "the feelings of guilt from hundreds of thousands of readers" by allowing them to feel that sexual phenomena like orgasm and homosexuality were normal, natural, and therefore moral, simply because they were prevalent. Much as Flo had criticized Karl for embracing the selfish if increasingly pervasive immoralities of the day by divorcing Grace, he was attacking Kinsey for equating prevalence with normality and normality with morality.[64]

Flo's influence on the essay went further, helping us to understand Karl's inconsistency in attacking Kinsey's book on female sexual behavior while avoiding equally applicable criticism of the volume on male behavior. Clearly, female sexual interests and activities troubled Karl far more. Indeed, while his essay was titled "What the Girls Told," he never alluded to what women actually had to say to Kinsey and his colleagues. The closest he came was to report that though he had "no adding machine in my office" when he talked to women patients, he would put the incidence of female adultery lower than Kinsey had and the frequency of frigidity much higher. There was almost a prudery in Karl's discussion. It was as if Flo were looking over his shoulder as he wrote and admonishing him that sexuality (above all, female sexuality) was a subject best left undiscussed. If discourse on male sexuality also ran against Flo's austere nineteenth-century evangelical values, women as moral guardians of the hearth had nothing to tell investigators of Kinsey's ilk.[65]

Taken together, "A Psychiatric Fable" and "What the Girls Told" indicated where Karl stood in 1953 when he assumed his chief of staff duties. He seemed to be retreating from those "modern" and "liberal" professional and personal values that became increasingly evident during the postwar decade. Both essays also represented affirmations of his parents. They pointed to Karl's effort, quite late in middle age, to somehow piece together values and standards Charles and Flo had given him, in order to build an integrated sense of selfhood.

It was a most difficult task, for neither essay represented an unmitigated affirmation of his parents' values. Both included elements of tenta-

tiveness, which characterized a mind in flux. Karl was not about to eliminate the values of psychiatric professionalism, "John Smith" and Charles
Menninger notwithstanding. Nor was he ready to mandate "religious
training" and Flo's moral standards as a precondition for permissible
sexual activity. In a way typical of his more popular earlier writings, Karl
decidedly overstated his case. Below the seeming certitude of the essays
there was a struggle to arrive at satisfying compromises between his
parents and contemporary values.

Only months before his critique of Kinsey, Karl delivered a paper to
a conference of rabbis in Saint Louis, which underscored the importance
of these compromises. Titled "Psychiatry Looks at Religion," the paper
sought to reconcile modern psychoanalytic psychiatry with Judeo-Chris-
tian traditions and values. Karl wrote in an equivocal tone and made one
vague pronouncement after another. He spoke, for example, of an overlap between the functions of modern psychiatrists and traditional clergy:
"Both of them are actually dedicated to the same purpose and, to a
considerable extent, use the same methods insofar as both appeal to the
intelligence of suppliants. Both of us combat trouble in the individual."
Indeed, the only part of the paper that reached beyond vague if reassuring rhetoric was where Karl felt compelled to acknowledge Freud's claim
that religion was merely an illusion. But even here, Karl's commitment
to reconciliation precluded a cogent and significant assessment. He noted
instead that "an illusion is not a delusion" and that art and music also
conveyed illusions. He insisted that "Freud did not mean to say that the
religious experience was negligible or that it was false, or that it was
nonexistent." In the end, Karl had to acknowledge that Freud was against
"certain forms developed in the name of religion," but so were Isaiah,
Jeremiah, and Jesus.[66]

Fortunately, most of Karl's energy went into clear and sincere efforts
to weave his parents' values into an integrated sense of himself. For the
most part, he affirmed verbally what Charles and Flo had exemplified,
while adapting to certain pervasive practices and eschewing efforts to
reconcile the two.

It was these preoccupations with the values of his parents, the professional aims of the foundation, and the moral dimensions of modern
society that explain why it was so difficult for Karl to cope with his duties
and to establish a presence on the home campus, however important his
responsibilities there were. A senior hospital psychiatrist complained that
Karl was "out of touch" with the campus. A staff psychologist observed
that Karl's extra time and energy were channeled into reading, writing,
and discussing more general matters of modern culture and ethics. Much

like the 1930s, between publication of *The Human Mind* and *Man Against Himself*, Karl was conserving his energy for deeper reflections.[67]

Consequently, the year 1953 ended with some conspicuous absences on the home campus. John Stone and Robert Knight were no longer there. Will was spending most of his time on the road. Charles had died in November. Karl was a visible reminder that Menninger was still a family institution, but his thoughts were elsewhere. It was almost as if the Menningers had vacated their grounds.

CHAPTER NINE

The Rapaport Group

As the presence and the authority of the Menningers on the home campus receded, the efforts of Lester Roach's administrative team to coordinate budgets and operations became crucial. But research psychologists also became an increasingly important factor in these years of transition.

During the war, David Rapaport had assembled a small group of young research-oriented psychologists. The group quickly transformed postwar psychological services into a vibrant department. Rapaport and his followers also established a separate research department, which made clinical and even experimental research important parts of foundation operations. Perhaps the major contribution of Rapaport's circle, however, was to provide national leadership in transforming the role of psychologists outside academia.

Before 1941, psychology had been an academic science concerned with the understanding of human behavior. The profession had attracted only a small wing of practitioners who were attentive to the treatment of mental disorders in a clinical setting. During World War I, some psychologists had been called upon to administer intelligence tests as screening devices in determining whether military recruits were fit to serve. And during the interwar period, a number of psychologists left academia to become full-time administrators of mental tests within clinical facilities under the supervision of psychiatrists. By the late 1930s, some clinical psychologists had even assumed modest roles in patient therapy; a few conducted psychoanalysis. But these therapeutic ventures provoked a backlash, as psychiatrists grew apprehensive of the diagnostic skills and of the potential for independent practice among the psychologists they supervised. On the eve of World War II, several prominent psychiatrists lobbied for stricter control and limitations on clinical psychologists.[1]

As America entered the war and Rapaport began to organize his group, however, conditions undermined this lobby. Thousands of troops required treatment. The armed forces had no choice but to allow psychologists to move beyond their traditional testing functions and become active partners with psychiatrists in the treatment process. Will was among the most ardent advocates of a strong clinical psychology presence on military psychiatric treatment teams, on discharge boards, and in therapy review agencies. By March 1944, he wrote with elation to Catharine that he had finally succeeded in getting "psychologists included in the table of organization of our larger [army] hospitals." Karl endorsed Will's army reforms and extended their spirit to the Menninger hospital while Will was away. With far too few psychiatrists and nurses to treat patients, Karl allowed several of his clinical psychologists to assist in the treatment process. Because they had few qualms about assigning increased responsibilities to psychologists, neither brother stood in the way as Rapaport and his colleagues moved into the treatment realm.[2]

The Rapaport group hired additional psychologists and encouraged them to become active in most phases of the treatment process. Indeed, after Rapaport established the Menninger School of Clinical Psychology as a component of the MSP, his group recruited trainees from all over the country. When both the Veterans Administration and the National Institute of Mental Health began to provide financial incentives for institutions that trained clinical psychologists, the Menninger Foundation became a beneficiary of that largess. By the late 1940s, as clinical psychology and psychological counseling came to account for over 40 percent of all psychology positions in the United States, Menninger was recognized as one of the major training facilities.[3]

But if the Rapaport group turned Topeka into a center for practice and training in clinical psychology, members did not forsake the tradition of the psychologist as scholar. Rapaport was a scholar's scholar. He demanded from his associates precise and painstaking analysis of text, research from primary sources, and publication in respected scholarly journals. Members published some of the landmark studies on perceptual styles, the psychology of infancy, alcoholism, psychological testing, hypnotherapy, and even the selection of candidates for psychiatric residency. At the same time, Rapaport became perhaps the major systematizer of Freudian theoretical writings.

These scholarly ventures underscored a firm pledge to intellectualism. The commitment caused many in Rapaport's group to feel isolated on the home campus. John Stone acknowledged that the group's dedication to the life of the mind often made its members feel like outcasts.[4]

The group felt less isolated at Winter Hospital. The MSP fellows

there prized their values of intellectual inquiry and scholarship. Rapaport
was one of the most respected classroom instructors, and his circle's
training supervision in psychological testing and research techniques was
valued. But their popularity at Winter had its limits. Most fellows there
had chosen to be psychiatrists. Like doctors in psychiatric residency elsewhere, many were less than comfortable with the insistence of psychologists upon rigorous application of statistical analysis, control groups, and
other behavioral science techniques. Most ranked a fine psychiatrist-
therapist like Robert Knight above a psychology scholar and researcher
like Rapaport.[5]

Nevertheless, Rapaport's national prominence and grant-harvesting
potential gave the members of his group much political leverage. They
used it in ways that limited pressure from the Menningers and checked
some of the demands of the MSP program at Winter. Indeed, Rapaport
emerged as a "baron" dedicated to the advancement of his group and the
"territory" under group authority. He created a new leadership style at
Menninger.

I I

On July 2, 1940, Menninger employees received a formal staff announcement of a new appointment in the small Psychology Department. It was
to go to a young Hungarian émigré whom Karl had recently met at nearby
Osawatomie State Hospital. In the course of a demonstration, David
Rapaport had administered Rorschach and Szondi tests to Karl and provided a lengthy and sophisticated report on the results. Although Karl
was clearly taken by Rapaport, his credentials seemed strange to the
Menninger staff. He had earned a Montessori degree in kindergarten
teaching as well as a doctorate in psychology at Budapest's Royal Hungarian University. Rapaport had also taken a personal analysis with Theo-
dor Rajka. Hired to institute a new Menninger program in psychological
testing, he had only a philosophic and academic background to draw
upon. Rapaport learned diagnostic testing techniques almost entirely on
his own. Though a Freudian, he was attracted to Kurt Lewin's general
theory of psychological forces and its premise that intentions were inter-
mediate forces rooted in "wish dynamics" that sought out instinctual
satisfaction.[6]

In the months after Rapaport arrived in Topeka, staff discovered that
he was even less likely than his European predecessors to blend smoothly
into the "family spirit" of the place. He was intense and restless, worked
endless hours, and expected others to do the same. His badly damaged,

rheumatic heart led him to feel that his days were numbered, and he carried on as if life were a race against time. An insomniac, he read half the night and taught himself to make notes in the dark while tossing in bed. Like earlier émigrés, Rapaport spoke broken English, mixing it with Hungarian and Yiddish expressions. Staff members found him difficult to comprehend, and some patients could not understand him at all. Although not very religious, he was deeply attached to Jewish culture, studied the Talmud, related an endless collection of Yiddish anecdotes and jokes, and considered migrating to Israel. What impressed Menninger staff most was his obvious brilliance. To some, he was the equal of Karl. Those who became his close associates considered him to be Karl's intellectual superior. But neither the Menninger family nor its organization was quite ready for "another Dr. Karl."[7]

Rapaport had been invited to Topeka to assist and eventually replace Junius F. Brown, a Yale psychology Ph.D. who had taught full time at the University of Kansas since 1932. Brown began quarter-time duties as a Menninger research associate in 1936 and came to be referred to as chief Menninger psychologist in 1939, even though he retained full faculty status in Lawrence. He had administered intelligence and Rorschach tests to incoming patients but had never made testing crucial to hospital and clinical operations. Nor had he built a research staff. Karl realized that he could not count on Brown to establish a significant presence for psychology or research in the organization. Consequently, he hired Rapaport. Although Will acquiesced in the appointment and, like everyone else, considered the man brilliant, he sensed that Rapaport had "a lot of stiff European customs" that made him "either too stubborn or too opinionated to work with happily." Upstaged by the émigré who had taken the initiative in both the testing and the research programs, Brown soon resigned.[8]

Rapaport had begun to recruit his group before Brown left. Margaret Brenman had been working on a dissertation concerning hypnotic techniques under Brown at the University of Kansas. In the fall of 1941, she transferred to the Brown-Rapaport Psychology Department, where she was an assistant in psychological testing and in experimental work on hypnosis as a form of psychotherapy. When Brown departed the following year, Brenman became Rapaport's second in command, commenced a formal hypnosis research project, and helped find other psychologists who were interested in research. She and Rapaport recognized that this research would have to grow out of their clinical duties. The Menningers were willing to allow them to staff a psychology department, but only if the psychologists focused on clinical tasks, mainly testing.[9]

Working within this framework, Rapaport and Brenman discovered

Merton Gill, who, like them, was Jewish. In an organization that had hoped to limit the number of Jewish staff, this gave a unique social quality to the emerging group. Gill, besides his doctorate in psychology from the University of Chicago, had the advantage, within the physician-centered Menninger setting, of an M.D. degree from the University of Chicago Medical School. He had interned at Michael Reese and come to Topeka as a psychiatric resident. Gill also had the benefit of some analysis with Harry Levey. But like Rapaport and Brenman, he identified himself primarily as a psychological researcher and not as an analyst or a physician. He was eager to investigate aspects of psychosomatic medicine.[10]

In the summer of 1942, the Menninger executive committee assented to Rapaport's request for a formal Research Committee to promote the "concentration of research in the hands of a few investigators whose time will be mainly allotted to research." Rapaport chaired the committee and chose Robert Knight as a second member to bolster it within the organization. By appointing Merton Gill as the third member, he was tacitly recognizing that Gill had replaced Brenman as second in command of his group. The Research Committee became a separate department with a separate budget. More than the Psychology Department, it became the locus of Rapaport operations. It also provided an institutional mechanism within which to press for the hiring of psychologists with strong research potential. From the 1940s until at least the 1970s, Research Department psychologists exerted major influence upon the Psychology Department.[11]

Roy Schafer, Sibylle Escalona, and Martin Mayman were precisely the sort of recruits Rapaport sought for his informal group and his new Research Department. He brought Schafer from CCNY in 1943. Having only a bachelor's degree, Schafer came as a psychology intern. Rapaport soon came to love him like a son, appointed him a resident psychologist, and called upon him for assistance in the preparation of a massive book on psychological testing. Half a year after Schafer arrived, Escalona joined the group. She had fled with her parents from Germany in 1934 and had studied at Iowa under Kurt Lewin. When Rapaport questioned her as to her highest goal in psychology, she said she wanted to remain true to psychoanalytic ideas but never to use the word "instinct." "Very good; you're hired," Rapaport replied. He felt he could count on her to help him bring Freud's ideas into closer proximity to clinical data. He helped Escalona begin a research project on the psychological nature of infancy and was pleased that by working with psychiatrist Eunice Mary Leitch, Escalona drew the young Canadian physician into some of the group's activities. Rapaport was also pleased that Escalona championed "individual liberty" and mutual respect within his group; this represented a healthy check on his tendency toward overbearing leadership.[12]

Martin Mayman arrived in 1944. Like Schafer, he was a scholarly Jew from CCNY who came to Menninger initially as a psychology intern and then as a resident psychologist. More comfortable with academia than Schafer, he later took a master's degree at New York University and a doctorate at the University of Kansas. Because of Mayman's interest in early ego psychology, Rapaport felt that he, like Escalona, could help him to link Freud's diverse theoretical writings to clinical endeavors. During this period, Rapaport also expressed interest in some of émigré psychologist Paul Bergman's work on the way children managed anxiety. But certain of Bergman's reservations regarding psychoanalysis led to bitter clashes with Rapaport; he never had more than peripheral status in the group.[13]

The opening of the Menninger School of Clinical Psychology in the fall of 1946 brought fifteen doctoral students to Topeka and justified the hiring of several junior-level psychologists. A few of the new staff and certain of the students were incorporated into the Rapaport group. George Klein was the most highly prized among the newcomers. Rapaport had been pursuing him for several years. A Columbia University Ph.D., he was interested in experimental psychology but also fascinated with metapsychology. Although Rapaport was troubled by Klein's absent-mindedness and his disposition to procrastinate, he recognized that the psychologist could help his group to integrate psychoanalytic theory with quantifiable clinical data and experimental laboratory findings. So could Robert Holt, who had also come to Topeka in 1946. With a recent Harvard doctorate in psychology, Holt taught in the MSP clinical psychology program. He was slowly integrated into the Rapaport group through his skillful work in the Resident Selection Project. Lester Luborsky, his chief associate in that project, earned his doctorate at Duke, briefly taught psychology at the University of Illinois, and joined the Psychology Department in 1947. Two other, more junior figures, Philip Holzman and Herbert Schlesinger, completed their doctorates in the School of Clinical Psychology's cooperative program with the University of Kansas. The quality of their clinical work and the intriguing link between psychological theory and clinical data in their dissertation projects impressed both Rapaport and Klein. Schafer trained them in clinical techniques, and they slowly became immersed in the group spirit. They helped Klein build a laboratory for perception research, and the three became especially close. Finally, there was Milton Wexler, whose age and wide experience distinguished him from several of his associates. Wexler started out as a

New York lawyer in the 1930s, earned an M.A. degree in psychology at Columbia in 1940, taught for a few years at the University of Tennessee, and served as chief of the Test and Research Division of the Army Engineers during part of the war. He arrived in Topeka as a Winter Hospital psychologist in 1946 while completing his dissertation at Columbia. But Wexler quickly lost interest in academic psychology as he began to use new analytically informed techniques on Winter patients. He never regarded Rapaport with the reverence of the others and sometimes sought relief from the intensity of the group.[14]

Although the Rapaport group expanded to twelve after the war, it remained small and intimate. All but Escalona and Holt were Jewish. Women, especially Brenman and Escalona, were quite influential. Indeed, Brenman had an acolyte in psychologist Gerald Ehrenreich. According to Rapaport, Brenman was primarily responsible for "a personal warmth of human relation," while Escalona was concerned with members' rights. Other women, like Eunice Mary Leitch, Suzanna Reichard, Elaine Grimm, Louisa Holt (Robert's wife), and Winter staff psychologist Marilyn Barnard, were also welcome to join in some discussions, research projects, and social affairs. In part, this extensive female participation is explained by the greater proportion of women historically within the psychology profession than within psychiatry.[15]

The political tendencies of Rapaport's group also singled it out. Members were likely to support Henry Wallace's Progressive party, to oppose universal military service, to find fault with atomic bomb alert drills in the public schools, and to support sporadic efforts by segments of the Menninger organization to unionize. Rapaport, Brenman, and Gill helped to initiate a food cooperative. Strong academic backgrounds also distinguished the group from other parts of the Menninger community. As well, all members were analyzed—either before or in the course of their Topeka years. This was the source of no little prestige.[16]

Despite these common characteristics, members sometimes broke into distinctive social circles. Brenman, Gill, and Schafer were always close. Klein arrived later but was regarded as part of this "older" group. Because of their work on the Selection Project, Holt and Luborsky became close. As postwar doctoral students with shared interests in perception research, Holzman and Schlesinger met often. However, these social bonding patterns were dwarfed by the power of Rapaport's leadership, which was the major factor behind group cohesion. Merton Gill found that the direct personal connection that members of the group had to Rapaport was their most thrilling and compelling influence at Menninger. Reflecting on life in Topeka a few years after he left, Rapaport agreed. The group there "was based always on direct personal contact of mine with anybody and everybody."[17]

Indeed, Rapaport based his leadership on meticulous attention to each of his associates. Individuals recalled how he asked them into his office before departing in the evening and read each a special poem, an insightful paragraph from Freud, or some passage that he found inspirational. Members also experienced what may have resembled paternal qualities in Rapaport's disposition to protect them against Karl's periodic and sometimes disconcerting intrusions. And he assisted generously with career advancement and even personal needs. George Klein observed that Rapaport prized connectedness—personal and professional—to his associates.[18]

At the same time, several of the group found his European manner overbearing. Rapaport demanded propriety and formality in personal relationships. He insisted that colleagues address one another by professional title and surname, became angry when this standard was breached, and took years to reach a first-name basis with those closest to him. Associates rarely got to see Rapaport after hours. He worked incessantly and had almost no social life.[19]

Rapaport's preference for formal titles befitted the authoritarian manner in which he directed his group. Although he professed to abhor discipleship and remarked that "I'm just a little Jew from Budapest," he carried himself as though he were a venerable sage—a brilliant tyrant. According to Mayman, "He was the house intellectual . . . and what he said people accepted as the voice of authority." Whenever he made a major point, Brenman noted, he pronounced it in a loud, evangelical, and absolutely authoritarian tone that hardly promoted discussion. Holt agreed, recalling that however experienced a psychologist might be in a particular clinical or research operation, when he worked with Rapaport he relearned the technique Rapaport's way. "I was content to be Rapaport's boy," Gill remembered; one did not question or oppose the leader. Frederick Hacker felt that he never became part of the group because he was outspoken and insufficiently submissive to the leader.[20]

In his demeanor, Rapaport resembled a Prussian taskmaster. He criticized loose thinking, expected data to be collected with the utmost care, wanted reports rewritten until they were flawless, and required that all assertions be supported with precise and abundant references. Even in casual conversation, Rapaport felt his associates should be able to cite technical details from memory, as he could. He insisted that they recall page numbers for key passages in scholarly texts and remember patients' test results. In the lore of the group, there is the story of Rapaport providing a new psychology student with a two-inch pile of papers. He instructed the student to "read them so carefully that if I should stick a pin through these papers you could tell me what word the pin is piercing."[21]

The group was almost totally dependent upon Rapaport's leadership. "It was usually I who picked up the ideas of others and took the initiative and action, or helped to implement them," Rapaport recalled. He drew upon the findings of each of his associates, integrated them with those of other colleagues, and in this way "remained the motor of execution" for projects and findings—the group's major research contributions. "There is no question that . . . Rapaport was the creative energy and creativity for most of our decisions," Brenman recalled. He was "the one who could always see where the original observation point fit." Without Rapaport constantly looking over his shoulder, Holt felt, he was "skating on thin ice" in his research. He could not connect it well to broader conceptual and factual findings. According to Escalona, Rapaport nurtured all members of the group, showing them how to establish connections between their findings and those of colleagues (and scholarly literature generally) in an intricate and satisfying weave. Cautious in his published papers, he encouraged his group "to express in conversation the most wildly and wonderfully creative ideas." By keeping "contact with everybody and their work," Rapaport was a wonderful facilitator. Guiding each member of the group, he built a viable unit by placing the individual's work in a fundamentally important collective context.[22]

Rapaport effected within his group a result entirely compatible with a trend in American psychological research during the 1940s. Eschewing an earlier tradition in which the psychologist conducted investigations primarily on his own, leading research psychologists of the decade came to embrace coordinated and cooperative ventures. The benefits were the reduction of the personal and idiosyncratic biases of the investigator, and more specialized and efficient division of labor. Rapaport embraced these goals and felt comfortable promoting leadership and cooperation within his group.[23]

III

Clearly, David Rapaport was not the sort of staff associate the Menninger brothers were accustomed to. Until now, Karl and Will had developed all Menninger institutions. But Rapaport was an institution builder in his own right. In creating and superintending his informal research group (which gave leadership to the research and psychology departments), he put a capstone on the first Menninger "barony."

Neither brother felt entirely comfortable with Rapaport's leadership and ambitions. Will was the more tolerant, although he could feel "a bit worn down after an interview with him"; conversations tended to be "tense, difficult affairs because Dave always feels so strongly and intensely about things." Will also resented Rapaport's strong and almost threatening tone in negotiating money matters for himself, for his two departments, and especially for his group. Yet he knew that "Dave is a stimulating fellow," with admirable "industry and ability," who had contributed much to the prestige of the foundation. For this reason, he was disturbed when in 1948 Rapaport announced his resignation: "we will miss you very, very much and I shall always feel that you are a part of us."[24]

In contrast, Karl never considered Rapaport entirely "a part of us." From his first meeting with Rapaport at Osawatomie, he was attracted primarily by Rapaport's mind and his professional ability. "We have a great and constantly increasing respect for the results of Doctor Rapaport's testing," he told Ruth Mack Brunswick. Owing to his testing skills and his brilliance, Rapaport was "probably the best clinical psychologist in the United States," Karl boasted in 1944. Two years later, he and Rapaport coauthored a paper for the annual meeting of the American Psychiatric Association on the importance of psychological testing for clinical diagnosis. Such direct and visible cooperation between a leading psychiatrist and a prominent psychologist was significant. It contrasted with the growing fears of psychiatrists that if psychologists continued to enter the clinical realm, medical degrees would count for little. As a measure of Karl's initial respect for Rapaport, he had urged his oldest daughter, Julia, to learn psychological test procedures from him in the hope that she might become one of his associates.[25]

Acknowledging Rapaport's remarkable skill in psychological testing and recognizing his ability to develop new programs, Karl gave him a free hand in building new departments and cultivating his informal research group. Karl recounted how he and Rapaport remained very close until the mid-1940s, when Rapaport gave him the draft of his manual on psychological testing to critique. Rapaport had used the term "subtest" to describe parts of the Wechsler Adult Intelligence Scale. Contemptuous of professional jargon, Karl asked, "What kind of test can be a 'subtest,' either it's a test or it's not a test." Rapaport became enraged at this criticism, Karl recalled, and never forgave him.[26]

The basis for a rift between the two men went deeper, of course.

Unlike Karl, Rapaport did not characterize that incident as cause for a fundamental erosion in their relationship. Half a decade after he departed from Topeka, Rapaport noted that "in Karl I had a support which, irascible and unreliable as it was, sustained me through the worst times."[27] Like many others in the organization, he was accustomed to Karl's mercurial temperament and his disdain for technical language.

The rift was rooted in the fact that David Rapaport and Karl Menninger were very much alike. Each regarded the other as stormy and stubborn, yet intellectually profound. To his friend Lawrence Kubie, Karl described Rapaport as "a little turbulent" and unyielding in his demands but "a real thinker." Conversing with Margaret Brenman, Rapaport described Karl as brilliant but temperamental and advised her how to get along with him: "You have to do like in Germany. You kiss the one above. You kick the one below." Another member of the group (who prefers to remain anonymous) characterized both leaders as "brilliant tyrant[s], impulsive & often maddening." Robert Holt concurred; both men were "second to nobody" and were "deferred to" through their vast intellectual and emotional power. When he visited Topeka in the mid-1940s, Erik Erikson predicted a falling out because both Karl and Rapaport were hotheaded thinkers and neither would defer to the other when differences arose.[28]

Considering their personalities, conflict was inevitable. Rapaport could be enraged when Karl monopolized the time of distinguished visitors like Erikson. Similarly, Karl became furious when he learned that Rapaport, in a characteristic display of elitism, sought to restrict hospital seminars to staff psychologists. Tensions reached the point where Rapaport felt it necessary to write accounts of each of his meetings with Karl in order to protect himself against potentially unwarranted charges. Similarly, Karl periodically felt compelled to break off contact with Rapaport for months at a time.[29]

In addition to temperamental incompatibilities, there was a structural dimension to their increasing inability to get along. Karl assumed that all vital foundation matters were to be coordinated through him. Even though MSP fellows developed a strong culture of their own, for example, he was determined to curb independent dimensions of student activity. He felt more directly threatened by Rapaport's overtly territorial maneuvers for his group. More than a personality squabble, the deepening division derived from competing concepts of institutional leadership.

Rapaport had not been at Menninger a year before he was fighting with the executive committee for more office space and an enlarged allocation for expenses. By early 1944, he had successfully persuaded the brothers to help pay for a research building consisting of fourteen offices plus laboratories and classrooms to house his staff. This occurred despite the difficulty of construction amid wartime shortages. Four years later, he requested even more office space for the Research Department, although there was an acute drain on home campus work space.[30]

Rapaport also fought successfully to recruit staff with research potential. He saw to it that talented researchers, especially those within his group, had time free from clinical duties for their investigations. Rapaport's vigorous recruitment efforts and his capacity to free up his staff for research reached the point where the executive committee (prodded by Karl) passed a resolution in June 1946 barring him from assigning clinicians to research projects without the approval of the chief of staff.[31]

Rapaport's success in accumulating resources and personnel without answering directly to Karl came largely because he made members of his group indispensable to clinical operations. Realizing that involvement in these operations enhanced his bargaining power for research needs, he saw to it that psychological testing of every incoming patient by his colleagues became an established routine at both Menninger and Winter. When physicians were in short supply on the home campus, the psychological test sometimes even replaced the initial psychiatric examination. Clinical operations could hardly proceed without the Rapaport group, and Karl knew it.[32]

The clearest sign of Rapaport's success, however, was in the formal training analysis, which was important to power and prestige in the Menninger psychiatric community. Without access to that analysis, it was almost impossible to retain skilled clinical psychologists; Rapaport would not have been able to keep promising staff like Brenman and Schafer. Yet there were only a handful of training analysts at Menninger, and each of them had a long waiting list of MSP residents. It was a measure of Rapaport's political skill that he circumvented not only Karl but the American Psychoanalytic Association ban on lay analysis by arranging training analyses for all members of his group who sought them.[33]

Given Rapaport's accumulation of power, it is small wonder that his relationship with Karl grew strained. This was unfortunate, for it undermined the potential for close collaboration between the two leading intellectuals of the organization. In *Man Against Himself,* Karl had begun to rethink the traditional psychiatric dichotomy between mental sickness and health. With far more detail than any other prewar Freudian, he had characterized a continuum on which people moved between illness and health. By 1947, Rapaport fully embraced this perspective; the normal and the psychopathological were "parts of the same continuum." Realizing that they were very close in perspective, the two men talked of serious scholarly collaboration. Karl recalled that they even considered "making research our main activity," since the MSP program had "put at our disposal so much more clinical material." But enmity prevailed, and major collaborative projects were never undertaken. Perhaps as a result, education more than research was the major emphasis at Menninger during the postwar years.[34]

IV

Although it never received the acclaim accorded the MSP training program, Rapaport's group was in the forefront of perhaps the most fundamental transformation of the psychological profession in twentieth-century America. In a 1946 paper, Rapaport and Schafer underscored just what they and others in their group sought to achieve. They felt that psychology, growing out of philosophy, remained too much a reclusive profession, operated within the protective walls of academia. Academic psychologists focused upon abstract comprehension of personality but were hardly committed to relieving mental suffering. "Academic university courses are too remote from everyday clinical work," they added. These courses emphasized traditional philosophic issues and behaviorism, belittling psychoanalysis and a myriad of issues that concerned the clinician. But this did not mean that Rapaport and Schafer were pleased with those psychologists who somehow found their way into the treatment clinic. Rather, they charged that most were mere technicians. They recorded "lifeless numerical-test results," usually of intelligence tests. But they were impervious to "living clinical dynamics"—to "the qualitative analysis of test results."[35]

In a book published that same year, Rapaport, Schafer, and Gill advanced a proposal to inject new vigor and relevance into clinical psychology. The tester was to eschew practice limited to the technicalities of intelligence testing, becoming instead a full-time clinician with a rich sense of the therapeutic setting. This could be achieved if he devised and administered batteries of both structured and projective tests of intellect and personality in ways that would give him a sense of what ailed the patient. From his findings, he could propose potential remedies. The clinical psychologist also had to become a personality theorist, for clinical testing was not to be detached from general theory. Theories (preferably psychoanalytic) were to inform the design and administration of the test battery. Conversely, data obtained from testing was to enrich theories of personality.[36]

Rapaport, Gill, and Schafer advanced an ambitious agenda for the clinical psychologist of the future. He was to enlarge the scope of psychological testing so that it became integral to treatment and contributed to personality theory through the data gathered. These two pioneering tasks became the broad goals of the Rapaport group. By 1948, they had achieved both goals at Menninger. They demonstrated to colleagues throughout the country that the psychologist could make major contributions as both a treater and a theorist.

At first, the Rapaport group's venture into clinical forms of psychological testing found considerable support at Menninger. Karl warmed to Rapaport's pleas for extensive testing and for integration of the results into all case conferences. Will, with his preference for the specific and the systematic, also encouraged Rapaport's venture. Diagnostic testing held out the hope for "specific measurements for certain aspects of personality in place of appraisals made intuitively or experimentally." Staff psychiatrist Carl Tillman found his colleagues interested in Rapaport's claim that psychological tests could be used for objective data to shore up psychoanalytic constructs. But certain members of the staff, apprehensive of a reduction in their clinical duties, charged that the Rapaport associates were testing too often and too comprehensively; after all, they were only psychologists. Opposition was ineffective. By 1944, Rapaport and his associates had conducted 1,720 tests. They used the relatively new Wechsler-Bellevue intelligence test, the Rorschach and Thematic Apperception tests, the Hanfmann-Kasanin tests, the Babcock Deterioration and Word Association tests, and others that seemed promising.[37]

To carry on an extensive testing program in the clinic, the hospital, and Winter, Rapaport needed a great deal of help from his associates. Although he insisted that those who administered tests be familiar with the clinical and psychological functions that yielded the test data, Rapaport felt awkward working with patients and was not entirely effective. This distinguished him from Karl, who usually showed empathy for and understanding of his patients. Almost always, Rapaport displayed a superior and distant manner toward those he tested.[38]

Rapaport recognized his shortcomings. He imparted his knowledge of the testing process to Roy Schafer and Sibylle Escalona and had them train others in his group. Above all, he taught them to overcome the original conception of psychological tests as x-rays of the mind, which had simply to be reported. That is, they had to do more than summarize test results in descriptive statements or statistical tabulations, for these revealed only surface aspects of deeper psychic structures. It was imperative that they fathom these structures through broad interpretive observations informed by psychoanalytic assumptions. Schafer proved to be perhaps the most skilled clinician-tester of the group. Even Karl was pleased by his clinical manner and his test reports, written in clear English. Despite Schafer's loyalty to Rapaport, Karl was willing to have him teach testing technique and case report writing to the MSP fellows.[39]

Through Schafer's supervision of a much expanded testing program, the Rapaport group influenced clinical operations at Menninger and Winter in striking ways. Rapaport felt he was helping to foster in these facilities an atmosphere "which will introduce academically-trained people to clinical problems and . . . clinical people to clear theoretical systematic thinking. Only this coupling can assure substantial development in psychiatry and clinical psychology."[40]

Rapaport stressed that his group should be committed to learning the terminology, diagnostic skills, and theoretical assumptions of the doctor on the psychiatric ward. By mastering them, the psychologist could develop new testing procedures that would yield superior information and theoretical insights to ward psychiatrists. Since at Menninger, psychiatrists continued to follow the psychoanalytic theory represented in Will's guide to the order sheet, Rapaport drafted test reports consistent with Will's formulations. He explained to his associates that, at least in Topeka, this was the way to bridge the traditional communication gap between psychologist and physician.[41]

Similarly, Rapaport explained to members of the Menninger medical community—psychiatrists, above all—that they had to become more receptive to test reports. Traditional medical diagnoses were too subjective. In the comprehensive test battery, "standard scoring systems provide an organization of the data which is relatively free from such subjective factors." To avoid subjectivity, Rapaport urged his associates to interpret test results blind (without the patient's name). In this way, they would focus on the objective data of the tests and not on the more fallible impressions inherent in the psychiatric examination. By being more objective and thorough in diagnoses, the psychological tester could fathom certain personality disorders that the psychiatric examiner might miss. Indeed, psychiatrists would do well to rely more upon psychological tests and get on with administering therapy rather than delay the therapeutic process through their long, tedious, and often unreliable diagnostic examinations.[42]

Rapaport was virtually arguing for the testing psychologist as an indispensable member of the treatment team. Unlike Adolf Meyer and William Healy, who decades earlier had also pressed for the psychologist to participate on the team, Rapaport conceived of no rigid separation between the psychologist's testing functions and the psychiatrist's psychotherapy responsibilities. When he first came to Topeka, Rapaport had invited himself to patient case conferences. Soon his testing reports constituted an important part of each conference. As he hired other psychologists, he saw to it that their reports were treated similarly. In time, Rapaport insisted that whenever a patient was admitted at Menninger, he was to be assigned to a single psychologist, who would carry him through the full testing process, prepare the testing part of the case report, and interpret test results at the conference. With this opening into treatment, Rapaport's colleagues pressed further. By 1944, two of them were conducting psychotherapy.[43]

Far beyond the role that Meyer and Healy had envisioned for the clinical psychologist, the progress of Rapaport and his colleagues in treating patients was historically unique. Robert Knight observed that they were cultivating the borderland between psychology and psychiatry. Fortunately for Rapaport's group, both the Veterans Administration and the United States Public Health Service provided ample funds in the immediate postwar years to irrigate this borderland.[44]

Nevertheless, most American psychiatrists continued to look down on clinical psychologists and to claim that they had insufficient medical training to participate fully in patient care. Owing to this resistance, psychologists came increasingly to assume that if they were ever to have meaningful roles within the clinical setting, they would have to become autonomous, self-sufficient therapists. Rejecting what the Rapaport group had accomplished as unworkable elsewhere, other clinical psychologists usually had to settle for the "Boulder model," outlined at the American Psychological Association conference in that city in 1949. According to this model, psychology graduate students could for the first time be trained by senior psychologists in entry-level skills necessary for clinical practice after they had received a thorough grounding in general psychology and research. (They had to acquire more advanced clinical skills on their own after they completed graduate studies.) Reaffirmed by other association conferences in the 1950s and 1960s, the "Boulder model" represented a limited opening for formal clinical training in psychology. But it was hardly comparable to the rich interdisciplinary psychologist-psychiatrist tradition that developed in Topeka.[45]

If Rapaport and his group were desirous of becoming integral participants in clinical diagnosis and therapy, they also tried to take testing data and other information obtained through clinical experience and use it to reshape psychological theory. Rapaport taught his associates to use his standard battery—intelligence as well as projective tests—to observe precisely where the patient's impulses intruded or broke through upon his formal thought processes. Marking these points, his colleagues were to describe as precisely as possible how the patient's ego or adaptational defenses dealt with the drive pressures. In this way, they would be offering explanations for personality dynamics that stressed ego functions and would not simply be reporting diagnostic labels or statistical representations on test scales. They would be pioneering in psychoanalytic ego psychology and thereby helping to bridge the long-standing gulf between clinical psychometrics and academic psychology's perennial search for laws governing the organization of thought. At the same time, they hoped to resolve the traditional dichotomy in Freudian circles between the concrete narrative account of the patient's problem and the broader, more abstractly interpretive analytic account. They became involved in the controversy over metapsychology.[46]

The fact that Rapaport and his colleagues used testing to integrate psychometric data with the latest currents in psychoanalytic personality theory contributed to their involvement in this controversy, which would separate the leader from his followers. Rapaport encouraged his group to become involved in clinical work, particularly broad-range testing. But after he published *Diagnostic Psychological Testing* in 1946—a massive and monumental textbook linking psychometric testing with personality theory—he seemed to lose interest in general clinical endeavor. During the late 1940s, abstract metapsychology became almost his all-absorbing preoccupation. Struggling principally with the seventh chapter of Freud's *Interpretation of Dreams* plus Freud's essays "Two Principles of Psychic Functioning," "Unconscious," "Repression," "Negation," and "Instincts and Their Vicissitudes," Rapaport hoped to demonstrate an order and a system to psychoanalytic theory that Freud himself may never have provided. If he succeeded, Rapaport felt he would demonstrate that psychoanalysis was more than "a practical discipline"—that it was "a scientific and rational therapy" and was therefore consistent with the established principles of psychology. Such an accomplishment would cause even the harshest skeptic to admit that psychoanalysis was a science, which offered legitimate paths to an understanding of one of Rapaport's most abiding interests—how people think.[47]

Students of psychological and psychoanalytic literature may be all too cognizant of the rebellion against psychoanalytic metapsychology on the ground that it was too detached from clinical data. The rebellion began in the late 1950s, before Rapaport died, generated numerous publications, and subsided in the late 1970s. Several of the most conspicuous rebels—Gill, Schafer, Klein, Mayman, Holt, and Holzman—belonged to Rapaport's group in the 1940s. Although Mayman regarded

Rapaport as his first mentor, he subsequently attacked "Rapaport's more abstract metapsychology" for sealing itself off from the experience of the consulting room or the hospital. He charged that Rapaport never came to grips with "qualities of self-experience"—the way patients actually felt and behaved. Holt concurred, noting that he, Klein, and others who worked together in Topeka generally waited to publish their attacks on Rapaport's metapsychology until after his death in 1960. But in the 1950s, Holt recalled, a few of them had confronted Rapaport with "increasingly pointed questions about metapsychology, and I didn't find his answers very satisfactory."[48]

The professed ground for this disenchantment and eventual revolt against Rapaport was that he had never given his students a genuine "middle language" to link Freudian metapsychological abstractions with concrete clinical data. In actuality, several students charged that what Rapaport had characterized as a "middle language" to bridge concrete clinical information with psychoanalytic abstractions was itself abstract metapsychology. Consequently, they had been misled.

Few of those who constituted Rapaport's circle will acknowledge that their crusade against metapsychology had its roots in Topeka in the 1940s, when he brought them together. Yet they cite precious few developments to explain what could have caused it in the period between the disintegration of their Topeka circle in the late 1940s and their first published assaults on metapsychology several years later. In fact, there is good evidence that the challenge to metapsychology manifested itself in Topeka in subtle but significant ways that had to erupt as members of the group matured and became more confident.[49]

The key to the slow genesis of the metapsychology debate was in subtle changes over time within both Rapaport and his associates. Several of his young researchers were impressed with the tremendously varied psychological qualities of people they observed and tested within the clinical setting. Working with Rapaport on *Diagnostic Psychological Testing*, Schafer and Gill were struck by the fact that psychological test data underscored enormous differences among people. These differences did not cause the two junior authors to discount the universal characteristics that either psychoanalysis or other theories of personality had postulated. Rather, they simply became uncomfortable at the disparity between their data and general theory. As Escalona progressed with Leitch in a long-term study of infants, she, too, became disquieted. Escalona and Leitch detected overwhelming evidence of psychological differences among healthy babies; each seemed to have his own unique constitution. From this, it seemed to follow that there was no right way to raise a baby, no normal and regular stages in children's psychosexual development. This suspicion did not cause Escalona to assume that Freud or any other theorist was wrong. Rather, "the extreme differences among healthy and well-developing babies" required the investigator to consider a vast "constellation of environmental variables" before postulating any theory. More than any other member of the group, Klein was taken with the varieties of personality that clinical and laboratory investigations seemed to yield. Initially, Rapaport urged him to devise statistical methods to represent the difference in Rorschach protocol responses and to cast these differences into broad patterns of mental disorders. But Klein went on to establish a research laboratory at Menninger, in which he conducted tests on human perception and diverse physiological functions as well as analyzed statistics. Although he sought out broad patterns, as Rapaport requested, Klein realized that this often involved reducing complex data and leaving all sorts of clinical variables unexamined. He became less concerned with Freudian or other metapsychological abstractions and more attentive to a myriad of methodological complexities in making any general psychological statement about people. Others in the group, particularly Holt, Holzman, and Schlesinger, were very much influenced by Klein's apprehensions about broad theoretical statements on personality.[50]

From time to time, members of the group talked among themselves—and sometimes with Rapaport—about how their clinical investigations were making them more attentive to specificity, variety, and complexity within human psychology. To be sure, all remained students of Freudian metapsychology. (This was especially true after Rapaport discussed with them the essays of major theorists that marked the emergence of psychoanalytic ego psychology.) But in late 1946 or early 1947, Klein and Holt began to urge their colleagues to consider extensive experiments to determine whether Freudian theory was empirically verifiable. In this way, their clinical work might connect more appropriately to their interest in psychoanalytic theory. Holzman and Schlesinger were sympathetic with the proposal.[51]

Initially, Gill, Escalona, Mayman, and Schafer disagreed with Holt and Klein. The most clinically oriented and least experimental members of the group, they insisted that psychoanalysis was not the subject of scientific corroboration. Brenman sympathized with these objections. Slowly and almost imperceptibly, however, those who balked at the Holt-Klein suggestion began to modify their opinion, and it is important to determine why.

When Rapaport schooled the group in the imperatives of psychological testing, he stressed that they had to move cautiously from specific test results to general theoretical observations concerning each patient. Speculation was to be minimized. Theoretical assertions had to be verifiable in hard clinical data. As a bridge between theoretical abstraction and concrete clinical data, Rapaport initially encouraged his colleagues to struggle with a "middle language." Through this "language," Freudian and other theory was to be worded somewhat more concretely, while clinical data "reached" for it by becoming somewhat more general. One did not speak of the patient's id, for example, or of particular muscular contractions, but tried to bridge the abstract to the concrete through "middle language," detailing varieties of the patient's impulsive behaviors. As the group discussed the Holt-Klein proposal for scientific corroboration of Freudian theory, those who had resisted it shifted gradually to the position that the proposal might help to determine how far and how adequately Rapaport's suggested "middle language" could connect clinical data to psychoanalytic abstraction. Mayman, for example, had been one of the doubters. But he became more receptive to Klein and Holt as he came to believe that their proposal offered a way to test the value of "middle language." Mayman had sensed increasingly in his clinical work that there was a "self" in each patient—a complete social being that neither specific psychological tests nor abstract Freudian metapsychology seemed to capture very well. He was sure that a "middle language" was the means to describing this "self."[52]

As doubters like Mayman embraced the Klein-Holt proposal, they discovered that Rapaport was not in accord. When Mayman approached him with his concept of the "self," Rapaport not only spurned it but dismissed his colleague's entire preoccupation with a "middle language." Although Rapaport did not reject the Klein-Holt proposal outright, he indicated to Mayman that he was hardly overjoyed that anyone wished to pursue it. "I felt myself turning away from what Rapaport was telling us," Mayman noted. Recalling how the group responded to Rapaport's disinterest in "middle language" and the Klein-Holt proposal, Mayman felt that the first seeds of the crusade against metapsychology had been planted: "You could see some of the germinal beginnings of it." What made the assault on metapsychology almost an inevitability was that just as the group became committed to a "middle language" and to testing of Freudian theories, Rapaport found their agenda unrewarding.[53]

Klein, Holzman, and Schlesinger—those in his group least involved with clinical therapy and most attentive to experimentation with perception—were not as distressed as their colleagues over Rapaport's lack of interest in bridging psychoanalytic abstraction with clinical detail. They recognized that much of Rapaport's impetus for building a psychoanalytic metapsychology was to outline deep-seated laws that explained how the mind worked. He considered their perceptual research along broadly psychoanalytic lines to be fully consistent with this aim. In contrast, the more explicitly clinical investigations of Mayman and others were geared toward recording and interpreting patient behaviors—the outcomes of mental processes—which interested Rapaport much less.[54]

By mid-1947, and perhaps earlier, Rapaport began to despair over the clinical orientation of most of his group. Like many European émigrés of the 1930s schooled in both psychoanalysis and classical philosophy, he realized that in the New World, theory occupied a back seat to practical endeavor. But he nurtured his European grounding in theories of thought (Kant's in particular) as he proceeded to become proficient at psychological testing: "I came to testing partly as a matter of getting my bread, and partly because of my interest in thinking." By late 1944, his Menninger associates did most of the testing and other clinical work. This allowed Rapaport to concentrate on theoretical pursuits. Although the establishment of the MSP in 1946 increased his supervisory and teaching duties, it did not require him to do much clinical work.[55]

As Rapaport grew increasingly distant from clinical operations, he departed from Freud in one important particular. Whereas Freud and his close associates, as clinicians, considered theory as a useful way to communicate their concrete clinical experiences, Rapaport now had fewer direct clinical observations upon which to draw. He tended increasingly to view psychoanalysis and theories of thought and motive as a compendium of general laws that required explication and tidying.[56]

The parallel between Rapaport and another European émigré, T. W. Adorno, is striking. In his monumental study, *The Authoritarian Personality*, Adorno drew extensively upon quantitative and survey research based on data of American experimental psychologists. Similarly, Rapaport borrowed heavily from the data generated by his associates and by other clinical and experimental researchers. Adorno then superimposed his full philosophic system upon the data, as if his book could have been written without it. By 1946 and 1947, Rapaport was conducting himself in much the same way.

The primary theoretical problem with which Rapaport had become enchanted in Europe and that preoccupied him in America was the formulation of an alternative to both Descartes and Locke. He rejected Descartes's view that man was wholly dependent on native forms within his mind, as well as the Lockean conviction that man was a clean slate on which external experiences "write" or create. Instead, Rapaport turned to Kant's perspective that experience is used to construct knowledge of the world, with the inherent form of the mind constraining the form of construction. That is to say, Rapaport sought out a unified theory of thinking and learning that would indicate how experiences within and outside the self were codetermined.[57]

Even before he left Europe, Rapaport felt that psychoanalytic theory offered the most fruitful possibility for demonstrating that Kantian code-termination. Intersection of inner drives and external superego constraints made this apparent to him. The problem was that Freudian writings, particularly the major metapsychological papers, had to be systematized, amplified, and then linked to the rest of psychology and to science at large. By the mid-1940s, Rapaport assumed that this task would constitute his principal work. It was an enormous undertaking, for it was by no means certain that the corpus of Freud's writing had internal consistency and was capable of systematization. In 1947, Rapaport proclaimed that "the only school of therapy which has attempted systematically to build a theory of personality is psychoanalysis." Unfortunately, psychoanalytic theory had never been elaborated fully and systematically, and "its fund of knowledge and theory" had not been integrated into the broader science of psychology. "The completion of this job awaits the clinical psychologist," he concluded, leaving little doubt about who that psychologist would be. Against this task, the Klein-Holt proposal, Mayman's notion of the "self," and a "middle language" for clinicians paled in significance for Rapaport. Many of the basic concerns of his group had become secondary.[58]

Rapaport had always felt comfortable with Freud's fundamental concepts of drive and drive restraint. Sharing with Freud a tragic view of the human condition, he agreed fully that intrapsychic conflict was inevitable. He nevertheless recognized that these constructs were of little interest to most American, or even many European, academic psychologists. They prized vigor, flexibility, and adaptational capacities in the human character; their primary concerns were intellectual mastery, conceptual development, the nature of play, and the quality of mental synthesis. Rapaport wondered how he might command the attentions of these psychologists without forsaking Freudian drive theory.[59]

Freud's associate Heinz Hartmann had published *Ego Psychology and the Problem of Adaptation* in 1938, and it provided a way out of Rapaport's bind. There was room in this essay to affirm traditional drive theory; Hartmann saw "primary ego adaptation" as consisting in the ego's constant working to check the id. Hartmann also provided Rapaport with a means of addressing the interests of academic psychologists; he referred to "secondary ego adaptation," or a conflict-free sphere of "ego strength," where restraint of the id was not the central pursuit. Instead, the ego summoned up "perception, intention, object comprehension," and like mental qualities to facilitate a sort of positive adaptation to the environment, during which time the psyche was not consumed by intrapsychic conflict.

Although Rapaport had not read Hartmann's essay in 1942, when he presented a paper on "The Psychoanalytic Concept of Memory" to the Topeka Psychoanalytic Institute, he came close to elaborating the nature of "secondary ego adaptation." No later than 1946 (perhaps a year or two earlier), Rapaport read the essay. He embraced Hartmann's concept of "a functional autonomy of the ego" as a way to understand thought processes, intentions, learning, play, and other phenomena of interest to academic psychologists, while preserving the Freudian concern for preemptory drive and intrapsychic conflict. The pressing need, Rapaport recognized, was to examine and flesh out systematically Hartmann's own amplification of Freud. Although *Ego Psychology and the Problem of Adaptation* was an abstract essay, Rapaport did not propose to link it to the clinical data that his colleagues and other clinicians were generating. Full systematization and elaboration of Freudian metapsychology had become his overriding concern. Rapaport felt that there simply was not sufficient time to corroborate any major aspect of psychoanalytic thought clinically while expanding it conceptually and systematizing it; at least, there was not time in his life. To Merton Gill, he confided a fear that clinical data might not prove compatible with Hartmann's and his own metapsychological endeavors. In that event, Rapaport felt, the clinical data was secondary. Gill believed otherwise.[60]

V

There can be no doubt that at least a modest rift existed by 1948 between Rapaport and his group. Members continued to admire him enormously and were hardly willing, even in private discussion, to challenge his tendency toward pure metapsychological elaboration. But the leader and his associates were heading toward open conflict. Rapaport began to distance himself from the group and spent less time fighting for group interests within the larger Menninger organization.[61]

It is curious, then, that in 1948 he departed for the Austen Riggs Center with his most prominent clinical research associates—Gill, Brenman, and Schafer. This exodus conveyed the image of a group with its most influential members still close. Yet this was hardly the case. Although the exodus stemmed from a variety of factors, the subtle rift between Rapaport and his associates was germane to an explanation of this signal event in Menninger history.

The most obvious factor was a grant application that Rapaport, Gill, Brenman, and Schafer had prepared for the Rockefeller Foundation. They had been notified late in 1947 that the grant was about to be awarded. It was for $35,000 annually over a five-year interval, with the Menninger Foundation pledged to provide a matching appropriation. The idea behind the proposal was to allow the Rapaport associates to concentrate on research projects and to limit their teaching and clinical duties. If they accepted the grant, Rapaport and his three colleagues would have been committed to remain at Menninger for another half decade.[62]

As the time approached for the Rockefeller grant to be awarded, they discovered that they had the opportunity to move to Austen Riggs. Even though Robert Knight had accepted the medical directorship of the Stockbridge, Massachusetts, facility in February 1947, it remained one of the less distinguished "new psychiatry" centers. To enhance Riggs's visibility, Knight advanced attractive offers to the four prominent clinical psychologists. Realizing that Rapaport wanted to devote the majority of his time to systematizing and elaborating Freudian metapsychology, Knight promised him a full-time research position with no clinical duties. And knowing that Brenman, Gill, and Schafer desired a hand in the treatment process but also craved considerably more time to write, he offered them part-clinical, part-research appointments.[63]

Schafer was the first to accept. He became chief psychologist at Stockbridge in the fall of 1947. This put pressure on Rapaport, Gill, and Brenman, who felt they would have to stay or go together.[64]

Menninger observers have often assigned responsibility to Karl for the exodus. Karl had been jealous of Rapaport, uneasy over his national prominence, and distressed by the fact that he had shaped a new role in the foundation. As a power-conscious "baron," Rapaport would not allow Karl to influence members of his research group or the psychology and research departments in his accustomed way. In turn, Karl had turned a deaf ear to their pleas for more time to conduct research uninterrupted by clinical and teaching duties. But this is not to say that Karl pushed the four out of Topeka. When he discovered that the exodus was about to occur, he tried to stop it by accusing Knight of professional impropriety. After the four left and the Rockefeller grant was lost, he characterized the exodus as "a terrific disappointment to me." With the

MSP transforming the foundation into a national center for psychiatric education, Karl had counted on the Rapaport group to turn it simultaneously into a national research center. After the departure, Karl knew "that it was rather hopeless."[65]

About a year earlier, Rapaport had told Will that unless all within his circle were given more time and financial support for their research, their scholarship would remain meager. Under present conditions, there was no future for them in Topeka: "we may end up like the gypsy who trained his horse slowly to go without food only to find the ungrateful creature dead on the very day when he reached the pinnacle of his hopes." Indeed, from the opening of the MSP until his decision to relocate, Rapaport argued that increased teaching, administrative, and clinical duties at Winter Hospital were cutting significantly into research time. Brenman wrote to Will underscoring Rapaport's claims; she and her colleagues were so busy with other duties that they made "a frantic attempt to meet the research commitment on over-time with the constant feeling that we are doing a poor job."[66]

In response, Will pointed out that Rapaport and his colleagues had brought on much of the expansion of their nonresearch duties. They had offered to teach and supervise the MSP fellows in psychological testing. Rapaport had asked to run the new Research Department, and Gill had been happy to serve as his assistant. Brenman and Schafer had volunteered to work with patients at both Menninger and Winter hospitals. The four "built up just what they have, and I thought were so enthusiastic about," Will added. Moreover, the suggestion that insufficient research time was behind the exodus does not square with the precise circumstances late in 1947. As John Stone noted, the five years of Rockefeller-Menninger funding would "make possible the formation of a nucleus of full-time research workers" and "permit them to be free of routine duties." Will was equally puzzled that the four would leave for Stockbridge just as the research conditions they claimed to need were about to materialize.[67]

To further understand the exodus, one cannot overlook the social dynamics of the Rapaport group, for they help to explain why the leader and three members left, while the rest received no job offers and remained. It is germane to recall the subtle rift between Rapaport as group leader and his associates over his increasing immersion in metapsychology. This rift was rendering the group leaderless in an institutional climate where aggressive direction had secured for its members the exciting research projects, social cohesion, and other benefits they prized. With his new focus, Rapaport ceased to provide unlimited enthusiasm and support. In fact, he wanted to end all administrative responsibilities.

Rapaport confided to Menninger trustee Mary Switzer, after deciding to leave Topeka, that he was going to a place where his "first fruits" (scholarship) could ripen because he would not have to continue as a leader-administrator.[68]

The fact that the rift in the Rapaport group was accompanied by a leadership gap helps to explain why Brenman, Gill, and Schafer left for Stockbridge. The three knew that Rapaport was the only figure in Topeka with the stature and forcefulness to create an independent research operation. Also, Robert Knight had been understanding and extremely helpful not only to Rapaport but to each of them personally. A scholar himself, Knight supported Rapaport's efforts to enhance Menninger research and publication. A clinician as well as a theorist, Knight (unlike Rapaport) was consistently sympathetic with the quest of the three to examine, corroborate, and modify psychoanalytic theory through clinical investigations. By moving to Stockbridge, they were therefore trading off Rapaport's increasingly questionable leadership at Menninger for Knight's solid and promising leadership at Austen Riggs.[69]

Although Knight had funds to recruit more staff than Brenman, Gill, and Schafer, he was apprehensive of charges of ethical impropriety if he hired Rapaport's entire group. Perhaps the most important reason he sought out the senior associates, however, was that he seemed bound to them and they to him through the hazardous emotional indebtedness that can develop within the training analysis. Knight had apparently talked extensively with Schafer before Schafer came to Stockbridge. He wanted very much to have Schafer—a talented clinician whom he viewed as a protégé—as his analytic candidate. In turn, Schafer was excited at the prospect of securing his training analysis with the man long regarded as Topeka's foremost therapist and analyst. Thus, Schafer followed Knight to Stockbridge and commenced his analysis shortly after arriving.[70]

The analytic bond linking Knight, Brenman, and Gill was even stronger. In 1943, Knight had commenced training analyses of Brenman and Gill, and had even accepted Gill's wife. By 1946, Gill and Brenman were in the concluding phases of their analyses. Both were struggling with unresolved transference to Knight. In turn, he was experiencing strong countertransferences to them. Neither could let the other go. At the same time, Gill and Brenman (both married to others) maintained a close personal relationship with each other, while Knight's marriage had been strained for years. Quite understandably, Brenman characterized the whole interval as "incestuous."[71]

One day during a concluding phase of his analysis with Brenman, Knight confided that he had been offered the directorship of the Austen

Riggs Center and intended to accept. "I am leaving Topeka within the year." When she protested, expressing a feeling of abandonment, Knight voiced hope that Brenman and her husband "will come along with me." He left no doubt about his feeling toward her. At the time, Knight may also have intended to invite Gill and Rapaport to join him, but it is instructive that he approached Brenman first. "That won't work unless David [Rapaport] and Merton [Gill] can come along too," she replied to his offer. Knight reflected for a few moments. Then he answered positively: "Maybe that can be worked out as well."[72]

Knight and Gill had begun divorce proceedings soon after the move to Stockbridge, while Brenman's husband (playwright William Gibson) had immersed himself in the New York theater world. Retrospectively, Brenman later warned that "wherever possible such an incestuous training should be avoided." But the kind of training analysis that she received, where personal and organizational affairs intruded, was hardly uncommon at Menninger.[73]

VI

Something of a group tradition survived among those in Rapaport's circle who remained in Topeka, yet in the aftermath of the exodus, they increasingly prized autonomy.

The appointment of Sibylle Escalona to head the Research Department promoted this tendency. Because of her administrative experience in the School of Clinical Psychology and as director of the large, federally supported Menninger Infancy Research Project, she had been recommended by Rapaport to take charge of the department on an interim basis. Will was so taken with Escalona's stewardship that after six months he named her permanent director.[74]

Bright, creative, but a loner, Escalona was not as territorial as Rapaport and not nearly as aggressive. Unlike Rapaport, she allowed the director of the Psychology Department to assume more than nominal authority. Although both Escalona and others within Rapaport's group continued to exercise substantial influence over Psychology Department operations, she seemed to be directing the primary focus of the group to the Research Department.[75]

In 1953, Rapaport compared his own authoritarian administration during his Topeka years with the Escalona leadership. In contrast to his emphasis on group cohesion and singularity of focus, he found Escalona stressing "a principle of respect for individual liberty." She tried to maintain an independent research agenda within her infancy project during years when most other participants in his group felt compelled to focus first on issues of psychological testing and then on the merits of metapsychology. Upon replacing Rapaport, she was determined to ensure substantial autonomy for remaining members of his group and for all investigators who joined or cooperated with the Research Department.[76]

By all indications, Escalona succeeded. Klein felt that the pressure and intrusiveness characteristic of Rapaport almost entirely ceased when Escalona became director. Although he missed Rapaport, he felt a sense of relief that he could pursue his perception project with considerably greater freedom. Escalona also encouraged Paul Bergman, an occasional participant in Rapaport group discussions, to extend the scope of his investigation by studying the consequences of psychotherapy. Quite unlike Rapaport, she urged Bergman to join with Menninger clinicians outside the Research Department in order to cultivate broad support for his endeavor. Bergman did, and the well-known Psychotherapy Research Project came into being. Escalona also hired Lolafaye Coyne, a mathematician who had just completed her master's degree at the University of Kansas, to establish a statistical laboratory, with resources from which all researchers could draw. Escalona's interests, broader and more eclectic than her predecessor's—she was willing to promote research that had no direct links to psychoanalytic theory—led her to encourage investigations in biochemistry, physiology, and neuroanatomy. When Escalona left Menninger in 1952, she justifiably claimed credit for facilitating a new era in which neither the Research Department director nor any department members felt compelled to "fit into existing patterns."[77]

Even with Escalona as formal director, George Klein might eventually have replaced Rapaport as charismatic leader of the old group and the entire Research Department. Klein was admired deeply for his scholarship, his brilliance, his relaxed manner, and his eagerness for direct involvement in clinical and laboratory activities. In the spring of 1950, however, he departed for a one-year position as visiting professor at Harvard, which he extended into a second year. In 1952, Robert Holt joined him at New York University, where the two established a psychoanalytically oriented clinical laboratory—the Research Center for Mental Health. From New York, Klein made arrangements to coordinate his perception research with Holzman and Schlesinger, who remained in Topeka. He returned to Topeka periodically to try to keep the perception project afloat. During these visits, he sometimes felt that he could "taste the flavor of clinical thinking which I deeply miss." But academia and the Northeast now had greater appeal to Klein. The longer he stayed away, the more his project colleagues became distressed with him for delayed communications and for losing vital materials; they construed these actions as Klein's way of separating from them. Late in 1951, they took their grievances to Escalona. She reprimanded Klein severely, and this made him even less committed to Topeka.[78]

As if the Stockbridge exodus and Klein's departure were not enough, those from Rapaport's circle who remained received another blow. After Escalona spent two years rebuilding the Research Department, Karl invited Alan Gregg, director of the Rockefeller Foundation's Medical Science Division and a longtime friend, to Topeka. He hoped that Gregg, impressed with Escalona's efforts, might award significant sums for further improvement of the department. Gregg spent three days in Topeka in 1950 and was unimpressed. In a conversation with Will and in an informal report to the foundation, he offered a disturbing critique. Gregg charged that clinical research would be carried out successfully only by professionally trained investigators operating in a well-funded and independent research unit. The Menninger organization had not let such a unit materialize during the Escalona years. Those with research training and potential remained distracted by heavy clinical duties, while other staff had no idea what genuine research involved.[79]

Escalona tried to offer a balanced assessment of Gregg's observations and report. Although the Rockefeller official had "a favorable impression of the research group and its work," she explained, he had a most "unfavorable impression of the intellectual and emotional climate of the Foundation as a whole." Escalona could not deny that other private philanthropies would get word of Gregg's evaluation and probably judge Topeka similarly. The potential for philanthropic support for the Research Department would be slim over the next several years. Nonetheless, Escalona cautioned Karl and others in Topeka not to rail against Gregg for the damage he seemed to have caused. It was prudent to avoid burning bridges.[80]

Responses at Menninger to the Gregg report were predictable. Senior hospital physicians like Lewis Robbins and Bernard Foster cited it to try to dismember the Research Department. They argued that all clinicians should be backed in their research; Gregg would have a few elite researchers entirely supported by hospital revenues, and this flew in the face of Menninger tradition. The Medical Council insisted that Gregg did not understand how clinical investigation by hospital staff constituted research. Karl took Gregg's report on a more personal level, coming as it did from a trusted friend. At the time it was issued, he was wrestling with the very values of professionalism that he once so fervently embraced. Gregg's report cast doubt on his own eclectic research endeavors. All his life, he maintained, he had dabbled in many areas. Indeed, there were "thirty or forty projects that I wanted some day to look into and I felt that Dr. Gregg's position practically meant that this sort of curiosity of mine had no value whatsoever."[81]

By early 1951, Escalona perceived that the conditions for psychological research at Menninger had become uncertain, even precarious. Staff outside her department claimed that they, too, were researchers and entitled to time to pursue their investigations. And the Menninger brothers opposed giving staff inside her department the full-time research days that Gregg recommended. In an atmosphere where her trained researchers were resented and worked under difficult conditions, Escalona knew that the most active among them would leave. Holt was to join Klein at NYU; Wexler was evaluating job offers; Rapaport was trying to recruit Holzman to Austen Riggs; while Luborsky was considering a move back to academia. Personal considerations also influenced Escalona. She felt her social life in Topeka was inadequate "for an unattached woman." And she had come to dislike administrative work: "I need to narrow down to the field in which I work—child development—and acquire depth there instead of increasing glibness about lots of things."[82]

Escalona told Will she expected to leave the foundation during the first half of 1952. A successor, Gardner Murphy, was hired. Because Murphy could not assume his duties before September 1952, Escalona agreed to serve until he arrived. But she became ill, and an acting director had to be appointed. When Escalona recovered, she assumed a position at another "new psychiatry" center, the Institute of Living, formerly the Hartford Retreat, relocated in New Haven.[83]

It was unfortunate that Escalona left Topeka physically weak and emotionally discouraged. Through diplomacy, she had maintained the relative independence of the Research Department. She had also done much to maintain the Rapaport tradition of rigorous scholarship, and a clinical setting where psychologists remained very nearly the equal of psychiatrists. Moreover, two traditions of her own became hallmarks of the Research Department: she gave the researcher the leeway to pursue ideas, and she allowed the group to mount a large number of varied projects. After Rapaport, research at Menninger ceased to be dominated by the "family spirit." After Escalona, researchers had the freedom to question psychoanalytic premises and to develop their own projects.

PART THREE

The Passing of the Founding Generation

The non-Menningers? Well, they're pretty brave or they wouldn't come into a family web as definite as ours.

KARL A. MENNINGER, 1975

CHAPTER TEN

"In the Hands of the Barons"

Midway through 1954, renovation of the two separate wings of the Menninger hospital—East Lodge and West Lodge—was completed. The wings were joined by a large new addition, to form a modern complex. Mildred Law had been assigned to plan the renovation. She had roughly $1.5 million at her disposal, much of it from Will's fund-raising. Over one third came from the federal government through the Hill-Burton Act to facilitate hospital construction. Law was intent on making the facility an edifice for the future.

Dedicated as C. F. Menninger Memorial Hospital, this complex was to increase bed capacity from 67 to 113. Breaking from the tradition of sex-segregated patient wards, it would be one of the first psychiatric facilities in the country to allow male and female patients to mix together outside their rooms. Law planned large and airy rooms, open to "bright sunshine and brighter hopes." She tried to disguise essential provisions for patient safety. Drapes were installed with undersized brackets so they would collapse under modest pressure, deterring suicide by hanging. Electric outlets were placed far enough away from water basins to avert electrocutions. Solid windowpane separators appeared decorative but could not be bent or broken to facilitate escape, nor could the reinforced screens be torn away.[1]

But Law lacked training in medical architecture and had not planned for the future. The buildings could not readily be enlarged to increase bed capacity. Therefore, many prospective patients would have to turn to other institutions. Will's milieu therapy approach, with its emphasis upon high staff-to-patient ratios, predisposed Law to design the new facility so staff would have to be increased disproportionately to the enlarged patient population. Necessarily labor intensive, the new hospital was saddled with a large built-in cost, which other hospitals circumvented.[2]

These hospitals emerged more rapidly than anyone at Menninger anticipated. During the 1950s, a number of institutions established strong residency programs and research capabilities as well as reputable treatment. Most of the competition came from cities on the east and west coasts. So long as Menninger was practically the only location for well-regarded, psychoanalytically oriented psychiatric residencies and training in clinical psychology, the geographic isolation of eastern Kansas had not been a factor. Now it was. Former Menninger psychiatrists carried the milieu therapy program to the Pinel Clinic in Seattle and Hillside Hospital in Long Island. As psychiatrist in chief at McLean Hospital near Boston, Alfred Stanton had strengthened its Harvard Medical School affiliation, transforming it from a custodial facility to a respectable treatment center. In San Francisco, Karl Bowman was drawing upon the resources of the University of California Medical School (of which it was a part) to make the Langley-Porter Clinic an attractive psychiatric residency and treatment alternative to Topeka. And in Philadelphia, Lauren Smith was developing the Institute for Mental and Nervous Diseases into a superior teaching and treatment unit within the Pennsylvania Hospital by drawing upon distinguished associates like Earl Bond, Edward Strecker, and Kenneth Appel.[3]

The rise of competition was not lost on Menninger staff. As early as 1951, George Klein had observed that "a certain kind of psychiatric poverty over the country *fostered* the [Menninger] clinic's growth." The problem was that Menninger was being "duplicated more and more"; consequently, it was less and less "an oasis nor *unique* in American psychiatry." Will found that there was keener competition for funds. By the mid-1960s, psychologist Harry Levinson remarked pessimistically: "Our drawing area tends to be more regional than national," a process that "is likely to continue as more and better facilities are created elsewhere."[4]

In addition to competition, Menninger was forced to confront other serious developments. The introduction of psychotropic drugs like Thorazine was touted to avert psychotic episodes and restrain thought disorganization. American pharmaceutical firms like Smith Kline & French won Federal Drug Administration approval to market these drugs commercially. State mental hospitals began using them. The drugs allowed staffs to maintain calm on disorderly wards without traditional physical restraints; indeed, they could discharge large numbers of patients. Private hospitals, with better staff-patient ratios than the overcrowded state facilities, tended to dispense the drugs more as supplements to interpersonal therapy than as replacements for it. But though psychotropic drugs did not substantially reduce patient populations, particularly at facilities like Menninger and Austen Riggs, the unprecedented effects of the new medications forced these institutions to rethink their therapeutic goals. Milieu therapy and other forms of psychologism were put on the defensive as psychopharmacology and biopsychiatry gained recognition and respect. Like its competitors, Menninger felt compelled to experiment with Thorazine.[5]

The community mental health movement and the concomitant policy of reducing state hospital patient populations also challenged the Menninger style of operations. The popular outcry against overcrowded and largely custodial state hospitals promoted the demand for community clinics as humane alternative treatment centers. Politicians, celebrities, social scientists, and conservative and liberal figures endorsed the efficacy of federal and state appropriations to establish community clinics. With such bipartisan support, state legislatures had begun in the late 1940s to increase appropriations for such community facilities. Consistent with the actions of state legislatures, the privately sponsored and widely esteemed Joint Commission on Mental Illness and Health issued a report in 1961 which, while favoring state hospitals as chronic care institutions, underscored the efficacy of community mental health clinics. Finally, through the 1963 Mental Retardation and Community Mental Health Centers Construction Act, Congress pledged itself to between one third and two thirds the cost of constructing community centers with but vaguely defined functions. Although these centers were not required to care for patients traditionally assigned to state hospitals, Congress committed no new federal funds to those hospitals. Under these circumstances, superintendents of the state hospitals felt that they had no choice (especially after 1965) but to reduce costs by discharging large numbers of patients. But the unexpected happened. Instead of ending up in new community centers, the majority were shifted into Medicaid-funded old age and nursing homes. Federally supported nursing homes assumed the clientele of state-funded hospitals, and the much touted community clinics treated a less incapacitated, wage-earning clientele.[6]

Because Menninger was primarily a privately funded institution with prosperous patients, the community mental health movement and the lateral transfer of poor and middle-class mentally ill from state hospitals to nursing homes did not directly affect its operations or its orientation. Nonetheless, these changes occurred in a climate of public concern for humane community-based treatment that could hardly have gone unnoticed within the foundation or among its rivals. Indeed, the leading proponents of community clinics shared a social orientation with Will's generation of military psychiatrists. Both groups felt that conditions rooted in the community, such as poverty, poor nutrition, and discrimination, were at least as significant in mental illness as personality malfunctions. The media and ambitious politicians also clamored for community-based reforms. With the convergence of these circumstances, private institutions like Menninger felt compelled to depart (if modestly) from their traditional medical perspective. National media recognition, donations, and grants came more readily if the "new psychiatry" facility offered social, community-based measures to prevent or alleviate mental illness. MSP fellows were especially attentive to this; some threatened to move to those training centers that followed current trends in community psychiatry, unless the Menninger Clinic rose to the occasion.[7]

Three and a half decades after psychotropic drugs were introduced, their harmful side effects have come to be recognized despite obvious benefits. And the passage of time has made it clear that custodial (sometimes dreary) nursing homes rather than innovative community clinics have assumed the primary burden of the state hospitals. But at the time, the Menningers and their staff felt enormous pressure to modify their activities. To retain a reputation for innovation that they were in danger of losing to competitors, they became more attentive to somatic variables suggested by the new drugs and social factors in psychiatric practice underscored by the community mental health movement. National developments had promoted a somewhat less self-confident era in Menninger history.

I I

The first official foundation-wide recognition that there had to be a concerted response to new circumstances came in October 1953. The trustees met with the recently established (and largely honorary) board of governors to adopt a Ten Year Plan pledging to raise $17 million for the organization. The money was to be used to double the faculty of the MSP and to quadruple the research staff. Within these two recruitment areas, staff were to be hired who had reputations in biopsychiatry and familiarity with the new psychotropic drugs. Most of the $17 million was to be used to facilitate work in "the social applications of psychiatry" and particularly in the "science of prevention," by training personnel to work with industries, schools, and community agencies.[8]

That the Menninger brothers would sell this Ten Year Plan to both boards was predictable. Bold shifts in foundation orientation had historically come from the family, which prided itself on its forward-looking spirit. Karl had warned the trustees and others that if the organization "didn't continue to grow, I think we will die." The foundation had to move more fully into biopsychiatry and especially into community mental health programs, Karl insisted; in the future, there had to be less involvement in inpatient hospital treatment and more "in extramural situations and in extramural patients." Will concurred. Encouraged by the reforms he had promoted in the army and then in the APA, he appeared more confident than Karl about the capacity of the foundation to adjust to change.[9]

Staff leaders justified the Ten Year Plan. "We are no longer in the forefront of psychiatry," charged child psychiatrist J. Cotter Hirschberg. He warned that with the advent of social and biological psychiatry, "We simply cannot afford to have individual [psychoanalytically informed] treatment as our primary focus." Hospital section chief Joseph Satten agreed, bemoaning the "virtual absence of a social science dimension in our clinical and educational programs." "With the advent of Community Psychiatry, the growth of many clinics throughout the country," Philip Holzman warned, "the small private mental hospital is not going to gain support." It had to reorient itself.[10]

In the years following passage of the Ten Year Plan, the brothers continued to press for a dramatic shift in Menninger Clinic priorities. Social but also biological solutions for community social problems were to be developed. As Elmer Southard's student, Karl found no difficulty in attaching new importance to biopsychiatry. Southard had also pioneered in research concerning psychiatric interventions in the industrial workplace. After working with Southard, Karl always insisted that industry was a key element in the community and that the community needed skillful psychiatric remedies.[11]

Will was even more determined to update the foundation. He encouraged Thorazine research and sought funds to recruit biopsychiatrically oriented researchers. On the subject of social psychiatry, Will's enthusiasm could hardly be contained. He looked upon this field as an extension of the preventive social programs he had championed in the army: "The pressure of circumstances led us to seek preventive measures . . . we needed to locate many, many more of our psychiatrists in the field rather than assigning them to hospitals." He supported programs to aid "the personnel working in courts and prisons, in churches, and in our schools." In 1950, Will created a Department of Social Applications to help these community agencies with Menninger consultants and staff trained in preventive social psychiatry. By 1960, the department had been responsible for a doubling of the programs that the foundation sponsored and for much of its emphasis on community psychiatry.[12]

By borrowing staff from other parts of the foundation and hiring specialists, the Department of Social Applications established programs in marriage counseling, mental health in industry, law and psychiatry, pastoral care and counseling, and school mental health. Although these programs were characterized as outreach measures for all classes of society, in practice they were compatible with the Menninger tradition of serving a wealthy and often professional patient clientele. They were provided at such steep fees that few other than the wealthy and those patronized by the prosperous could afford them. For example, the Industrial Mental Health program serviced mainly the corporate rich and their highest managerial class. And though Pastoral Care trained middle-class clergy in counseling techniques, few could absorb the steep fees without special corporate subsidies. The new social orientation in no way contradicted the practice of balancing foundation account books through payments from the affluent.[13]

The first of the new curricula launched under the Department of Social Applications was a Marriage Counseling Service. In 1950, the W. T. Grant Foundation provided Menninger with $97,500 as seed money to inaugurate a training program for marriage counselors. Fellowships enabled counselors and pastors to come to Topeka to update their skills. Will selected Robert G. Foster to head the marriage service. Foster's wide-ranging background included a doctorate in rural sociology at Cornell, postdoctoral work at Yale's Institute for Human Relations, and the direction of marriage and family counseling programs at both the Merrill Palmer Institute in Detroit and the University of Kansas. Will—who had hoped that bickering between psychiatrists and other mental health professionals could be averted in the familial hospital he had founded—was distressed when psychoanalytically oriented hospital physicians objected to Foster. They charged that he lacked medical training and seemed more interested in relieving marital distress than in rendering fundamental personality changes. Opposition to Foster hurt the marriage counseling program, and it never flourished. By 1959, trainees were limited to armed forces chaplains on military subsidies. Therefore, it made sense to transform the service to Pastoral Care and Counseling.[14]

That program found much greater support. Karl backed it enthusiastically. Since 1954, he had organized short conferences with about thirty participants, mental health staff and theologians of all faiths, on topics like "Suffering," "Freedom," and "Healing," to draw closer together these two seemingly disparate callings. Within a few years, a wealthy foundation governor from Indianapolis, Edward F. Gallahue, donated $100,000 to increase the size and scope of the gatherings. A $275,000 five-year grant from the Danforth Foundation, plus other funding, helped to buttress the program. Support also came from senior staff psychiatrists, psychologists, and social workers. The program originally trained clergy to counsel those with family problems. By 1963, it also taught them to deal with the mentally retarded and with convicted felons. By 1964, Pastoral Care had trained forty-four theology students and seventy-three clergy through three-month clinical programs. With Karl's backing, program leaders like Thomas Klink and Paul Pruyser became influential in Menninger affairs. Karl conceived of himself as the founder of the program and felt that his mother would have been pleased with its success as an exercise in "practicing Christianity."[15]

The Division of Industrial Mental Health was an even more powerful component of the Department of Social Applications. Whereas Pastoral Care was regarded as part of Karl's domain, Industrial Mental Health belonged to Will. He had made plans for it in the early 1950s, but as fund-raising duties created greater demands upon his time, he felt compelled to turn further planning and administration over to Harry Levinson. Levinson, investigating ways in which American industries responded to employee mental health problems, concluded that these responses were usually inadequate. Corporations tried to manage their workers without knowing much about the individual employee and his relationships, experiences, and desires.

Levinson and Will received a Rockefeller Brothers Fund grant to support a proposed Division of Industrial Mental Health, $105,000 over a three-year period. Under Levinson's direction, the division organized teams of psychiatrists, psychologists, and occasionally a sociologist. Each group studied the staff of a particular company and prepared a report on its findings to guide the company. But the major activity of the division was a five-day seminar, to which corporations sent high-level managers and even some staff physicians, with the expectation that they would learn how to deal with corporate personnel more effectively. Assisted by a few psychiatrists, psychologists, and even one or two of Lester Roach's administrators, Levinson tried to show corporate managers that they could better direct others if they were in control of their own emotional lives. By the end of 1964, Industrial Mental Health had worked with 372 executives and 280 industrial physicians. The seminars' high fees, together with donations Will secured from large corporations like AT&T, International Harvester, and General Electric, provided income. Menninger public relations staff underscored the fact that Industrial Mental Health was backed financially by some of the most influential companies in the nation and worked with hundreds of employees from the private sector.

They portrayed Menninger as an organization that responded to social problems. The financial support and publicity benefited Levinson. By the mid-1960s, he had accumulated a level of influence and power approaching David Rapaport's in the 1940s.[16]

Two other new programs or divisions were considerably smaller than Pastoral Care and Industrial Mental Health. A grant from the Scaife Foundation and support from Karl allowed hospital psychiatrist Joseph Satten to create the Division of Law and Psychiatry. Satten established consulting relationships between staff and agencies like the Federal Bureau of Prisons, the Topeka Police Department, the Topeka Juvenile Court, county courts throughout Kansas, and state law schools. His efforts to establish a research center within his division to focus on psychiatric solutions to crime and delinquency never materialized. Instead, the mainstay of his program became courses in the MSP that instructed fellows on issues of child custody, divorce, and crime. The Division of School Mental Health was even smaller. Psychiatrist Edward Greenwood, who as early as the mid-1940s had consulted with area schools on mental health issues, was permitted to form a special division in 1964. Under Greenwood's sponsorship, MSP fellows in child psychiatry were sent to local schools, while seminars were arranged for guidance counselors, principals, and teachers.[17]

A geriatrics program was established in 1960, as a division of the hospital, not of Social Applications. Encouraged by Karl, psychiatrist Prescott Thompson surveyed geriatric centers in other parts of the country and secured internal funding to open a facility that would deal with the emotional problems of aging and retirement. Emphasis was placed on short-term psychiatric treatment. But the program was abandoned in the mid-1960s for lack of patients, among other reasons. It was an idea whose time had not yet come.[18]

Despite the importance of biopsychiatry in the Ten Year Plan, almost all of the new programs concerned community social psychiatry. No unit within the Department of Social Applications focused upon biological and pharmacological developments affecting mental health. The hospital sponsored modest research on the effects of Thorazine, and a few Research Department projects dealt explicitly with biomedical issues. But no more was done in this area. The foundation's psychoanalytic traditions plus the absence of abundant data and experience to encourage staff to move in biological directions explain some of this reluctance. The preference of both brothers for holistic, unified personality theory and social activism over somatic concerns was also relevant. So was the role of the brothers' good friend Robert H. Felix, founding director of the

National Institute of Mental Health. During his tenure from 1949 to 1964, Felix consistently assigned funding priority to institutions and research projects that stressed the social roots of mental disorders. He rarely attached much importance to biomedical research, and ambitious young program builders at the foundation, like Levinson and Satten, were not unmindful of this.

Although it was understandable and hardly censurable, this failure of the brothers and their staff to do much with biological aspects of research and treatment would be telling. Even in the immediate postwar years, when their psychodynamic approach to treatment of the individual patient had gained wide acclaim, that recognition rested upon a tenuous foundation. Any individualized path to cure could reach only a small number of mental patients at a substantial cost. By the late 1950s and early 1960s, psychiatric centers in large regional university medical school complexes returned increasingly to biological over psychodynamic perspectives. As new psychotropic drugs emerged, capable of reaching millions of potentially needy patients at a fraction of the cost of interpersonal therapy, they necessarily reinforced the biopsychiatry trend. This meant that eventually Menninger's reputation in the forefront of psychiatric leadership had to slip.

Over the short term, it was possible for the brothers and others to misjudge the shift toward biopsychiatry and to take pride in their new, well-funded, and widely recognized social programs. According to psychiatrist William Robinson, these programs had transformed the foundation from a clinical treatment "specialty shop" to "an all purpose department store."[19] The advent of such an "all purpose" workplace decidedly influenced internal power relationships. As late as 1953, it was possible to list four people as major power brokers. Lester Roach managed a team of professional administrators. David Rapaport's successors, Sibylle Escalona, then Gardner Murphy, directed the Research Department. Will was chief foundation fund-raiser; and Karl was chief of staff. By the middle 1960s, however, power had become considerably more dispersed. Each program, division, or operation was headed by a leader determined to expand his or her domain and to ward off the claims of leaders within rival power centers. Consequently, Menninger seemed to lack a single core institution. Moreover, although it had been moving steadily away from the "family spirit," neither the brothers nor their senior staff offered a clear vision of what the organization was becoming as that spirit receded.

III

In 1951, Paul Bergman, émigré psychologist and sometime participant in the Rapaport group, analyzed the Medical Council, which consisted mainly of senior psychiatrists. He noted that these psychiatrists were trying to turn the council into a vehicle to counter the weight of the Menninger brothers, just as Rapaport had worked to establish his own power base. What this meant, Bergman claimed, was that power had gradually been and would continue to be "taken from the emperor & put in the hands of the barons!" Bergman was arguing that the brothers no longer represented the primary impetus behind most foundation activities. Instead, power had "tended to centrifugally retreat" into particular "circles of congenial people." Most of these "circles" were unified by a leader, or "baron." Bergman's immediate complaint was that only those "barons" who happened to be psychiatrists had gained entry into the Medical Council.[20]

Bergman's analysis comported with a developmental model that has been outlined by social theorist Larry E. Greiner, according to which an organization may experience a relatively fluid and creative founding stage that is followed by a more closely managed second stage of directive leadership. The Menninger Clinic evidenced these stages in its shift from the fluid, evolving, pioneering organization of the 1920s and 1930s, governed by a somewhat amorphous "family spirit," to the postwar years, when the Roach-Sheffel management team instituted detailed administrative procedures and policies. Greiner's third stage is decentralization: autonomous field managers seek to run the affairs of their separate constituencies. Thus Bergman's "barons," promoting the interests of their departmentally and programmatically based "baronies."[21]

Bergman considered the "barons" scarcely able to consider the needs of the organization as a whole. Roach and Sheffel were aware of this hazard and encouraged the development of general committees like the Medical Council in order to draw the leaders into closer cooperation and to provide them with broader perspectives. With their prompting and the brothers' support, a Research Council, an Educational Council, a Clinical Council, and even a Coordinating Council were organized, to be "looking at problems from the point of view of the Foundation as a whole." And yet all such efforts at coordination failed dismally, as one council replaced or supplemented another. By 1956, Karl felt the Menninger community had become so large and fragmented that there was no longer much point in continuing his monthly meetings with the professional staff. The only people with whom it seemed helpful to communicate were the department and program heads, but through direct individual encounters rather than within special councils.[22]

What Bergman referred to as a drift toward "baronies" and Karl saw as fragmentation was described by other staff veterans. Psychiatrist Harlan Crank spoke of "balkanization." Robert Holt referred to "metastatic menningeritis," in which new leaders for new programs were emerging. Psychiatrist Herbert Modlin, an influential figure at the MSP, felt that staff generally came to direct their loyalties more toward their particular department and program heads than toward the Menningers. By the mid-1960s, Philip Holzman could outline a "fiefdom" structure: "Each Department Director seems to have the total autonomy and discretion as to where he wants to go with his department, but there is no one to stop him, or check and see whether this is consistent with where The Foundation wishes to go." Organizational power appeared to have shifted decidedly, with the proliferation of divisions, programs, and general organizational complexity, into "the hands of the barons."[23]

New staff as well as veterans from the era of a strong "family spirit" noticed the change. Research psychologist Lois Murphy, who had arrived in Topeka in 1952, felt that by the 1960s it had become "too overwhelming" to seek to know and work with staff "outside of one's own area." The longer she stayed at Menninger, the more she felt anonymity outside the Research Department and the Children's Division. Many called for a return to a single integrated facility like the original Menninger Clinic and for a foundation house that would convene in one place the diverse strands of the organization. Margaret Mead, a Menninger visiting scholar and consultant since 1942, was particularly disturbed by this new age of programmatic diversity and semiautonomous leaders. She underscored her difficulty in detecting a center or a common denominator within the organization.[24]

However, there could be no dismantling of the structure of operations. The new programs had been responses to national trends. They necessarily intensified competition for resources among departmental and program heads; it was futile to expect such competition to disappear. Indeed, despite their misgivings over the passing of the old order, neither Lewis Robbins at the hospital nor Cotter Hirschberg in the Children's Division was ready to give up the substantial salary and prerogatives that came with his position. Nor could either explain how to restore the unifying traditions of the "family spirit."[25]

One functioned, then, primarily for a particular "barony" and secondarily for the foundation. To grasp fully how this had become perhaps the most important fact of organizational life, it is instructive to explore the three most powerful "baronies" of the period: the hospital, the Children's Division, and the Research Department. Most Menninger staff worked for at least one of them. Collectively, the three received the lion's share of foundation income and accounted for most of its expenditures.

I V

Because the hospital had long been the major institution, senior staff were particularly disturbed by the emergence of rival power centers that were a potential drain on hospital resources.

Despite the national trend toward community clinics, the hospital had expanded from sixty-seven beds in 1949 to one hundred fifty beds in 1966. Although private psychiatric hospitals ran at an average occupancy rate of 77 percent, Menninger consistently operated closer to capacity. In addition, hospital staff often treated outpatients and were responsible for those in the new day hospital, which enrolled an average of thirty-four patients by 1957. With this substantial increase in the adult patient population, the hospital generated an increasing proportion of foundation revenue. By 1960, it earned nearly three fourths of total Menninger income, so its staff was less than enthusiastic about many of the new programs. Several charged that they channeled hospital earnings into nonhospital ventures; the new programs spent their money. This was a misunderstanding, for most of the programs were supported either by government grants and grants from private philanthropies or by unrestricted donations solicited by Will. Hospital staff were particularly indignant with the Research Department: the research director had supposedly managed to use some of their doctors and psychologists for help with leisurely non-income-producing departmental investigations while remaining staff were overworked.[26]

The loss of cohesion and "family spirit" within the hospital was also distressing. In the postwar decades, the guide to the order sheet gradually fell into disuse, and with it went the integration of internal operations and the underlying sense of community. Several developments account for the gradual undermining of the guide, including the increased size of the hospital and the volume of its operations. The guide had been workable in a sanitarium of twenty-five or thirty patients. But as the number of inpatients increased to one hundred fifty (plus day patients) and as hospital staff grew at an even faster rate, the close communication that the guide required to coordinate staff attitudes toward patients became impossible. Moreover, hospital directors after Will never felt the same personal and professional stake in the guide; they often failed to instruct new staff on how a seemingly rigid document could be used flexibly. Finally, several new doctors excused themselves from guide traditions on the ground that it had been based on Freud's drive theory, whereas the new emphasis in psychoanalytic therapy required attention to ego psychology. Under the guide, some of them maintained, the patient had often failed to develop the ego strength or adaptational capacities to adjust to conditions of everyday life when he left Menninger.[27]

With the guide to the order sheet used less and less, the cohesion of the milieu therapy program began to dissipate. To restore the unity of an earlier era, the hospital administrative council called in 1959 for an abbreviated version of the guide. The following year, hospital director Herman Van der Waals conducted informal discussions with three senior therapists, psychiatrist Ann Appelbaum and psychologists Herbert Schlesinger and Philip Holzman. They tried to revise the guide so that it would be compatible with a large hospital oriented toward ego psychology and without Will to supervise operations. The task proved impossible, and the guide was invoked even less.[28]

If there was interest in somehow strengthening guide traditions, there was also reliance upon a professional chain of command based upon pervasive notions of medical hierarchy. With or without reference to the guide, the hospital director and his assistants passed orders to section chiefs. In turn, the section chiefs directed doctors under them, and these doctors directed nurses and attendants. It is important to see how this mix of the heavily familial guide with a hospital run increasingly according to notions of medical professionalism and hierarchy colored the experiences of one hospital director after another from the late 1940s through the 1960s.

When Will appointed Lewis Robbins to head the hospital in 1949, he hoped that it might once more become the intimate and efficient facility it had been in the 1930s. After all, Robbins had learned hospital psychiatry from him as a young resident and had worshiped guide traditions and the prewar "family spirit." He consciously modeled himself after Will as an efficient, knowledgeable, and paternal supervisor of a tightly knit hospital unit. Like Will, Robbins insisted that hospital staff (regardless of rank) communicate directly with him. And also like Will, Robbins made all vital hospital decisions himself.[29]

Robbins felt that if he pressed constantly for guide to the order sheet tradition and "the basic truths on which it was based," he could resurrect the hospital of the 1930s. Ironically, the facility became even less intimate and cohesive. Younger physicians complained that the hospital had become far too large for any director to supervise implementation of the guide approach to milieu therapy as Will had. Several resented Robbins's paternalism and insisted that any hospital approach to treatment had to be implemented loosely, owing to new staff, who had not been trained under the guide, and to different treatment circumstances in the postwar period. Robbins never acknowledged any validity in these criticisms. However, he found that he could improve morale and enhance supervision procedures if he delegated significant responsibilities to captains of separate treatment teams. Among other responsibilities, each captain might determine together with colleagues on his team how fully the guide was to be implemented.[30]

By 1953, when Robbins was replaced, he finally admitted that because of the hospital's size and staff composition, he had had no choice but to decentralize operations, to delegate authority, and to allow the guide to become less significant in the treatment process. But Robbins felt even more disheartened by another loss. Whereas all Menninger institutions had formerly been subsumed under the hospital, this had ceased to be the case. Unlike Will, he had felt compelled to fight constantly for "turf" (for more staff and other resources) in order to retain hospital influence within the larger organization. Robbins had become the first hospital "baron."[31]

Irving Kartus replaced Robbins as hospital director and held the post until 1959. He was succeeded by Herman Van der Waals, who ran the hospital until 1962. From the standpoint of their approaches to hospital management, Kartus and Van der Waals were very different. A member of the first MSP class, of 1946, Kartus, like Robbins, had been taught by older staff to cherish the traditions of the guide and milieu therapy procedures. Like Robbins and Will, he prized precisely written case reports and a noninstitutional air about the hospital. But unlike the men upon whom he sometimes modeled himself, Kartus was never particularly comfortable as director. Relaxed and accommodating, he delegated responsibilities easily and allowed the patients to drink wine, carry food about, and sleep at odd hours.[32]

Van der Waals, a prominent and aristocratic Dutch analyst who had fled when Hitler invaded his country, had none of Kartus's American informality. He disliked popular culture and prided himself on a scholarly understanding of Van Gogh and classical music. When he assumed the directorship, he announced that the character of the facility was to change. Patients were not allowed to stay up all night drinking coffee, watching television, or listening to popular music. To encourage marketable vocational skills, Van der Waals promoted programs to train patients in trades like upholstering and bookbinding. These, and not leisure pleasures, were to constitute the core of the activities programs.[33]

Despite their different approaches, both Kartus and Van der Waals fought zealously for the interests of the hospital. Both assumed that their primary responsibility was to augment hospital resources at the expense of other foundation operations and to conduct themselves as independently of the Menninger family as was possible. As well, Kartus and Van der Waals never actually ran internal hospital affairs. Both delegated the practical direction of the hospital to assistant director Peter Fleming. Although he was formally designated director from 1962 to 1968, Fleming essentially headed the internal operations from the last years of the Kartus administration.[34]

Like Kartus, Fleming had been an MSP resident in the class of 1946. Born in New York City and raised under difficult economic and social circumstances, he attended the University of Alabama as an undergraduate and completed medical school at Washington University in Saint Louis in 1941. During the war, Fleming served in an army parachute infantry regiment in the South Pacific. He finished his MSP residency at Winter in 1948 and rose rapidly through the ranks at Menninger. He was a junior-level hospital staff associate until 1952, an intermediate-level physician to 1955, the most influential hospital section leader from 1955 to 1958, and a senior psychiatrist and assistant hospital director from 1958 to 1962, when he finally assumed the formal title of director. Fleming's capacity to secure resources for the hospital was enhanced by the significant positions he occupied in other foundation power centers. After completing a training analysis with Karl in 1958, he became active in the Topeka Institute for Psychoanalysis. He also sat on the executive committee that directed the MSP.[35]

Fleming's administrative style demonstrated a full transition from Will's "familial" sanitarium. He recognized that while it was prudent to defer to the guide and Will's sanitarium program, he had to work within a large and complex multiprogrammatic organization. Like Robbins, Fleming assumed that if the hospital was to thrive, other departments and programs would have to be diminished. After Rapaport departed, Robbins had tried to collapse the Research Department and bring its resources into his hospital. Fleming revived this strategy after Gardner Murphy ceased to be research director in 1964. Without Murphy's distinguished leadership, he argued, research activities should be "brought in closer to the clinical workings of the place"—i.e., as part of his hospital. Similarly, Fleming recognized the subtle power that TIP exerted over his hospital because senior institute training analysts had analyzed and were analyzing his doctors and psychologists. More than most psychiatrists, Fleming understood the role of psychoanalysis in foundation politics and fought back. To reduce the control of TIP training analysts, he forbade them from working with those of their analysands who happened to be on his staff.[36]

Fleming was a tough autocrat and invoked none of Will's gentle and familial forms of governance. He alone was to decide key policies and procedures. Hospital section chiefs were expected to implement *his* decisions, and they were instructed to issue orders to their underlings in much the same authoritarian fashion. All section chiefs were physicians. The most influential members of treatment teams were also physicians. Physicians dictated how nurses and attendants worked with patients. To further erode what was left of Will's practice of consulting the nursing staff, Fleming sought to fuse nursing and activities therapy departments into one administrative entity and to blur differences between their responsibilities. Apprehensive that respected psychologists like Holzman and Schlesinger might impede his quest to place ultimate authority in the hands of physicians, Fleming even attempted to install the social worker above the psychologist in his hierarchy on the treatment team.[37]

Consummate diplomacy and political skill were required for an assistant hospital director to exert more authority than the director. Fleming may have been the most skillful of the "barons" during the 1950s and 1960s. He was something of a prankster and mixed freely with all levels of his hospital staff, rarely missing social activities. Since his policies were sometimes unpopular, Fleming tried to distance himself from them by requiring a close associate, like senior psychiatrist Harvey Schloesser, to announce them. Nor was he above appealing to the preferences and fears of particular staff when he needed their support. Above all, Fleming demonstrated his political skill through the way he accommodated Karl, who had been his training analyst. He invited Karl once a week to a case conference and treated the visit as a great honor to the staff. Perhaps understanding Karl's sense of inadequacy better than Karl understood his analysand, Fleming found that he was able to reduce Karl's intervention in hospital affairs.[38]

Despite his considerable political skill, Fleming could not have enjoyed such a long tenure without keen understanding of the hospital treatment program. He recognized that because of the foundation's treatment orientation, the success or failure of its clinical program rested upon supervision of all aspects of the patient's day. Consequently, a heavy staff-patient ratio was imperative. He saw to it that by 1967 the total hospital ratio exceeded that of all competitors. Menninger especially outflanked its long-standing "new psychiatry" rivals in the proportion of regular (nonresident) physicians, activities therapists, and social workers who labored full time on hospital wards.[39]

Fleming was also a talented administrator. He rarely failed to appoint adept psychiatrists as his section chiefs, and he passed on many practical suggestions to attendants. Quite consciously, he tried to set an example for the doctors under him by spending a lot of time with patients. The doctor had to know the patient so well, Fleming insisted, that he should share the patient's sense of reality and feel nearly responsible for the patient's failures. This intensely individualized approach to treatment resembled Will's prewar approach in certain respects. But Fleming was no admirer of the "family spirit" and had qualms about a hospital doctor or nurse giving preference to staff "family" over the family at home. He also felt free to think the unthinkable about clinical procedures, much as Karl had often done. He asked quite openly, for example, why certain patients who had left the Menninger Clinic had improved in hospitals that most psychiatrists considered professionally inferior.[40]

Fleming's term ended in July 1968. Following various interim arrangements, Otto Kernberg replaced him a year later. In Menninger lore, Kernberg has been credited with having reversed Fleming's centralized rule. He established a hospital council of section chiefs and department heads, and asked them to decide major policies, which Fleming had formerly determined. Kernberg also decided that all hospital sections and professional disciplines were to have considerable autonomy in managing their own affairs. But long before Kernberg took over, forces were at work that promoted autonomy for the staff and even more freedoms for patients. Years earlier, these forces had made it increasingly difficult for any head of the hospital (including Fleming) to concentrate power in his position as Will had.[41]

Growth in the staff and patient population was one of the most important forces. When Robbins became hospital director, he found that he had to divide staff into three interdisciplinary treatment teams. After the enlarged physical plant became operational in 1954, several more teams were authorized. Although Fleming wanted to centralize power, each team required considerable autonomy to function effectively. He had to settle for passing orders to each of several section chiefs, who communicated to captains of the teams under their jurisdiction.[42]

The specialization of knowledge within mental health disciplines also militated against a centralized command. Team captains often found themselves more dependent upon specialists within their unit than upon the advice of their section chiefs or upon Fleming. Only the team's social worker had been trained to take family histories and to link data from these histories to behavior. Only the team psychologist knew how to administer tests proficiently or to extrapolate from them for treatment recommendations. And only the team activities therapist, whose training differed fundamentally from the doctor's psychotherapeutic approach, knew how to plan and revise many aspects of the patient's activities schedule. In spite of Fleming's efforts, physicians often lacked authority. Few were willing to press their perspectives on their colleagues, and it often happened that someone other than the doctor—a senior psychologist or social worker, for example—became the real leader of a team. Although the teams acknowledged the pronouncements of the director and the section chiefs, the social relationships and specialty skills of particular team members were often far more important to operations than orders from above.[43]

The drug revolution also placed a subtle check on Fleming's fondness for power. His allegiance to psychoanalytically informed milieu therapy made him skeptical of the new psychotropic drugs. He insisted that the beneficial effects of the drugs had to be measured against their side effects. Accordingly, Kartus began a research project on the effects of Thorazine. It was administered to a limited number of patients, and several became sufficiently tranquil to leave the more restricted hospital wards and join activities programs. Nurses and attendants were pleased, for the patients were easier to manage. Some younger doctors and several psychologists were also impressed; they recommended greater use of Thorazine and new research programs on other psychotropic drugs. By the early 1960s, Fleming felt compelled to allow recruitment of psychiatrists whose orientation was more biological than psychoanalytic. Although he would not appoint any of them to head a treatment team, he permitted, and in time encouraged, a fundamental diversity in psychiatric orientation in the foundation's largest institution.[44]

Finally, Fleming's authority over his hospital was limited by a perspective that mandated greater patient autonomy. First articulated in England after the war, this was amplified by Maxwell Jones in *The Therapeutic Community* (1953), which held social environment to be the key to the onslaught of mental illness and therefore basic in combating it. An effective mental hospital became a therapeutic community where patients prompted one another to function according to healthy yet common social norms. Patients learned from one another to adopt the tenets of their community. Reducing social dissonance in this way, the patients essentially cured one another.[45]

"New psychiatry" facilities like Austen Riggs and the Institute for Living, drawing heavily upon Jones's concept, found that because psychotropic drugs reduced violent mood swings and thought disorders, they permitted patients to become active in determining their own communal rules. Although Fleming was no devotee of Jones's theory, he did not feel Menninger could afford to be overtaken by its competitors and allowed elements of the therapeutic community to be implemented. Patients were encouraged to hold formal meetings, to establish governing bodies, and to elect officers. They were even permitted to propose measures to modify hospital life. A hospital-wide Patient Council, an Outpatient Club, and social and recreational groups were formed. Patients drafted constitutions that underscored their rights and responsibilities. At times, the Patient Council met with the hospital director or assistant director to voice grievances. Council requests were difficult to disregard. According to "Years of Change," a remarkable account by a Menninger patient, the emergence of new freedoms and opportunities for patients was the most important development in the facility during her stay. Whereas patients had been perceived paternalistically under the prewar milieu therapy program, introduction of the therapeutic community concept influenced hospital policy to regard patients as adults.[46]

If the hospital under Fleming lacked the certitudes of the old "family spirit," both staff and patients therefore had increased freedom. Much more than before, staff spoke of the importance of "self-expression," of "using our best judgment, each of us, no longer being guided by some [hospital] document." There were unprecedented demands for more participation of staff in the decisions of the hospital. Patients, too, requested greater autonomy, and their demands were taken seriously. When "Stephanie Michaels" was admitted to the hospital in 1953, attendants insisted that she and other patients play Pin the Tail on the Donkey and similar depreciatory games. By the end of the decade, Michaels felt that a viable patients' rights tradition had changed all that. The childish games had been put away, and wine bottles appeared occasionally at tables.[47]

Greater staff freedom and enhanced opportunities for patients did not necessarily make for improved treatment results. It is difficult to compare statistics on cure rates under Fleming with other stewardships, because of changes in the characteristics of the patients themselves.

Most continued to be quite wealthy. Monthly fees averaged $1,400 in the mid-1950s and nearly $2,000 a decade later, but special reductions or foundation subsidies were rare. Despite the spread of health insurance coverage, the average patient recovered only about 25 percent of that amount from third-party payments and had bills to pay for at least a year, because stays were longer than at most other facilities. Therefore, it is hardly surprising that by 1965, the average annual family income of a patient exceeded $20,000. Consistent with the past, patients in the Fleming hospital tended to be well educated. Over half had some college experience. The majority had traveled widely, were culturally sophisticated, and came from professional families. An important difference between them and patients from earlier eras was that most were adolescents or young adults. This reflected a national reduction in age within private facilities. Another departure was that the proportion of patients with character (personality) disorders increased steadily under Fleming. During the 1961–62 fiscal year, they accounted for 36 percent of patients released. A character disorder was difficult to treat in any setting, but since the disorder often made it impossible for the patient to develop a transference relationship with his therapist, it was especially difficult in a psychoanalytic facility.[48]

The high percentage of patients suffering from character disorders and of those who had had prior hospitalizations countered successful treatment outcomes. But youthfulness, which signaled greater treatment potential, may have been a more important variable, for statistics under Fleming yielded a rather optimistic picture. Whereas the percentage of patients categorized as "improved" on release only slightly exceeded the percentage "unimproved" during the immediate postwar years, the gap widened under Fleming. In the 1957–58 fiscal year, for example, 84 percent "improved"; only 16 percent were "unimproved." In the 1960s, these promising figures were lowered somewhat (66 percent "improved," 34 percent "unimproved," in 1964–65). But even this was encouraging, because less than 12 percent of the patients had entered the hospital with an "overall good" prognosis. Whereas more patients left "improved" than anytime in the past, the readmission rate was nearly cut in half between 1953 and 1960.[49]

The most reliable statistical information on patients under Fleming came from the Psychotherapy Research Project. The PRP carefully accumulated vast amounts of information on forty-two patients. Of the twenty-two in psychoanalysis, eight (36 percent) showed "really good improvement," six (27 percent) represented "failure," five (23 percent) "moderately improved," and three (14 percent) showed "equivocal improvement." The twenty in supportive therapy had somewhat better outcomes: nine (45 percent) showed "really good improvement," five (25 percent) "failed," three (15 percent) made "moderate improvement" and three made "equivocal improvement." Despite the limited number of PRP patients, it is significant that between two thirds and four fifths of them "improved."[50]

However, Fleming's hospital did not compare well to several rivals. The psychiatric research group of Robert L. Kahn, Max Fink, and Nathaniel Siegel published a systematic comparison for 1959 of Menninger with the Massachusetts Mental Health Center. Although MMHC had a far inferior staff-patient ratio, a less comprehensively trained staff, and considerably fewer funds to enhance treatment, its patients enjoyed shorter stays and seemingly more successful results. Menninger patients often had to be hospitalized for more than a year, after which 19 percent were rated "unimproved." In contrast, MMHC patients stayed only a few months (often less) and only 10 percent left "unimproved." Linda Hilles, a former Menninger Clinic psychiatrist practicing at San Francisco's Mount Zion Hospital, published a comparison of Menninger with Topeka State Hospital for 1965. Hilles noted that the initial prognosis for patients in both facilities was poor. There was only an 11.7 percent chance for an "overall good" outcome at Menninger and 15.4 percent at Topeka State. However, whereas 55.3 percent of Menninger patients were advised to seek additional treatment in other hospitals, only 11.3 percent were so advised at Topeka State. And despite the superior financial resources and staff-patient ratios at Menninger, the percentage of patients labeled "unimproved at discharge" (34.2 percent) was comparable to the "unimproved" rate (39.4 percent) at Topeka State.[51]

Both studies were potentially misleading. At MMHC and at Topeka State, "improvement" tended to be equated with symptom relief and the patient's ability to resume work. Menninger required far more. Fleming's staff insisted that the patient had to "develop insight" and evidence a capacity to "work through" his problems. In addition to the acceptable behavior patterns that MMHC and Topeka State required for the "improved" category, Menninger demanded convincing signs of intrapsychic change. Nonetheless, in a period when the health insurance industry, state legislatures, and private donors took increasing stock in short hospital stays and high if superficial "improvement" rates, Fleming and his colleagues knew that the conclusions of the two studies would not enhance their image.

An exhaustive statistical study prepared by Charles K. Kanno and Raymond M. Glasscote—*Private Psychiatric Hospitals: A National Survey*—provided more cause for concern. Published by the Joint Information Service of the American Psychiatric Association and the National Association for Mental Health, this 1966 document had almost official status. Reporting only aggregate results and never revealing individual hospital responses to their questionnaire, the survey indicated that other private facilities were experiencing the same changes in patient clientele as Menninger. Patients in most private hospitals were younger than before and suffered more often from character disorders. Unlike Menninger, however, three quarters of the hospitals reported an average patient stay of less than two months. And whereas 55.3 percent of Menninger patients discharged for 1965 were referred to other hospitals for further treatment, this compared to a 6 percent referral average for private hospitals generally. To be sure, the standards for improvement and cure at Menninger were probably far more demanding than those of several private competitors. But Fleming's staff would have had trouble making this case against similar, psychoanalytically oriented clinics, like Chestnut Lodge and Austen Riggs.[52]

In general, then, treatment results in Fleming's hospital seemed to have improved markedly over previous regimes. But it was less than apparent that the staff outperformed their "new psychiatry" rivals, despite better staff-patient ratios.

V

In 1958, Peter Fleming's hospital was the largest component of the Menninger Clinic, with nearly six hundred full-time employees and a budget approximating $2 million. However, the Children's Division had begun a period of unprecedented growth, and by the mid-1960s, it had become the second-largest Menninger institution and a major "barony."

In 1952, the organization appropriated money to remodel several decrepit buildings that had housed the Children's Division. It also purchased a ten-acre parcel for future expansion. At the same time, it committed itself to attract distinguished professional leadership. Negotiations commenced to recruit J. Cotter Hirschberg, one of the most prominent child psychiatrists in the nation. At the Denver Mental Hygiene Clinic, a child guidance facility of the University of Colorado Medical Center, Hirschberg had designed a widely heralded program to train child psychiatrists, psychologists, and social workers. Several of his students were emerging as leaders in child psychiatry. To relocate, Hirschberg made substantial demands. He sought a higher salary than any Menninger senior psychiatrist, a firm commitment to reorganization and expansion of the Children's Division, plus attractive job offers for Denver associates so that they could move with him. Despite some misgivings, the foundation met all of Hirschberg's requirements.[53]

The primary motivation for this sudden attention to the children's facility, after Southard School's troubled beginnings, was institutional self-interest. With the mean age for mental patients decreasing, more adolescents and adults in their twenties filled the hospital. Foundation officials assumed that large numbers of children might soon be candidates for Menninger services. They increased their chances for an enlarged clientele and lower per capita costs through economies of scale if they improved the physical plant and recruited a distinguished director. Moreover, influential Menninger trustees Mary Switzer and Marion Kenworthy offered to raise funds to cover increased expenditures for the physical plant and personnel and to enlist other trustees in fund-raising, even if long-term profits did not eventuate.[54]

Karl and Will favored expansion and improvement. Both recognized that this could benefit the Research Department and the MSP in important ways. A large and vigorous Children's Division could provide a data base for various Research Department projects and a training center in child psychiatry for MSP fellows. Because of his growing interest in preventive psychiatry, Will found himself attracted to the notion of treating the child to avert problems in adult life.[55]

Therefore, Cotter Hirschberg arrived in Topeka in mid-1952 with firm pledges of support, more prestige than any other Menninger psychiatrist, and promises of unprecedented autonomy. He had another advantage. Since Hirschberg was allowed to bring with him staff associates, such as social worker Arthur Mandelbaum, his authority was less likely to be diminished by colleagues with primary loyalties to the Menningers or to other foundation directors. Indeed, he came to Topeka determined to develop the sort of "barony" within the Children's Division that Rapaport had built in the Research Department and Robbins and others were fashioning in the hospital.

Much more than any of his predecessors, Hirschberg stressed a medical approach that focused upon the individual child. He drew the division away from its traditional emphasis on educational and recreational programs where the child was approached as a member of a classroom or play group. Instead, he created procedures intended to locate and track the specific physical and psychic impediments of each child. Careful diagnosis was especially important, because disturbed children rarely display clear and stable symptoms; many "show different symptoms with different persons in the same setting." More than adults, children evidence "wide variations in etiological factors in the resultant adaptive patterns." Once the causal factors behind the child's malady and corresponding adaptive patterns were diagnosed, Hirschberg promoted a team approach to treatment. It was necessary for the psychiatrist, the neurologist, the psychologist, and the social worker to exchange observations regularly and to record how the child was progressing with "intensive individual therapy."[56]

Although this approach was to be "based on classical psychoanalytic theory," Hirschberg emphasized that the mental lives of children were much more unstable than those of adults. Among children, there were "less definite clear-cut neuroses and psychoses." Therefore, it was essential for staff to "modify classical analytic techniques according to the needs of the therapeutic situation with the specific problem presented by each child." Concrete medical, social, and psychiatric observations on the way the child responded to specific therapy were to be emphasized over classical theory and techniques. Like Klein, Holt, and other members of Rapaport's former research group, Hirschberg urged his colleagues to trust clinical observations over traditional psychoanalytic abstractions, even over Freudian clinical techniques.[57]

Hirschberg's approach brought him into conflict with émigré analyst Rudolf Ekstein, who was more deeply committed to psychoanalytic theory and technique in children's work. Ekstein often used his staff seminar to criticize Hirschberg. He insisted that a child's organic life and his interaction with his social milieu could not be understood without classical psychoanalytic insights. In some sense, this Ekstein-Hirschberg debate duplicated the discussions within the Rapaport group on the utility of Freudian metapsychology. Will felt that it promoted a serious "split in staff allegiance" among child care workers.[58]

Conflict emerged, too, between the professional and the nonprofessional staff (cooks, janitors, and attendants). The latter considered themselves overworked because of Hirschberg's focus on the individual child. Children had been easier to cook for, to clean up after, and to care for when they had been required to follow a common schedule and to express themselves in the same socially sanctioned ways. Moreover, the very jobs performed by most nonprofessional staff had evolved out of the inpatient character of the children's operation—i.e., around-the-clock services. As Hirschberg pressed for increased outpatient services, there was fear that some positions would be phased out.[59]

So Hirschberg found himself confronted by both Ekstein and nonprofessional staff. To add to his troubles, he lost the support of Lester Roach and both Menninger brothers, because he demanded conditions that did not exist elsewhere in the foundation. He insisted that though his staff's work week fell short of the standard forty-eight hours, they were not to compensate with time at the hospital. Hirschberg also limited the number of adolescent patients despite his operating deficit, because "the broad spread in age groups interfered with efforts to establish a unified program." Roach chided Hirschberg for "running such an esoteric center that we don't admit anybody."[60]

Hirschberg claimed that these provisions were essential to "the special problems of child psychiatry" and insisted that they "are not required to bear any relationship to patterns elsewhere in the Foundation." Roach advised Will to replace Hirschberg. Will agreed that Hirschberg did not seem to be able to deal with budgetary realities. Karl (who was distressed that Hirschberg knew little about his Jewish heritage) liked some of his "exotic" treatment measures but was displeased by their cost.[61]

If Hirschberg prompted too much ill will throughout the foundation and among his staff to establish a powerful "barony," he nonetheless transformed his division into a renowned center for child psychiatry. One of his innovations was particularly significant. He did not allow parents simply to leave a child in his lap, for a problem of family dysfunction often accounted for the child's maladaptive conduct. Although the family therapy movement had hardly commenced in the early 1950s, Hirschberg insisted that the whole family go through intensive interviews before a child could be admitted. After admission, parents were pressured to enter therapy in their hometowns and were required to return to Topeka for family therapy sessions with their child at least every two months. In addition, social workers were assigned to meet and correspond with the parents and to explain to the treatment team the family's psychological patterns. Senior staff claimed that "a major part of our work is concerned with helping the parents themselves with hidden feelings which deter them from seeking constructive solutions to the task of helping their child."[62]

Another innovation concerned scholarship funding. Karl had always warned that his organization served only a wealthy clientele. Hirschberg was determined that his division would cease to be a center for the affluent. He persuaded the brothers and the trustees that scholarships for children who could not afford the $650 monthly fee would only modestly increase costs, significantly enhance enrollment, and encourage philanthropic donations. A few months after the scholarship program was in place, Hirschberg reported that enrollment had risen to the capacity of sixteen and that there was a waiting list of "scholarship cases." Indeed, Will found it easier to solicit donations once the class bias had been addressed. After adoption of a policy through which all staff publication royalties were channeled into the scholarship fund, the Seeley Foundation took the lead among private philanthropies in contributing to the fund.[63]

One of the ironies of the treatment reforms and the scholarship plan was that when Hirschberg stepped down as divisional director in 1957, he left to his successor a large, well-financed, nationally recognized children's program. If he did not preside over it with a powerful air of command, he had provided the resources for his successor to do so. Indeed, Hirschberg's final innovation was to initiate plans for a new Children's Division campus, half a mile from other Menninger facilities. A school, an activities center, and residence buildings were to be constructed there, to serve as many as fifty children.

There were several reasons for the Menningers' acquiescence to Hirschberg's proposed campus. After the scholarship program was instituted, a long waiting list indicated that more children could be admitted if there were facilities for them. Many on the list were adolescents; youth treatment might become a new specialty area. A young patient clientele was appealing, for the climate of "deinstitutionalization," the rise of community mental health centers, and the use of new drugs might eventually decrease the number of adult patients. Finally, financial appeals for children's facilities found a level of support nationally that had not been evident in the past. Will secured $500,000 from the Good Samaritan Foundation, for example, and $900,000 in federal funds under the Hill-Burton Act. So construction on the new campus began in 1959, and the division moved there two years later.[64]

It did so under a new director, Robert Switzer, a former navy medical officer. He had received his medical degree at Indiana University School of Medicine, then completed a psychiatric residency in the U.S. Naval Hospital at San Diego, where he met Hirschberg. Switzer took a second residency at the Colorado Psychopathic Hospital in Denver and ended up training under Hirschberg, but he continued to work at naval hospitals until early 1956, when he accepted Hirschberg's offer to join the Children's Division. In Topeka, Switzer still regarded Hirschberg as a mentor. Becoming inpatient director, however, he demonstrated administrative capacities superior to Hirschberg's, particularly in financial management.[65]

In 1957, Roach and the Menningers asked Hirschberg to serve as director of training in child psychiatry. They made Switzer divisional head, because they wanted "somebody who really wants to be an administrator" and felt that Switzer would be a tough manager who, while perpetuating the reforms of the Hirschberg era, would force a growing staff to live within necessary budget constraints.[66]

Switzer kept close tabs on divisional finances. He cut costs by forcing the Equitable Life Assurance Company into a precedent-setting settlement that required Equitable to issue hospital insurance to his division even though it had no operating room. Switzer increased physician referrals and contributed significantly to fund-raising efforts. He also reorganized all Children's Division departments to enhance their efficiency.[67]

The biggest staff objection to Switzer was that he ruled with such a strong hand that discussion was inhibited. Playing the part of the naval captain, he often issued orders without consulting staff. Disagreement with those orders "does not necessarily mean disloyalty," child psychiatrist Tarlton Morrow tried to explain to Switzer. Others underscored the point, but with little effect. And when they urged him to hire experienced senior professional staff to keep pace with the growth of the patient population, the budget-minded director recruited less costly child care support workers.[68]

Although most of the staff preferred Hirschberg's conciliatory manner to Switzer's authoritarian rule, they appreciated the latter's strength when he defended the division's resources. Under Hirschberg, they had feared that Fleming might turn children's work into an adjunct of the adult hospital. But with Switzer's more assertive leadership, their fears receded. He defeated Fleming's attempt to integrate children's outpatient work with adult outpatient services until 1964, when Fleming prevailed on the grounds of avoiding wasteful duplication. But Switzer reversed the merger, with the claim that it promoted inefficiency and heightened staff tensions.[69]

As Fleming's equal in territorial conflicts, Switzer saw to it that his staff kept abreast of national developments in child psychiatry. He considered the drug trend as the beginning of a shift nationally toward biopsychiatry and insisted that even a facility with strong Freudian traditions ignored the trend at its peril. If psychotropic drugs calmed troubled children without adverse side effects, his staff would have more time and energy for depth psychotherapy; they would not have to waste staff hours with discipline problems. Despite considerable staff resistance, Switzer succeeded in increasing drug therapy.[70]

The division's developing reputation for therapeutic excellence derived, too, from its concern for family relationships. More even than Hirschberg, Switzer pressured divisional staff to see the child as part of a family constellation. He had his associates devote much of their time to family life, on the grounds that family relations contributed significantly to a child's illness. Staff were also urged to research and publish on the role of the family. The program furthest from the prewar "family spirit" now led the foundation in its understanding of family issues.[71]

Despite these accomplishments, divisional staff never warmed to Switzer and he never exhibited much pride or affection for most of them.

Several blamed him for their difficulties with an increasingly adolescent clientele; he admitted fourteen-to-sixteen-year-olds, which few hospitals were willing to treat. Switzer retorted that staff treatment was somehow lacking; only about a third of the children they worked with were able to cope effectively after returning to their families.[72]

This atmosphere of mutual distrust and conflict differed markedly from conditions at the hospital. Although many factors contributed to these contrasting climates, differences in the scale of operations and the sensitivity of the directors were among the most important. The adult hospital had become so large and complex that centralized directives never came across with quite their original force or content. Fleming recognized that this was inevitable and rarely pressed for closer compliance. In contrast, the Children's Division staff was much smaller and more concentrated; Switzer could determine more easily when his orders were breached. But unlike Fleming, he never understood that it was often best to permit departures from his commands.

V I

When Gardner Murphy arrived in Topeka in 1952 to become the new Research Department director, there was little prospect that Research could approximate the hospital as one of the most powerful foundation "baronies." Its strengths had diminished significantly with the Stockbridge exodus.

The successful recruitment of Murphy revived the spirits of the department as no other event could have. Born in Chillicothe, Ohio, in 1895, the son of a nationally prominent Episcopal minister and educational reformer, Gardner Murphy did his undergraduate work in psychology at Yale and received his master's degree at Harvard and his doctorate at Columbia. Murphy also worked briefly at two Massachusetts "new psychiatry" facilities, McLean and Boston Psychopathic. Using word association tests on Manhattan State Hospital patients in the early 1920s, he anticipated Karl's concept of a continuum between normal and pathological mental states. Murphy taught in the Columbia Psychology Department during the 1930s and moved to the Psychology Department at City College of New York in 1940. His book *Experimental Social Psychology* (1931) employed an empirical approach to a subject area that had not yet been accepted in academic psychological circles. His next volume, *Approaches to Personality* (1932), explicated the tenets of psychoanalysis and of other modestly heretical branches of personality theory. With broad interests that extended even into parapsychology, he conducted several important studies of perception.[73]

At CCNY, Murphy supervised the studies of George Klein, Roy Schafer, Martin Mayman, and Philip Holzman. He also worked with Rudolf Ekstein. Having met David Rapaport through his interest in assisting refugee intellectuals, Murphy was impressed by his brilliance and helped him to find employment at Osawatomie State Hospital. After Rapaport moved to Menninger, Murphy told Klein, Schafer, Mayman, and Holzman that they would benefit by working with him. Although he had reservations about Rapaport's insistence on a common perspective among his Topeka researchers, Murphy nevertheless played an important part in the formation of the Rapaport group.[74]

By hiring Murphy in 1952, the Menningers anticipated that even if he failed to rebuild Research, some of his enormous prestige would reflect on the foundation. Here was a man who had been chair of the Society for Psychological Studies of Social Issues and president of both the Eastern Psychological Association and the American Psychological Association. Columbia University had awarded him the esteemed Butler Medal for his work in experimental social psychology, while the United States Department of Agriculture used him as a consultant.[75]

Through a strange lapse in the recruitment process, neither the Menningers nor many foundation officials knew that Murphy lacked clinical experience, especially after the 1920s. Nor did he have training in psychoanalysis. Although he read widely on almost all phases of psychological research, by the early 1950s Murphy was no longer involved in psychological investigations of any sort. Escalona and Klein represented a minority on the staff in recognizing that from the standpoint of age, as well as of psychological orientation, he was very different from Rapaport.[76]

The contrast between Rapaport and Murphy was especially striking in terms of their perspectives on psychoanalysis. Rapaport came to regard his principal contribution as one internal to the psychoanalytic movement—systematization of Freud's theoretical writings. Acknowledging "I simply don't know very much about psychoanalytic theory," Murphy knew enough to feel that Freudians were too preoccupied with internal concerns. "The secularism, or provincialism of psychoanalysis bothers me, as usual," he said. He felt that analysts had not kept up with new research in cognitive psychology, behaviorism, and other important areas of psychological inquiry. Indeed, too few psychoanalytic loyalists understood the breadth of Freud's own conceptions and how they overlapped with phenomenology, gestalt theory, and diverse biochemical and sociocultural systems of thought. Murphy was also convinced that if psychoanalysis hoped to become rigorous and systematic in its language and observations, adherents would have to move beyond Freud's formulations. These were too "socioculturally stained" by Freud's time and place to carry the modern scientific researcher very far. Finally, Murphy was sure that psychoanalysis was inattentive to the "problems of the different structural composition of groups." Psychoanalysis had to adopt a social psychology that would enable it to focus on the structures of those cultures and institutions that shaped individual lives.[77]

It is somewhat surprising that Murphy accepted a Menninger offer, for he knew he did not share the foundation's clinical and psychoanalytic orientation. However, he sensed that certain foundation researchers were ready to break with tradition in favor of a more eclectic investigatory program. And his interviews in Topeka fanned that flame. Moreover, his wife, Lois, was eager to move to Topeka. A psychological researcher at Sarah Lawrence College, she was promised the records of Escalona's infancy project if she came. This would enable her to investigate systematically the emotional lives of these children as they grew up.[78]

Gardner Murphy soon realized that it would be more difficult to develop the Research Department than he had anticipated, even though Will consistently supported him. Lester Roach encouraged Murphy in his willingness to undertake biomedical topics and other research projects that the foundation traditionally avoided. Together, Will and Roach promised added resources, considerable flexibility, and even a special Research Department building. Murphy's problem was Karl.[79]

Karl felt that Murphy was on his brother's "side." Although he respected Murphy enormously, he was also jealous of a man whose national reputation rivaled his own. Karl was particularly irked by Will's pledge to give Murphy two months off every summer and to hire his wife. Periodically antagonistic to Murphy for these and other reasons, Karl sometimes taunted the Research Department staff for failing to produce better and faster than the new director required. Karl's behavior distressed Murphy beyond measure. Four years after arriving in Topeka, he was exploring the possibility of returning to CCNY.[80]

By 1954, Murphy realized that the Research Department would remain less than vital to the foundation without support from clinically oriented psychiatrists. So he appointed Robert Wallerstein, an ambitious and energetic MSP psychiatric graduate, as assistant research director. Wallerstein had demonstrated clinical talent as chief of psychosomatic services at Winter Hospital. He also had a commitment to psychoanalysis; Murphy hoped that this might provide a balance against his own reservations about Freud's theories. Finally, Wallerstein had shown himself to be an aggressive and territorial leader. Murphy was certain that he had made the right choice, especially after he and Lois became close friends with Wallerstein and his wife.[81]

Soon after he joined Murphy, Wallerstein established the Psychotherapy Research Project as the major departmental undertaking. It was to be "the largest single feather in our cap." One of the first large-scale investigations of the psychotherapeutic process anywhere, the project evolved out of Paul Bergman's informal research group. In 1946, Bergman had begun a review of Freudian, Jungian, Rogerian, and other psychotherapeutic schools to determine how the theories of each translated into clinical practice. He also began to collect data on the relative success of his own diverse treatment approaches to Menninger patients. By 1949, Bergman had assembled an interdisciplinary committee to join him in reading about and discussing results of various therapies. Consisting of hospital physicians, training analysts, and psychologists, the Bergman committee linked the Research Department with staff elsewhere in the organization. Other than a Health-Sickness Rating Scale, with which the mental health of patients could be compared, however, Bergman's committee produced no major documents. When Wallerstein became Murphy's assistant, he recognized that an expanded committee pledged to a formal study and major publications was the best way to make Research relevant to the rest of the Menninger Clinic.[82]

With considerable political skill, Wallerstein went about formalizing and enlarging what Bergman had initiated. He invited Lewis Robbins, still a powerful presence in the hospital, to become the cochair of the Psychotherapy Research Project. Wallerstein also saw to it that other prestigious physicians had important roles in this venture. Mindful, too, that senior training analysts were influential figures and potentially serious adversaries, Wallerstein recruited several for PRP roles.[83]

Next, Wallerstein drafted various research proposals. He secured a start-up grant from the New York Foundation and then one from the Ford Foundation. Soon the Research Department was paying the salaries of between fifteen and twenty PRP investigators. As the financial base for and prestige of the PRP expanded, several adversaries became strong defenders.[84]

To perpetuate these political gains and ensure continued funding, Wallerstein realized, an elaborate, scientifically respectable design for the measurement of psychotherapeutic outcomes would have to be devised and implemented. Yet he recognized that Menninger staff, aside from a few Research Department psychologists, lacked experience with rigorous procedures for tests and measurements.

To help remedy this deficiency, Wallerstein found psychologist

Helen Sargent of incalculable value. Sargent agreed to oversee methodological aspects of the PRP. She decided to focus the project on forty-two
adult patients who started therapy between 1954 and 1958. All were
evaluated by PRP staff at three crucial points: when they entered treatment, when their treatment was terminated, and during follow-up inquiries several years later. After noting many of the assumptions implicit in
the psychoanalytic theory of therapy, Sargent drafted with colleagues
roughly two thousand predictions. PRP staff were to choose from among
the predictive statements and assumptions as they worked with patients.
The staff member was to assign a number on a numerical scale that
corresponded with how fully a predictive statement or theoretical assumption applied to a patient at a designated point in time. In this way,
Sargent succeeded in installing the Guttman Scale and other means to
measure quantitatively the changes in each of the patients before, during,
and after therapy. As a result, the project yielded statistical information
on the relative utility of various forms of therapy that scientific researchers elsewhere took seriously.[85]

As work on PRP progressed, Sargent, Wallerstein, and other key staff
worked to perfect their techniques and data. It took a dozen years before
they felt that they could release even a preliminary formulation of their
major finding—that a patient's ego strength was a crucial variable in the
treatment process. Only patients with strong initial ego strength would
do well with relatively orthodox, highly unstructured, and therefore
rather expressive psychoanalytic treatment. Those with low ego strength
would do better with more structured and supportive therapy. Although
this conclusion was hardly earth-shattering, it had never before been
sustained with such a massive array of statistical data. Predictably, the
number of orthodox analyses of Menninger patients with low ego
strength declined substantially in the years after the basic PRP conclusion
was released. But despite this tangible result, psychoanalytically oriented
therapists elsewhere in the country found the PRP conclusion too commonplace to merit extensive discussion. It seemed merely to reinforce
Freud's feeling that full-scale psychoanalysis would be ineffectual with
psychotics or with those heading toward psychoses. As PRP researchers
recognized that they were saddled with this mundane finding, they became even more preoccupied with questions of methodology. The preponderance of PRP publications concerned specific remedies for dozens
of methodological impediments to scientific measurement of the therapeutic process.[86]

As the PRP dragged on, terminating officially in 1972, support for
it within the foundation began to fade. Even members of the Research

Department lost interest, except for those involved with methodological subtleties. Nonetheless, for most Menninger clinicians, the PRP established the utility of the Research Department. The extended PRP investigations removed much of the mythology and mystery from psychoanalytically informed psychotherapy. At the same time, they helped some staff to see more clearly that psychoanalysis had important treatment limitations. Psychoanalysis could feed upon its own theoretical premises and jargon, and isolate itself from knowledge in other fields of inquiry.

As Wallerstein busied himself with the PRP, Gardner Murphy was determined to move the department beyond Rapaport's psychoanalytic preoccupations. He had long believed that human personality was best understood by focusing on the interaction between emotional life and the environment. This interaction would best be assessed by linking three approaches to personality—the biological, the psychological, and the sociological. Such disciplinary interactionism would do more than broaden the scope of psychoanalysis; it would enhance all personality theories. To promote interactionism, the Research Department had to recruit staff with innovative biological and sociological approaches, including some with nonpsychoanalytic perspectives. "We should be building a *system* of interrelated projects," Murphy insisted.[87]

For developing a biological orientation, Murphy had no compunction about hiring a neuropsychologist like Phillip Rennick, who studied brain lesions and evaluated human motor capacities. Joseph Kovach, an ethnologist trained in the American biopsychological tradition, was retained to study birds. A thyroid gland dysfunction project was organized to investigate the psychological and endocrine functioning of people with overactive nodules within the thyroid. Murphy also pushed, often unsuccessfully, for staff and research projects involving genetic and pharmacological factors in personality. He hired Elmer Green, a psychologist who had been trained in engineering, to open a laboratory filled with machines that could measure psychophysiological responses to stimuli and to pursue biofeedback techniques.[88]

Murphy's efforts to spur investigations in social psychology were less extensive but hardly insignificant. He created a social science division, which studied how those Topekans who had been relocated because of a federal urban renewal project fared psychologically. It also examined psychological effects of a 1966 tornado that devastated Topeka, and it investigated why low-income families in the city responded poorly to psychotherapy. Researchers assigned to these and other projects within the division became proficient in survey research, demography, cultural geography, and urban economics.[89]

Whatever their orientation, Murphy was supportive to his researchers. Reflecting on his Menninger Clinic years, he acknowledged that he had been "very good at nurturing research." Quite unlike Rapaport, Murphy took "the utmost pains to avoid domination of any person or imperialistic interference with any research idea which germinates anywhere." Admitting that his days as a researcher had passed, he willingly assumed the midwife role of encouraging those with potentially significant research projects. He cut red tape, helped researchers to circumvent cumbersome foundation procedures, and tried to ensure a ready supply of funding for each project. At the same time, Murphy maintained a benign pressure on all his investigators to write, to publish, and to learn how to acquire grants in an age of vastly improving external funding opportunities. For the most part, he was pleased with the results of his efforts; his department was productive. Wallerstein humorously compared him to a gardener "who cares for every single sprout in the hopes that a couple will bloom into flowers." Psychologist Charles Solley likened Murphy, in his support of theoretically conflicting research orientations, to "Walt Whitman, who declared 'I am immense, I contain contradictions.' "[90]

Although Murphy was more supportive of his staff than Switzer or even Fleming, he was less successful in uniting his department. His policy of interactionism was supposed to promote unity. Researchers from various projects were to provide those in other projects with fresh data and ideas; the entire departmental research effort would be enhanced by a cooperative spirit. This vision never materialized. Murphy did not understand that in an age of increasing specialization, where professional recognition accrued primarily to those with particularized research, it was unreasonable to expect his heterogeneous staff of investigators to interact. As Richard Siegal, one of his young researchers, explained to Murphy in 1967, interactionism never had any prospect of succeeding.[91]

Even before his discussion with Siegal, Murphy recognized that interactionism had failed. When he became research director in 1952, his department had perhaps a dozen investigators working on four different projects. By the mid-1960s, the staff had grown to ninety and was undertaking thirty-five separate projects. As staff increased and projects proliferated, communication with departmental staff in other projects decreased. To reverse this trend, Murphy and Wallerstein met with the investigators of particular projects to encourage them to build bridges with colleagues. But it soon became clear that neither had the precise technical knowledge to communicate to an investigator of thyroid nodules, for example, how a particular aspect of his work linked to that of a specialist on brain lesions. Projects had become so specialized that neither Murphy nor Wallerstein could know enough to recommend viable interproject connections. Wallerstein cogently observed that the Research Department remained "a loose conglomeration of people and programs and groups."[92]

The department had no choice but to remain a "loose conglomeration," because of the imperatives of external funding. During Murphy's tenure, the number of federal grants for medical and psychological research multiplied, and he pressed his staff to win them. By 1965, roughly two thirds of the department's budget came from federal grants, with the National Institute of Mental Health providing much of the money. But neither the NIMH nor most other agencies gave much support to institutions or departments. Agencies favored disparate conglomerations of units and people dedicated to the production of discrete bodies of knowledge. Consequently, the preponderance of Murphy's departmental income was pegged to particular people and specific projects.[93]

The "loose conglomeration" of researchers and projects that characterized their department did not prevent Murphy and Wallerstein from pressing hard for Research interests in the affairs of the foundation. By 1953, Murphy had achieved a seat on the executive committee of the board of trustees. Next, he and Wallerstein persuaded the trustees and governors to commit funds toward a Research Department building—a counterpart of sorts to hospital and Children's Division building complexes. Murphy could also increase research resources through federal grants for particular projects. This created a certain independence for Research that the hospital and Children's Division lacked.[94]

But Murphy and Wallerstein also experienced defeats. Realizing that a prominent university with its medical school and its affiliated teaching hospital stood at the apex of all regional medical activities, they sought to enhance Research Department affiliations with the University of Kansas. They assumed that such ties would broaden research opportunities and provide a large pool of psychology and medical students and faculty with whom they might collaborate. But the Menninger brothers continued to fear that a firm academic affiliation might eradicate the foundation's unique identity. Another defeat came when Fleming and his colleagues balked at committing hospital staff and resources to Research Department projects beyond the PRP. Fleming even vetoed Murphy's proposal for a twenty-five-bed hospital wing where patients would be in close contact with biochemical and psychophysiological laboratories conducting Research Department projects.[95]

As time passed, Murphy grew discouraged. Because of his staff's

success with grants and investigations, he had expected other parts of the
foundation to be more supportive of Research. Karl's periodic interventions were also irritating; Murphy expected the same autonomy in
Topeka he had enjoyed at CCNY. And he became increasingly distressed
with "the fragmentation of my time" and his inability to accomplish much
reading or scholarship. He thought increasingly about a return to
academia.[96]

By the early 1960s, it was obvious that the seventy-year-old director
was weary of power struggles. Ernst Ticho of the Topeka Institute for
Psychoanalysis charged that Murphy was washed up and should resign.
Neither of the brothers was averse to the suggestion. Both sensed that
because Wallerstein was an analyst and a clinician, he could replace
Murphy and steer the department back to the psychoanalytic and clinical
emphasis of Rapaport and Escalona. Evidence conflicts on whether Murphy resigned in 1964 or was asked to step down. The following year, Will
picked Wallerstein as Research director; he announced that Murphy
would continue in an endowed foundation chair and would direct a research project on reality testing. Wallerstein left for a position in San
Francisco within months of his appointment. Embarrassed, Will called on
Murphy to serve as acting director during a search process. In 1967,
Murphy resigned and moved from Topeka.[97]

Despite the unpleasantness that marked Murphy's termination, Research evolved during the 1950s and 1960s into perhaps the most cosmopolitan part of the foundation. In some measure, this happened because
the department was oriented toward external funding agencies and national research currents as well as toward internal competition. But Murphy's and Wallerstein's leadership should not be discounted, for they
promoted full freedom for investigators to pursue diverse interests and
methodologies. What most distinguished them not only from Rapaport
but from Fleming and Switzer was that they made Research the strongest
center in the foundation for unrestricted inquiry and professional values.
Neurologists, statisticians, sociologists, and others were eagerly recruited, regardless of their perspectives on psychoanalysis or their loyalty
to familial aspects of the Menninger heritage.

VII

Attention to those who ran the three major foundation institutions tends
strongly to confirm Paul Bergman's view that power had come to reside
"in the hands of the barons." This is not to say that Fleming, Switzer, or

Murphy totally dominated his division or department. The imperatives of administrative efficiency in the face of rapid expansion of facilities, staff, and patients made it expeditious for directors to allow a measure of staff autonomy.

Directors were also constrained by the fragmentation and specialization of knowledge. Samuel Hays, Robert Wiebe, and other students of the social history of professional knowledge have underscored a trend, commencing at the turn of the century, toward national and regional affiliation of experts in aspects of urban industrial life. Those who identified with others possessing specialized knowledge like their own (e.g., lawyers, doctors, and engineers), and who were concerned more with broad national and regional issues than with immediate local concerns, formed societies to promote their sense of identity and to advance their collective interests. Regional and national affiliation was particularly evident within the mental health professions during the first four decades of the century. Based upon their job categories and their command of special bodies of knowledge, psychiatrists, nurses, clinical psychologists, psychiatric social workers, and even occupational therapists cultivated identities through separate professional affiliations.[98]

By the 1950s, it was perilous for directors at Menninger to make light of discrete bodies of expert knowledge that unified professions. Fleming found that members of local treatment teams in his hospital would not cooperate unless he allowed them to represent fully the knowledge and perspectives of their professional specialties in team decisions. Murphy and Wallerstein also had to accept a department consisting of similarly trained researchers banding together in highly specialized investigatory projects. Even Switzer acknowledged the propriety of a treatment team of experts from the various disciplines.

Administrative pressures to decentralize, professional identifications, and fragmented knowledge were elements evident in a variety of large institutions that limited the authority of department directors. In Topeka, "barons" faced three other formidable checks. They had to contend with the Topeka Institute for Psychoanalysis, with Roach and his administrative team, and, above all, with the Menninger family.

Senior training analysts who ran TIP had the capacity to limit the "barons." They held out firmly against the old "family spirit," maintained important leverage over MSP fellows in analysis, and even won substantial pay increases through a work stoppage. Anna Freud, concluding a ten-day visit to Topeka in 1962, described the institute as no mere subsidiary of the foundation. It was "the innermost circle" in a series of "concentric circles" that provided policy and direction within the Menninger psychiatric community. Lewis Robbins concurred. He characterized TIP's senior training analysts as "our major caste," with unapproachable status and influence throughout the foundation.[99]

It is one thing to acknowledge the power of TIP's senior analysts. It is another to explain how that power limited the authority of Menninger "barons." The analysts held themselves to be "a rather mysterious, aristocratic, and quite arbitrary body"; they appeared as the ruling elite of the most exclusive club in the foundation. After the 1951 strike, they were among the highest-salaried members of the staff. Senior analysts demanded deference from all on the basis of their age, wisdom, and experience, and they grumbled when it was not forthcoming. Will complained that some of them had taken "me to pieces, condemning my policies, in a sarcastic vein." At the same time, they tended to keep TIP's "scientific discussions" to themselves. As Paul Bergman noted, they "tended to centrifugally retreat into small circles of congenial people." In these circles, senior analysts often reaffirmed their faith in Freudian orthodoxy and spoke bitterly of ventures like the PRP, which questioned the utility of traditional analytic techniques. Whether very junior staff or powerful figures like Wallerstein, those closest to these unorthodox ventures were sometimes singled out for retribution.[100]

Retribution could involve restricted access to the innermost circles of TIP decisionmaking. Paul Pruyser rose by the early 1960s to become director of the Department of Education and exerted "baron"-like power over the MSP. But senior analysts never allowed him to pursue a didactic analysis. Consequently, Pruyser was not able to become a training analyst (a requisite for "full" TIP membership). Similarly, although psychiatrist Harvey Schloesser became Fleming's right-hand man, he was denied membership in the institute because certain members were suspicious of him. One ground for suspicion was that Schloesser's wife worked full time while raising children.[101]

Another form of retribution came from what senior analysts learned about staff families through the analytic process. This was a strong weapon in an organization where, as Lewis Robbins noted, "the wife of one staff member is being treated by another staff member who is being controlled [through training analysis] by a third staff member whose sister is in analysis with the first person whose wife is in analysis." Those in TIP's inner circle often shared this very personal information. The fact that they "knew all" was usually sufficient to intimidate many on staff. According to Bergman, this knowledge alone held "our [analytic] candidates in servitude." Despite the eminence of researchers who had belonged to Rapaport's group, for example, all of them avoided controversy with Rudolf Ekstein, their training analyst. Winter Hospital director R. C. Anderson, outspoken and temperamental, never lost the capacity for deference in the presence of his analyst, Otto Fleishmann. Even Karl periodically deferred to Ishak Ramzy, the senior TIP official who had analyzed his son, Robert, despite the fact that Ramzy honored the code of confidentiality.[102]

Breaches in that confidentiality constituted another formidable weapon for TIP's senior analysts. In making the decision to accept someone on staff for training analysis, for admission into or even for graduation from TIP, ethical standards of the day permitted discussion of personal data that had been revealed on the analyst's couch. But these standards did not allow the analyst to use that data for political purposes. Yet this sometimes happened. Breaches of confidentiality by training analysts help to explain why certain candidates never received responsible positions within the foundation, despite their proficiency and sometimes despite the backing of a "baron." One analyst was formally charged with "old womanish gossip" about his candidates and with talking to his candidates about foundation officials. Perhaps reflecting his own analyses with Franz Alexander and Ruth Mack Brunswick, Karl was hardly exempt from significant breaches in confidentiality. It was not uncommon for him to press other analysts for personal data on candidates and to use this information in politically advantageous ways. Lester Luborsky had to plead with Karl not to volunteer data concerning analysands on staff to the Psychotherapy Research Committee. When the chief of staff breached confidentiality so blatantly, this weakened standards of trust throughout the entire Topeka Institute.[103]

Karl's breaches underscored still another source of power for senior analysts. Like Karl, most held other authoritative positions; they were department heads, clinical supervisors, MSP instructors, and members of key foundation councils. Wallerstein observed that "the training analysts were all over the place" and, in this way, were "thoroughly integrated into the life of an institution." A senior analyst like Herman Van der Waals might unintentionally command unresolved transferences from one of his analysands on staff and thereby enhance his position as hospital director against assistant director Fleming. A significant supervisory position could augment the authority of the senior analyst in places distant from his office.[104]

The power of the senior TIP analyst over the "baron" or prospective "baron" is well illustrated by the search to replace Murphy and Wallerstein. Supported by Karl, Philip Holzman of the Rapaport group was the favorite for Research director. Holzman was a widely respected therapist and a nationally prominent researcher. But he had given a junior-level psychiatrist ideas for future investigations, and the psychiatrist discussed the ideas in his analysis with a senior TIP official. Owing to an analytic lapse or through intent, the psychiatrist reversed the facts; he claimed that Holzman had stolen research ideas from him. Opposing Holzman's candidacy, the TIP official urged his analysand to inform others of Holzman's misdeed. The psychiatrist obliged; he went to the Research Directorship Search Committee and to foundation president Roy Menninger with his story. When he learned what had transpired, Holzman demanded that the psychiatrist recant the falsehood or face a lawsuit. The psychiatrist went public with the truth, but the Holzman candidacy was badly damaged. Along with other factors, the TIP official's use of the analytic relationship for political purposes explained why Holzman never succeeded Murphy and Wallerstein.[105]

If the limitation upon "baronial" power imposed by TIP analysts was often subtle and circuitous, a second restriction, unique to the Menninger setting, was quite direct. Lester Roach, in his capacity as chief foundation administrator, routinely curbed department directors. Initially, Roach accumulated power through his relationship with Will. When Roach arrived in 1948, the two became close friends and worked together to limit the drain of Karl's MSP projects on home campus resources. When Will became foundation fund-raiser and absented himself from Topeka, Roach claimed to be acting under Will's authority as he enlarged his responsibilities. By 1957, when the trustees gave Will the title of president to bolster his stature, Roach controlled all internal budgets and exercised policymaking powers that went with control of the purse. "I ran the place when he was gone," Roach said. He was exaggerating. But men like Fleming, Switzer, and Murphy had to consider him before launching initiatives.[106]

Beyond his tie to Will, Roach accumulated authority by instructing his administrative staff, working within all departments and programs, to master budgets and work routines. This gave him in-house operational detail that was second to none, which helped him in his relations with the trustees. More than to any other foundation official, trustees looked to Roach for recommendations on financial and managerial policy. Although a department head might oppose him on specific policies concerning his unit, Roach usually spoke to the trustees more convincingly because he had a foundation-wide economic perspective.[107]

Roach also increased his power by allying himself with his chief associate, Irving Sheffel, in managing the contentious relationship between the brothers. Only when "Les and Irv both joined us," Will acknowledged in his diary, was it possible to have a "very good session with Karl." Before each session, Roach and Sheffel determined what they wanted to accomplish. Afterward, they decided how to implement measures they had persuaded the brothers to accept. Thus, Roach and Sheffel could speak authoritatively in behalf of Karl and Will. But they never regarded the brothers as their puppets. Rather, they worked to advance the interests of the family at all levels of organizational decisionmaking. In meetings with Karl and Will, they delineated battle lines with powerful department heads and made their allegiances clear. They also tried to restrict as many important financial decisions as possible to themselves, the brothers, and the trustees—bypassing department directors. Although Karl never shared Will's fondness for Roach, he, too, recognized that the chief administrator served the interests of the family.[108]

This is not to say that Roach's relationship with department heads was always adversarial. An astute diplomat, he usually got on well with them. Sometimes he helped them deal with Karl. When Murphy sought an additional month of vacation pay to travel to India but knew that Karl would veto the request, he went to Roach, who quietly bypassed Karl and got Will's approval. Roach also instructed Sheffel that Fleming was best managed with a carrot—promises of financial support for the hospital. But the chief administrator was as adept with a stick. When Switzer demanded more authority and resources, Roach frightened him with vague threats of divisional budgetary cuts and a lower salary.[109]

If department and program heads were thwarted by TIP's senior analysts and by Roach, they usually found those checks less distressing than those imposed by the Menningers. Above all, they felt devastated by certain of Karl's interventions in his capacity as chief of staff.

In the course of the 1950s, Karl shed the doubts and ambivalence he had when he assumed that position; he regained his desire to command. According to Irving Kartus, "his motto seemed to be let's make changes, let's be different, let's not get in a rut even when things are going well." Martin Mayman agreed: "He never settled for what was. He was always restlessly looking to see whether there was some way to do it better—to do it differently." The problem was that no one person could keep an eye on all or even most components of the organization. There were so many departments, programs, and professional cleavages that even a compulsively methodical man like Will could not keep tabs on the much expanded scale of operations.[110]

Karl's temperament made it impossible for him to display even a measure of the steadiness and thoroughness that his difficult job required: "You are ebullient one day (or moment), despondent the next,"

Albert Deutsch warned him. When Will's eldest son, Roy, returned home in 1961, he made some effort to grasp how staff perceived his sixty-eight-year-old uncle. Roy concluded that they pictured Karl as "a roving, restless spotlight," who could focus closely on certain people and operations only at particular times. This characterization was not very different from the way Karl described his daily routine: "my life consists chiefly in keeping tab on a lot of activities around here, rushing to any trouble spots when they develop." More often than not, those "trouble spots" were the "baronies," and this caused Fleming, Switzer, and Murphy no little anguish. At those moments when Karl focused upon them, their power dissipated; only when the "spotlight" moved on did they regain their authority.[111]

Karl's contact with the hospital was a case in point. He rarely spent more than two hours a day on the hospital grounds. In fact, all that the director could count on was that Karl appeared at one staff case conference a week. Although he could often be friendly, cooperative, and exceedingly helpful at this conference, he could also be outspoken and critical.[112]

Often so disruptive that his capacity for remarkable diagnostic sensitivity could be forgotten, Karl proved overpowering when he chose to assert his presence. Keenly aware of this, Robbins instructed his secretary that he would not tolerate interruptions in his sessions with analytic patients—with two exceptions: his wife and Karl. Karl felt free to replace Robbins's successor, Kartus, as hospital director with Van der Waals and Van der Waals with Fleming on short notice and from caprice. Although Fleming was the strongest of all hospital leaders, he, too, melted before an angry and probing chief of staff but was ebullient when Karl praised.[113]

Even if Karl could dominate a case conference and overpower the director almost at will, his interventions were sporadic. This is a salient point. As Karl's attentions shifted to other parts of the foundation (often within hours and sometimes within minutes), the hospital director and his staff quickly recovered.[114]

Karl focused less frequently upon the Children's Division than upon the hospital. His discomfort with emotionally disturbed children had not abated. He rarely appeared on the Children's grounds and dealt with divisional problems from a distance. Although Switzer, like Hirschberg before him, felt devastated by Karl's bursts of criticism, he cautioned his staff that normalcy would soon return as Karl's attentions shifted.[115]

Karl's "spotlight" penetrated the Research Department scarcely more than the Children's Division. But it was not taken lightly. His periodic comments critical of departmental operations disturbed Murphy and

Wallerstein deeply. Wallerstein was also upset when Karl voiced doubt (along with insightful suggestions) concerning aspects of the Psychotherapy Research Project.[116]

Clearly, Karl could curb the authority of even the most powerful Menninger "baron" at any point in time. When he boasted of his power during a visit with Mayo Clinic officials in 1956, they were unimpressed. A few hinted to him that his organization had become too large and complex, too dependent upon intricate cooperation between specialists, for such displays of one-man rule. They may also have reminded him that Mayo's managerial officials retired at sixty-five. But such advice would have had no impact on Karl; he would not concede his authority. When Walter Cronkite came to Topeka five years later to produce an episode about the foundation for CBS television's "Twentieth Century," Karl was pleased that Cronkite referred to it as "your institution."[117]

Yet it was not Karl's institution as it had been before the war, for his impact upon a department or program lasted only as long as he could maintain his "spotlight" upon it. Because his contact with the MSP had decreased markedly, consultant Seward Hiltner felt that by 1957 Karl could not shift the fellows from an increasingly dogmatic Freudianism. Long-term control over daily affairs in the school and elsewhere remained "in the hands of the barons." Will challenged this pattern of authority even less, owing to his full-time travels as foundation fundraiser. But despite their diminished roles, both brothers placed heavy pressures upon their sons to train in psychiatry and return to Topeka, ensuring a continuing family presence in the workplace. Between the mid-1950s and the mid-1960s, the sons returned. Although their influence was hardly what their fathers' had been before the war, no director could afford to ignore them. As this third generation of the "first family" became increasingly conspicuous, all directors felt new constraints.[118]

Despite Robert Menninger's strong interest in veterinary medicine, Karl pressured him to attend medical school and to take his residency in the MSP program. Robert rose rapidly through the hierarchy of Fleming's hospital. By 1959, three years after completing his residency, he was a section chief and day-hospital director. He had also been pushed to the top of a crowded waiting list for his TIP training analysis and was appointed to the Menninger board of governors. In 1965, Robert was also named director of Outpatient Diagnostic Services. Usually, Karl and Will lobbied for these advancements; sometimes department and program directors and trustees wished to please the brothers.[119]

While advancing Robert's career, Karl complained that his son was insufficiently assertive in foundation affairs; he lacked ambition. Karl was especially disappointed that Robert did not aspire to run the organization. Will tried to ease Karl's disappointment: "Bob is such a level headed, even keeled fellow and I think an enormous asset to us." But Will knew that the "level headed" quality was an aspect of passivity. Colleagues complained that Robert was inattentive, that he avoided difficult treatment and managerial issues.[120]

Beneath Robert's passivity, indignation mixed with sadness that others (especially Karl) made important decisions for him. Occasionally Robert's anger surfaced, as when he told a hospital activities planning committee that Karl could not understand the needs of patients "when he only thinks about it for one hour when he is here on Sunday mornings." More typically—as when Karl customarily passed on to him an unwanted lecture invitation or a gift—Robert turned the anger inward and sulked. But though his dispirited periods were frequent, he was hardly a secondary figure in foundation affairs. Strategically, Robert was involved in a power conflict between TIP, where he had been analyzed, and Fleming's hospital, where he worked. The training analysts and Fleming would manipulate him, one against the other. Sometimes he resisted, invoking his family name and his access to Karl and Will. Unlike other junior psychiatrists, Robert was able to foster apprehensions, at these times, in both Fleming and senior training analysts.[121]

Robert's older sister, Julia, the bright and energetic wife of an MSP resident, supported and encouraged him in foundation affairs. His younger sister, Martha, was less attentive to campus politics. Accepting the family's strong patriarchal traditions, both women assumed that their influence on the workplace came through Karl and Robert. Will had the advantage of three sons (he had no daughters). Philip, the middle son, an undiagnosed dyslexic, never attended medical school and, like the middle son of the prior generation (Edwin), conceived of himself as the odd sibling out. Will installed Philip in various secondary administrative positions; unlike Karl's daughters, he was on staff.[122]

Will's oldest son, Roy, and his youngest, Walter, were psychiatrists and represented more formidable figures. It was no small achievement for Will to have drawn Roy back to Topeka; father and son had never been close. Rather than wait for Will's approval, Roy sought some measure of independence and geographic distance. After graduating from Cornell Medical School, he took a residency at Boston Psychopathic Hospital and became a staff associate at Peter Bent Brigham Hospital near Cambridge. He intended to settle in the Boston area; his wife opposed leaving Boston for Topeka. But Karl visited Roy to coax, and Catharine stressed how much his return would mean to her. Will wrote that "this place is ours—yours—which no other kind of job would even be in the same sense."[123]

When Roy returned, half a decade after Robert, senior staff (including "barons" and their associates) became apprehensive that they might be displaced by the Menninger sons. This was particularly true after Karl and Will saw to it that Roy was advanced despite a less than promising clinical record in Fleming's hospital. Will asked outpatient director Bernard Hall to keep a special eye on Roy and to cover for his clinical misjudgments. By 1964, Will seemed to have recognized that Roy's future was not as a clinician. He appointed him as cochairman of the new Division of School Mental Health, one of many community-oriented social programs in the influential Department of Preventive Psychiatry (the former Department of Social Applications). The brothers intended to make Roy department director when the position became vacant, and this occurred in 1965. Roy proved to be a proficient administrator, and staff predicted that even higher appointments would come his way in the years ahead. After all, he had already moved higher and faster than Robert, despite his clinical record and the refusal of the Topeka Institute to accept him for training analysis. Roy had certain qualities Robert lacked—managerial and political skills, plus a father who was a consummate diplomat.[124]

Clearly, the third generation of doctors Menninger was being advanced within the foundation hierarchy. If they did not enjoy power comparable to Fleming's or Switzer's, they could not be taken lightly. Few could doubt this by 1964, when Walter Menninger, who had taken his residency in the MSP program, returned from the Peace Corps to become a hospital staff psychiatrist. Unlike Roy, he had always felt close to his father; his highest ambition had been to join Will in clinical practice. Whereas Roy felt ambivalent about being a Menninger and working on the home campus, Walter did not. He believed that the family name was a liability as well as an asset: if he was to be saddled with the drawbacks, he had a right to the advantages. As a third son, Will identified with Walter and was enormously pleased when he announced his plans to join the hospital staff. Above all, Will confided to Karl, "I am so pleased really . . . that he would so deeply identify with the Foundation as to feel very cheated if he didn't get to the annual meeting." This was especially cheering since Will did not expect to continue his current pace as a fund-raising president for many more years.[125]

When Walter joined the hospital staff, Fleming feared that he had aspirations to take charge of the entire facility. He warned Walter to remember that he was a very junior staff member—that he must not stand out if he valued his career in the hospital. But Walter knew that if Fleming circumscribed his activities excessively, Will and even Karl would assist him. Unlike Roy, he showed himself to be a proficient clinician and was accepted for a TIP training analysis. Yet despite this good fortune, Walter confessed during his analysis to feeling like the little puppy within the larger family who had, somehow, to prove himself—especially in the workplace that he had neither created nor developed.[126]

If Karl's "spotlight" was more visible and formidable than the activities of the three younger doctors Menninger, it would grow dimmer as time passed. But in view of the positions Robert and Roy quickly assumed, and considering Walter's ambitions, directors like Fleming realized that the sons would offer more serious long-range challenges to power "in the hands of the barons."

VIII

Observing the transformation of the Menninger Clinic into a multiprogrammatic institution, its largest and best-funded divisions run by men like Fleming, Switzer, and Murphy, one would assume that power had shifted from the family to the "barons." But this appraisal has to be qualified, for there were decentralization pressures and professional staff divisions within each department, and sometimes senior TIP training analysts or Roach constricted the authority of department directors. Moreover, Karl's "spotlight" on particular departments as well as the Menninger sons' advancement points to the family's continuation as a force to be reckoned with. In essence, power shifted in and out of a "barony" from time to time and from situation to situation.

With the decisionmaking process so complex and variable, Menninger leaders had to be attentive to internal events, moods, and rumors if they were to have some sense of potential dangers and opportunities within the organization. Consequently, they could often glance only hurriedly at crucial national trends like the turn toward biopsychiatry, the discovery of psychotropic drugs, and the community mental health movement. It was difficult even to leave Kansas for a few days to visit rival "new psychiatry" centers. So much energy and attention had to be devoted to internal affairs that leaders did not direct their colleagues to national changes and the needs of potential patient constituencies, as they might have under different circumstances. Although few saw cause for alarm, Menninger appeared gradually and subtly to be victimized by its own complex patterns of power disbursement.

As long as Roach and Sheffel could keep the Menninger brothers acting in concert on basic policies despite their mutual animosity, so long as the power abuses inherent in training analyses did not become too heavy-handed or conspicuous, and as long as the competition among department heads precluded their concerted action in retaliation against Karl, the organization functioned with some stability. Leaders could look upon the foundation's respectable financial balance sheet and its continuing national recognition as a major psychiatric institution, and they could voice guarded optimism about its future. During a week in April 1965, however, some of these essential preconditions for optimism ceased to obtain. As a result, the most traumatic chain of events in Menninger history began to unfold. Some of those who survived refer to these events as the "palace revolt." Others characterize the events as the "revolution."

CHAPTER ELEVEN

The Palace Revolt

The events of April 21–27, 1965, were more crucial to the Menninger organization than any other in its history, pressing themselves indelibly on the minds and spirits of all participants. Most who were involved recorded the details on cassette tapes, in diaries, and on memorandum pads. All had been close to Menninger psychoanalytic tradition and knew of the danger of repressing knowledge of vital events. Yet many hid their recorded accounts of the occurrences of that week, locking them away for nearly a quarter century in file cabinets, in unopened bank vaults, and in dusty attic trunks. Nor have the participants candidly discussed the events with their colleagues. Research psychologist Donald Leventhal and psychiatrist Ray Bullard had some vague sense of a replay of Freud's *Totem and Taboo* ritual: the founding father (Karl) was being "slain." But they were apprehensive about learning more. This spirit of silence and restraint continued in the years that followed. Many who joined Menninger after 1965 never heard of the palace revolt.[1]

The chain of events began Wednesday evening, April 21, when Lester Roach telephoned Will and announced that he was resigning as chief administrator. For weeks, Roach had known that Karl was intent on replacing him with Colonel Donald Vivian, a skillful administrator at nearby Forbes Air Force Base, who had suggested ways to reform the foundation's managerial structure. Will had met with Vivian earlier that day and had been impressed with his observations on an organization that had more than doubled its staff and quadrupled its budget over the past fifteen years but had failed to modify its managerial system. After his discussion with Vivian, Will spoke with Roach to indicate that he was taken by Vivian. Roach, knowing the younger brother's tendency to acquiesce when the older was insistent, went home convinced that Will would accede to Karl's effort to replace him.[2]

That evening, Roach drove to Irving Sheffel's home to discuss the day's events and then visited with Basil Cole, another close member of his administrative team. He returned home, considered his options, and called Will to report his decision to resign. Roach said that he was no longer going to take Karl's abuse and that Sheffel was resigning too. He would not resume his duties unless Will "took over the running of things at the Foundation." After Roach hung up, Will called Sheffel in panic, saying that he could not function as president without Roach and his administrative associates. Sheffel tried to calm Will, assuring him that he had no plans to resign, and made an appointment for early the next morning.[3]

The two met after a virtually sleepless night. Sheffel recommended that Will not allow Karl to replace Roach with Vivian. If that happened, the senior staff would be disturbed, the administrative structure would fall entirely into Karl's hands, and Sheffel, like Roach, would resign or be replaced as Vivian appointed his own administrative team.[4]

Desperate to get Roach back and retain Sheffel, Will called a meeting later that morning. He invited associates he knew fairly well and regarded as the most influential figures among the staff. Robert Switzer was unavailable, but Herbert Schlesinger, chief clinical psychologist at the hospital, came. His superior, Peter Fleming, also arrived. So did Paul Pruyser, a psychologist who directed the Education Department and the MSP program. Karl had been fond of Pruyser. He had been even fonder of Outpatient Services Department director Bernard Hall, who also came to the meeting. Since Gardner Murphy had ceased to be a regular departmental director and Robert Wallerstein was away on leave, Research was not represented.[5]

The meeting took up most of the morning and a brief period following lunch. The four senior staff spoke generally and rather indirectly of their discomfort over the current state of affairs. They were apprehensive that if Vivian replaced Roach, it would be even more difficult for them to work with Karl. Successful in removing Roach, Karl might even consider terminating one of them. All four therefore gave Will advice he must have anticipated: he should keep Roach. As one of his conditions for returning to work, Roach had told Will that he would report only to him, no longer to Karl. When Fleming, Pruyser, and Hall learned of Roach's stipulation, they implied that they, too, wanted to report exclusively to Will. Essentially, they were appealing to him to couple his duties as president with his brother's position as chief of staff. Although Will gave no clear sign that he was ready to assume Karl's duties, he was determined to retain Roach and to consider "a shift in our functional alignment in the Foundation." After lunch, he asked Sheffel to join the

meeting and was pleased when Sheffel and the other four decided to visit
Roach later that afternoon to plead with him to return. Within fourteen
hours of Roach's resignation, Will seemed to be developing an alliance
between Roach and Sheffel, the most powerful department heads, and
the office of the president. Together, they might summon the emotional
and material resources to confront Karl.[6]

The next day, Will took measures to keep the constituents of his
alliance together. He urged Sheffel to visit Roach and persuade him to
return. Then he met again with Pruyser, Fleming, and Hall, who were
joined by Switzer. Karl was resorting to his periodic role as tyrant, Switzer
charged, by trying to replace Roach with Vivian, whom he hoped to
control. Schlesinger, who had been considerably less militant than his
colleagues, had left for a meeting in Chicago. Thus, his conciliatory voice
was replaced by Switzer's vehemence. However, no one demanded more
than rehiring Roach and imposing some limitations on Karl's duties.
Fleming, mindful of Freud's discussion of the patricidal myth, in which
the sons united to kill off the primal father, warned of a disaster if the
group pressed Karl too far. "Each of us will pay a price for this," he
warned. "As we shoot down the father now—that also will be our fates."[7]

Hours after this second meeting, Will telephoned his brother and
conveyed some idea of what had transpired. Karl was distressed that Will
had conducted both meetings without him. He was particularly hurt by
the apparent disloyalty of Hall and Pruyser. When he visited the Forbes
Air Base Officers Club to dine with Vivian that evening, Karl ran into
Switzer (a reserve admiral) and delivered a short but firm reprimand. At
dinner, Vivian told Karl that he sensed Will had reservations about him
and that, at any rate, he would not accept an appointment. However, Karl
did not allow Vivian's decision to resolve the crisis. Late that night, he
and Jeanetta visited Hall. They reviewed recent events with him and
demanded that he continue to support Karl. Karl was confident that Will
and his colleagues would back down once he demonstrated his extreme
displeasure.[8]

On Saturday morning, Will called a third meeting, with Fleming,
Hall, Switzer, and Pruyser in attendance. Sheffel was also present, as was
Bennett Klein, an independent consultant friendly to Roach and Hall,
who occasionally advised the foundation. Karl had been invited but did
not appear. There was strong concurrence that Karl would have to exercise his responsibilities with more equanimity.[9]

At this point, Will agreed to allow the department heads to start
reporting to him unless Karl was willing to reform. Then he telephoned
Karl to say that they were waiting for him. Karl arrived with Leo Bar-

temeier, a prominent Detroit psychiatrist and longtime foundation trustee, who was in Topeka as a visiting MSP instructor. Karl indicated that he would not conduct himself differently. Extremely upset, he charged that he was a prudent chief of staff, that he had not badgered Roach, and at any rate, Roach could stay on, because Vivian was uninterested. He felt there was no basis for legitimate grievances. For the first time, Fleming and Pruyser disagreed openly with Karl. They reminded him of his refusal to countenance any measure of departmental autonomy or to allow staff agencies like the Senior Council to function effectively. When Karl dismissed these comments as nonsense that covered a more basic desire to strip him of his responsibilities, Will, hitherto firmly in control of the meeting, turned gray. Sheffel felt that Will was on the verge of an emotional breakdown. In his diary, Will emphasized "what a difficult time it was for me."[10]

When the group reconvened briefly in the afternoon, Will seemed more composed. Bartemeier warned him against stripping Karl of power. When the gathering adjourned so that Karl, Hall, and Klein could attend the wedding of the daughter of a foundation donor and trustee, it was apparent that Bartemeier had not prevailed. Both Will and the department heads felt that unless his authority was circumscribed, Karl would retaliate against all of them. At the wedding, Karl was very cold to Hall and complained to other guests that he had been fired. Jeanetta called Klein a "father killer." Will skipped the wedding. When he arrived home, he told Catharine that he had just chosen between the well-being of the foundation and the wishes of his brother; he was siding with the foundation. Catharine sensed that Will was suffering.[11]

By Sunday, Will was acting as chief of staff and president. He announced that on Monday all department heads were to explain to their staffs the nature of the administrative change that had occurred. Bartemeier tried desperately to reverse this turn of events. He met with Fleming, Hall, Pruyser, and Switzer, urging them to give Karl another chance. All four refused, maintaining that Will had properly become their immediate superior. When they met that day with Will, they warned him that Karl, in a bid to regain his position, might report the revolt to MSP alumni, trustees, and former staff at the approaching meeting of the American Psychiatric Association. They had grounds for apprehension. Even Bartemeier conceded that Karl was "in an absolute frenzy" and that his behavior seemed psychotic. At lunch that day, Karl had told Bartemeier that Hall and Roach were spearheading a conspiracy against him. Early in the evening, Karl pleaded with Pruyser to desert the group that was conspiring against him. Karl warned that as Pruyser was a psychologist among psychiatrists (Fleming, Hall, and Switzer), the three would remove him from their coalition once they eliminated a chief of staff who supported psychologists.[12]

By Monday, when Roach returned to work, a new chain of command was in place. All lines of communication ran from department directors to Will. Roach reported only to Will, as he had demanded. When Sheffel appeared at Karl's office for their regular 8:30 A.M. meeting, he learned that Karl had cleaned out his desk over the weekend, leaving a note for his secretary to forward his mail and his remaining belongings to the office he continued to maintain at the VA hospital. A stack of chief of staff files was to be forwarded to Will.[13]

An hour later, Sheffel came across Bartemeier and Roy Menninger. The three agreed to drive to Karl's office in the VA facility. Arriving, they explained to him that the administrative change would make the foundation a stronger organization. Ultimately, the shift would transfer power from the brothers to department directors, who had greater knowledge of their particular operations. Karl disagreed and insisted that Roach and Hall had been plotting for some time to take over the foundation. But he seemed less agitated than he had been. Sheffel was conciliatory. He suggested that Karl might call on Vivian for various administrative services. Both Sheffel and Bartemeier were assured that Karl would not make inappropriate remarks at the APA meeting in New York. Although Karl was bitter, he did not seem eager to continue the fight.[14]

Nevertheless, when Sheffel had lunch with Jeanetta and Karl that day, he sensed that she wanted her husband to persist. Robert also sought to encourage his father's combativeness. Hall had excluded Robert from an Outpatient Department staff meeting held that afternoon to explain the new chain of command. Robert, failing to understand that Hall had done this to avoid embarrassing him, complained to his father as they drove to the railroad depot that evening. Karl was going to Chicago and then to New York. If he mentioned at the APA that a junta had deposed him, the reputation of the foundation could suffer considerably.[15]

By April 27, it seemed obvious that whether or not Karl went public, a crucial sequence of events was over. Will met regularly with department heads and Roach. Tired from years as a fund-raiser and nostalgic for the home campus, he was ready to manage internal operations again. For the most part, Will seemed satisfied. But there had been a price. Ever since he watched Karl castigate Fleming and Pruyser and lash out at others in his coalition, he had often felt almost numb.

Will experienced that feeling when Karl telephoned from Chicago and charged him with participating in a plot to push his older brother out of the organization. This was the first time Karl explicitly accused Will of being allied to the department heads. During a pause in the conversation, Will faintly heard Jeanetta's voice in the background. It dawned on him that she was coaching her husband. Karl insisted he would struggle to continue as chief of staff. When he hung up, Will was both sad and uncertain. He knew that Karl preferred to hold Roach and Hall—and perhaps Fleming, Pruyser, and Switzer—responsible. But Jeanetta, who had never been comfortable with Will or his family, was doing her utmost to steer Karl's "spotlight" his way. Will realized that he might be portrayed as a major instigator of the palace revolt.[16]

I I

An eruption within the Menninger family and the foundation had been bound to occur, although it did not necessarily have to take the shape it did in the spring of 1965. Will accurately explained to the trustees that fall that "the events of last April were a revolutionary twist to the tail of an evolutionary process, long since in motion."[17]

The process would never have been set in motion if the brothers had been on good terms and able to share power amicably. To be sure, tensions had been reduced by Will's pursuing a fund-raising career while Karl remained in Topeka. But Will acknowledged privately that "this business of having a sense of two heads—KAM here and myself away— isn't very good, the more so because I don't know who it is that is really going to make some firm decisions and keep them." Yet periodic meetings between the brothers to make decisions proved troublesome. Will explained what he was up against: Karl "gets so intent on little things and then he insists that I don't understand or I won't listen or somehow or other I can't raise questions because then that seems to make him feel I don't trust him." On certain of the more acrimonious occasions, when Karl became angry, suspicious, and ready to walk out, Will came close to tears. At times, he responded that Karl was taking away his authority by pressuring him constantly to acquiesce. Both brothers found it easier to become very "busy" so that they could "spend very little time [meeting] together." Cooperation between the president and the chief of staff occurred on Karl's terms or (more often than not) it simply did not happen.[18]

Despite their difficulties in communicating and cooperating, each brother characterized the other's strengths as complementary to his own. In speeches before state legislatures considering mental health appro-

priations, Will regularly lauded Karl for "vision and guidance and energy" far beyond his own. He was a promoter and implementing arm for
his brother's ideas. And Karl acknowledged publicly that the Menninger
Clinic's success was contingent on a balance between Will's "orderly and
systematic structure," his capacity to promote "stability" in institutional
affairs, and his own "more libertarian and untrammeled thinking" and
interest in "growth."[19]

The balances and imbalances of the fraternal relationship influenced
Karl as he prepared *The Vital Balance: The Life Process in Mental Health and
Illness* (1963). The volume was dedicated "To My Brother." He attributed
"its inception to the year 1943, when my brother Will, then assistant to
the Surgeon-General, was wrestling with the difficulties caused in the
Army medical service by the incompatibility of medical facts and nosolog-
ical [disease classification] traditions."[20]

The primary theoretical endeavor in *The Vital Balance* was to argue
for the replacement of rigid psychiatric classifications with more dynamic
perspectives. Karl expanded upon a notion that he had advanced a quarter century earlier in *Man Against Himself:* that people tended to shift to
different positions on a broad emotional-mental continuum between the
life wish and the death wish as they responded to their inner urges and
to external stimuli. Unlike the earlier book, the new one stressed the
importance of a well-functioning ego to avert a continuous movement
toward the death wish. Among other qualities, a strong ego restored
internal equilibrium or stability (homeostasis) by responding and in some
measure adjusting to disruptive (heterostatic) impingements.[21]

When Karl first presented his continuum perspective in 1938, it
represented a compelling extension of suggestions by Freud, William
James, Adolf Meyer, and other challengers of the nineteenth-century
paradigm that mental health and mental disease were fixed entities. By
1963, however, this view was widely accepted in mental health circles. So
was the focus upon ego adaptation. The only innovative element in *The
Vital Balance* was Karl's skillful merger of his discussion of the ego as a
mechanism to restore equilibrium with Ludwig von Bertalanffy's general
systems theory.[22]

If *The Vital Balance* was no groundbreaking study, it had helped Karl
fathom the troubled relationship between himself and Will. As he developed the concept of homeostasis, he was describing Will, the "conserva-
tor": "He likes to have things definite and sane and safe and careful." In
contrast, Karl considered himself a primary force for heterostasis or
disequilibrium: "I, on the other hand, have been expansionist all my life.
I don't care about things being so rigid, so firm." Consequently, just as

stability and change were both essential to human development, the Menninger family and the foundation required the efforts of each brother. The two men needed each other: "Will needed me and I needed him. . . . He made even my crazy ideas seem sensible and sane."[23]

What Karl seemed to be searching for in his relationship with Will was the equivalent of a well-functioning ego—a regulatory or balancing mechanism that assured constant shifts between equilibrium and change. At some level, Roach, Sheffel, and even Charles acted as "balance wheels" between the brothers. But with Charles's death in 1953 and Karl's increasing distrust of Roach, tensions between Karl and Will mounted.

At the time *The Vital Balance* was being completed, the rapport between the brothers had reached its nadir. When Walter Cronkite arrived in Topeka to develop his program on foundation accomplishments, he tried to film a conversation between himself and the brothers. As soon as it became clear that Karl and Will would not sit together, Cronkite's staff was reduced to camera tricks to make it appear as if all three were conversing around a table.[24]

Will grew depressed over the future of his partnership with his brother and with his professional life generally. Seeking to reestablish ties to the home campus, he took a special interest in the Preventive Psychiatry Department, which he had inaugurated, particularly its industrial mental health program. However, by 1964, Karl pressured Will to transfer the department to his jurisdiction. Though Roach urged Will to stand up to his older brother, Will's resistance was a tearful and scarcely militant plea: "You know you are taking away the last program I have in the Foundation." It seemed as pointless as it was painful to oppose Karl. Catharine recalled that Will was deeply wounded and very nearly in despair as Karl assumed jurisdiction over his most prized connection to the campus.[25]

Roy, a leader in the Preventive Psychiatry Department, agreed with Catharine. Indeed, by early 1965, Roy was sure that his father suffered from a clinically diagnosable depression. Karl concurred that Will was becoming increasingly dejected. On those rare occasions when he met with his brother, Karl noted, "you clam up and stare me away and tell Roach not to mention the matter." Karl was so disturbed at Will's silence that he described it as "a passive war . . . a passive blockade," which was contributing to "your bronchitis and I am sure it has something to do with my frequent sleeplessness." From the "passive war" of late winter, something like the more active "war" of April was predictable. Will would eventually strike back.[26]

Even more than the controversy over Preventive Psychiatry, tensions between the brothers were aggravated by land acquisitions. A major dispute over real estate parcels had evolved out of endless discussions concerning the wisdom of the foundation's purchasing a 372-acre site on Martin's Hill, a few miles west of the campus. The grounds included what had once been a two-hundred-bed hospital building and six smaller adjacent structures. Karl felt that the site would make an excellent home for new programs in delinquency, geriatrics, mental deficiency, and kindred ventures. Neither Will nor Roach opposed the purchase; they felt that the social programs established during the 1950s were contributing to an overcrowded home campus. But the $2.61 million sale price and an estimate of $1 million for repairs had given them pause. Through Karl's prodding, a special corporation was established to help with this financial burden, a paper organization financed by wealthy friends of the foundation, who stood to benefit by tax write-offs and appreciated land values. The corporation secured the forty acres of the site upon which all buildings were located, took out an option to purchase the remaining land, and bought all of it in 1960. Then the corporation donated its stock holdings to the Menninger Foundation and dissolved.[27]

Even before the corporation completed its transactions, Karl laid claim to the land as if it were his own. Carpenters were still refitting the former hospital building—a replica of Independence Hall in Philadelphia—for occupancy when he moved his office there. New programs like Industrial Mental Health, Marital Counseling, and Religion and Psychiatry quickly followed. So did the Research and Education departments. Fleming's hospital filled much of the vacated east campus space. Sheffel followed Karl to the new west campus and took an office near him. As one program and department after another moved to the west campus, Will insisted that traditional clinical services remain where they were. By the mid-1960s, Lois Murphy articulated a pervasive sense on the staff that Menninger had essentially been transformed into two very different and to some extent rival campuses. The center for older, more traditional psychiatric services—where Will and Roach retained their offices—was perceived to be for profit-making programs. In contrast, Karl's campus consisted of programs that were often regarded as spending those profits on new ideas. In a visit to this new campus, Margaret Mead looked out and saw "one of the few places . . . in the whole United States where vision is matched with space in which to express it."[28]

Each brother, on his respective campus, began to struggle over new land. Between 1962 and 1965, the primary issue between them was whether the foundation should purchase parcels in areas where Topeka was expanding beyond the west campus. Karl wanted that acreage to be bought quickly before it became as difficult to acquire as land in settled neighborhoods adjacent to the east campus. He sought out available parcels on the far west side of Topeka, particularly those that had not been converted into costly residential developments. Karl insisted: "We *can* afford it, of course, if we continue to grow and if the city population continues to grow, which seems inevitable." Landowners quickly recognized Karl's insatiable quest for acreage and demanded top dollar for their parcels. The foundation had to pay anywhere from $1,200 to $3,700 for each new acre. Once sufficient land was purchased, Karl planned a two-hundred-room international hotel for foundation guests, a manufacturing plant to serve as a research base for the Industrial Mental Health program, a deluxe restaurant, a marina for patient recreation, tennis courts and horseback trails and a summer camp for hospitalized children, a ranch for delinquent youth, a halfway house, an arboretum, and a luxurious apartment complex, with rents beyond the reach of his senior physicians. The west campus would become a world-renowned center for professional gatherings, for research, education, and prevention programs, and for affluent living. The missionary tradition kindled by his mother would take on new proportions. That, at least, was Karl's dream. The older and more traditional east campus could be the province of consolidators and managers like his brother.[29]

The dream was never realized. Karl had difficulty buying several costly parcels near the west campus. Moreover, he was not able to purchase hundreds of additional acres that he considered essential, because Will, supported by Roach, Fleming, and several of Will's friends among the trustees, strongly opposed these acquisitions. Whereas Karl insisted, "we ought to be buying every bit of real estate we can get our hands on at the right price," Will felt that would place impossible fund-raising demands on him. He did not "want to spend the money for land" when "it is so darned hard to get money" to support existing operations. He preferred to conserve funds for a large endowment that earned substantial interest, thus easing the burden on his tired fund-raising shoulders. In refusing, quite uncharacteristically, to acquiesce to Karl's demands, Will would not confront Karl directly but instructed Roach to quietly block land purchases. Roach insisted that the trustees had to approve many of Karl's proposed acquisitions before he could authorize foundation money for them. At the same time, Roach cultivated the already considerable trustee opposition to new land. Karl, thwarted, kept reprimanding the trustees, Roach's administrators, various department heads, and Will for failing to see that "our younger men will continue to grow, will continue to have ideas, will continue to develop projects. . . . It would be a great tragedy, in my opinion, to inhibit the development of their ideas and inventions by failing to lay a proper real estate foundation for a very considerable development."[30]

At this juncture, when conflict between the brothers was more intense than ever before, and when Will was building a base of support, various senior staff began to talk among themselves about restructuring the foundation. Philip Holzman, for one, felt that some tinkering with governance at Menninger was necessary if it was to survive the tension between the brothers and the competition between departments. Through reforms that produced stronger staff commitments to the well-being of the foundation, Holzman speculated, it might be possible for the brothers, the department heads, and other employees to deal better with the internal conflicts. No champion of the prewar "family spirit," he advocated reforms that would promote a spirit of disinterest and dedication to the large and complex entity the foundation had become.[31]

When Karl and Will consented in 1961 to the formation of a Coordinating Council consisting largely of senior staff, Holzman and like-minded colleagues had been mildly optimistic. They hoped the council would rise above the conflict between the brothers and the battles between department heads, devising policies of general benefit. However, many of the staff were not accustomed to thinking beyond "baronies." And because the brothers rarely took the council seriously, it seldom met. Karl revamped it early in 1963 as the Senior Council. He insisted that it meet regularly to devise solutions to major foundation-wide problems; he and Will would implement these solutions. Karl also held out the hope that members of a successful council might eventually run the organization—that the experience might "prepare them for leadership when Dr. W & I would no longer be able to supply it." But within a year, the Senior Council was almost moribund, as Karl disrupted substantive discussions with trivial and unrelated matters. At times, he appeared so disoriented that some members of the council suspected he had suffered a stroke.[32]

Department heads and other high staff were apprehensive because the Senior Council was failing like its predecessor. They felt that because Karl did not let it become an important governing body, he would never allow its members or other senior staff to occupy the top positions in the organization. The brothers would choose their sons as their successors. Their eldest sons were already occupying significant roles in the foundation and seemed destined for even higher positions. From time to time, Karl had tried to oust Fleming as hospital director and replace him with Robert. Although Will was more discreet, he awaited an opportunity to appoint Roy director of the Department of Preventive Psychiatry. Increasingly, senior staff feared that they would never advance beyond their current positions and might even be demoted as the Menninger sons rose in the ranks. The only hope, they felt, was to curb Karl and to arrive at an accommodation with his more approachable brother. As department heads and other high staff came to view Karl as the principal obstacle to their careers, some began to wonder aloud whether he simply should be asked to leave. The dissension was not lost on Will. By early 1965, he had begun to contemplate ways to transform disgruntled senior staff into potential allies.[33]

The opportunity presented itself when Roach resigned on April 21. Will established a coalition that included Sheffel (standing in for Roach) and the most powerful senior staff. Within a week, this alliance essentially removed Karl as chief of staff. But that did not conclude the palace revolt. There was an important aftermath. For the next several years, the foundation would struggle to determine Karl's new place in the organization and to develop a new structure of governance.

III

Karl spent the first week of May at the American Psychiatric Association meeting. Sheffel accompanied him, relieved that Karl kept quiet about the revolt.[34]

Meanwhile, Will busied himself with a new structure for the foundation. Accord in his coalition with department heads and Roach's administrators was reached on three essentials. Karl was to be eased into an elder statesman role with no formal authority. The Senior Council and various subsidiary councils were to be dissolved. In their place, Will would rely directly upon senior staff for advice. And authority was to be decentralized. Each department and program head would be given specific but extensive jurisdiction over his unit. Thus, Will was recognizing the supremacy of the departments as a fact of organizational life. He hoped that each head would share responsibilities with various underlings. In this way, he explained to the trustees that October, there might be greater staff participation in decisionmaking.[35]

"Barons" like Hall, Pruyser, Fleming, and Switzer were pleased with Will's plan. But Karl argued that the centralized structure that had characterized his shared leadership with Will and the Senior Council had been the key to organizational growth and innovation. Opposing Will's policy of "departmental laissez faireism," he felt that "the Foundation as a whole should come first" and that Will's policy legitimized the self-ag-grandizement of department heads who had risen against him. For Karl, these men clearly lacked leadership potential. Desperate to turn back the course of recent events, he offered a number of proposals predicated on his returning to a leadership position. Under one, he would run a west campus nonprofit foundation committed to innovation, while Will could take charge of a profit-making east campus clinical partnership. According to another, the brothers would be joined by a third man, who might succeed them; a triumvirate would rule. Karl also proposed that both brothers retain their former positions while a council of vice-presidents would oversee most foundation activities.[36]

As Karl attacked Will's plans and proposed alternatives, a hitherto unorganized and unrecognized staff constituency devised plans of its own. The Professional Staff Organization had originated as an informal group of senior therapists in various departments; they met to resolve problems in the therapeutic services. When they learned that Karl had been deposed, the PSO quickly shifted its focus to the governing structure of the foundation.[37]

At a meeting two and a half weeks after Karl's removal, the PSO chose to deemphasize the role of department heads. Instead, it recommended that the full professional staff be given a voice in the process of change "from an organization administered by two of its founders to an organization which required the measured and creative thinking of its entire staff." According to Lois Murphy, this was a call for "a certain kind of blossoming of talents which had been submerged under the previous extremely autocratic regime." Within months, the PSO grew from a group of senior staff to a large body of physicians, psychologists, social workers, and even administrators who had been with the foundation for at least three months. It was to bridge differences rendered by specializations within the staff. Ad hoc PSO committees were established to prepare position papers on foundation identity and goals, clinical activity, psychoanalysis, personnel practices, and fund-raising. By April 1966, the PSO had mobilized 127 staff, 118 of whom voted at an election of officers. Psychologist Howard Shevrin felt that "a widespread rejuvenation" had taken place within a staff that had never before participated significantly in organizational affairs.[38]

The PSO recognized that the "administrative leadership given by Doctor Karl and Doctor Will admirably suited the Foundation during the years of its inception and growth." But the current need was to go beyond that patriarchy and "give younger staff the opportunities to develop their administrative and leadership abilities." Otherwise, the foundation would continue "to foster an infantile dependent role" in its employees. Committed to far-reaching democratic aims, the PSO opposed not only Karl's efforts to retain autocratic control but, indirectly, Will's attempts to decentralize and rule in alliance with high senior staff. Therefore, the PSO held itself out to the trustees as an alternative both to the "barons" and to the brothers. It alone stood for broad staff participation in the foundation's planning and decisionmaking.[39]

Although the PSO functioned through the late 1960s, it never emerged as an effective force. Most members and even key leaders like Prescott Thompson and William Tarnower had almost no experience in foundation politics. They lacked the knowledge and skills to outflank either the department heads or the brothers. And while they opposed Menninger patriarchy, they sometimes acknowledged continuing to "feel in some ways like members of the [Menninger] family." This was why Will's courting of various PSO leaders and his public reference to them as a "valuable reservoir for leadership and counsel" tended often to head off militant outcries. Indeed, Thompson presented the PSO to the trustees as an agency akin to a university academic senate, capable of submitting advice but not designed to make final decisions. Along with reticent leadership, the PSO was ineffective because it presented its case for staff participation within vague and often ambiguous guidelines. It could do no more because precise recommendations for action and structural changes would have splintered the group. If differences between specialists had already partially fragmented departments, precise recommendations on governance and treatment issues might have destroyed the coalition that made up the PSO. In fact, tensions running along the lines of specialty groups often made it difficult for PSO committees even to meet on a regular basis.[40]

By late 1966, Gardner Murphy, a PSO activist after resigning from his Research Department directorship, observed that the group could hardly govern itself. It represented no real challenge to the status quo. "I was foolish enough to believe that the PSO would not only talk," Murphy acknowledged, "but get issues to a point of demanding action, and would either persuade or apply pressure so that there would really be action."[41]

He may have been too hard on the PSO. Its many position papers and declarations represented a blatant and organized demand for expanded staff participation. Trustees saw for the first time that neither the Menningers, the department heads, nor Roach's administrators had a monopoly on knowledge. Staff at large also came to acknowledge that neither their department directors, nor Roach, nor the brothers necessarily considered their interests. Indeed, the PSO represented one more slow and halting step away from the "family spirit" and toward greater staff freedom. "In various and sometimes personal ways," a PSO study group proclaimed, "we are grateful to Drs. Karl and Will *but . . .* identify ourselves with our own lives, not theirs."[42]

I V

Concrete actions were more important than the proposals that the brothers and the PSO issued in the months following the palace revolt. No actions were more significant than Karl's. Rumors spread about how he would deal with Will and the department heads. In an organization where commitment to psychoanalytic premises remained keen, there was general apprehension that a patricidal revolt had transpired and would run its full if tangled course. The father had been wounded but not slain. Most expected him to do far more than inveigh against Will's proposals.

Initially, Karl responded indecisively to the revolt. Martin Mayman expected him simply to fire the rebel department heads, reprimand his brother, and inform the trustees that nothing was changed. After all, Will had always backed down when Karl opposed him before the trustees. Yet Karl did not strike out in this characteristically aggressive manner when he returned from the American Psychiatric Association meeting in New York. In the past, Karl had sometimes disarmed potential adversaries with pats on the back or inquiries concerning their grievances. If he had been conciliatory, Will and frightened department heads like Fleming and Switzer might have tried to accommodate him. This time, however, Karl seemed ambivalent, with strong mood swings. Will complained in his diary that his brother "won't stay hitched—he has one idea today and another one tomorrow and keeps us sort of on the edge of the seat all of the time as to what he is going to do or say next." At some moments, Karl played the part of Lear, charging that he had been betrayed. He would cite *Totem and Taboo,* asking if the rebels knew of its fateful implications. At other moments, he appeared submissive. The day he returned from the APA convention, he called a meeting of three influential psychologists: Philip Holzman, his strong supporter; Herbert Schlesinger, the most moderate and conciliatory of the rebels; and Paul Pruyser, perhaps the most militant. For two and a half hours, Karl quietly reviewed the events of April and agreed to follow whatever advice the three might offer.[43]

As weeks and then months passed, Karl's pattern of behavior appeared even more erratic. He seemed to be operating on several different levels. On one level, he completely denied that anything significant had occurred, owing to his and Will's "vested rights to authority." Even though department directors were reporting to his brother, he remained chief of staff and chairman of the trustees until he decided to step down. In October 1965, he openly proclaimed to the trustees: "I will continue as your Chairman and as Chief of Staff." In those capacities, he had quite properly sought an "effective and responsible administrator" like Colonel Vivian to replace Roach. When close staff associates like Sheffel tried to reason with him, explaining how his brother had invoked presidential prerogative and assumed his chief of staff functions, Karl retorted that the foundation was in an all-or-nothing situation; he would continue the forty-year partnership with Will, or there would be no Menninger organization at all.[44]

While he insisted that he was still chief of staff, Karl, aided by Jeanetta and by Robert Anderson, his attorney, was negotiating with the foundation for money and responsibilities that would accrue to him if he agreed to relinquish his title. Will, Roach, and the trustees wanted contractual guarantees that Karl would never lend his name to any other hospital or professional group. They realized it was essential to continue his formal affiliation with the foundation, or fund-raising and patient admissions would be jeopardized. Karl said he would relinquish his position and sign a contract to continue his Menninger affiliation if the foundation agreed to pay him $50,000 annually for the rest of his life or $25,000 a year to Jeanetta if she survived him. In addition, the foundation would have to give him office space and secretarial services. If these had been the only provisions he sought, a contract might have been drafted and signed with dispatch. Prodded by Jeanetta, however, Karl insisted on the right to represent the foundation, thus perpetuating to outsiders the myth that he ran the organization. Sometimes he also sought authority over the foundation's small museum, archives, and library. On still other occasions, he requested contractual terms guaranteeing him supervision over west campus landscaping, control over the *Bulletin of the Menninger Clinic,* or continuation of his car and travel allowances. Although negotiations frequently broke off, they always resumed because the foundation had to tie Karl down legally as an official of the organization. When Will or Roach or another administrator balked at one of his less reasonable demands, Karl usually got his way simply by proclaiming that he could not "permit the use of my name to any organization which I disapprove and in which I have no voice." He showed himself to be a shrewd and resourceful negotiator.[45]

However, sometimes he acted without much shrewdness. One of Karl's responses to the revolt was to meet secretly with relatives as part of a naive and desperate effort to reestablish a united family. He urged Will to admit to mistakes during the revolt. Indeed, he never ceased to believe that Will would reunite with him if only he could somehow free himself from the "corruption" of "his wife Kay, & his impulsive sons Walter & Phil. Will & I should never have been parted, even tho we disagreed on some policies." Karl also drew Robert and Roy into his discussions with Will. In these meetings, Karl warned that if the family did not work together and reverse the course of recent events, the department heads would eventually control the foundation. They would topple Will as they had overthrown Karl and would deny their sons the leadership positions they deserved. Robert usually supported his father in these meetings, but Roy warned that other Menningers would suffer Karl's fate if they, too, ruled autocratically. Will rarely spoke, and the four always parted without agreement. The Menningers had ceased to be the Karl-centered family of old.[46]

All the while, Karl also acted on the conflicting counsel of two small groups of colleagues—the first consisting of émigré analyst Michalina Fabian plus Holzman and Mayman. All three were experienced clinicians who felt that Karl's intellectuality and charisma made him the natural leader of the foundation. Other staff shared their love for him, they believed, but some were momentarily elated over the prospect of wider participation in foundation affairs. They urged Karl to bide his time; eventually, a groundswell of support would restore him to power. Karl deeply respected these colleagues and often abided by their admonitions for wise silence, distancing himself from foundation activities. But at other times he turned to a second and even more trusted group of loyalists—Jeanetta, former Menninger psychiatrist Frederick Hacker, who served as a visiting scholar and consultant, and former Parsons College history professor Lewis Wheelock, who had managed the foundation's museum and archives. The three flattered Karl for his "creative genius." They insisted that his opponents knew well that unless they allowed him to function to the fullest extent, they would be promoting "institutional suicide." Sometimes they succeeded in persuading Karl to tell particular donors and friends of the foundation precisely what had happened to him. With threats of reduced money and support, Will and the department heads would have no choice but to restore Karl's power.[47]

Clearly, Karl was moving along very different paths. The effect of his various responses to the revolt was probably to keep Will, the rebels, and other concerned parties more off balance than any single, concerted course would have done. They rarely knew what to expect. But there is nothing to suggest that Karl's diverse responses were components of a political strategy to unsettle others as he extricated himself from a difficult situation.

Late in 1965, W. Clement Stone complicated matters further. Some months earlier, this millionaire Chicago insurance executive had joined with Paul W. Brandel, a prosperous lawyer and developer, to purchase Chicago's St. Luke's Hospital complex. Together, they would turn the facility into a massive community medical complex—the Stone-Brandel Center—with psychiatry representing one of twenty-two medical specialty units. Stone invited the Menningers to help him establish the psychiatric unit. Although formal ties with the Stone-Brandel Center offered the brothers the opportunity to link the foundation with the fashionable field of community mental health, Will felt he first needed to sort his way through the Menninger organization's internal crisis. Moreover, he regarded Stone as a right-wing "eccentric," who wrote "amazingly asinine books" propounding mind-cure perspectives much like those of Norman Vincent Peale. Will told Stone that his Chicago center was too large and too distant from the foundation for him to assume an active role.[48]

Karl, however, took a number of trips to Chicago. He talked with Stone and Brandel about transforming the center's psychiatric unit into one of the largest, most comprehensive, and most innovative mental health facilities in America. As he advanced his proposal, Karl disclaimed that any "divorce between me and the Foundation" was pending; he was simply considering whether "to put into practice [in Chicago] some of the things the Menninger Foundation has always believed in and stood for." He acknowledged that "it would have been my preference to have spent the latter years of my life developing certain projects and dreams in Topeka." Unfortunately, the foundation's trustees and staff did not seem to want him to do so, while Brandel and especially Stone begged him to serve as a senior consultant. He was disposed to accept their offer.[49]

Much more than Brandel, Stone was the moving force behind the new center. In view of what they knew about Stone's conservative political ties and his rapport with Chicago Mayor Daley's political machine, neither Will, Roach, department heads, nor the more active trustees could fathom why Karl was interested. They wondered whether he was using Stone's overture for leverage to negotiate a better contract with the foundation, to return as chief of staff, or to prompt outsiders to intervene in his behalf.[50]

Karl and Stone reached an agreement in August 1966 that the Menninger Foundation accepted as contractually binding. The document provided that the Stone-Brandel Center would send $37,500 quarterly to the foundation to cover Karl's salary and that of any assistants he might hire, $5,000 additional as a one-time-only first-year bonus, plus $15,000 annually to cover Karl's office, secretarial, and other operating expenses. Although the contract did not specify more, Karl assumed that he would be assisting the center for perhaps two thirds of each year. During that interval, he planned to reside with Jeanetta at the University Club and had been assured that his life style would approximate Stone's and Brandel's (including daily chauffeur service plus tickets to Chicago Symphony concerts and Art Institute galas). For the remainder of the year, he would return to his Topeka home, lecture occasionally at the University of Kansas, and perform the essentially honorary functions of MSP dean and Menninger board chairman.[51]

Despite the generous terms of the contract, the duration and extent of Karl's participation in the Stone-Brandel Center was difficult to forecast. Stone provided enormous reassurance and support for Karl at a time in his life when he was certain that many friends had abandoned him. Indeed, Stone's money, praise, and encouragement to build a major psychiatric unit assuaged Karl's always fragile sense of self-worth. But the new undertaking was risky. Moving through the Stone-Brandel Center would be officials from Stone's large and interlocking enterprises whose fundamental loyalties were to managers other than Karl. Although the Menninger Foundation had become uncomfortable for him, an organizational complex in which much of the staff voiced the self-help slogans of W. Clement Stone could become even more distressing. To add to the complications, when the building complex was purchased, considerable back taxes remained unpaid. Despite Stone's close ties to Mayor Daley, insistence by the city on full payment of past and present taxes, as well as changes in the tax laws, could turn the center into a serious financial liability for the two partners and force liquidation.[52]

Karl's agreement with Stone and Brandel placed him partly within and partly separate from the Menninger Foundation. This mirrored the acute ambivalence he had felt toward his organization since the palace revolt. Karl's ambivalence might be characterized by the final stage in Erik Erikson's epigenetic chart of the human life cycle—ego integrity versus despair. Erikson postulated that in later adulthood, those who adapted themselves to the disappointments as well as the triumphs of existence found order and meaning in their lives. Those who did not, fearing death and feeling that life was too short to start anew, despaired. But in Erikson's model, many older adults struggled between the poles of integrity and despair, and Karl may have been one of them. As he sought to maximize his role in foundation affairs after the revolt, he appeared to despair for the meaning of his life; there was still much at Menninger he had not accomplished. On the other hand, by taking strides to withdraw from internal foundation affairs, Karl may have shown a measure of ego integrity, recognizing the end of his role in the organization.[53]

Clearly, Karl's course in the year and a half after the revolt was complex and changing. His struggle may have represented his way of retiring.

V

On several occasions during the months following the revolt, Karl proclaimed that those who conspired against him should have learned from Freud that the sons of the tribe could not overthrow the father without bringing disaster upon themselves. Will and the rebels of April characterized this reaction as no more than fanciful rhetoric. But they were all too familiar with the story of the inglorious contest in which, after killing the primal father, the sons struggled among themselves to determine who would succeed him. They felt that they had to support each other if they were to resist such a fate. Despite this determination, each suffered enormously in his own way.[54]

Although Fleming had accrued great power as director of the hospital, he was distressed about the potential consequences of his role in the coup. Karl had been his training analyst as well as his immediate superior. Fleming realized that Karl sometimes used personal data revealed during analysis to get his way in political squabbles, and he feared that Karl might use this confidential information against him. Indeed, when he told Karl, after the events of April, that his hospital functions had ceased, Karl denied Fleming's authority in a devastating way. With obvious reference to a sense of personal inadequacy that Fleming had conveyed to him during analysis, Karl asserted that "Dr. Fleming need feel insecure ONLY on the basis of the quality of his work."[55]

Fleming began to drink heavily after the revolt. He thought constantly of Freud's patricidal myth and worried "that if you kill off the chief then the time would come when you yourself would be killed off." In the course of a physical examination that fall, doctors discovered a spot on Fleming's right lung. Although malignant, the growth had not spread to any lymph nodes. The upper lobe of the lung was removed, saving his life. But the quality of his work thereafter was not what it had been before the revolt. In April 1968, he was replaced as director of the hospital and was assigned the honorary title of Senior Consultant for Clinical Services.[56]

Outpatient director Bernard Hall also augmented his drinking after the coup. Like Fleming, he thought obsessively about the fate of sons who rose against the father, particularly because he had long been one of Karl's favorites. Even more than Fleming, Hall had been pained that Karl refused to talk to him in the aftermath of the revolt. "KAM spoke to me for the first time in 5½ months," he wrote in October. But this did not assuage Hall's guilt, particularly after Karl refused to forgive him and after Karl's daughter Julia called Hall "a power grabber." The worst was yet to come. There was concern that Hall's homosexuality was becoming too obvious. In 1970, the evidence was unmistakable that along with uncontrolled drinking, he had made persistent homosexual advances to two Menninger patients. Although no legal action was taken, Hall went on annual leave and was not permitted to return.[57]

Education Department director Paul Pruyser may have suffered less than Fleming and Hall. He had never been analyzed, and he insisted that nothing akin to a patricidal revolt had been staged. Rather, he and other rebels had participated in an administrative adjustment in the interests of organizational efficiency. This explanation for the events of April seemed to give Pruyser a measure of strength that Fleming and Hall lacked. After a staff meeting with Karl in the fall of 1965, Pruyser saw that Menninger had taped on his office wall a page from his April desk calendar on which he had written: "The Day Karl Menninger was Killed." Pruyser characterized this as "a flagrant accusation of all of us. And you are not entitled to it." Then he told Karl to take the paper off the wall and destroy it, and Karl obliged. Pruyser's struggle to downplay the psychological import of the revolt was aided by the fact that he remained cooperative with Karl's closest staff supporters. He may also have felt fewer apprehensions and self-doubts because he could talk openly with Karl about how they both needed to put aside ill feelings. Nonetheless, his closest colleagues acknowledged that Pruyser took an emotional beating. Survival as a member of the staff came at the cost of the enormous repression and intellectualization that were required in characterizing the emotion-laden revolt as an administrative adjustment. Pruyser aged precipitately and developed a facial twitch. Shortly after he was removed as Education Department director in 1971, he wrote to Karl, "hoping" that he would "appraise the last ten years as a period in which I have not only kept your great heritage, but nurtured, fostered and expanded it, with the help of able and loyal colleagues."[58]

Children's Division director Robert Switzer was less active in the coup than Fleming, Hall, and Pruyser. Afterward, he acknowledged that there may have been some merit to Karl's effort to replace Roach. Karl was willing to converse with Switzer but chiefly asked why the man had cooperated with the other "assassins": "Switz how did you do it?" Karl never forgave him, and Switzer never pushed for a reconciliation. He continued in his post until he was asked to step down in 1973.[59]

Herbert Schlesinger fared considerably better than the others. He continually counseled the rebels and the Menningers in moderation and conciliation, and as a result, all parties talked freely with Schlesinger, regarding him as a trusted colleague. Though some called him "wishy-washy" and accused him of "walking both sides" of the controversy, for the most part everyone appreciated that he favored a cautious, evolutionary transition toward greater staff autonomy while preserving for Karl a meaningful tie with the organization.[60]

This is not to say that Schlesinger emerged as the unruffled statesman of the revolt. Ever since his training analysis with Rudolf Ekstein, associates had attributed to him qualities of indecision, self-doubt, procrastination, and thinly disguised anxiety. His moderation during and immediately after the revolt may have been rooted in an inability to arrive at conclusions and to act on them. Whatever the source, it was obvious that the events of April troubled him deeply. He kept detailed records of the course of developments and collected additional evidence. But though he reviewed his files periodically in the privacy of his office, Schlesinger was unwilling to share or to discuss most of them. The past was to remain buried—partially, at least. All the while, he felt obligated to assure Karl that the "insights and points of view that I learned from you" seemed "as fresh and brilliantly illuminating to my students as they did to me on first learning."[61]

Of all those who suffered the consequences of challenging Karl, none suffered more than Will. His health had not been good since the early 1950s, when he began to travel. He smoked two packs of Chesterfields a day, lived a sedentary life on trains and in hotel rooms, and drank socially a good deal. Eventually, he developed erosion of the spinal vertebrae, chronic bronchitis, and emphysema. In addition, he became increasingly depressed, as he found it more and more difficult to communicate with Karl. Yet physicians assured him that these were not serious maladies. A chest x-ray taken a few months after the revolt was negative. So were other medical tests. To be sure, Karl's behavior after April— acquiescence one day and belligerence the next—irritated Will. "There is something new every day in connection with Karl's hopes or aspirations, wishes or intentions," he noted in despair. But though during periods when contact with Karl seemed particularly distressing he considered following his brother into retirement, at other times he exhibited optimism and genuine pleasure in running the foundation.[62]

Two days before Christmas, however, Will learned that his recent x-rays revealed a large mass in one of his lungs and there was a strong possibility that it was a carcinoma. In his diary that night, he wrote: "I was awfully shaken, knowing damn well the handwriting was on the wall." After Christmas, he went to the Mayo Clinic, where tests confirmed the presence of a lymphoma or a small-cell carcinoma, the size of a grapefruit. X-rays and chemotherapy administered in the months that followed produced mixed results. In the course of treatment, Will had had hopes of living another "year or two or three," but he died on September 6, 1966.[63]

Julia Menninger maintained that the cancer occurred because her uncle "never learned to cope with his violent feelings" and turned them inward on himself rather than toward the complex and often aggressive conduct of her father. Julia's explanation finds support in Will's characteristic acquiescence, even during the early months of 1965. But in the course of the revolt, Will did fight back; he manipulated many of the events that removed Karl from power.[64]

Will's friend and colleague Harry Levinson, a specialist in the psychology of organizational behavior, cited the pattern of many family-run businesses. When the younger brother attacks and displaces the older, he often feels enormous guilt for the assault and for usurping the older brother's seemingly rightful historic role. Levinson recalled that Will felt extremely guilty about the events of April, and several of Will's closest associates agreed.[65]

Will's funeral at the First Presbyterian Church was one of Topeka's largest of the decade. Menninger Clinic Chaplain Thomas Klink told a congregation of approximately fourteen hundred how Will had been "a man of dignity and deep feelings" and "an evangelist for holy causes." The medical director of the American Psychiatric Association attended. So did several corporate executives Will had met as a fund-raiser. Kansas was represented by the governor, the chancellor of the University of Kansas, and the attorney general. All of the family was there except for Edwin, who remained in Florida. Will Kercher, a boarder in the early Menninger household, came. William L. White, editor and publisher of the *Emporia Gazette,* made the trip to Topeka and later wrote a column describing the church service as a tribute to one of two brothers who "have made Kansas known around the world, although those Kansans who know or care may be all too few."[66]

After the service, Will's casket was lowered into a grave adjacent to his parents'. That day and during the week that followed, obituary notices on the 66-year-old leader appeared in newspapers throughout the country. Letters of condolence emphasized Will's importance and his personal worth. Chancellor W. Clark Wescoe of the University of Kansas called him "a giant in American medicine," Governor John Volpe of Massachusetts stressed "the warmth of his character," and APA president Harvey J. Tompkins asserted that "No psychiatrist ever had so many friends and admirers." Anna Freud wrote that she would "never forget the smile on his face."[67]

Karl sat attentively through the funeral service and read carefully much that was written about his brother. Weeks passed before he could summon the energy to prepare a tribute. Finally, he wrote a two-page introduction to a short foundation pamphlet, "In Memoriam for Doctor Will." He began by underscoring "the great emptiness left by my brother Will's departure. A different world surrounds us, a sense of hesitation and brooding sadness pervades our hearts." Lightly, he alluded to one of Will's shortcomings: "He did not pursue theories or issues or new projects," but he "supported me." Through most of the tribute, Karl emphasized Will's personal qualities. Will "was a calm, amiable, level-headed" person who made "nearly everyone he talked to feel that he, Dr. Will, was interested in what they were doing and how they were getting along." Consequently, people were happy to follow Will and to cooperate with him in reform causes. For Karl, this meant that Will "exemplified a mental healthiness which goes beyond all the definitions which he or anyone else ever wrote." The implication was that Karl, who had sometimes reprimanded his brother for the coup as Will lay dying, had exemplified less.[68]

V I

Will's terminal illness had created widespread distress through the foundation. Patriarchal and psychoanalytic traditions converged as thoughts turned toward a new leader.

Will hinted at his preference when he asked the department directors to nominate Roy to chair their coordinating committee in his place. He had only recently appointed his thirty-nine-year-old son director of the Department of Preventive Psychiatry; Roy was the least experienced administrator on the directors' committee. By proposing him for interim chair, Will breached a long-standing understanding with Karl that if one of them became ill or died, the other was to take charge. He had also slighted the seniority of Karl's son, Robert, who had recently become director of Outpatient Diagnostic Services.[69]

The department directors, closely allied to Will since the revolt, accepted his proposal and formally nominated Roy to be interim chair. Because Will foresaw potential opposition from the PSO and others, he stopped short of recommending that Roy also succeed him as president. When Roy accepted the appointment, he stressed that it had no long-term implications; he was not president designate. In the days that followed, Karl argued that Robert would have been a more appropriate choice as chair. PSO leader Prescott Thompson voiced dismay that his group had not been consulted.[70]

Early in 1966, when Will left for treatment at the Mayo Clinic, he instructed Roy to conduct himself in the interim chair position as if he were president: "I don't want the Trustees looking around for someone else to come in there and head the Foundation," on the assumption that "your job is very restricted and limited." Roy followed his father's advice. By the middle of the year, he was essentially deciding policy, meeting three times a week with a special advisory committee consisting of department heads, a senior psychologist, a senior social worker, Roach, Sheffel, and Dolgoff for the central administration, plus two senior training analysts to represent the Topeka Psychoanalytic Institute. In this way, Roy cemented a working relationship not only with department directors but with other high-level staff members and administrators.[71]

Roy was especially attentive to the ideas and needs of the former rebels, Roach, and Sheffel. He acknowledged to these colleagues that the PSO would not be allowed to weaken the authority of department directors or the office of the president. But at sessions with the PSO, Roy talked vaguely of the need to shift power from a small group to the foundation staff; he favored "involving the staff and using the combined talents of all." Through his politically astute and conciliatory approach, Roy earned support as a competent and efficient chairman of all committees and subcommittees over which he presided. If he failed to build a rapport with Karl, he nonetheless managed to assure Robert that "the sins of our fathers were not visited upon the sons."[72]

Because Roy demonstrated administrative facility while he fortified his father's alliance and worked to conciliate potential adversaries, he quieted much of the discontent that accompanied his appointment. After Will's death, the trustees named one of their number, R. Charles Clevenger, as interim president, and none objected to Clevenger's delegating "all operational responsibility and authority to Roy Menninger."[73]

Once it was evident that Will had only a few months to live, the trustees established a procedure for selecting the next president. A search committee would be formed, consisting of six trustees and four staff members (plus an alternate). Two of the four were to be chosen by management (Roach and the department heads). Consequently, only two seats and one alternate on the committee would represent the majority of staff.[74]

Although he had essentially assumed his father's role, Roy publicly disavowed any interest in becoming president when the search process began. Privately, he was torn. Unlike Walter, he had not modeled himself entirely on his father and was not sure he would be comfortable in the position on a permanent basis. As the months passed, his confidence increased. But despite encouragement from his wife, strong doubts remained.[75]

Will, less ambivalent, felt that the Menninger name was essential for fund-raising purposes and to perpetuate the family legacy. In time, he came to think that because of Roy's evenhandedness as chair of the directors' coordinating committee, he was better suited for the job than Walter or Robert. With this in mind, Will instructed Clevenger that "the President ought to be a physician and preferably of course a psychiatrist," in view of the medical character of the organization. He also told Clevenger to make sure that he appointed "staunch friends" like Arthur Mag and Willard King as trustee representatives on the search committee. He asked Roach to choose Sheffel as one of the two management representatives, so that Sheffel might end up "playing quarterback" and directing the proceedings. Through Will's discussions with Sheffel during the early months of the search process, he continued to exert substantial leverage for his oldest son.[76]

Before the search formally commenced, a clear majority of the trustees supported Roy. Most of them were prosperous businessmen and professionals whom Will had met during his fund-raising trips. They owed their appointments to Will, felt closer to him than to anybody in the organization, and were more than willing to give him the successor he preferred. Moreover, almost all trustees felt the next president had to be a Menninger. So it was hardly surprising that when the search committee polled the twenty-two trustees for nominees, a decided majority suggested various Menninger sons, mostly Roy but also Robert and Walter.[77]

Because Will had cemented an alliance between the office of the president, the Roach administration, and the department heads, and because Roy had committed himself to that alliance, there was little doubt whom these men would support. Indeed, the rebels from the April revolt felt that just as Will had been a pillar of support when they confronted Karl, his son was likely to be their strongest ally if Karl challenged their authority. Consequently, Fleming, Hall, Pruyser, and Switzer invoked the substantial power of their departments to influence the search committee.[78]

Otto Kernberg and Ernst and Gertrude Ticho, who jointly exercised power within the Topeka Psychoanalytic Institute, urged the committee to select Roy for somewhat different reasons. Because of his youth and inexperience, they calculated that he would become a figurehead president and they could become the real powers behind that office. Robert Wallerstein, who was about to leave for a position in California, was the only major staff figure who failed to support Roy. He spoke of the need for moving beyond a family dynasty, as the Mayo Clinic had, in order to facilitate new patterns of growth and new ideas. Roach, with his strong loyalty to the Menninger family, felt that Roy had to be president, even though "he's too democratic and tries to listen to too many people." But Roach was apprehensive that Roy might not listen to him for advice as exclusively as his father had. He represented the most equivocal vote of support for Roy within Will's old alliance.[79]

Because of Will's traveling, the presidency had become a post with very little direct bearing upon internal affairs. Roach's administrative team, department heads, and other high senior staff had taken charge of day-to-day management. But the events of April had led them to regard the presidency as far more than the ceremonial, money-raising position it had become. They conceived of the chief executive as an indispensable officer because he alone could hold Karl in check and preserve the gains of the palace revolt.

They may have overestimated Karl's capacity to regain authority. If his conduct immediately after the revolt did little to restore his influence, his actions during the presidential search ensured his remaining on the periphery of power. He told the search committee and others that Roy was unfit for the presidency. His nephew was not a psychoanalyst, he had not been trained in the MSP, and he had not proved himself in any position within the foundation. Karl's son, Robert, however, had all these qualifications. Encouraged by his less than judicious adviser, Lewis Wheelock, and by his daughter Julia, Karl supported Robert for the presidency. This was a major blunder, for even those on the staff who would not support Roy felt that Robert was not a viable candidate. He had been indecisive and unable to provide serious leadership. While Karl went on record in Robert's behalf, moreover, Robert negotiated privately to assume his father's former position in a Roy Menninger administration. Neither Karl nor Robert showed any comprehension of the one tactic that had some chance of stalling Roy's bandwagon. Instead of trying to appeal to the considerable sentiment within nonmanagerial circles for a genuinely wide-ranging search process, Karl and Robert proclaimed quite openly (as Roy wisely had not) that the foundation belonged to "the family."[80]

Karl eventually realized that by championing Robert's candidacy he was hardly blocking Roy's path to the presidency. Like a good many others early in 1967, he felt that Roy's selection was almost inevitable. In some sense, he preferred Roy to a non-Menninger. But he continued to feel that his nephew was the weakest of the candidates. Karl knew that the committee had been impressed by James Allen McCain, the experienced and capable president of Kansas State University, who had taken major initiatives in behalf of international education exchanges. He praised McCain as an alternative to Roy. Since McCain was elderly, Karl suggested to committee members that they could select him on the ground that this would give his nephew time to grow into the job. What Karl failed to say but could hardly conceal was that a short McCain presidency might give him time to turn his own son into a more credible candidate. The search committee was not eager to present him with that opportunity.[81]

The Professional Staff Organization was hardly more effective in forestalling Roy's candidacy. A great many PSO position papers underscored the importance of an extensive and open search, but they did not sway votes on the search committee or rouse support among the trustees. Because the PSO considered itself a professional rather than a political organization, it did not seek to mobilize the widespread staff feeling that Roy was too young and inexperienced to be president. It neither circulated petitions among the staff against Roy's candidacy nor went firmly on record in opposition. The PSO remained as impotent during the presidential search as it had been in the months following the April revolt.[82]

There was no effective voice for a search process through which professional qualifications and experience could be valued above the family name. It seemed clear that Will's alliance would dictate his successor. But Roach had been crucial to that alliance, and he had serious qualms about Roy's talent. Out of friendship and loyalty to Will, he supported Roy. But after Will died, Roach felt less duty-bound to deliver the presidency to his son. Indeed, he seemed modestly receptive to a last-minute plan to prevent Roy from securing the position.[83]

The plan had been devised by senior research psychologist Howard

Shevrin, the search committee's most adamant opponent of Roy's candidacy. Shevrin had gathered support from several senior associates in the Research Department, particularly Gardner Murphy, Robert Wallerstein, and Philip Holzman. With Murphy stripped of the department directorship in 1964 and Wallerstein intent on leaving the foundation, Research leaders had been conspicuous for their refusal to line up with high staff elsewhere. Shevrin and his group proposed John Sutherland, the experienced former director of the Tavistock Clinic and a well-regarded consultant to the foundation, as a transitional president. They noted that Sutherland's international stature approximated Will's. All of the Menningers liked Sutherland and would hardly view him as a threat to family hegemony. By holding office for perhaps five years, they pointed out, Sutherland could train Roy to become an effective president. Among themselves, however, Shevrin and his colleagues calculated that a Sutherland presidency might eliminate the vestiges of the "family spirit." If they broke a succession pattern for the foundation's highest office, even on the claim that it was temporary, both trustees and staff would be able to see that the organization could survive and prosper without the Menningers.[84]

Although the Sutherland candidacy represented an eleventh-hour proposal, it had some prospect of success. Will was not alive to fight it. If influential trustees would back it, Roach seemed ready to do so too. Willard King, chairman of the search committee, was ready to mobilize fellow trustees for Sutherland. King recalled how Will had conceded to him a year earlier that Roy needed a few years of seasoning. If King had convinced trustee Arthur Mag, if Shevrin had secured support from a second staff member, and if Roach had instructed Sheffel, there might have been enough votes on the committee for Sutherland. However, before this prospective alliance could solidify, Sutherland told the committee he would not accept the post: he had obligations at Tavistock, it would be problematic for a foreigner (he was Scottish) to preside over an American foundation, and the job would place him in the middle of obvious conflicts. At this point, King seemed willing to back an alternative interim appointment, Mayo Clinic psychiatrist and staff president Howard Rome. But Mag convinced him that after the Sutherland gambit, it would be hazardous if the trustees failed to close ranks behind Roy. The initiative dissolved, and Roy was assured the presidency.[85]

Early in April 1967, the search committee convened to make its nomination to the trustees. The committee had narrowed its short list from nineteen candidates to five. Four of them—James McCain, Howard Rome, Robert Wallerstein, and MIT social scientist and management consultant Donald Schön—were far more prominent and experienced than Roy. The six trustees and two management representatives voted for Roy, while the two nonmanagerial staff representatives voted against him. With an overwhelming majority for a Menninger to continue in the presidency, King reported Roy's nomination formally to the board. At this point, Catharine, who had known of the Sutherland gambit, played her trump card. She warned the trustees that any further reluctance to accept her son would represent a betrayal of Will's legacy.[86]

The trustees accepted the nomination with minimal discussion, and Roy's administration officially began. Although the "family spirit" was not as significant in 1967 as it had been in the past, and though the tensions between Karl and Will had seriously divided the family, the Menningers were still a force to be reckoned with. If they no longer had much direct impact over the life of most staff, they still had significant input at high levels of decisionmaking. The third generation had succeeded the second.

CHAPTER TWELVE

Roy Menninger's Presidency

Roy Menninger's presidency commenced with an unanticipated event. Karl insisted on introducing the new president to the foundation trustees at their spring meeting in 1967, claiming that the foundation would be better served if he, rather than interim president R. Charles Clevenger, made the presentation. Although Clevenger feared that Karl might use the occasion to proclaim a counterrevolt, he was unwilling to protest.

In his introductory remarks, Karl implied that he had played a role in the selection of his nephew. He charged that the continued viability of the organization was of the utmost importance to mankind. Consistent with the well-being of the foundation, he wholeheartedly approved of Roy as president and urged all staff to unite behind the new leader. Roy compared the honeymoon interval that followed to feudal times, "when all the knights and barons from the countryside would come into the castle to swear fealty to the new king." Despite a certain cynicism, he responded cordially to staff support. He also recognized that those who made him president had done so largely out of respect and affection for his father; he alone could not have earned their unqualified fealty.[1]

During this transitional period, Roy hired consultant firms to examine the foundation and to recommend long-term reforms. Karl and Will had rarely drawn upon such outside advice, but Roy felt that those insular days had passed. His organization was nearly half a century old, and its psychoanalytic heritage was hardly cause for smugness in an emerging age of biopsychiatry. Moreover, Roy recognized that he was not a pioneer or an innovative, charismatic leader, as his uncle and his father had been. Like Karl, he acknowledged that he felt within himself "the normative drive of a first-born to achieve, to compete and control." But he admitted that he lacked Karl's capacity for profound insights and for creative leadership. Roy also described how he had been deeply impressed by "the example of a third-born father whose cognitive style emphasized affiliation, good feeling, and consensus." Yet he knew that others did not love or respect him as deeply as they had Will. Lacking Karl's full power of creative command and Will's full capacity to cultivate personal loyalty and agreement, Roy had a "difficult on-going task" of balancing what he possessed of these contrasting qualities. But he feared he was unequal to the task. Consequently, he needed the help of consultants if he was to preside successfully over a large and complex organization.[2]

Based upon their advice, Roy moved quickly on a particularly pressing problem. The presidential search process had accentuated the role of the trustees, and members of the board of governors began to question the utility of their own body. Roy ordered a redrafting of the foundation bylaws so that the board of governors was abolished and current governors were offered positions on the new hundred-member board of trustees. Because a body of that size could hardly deal with vital problems, a fifteen-member executive committee was established. The committee would meet at least four times a year and execute "most of the functioning authority and responsibility" of the board. Since the president was to select executive committee members, Roy was able to constitute a committee compatible with his outlook and values at the very beginning of his administration.[3]

In the months after he took office, Roy found that operating expenses were significantly in excess of revenues. At the close of the 1967–68 fiscal year, the first annual deficit in several decades forced him to draw upon the foundation's modest endowment. As American involvement in the Vietnam War accelerated, federal mental health grants began to decline. At the same time, several long-standing donors were not eager to contribute to Will's successor. Roy therefore instituted stringent controls over expenses, increased patient fees, and assigned several staff (including his brothers and Robert) to solicit financial contributions. He was grateful for a large life insurance policy that the foundation had taken out on Will. Although the deficit was less substantial by 1972, contributions and grants were dwindling, and apprehension over economic survival persisted.[4]

The onset of a financial crisis within a year of his father's death underscored a basic problem for Roy. How was he to follow in the footsteps of Karl and Will, who were among the most prominent and influential psychiatrists of the century? Comparisons were inevitable, especially during crises. Consultants like Seward Hiltner and John Sutherland warned him that he should not aspire to compete with his uncle and father. They advised him to be understated, to appear confident and competent, and to stress group responsibility as the key to organizational success.[5]

Indeed, Roy felt more natural with a leadership style that conformed to their recommendations rather than to that of his predecessors. While he praised his father and his uncle, he insisted that "we have expanded beyond the length and breadth of their shadow." The staff "must begin to fill some of the places previously filled by the Founders." The president and the staff together had "to replace our charismatic leadership of the past with a more systematic and organized corporate structure." "It is not a one-man organization. It is not a one-family organization," he insisted. "It *is* a group. And the task is to mobilize the efforts of all of us to move forward." He resorted to group relations conferences to influence staff who were "psychologically handicapped" by traditional deference to Will and Karl. Recognizing that the "family spirit" had contributed to the "dependency culture" of the staff, he took pains to "de-emphasize the family aspect of this organization."[6]

To some extent, Roy's focus on group process was self-serving. If he downplayed the importance of personality and emphasized collective competence, he stood to be blamed less for the financial crisis and other problems. Nonetheless, his message was well received. For the first time, the most powerful Menninger was allowing staff to discount the founding family. Although Roy privately qualified his statements, indicating that "I could not go along with a shift so great as to deny that the family has anything to do with it [the organization]," he conveyed that there was plenty of room for staff ideas and opportunities for moving up to the higher echelons of authority.[7]

During the first few years of his presidency, Roy reversed the family practice of giving relatives major positions. His brother Walter, who had clinical talents that Roy lacked, coveted Roy's position. Roy assigned him to Topeka State Hospital for long-term supervisory duties, without inquiring whether or not he wanted to leave the home campus. He allowed Robert to continue until 1971 as director of Outpatient Diagnostic Services. But beyond this, Roy balked at giving "Bob a real job to do." Indeed, he kept him out of all high-level decisionmaking and excluded him from meetings with large foundation donors.[8]

A more significant measure of Roy's efforts to mute the role of the founding family was his success in restricting Karl to a ceremonial role as elder statesman. W. Clement Stone helped by enticing Karl to Chicago as a psychiatric consultant to the Stone-Brandel Center. Roy considered himself fortunate to have Karl several hundred miles away. He was able to consolidate power, to make his own appointments to key positions, and to encourage the departure of some of Karl's loyalists. When Karl protested several of these actions, Roy acknowledged his uncle's opinions and proceeded to ignore them. When the Stone-Brandel Center collapsed because of tax complications, Karl continued to use office space and staff at Stone's expense. But he spent more and more time in Topeka, and by 1971 his return was complete. Roy drafted a carefully worded staff announcement to minimize Karl's return. According to the announcement, Karl was retiring. He would be "pursuing his special interest in writing," and "he will be doing a good deal of traveling to other psychiatric centers on behalf of the Foundation." But he would have no official position, save for the chairmanship of the board of trustees.[9]

Although Karl marked up his copy of the announcement with "no," "no such," and other denials, he had no significant support within the foundation and could not fight back. He had not played a visible role in the organization since the palace revolt. No former staff associates were willing to join him in a crusade against his nephew. Even if they had been willing, it was unclear whether or not Karl had the determination to lead them. Much as he resented the fact that Roy proclaimed his retirement to the staff, Karl realized he had not emerged as the indispensable leader of the Stone-Brandel Center, and now, in his late seventies, he seemed hardly prepared for more than a gadfly role within the foundation.[10]

The diminished roles of Walter, Robert, and Karl underscored a weaker "family spirit" in the workplace. That was illustrated even more clearly by the way staff regarded Roy's divorce in 1971. In contrast to Karl's, no one voiced concern about the stability of the foundation. Of course, divorces were far more commonplace by the early 1970s. But it is also relevant that Roy kept his personal life much more private than had his uncle, who encouraged staff to consider him and his family very nearly inseparable from the organization. In addition, staff were far less likely to feel that a young and relatively unknown psychiatrist could threaten the survival of the organization. Roy issued a memorandum noting that despite the divorce, "the business of the organization will proceed without interruption," and few had cause to assume otherwise.[11]

If Roy was determined to curb a "dependency culture" and downplay the founding family, his commitment to staff autonomy and freedom had distinct limits. This was demonstrated by his dealings with the Professional Staff Organization, which was pleased that he agreed to the principle of regular consultation with its representatives on policy matters. Roy was perturbed over a demand in 1968 that there had to be significant staff representation on search committees for important positions and that the PSO would appoint the committees. Angry that PSO leaders had "no realization that they were preempting my responsibility," Roy ceased to meet regularly with them. Instead, he instructed Lester Roach to designate various tasks for the PSO. But the group's president, Leonard Horwitz, balked, complaining to Roach that the prescribed tasks were busy work designed to render the organization ineffective.[12]

Over the next year, Roy and Roach agreed to compromise with the PSO concerning search committees, assuring its leaders that staff would be represented in selecting department directors. But neither Roy nor Roach responded to other major proposals, and PSO representatives found it increasingly difficult to schedule appointments with them. A sense of futility prevailed, and the PSO ceased to meet.[13]

Whereas Roy gave lip service to increased staff participation, he was more zealous than Will at shoring up the president's power. During his first years in office, he quietly reduced Roach's power and that of the most influential senior staff. Their resignations were inevitable.

Roy did not feel tied to Roach in the way his father had. He often chose to bypass Roach and go directly to the department directors. Soon he appointed two young administrators to serve as his links with departmental and program heads. Roger Hoffmaster was to oversee west campus departments and programs, while Duane Swanson would attend to the east campus. Roy also departed from Roach's ideal of the all-purpose administrator. Consistent with a nationwide trend, he hired administrative staff with expertise limited to specific functions, like finance or personnel management. By the early 1970s, various administrators had absorbed many of Roach's functions and responsibilities. Sheffel and Dolgoff recognized that they, too, would lose influence unless they became more directly supportive of the new president. While they did not repudiate Roach, they tried to be of greater value to Roy. The inexperienced young president was showing a talent for consolidating his authority. Roach resigned in 1975.[14]

While he bypassed Roach, Roy dismantled the alliance with department heads initiated by his father. Peter Fleming recovered from his bout with cancer, but Roy supplanted him because Fleming experienced constant "difficulties carrying on the responsibilities" of hospital director. Bernard Hall served temporarily in that position but was replaced. Robert Switzer was removed after Roy accused him of circumventing the office of the president and allowing the Children's Division to disintegrate into "a set of isolated baronies." Asked to serve as a fund-raiser and consultant, Switzer realized that he had ceased to have important duties and left. Herbert Schlesinger resigned for a professorship at the University of Colorado Medical School. Only Paul Pruyser managed to retain a significant position, though his influence as Education Department director had been circumscribed. With subtle pressure from Roy, he resigned, accepted an endowed Menninger professorship, and became a resident teacher-scholar.[15]

I I

By rendering his family, Roach, members of Will's alliance, and the PSO powerless, Roy established uncontested authority. At the beginning of his presidency, he also sought to create opportunities at lower echelons of the staff by proclaiming decentralization as his central goal:

> With our beginning attempt to decentralize some of the decision-making and power, it becomes important to recognize that the assumption of new responsibilities is a vital part of making this shift work. Automatic referral of all decisions to the top sharply enhances a sense of dependency, and increases the feeling of helplessness which we seek to minimize.

Early on, staff were instructed to make basic policy decisions over matters that concerned them cooperatively with their colleagues.[16]

Roy recognized that for decentralization to work, staff had to feel free of censure within their programs and departments. Moreover, their ideas had to reach him. To facilitate this end and to promote foundation-wide cooperation, Roy replaced the Department Directors Committee with the Interdepartmental Council. A ten- or eleven-member executive cabinet of unit heads, the IDC was to encourage and coordinate local decisionmaking and to promote cooperation between departments and programs. He also created the Monday Luncheon Forum of managerial staff, to talk more generally with him about decentralization and other concerns.[17]

However, Roy had only modest success at prompting staff to be candid and to take the initiative. Old habits persisted; staff in the larger departments still tended to defer to their directors. The directors appointed by Roy behaved like their predecessors. Some interpreted Roy's decentralization crusade as authorization to take their own initiatives rather than to implement staff decisions. Several seemed to compete with rival department heads even more intently than had those they replaced. Roy urged the directors to consider the general interest of the foundation: "We cannot be simply a set of confederated functions basically competing with each other for light in the sun." But his words did not prompt change.[18]

By 1969, Roy acknowledged that his vision of a new era of decentralization and interdepartmental cooperation was not coming to pass: "Our present structure is like the elephant—each of us has a different piece of it and each has a different perception of the nature of the organization."

He bemoaned the fact that foundation operations were characterized by "private negotiations" between individual staff and department directors, with all parties seeking to increase their power; few thought of the good of the foundation as a whole. Other officials spoke of the "unrelatedness" of the organization's operations; the various parts of the foundation simply did not "cohere." However, the president continued to promote "coherence," scheduling regular appointments with every administrator and department director. He also drafted plans for structural reforms. And he hired group therapy consultants to hold special discussion sessions designed to modify staff attitudes.[19]

Nevertheless, Roy soon felt pressed to back down on his campaign for decentralization and cooperation. Financial advisers warned him that for serious inroads to be made against a troublesome deficit, a delicate balance had to be maintained between the inpatient census, donor contributions, salaries, and staff scheduling. They insisted that a centralized perspective from the office of the president was necessary to coordinate these variables. Despairing of the IDC, whose directors behaved "like feudal barons contesting with each other," Roy replaced it in 1973 with a small Central Management Committee. Consisting of administrators and senior staff he considered loyal to him, the CMC was to make recommendations on planning and budgeting from a foundation-wide perspective. Even under the CMC, however, department directors had more input on operating budgets, salaries, and personnel matters within their units than under Karl and Will. Decentralization had carried that far.[20]

After half a decade under Roy, then, the foundation consisted of "barons contesting with each other," in tandem with a surprisingly active and assertive young president. Preoccupied with internal affairs, Roy rarely concerned himself with psychiatric developments elsewhere or with changing federal and state mental health policies. This provincialism, evident even under Karl and Will, was partially rooted in the foundation's location. The western Midwest remained fundamentally segregated from the coastal centers of medical research and innovation. A partial remedy might have been realized if the Menningers had better understood the nature of "hierarchical regionalism" in medical services. After World War II, university medical schools and their affiliated teaching hospitals became the centers of medical activity for particular regions of the country. The Menninger Foundation suffered because it excluded itself from association with the important University of Kansas medical complex and its affiliated hospitals and programs in Kansas City and Lawrence. The major connection—a cooperative Menninger–University of Kansas doctoral program in clinical psychology—had lapsed in 1949.[21]

Roy recognized that closer ties with the university might improve the foundation's fortunes. But even before he was formally installed as president, he had found himself "so swamped by the responsibilities that have accrued to me since Dad's death that there seems to be little time to think deep thoughts; mostly just time to put out fires." Consequently, Roy could only encourage associates to pursue a comprehensive academic-medical affiliation. At one point, he wondered aloud whether that affiliation might be advanced if he moved the foundation to Kansas City. However, he lacked the time or the energy to reply to overwhelmingly negative staff responses. Failing to cultivate links with the University of Kansas, the foundation negotiated a small tie with an undergraduate liberal arts institution, Antioch College, in Yellow Springs, Ohio. Through the efforts of Menninger psychologist Howard Shevrin, a small number of Antioch undergraduates began in 1972 to take six-month clinical internships at the foundation as part of their work-study program. But as useful as the Menninger-Antioch connection proved to be in the experience of undergraduate psychology majors, it hardly represented the asset of a regional medical center. So there persisted a troublesome situation that one senior psychiatrist characterized as a " 'magic mountain' atmosphere" of medical-professional isolation.[22]

I I I

Tangible successes eluded Roy during his first years in office. His decentralization campaign fell short of his expectations, and he launched no initiatives to rescue the foundation from its professional isolation. A few years into his presidency, he faced a more immediate problem. Three of the seven members of his Central Management Committee (European émigrés Ernst and Gertrude Ticho and Otto Kernberg) sought to outflank him and run the foundation.

The Ticho-Kernberg alliance evolved during the 1960s. Initially, the three joined with former hospital director Herman Van der Waals and others to form the ruling faction in the Topeka Institute for Psychoanalysis. While Bernard Hall remained at the foundation, he befriended them. So did Lester Roach; he recognized the strong support network that sustained Gertrude Ticho's long reign as Topeka Psychoanalytic Society and then TIP president. By the mid-1960s, Kernberg and the Tichos dominated the Topeka society and the institute, but they wanted to broaden their influence. They backed Roy to succeed Will because he was "lacking in experience" and would need to be assisted "by some kind of senior council or cabinet" (namely themselves). Ernst Ticho hoped to become senior vice-president, while Kernberg counted on the Research Department directorship. With the control of the Topeka Institute, Research, and the vice-presidency, plus the close ear of a young and inexperienced president, the Tichos and Kernberg anticipated that they would determine the foundation's future. The restoration of psychoanalytic thought and practice to the primacy that it once held was critical to their vision of that future. But a zest for political strategy and authority was no less important.[23]

They received their first setback when Roy failed to create a special vice-presidency for Ernst Ticho, despite his tenure as head of the Psychotherapy Service. Although Roy was willing to let Kernberg become director of the Psychotherapy Research Project when Wallerstein left, he refused to select him as the new Research Department director. If the Tichos and Kernberg were not overjoyed with Roy's initial appointments, they calculated that as long as he followed their advice, a formal vice-presidency and a Research Department directorship were unnecessary. They were pleased when he congratulated Gertrude Ticho for her reelection as director of the Topeka Institute—"I am delighted (and relieved)"—and allowed Ernst Ticho to solidify his authority as director of the Psychotherapy Service. And Roy's decision to appoint Kernberg as Fleming's successor more than atoned for his refusal to name him head of the Research Department. So the three dominated Menninger treatment services and TIP, and counted on gradually expanding their influence. Like other staff, however, they underestimated Roy's political astuteness.[24]

Roy had never been a champion of TIP or of psychoanalysis generally. He favored a more eclectic and pragmatic approach to hospital psychiatry, which included considerable recourse to group therapy. Moreover, he considered new programs like Industrial Psychiatry and School Mental Health, which applied psychiatric knowledge broadly to community social problems, as the most innovative operations in the foundation. Much more than psychoanalysis, Roy looked to these programs to restore Menninger's flagging reputation.[25]

Differing visions of the foundation's future drove the first serious wedge between Roy and the Ticho-Kernberg alliance. Roy had been president only two years when he proposed a substantial cut in the TIP budget. Much alarmed, the Tichos protested and called upon officials from the American Psychoanalytic Association to mediate the dispute. Roy added to tensions by reprimanding Ernst Ticho for refusing to promote alternatives to traditional psychoanalytic psychiatry. He was particularly displeased that Ticho did not encourage clinical staff to use new group therapy techniques. The president's proposed budget cut and reprimand enraged the Tichos and Kernberg. They feared that he was intent on uprooting the foundation from its psychoanalytic mooring.[26]

Before they could marshal their resources, however, Roy effectively turned them against one another. He told Kernberg that he had a mind to reinstitute the chief of staff position and wondered whether Kernberg might be interested in assuming the post. Kernberg replied that he was. Roy told him to talk it over with the Tichos. Kernberg did. They were angry with Roy for considering Kernberg over Ernst Ticho, who was older and had eight years seniority at Menninger. And they were shocked and hurt at Kernberg's willingness to assume a position that properly belonged to the director of the Psychotherapy Service. Almost instantly, the Tichos and Kernberg became divided, and their alliance disintegrated. They could only watch dejectedly as Roy then reversed himself, announcing that he would not appoint Kernberg chief of staff but would install Irving Sheffel as the foundation's first vice-president. At odds with one another and with their ambitions crushed, Kernberg left Topeka in the fall of 1973, while the Tichos departed a few months later.[27]

If Roy demonstrated considerable sagacity in his struggle with Kernberg and the Tichos, his maneuvering never captured much staff support. Indeed, none of Roy's activities during his first six years in office commanded a level of staff enthusiasm comparable to that for Will and Karl. Staff came increasingly to recognize Roy's ability to enhance his power, but few considered him an inspiring leader. Some even characterized him as vacuous. Although Roy denied that he lacked substantial vision, he had always acknowledged that he was not charismatic like his father and his uncle.

The contrast carried further. If charisma is considered from Max Weber's perspective—the pervasive belief in the extraordinary power of leaders—Roy's presidency marked the end of an era. By the time he dismantled the Ticho-Kernberg alliance, he presided over an organization that exhibited qualities of a bureaucracy in which legal-rational jurisdictions and formal rules and procedures appeared to be replacing personal leadership. Like many bureaucratic orders, this one seemed to be oriented toward the maximization of staff efficiency and the rule of financial balance sheets.

With thirty-nine buildings spread over two campuses, approximately nine hundred staff, and an annual budget for 1973 not far from $15 million, it was nearly impossible for the foundation to function without bureaucratic procedures. Phrases like "core management group," "maximum productivity," and "segment of the management system" pervaded staff communications. Such terms—which often originated with Roy—structured approaches to many of the organization's most crucial issues and even helped to determine them. "The basic question we must attempt to answer as we plan for the future," according to one of Roy's assistants, was "to what extent will contributions and grants from the private sector compensate for the continuing reduction of Federal support of psychiatric education and research."[28]

Although bureaucratic imperatives had become more evident, they do not account fully for Roy's administration. His focus on structure, coordination, and efficiency was also that of a psychiatrist intensely interested in group psychological processes. Influenced, too, by his undergraduate years at Swarthmore, he conceived of the president as the convener of a therapy session that had qualities of a Friends Meeting. Roy regarded himself more as a facilitator-healer of a "dependency culture" than as a tough manager attentive to balance sheets. He preferred to construct graphs of the kind that correlated highly personal, nonquantifiable events like the death of his father with the general level of staff unrest and the aesthetics of home campus buildings and grounds.[29]

A 1973 event underscores the difficulty of describing Roy solely as a bureaucrat. A group of influential senior staff asked him to arrange a meeting between themselves and some members of the trustees' executive committee to discuss foundation policy. By requesting direct communication with the trustees, they were jumping the organizational chain of command. Nevertheless, Roy asked no questions about their agenda and arranged the gathering.[30]

At the meeting, the staff presented many grievances against Roy. They charged that he was a poor fund-raiser, sought weak and unimaginative yes-men as top advisers, was unable to keep capable senior staff, and failed to foster conditions that would draw nationally recognized professionals to Topeka. Despite their candor and harshness, however, the group did not maintain that Roy was bureaucratizing the organization. Rather, they insisted that because he had no goals, he could not move Menninger in any clear direction. Although Roy was angry when he learned of these complaints, he never punished or castigated any in the group. Most rose to fairly prominent positions in the foundation and continued to speak out against him when they felt it was appropriate.[31]

If this episode illustrates that Roy could dispense with rigid, bureaucratic procedures, his approach to the hospital suggested that he was not excessively cost-conscious. Because the hospital produced most of the foundation's clinical income, it was crucial to all calculations of a balanced budget. In both 1967, when he took office, and 1975, after he and his advisers established cost-accounting guidelines, the ratio of hospital staff to patients at least equaled and very possibly exceeded that of all other private hospitals in the country. This was despite an unprecedented deficit. From the standpoint of high-salaried senior psychiatrists, the hospital patient/staff ratio was more generous than at any comparable facility. Nor were there rigorous efforts to reduce senior staff or to invoke other procedures to trim hospital expenses.[32]

A psychiatric hospital cannot simply buy exemplary treatment. There were at least modest benefits from Roy's costly staffing commitments, however. If in-house statistics on patient outcomes were based on impressionistic observations, they at least suggested that patients responded well to treatment. In the decade before Roy took office, between half and two thirds of all patients had been released after "moderate" to "good" improvement. Between 1967 and 1974 (with the same essential mix of patients and diagnoses), better outcomes were reported. In 1971–72, for example, 66 percent of all terminating patients were categorized as "improved" on release. By 1972–73 and 1973–74, this rate had risen to 71–72 percent. Data for difficult-to-treat disorders was even more encouraging.[33]

Despite the comparatively extravagant staffing costs and the encouraging statistics on treatment outcomes, however, foundation officials openly admitted that the organization's stature had obviously declined, and this troubled the president. At a department directors' retreat, a staff veteran proclaimed that Menninger "once had impact and influence. [We] Don't have it now." Another charged that the foundation had isolated itself from the innovative centers of mental health professionalism. The consulting firm of Brakeley, John Price Jones echoed these points in 1972 after a detailed investigation: "the Foundation does not enjoy full preeminence in either professional or lay circles today." If the image of professional excellence was not restored, Roy felt, he might eventually be presiding over a dying institution.[34]

I V

Beginning in the mid-1970s, Roy devoted much of his time to improving the foundation's image. With Kernberg and the Tichos gone, and with minimal challenges to his leadership from Karl, Robert, or Walter, his focus shifted from internal politics and policy to external diplomacy and publicity. By 1988, Roy felt that redirection of his efforts had yielded

mixed results. He could refer to a "nationally respected name and reputation for quality services" as one of Menninger's major strengths. But he
had to acknowledge "insufficient visibility and influence among our
peers." His public relations efforts had contributed to the popular reputation for "quality services." However, mental health professionals in an
age of biopsychiatry continued to be skeptical.[35]

Roy considered an extensive travel schedule, much like his father's,
essential to his effort to enhance the Menninger image. He traveled to
make public appearances almost as much as to solicit funds; favorable
receptions facilitated solicitations. Bev, his second wife, recalled how "he
rushed off to moderate a symposium in New York the day before our
wedding, and flew off . . . to Hollywood the day after to appear on the
Merv Griffin show." Roy also used mass mailing appeals, public relations
publications, and press releases. He came to rely heavily upon Patrick
Burnau, director of his Office of Public Affairs. Burnau preferred to focus
much of the foundation's publicity and solicitation on the affluent
through well-catered informational seminars and luxurious banquets. He
also emphasized slogans like "the caring society" and "the best for quality care" to describe Menninger treatment. In 1984, Roy appointed Burnau senior vice-president for public affairs, in charge of fund-raising and
marketing.[36]

Roy's and Burnau's efforts yielded tangible results. The magazine
Menninger Perspective was cited for its effectiveness in public relations by
the International Association of Business Communicators and the Kansas
chapter of the Public Relations Society of America. Both the hospital and
the Children's Division were directed to pursue aggressive marketing
strategies. The Office of Public Affairs offered thousands of medical
professionals favorable reports on Menninger services. It also conducted
systematic studies of competitor facilities and marketing conditions. By
the mid-1980s, after several years of intense public relations efforts,
Menninger came to be named as America's finest psychiatric hospital in
publications like *Family Circle, Good Housekeeping,* and *Town & Country.* If
mental health professionals like John Sutherland recognized that new
MSP residents were sometimes recruited from second-rate medical
schools and detected other professional shortcomings, the popular
media did not.[37]

Roy and Burnau were less successful at raising funds. Whereas Will's
efforts plus income from grants had accounted for roughly a third of the
foundation budget in the mid-1960s, donations and grants had dwindled
to 6 percent by 1983. Third-party insurance payments represented an
increasing proportion of the organization's income. However, by the

mid-1980s, insurance companies were becoming increasingly reticent about paying for long-term mental health services. With major federal grants more difficult to acquire in the face of the budgetary reductions of the Ford, Carter, and Reagan administrations, Roy and Burnau were desperate for a few large private donations like those Will had secured in difficult times. When he traveled to California, Roy sometimes called upon Beverly Hills oil heiress Liliore Green Rains. She died in 1986, leaving $40 million to the foundation—the largest single grant in Menninger Clinic history. Incorporated in the foundation's endowment, it earned income that relieved strained educational and research budgets. The Rains bequest also strengthened Roy's never entirely secure presidency.[38]

In publicizing the foundation, Roy and Burnau emphasized programs and services. These proliferated widely. Research projects on psychosomatic conditions like migraine headaches and hypertension were initiated. Outpatient treatment was offered for eating and sexual disorders, and for emotional problems inherent in job displacement. Group homes were established for abandoned and emotionally troubled children, while an infant and early childhood center was developed. Marital and family therapy services were enlarged, and centers to train therapists were opened in Kansas City and Saint Louis. In 1984, Roy launched plans to develop clinics and other treatment facilities outside Topeka so as to "seek out patients" and enhance revenues. Menninger outpatient clinics were opened in Albuquerque and Kansas City, and an inpatient facility was established in Phoenix's St. Joseph's Hospital.[39]

Roy considered public relations, fund-raising, new programs, and out-of-town centers as cornerstones of his administration. But he regarded as his signal accomplishment the abandonment of the original east campus, the shift of all hospital operations to the west campus, and the construction there of a series of hospital buildings. At a groundbreaking ceremony in 1980, where soil from the older campus was transferred to the west campus to symbolize a move that would occur in 1982, Roy characterized a foundation "emerging from under the shadow of two giants" and changing "from a generation of founders to a generation of institution builders." By moving from the campus established by Will and Karl, Roy hoped his presidency would finally be freed from comparisons with the leadership and accomplishments of the founders.[40]

He also had specific justifications for the move. East campus buildings were termite-ridden, with leaking roofs, and were not serviceable as modern treatment centers. The cost of ad hoc modernization of these facilities would have been extensive and less than satisfactory over the long term. It was more expeditious to raise $27 million so that all Menninger operations could be consolidated on one modern campus. To help cover costs, Roy and Burnau undertook a cross-country fund-raising tour. Shawnee County issued tax-exempt revenue bonds to complement donations.[41]

The advantages of a modern, unified campus were obvious. Staff no longer had to drive back and forth between two grounds, program coordination was facilitated, and fewer incidents of violence, attempted suicide, and unauthorized departure of patients occurred. There were also liabilities. The remodeled houses, barns, and garages of the old campus had been filled with powerful memories. The more modern and functional buildings of the new campus carried, instead, a significant financial burden—revenue-bearing bonds requiring high interest payments, and a string of major if unanticipated expenses as staff and patients settled in.[42]

After the Rains bequest eased financial pressures, Roy proclaimed that the move, together with his other initiatives, marked "the end of a long and very difficult transition . . . a change in leadership, a change in style, a change in strategies—without changing the values and beliefs which we had inherited." However, several older staff insisted that the values and beliefs had changed. They recalled how Will invoked the slogan "Brains before Bricks" to show that he valued well-trained staff over buildings. But Roy and Burnau changed it to "Brains and Bricks" in their campaign for hospital construction funds. What this signified, some whispered in the Menninger cafeteria and in the privacy of their offices, was a new era of "Bricks before Brains." A vacuous leadership dedicated only to construction and promotionalism had (supposedly) substituted for two inspiring crusaders for psychiatric excellence.[43]

By 1987, the organization was divided legally into four institutions—a parent Menninger Foundation corporation and three subsidiaries: the Menninger Clinic would encompass all programs in treatment, education, research, and prevention; the Menninger Fund would manage the foundation's endowment; the Menninger Corporation would sponsor any future for-profit programs. Some lawyers among the trustees argued that with these legal divisions, it would be more difficult for litigants to win large shares of Menninger assets. Others disagreed, but the board decided against them. The divisions created a nightmare for Menninger accountants. While he acknowledged that the change was more a legal maneuver than a functional shift, Roy lauded it as an effort "to meet the needs and challenges of our times."[44]

Few trustees slighted the accomplishments of Roy's presidency. None seriously considered removing him, despite periods of staff dissension. Still, some of the older trustees had been impressed by the shared leadership of two founding brothers during a more prominent era in Menninger history. By the late 1970s, several trustees pressured Roy to share responsibilities with Walter. Walter had demonstrated his skill as a clinical supervisor and director of the residency program at Topeka State Hospital. He had also served on the prestigious National Commission on the Causes and Prevention of Violence, lectured widely, and written a nationally syndicated newspaper column. Karl and Catharine joined in pressing for Walter's return and for his assuming leadership responsibilities; such was his "family inheritance." In 1981, Roy yielded somewhat by appointing Walter director of the small Division of Law and Psychiatry. The pressure persisted. Early in 1984, he made Walter director of the important Department of Education. A few months later, he also gave Walter Karl's old chief of staff position. Roy was quite conscious, at this point, that he was establishing a division of authority that replicated the relationship between Karl and Will. Walter was exceedingly ambitious, and the brothers rarely got along. Consequently, Roy feared a major upheaval like that of 1965. Because he had never developed an enthusiastic following, he suspected that a revolt might involve Walter's pitting senior staff against him.[45]

V

Confined to a gadfly role throughout Roy's presidency, Karl was discouraged about the direction of the foundation and pleaded for more responsibilities. He told Roy about a dream he had after Jimmy Carter won the presidency. Karl was consulted by the new administration. But Roy restricted Karl to the ceremonial role of chairman of the board of trustees, and Karl made his displeasure known. When he saw an architect's model for hospital construction on the west campus, he spoke of Roy's "magnificent erection." At the ground-breaking ceremony in 1980, he proclaimed, "I belong to the past." Karl also scored Roy for "several very serious blunders of management which have cost the Foundation millions in dollars, and much impairment of function and reputation." He complained bitterly that under Roy, the workplace had nearly ceased to be "a family foundation." "Did The Foundation begin to dissolve on April 23, 1965?" he wondered.[46]

When Walter returned from Topeka State, Karl embraced him as an ally. Together, they might compel Roy to increase their responsibilities; if he refused, they could work together to terminate his presidency. Karl and Walter admitted to each other their frustrations over their roles at Menninger. Karl prized these conversations because Walter informed him of significant foundation developments. But after Walter's promotions in 1984, Karl noticed that he seemed less candid. If Walter had any plan to augment his power and challenge Roy, it was not to involve his uncle.[47]

Even if Karl had been given important tasks, he was becoming less capable of doing them. He underwent surgery in 1976 to remove a nonmalignant brain tumor; the operation left him with a partial facial paralysis. In 1984, he had a major bout with bronchial pneumonia and a stroke. Milder strokes followed. A pacemaker was required to stabilize his heartbeat. Walking became difficult, even with a cane.[48]

When Karl turned ninety-five, in July 1988, the foundation scheduled an awards ceremony. A dozen people presented him with special gifts, including citations of merit, a new biography of Freud, and five cherry trees. The major gift was a three-volume loose-leaf collection of letters written by well-wishers. Although Karl enjoyed the attention, he would have preferred an invitation into the higher circles of decision-making.[49]

This sense of detachment from the organization he created was conveyed again and again during two days of continuous conversation. Karl and I met at his home six weeks after his birthday to explore his attitudes at ninety-five. "I haven't gotten used to this business of being completely superfluous to the foundation," he emphasized. "They've bumped me out of the wagon." When we greeted trustee David Neiswanger, Jr., at lunch, Karl said he no longer belonged to the organization he had created.[50]

Yet Karl felt that the foundation had fallen upon hard times and desperately needed him. He criticized Roy for hiring too many staff, particularly training analysts, and for excessive staff salaries. It was small wonder that the organization failed to turn a profit for the latest fiscal year. Karl charged that Roy had failed as a manager because he relied upon dull and limited advisers like Burnau, who worked only to enhance Roy's image and cover for Roy's misdeeds: "Take Burnau out of my sight." Karl was especially bitter because Roy and his advisers refused to consult Robert or to give him significant responsibilities: "Bob's the smartest one in the family."[51]

Karl claimed that he and his son could restore Menninger to its former greatness by drawing upon the few truly talented senior staff who remained. With these veterans, he could increase support for innovative programs like biofeedback and family therapy, and develop creative new programs. He could install an ecumenical religious studies department and a special criminology institute where convicts would be assigned to productive and rewarding work experiences. Above all, he could establish a children's institute with a hospital, a nursery school, and a day care center.[52]

As Karl reviewed birthday letters and talked, hour after hour, about the alleged failings of Roy's presidency, there was a sense that one of his most characteristic qualities was missing. Although he was alert and articulate, he posed none of the original and penetrating if unfashionable questions about people and events that had been his trademark for decades. He lacked intellectual vitality. He read Charles Lamb's poem "The Old Familiar Faces," in which "the leaves of life keep falling," and noted that few of the birthday letters hinted at his death.

If Karl felt disconnected from the foundation, he emphasized that he was still important to The Villages—small groups of foster homes for neglected, abused, and homeless children in Topeka, Lawrence, Indianapolis, and a few other locations. Although Karl had refused to serve on the board of The Villages Corporation when it was founded in 1964, he became active on it after the palace revolt. Honored by The Villages' directors and staff as the founding father, he became increasingly devoted to that corporation the longer Roy kept him from power. The day before the Menninger awards ceremony, the Topeka Villages of four group homes threw a party, which touched him deeply. The children greeted Karl with a hand-painted eight-foot birthday card, a giant birthday cake, and two stained-glass windows inscribed "Dr. Karl Menninger, Founder —The Villages Inc." A few of the children came up to talk with him and to sit on his lap, and they released ninety-five helium balloons, each carrying a packet of wildflower seeds and instructions to the finder to plant them in honor of Karl's birthday.[53]

As he reviewed his birthday letters with me, Karl stressed that all his life he had wondered whether he had any true friends; he now felt he had. Then, as he compared his less than joyous memories of the Menninger awards ceremony with the "gaiety" and warmth he had felt at The Villages party, Karl remarked that many of his friends—children and staff—were from The Villages. He also talked about his dream of that happy party. In a letter to an old friend, Lawrence Wagner, he had written: "I even dreamed about it recently, only they were angels, instead of being little boys and girls . . . lots of smiling people moving around." Karl had dreamed of dying and going off to heaven past a "cloud of 95 balloons." He finally felt assured that his life had been validated.[54]

Flo Menninger's oldest child found peace of mind in a heaven connected to The Villages far more than to the institution he and his father
had begun seventy years earlier. For Karl, the connection between family
and clinic seemed almost to have been severed.

Notes

Abbreviations Used in Notes:

M
: The Menninger Archives, Topeka, Kans. (This encompasses all historical materials within the Neiswanger Building, which houses the archives. It includes sundry organizational files, like the papers of the Topeka Institute for Psychoanalysis, Karl Menninger's professional and private papers, Menninger family papers, the Gardner Murphy papers, and diverse other "collections." Materials in these "collections" overlap extensively. Moreover, much within the archives has been misfiled and much remains unfiled. Investigators may therefore wish to consult with me for assistance, for I have maintained extensive notes on the contents of each file in the building, plus a substantial and fully organized collection of photoduplicates.)

MMR
: The Menninger Medical Records Office, Topeka, Kans.

MT
: The Menninger Trustees Papers, Tower Building, Topeka, Kans.

Libraries

AHAP
: Archives of the History of American Psychology, Akron University, Akron, Ohio.

APA
: American Psychiatric Association Archives, Washington, D.C.

JHMS
: Chesney Medical Archives, Johns Hopkins Medical School, Baltimore, Md.

KHS
: Kansas State Historical Society Archives, Topeka, Kans.

LC
: Library of Congress, Manuscript Division, Washington, D.C.

NA
: National Archives, Washington, D.C.

NYPsa
: New York Psychoanalytic Institute Library (Brill Library), N.Y.C.

PTS
: Princeton Theological Seminary, Speer Library, Princeton, N.J.

RFA
: Rockefeller Foundation Archive Center, Pocantico Hills, North Tarrytown, N.Y.

SCPsa
: Southern California Psychoanalytic Institute Library, Los Angeles, Calif.

TSH
: Topeka State Hospital Library, Topeka, Kans.

Private Collections

IK	Irving Kartus Papers, home of Irving Kartus, Leawood, Kans.
RPK	Robert P. Knight Papers, home of Adele Boyd, Stockbridge, Mass.
AM	Arthur Marshall Papers, home of Wendy Greene, Woodland Hills, Calif.
WCM	William C. Menninger Papers, home of Catharine Menninger, Topeka, Kans.
LLR	Lewis L. Robbins Papers, Hillside Hospital, Long Island, N.Y.

Interviews

TI	Transcript of tape-recorded interview
TRI	Tape-recorded interview
PI	Personal interview (notes)

Names

LJF	Lawrence J. Friedman
CFM	Charles F. Menninger
CWM	Catharine W. Menninger
EAM	Edwin A. Menninger
EAMJr.	Edwin A. Menninger, Jr.
FVM	Flo V. Menninger
JLM	Jeanetta Lyle Menninger
KAM	Karl A. Menninger
RGM	Robert G. Menninger
RWM	Roy W. Menninger
WCM	William C. Menninger

Journals

AJP	*American Journal of Psychiatry*
AJPT	*American Journal of Psychotherapy*
BHM	*Bulletin of the History of Medicine*
BMC	*Bulletin of the Menninger Clinic*
BJP	*British Journal of Psychiatry*
FR	*Family Relations*
HGP	*Heritage of the Great Plains*
IJP	*International Journal of Psycho-Analysis*
JAH	*Journal of American History*
JAMA	*Journal of the American Medical Association*
JAPA	*Journal of the American Psychoanalytic Association*
JCP	*Journal of Consulting Psychology*
JHBS	*Journal of the History of Behavioral Sciences*
JHMAS	*Journal of the History of Medicine and Allied Sciences*
JMF	*Journal of Marriage and the Family*
JP	*Journal of Parapsychology*
KH	*Kansas History*
MQ	*Menninger Quarterly*
OTR	*Occupational Therapy and Rehabilitation*
P	*Psychiatry*
PI	*Psychological Issues*

PQ   *Psychoanalytic Quarterly*
SMJ   *Southern Medical Journal*
SR   *Social Research*
TNHR   *Trained Nurse and Hospital Review*
TPR   *T(emperature), P(ulse), R(espiration)*
WMJ   *Wisconsin Medical Journal*
WQ   *Wilson Quarterly*

CHAPTER ONE: *The Menningers of Topeka*

1. The polarized characterizations of Kansas are discussed and quoted in Arthur M. Schlesinger's introduction to Joanna L. Stratton, *Pioneer Women: Voices from the Kansas Frontier* (New York, 1982), and Burton J. Williams, "Kansas: A Conglomerate of Contradictory Conceptions," *HGP* 19 (Summer 1986): 3–11. See also Carl Becker, "Kansas," *Essays in Honor of Frederick Jackson Turner* (New York, 1951), 110; White's editorial in the *Emporia Gazette,* Aug. 15, 1896; and Walter Bromberg, *Psychiatry Between the Wars, 1918–1945* (Westport, 1982), 16, quoting Mencken.

2. Stratton, *Pioneer Women,* 12, quoting Becker; Thomas Bonner, *The Kansas Doctor: A Century of Pioneering* (Lawrence, 1959), esp. 94, 120, 199, on Kansas medical achievement in this reform era.

3. KAM to Julia Gottesman, June 20, 1966, KAM papers, M, on Topeka's local college and Kansas institutions like it as "a monument to mediocrity"; *To the Stars* 5 (Sept. 1950): 7, quoting KAM on "Its alert and energetic people"; KAM, "Why I wrote *The Human Mind,*" 1930, Historical Scrapbook (H.S.) 14, M, on the "country doctors of Kansas."

4. KAM, TRI by Frederick Hacker, Topeka, Mar. 18, 1971, M.

5. CFM to Eric Menninger Von Lerchenthal, Jan. 30, 1934, H.S. 20, M; Claire Menninger to RWM, Mar. 13, 1979, Family Room, M; KAM to Gerda Norgel, May 26, 1954, Family Room, M.

6. *Tell City News Centennial,* Aug. 8, 1958; KAM to Gerda Norgel, May 26, 1954, Family Room, M; Walker Winslow, *The Menninger Story* (Garden City, N.Y., 1956), 32.

7. Winslow, *Story,* 33; CFM to Eric Menninger Von Lerchenthal, Jan. 30, 1934, H.S. 20, M; CFM to Thomas Amory Lee, July 5, 1921, Family Room, M; KAM, PI by LJF, Topeka, Jan. 14, 1985; CFM, TRI by Walker Winslow, 1952–53 (cylinder 25), M; Flo V. Menninger, *Days of My Life: Memories of a Kansas Mother and Teacher* (New York, 1940), 250, 257; CFM to WCM, May 7, 1920, WCM Papers (private), for the fullest explanation of Charles's decision to go to Campbell College.

8. Melvin H. Knisely to KAM, Apr. 10, 1946, Family Room, M; "Heikes Family" in *Clay Center Dispatch,* May 28, 1983; FVM, *Days,* 54, 58–9, 103; "Flora Vesta Knisely Menninger, April 23, 1863–February 9, 1945," n.a., n.d., 1 (in FVM Papers, M); Lola Flack, Helen Gilbert, Vera Olsen, *The Heikes-Augaty Family* (Wayne, Neb., 1968), 21, 35–6, 50; KAM, PI by LJF, Topeka, Mar. 10, 12, 1986.

9. EAM, "Midwest Magnificence" (unpub. ms., 1948), 75, 120, M; KAM, TI by Harold Maine (pseud. Walker Winslow), Aug. 20, 1952, Topeka, 14, M; KAM, TRI by Hacker, Apr. 18, 1971, M.

10. FVM, *Days,* 198–209; EAM, "Midwest Magnificence," 93; Bonner, *Kansas,* 202, on the emergence of women as Kansas physicians.

11. CFM to Thomas A. Lee, Jan. 5, 1921, H.S. 5, M; and *Stuart* (Fla.) *News,* Dec. 3,

1953, on Charles Menninger's teaching duties at Campbell College; FVM, *Days,* 292, "My dream."

12. FVM, *Days,* 212–14; see also FVM to KAM, Jan. 15, 1934, KAM Papers, M; CFM, TRI by Walker Winslow, Topeka, 1952–53 (cylinder 22), M.

13. FVM to KAM, Jan. 15, 1934, KAM Papers, M; FVM, *Days,* 214.

14. FVM, *Days,* 220–33, 243–6; see also KAM, TRI by LJF, Abilene, Mar. 13, 1986, on the couple's church preferences.

15. Bonner, *Kansas,* 111, on the economic status of late-nineteenth-century Kansas physicians; FVM, *Days,* 230, on Charles's going to medical college and eventually being able "to earn a home."

16. FVM, *Days,* 232–6, on the decision to locate in Topeka and on Flo moving there to teach. For descriptions of Topeka in the late 1880s and early 1890s, see Lucy Freeman, ed., *Sparks: Karl Menninger, M.D.* (New York, 1973), 2–10; Winslow, *Story,* 89, 91, 98, 105; Barbara Hauschild, *On the Avenue of Approach* (Topeka, 1979), 1–2, 13–15; CFM to Thomas A. Lee, Jan. 5, 1921, H.S. 15, M. The most detailed information on Topeka society and life at the time is the wonderfully comprehensive *Radges' Directory of Topeka and Shawnee County. And Gazetteer of General Information* (Topeka, 1891).

17. CFM, TRI by Winslow, 1952–53 (cylinder 9); *Radges' Directory.*

18. Bonner, *Kansas,* 73–5, on Menninger following Roby's lead and turning from homeopathy. See also CFM, "The Origin of the Menninger Clinic and Sanitarium," n.d. (1926), 1, H.S. 10; CFM, TRI by Winslow, 1952–53 (cylinder 4); Mildred Law, TRI by CWM, Sept. 26, 1969, M; B. H. Hall, ed., *A Psychiatrist for a Troubled World: Selected Papers of William C. Menninger, M.D.* (New York, 1967), I, 282; Alice Dangerfield, "Biographical Sketch of Charles Frederick Menninger, M.D., December, 1942," 12, H.S. 43, M.

19. CFM, TI by Winslow, Sept. 4, 1952; FVM, "Dear Folks," Jan. 28, 1940, FVM Papers, M; KAM, TI by Winslow, Aug. 18, 1952, 2; EAM, "Midwest Magnificence," 75, 110.

20. FVM, *Days,* 246–7.

21. FVM, *Days,* esp. 254–5; FVM, "Baby Book" (diary), esp. July 13, 1895, KAM Papers, M.

22. Winslow, *Story,* 98–100.

23. Quoted language in FVM, *Days,* 291. See also *Days,* 295–300; *TPR* 26, no. 1 (Nov. 1966): 10–11; EAM, "Midwest Magnificence," 116; FVM, "Dear Folks," Jan. 28, 1940, FVM Papers, M.

24. For observations of Flo Menninger after she became a leader in Bible study classes, see Pearl Boam, TRI by CWM, Topeka, Sept. 25, 1968, M; and EAMJr., TRI by LJF, Lillington, N.C., Aug. 17, 1985. Cogent analysis of the women's club movement is to be found in June Underwood, "Civilizing Kansas: Women's Organizations, 1880–1920," *KH* 7 (Winter 1984–85): 296–7.

25. Winslow, *Story,* 188. RGM, PI by LJF, Topeka, Feb. 27, 1984, on the development of Charles's hobbies; CFM to Pearl Boam, July 30, 1926, WCM Papers (private), "She is sitting here"; KAM diary for 1906, Feb. 23, 1906, KAM Papers, M; CWM, PI by LJF, Topeka, July 30, 1984.

26. EAM, "Midwest Magnificence," 111, "peace at any price": *ibid.,* 76, on the check account controversy; *ibid.,* 110, on the malpractice suit; KAM, TI by Harold Maine, Aug. 18, 1952, Topeka, 10–11, on the people's harvests. See also EAMJr., TRI by LJF, Lillington, Aug. 17, 1985.

27. CWM, PI by LJF, Topeka, July 30, 1984, on the "Charlie" salutation and the handkerchief gifts; FVM to KAM, July 22, 1937, KAM Papers, M, on traveling with Charles.

28. KAM to RGM, May 15, 1940, KAM Papers, M, on Flo's fear of losing Karl as she lost her father; FVM, "Karl A. Menninger" (1893–94—first-year diary), KAM Papers, M, n.d., on refusing to eat for a day; FVM, "Baby Book," Apr. 24, 1895, KAM Papers, M, on the parlor lamp; FVM, "Karl A. Menninger" (first-year diary), n.d., on the food that did not taste right.

29. FVM, "Baby Book," KAM Papers, M, Oct. 26, 1896, Jan. 21, 1897, and May 8, 1895, contain the quoted expressions of anxiety, while Dec. 15, 1895, entry notes why she encouraged Karl to nap.

30. FVM, "Baby Book," Jan. 11, 1898, and Feb. 9, 1897, on love and "fear" of Karl; April 29, 1895, "a mind of his own"; July 24, 1896, "like me in many ways."

31. Alice Miller, *The Drama of the Gifted Child* (New York, 1981), 32, 35, 45, affords a brilliant analysis of the mirror image in child development.

32. KAM, "The Middle of the Journey: Dragons and Grails," *BMC* 40 (July 1983): 308, identifying with Flo's sibling position; KAM to Ella W. Brown, Feb 17, 1945, "oldest problem child"; KAM, TI by Stannie Anderson, Topeka, Aug. 12, 1974, M, "allergy to . . . faking"; KAM to FVM, n.d. (1914), KAM Papers, M, "please mamma"; FVM to KAM, n.d., KAM Papers, M, "You have always been fine."

33. KAM to Julia Gottesman, Apr. 5, 1961, KAM Papers, M, "most determining influence"; KAM, TI by Maine, Topeka, Aug. 18, 1952, 1, M, and KAM Diary, 1906, KAM Papers, M, May 7, 1906, on Flo doing things to please him; KAM Analysis Notes, 1930–32, KAM Papers, M, Jan. 29, 1931, recalls the enemas, while KAM to Martha Nichols, Jan 13, 1955, KAM Papers, M, notes the Christmas bells when he was only one and a half years old; KAM, TI by Maine, Topeka, Aug. 18, 1952, on Flo's depression and outbursts against Charles; KAM Diary, 1906, KAM Papers, M, Feb. 26, 1906, on mother leaving the house.

34. KAM, *The Human Mind* (New York, 1930), 200; KAM, TI by Verne Horne, Topeka, Mar. 4, 1986, M.

35. Winslow, *Story,* 153, quotes Karl on deciding to go into medicine; KAM Analysis Notes, 1930–32, KAM Papers, M, Feb. 18, 1931, contains his feelings toward Flo during analysis; FVM, "Baby Book," July 21, 1930, 253, 255, KAM Papers, M, "too much mother."

36. FVM, *Days,* 257–9, on Edwin's birth, temperament, and dietary habits.

37. FVM, "Baby Book," Aug. 5, 1899, "sunbeam," July 21, 1930, "Dear little Edwin," "poor Karl"; FVM Diary, Aug. 5, 1899, 228, Family Room, M, Charles offering boys a ride.

38. EAM, "Midwest Magnificence," 54, on Karl-Flo bonding; FVM, "Baby Book," Aug. 23, 1896, on Karl assaulting Edwin; FVM Diary, July 6, 1899, 223, "Edwin and Mama."

39. FVM, *Days,* 265, on wanting a girl; EAMJr., TRI by LJF, Lillington, Aug. 18, 1985, recalls Flo calling him "Claire" through the 1930s. FVM, "Dear Folks," Aug. 14, 1938, KAM Papers, M, minister consoling her on no daughters and Will's reply.

40. On adolescent dating, see WCM, "Some Impressions of My Childhood," 1953, 8, in Introd. to WCM Diary, 1910–39, WCM Papers (private); WCM to FVM, CFM, Pearl Boam, KAM, Julia Menninger, Apr. 3, 1921, on Sunday hikes, Mar. 20, 1921, on clothes repairs (both in KAM Papers, M); WCM to FVM, June 3, 1921, on clothes repair, June 8, 1922, on being the "baby" of the family, KAM Papers, M.

41. In his interview of CFM, Aug. 29, 1952 (TI, M), Harold Maine speculates sensitively on Will's unique and more distant spot in the sibling order; WCM, "Some Impressions of My Childhood," 1953, 8, on the stealing incident; see also EAM, "Midwest Magnificence," 77; WCM Diary, Apr. 5, 1941, on cooling toward church service. WCM, "Some Impressions of My Childhood," 6, on musical instrument practice.

42. An unpublished biography of Karl Menninger by Lewis Robbins and Melvin Herman stresses Flo's comparing Will to Karl in this way. But I have found far too little evidence to characterize it as a persistent pattern. Virginia Eicholtz (TRI by LJF, Topeka, Sept. 10, 1985), a neighbor and friend of Flo Menninger during World War II, holds to a more balanced view of this lifelong pattern. Eicholtz notes that Flo put Karl down regularly, but did not always compare his progress to Will's when she did so.

43. KAM, TRI by Frederick Hacker, Apr. 18, 1971, M, on the meal pattern; KAM, "To my Father on the occasion of ninetieth birthday," July 11, 1952, H.S. 83, M, on Charles studying after dinner; Winslow, *Story,* 152, on Charles's greater interest in his sons as they grew older; KAM Diary, Apr. 7, 1906, notes Charles offering to let the boys ride with him during medical visits. His advising the boys on horse-and-buggy matters is noted in Preston O. Hale and Pauline D. Beatty, eds., *Aristocratic Topeka Avenue and Its Environs* (Topeka, 1979), 41–2.

44. WCM, "Some Impressions of My Childhood," 6, "family orchestra." See, e.g., CFM to WCM, Oct. 9, 1922, H.S. 6, M, advising Will on diversions during medical studies, and CFM to WCM, Apr. 28, 1920, H.S. 4, M, "looking forward" and "I love you very dearly."

45. The quotes in this paragraph and a wealth of similarly illustrative material are found in WCM Diary, Nov. 28, 1953, and WCM, "Some Impressions of My Childhood," 9.

46. FVM to WCM, Feb. 25, 1920, WCM Papers (private); KAM to EAM, Sept. 15, 1966, KAM Papers, M; EAM in *Stuart* (Fla.) *News,* Dec. 3, 1953; EAM in *TPR* 3 (July 1–31, 1942): 63; CFM to EAM, July 10, 1908, EAM Diaries, 1908, Family Room M; EAM, "Midwest Magnificence," 33.

47. On Charles's ninetieth birthday, Karl referred to his father as "a Solomon" who "was good to everyone" (*Washington Post,* July 25, 1983). Winslow, *Story,* 153, and KAM to Harold Maine, Nov. 25, 1953, Maine Papers, M, recounts Charles's response to Karl's deciding to become a doctor.

48. KAM to Franz Alexander, Oct. 28, 1933, KAM Papers, M, and KAM Analysis Notes, 1930–32, 8 (Feb. 11, 1931), KAM Papers, M, on Karl's sibling jealousy toward Will; FVM to KAM, Sept. 30, 1939, KAM Papers, M, recounts the algebra lesson and the sermon outline incidents.

49. KAM, TI by Maine, Aug. 20, 1952, contrasts Karl's relationship with Flo and with Charles; KAM to Harold Maine, July 7, 1954, on him and his mother as more "sensitive" than Charles (and, by implication, Will); KAM Analysis Notes, 1930–32 (Apr. 2, 1931), on his inability to identify with Charles. There is considerable scholarship on gender roles in Victorian prescriptive literature. Nancy F. Cott, "Passionless: An Interpretation of Victorian Sexual Ideology, 1790–1850," *Signs* 4 (Winter 1978): 219–36; Barbara Welter, "The Cult of True Womanhood, 1820–1860," *American Quarterly* 18 (Summer 1966): 151–74; and Ronald W. Hogeland, "The Female Appendage: Feminine Life-Styles in America, 1820–1860," *Civil War History* 17 (June 1971): 101–14, are especially helpful.

50. Winslow, *Story,* 121, and EAM, TRI by LJF, Lillington, Aug. 18, 1985.

51. FVM, *Days,* 308, on the brothers being apart from 1914 to 1935; Walter Toman, *Family Constellation: Its Effects on Personality and Social Behavior,* 3rd ed. (New York, 1971), 18, 156–7; WCM to CFM and FVM, May 25, 1922, KAM Papers, M, "mental bath"; WCM to Bernard Hall, May 10, 1966, WCM Papers, M, on writing professionally; WCM to KAM and JLM, Dec. 20, 1947, KAM Papers, M, "good cry."

52. Toman, *Constellation,* 153, on older brother expecting younger brothers to be loyal; KAM, *Sparks,* 24, "attached to me like a son"; KAM, TI by Stannie Anderson, Aug. 12, 1974, M, on Will imitating him and on Karl acknowledging Will's independent, stubborn qualities.

53. EAM, "Midwest Magnificence," 17; Hazel Knisely Bowyer, TRI by LJF, Mar. 13, 1986, on the Knisely farm; KAM to WCM, June 6, 1922, unclassified, M, on Will's school work; KAM to WCM, Dec. 5, 1921, unclassified, M, offering to help Will's missionary endeavors; KAM to WCM, Oct. 13, 1920, KAM Papers, M, on medical career choices; KAM to WCM, Sept. 24, 1924, KAM Papers, and KAM to WCM, Oct. 28, 1929, H.S. 13, M, on career study, activities for Will's wife.

54. *Topeka Daily Capital,* Mar. 3, 1915, reporting the facts of the incident. Edwin Menninger, Sr., confirmed to me the correctness of these facts (see Edwin's notations on my letters: LJF to EAM, Jan. 23, 1985, Feb. 6, 1986). See also CFM, TI by Walker Winslow, 1952–53 (cylinder 15), M; Winslow, *Story,* 158–60; EAMJr., TRI by LJF, Lillington, Aug. 17, 1985.

55. My taped interview with Edwin Menninger, Jr., Lillington, Aug. 17–18, 1985, was the most comprehensive source of data on Edwin's life from the time he left Topeka; FVM to WCM, n.d. (Aug. 1922), WCM Papers (private), on Flo and Charles not quite knowing what to do for Edwin after the accident.

56. KAM, TI by Stannie Anderson, Topeka, Aug. 12, 1974, M, recalls Edwin Menninger repeatedly away from home and TI, July 15, 1974, notes Edwin burning his hand; FVM, "Baby Book" (Sept. 27, 1900), 246, on Edwin cutting his thumb off; Winslow, *Story,* 157, notes Edwin's carelessness with chemicals.

57. Excellent discussions of sociological research on the middle-born are provided by Jeannie S. Kidwell, "The Neglected Birth Order: Middlesons," *JMF,* Feb. 1982, 225–35, and Toman, *Constellation,* 22.

58. KAM noted the "belonging quality" of family life in *Los Angeles Times,* Oct. 30, 1983, 16; EAM, "Midwest Magnificence," underscores the religious dimension of Menninger family routines. See also Winslow, *Story,* 113–14, and FVM, "Baby Book," Nov. 4, 1896.

59. Winslow, *Story,* 84–8, 93–100, 152–3, 229–33, 251–5, 305–9.

60. Winslow, *Story,* 33, on August Menninger taking in homeless children; FVM, *Days,* 95, recalls "grandfather Heikes" taking in the needy, and p. 163, on the Coulsons; Hazel Knisely Bowyer, TRI by LJF, Abilene, Mar. 13, 1986, on Amanda Knisely boarding the local teacher.

61. The nature of the nineteenth-century boardinghouses and the transition from boarders to lodgers is discussed in Mark Peel, "On the Margins: Lodgers and Boarders in Boston, 1860–1900," *JAH* 72 (Mar. 1986): 814; Bonner, *Kansas,* 90–3, on several late-nineteenth-century Kansas "hospitals" as essentially boarding institutions for the poor; FVM, *Days,* 219, 222–3, on Amanda's boardinghouse (p. 222 contains the quote on profit). See also Winslow, *Story,* 43, and Virginia Eicholtz, TRI by LJF, Topeka, Jan. 9, 1985, on the boardinghouse.

62. Winslow, *Story,* 57, on Flo helping families of Branner School children.

63. For a good general discussion of the heightened late-Victorian sense of kinship obligations, see Steven Ruggles, *Prolonged Connections: The Rise of the Extended Family in Nineteenth-Century England and America* (Madison, 1987). FVM, *Days*, 249, on taking in Dave Knisely and his family. For data on Will Kercher and Charlie Menninger as boarders, see KAM to Harold Maine, July 7, 1954, KAM Papers; FVM, *Days*, 257, 285; Winslow, *Story*, 94; KAM, PI by LJF, Topeka, Jan. 14, May 18, Sept. 11, 1985. My interview with EAMJr., Lillington, Aug. 18, 1985 (TRI), was particularly fruitful on the particulars of the contacts between Flo and Charles Menninger and their families in Tell City, Pennsylvania, and Abilene. See especially Murray Bowen, *Family Therapy in Clinical Practice* (New York, 1978), 538, for cogent observations on the need to forge substitute families.

64. For a good analysis of the economics of boarding, see John Modell and Tamarah K. Hareven, "Urbanization and the Malleable Household: An Examination of Boarding and Lodging in American Families," *JMF* 35 (Aug. 1973): 467–79. For data on economic reasons for taking in Will Kercher, see FVM, *Days*, 257, 261; periodic references in FVM, "Baby Book," and KAM, PI by LJF, Topeka, May 18, 1985. In this interview, Karl noted Frank Delancey, while FVM, *Days*, 274, noted Frank Preer. For data on Foy Ernest, see FVM, *Days*, 259–60, 269; Winslow, *Story*, 95 and penciled notation on 114 by KAM on copy of this book at M. See also KAM to Harold Maine, July 7, 1954, KAM Papers, M, on Kercher and Ernest as laborers, and KAM to CWM, Oct. 16, 1985 (in possession of CWM), on labor from other boarders.

65. For information on Bible authorities as boarders, see FVM, *Days*, 297, and KAM, TI by Harold Maine, Topeka, Aug. 18, 1952, 2, M. For data on "artist" boarders, see EAM, "Midwest Magnificence," 66, 120; FVM, *Days*, 263–4; Winslow, *Story*, 101–2; KAM, PI by LJF, Topeka, May 18, Sept. 9, 1985; KAM to CWM, Oct. 16, 1985 (in possession of CWM); notes dictated to CWM by EAM, June 27–29, 1979 (also in possession of CWM).

66. *Lamps on the Prairie: A History of Nursing in Kansas* (reprint, New York, 1984), 135, on the 1903 Kaw River flood and its impact on Topeka. For coverage of relief effort by the Menningers, see EAM, "Midwest Magnificence," 5–9; FVM, *Days*, 273–4; and Winslow, *Story*, 118–19.

67. For data on the efforts to adopt Grace Tanner, EAM, "Midwest Magnificence," 9–10; WCM Diary, Mar. 13, 1956, WCM Papers (private); KAM to Grace Tanner, Dec. 17, 1951, Family Room, M; KAM, PI by LJF, Topeka, May 18, 1985; KAM to Harold Maine, July 7, 1954, KAM Papers, M. In EAM, TI by CWM, June 1979, 2–3 (in possession of CWM), the middle son conveyed many of his feelings about Grace Tanner. He claimed that her parents were still alive at the time of the adoption but too poor to care for her. However, I have found no evidence to support this assertion and much to contradict it.

68. FVM, *Days*, 286–7, on Pearl's operation and coming to stay with the Menningers. See also Winslow, *Story*, 167–9; Josephine Boam, TRI by LJF, Feb. 27, 1984, and CWM's recollections of Pearl Boam, Jan. 17, 1974 (TRI, M). In my taped interview, Lillington, Aug. 17, 1985, EAMJr. noted (as a boarder himself during the 1930s) that Charles always referred to Pearl as his daughter.

69. Several interviews I conducted best characterize the emerging rapport between Pearl Boam and the Menningers: Josephine Boam, Topeka, Feb. 27, 1984 (TRI); Julia Gottesman, Los Angeles, Jan. 3, 1984 (TRI); CWM, Topeka, Mar. 9, 1985 (PI); Virginia Eicholtz, Topeka, Jan. 9, 1985 (TRI). See also FVM, *Days*, 289–90.

70. FVM, *Days,* 284; Winslow, *Story,* 190.

71. Winslow, *Story,* 13–16, and CFM, "The Origin of the Menninger Clinic and Sanitarium," n.d. (1926), Family Room, M, on his 1908 visit to Rochester. CFM, "The Origin," esp. 1–2, on his two trips to Joslin, the second being "when insulin came." Winslow, *Story,* 170–1, also notes the trips to Joslin and the lesson from the student who left. I have learned a great deal from former Joslin Foundation president and physician Alexander Marble about Elliott Joslin: Alexander Marble to LJF, Nov. 7, 21, 1985; Marble, "Evolution of the Joslin Diabetes Center," unpub. ms., Dec. 21, 1984; Marble, "Elliott Proctor Joslin," *Transactions of the Association of American Physicians,* 75 (1962): 25–9; Marble et al., "Elliott Proctor Joslin," *Harvard University Gazette* (Sept. 29, 1962), 19–21. For CFM's remark on the loneliness he felt practicing medicine by himself, see CFM, "Chicago Meeting, Nov. 30, 1950," H.S. 79, M. KAM, "The Birth of the Menninger Clinic," n.d., 5, KAM Papers, M, on Charles's desire for "a group like a family."

72. WCM to KAM and JLM, Dec. 20, 1947, Historical Notebook, M; Winslow, *Story,* 142–3; WCM to CFM and FVM, n.d. (Dec. 1920), KAM Papers, M.

73. KAM Analysis Notes, 1930–32 (Apr. 2, 1931), KAM Papers, M, "world adulation." JLM, TRI by LJF, Topeka, Jan. 7, 1983, and Bernard Kamm, TRI by LJF, Chicago, Feb. 4, 1984, were both exceedingly helpful in detecting the beginnings of the increasing centrality of Karl in family affairs.

74. Winslow, *Story,* 151–3, on general background to Karl's career decision, the visit to Dr. Koester, and Karl's "I am going to become a doctor" remark. KAM to Harold Maine, Nov. 25, 1953, Maine Papers, M, gives Karl's account of the career decision; he stresses Grace Gaines's role when he decided against the ministry.

75. In 1940, Karl recalled Southard's November 1908 advice in "KAM's Experiences in Kansas City General Hospital and Boston Psychopathic Hospital, 1918–1919," July 29, 1940, H.S. 2, M. This has been the basis for the traditional account of the origins of the Menninger partnership. See, e.g., Lewis L. Robbins and Melvin Herman, "Karl Menninger—Still Ahead of His Time," *BMC* 42 (1978): 295. Winslow, *Story,* 169–71, on Charles trying to draw his son back to Topeka.

76. In KAM, PI by LJF, Topeka, May 18, 1985, Karl acknowledged that the early Menninger household was more fundamental to his mental health interest than his studies under Southard. In the Menninger Archives copy of Winslow, *Story,* p. 114, Karl made a note in 1980 on his reading with Ernest during the 1902 quarantine.

77. KAM, *BMC* 47 (July 1983): 308–9, is his fullest account of the Phi Delta rejection and contains his remark on organizing his own groups. See also Winslow, *Story,* 139–40; KAM, TI by Harold Maine, Topeka, Aug. 18, 1952, 7–9; KAM, PI by LJF, Topeka, May 21, 1985; Lewis Robbins, TRI by LJF, New York, Aug. 23, 1983.

78. KAM, TI by Harold Maine, Topeka, Aug. 18, 1952, 9, for insistence that the Phi Delta rejection did not fully commit him to a neuropsychiatric career. CFM, TI by Walker Winslow, 1952–53, n.d. (cylinder 1), M, contains Charles's remark on choosing Harvard for Karl.

79. See "Harvard Medical School. Record of K. A. Menninger" in H.S. 2, M, for Karl's Harvard grades and scores. For useful information on Karl's stay at Harvard and his exposure to Freud, see KAM, "Reading Notes," *BMC* 47 (Jan. 1983): 79–80, and KAM to Mr. and Mrs. Max Epstein, June 16, 1950, KAM Papers, M.

80. KAM to Thomas F. Miller, Jan. 29, 1917, H.S. 2, M, on the arrangements for Karl going to Kansas City General Hospital for his internship.

81. For Karl's experience with mental patients at Kansas City General, see KAM, "20th Century Interview," Sept. 15, 1961, transcript, 3, WCM Papers, M.

82. For Karl's lessons from Southard, see "KAM's Experiences in Kansas City General Hospital and Boston Psychopathic Hospital, 1918–1919," July 29, 1940, H.S. 2, M; KAM, PI by LJF, Topeka, Sept. 11, 1985; Lewis Robbins, TRI by LJF, New York, Aug. 23, 1983; KAM to WCM, Sept. 24, 1924, WCM Papers (private).

83. B. H. Hall, ed., *A Psychiatrist's World: The Selected Papers of Karl Menninger, M.D.* (New York, 1959), II, 815, on Southard as "superficialist." KAM, PI by LJF, Topeka, May 21, 1985, on his dissatisfaction at the time with Southard's use of diagnostic labels. *Sparks*, 114, on turning to Jelliffe on the death of Southard. Smith Ely Jelliffe to KAM, Feb. 15, 1920, KAM Papers, M, on Southard as never getting below the skin. See also KAM, TRI by LJF, Topeka, Nov. 8, 1987, and KAM to Gregory Stragnell, Sept. 19, 1921, KAM Papers, M, on Karl reaching for Freudian literature throughout his medical education.

84. Karl's personal tie with Southard is revealed in KAM, "Anecdotal Material," July 22, 1946, H.S. 54, M; Hall, ed., *A Psychiatrist's World,* II, 814; KAM to Frances Whiting, Nov. 15, 1929, and to Frederick P. Gay, Jan. 21, 1935, both in KAM Papers, M.

85. KAM to Harold Maine, July 15, 1954, M (unclassified), on Southard's poor marriage, his evenings with Karl, and Karl's reminiscence. See also KAM to TMF Museum, n.d., KAM Papers, M, claiming anorexia nervosa early in his marriage to Grace, and Julia Gottesman, TRI by LJF, Los Angeles, Jan. 3, 1984.

86. Karl seemed best to convey the complex emotions on whether to return to Topeka or to stay with Southard at Boston Psychopathic Hospital when talking to Walker Winslow (pseud. Harold Maine). See especially KAM to Harold Maine, July 14, 1954, CFM Papers, M; and KAM, TI by Harold Maine, Topeka, Aug. 18, 20, 1952 (transcript in H.S. 84, M).

87. Karl's process of recall of past rapport with his father after his conversation with Southard is indicated, if rather obliquely, in his diary (KAM Diaries, 1906–1919, KAM Papers, M) and in certain of his reminiscences (see, e.g., "To My Father on the Occasion of His Ninetieth Birthday," July 11, 1952, KAM Papers; "KAM's Experience in Kansas City . . . ," H.S. 2, M; KAM, TI by Harold Maine, Topeka, Aug. 18, 20, 1952). Winslow, *Story*, 153, on Charles's response to Karl's decision to become a doctor.

88. KAM to CFM, June 30, 1918, H.S. 2, M, his letter of advice to his father on the medical practice, contains the "nowhere in the world" remark. "KAM's Experience in Kansas City," H.S. 2, M, reveals that Charles took the letter graciously and respectfully, and implemented a number of the suggestions. Interestingly, KAM Diaries, 1906–1919, KAM Papers, M, indicates a predisposition to work with Charles as early as July 11, 1916.

89. KAM to editor of *Washburn Review*, Feb. 5, 1921, H.S. 5, M, "probably the leading man."

90. C. F. Menninger, "The Insanity of Hamlet," Oct. 18, 1890, CFM Papers, M. See also CFM in *Topeka State Journal,* June 16, 1952, and CFM, "Nursing History," Nov. 16, 1941, Inst. Archives, M, for indications of Charles's early interest in psychiatry. CFM, "Chicago Meeting, Nov. 30, 1950," H.S. 79, M, quotes Charles on his medical practices supporting the partnership while they pioneered in psychiatry.

91. CFM, "The Origin of the Menninger Clinic and Sanitarium," n.d. (1926), H.S. 10, M, "I concluded."

92. KAM to Harold Maine, July 14, 1954, CFM Papers, M, on his 1919–20 trips to Boston.

CHAPTER TWO: *Family Configurations*

1. More than any other source, scholars are indebted to the prodigious research and persuasive argument within Gerald N. Grob, *Mental Illness and American Society, 1875–1940* (Princeton, 1983), for an understanding of the turn-of-the-century crisis within the psychiatric profession. Chapters 2 and 5 are particularly helpful.

2. Grob, *Mental Illness*, is also the best source on efforts to resolve the psychiatric crisis, especially Chapters 3, 5, 6, 9. See also Leland V. Bell, *Treating the Mentally Ill: From Colonial Times to the Present* (New York, 1980), 81, and David J. Rothman, "Social Control: The Uses and Abuses of the Concept in the History of Incarceration," *Rice University Studies* 67 (1981): 18–19. I. S. Wechsler, "The Legend of the Prevention of Mental Disease," *JAMA* 95 (1930): 24–6.

3. See Philip Rieff, *Freud: The Mind of the Moralist* (Garden City, 1961), 390, for an insightful discussion of the twentieth-century hospital as comparable symbolically to the church and the legislative hall. Grob, *Mental Illness*, 135–7, on the emergence of psychiatric specialty wards in general hospitals.

4. St. Elizabeths Hospital is discussed in Bell, *Treating*, 126–7; Dwight Macdonald, "The 'Nervous Breakdown,' " *Fortune* 11 (1935): 85.

5. L. Vernon Briggs, *History of the Psychopathic Hospital, Boston, Massachusetts* (Boston, 1922); Grob, *Mental Illness*, 139; Grob, *The State of the Mentally Ill: A History of Worcester State Hospital in Massachusetts, 1830–1920* (Chapel Hill, 1966), 333–4.

6. *Patients in Hospitals for Mental Disease 1923* (Washington, D.C., 1926), 11—the U.S. Census breakdown for public and private hospitals and patients. Walter Bromberg, *Psychiatry Between the Wars, 1918–1945: A Recollection* (Westport, Conn., 1982), 131. Macdonald in *Fortune* 11 (1935); esp. 195. KAM, PI by LJF, Topeka, Sept. 29, 1983, May 21, 1984.

7. General discussions of Meyer's approach at the Phipps Clinic are found in *Fortune* 11 (1935): 85; Bell, *Treating*, 84–5; Grob, *Mental Illness*, 138–9. Adolf Meyer to Harvey Cushing, Apr. 26, 1919 ("inadequate feeding"), and Meyer to David T. Lyman, Jr., June 21, 1922, both in Adolf Meyer Papers, JHMS. KAM, PI by LJF, Topeka, May 21, 1984.

8. *Fortune* 11 (1935): 196–200; Lawrence S. Kubie, *The Riggs Story: The Development of the Austen Riggs Center for the Study and Treatment of the Neuroses* (New York, 1960), 18–20; Francis J. Braceland, *The Institute of Living: The Hartford Retreat 1822–1972* (Hartford, 1972), 149; Walter Freeman, *The Psychiatrist: Personalities and Patterns* (New York, London, 1968), 244–5, on Chestnut Lodge.

9. *Fortune* 11 (1935): 197–200; Bliss Forbush, *The Sheppard & Enoch Pratt Hospital 1853–1970* (Philadelphia, Toronto, 1971), 54, 127.

10. Forbush, *Sheppard-Pratt*, 63, 68; Helen Swick Perry, *Psychiatrist of America: The Life of Harry Stack Sullivan* (Cambridge, Mass., 1982), 187–95 (Sullivan at Sheppard-Pratt); *Fortune* 11 (1935): 197–200, on Austen Riggs, Craig House, and the Hartford Retreat; Braceland, *Institute*, 149; William Logie Russell, *The New York Hospital: A History of the Psychiatric Service 1771–1936* (New York, 1945), 392–8, 453–4, on Bloomingdale; Kubie, *Riggs*, 27–8.

11. Russell, *New York Hospital*, 453–4; *Fortune* 11 (1935): 197–200; Freeman, *Psychiatrist*, 244–5; Forbush, *Sheppard-Pratt*, 103; S. B. Sutton, *Crossroads in Psychiatry: A History of the McLean Hospital* (Washington, D.C., 1986), 209.

12. Copp as quoted in Braceland, *Institute*, 153. The Bloomingdale annual reports for 1912 and 1914 are excerpted in Russell, *New York Hospital*, 400, 414.

13. KAM, "1935 Annual Report to Directors," Historical Scrapbook (H.S.) 22, p. 7, comparing the Menninger facility with other elite private hospitals. See also KAM, PI by LJF, Topeka, May 21, 1984.

14. *Lamps on the Prairie: A History of Nursing in Kansas* (reprint, New York, 1984), 90–1; Thomas N. Bonner, *The Kansas Doctor: A Century of Pioneering* (Lawrence, 1959), 192; KAM, "Nursing History," Nov. 15, 1941, H.S. 42; KAM, PI by LJF, Topeka, July 29, 1983, June 19, 1986. Grob, *Mental Illness,* 198, notes that the very existence of state mental hospitals in the early twentieth century discouraged serious exploration of alternatives for mental health care.

15. Bonner, *Doctor,* 192, on the plight of private hospitals in Kansas.

16. Bonner, *Doctor,* 120–71, 207–21, provides excellent coverage of the Kansas medical profession during the Progressive period and (in contrast) during the postwar years. Mary S. Rowland, "Social Services in Kansas, 1916–1930," *KH* 7 (1984): 215–16, 224, on pervasive beliefs in mental disease as hereditary.

17. KAM to LJF, Nov. 26, 1985 (letter); KAM, PI by LJF, Topeka, May 21, 1984, Mar. 11, 1986; G. L. Harrington, Jr., TRI by LJF, Los Angeles, May 10, 1984.

18. FVM to CFM, Feb. 25, 1920, WCM Papers (private); KAM Diaries, 1906–1919, entry for Sept. 1, 1914, KAM Papers, M; Walker Winslow, *The Menninger Story* (Garden City, N.Y., 1956), 156; Julia Gottesman, TRI by LJF, Los Angeles, Jan. 3, 1984.

19. Early office facilities are noted in "Excerpts from Dr. C. F. Menninger's Talk at Annual Meeting," Feb. 16, 1924, 1, Inst. Archives, M. KAM, PI by LJF, Topeka, July 30, 1982, on Charles letting Karl take the largest office. CFM, TRI by Walker Winslow, Topeka, 1952–53 (cylinder 9), M, on Karl replacing Charles's secretary. KAM, "Psychiatric Approach to the Nervous Patient," Apr. 20, 1936, 9, Inst. Archives, M, on the Wassermann test. KAM, TI by Harold Maine (pseud. Walker Winslow), Topeka, Aug. 20, 1952, 16–17, M, and KAM to John E. Wattenberg, Nov. 10, 1919, KAM Papers, M, on Karl taking the larger salary.

20. CFM to KAM, June 2, 1921, H.S. 5; KAM to WCM, Sept. 24, 1924, WCM Papers (private); KAM, TI by Walker Winslow, Topeka, Aug. 20, 1952, M; KAM, PI by LJF, Topeka, Jan. 12, 1985.

21. CFM, TRI by Walker Winslow, Sept. 4, 1952, M, on Charles purchasing Oakwood and thinking of retiring. FVM to "My Dear Mother & Sister," Nov. 16, 1924, WCM Papers (private), on Charles feeling he was "falling down."

22. KAM, TI by Harold Maine, Topeka, Aug. 20, 1952, M, on KAM traveling all over Kansas. KAM to WCM, Nov. 19, 1924, KAM Papers, M, on the branch offices. *TPR* 5 (Nov. 17, 1944): 1, on Charles urging Karl to take off a month each year. KAM to WCM, Apr. 4, 1924, "running around." For cogent discussion of sons needing to outdo fathers in the nineteenth-century success ethic, see John Demos, "Oedipus and America," in *Our Selves/Our Past,* Robert J. Brugger, ed. (Baltimore, 1981), 301.

23. KAM to Orville Reed, Feb. 21, 1921, KAM Papers, M, on neuropsychiatric work in China. KAM to WCM, May 2, 1924, unclassified, M.

24. For general data on early staffing of the Diagnostic Clinic, see "Where Knowledge Is Gained, It Should Be Shared," *Menninger Perspective* 5 (Winter 1974–75): 15; KAM, "Termination of the Diagnostic Clinic," July 29, 1920, H.S. 4, M; Winslow, *Story,* 174, 181–2; KAM, PI by LJF, Topeka, Mar. 13, 1985; E. W. Netherton to KAM, Aug. 26, 1940, H.S. 40, M. *Topeka Daily Capital,* Sept. 20, 1953, provides biographical data on Mildred Law. Karl's recollection of Law as "family" is contained in his speech to Menninger Foundation trustees (handwritten), May 20, 1976, unclassified, M.

25. For John Stone's background, see *Topeka Daily Capital,* Jan. 12, 1949; misc. notes

for Dec. 1920 in H.S. 40, M; KAM, "Searches in Old Archives," n.d., unclassified, M; Norman Reider, TRI by LJF, San Francisco, Dec. 28, 1983. KAM to John R. Stone, Feb. 4, 1925, Stone Papers, M, on Karl breaking off Stone's analysis on financial grounds. KAM to Harold Maine, July 14, 1954, KAM Papers, M, on Charles's suspicion of Stone and Stone's postanalysis personality. KAM, TRI by John Fitzpatrick, Apr. 9, 1980, M, "changed boy." For other useful data concerning the impact of Stone's initial analysis on his relationship with the Menningers, see KAM to John Stone, Oct. 7, 1924, Feb. 22, 1925, in Stone Papers, M.

26. KAM, PI by LJF, Topeka, July 25, 1984, Jan. 12, May 21, 1985; KAM, "Birth of the Menninger Clinic," Mar. 16, 1983, 2, KAM Papers, M; "Laboratory," Apr. 26, 1940, H.S. 39, M; KAM to Mamie Johnson, Oct. 23, 1923, H.S. 7, M; Mildred Law, TRI by CWM, Sept. 26, 1969, M; KAM, "Summary of Business for May 1924," Inst. Archives, M.

27. Grob, *Mental Illness*, 188–9, provides a good historical survey of scientific research on syphilitic infection as a cause of mental abnormality. For early Menninger treatment of syphilis, see *Topeka State Journal*, June 16, 1952; "Talk by C. F. Menninger at Board of Governors Meeting," Apr. 6, 1952, 4, M; KAM, PI by LJF, Topeka, July 25, July 28, 1984.

28. Bernard H. Hall, ed., *A Psychiatrist's World: The Selected Papers of Karl Menninger, M.D.* (New York, 1959), I, 107–66, houses Karl's early papers linking influenza to serious mental disorders. Most important among them is the 1921 paper, "Reversible Schizophrenia," 126–33, which ends with the "Diagnosis is chiefly useful" remark. See also KAM to G. H. Black, July 17, 1919, MMR; and KAM, PI by LJF, Topeka, July 25, 1984. Timothy J. Crow notes Karl as a pioneer formulator of the viral hypothesis in "A Re-evaluation of the Viral Hypothesis," *BJP* 145 (1984): 244.

29. For Karl's early 1920s experience conducting psychoanalysis, see, e.g., KAM to Gregory Stragnell, Aug. 29, Sept. 19, Oct. 4, 1921, KAM Papers, M; KAM to Smith Ely Jelliffe, Nov. 25, 1922, Feb. 15, 1924, KAM Papers, M; KAM, PI by LJF, Topeka, July 25, 28, 1984. In "Minutes, 9-15-24," Inst. Archives, M, Karl notes spending 92 hours doing psychoanalysis in August. In KAM, PI by LJF, Topeka, July 28, 1984, he recalled how he had developed the neurotic-versus-psychotic characterization of his early analytic patients.

30. "Articles of Agreement, the Topeka Clinic," Apr. 19, 1919, H.S. 3, M, "equal suffrage."

31. John Stone to KAM, Feb. 10, 1932, Stone Papers, M, "more like a family." KAM to WCM, Sept. 24, 1924, KAM Papers, M, on the clinic's departures from the Southard model.

32. KAM, TI by Spafford Ackerly, Sept. 9, 1974, M, recalling Lindsay's early experience and his propensity to follow Lindsay's measures. KAM, "Nursing History," Nov. 15, 1941, H.S. 42, M, and KAM, PI by LJF, Topeka, July 29, 1983, on the arrangement at the former attendant's home. For data on the Christ's Hospital arrangement, see CFM, "The Origin of the Menninger Clinic and Sanitarium," n.d. (1926), 4, H.S. 10, M; KAM to James Stewart, Aug. 2, 1921, KAM Papers, M; and KAM, PI by LJF, Topeka, Jan. 14, 1985.

33. KAM, "Nursing History," Nov. 15, 1941, H.S. 42, M; Winslow, *Story*, 193; John Stone to KAM, n.d., Stone Papers, M; KAM to F. A. Cogswell, Apr. 15, 1925, KAM Papers, M; KAM, PI by LJF, Topeka, Sept. 10, 1982. See also *Lamps on the Prairie*, 87, on the nineteenth-century custom of husband and wife as asylum caretakers.

34. For the details of the formation of the Menninger Sanitarium Corporation, see

CFM, "The Origin of the Menninger Clinic and Sanitarium," n.d. (1926), H.S. 10, M; Charles's comment in "Stockholders Meeting," Feb. 9, 1939, H.S. 34, M; and Winslow, *Story,* 194–5. *The Menninger Foundation Report of Progress for the Year July 1, 1962–June 30, 1963* (Topeka, 1963), 5–6, "like another brother." KAM to WCM, Sept. 24, 1924, WCM Papers (private), "practically control."

35. KAM to E. H. Skinner, Apr. 9, 1925, H.S. 8, M, on the purchase price for the farm. The house and grounds are described in *Topeka Daily Capital,* May 3, 1925; "The Menninger Psychiatric Hospital and Sanitarium: Circular of Information," May 1925, 1, H.S. 9, M.

36. For data on the early patient clientele, see KAM to CFM, Dec. 31, 1925, H.S. 9, M; KAM to W. J. Davie, Mar. 20, 1926, KAM Papers, M; KAM to E. K. Wickman, Sept. 23, 1926, Inst. Archives, M.

37. KAM to Board of Administration, Kansas State House, Apr. 5, 1926, H.S. 10, M, on the remodeled garage and the American Hospital Building facilities. For data on East Lodge, see *Topeka Daily Capital,* Jan. 1, 1928; *Topeka State Journal,* Jan. 6, 1928. Lucille Cairns, "A History of the Menninger Clinic of Topeka, Kansas, Up to the Time of Its Transfer to the Menninger Foundation, 1919–1945" (unpub. Ph.D. diss., George Warren Brown School of Social Work, Washington University of St. Louis, 1946), 50, on the Diagnostic Clinic moving.

38. KAM, PI by LJF, Topeka, Mar. 13, 1985; Cairns, "History," 43.

39. *TPR* 1 (Dec. 1940): 54; CFM, "Nursing History," Nov. 16, 1941, Inst. Archives, M; KAM, PI by LJF, Topeka, Mar. 13, 1985; Ruby White Woodford to LJF, Aug. 20, 1983 (letter).

40. Good characterizations of the Neeses and their managerial practices are found in KAM, "Nursing History," Nov. 17, 1941, H.S. 42, M; Ruby White Woodford to LJF, Aug. 20, Sept. 12, 1983 (letters); KAM to CFM, Dec. 31, 1925, Inst. Archives, M. KAM, *The Human Mind* (New York, 1930), 39, on the essence of a good therapist.

41. The daily routine of the Menningers at the sanitarium is sketched out in WCM, TI by Bernard Hall and Emlin North, Topeka, May 28, 1966, M. Karl's sanitarium class is covered cogently in Ruby White Woodford to KAM, July 18, 1983, KAM Papers, M, and Woodford to LJF, Aug. 20, 1983.

42. WCM, TI by Bernard Hall and Emlin North, Topeka, May 28, 1966, 20, M; Winslow, *Story,* 221; WCM Diary, Dec. 7, 1929, WCM Papers (private); KAM, PI by LJF, Topeka, July 29, 1983; "Nursing History: Notes on an Interview by Mrs. Brown of KAM," Nov. 17, 1941, M.

43. The board proceedings and discussions leading to the departure of the Neeses and their staff are noted in KAM, "Firm History," n.d. (1930), H.S. 14, M; WCM Personal Log, Jan. 23, Feb. 6, 1930, and WCM Diary, Jan. 23, 1930, WCM Papers (private).

44. "Nursing History," Nov. 17, 1941, H.S. 41, M, "final straw."

45. Will's designation as new sanitarium director is summarized in KAM, "Firm History," n.d. (1930), H.S. 14, M.

46. WCM, "Dr. William Menninger," Dec. 1925, H.S. 9, M, "because that was the place," and interest in foreign missions. Will's intense desire to be a medical missionary, especially after he met Catharine Wright, is also revealed well in WCM to CFM and KAM, Apr. 23, 1920, H.S. 4, M; WCM to CFM and FVM, June 1, 1922, WCM Papers, M; WCM, TI by Bernard Hall and Emlin North, May 25, 1966, 6, M.

47. CFM to WCM, Apr. 28, May 7, 1920, WCM Papers (private). Flo's letter to Will

is noted in WCM, "Line-A-Day Diary," Nov. 27, 1925, WCM Papers (private). KAM to WCM, Nov. 10, 1925, KAM Papers, M; KAM to WCM, Dec. 5, 1921, WCM Papers (private); KAM to WCM, Nov. 19, 1924, KAM Papers, M.

48. WCM, "Dr. William Menninger," Dec. 1925, H.S. 9, M; WCM, TI by Bernard Hall and Emlin North, Topeka, May 28, 1966, 15–16, M.

49. WCM, TI by Bernard Hall and Emlin North, May 28, 1966, 15–16, M, describes Will's basic duties Dec. 1925–Apr. 1930; Will's activities at St. Elizabeths Hospital, 28–31. WCM to CWM, Mar. 9, 1934, WCM Papers (private), "coerced," "physical-psychical relationships."

50. Through the 1920s, Charles and Karl were constantly seeking to make Will feel that he naturally belonged, with them, in the leadership of the Menninger organization. See, e.g., CFM to WCM, Apr. 28, 1920, CFM and KAM to WCM, Apr. 23, 1923, and KAM to WCM, Apr. 4, 1924, all in WCM Papers (private).

51. Will's official titles are noted in Minutes of the Board of Directors, Aug. 20, 1931, 1, MT. Winslow, *Story*, 210–11, and KAM, PI by LJF, Topeka, Mar. 7, 1983, on the construction of West Lodge. Owing to the stock market crash and the Depression, West Lodge temporarily remained empty while 29 patients crowded into East Lodge. Senior Council Meeting (minutes), Feb. 21, 1963, KAM Papers, M, "main thing."

52. CFM, TI by Harold Maine, Aug. 29, 1952, on Will's initial support in the hospital. Will's early medical publications and competencies are noted in Winslow, *Story*, 213; Bernard Hall, ed., *A Psychiatrist for a Troubled World: The Selected Papers of William C. Menninger, M.D.* (New York, 1967), I, xvi, 11–12. WCM to CFM, KAM and John Stone, June 6, 1933, H.S. 19, M, "the best."

53. John Stone to KAM, Feb. 10, 1932, Stone Papers, M, on how he told Will that the organization functioned like a family, with "protracted counselling."

54. For data on Ben Boam, see *TPR* 1 (Dec. 1–25, 1940); 54–5; *TPR* 13 (Oct. 15, 1952): i; Josephine Boam, TRI by LJF, Topeka, Feb. 27, 1984. Data on Hoover in *TPR* 1 (Dec. 1–25 1940): 57; TPR 6 (Sept. 21, 1945): 1,3; Winslow, *Story*, 257. Erickson's role, detailed in the next chapter, is discussed fully in William A. Roberts, TRI by LJF, Topeka, July 31, 1984.

55. Robert Knight's quick success at Menninger is noted in KAM to Robert Knight, July 2, 1937, Robert Knight Papers (private); Stuart C. Miller, ed., *Clinician and Therapist: Selected Papers of Robert P. Knight* (New York, 1972), 6–7. Robert Knight to KAM and WCM, Oct. 29, 1965, KAM Papers, M, "Menninger brother"; see also KAM to Robert Knight, July 2, 1937, Knight Papers (private). Bonner, *Doctor*, 245, on Menninger being one of the most completely staffed private hospitals with the addition of the six residents.

56. For Karl's increasing literary and speaking commitments, his desire for a personal analysis, and his need for free time, see KAM to Max A. Bahr, Aug. 10, 1931, H.S. 17; KAM to Ernst Simmel, May 5, 1933, KAM Papers; KAM, "Footprints," Nov. 30, 1958, 21, KAM Papers; KAM, PI by LJF, Topeka, Sept. 10, 1982, July 28, 1984.

57. KAM to Kathleen O. Larkin, Dec. 20, 1929, KAM Papers, and Mark I. West, "Missionaries for Mental Health," *Menninger Perspective* 15 (1984): 11, on how *The Human Mind* grew out of Karl's Washburn course.

58. KAM, *Human Mind*, 2, defining mental health. *Ibid.*, 428, on psychiatry displacing "existing legal methods." *Ibid.*, 355, "psychoanalysis as a research technique." *Ibid.*, 267, "growing up emotionally."

59. KAM, *Human Mind*, 95, 369.

60. KAM, *Human Mind,* 3.

61. KAM to Harold Voth, July 19, 1976, KAM Papers, "go home and reorganize" *The Human Mind.* KAM to Kathleen O. Larkin, Dec. 20, 1929, KAM Papers, on fretting about the book two weeks before publication. *Human Mind,* x, "I've had to put together this manuscript."

62. KAM, TI by Selma Robinson, 1930, H.S. 14 (1930), M, explaining the dedication of *The Human Mind.*

63. John Stone to KAM, Feb. 10, 1932, John Stone Papers, M.

C H A P T E R   T H R E E: *A Hospital Treatment Program*

1. Quoted in Bernard H. Hall, ed., *A Psychiatrist for a Troubled World: Selected Papers of William C. Menninger, M.D.* (New York, 1967), I, 360 [hereafter Hall, ed., *WCM*].

2. Will's recollection of the "scientific"-medical structure for the hospital relationships is noted in Bernard Hall's narrative of an interview with Will, "Philosophy of Treatment for the C. F. Menninger Memorial Hospital," n.d. (1968), Inst. Archives, M. Karl's contrasting recollection is quoted in KAM, "Menninger Foundation Hospital: A 40 Year Look Backward and a 10 Year Look Ahead," n.d. (Aug. 28, 1965), unclassified, M.

3. Interactionism is surveyed cogently in Anselm Strauss, "Sociological Theories of Personality," in *Current Personality Theories,* Raymond J. Corsini, ed. (Ithaca, 1977), ch. 10. Irving Goffman, "On Face-work," *Psychiatry* 18 (1955): 213–31.

4. Hall, "Philosophy of Treatment," Inst. Archives, M, reporting on Will's recall of his early quest for specific cures. This is the fullest account available on that aspect of Will's career.

5. Meyer and his therapy routine are discussed cogently in Gerald N. Grob, *The State and the Mentally Ill: A History of Worcester State Hospital in Massachusetts, 1830–1920* (Chapel Hill, 1966), 285–307; John C. Burnham, "Psychoanalysis and American Medicine, 1894–1918: Medicine, Science, and Culture," *Psychological Issues* V, monograph 20 (1967): 160–1; Richard S. Lyman's notes on Henry Phipps Clinic, 1939, 10 (Adolf Meyer Papers, JHMS); Seward Hiltner, "The Menninger School of Psychiatry," n.d. (1957), 11–12, Seward Hiltner Papers, PTS.

6. Bernard H. Hall, TRI by LJF, New York, Aug. 25, 1983, was particularly useful on the impact Charles had upon Will as the son forged his milieu therapy program. FVM, *Days of My Life: Memories of a Kansas Mother and Teacher* (New York, 1940), 256, notes teaching in a class for nurses in the mid-1890s. WCM to CFM, July 8, 1921, WCM Papers, M, on Charles's instilling in him a love for the out-of-doors.

7. KAM, PI by LJF, Topeka, Mar. 10, 1983, characterizing the problems that all psychiatrists of the 1920s (including Will) wrestled with. In *Menninger Quarterly* 12 (Dec. 1958): 3, David Neiswanger noted that Will's residency at St. Elizabeths Hospital was particularly important in making him aware of the general psychiatric dilemma of the 1920s. Will's apprehensions over Metrazol and other "active therapies" (i.e., organic) is illustrated in WCM, "The Results with Metrazol as an Adjunctive Therapy in Schizophrenia and Depression," *BMC* 2 (Sept. 1938): 140. For Will's commitments to auxiliary staff, see, e.g., WCM to KAM, Nov. 4, 1938, Historical Scrapbook (H.S.) 20, M; Hall, ed., *Psychiatrist,* I, 409; Sophia A. Schweers, "Biannual Report—Oct. 1, 1930 to April 15, 1931," Apr. 15, 1931, H.S. 16, M.

8. Ernst Simmel, "Psychoanalytic Treatment in a Clinic," *IJP* 10 (1929): 70–89; *BMC* 46 (Jan. 1982): 3–5.

9. For Will's 1933 contact with Simmel, see Simmel, "The Psychoanalytic Sanitarium and the Psychoanalytic Movement," *BMC* 1 (May 1937): 133; *BMC* 46 (Jan. 1982): 6–7; CWM, PI by LJF, Topeka, Mar. 9, 1985. In Hall, ed., *WCM*, I, 386, Will acknowledges Schloss Tegel as a model. Simmel, *BMC* 1 (May 1937): 135, on his 1936 visit to Topeka.

10. Staff Physicians Conference comparing Menninger to Schloss Tegel, Aug. 1, 1933, H.S. 19, M. In KAM, PI by LJF, Topeka, Mar. 16, 1985, Karl notes that when Simmel claimed in 1936 that Menninger was like Schloss Tegel, Karl knew otherwise. Using the example of tearing down an old building, Will makes clear that Simmel gave him a language and a theoretical framework (WCM, TI by Bernard Hall and Emlin North, Topeka, May 28, 1966, 23, M). See also Hall, ed., *WCM*, I, 379.

11. WCM, "The Specificity of Psychiatric Hospital Management," Jan. 20, 1939, WCM Papers, M. The analogy of prescribing therapy to prescribing medicines is found in WCM and Isabelle McColl, "Recreation Therapy as Applied in a Modern Psychiatric Hospital," *OTR* 16 (Feb. 1937): 15; and WCM, TI by Hall and North, Topeka, May 28, 1966. WCM, "The Functions of the Psychiatric Hospital," *BMC* 11 (July, 1942): 11, on prescribing staff attitudes and therapies exactly. WCM, TI by Hall and North, May 28, 1966, 36, on "scientifically controlled" relationships.

12. WCM, "Individualization of Psychiatric Hospital Treatment," *WMJ* 37 (Dec. 1938): 1087, "all the symptoms . . . represent disturbances." Hall, ed., *WCM*, I, 377, "mismanagement." Abbreviated Guide to Therapeutic Aims, June 23, 1937, Inst. Archives, M, "correct disturbances." The displacement and discharge aspect of Will's theory is discussed cogently in Alfred H. Stanton and Morris S. Schwartz, *The Mental Hospital: A Study of Institutional Participation in Psychiatric Illness and Treatment* (New York, 1954), 419.

13. This point is underscored in Lewis L. Robbins to Paul W. Pruyser, July 15, 1982, copy in LLR Papers (private); Lewis L. Robbins, TRI by LJF, New York, Aug. 23, 1983.

14. The best discussion of the role Will established for the prescribing physician is found in a special issue of *BMC* 46 (Jan. 1982), on the guide to the order sheet, esp. 3–11.

15. WCM to Ernst Simmel, June 24, 1937, WCM Papers, M, on Will's control over the design and revision for the guide to the order sheet. Harlan Crank, PI by LJF, Austin, Nov. 22, 1985, on Will's guide to the physician's case report.

16. Note 17 covers all sources for case conference practices. Interestingly, the most senior Menninger had no designated seat or role at the case conference table. Semiretired, with poor hearing, Charles attended only periodically and rarely spoke. Leo Stone, TRI by LJF, New York, Nov. 7, 1983, comments fully on Charles at case conferences.

17. Case conference practices are reported in Norman Reider, TRI by LJF, San Francisco, Dec. 28, 1983; Edward Greenwood, TRI by LJF, Topeka, Nov. 10, 1982; Lewis Robbins, TRI by LJF, New York, Aug. 23, 1983; Douglass Orr to LJF, Dec. 14, 1983 (letter); Orr, "Some Psychoanalytic Reminiscences, Part II," *CAPE News* 11 (Mar. 1981): 28.

18. Harlan Crank, PI by LJF, Austin, Nov. 22, 1985, on Will going over a physician's letter to the patient's family.

19. WCM, *WMJ* 37 (Dec. 1938): 1088, "rationale for the orders." Hall, ed., *WCM*,

I, 303, on auxiliary staff understanding drive theory. Garland K. Lewis to Bernard Hall, June 14, 1966, WCM Papers, M, on how Will insisted on physicians' attentiveness to nurses' daily notes. Norman Reider, TRI by LJF, San Francisco, Dec. 28, 1983, stressed the give-and-take between doctor and nurse.

20. In Hall, ed., *WCM,* I, 296, Will underscored the importance of auxiliary staff spending more time with the patient than the doctor. The importance attached to auxiliary staff, especially nurses, is revealed in Lewis Robbins, "Reflection 1940–1966," *BMC* 30 (July 1966): 193; Bernard Hall, TRI by LJF, New York, Aug. 25, 1983; "Nursing History: Notes on an Interview by Mrs. Brown of KAM, Nov. 17, 1941," Inst. Archives, M; Isabel Erickson, "The Psychiatric Nursing Care of Manic-Depressive and Schizophrenia Psychoses," *TNHR* 98 (June 1937): 589.

21. Particularly useful discussions of the purposes of activities therapy in Will's milieu program are found in WCM and Isabelle McColl, "Recreational Therapy as Applied in a Modern Psychiatric Hospital," *OTR* 16 (Feb. 1937): 21; Hall, ed., *WCM,* I, 301, 334, 372; WCM and Mildred Cutter, "The Psychological Aspects of Physiotherapy," *AJP* 93 (Jan. 1937): 910; Marion R. Medd, "Individualizing Occupational Therapy for the Mental Patient," *OTR* 13 (Aug. 1934): 248.

22. "The Menninger Hospital's Guide to the Order Sheet," *BMC* 46 (Jan. 1982): 37, "atmosphere created." This issue of *BMC* reproduced the full guide document; its "Attitude Therapy" sections list and explain the sundry staff attitudes from which the physician makes assignments. For the guide admonition on a "uniform attitude," see *BMC* 46 (Jan. 1982): 37. For Will's other warnings on attitudinal consistency, see WCM and McColl, *OTR* 16 (Feb. 1937): 19, and WCM, *SMJ* 32 (Apr. 1939): 350.

23. Hall, ed., *WCM,* I, 351.

24. Karl's activities during the 1930s that impacted the hospital are indicated in KAM, "Notes to the Business Department," June 5, 1937, M; KAM to Executive Committee, Dec. 15, 1941, H.S. 42, M.

25. In WCM, TI by Hall and North, Topeka, May 28, 1966, 43, Will is quoted for his version of the way the guide was drafted. He also elaborates on the remark.

26. William A. Roberts, TRI by LJF, Topeka, July 3, 1984, indicates that attendants like himself were excluded from the meetings. Peggy Ralston Shelton, TRI by LJF, Topeka, Sept. 13, 1985, concurs on attendant exclusion. She was an educational therapist who attended. Ms. Shelton also recalled that certain doctors attended some of the meetings. One doctor who periodically attended, Douglass Orr, made the quoted remark on Will "explaining" the guide (Douglass W. Orr letter to LJF, Ukiah, Calif., Dec. 18, 1983). See also WCM Diary, Mar. 19, 1940, WCM Papers (private).

27. The Menninger Archives holds a tape entitled "Old Timers," Topeka, Nov. 2, 1970, wherein veteran staff comment on the gender composition of the 1930s staff. "Statement of Research at the Menninger Clinic," June 18, 1938, in Index to Menninger Clinic Papers, M, on the informal executive cabinet. Harlan Crank to LJF, Austin, Dec. 16, 1985 (letter), on how physicians "felt constricted and restrained."

28. For criticisms of the 1930s hospital regime, see Ezra Stotland and Arthur L. Kobler, *Life and Death in a Mental Hospital* (Seattle, 1965), 239; Peter Hartocollis, "A Brief History of a Psychoanalytic Hospital," Newsletter, American Psychoanalytic Association (June 1975), 6; Ann Applebaum et al., "Dependency versus Autonomy: The Group Conference Method Applied to an Organizational Problem," *BMC* 39 (Jan. 1975): 51; Murray Bowen remarks in "Administrative Conference," Mar. 16, 1949, WCM Papers, M.

29. "Interpretive Guide to Physician's Order Sheet," 1943, Inst. Archives, 1; WCM, "Psychiatric Nursing: The Viewpoint of the Psychiatrist," *BMC* 2 (Mar. 1938): 36; "Abbreviated Guide to Therapeutic Aims," June 23, 1937, WCM Papers, M; WCM to W. Walter Menninger, Jan. 31, 1961, unpub. ms., M Special Collections Room (on John Dokes).

30. Norman Reider, TRI by LJF, San Francisco, Dec. 28, 1983.

31. In TI on the guide to the order sheet, Topeka, Dec. 4, 1982, M, James Pratt recalls the overprecise and laborious nature of the guide. Madeline Olga Weiss, *Attitudes in Psychiatric Nursing Care* (New York, 1954), 5–6, on the difficulty of maintaining "passive friendliness." Applebaum, *BMC* 39 (Jan. 1975): 51, cogently underscores the rationale for the tendency toward "loose" adherence to orders. Lou Davie Crank, PI by LJF, Austin, Nov. 22, 1985, on recreation therapists dividing their labors so as to feel "comfortable" executing orders.

32. Mildred Pratt, TRI by LJF, Topeka, Jan. 6, 1983; Mildred Pratt in TI on the guide to the order sheet, Topeka, Dec 12, 1981, M; Peggy Ralston Shelton, TRI by Irving Sheffel, Jan. 15, 1983; Peggy Ralston Shelton, TRI by LJF, Topeka, Sept. 13, 1985.

33. Will on a "model . . . community" and sketching out plans for elements in his "miniature community" in "Annual Report of the Medical Director for the Year 1938. Presented to Stockholders—Feb. 9, 1939," WCM Papers, M. "Annual Report of the Medical Director . . . Feb. 13, 1941," M, reports on the purchase of a nearby house to serve as a new "Nurses Residence." Harlan Crank, PI by LJF, Austin, Nov. 22, 1985, and "Employees Recall Changes during 35 Years at Foundation," *Menninger Perspective* (Feb.–Mar. 1971), 29, on the frequency of employees eating on the grounds. Will on holiday celebrations in *Roundabout* (Christmas, 1941), and *TPR* 2 (June 16–July 15, 1941): 105. KAM to Robert P. Knight et al., May 2, 1941, H.S. 41, M, on parties, picnics, etc.

34. Uses of the library are noted in Peggy Ralston, "Summary of Educational Therapy for the Year 1940," WCM Papers, M, and "Annual Report of the Medical Directors . . . Feb. 8, 1940," M; "Report to Stockholders for the Recreation Department, January 20, 1937," H.S. 26, on theatrical productions. For discussion of organizational publications, see KAM to Jean Lyle, May 1, 1936, Inst. Archives, M; WCM to Jean Lyle, Oct. 27, 1939, WCM Papers, M; KAM, "Executive Committee Proposal," July 11, 1940, H.S. 40, M; KAM, "To All Members of the Menninger Organization," July 23, 1940, H.S. 40, M. The exclusion of black patients is noted in "Report to Physicians Record Company, July 7, 1936," H.S. 24, M, Question 21. KAM to Ralph M. Fellows, June 14, 1940, KAM Papers, M, on the quota on Jewish physicians. Edward Greenwood, TRI by LJF, Topeka, Nov. 10, 1982, on a separate dining room for black staff in 1939 when he arrived, and possibly earlier.

35. For general references to familial and homelike aspects of the hospital, see, e.g., Olga Weiss to Bernard Hall, June 8, 1966, misc. M; "Psychiatric Examination. August 29, 1932. Answers to Question 10," H.S. 18, M; Julia Gottesman, TRI by LJF, Los Angeles, Jan. 3, 1984. The blood family and extended family notion is conveyed in Norman Reider, TRI by LJF, San Francisco, Dec. 28, 1983; Leo Stone, TRI by LJF, New York, Nov. 7, 1983; Peggy Ralston Shelton, TRI by Irving Sheffel, Topeka, Jan. 15, 1983. Voluntary staff leaves without pay are discussed in WCM Diary, Mar. 1940, WCM Papers (private); Peggy Ralston Shelton, TRI by Irving Sheffel, Topeka, Jan. 15, 1983. In *Roundabout* (Christmas, 1941), 2, Will refers to "our family."

36. KAM to Lionel Blitzsten, Aug. 31, 1932, KAM Papers, M.

37. The best accounts of Will's vigorous daily hospital routine are found in William A. Roberts, TRI by LJF, Topeka, July 31, 1984, and Lewis Robbins, self-recording of memoirs of his Menninger days, Feb. 2, 1980, transcript, 4, LLR Papers (private). Will's after-hours hospital activities are noted in *Roundabout* 9 (Sept. 25, 1941): 1; 10 (Apr. 23, 1942): 1; 10 (July 16, 1942): 2.

38. Garland K. Lewis to Bernard Hall, June 14, 1966, WCM Papers, M, on Will's calm manner on the hospital floors. For comments on Will's "good father" qualities of warmth and firmness, which made one feel loyal to him, see Peggy Ralston Shelton, TRI by LJF, Topeka, Sept. 13, 1985; Peggy Ralston Shelton, TRI by Irving Sheffel, Topeka, Jan. 15, 1983; Lewis Robbins self-recording, Feb. 2, 1980, transcript, 2–3; John R. Stone, "Interview with Harry Harwick," n.d., Inst. Archives, M; James Pratt, TRI by LJF, Topeka, May 27, 1983, "made you feel appreciated."

39. Leo Stone to WCM, Oct. 3, 1934, H.S. 20, M, exemplifies how Will kept a doctor on staff longer, while WCM Diary, Mar. 1940 (on Norman Reider), reveals how he made a departing doctor feel a bit like a betrayer. Lewis Robbins self-recording, Feb. 2, 1980, transcript, 4, and Garland K. Lewis to Bernard Hall, June 14, 1966, WCM Papers, M, on Will's rapport with auxiliary staff. Lewis's letter to Hall also recounts the attack incident by a patient.

40. Hall, ed., *WCM*, I, 303, on the duties of the staff physician. Douglass W. Orr to LJF, Dec. 30, 1982, Dec. 14, Dec. 18, 1983 (letters), on his role and Knight's in individual therapy. For data on how female physicians were regarded, see WCM Diary, Mar. 20, 1941; Lewis Robbins, TRI by LJF, New York, Aug. 23, 1983; KAM to WCM, Sept. 18, 1942, KAM Papers, M.

41. WCM, "Psychiatric Nursing: The Viewpoint of the Psychiatrist," *BMC* 2 (Mar. 1938): 33, on the importance of the many hours the patient spent with nurses as against the one hour spent with physicians. Olga M. Church, "The Noble Reform: The Emergence of Psychiatric Nursing in the United States, 1882–1963" (unpub. Ph.D. diss., U. of Illinois Medical Center, 1982), 206, on the traditional images of psychiatric nurses as mothers and ward hostesses that persisted as late as 1947. Will's views of psychiatric nurses as mothers are best revealed in his paper "Maladjustment in Nurses," 6–7, delivered at the Institute on Psychiatric Nursing in Oklahoma City, Apr. 16, 1939, Inst. Archives, M. Weiss, *Attitudes*, 15–16.

42. Erickson, "Psychiatric Nursing Care," *TNHR* 98, 588. WCM, "Maladjustment in Nurses," 15; WCM to A. B. Stewart, Nov. 14, 1936, WCM Papers, M.

43. Peggy Ralston Shelton, TRI by LJF, Topeka, Sept. 13, 1985, and Shelton, TRI by Irving Sheffel, Topeka, Jan. 15, 1983, on nurses and activities therapists being closely linked. WCM to W. Walter Menninger, Jan. 31, 1961, Special Collections, M. recalls his 1930s perspective on activities therapists resembling attendants.

44. Isabel Erickson, "The Nursing Problem in the Psychiatric Hospital," *Hospital* II (May 1937): 59, on attendants' employment problems. WCM to W. Walter Menninger, Jan. 31, 1961, Special Collections, M, on directions for the "dullest" attendants. Harlan Crank, PI by LJF, Austin, Nov. 22, Nov. 23, 1985, on suicides, litigation, etc., as a constant fear Will had from attendant misconduct. William A. Roberts, TRI by LJF, Topeka, July 31, 1984.

45. For staff imagery of patients as childlike and regressed, see, e.g., Hall, ed., *WCM*, I, 117; WCM, "Maladjustment in Nurses," 14; Robert Knight, "Psychoanalytic Treatment in a Sanitarium of Chronic Addiction to Alcohol," *JAMA* 111 (Oct. 15, 1938):

1445; Weiss, *Attitudes,* 33. WCM, "Information for Newly Arrived Guests," Mar. 2, 1940, H.S. 39, M, evidences rules for childlike adult patients.

46. Will's "Medical Report" for each year (M) indicated total admissions, discharges, and the degree of improvement of each discharged patient. Will on his patients' prominent backgrounds in "Annual Report of the Medical Director of the Menninger Sanitarium," Dec. 31, 1936, 1, H.S. 25, M. Occupational therapy director Nada Ballator makes the same point in "An Educational Therapy Program in a Mental Hospital," *OTR* 17 (June 1938): 148. General background of Menninger patients at the time is also to be found in Hall, ed., *WCM,* I, 333; Robert P. Knight, "Evaluation of the Results of Psychoanalytic Therapy," *AJP* 98 (Nov. 1941): 444–5; Mildred Pratt, TRI by LJF, Topeka, Jan. 6, 1983. The most valuable sources for patient social characteristics, however, are obviously the patient files for the period. I have been able to review 32 detailed files as well as random case notes on other patients by Menninger staff. But I cannot cite these materials for reasons of confidentiality. Some of these files were provided by the Menninger Foundation Medical Records Office and some were in the Foundation archives. Lewis Robbins, a hospital physician during the early 1940s, allowed me to review his own detailed case abstracts of the period. Although these materials collectively do not constitute a "representative sample," information in the 32 files was so heavily repetitious that I feel fairly secure in the generalizations that I have advanced. The file numbers for the 32 ranged from 4894 to 6687, with most concerning inpatients at the hospital between 1938 and 1942.

47. For examples of patient exposé of staff, see *Roundabout* 9 (July 31, 1941), on Homer Jameson, and 9 (Oct. 23, 1941), on Garland Lewis.

48. Dwight Macdonald, "The Nervous Breakdown—The Sanitariums," *Fortune* 11 (Apr. 1935): 202. The 32 sample case files again constitute the basis for most of the description of patient maladies. The hospital's monthly "Clinical Report" listing patients admitted and their "status" (Inst. Archives, M) provided a useful check on the "representativeness" of the 32 cases.

49. Hall, ed., *WCM,* I, 342, notes an average patient stay in 1941 of two months. Robert P. Knight, "Clinical Services at the Menninger Clinic and Sanitarium," July 26, 1944, H.S. 47, and Knight, *AJP* 98 (Nov. 1941): 444–5, provides figures on most patients being released as "improved." Hospital policy discouraging custodial patients is noted in Business (Committee) Minutes, May 18, 1938, Inst. Archives, M. The yearly hospital "Medical Report," Inst. Archives, M, lists patient discharges in "recovered," "improved," "unimproved," and "deceased" categories. It is interesting that this in-house document reported statistics on patient condition at discharge that were far less hopeful than the "Annual Report of the Medical Director," which was essentially a public relations document.

50. Hall, ed, *WCM,* II, 608. Minnie Harlow, "A System of Groups in the Hospital Community Dealing with the Social Functioning of the Patient Populations," Feb. 7, 1964, 4, Inst. Archives, M, fully explicates and critiques Will's argument for a protective atmosphere.

51. Harlan Crank, PI by LJF, Austin, Nov. 22, 1985, recalled the details of Robert Morse's critique of the Menninger Hospital from the perspective of Chestnut Lodge. Crank recalled other, very similar criticisms as well.

52. Harlan Crank, PI by LJF, Austin, Nov. 22, Nov. 23, 1985, details Will's private justifications for a closely regulated hospital—the avoidance of patient self-injuries—

and the "family spirit" public justifications. Ernst Simmel, "Psycho-analytic Treatment in a Sanitarium," *IJP* 10 (1929): 70–89, on hospitalizations prompting regressions.

53. CWM, PI by LJF, Topeka, Mar. 9, 1985, for the fullest account of the origin of the spouse exclusion policy. She cites 1927 as a probable date of origin. Having found no written documentation, I surmise the policy was an oral understanding. Julia Gottesman, TRI by LJF, Los Angeles, Jan. 3, 1984, provides added details on the policy.

54. John R. Stone to Executive Committee, May 6, 1941, H.S. 41, M. The thinking of the Menninger brothers and other doctors is recalled in CWM, PI by LJF, Topeka, Mar. 9, 1985, and W. Walter Menninger, PI by LJF, Topeka, Jan. 10, 1985.

55. CWM to RWM, Oct. 13, 1968, RWM Papers, M; Douglass W. Orr to LJF, Dec. 23, 1983 (letter); Harlan Crank, PI by LJF, Austin, Nov. 22, 1985, quotes Florence Knight on the "jealous mistress."

56. Douglass W. Orr to LJF, Dec. 23, 1983, recounts fully this episode and the resulting policy changes. The disagreement between the Menninger brothers is evident in KAM to Robert P. Knight, WCM, CFM, Douglass W. Orr, John R. Stone, May 2, 1941, H.S. 41, M. (Will's notations on this memorandum disagree with what Karl said.)

57. Douglass W. Orr to LJF, Jan. 12, 1984 (letter), "passes." CWM, PI by LJF, Topeka, Nov. 7, 1987, on physicians dancing with female staff at parties and on Margaret Stone's perception of that as well as her own. Lewis Robbins, TRI by LJF, New York, Aug. 24, 1983, on Charles Menninger. Peggy Ralston Shelton, TRI by Irving Sheffel, Topeka, Jan. 15, 1983, and Lou Davie Crank, PI by LJF, Austin, Nov. 22, 1985, on liaisons between nurses, activities therapists, and doctors. KAM to WCM, Oct. 26, 1933, KAM Papers, M, on Mildred Law. See also Gennie Fried to JLM, Apr. 15, 1939, Inst. Archives, M.

58. Karl's "they *knew*" remark is a marginal note that he made in May or June of 1980 in the M archives copy of Walker Winslow, *The Menninger Story* (Garden City, N.Y., 1956), 236. Karl's affairs will be discussed in some detail in Chapter 6. The notations he made during his first analysis with Alexander—"KAM's Analysis, 1930–32," KAM Papers, M—cover the Johnson affair. So does CWM, PI by LJF, Topeka, July 30, 1984. Harlan Crank, PI by LJF, Austin, Nov. 22, 1985, on Alexander encouraging analysands to have mistresses. JLM to KAM, Feb. 2, 1939, KAM Papers, M, explicitly acknowledges the second affair. It is recalled by Karl's daughter, Julia Gottesman, TRI by LJF, Los Angeles, Jan. 3, 1984. Relatively limited staff knowledge of either affair is indicated in Norman Reider, TRI by LJF, Topeka, Dec. 28, 1983; and Mildred Pratt, TRI by LJF, Topeka, Jan. 6, 1983.

59. Frances Rothman, "The Menningers: Memoirs & Memos," *The Week Ahead,* May 14, 1971, for CWM not wanting her husband to return to Topeka. WCM Diary, Jan. 3, 1927, on CWM's depression. CWM, "What Wives Can Do to Solve the Communication Problem," *Reader's Digest* (July 1969), 214–16, recounts her "humdrum existence" and Will's urgings for her to be a contented homemaker. WCM to Reinhold Hoffman, July 3, 1934, WCM Papers, M, evidences his interest in "pretty girls." Harlan Crank, PI by LJF, Austin, Nov. 22, 1985, recalls complaints by CWM of her husband putting in too much time at the hospital.

60. Will's remark divorcing his life from business is a notation on a memorandum by his brother (KAM to Robert P. Knight, WCM, CFM, Douglass W. Orr, John R. Stone, May 2, 1941, H.S. 41, M). Will's refusal to discuss hospital affairs at home and

his minimal contact at home with his sons is revealed in RWM, PI by LJF, Topeka, Jan. 5, 1983; Philip B. Menninger, TRI by LJF, Topeka, Jan. 14, 1985; and especially Philip B. Menninger to LJF, Oct. 21, 1985 (letter), which contains the remark on Will's "problems communicating" with his children. For details on the wedding on the hospital grounds, see CWM, PI by LJF, Topeka, Mar. 9, 1985, and Frances Rothman, *The Week Ahead,* May 21, 1971.

61. For Isabel Erickson's background, see TPR I (Dec. 1–25, 1940); and KAM, "In Memorial, Isabel Erickson, 1908–1958," *BMC* 22 (Nov. 1958): 232. William A. Roberts, TRI by LJF, Topeka, July 31, 1984, and WCM to KAM, July 1, 1943, WCM Papers (private), on Erickson coming to run most hospital auxiliary staff units with Will's help. The same point is acknowledged in Lou Davie Crank, PI by LJF, Austin, Nov. 22, 1985. In her interview on tape of Mildred Law, Topeka, Sept. 29, 1969, M, CWM recalls Erickson shining her husband's white shoes and putting a flower in his lapel. See also WCM to CFM, FVM, and Pearl Boam, Feb. 7, 1941, KAM Papers, M.

62. Harlan Crank, PI by LJF, Austin, Nov. 22, 1985, on seeing Will's car parked at Erickson's house and on accompanying the two to a funeral in Lincoln. For Will and Erickson attending the same professional meetings and staying at the same hotel, and attending other medical events together, see, e.g., WCM, "Grading Plan for Activities," n.d. (1938), WCM Papers, M; WCM to Jeanetta Lyle, Dec. 2, 1939, WCM Papers, M; *Newsletter of the Menninger School of Psychiatric Nursing* III (May 1939): 1. WCM to CWM, Feb. 4, 1935, WCM Papers (private), on Erickson visiting Will in Chicago for "a good time." CWM, PI by LJF, Topeka, June 21, 1987, on what Alexander told her and her husband about having affairs. *Reader's Digest* (July 1969), 212, on Catharine wishing to be Will's "mistress." Robert Knight to Loraine Nuzman, n.d. (Nov. 1944), Inst. Archives, M, for a subtle reference to the affair. The affair with Erickson is explicitly acknowledged by staff of the period; see, e.g., Mildred Pratt, TRI by LJF, Topeka, Jan. 6, 1983; Norman Reider, TRI by LJF, San Francisco, Dec. 28, 1983; Edward Greenwood, TRI by LJF, Topeka, Nov. 10, 1982. It is noted by Karl's daughter (Julia Gottesman, TRI by LJF, Los Angeles, Jan. 3, 1984). CWM to KAM, Oct. 9, 1944, KAM Papers, M, acknowledges it too.

63. Erickson, *Hospital* II, 58.

64. Mildred Pratt, TRI by LJF, Topeka, Jan. 6, 1983, and Lou Davie Crank, PI by LJF, Austin, Nov. 22, 1985 (both explain why they and many other staff remained silent while sensing the affair). Norman Reider, TRI by LJF, San Francisco, Dec. 28, 1983, conveys his own feeling on the efficacy of psychoanalysis and notes that it was shared by many staff. Edward Greenwood, TRI by LJF, Topeka, Nov. 10, 1982, on his own distress over the affair and on Karl voicing distress to Greenwood.

65. Harlan Crank, PI by LJF, Austin, Nov. 22, 1985, provides a very detailed and prolonged account of the confrontation with Will.

66. WCM to KAM, July 1, 1943, WCM Papers (private), on his intentions of returning to his old job and on Karl as inappropriate in "actively managing" the hospital. The leadership structure of the hospital when Will was gone is covered in WCM, "Plans for Hospital Operation during the Emergency," n.d. (1942), WCM Papers, M; *Roundabout* 10 (Nov. 19, 1942): 1; Peggy Ralston Shelton, TRI by LJF, Topeka, Sept. 13, 1985; KAM, "Staff Bulletin #9," Mar. 3, 1943, H.S. 44, M.

67. KAM to Grace Menninger, n.d. (1938), KAM Papers, M, on Alexander having not resolved his own marital problem. KAM to Grace Menninger, May 4, 1940, KAM Papers, M, "a certain insincerity." In addition to these letters, several of my personal

interviews with Karl from 1982 through 1987 (particularly those of Sept. 11, Sept. 13, 1986) dealt with Alexander and Brunswick. In those interviews, he suggested that he had (in some measure at least) been abused and betrayed by both of his analysts. The notes Karl maintained on his training analysis with Alexander (KAM Papers), especially for Dec. 5, 1930, Jan. 2, Apr. 2, June 23, 1931, and above all for Feb. 18, 1932 (his final session, where he was "concealing" memories), provide added evidence of this sense of the analytic process. KAM, PI by LJF, Topeka, June 22, 1987, on Brunswick's analytic irregularities. See also Steven Marcus, *Freud and the Culture of Psychoanalysis* (Boston, 1984), 215, on Brunswick's addictions and her distractive habits during analytic hours.

68. Robert P. Knight to WCM, July 4, 1943, WCM Papers (private), and Harlan Crank, PI by LJF, Austin, Nov. 22, 1985, on Worthington leaving his analysis and becoming depressed and withdrawn. Understandably, Worthington's letters to me have been less clear about his analysis with Karl (Worthington to LJF, Jan. 2, Mar. 4, 1984).

69. KAM to WCM, June 22, 1943, WCM Papers (private). WCM to CWM, June 30, 1943, WCM Papers (private), urging Karl to "clean house" or "quit meddling." KAM to WCM, June 22, 30, 1943, WCM Papers (private); Lou Davie Crank, PI by LJF, Austin, Nov. 22, 1985; and CWM, PI by LJF, Topeka, Mar. 5, 1983, on Karl going after powerful Will loyalists like Erickson despite Charles's protests. See also KAM to WCM, June 23, 1943, and WCM to KAM, July 1, 1943, both in WCM Papers (private).

70. John C. Whitehorn to Lewis H. Weed, Oct. 24, 1945, Whitehorn Papers, APA, on staff shortages at the Phipps Clinic. Bliss Forbush, *The Sheppard & Enoch Pratt Hospital, 1853–1970* (Philadelphia, Toronto, 1971), 131–2, on staff shortages. Karl's problems of wartime staff shortages are noted well in "Annual Report of Medical Director," 1942, 2–3, and 1943, 12–13; KAM to Ruth Mack Brunswick, Sept. 18, 1942, KAM Papers, M; Education Committee meeting, July 24, 1945, 2, Inst. Archives, M.

71. "Annual Report of the Medical Director, The Menninger Psychiatric Hospital, For the Year 1944," by KAM and Robert L. Worthington, H.S. 46, on temporarily assigning attendants to more patient care duties. Gerald N. Grob, *The Inner World of American Psychiatry, 1890–1940* (New Brunswick, N.J., 1985), 187–8, on Southard creating a social work program. The duties of early hospital social workers are discussed in Carol B. Douglas, "A Brief Study of the Change in Practice in Regard to Relatives in a Small Psychiatric Hospital," unpub. ms., n.d., 6–7, Special Collections, M. Richard E. Benson, TRI by LJF, Topeka, Mar. 14, 1985. Margaret Mead to KAM, Dec. 12, 1944, KAM Papers, M. See also KAM to Franz Alexander, Oct. 20, 1942, KAM Papers, M.

72. Francis J. Braceland, "Psychiatric Lessons from World War II," *AJP* 103 (Mar. 1947): 592, on early uses of group therapy in the military. Karl's pioneering efforts in group therapy are noted in KAM to WCM, June 30, 1943, July 28, 1944, Robert P. Knight to WCM, July 4, 1943, both in WCM Papers (private); *TPR* 6 (Aug. 3, 1945): 4.

73. Winslow, *Story,* 258, on Karl initially increasing the patient load. "Annual Report of the Medical Director, The Menninger Psychiatric Hospital, for the Year 1944," by KAM and R. Worthington, H.S. 46, M, on enlarging the psychotherapy staff, reducing the chronic patient population, and increasing individual therapy sessions.

74. Linda Hilles, "Changing Trends in the Application of Psychoanalytic Principles to a Psychiatric Hospital," *BMC* 32 (July 1968): 211, on the push for unorthodox

psychoanalysis. Innovative visitors are noted in Peggy Ralston Shelton, TRI by LJF, Topeka, Sept. 13, 1985, and *TPR* 4 (July–Aug. 1943): 28. KAM to WCM, July 28, 1944, WCM Papers (private), on the organization undertaking education and research activities.

75. Comparison of Annual Reports of the Medical Director of the Sanitarium under Karl and Will show the continuity in outcomes despite Karl's discharge in 1944 of many chronic patients. WCM, "Impressions of Problems as of this Date," memorandum, Sept. 10, 1946, 2, WCM Papers (private), "treatment standards." WCM to Robert Worthington (memorandum), Feb. 6, 1947, 2, WCM Papers, M, "broken down" milieu therapy. Edward Greenwood to WCM (memorandum), Aug. 12, 1947, WCM Papers, M. See also TI on "Guide to Order Sheet," Dec. 4, 1981, and WCM to Lester Roach, June 6, 1951, Inst. Archives, M.

76. For attacks by the Menninger brothers upon one another along the lines noted here, see, e.g., KAM to WCM, July 8, 1943, WCM Papers (private); WCM to KAM, July 1, 1943, WCM Papers (private); WCM, "Impressions of Problems as of this Date" (memorandum), Sept. 10, 1946, 1, WCM Papers, M.

77. WCM to KAM, CFM, and John Stone, n.d. (Dec. 1934), WCM Papers, M. See also Hall and North, TI of WCM, Topeka, May 28, 1966, 28.

C H A P T E R   F O U R: *Southard School*

1. JLM to Robert and Helen Morse, June 3, 1943, Robert Switzer Papers, M; KAM in "Minutes of Board of Trustees and Governors, Annual Meeting," Oct. 8–9, 1960, MT.

2. Dean T. Collins, "Children of Sorrow: A History of the Mentally Retarded in Kansas," *BHM* 39 (Jan.–Feb. 1965): 54; Thomas N. Bonner, *The Kansas Doctor: A Century of Pioneering* (Lawrence, 1959), 155–7; CFM, TRI by Walker Winslow (cylinder 12), 1952–53, M; Walker Winslow, *The Menninger Story* (Garden City, N.Y., 1956), 79, 181.

3. KAM to Henrietta Campbell, Nov. 8, 1926, H.S. 10, M, recalling Southard remarking, "Don't forget the children." L. Vernon Briggs, *History of the Psychopathic Hospital, Boston, Massachusetts* (reprint, New York, 1973), 158–9, concerning early children's work there. See Helen L. Witmer, *Psychiatric Clinics for Children* (New York, 1940), 160–1, 168, for cogent observations on Southard at Boston Psychopathic Hospital. See also Mel Herman and Lewis L. Robbins, "Karl Menninger and Ernest Southard," *Menninger Perspective* 14 (1983): 5.

4. See Kathleen W. Jones, " 'Straightening the Twig': The Professionalization of American Child Psychiatry" (unpub. ms., 1986), 18–41, and Jones, "As the Twig Is Bent: American Psychiatry and the Troublesome Child, 1890–1940" (unpub. Ph.D. diss., Rutgers University, 1988), for coverage of Healy and his early followers. See also Witmer, *Psychiatric Clinics,* 56–7, 62–3.

5. KAM, PI by LJF, Topeka, June 22, 1987.

6. Witmer, *Psychiatric Clinics,* 177–81, on the Iowa State Psychopathic Hospital mobile clinic program. KAM, TI by Spafford Ackerly, Topeka, Oct. 21, 1972, 11–12, M, on his visit to Lowrey's Iowa clinics. Lowrey's article "The Child Guidance Clinic," *Childhood Education* I (1924), esp. 100, suggests his turn toward Healy-like orientation.

7. Peter L. Tyor and Leland V. Bell, *Caring for the Retarded in America: A History*

(Westport, Conn., 1984), 124–9, on the trend in work with the mentally retarded. Fernald's commitment to outpatient work with the retarded is elaborated in Peter L. Tyor and Jamil S. Zainaldin, "Asylum and Society: An Approach to Institutional Change," *Journal of Social History* 13 (Fall 1979): 39.

8. The centrality of the outpatient approach in almost all innovative child psychiatry ventures of the period is elaborated in Robert H. Felix, "Education of Community Mental Health Concepts," *AJP* 113 (Feb. 1957): 674; Jones, " 'Straightening the Twig,' " 35–7, 54–5. For the Menningers' justification of their decision to open an inpatient facility, see CFM (form letter on Southard School), June 27, 1931, H.S. 16, M; KAM to E. K. Wickman, Sept. 23, 1926, and KAM to Henrietta Campbell, Nov. 8, 1926, both in Inst. Archives, M; KAM, PI by LJF, Topeka, July 22, 1987.

9. KAM to Harold Maine, July 14, 1954, CFM Papers, M; KAM to E. K. Wickman, Sept. 23, 1926, Inst. Archives, M.

10. CFM (form letter on Southard School), June 27, 1931, H.S. 16, M. KAM to E. K. Wickman, Sept. 23, 1926; KAM to Henrietta Campbell, Nov. 8, 1926; KAM to George Neuhaus, Oct. 16, 1929, all in Inst. Archives, M.

11. KAM to Henrietta Campbell, Nov. 8, 1926, Inst. Archives, M, on Stella Pearson's background. KAM to E. A. Farrington, Nov. 11, 1929, Inst. Archives, M, on Pearson bringing a child for consultation. Stella Pearson to KAM, Mar. 3, 1926, Inst. Archives, M, outlining her treatment approach. Stella Pearson to KAM, June 4, 1926, Inst. Archives, M, agreeing to move her school to Topeka.

12. KAM to E. A. Farrington, Nov. 11, 1929, Inst. Archives, M, "without any financial recompense." KAM to American Medical Association, Sept. 21, 1926, H.S. 10, M, "equal partnership." KAM to Henrietta Campbell, Nov. 8, 1926, Inst. Archives, M, and Robert E. Switzer, "The Evolution of a New Program and a New House" (unpub. ms., 1961), 1, M, on the capacity and initial enrollment of the school.

13. KAM to Henrietta Campbell, Nov. 8, 1926, "supervisory interest." Winslow, *Story,* 204–5, on Charles's and Stone's roles in the school. KAM, PI by LJF, Topeka, Jan. 14, 1985, and KAM and JLM, PI by LJF, Topeka, Sept. 13, 1986, on Karl's plans for Charles at the school.

14. KAM to George Neuhaus, Oct. 16, 1929, H.S. 13, M, on Pearson knowing "how to handle children," "has helped us to learn," and returning children to public schools. KAM to Leo Bartemeier, July 21, 1933, KAM Papers, M, on locking and tying children during visitations. KAM to Bartemeier, Sept. 17, 1931, KAM Papers, M, on Holcombe using "old" punishment methods. Lucille Cairns, "A History of the Menninger Clinic at Topeka, Kansas up to the Time of its Transfer to the Menninger Foundation, 1919–1945" (unpub. Ph.D. diss., Washington University of St. Louis, 1946), 52, on the sisters bringing Southard children in contact with school groups.

15. KAM to Leo Bartemeier, July 21, 1933, KAM Papers, M; KAM to E. A. Farrington, Nov. 11, 1929, KAM Papers, M; "Board of Trustees. Eighth Annual Meeting," Oct. 2, 1949, 38, Lester Roach Papers, M, on the $1,000 monthly profit from the sisters; KAM, PI by LJF, Topeka, Jan. 14, 1985.

16. KAM to Frederick W. Brown, Mar. 30, 1931, H.S. 16, M; KAM to Stella Pearson, Mar. 26, 1930, H.S. 14, M; Stella Pearson to KAM, Apr. 24, 1930, H.S. 14, M.

17. George Knoppenberger to KAM, Mar. 18, 1927 [1930?], unprocessed, M (the physician's letter on Pearson's condition). KAM to Frederick W. Brown, Mar. 30, 1931, H.S. 16, M; KAM to E. A. Farrington, Sept. 1, 1930, H.S. 15, M; KAM to John E. DuMars, Aug. 14, 1930, H.S. 15, M; KAM, PI by LJF, Topeka, May 21, 1984, Jan. 14, 1985.

18. WCM Diary, Aug. 30, 1930; KAM to Frederick W. Brown, Mar. 30, 1931, H.S. 16, M; KAM to George Stevenson, Aug. 29, 1930, H.S. 15, M; "Business [Committee] Meeting," Mar. 9, 1936, Inst. Archives, M; KAM, TRI by Verne Horne, May 30, 1972, M; "Children's Division—The Menninger Foundation," n.a., n.d. (1954), 1–2, Inst. Archives, M.

19. KAM to Frederick W. Brown, Mar. 30, 1931, H.S. 16, M; KAM to E. A. Farrington, Sept. 1, 1930; KAM to George Stevenson, Aug. 29, 1930; WCM Diary, Sept. 6, 1930.

20. KAM to John R. Stone, Aug. 28, 1930 (telegram), H.S. 15, M; KAM to Thomas French, Sept. 12, 1931, KAM Papers, M, on "prescriptions"; KAM to CFM, Aug. 14, 1935, KAM Papers, M.

21. KAM, PI by LJF, Topeka, Sept. 10, 1986, recalling his vision of the post-Pearson period. KAM to John Stone, June 13, 1939, Stone Papers, M, recalling his hope that Charles would assume a forceful presence at the school.

22. CFM to R. E. Wing, Mar. 8, Nov. 13, 1934, CFM Papers, M, urging "sympathy" with the children and continuing those who did well "at our expense." "Children's Division—The Menninger Foundation," n.a., n.d. (1954), Inst. Archives, M, on the emotional reeducation research project. CFM to Sydney V. Smith, July 8, 1936, Inst. Archives, M, on Ruth Shaw. CFM to Edna Batchilder, Jan. 13, 1932, H.S. 18, for his dealing with staff grievances. Simmel in *BMC* I (May 1937): 135.

23. *TPR* 1 (Dec. 1–25, 1940): 55, on Coffman's background. KAM to John Stone, Mar. 11, 1939, Stone Papers, M, "saved our School's life." The nature of the Coffman social group and its internal family-like qualities is revealed in KAM to CFM, Aug. 14, 1935, KAM Papers, M; "Notes to Harold Maine," Aug. 4, 1954, CFM Papers, M; JLM, PI by LJF, Topeka, Mar. 11, 1986; JLM, TRI by LJF, Topeka, Nov. 8, 1987.

24. Stella Coffman, "The Department of Education at Southard School," July 13, 1939, H.S. 35, M; KAM to CFM, Aug. 14, 1935, KAM Papers, M; KAM, PI by LJF, Topeka, Sept. 10, 1986; JLM, PI by LJF, Topeka, Mar. 11, 1986.

25. KAM to John Stone, June 13, 1939, Stone Papers, M, recalling how Charles lacked the "energy or the power." See also JLM, TRI by LJF, Topeka, Nov. 8, 1987.

26. "Meeting of Dr. C.F., Dr. Ackerman, and Miss Lyle, Minutes," Sept. 5, 1935, Inst. Archives, M, on problems with the Coffman group; KAM, PI by LJF, Nov. 11, 1984; JLM, PI by LJF, Topeka, Mar. 11, 1986, and JLM, TRI by LJF, Topeka, Nov. 8, 1987.

27. Jeanetta Lyle's new role at the school is noted in KAM, PI by LJF, Topeka, Nov. 11, 1984; "Business [Committee] Meeting," Feb. 8, 1936, WCM Papers, M. KAM to CFM and FVM, Aug. 20, 1935, KAM Papers, M, on Ackerman's good ideas and interest in children's work. Ackerman's theory for child therapy is best conveyed in his essay "A Plan for Maladjusted Children," *BMC* I (Jan. 1937): 68. See also KAM to CFM, Aug. 14, 1935, KAM Papers, M, praising Ackerman's strong leadership.

28. KAM, "Confidential Bulletin to Staff and Residents," June 4, 1936, H.S. 24, on admission of normal- and high-intelligence children. JLM, TRI by LJF, Topeka, Nov. 8, 1987, and Arthur Mandlebaum, "The Menninger Foundation Department of Child Psychiatry," 1956, 2, M, also discusses the changing patient clientele. "Emotional re-education" of the feebleminded through psychoanalysis is noted in "Southard School Publicity," Sept. 21, 1933, H.S. 19, M; KAM in *Kansas City Star*, June 17, 1934; KAM to Elizabeth M. Hincks, Mar. 9, 1931, Inst. Archives, M. Progressive teachers and departmentalized specialties in "Meeting of Dr. C.F., Dr. Ackerman, and Miss Lyle, Minutes," Sept. 5, 1935, Inst. Archives, M; "Business [Committee] Meeting," Feb. 8, 1936, Inst. Archives, M.

29. In "Board of Trustees, Eighth Annual Meeting, Minutes," Oct. 2, 1949, 38, Inst. Archives, M, Will recalled the $1,000 monthly under Pearson and how the "problem" of uncontrolled deficits arose when she left. KAM to Elizabeth M. Hincks, Mar. 9, 1931, H.S. 16, M, on "financial liability." See also KAM to CFM, Aug. 14, 1935, KAM Papers, M.

30. The breakdown of the Ackerman-Lyle management traditions in the late 1930s are noted in John Stone to KAM, Mar. 9, 1939, Stone Papers, M; Alden Krider, TRI by LJF, Topeka, May 24, 1984; Douglass Orr to LJF (letter), Dec. 30, 1983. Earl Saxe, TRI by LJF, New York, Aug. 29, 1983.

31. Alden Krider, TRI by LJF, Topeka, May 24, 1984; KAM to John Stone, Mar. 11, 1939, Stone Papers, M.

32. The rise of Geleerd, Hawkins, and Benjamin to power and influence at the school is documented in John Stone to Winifred B. Klinger, Apr. 23, 1941, Inst. Archives, M; Margaret Brenman to A. H. Maslow, Oct. 23, 1940, A. H. Maslow Papers, AHAP; KAM, PI by LJF, Topeka, Jan. 14, 1985; Earl Saxe, TRI by LJF, New York, Aug. 24, 1983; Douglass Orr to LJF (letter), Dec. 30, 1983. The 1944 statement of thanks in "Executive Committee Meeting," Nov. 6, 1944, Mildred Law Papers, M.

33. Hawkins's and Geleerd's extensive deployment of psychoanalysis is discussed in Benjamin's report to "The Menninger Foundation Meeting of Members," Oct. 6, 1942, 36–8, Inst. Archives, M; E. M. Leitch, "The Southard School Annual Report" (1944), 7, Inst. Archives, M. For the devotedness of the school leadership, see Benjamin, "Southard School Annual Report," 1942, 11, Inst. Archives, M; Sibylle Escalona, TRI by LJF, New York, Nov. 7, 1983.

34. The replacement of feebleminded and epileptic children with emotionally disturbed children of average or higher intelligence in KAM to CFM, WCM, John Stone, Mildred Law, Dec. 19, 1941, H.S. 42, M; *TPR* I (Dec. 1–25, 1940): 49; Cairns, "History of Menninger Clinic," 53. For the turn to superior-intelligence criteria, see Alice Dangerfield, "Plan of Action in Re-Education of Neighborhood about Southard School," May 21, 1943, H.S. 45, M; Anne Benjamin form letter, Dec. 16, 1941, H.S. 42, M. That form letter plus Earl Saxe, "Annual Report of Southard School," n.d. (1940), Inst. Archives, M, concern the shift in school staff. "The Menninger Foundation Meeting of Members," Oct. 6, 1942, on Hawkins's and Geleerd's heavily individualized therapy approach, with emphasis on transference.

35. KAM to CFM, Feb. 10, 1942, KAM Papers, M, on the $1,000–$1,500 deficit and "spending money so extravagantly." "Executive Committee Meeting," May 6, 1942, Mildred Law Papers, M, on the ultimatum to close the school. See also KAM to Lucy McLaughlin, May 7, 1942, MT.

36. The initial Hawkins proposal of 1940 and its fate is described fully in Earl Saxe to KAM, Sept. 5, 1940, Inst. Archives, M. See also Donna T. Love, "The Use of Boarding Homes as a Part of the Program of Southard School" (unpub. Ph.D. diss., Washington University of St. Louis, 1948), esp. 5–10, and Lewis Robbins, TRI by LJF, New York, Aug. 23, 1983. "Meeting of the Board of Directors of the Menninger School Corporation," Aug. 22, 1939, Inst. Archives, M, shows Karl and Will opposing a day school proposal even before Hawkins's plan.

37. Love, "Use of Boarding Homes," 9, 40; "Executive Committee Meeting," Feb. 6, 1942, Mildred Law Papers, M; KAM to CFM, Feb. 10, 1942, KAM Papers, M; Alberta Hillyer's report for Southard School in *The Menninger Foundation Second Annual Report, Fiscal Year July 1, 1942–June 30, 1943* (Topeka, 1943); JLM to Lillian Smith, Feb. 6, 1944, KAM Papers; Mabel J. Remmers, PI by LJF, Topeka, June 20, 1987.

38. Hillyer, *Menninger Foundation Second Annual Report;* Love, "Use of Boarding Homes," 40, 95–6; Lewis Robbins, TRI by LJF, New York, Aug. 23, 1983; Dorothy C. Wright, "The Role of the Social Case Worker in the Boarding Home Plan of the Southard School," *BMC* 8 (Nov. 1944): 214–15.

39. For social workers defending the program, see, e.g., Wright, *BMC* 8, 215, and Love, "Use of Boarding Homes," 95–6. JLM to Lillian Smith, Feb. 6, 1944, KAM Papers, M. Benjamin's posture is noted and rejected in "Executive Committee Meeting," Feb. 6, 1942, Mildred Law Papers, M.

40. KAM to John Stone, Apr. 1, 1939, Stone Papers, M, "constant male head." KAM to John Stone, June 13, 1939, Stone Papers, M, "masculine assertiveness." KAM to Julia Menninger, Jan. 19, 1940, KAM Papers, M, and KAM to Anna Freud, Jan. 30, 1940, KAM Papers, M, both underscoring Karl's gender preferences for school leadership. KAM, PI by LJF, Topeka, Jan. 14, 1985, and esp. Sept. 14, 1985, on his grievances over Benjamin, Hawkins, and Geleerd as Southard leaders and his memories of the early Menninger household.

41. Sibylle Escalona, TRI by LJF, New York, Nov. 7, 1983.

42. KAM to Frank H. Woods, June 14, 1944, KAM Papers, M, on Leitch's very long hours with little effective return. Hazelle Bruce, TRI by LJF, Topeka, Jan. 13, 1985, on the increasing disarray of school affairs. Cairns, "History of Menninger Clinic," 106, and Merle Hoover, "The Southard School: Report of the Treasurer at the Postponed Annual Meeting," Sept. 6, 1944, Inst. Archives, M.

43. Edward Greenwood, TRI by LJF, Topeka, May 24, 1984; Sibylle Escalona, TRI by LJF, New York, Nov. 7, 1983.

44. Dorothy Wright and E. M. Leitch, "The Use of Boarding Homes in Conjunction with a Private Psychiatric Residential School," *American Journal of Orthopsychiatry,* May 1945, 10, "home life had contributed." WCM to KAM, Mar. 18, 1935, unprocessed, M, considering possible "special" community children's services. KAM to Robert L. Brigden, Jan. 9, 1940, H.S. 38, M, delineating all the community services of Southard School and its participation in the City Free Clinic. Signs of the Menningers and others being disposed, increasingly, to a regular outpatient treatment service is suggested in Edward Greenwood, TRI by LJF, Topeka, May 24, 1984, and "Planning and Coordinating Committee," June 12, 1946, Mildred Law Papers, M.

45. Edward Greenwood, "Southard School, Children's Division" (1946), 1, Inst. Archives, M, and a 1946 diagram of the "Services of Patients" operation under Robert Knight (Inst. Archives, M) confirm the rise of an outpatient department and the old Southard School as the inpatient department of the new Children's Division. Edward Greenwood, TRI by RGM, Topeka, Apr. 5, 1977, M, on Karl's changing attitudes and particularly his proposal for cottages for parents of Southard children. WCM Diary, Oct. 19, 1949, on how the outpatient department still had not developed into a viable entity. S. A. Szurek, I. N. Berlin, and Maleta J. Bloatman, ed., *Inpatient Care for the Psychotic Child* (Palo Alto, 1971), viii–ix, on postwar inpatient-outpatient programs like Langley Porter.

46. WCM Diary, Feb. 21, 1942; CFM to KAM, Feb. 24, 1942, CFM Papers, M; KAM to Frank H. Woods, June 14, 1944, KAM Papers, M.

47. Paul Pruyser, James Pratt, et al., TI on guide to the order sheet, Topeka, Dec. 4, 1981, M, on the absence of a guide tradition in the school. For apprehensions over the preponderance of women and their nonmedical role, see, e.g., Earl Saxe, TRI by LJF, New York, Aug. 24, 1983; WCM Diary, Mar. 20, 1941. Southard staff frequently underscored the difficulty of working with disturbed children who often regressed and

exhibited very primitive fantasies as inpatients but did not verbalize well. See, e.g., Earl Saxe, "Typical Maladjustments," June 6, 1940, Inst. Archives, M; "Menninger School Corporation Executive Committee Meeting," Aug. 9, 1945, 2–3, Inst. Archives, M. Yet there was little sympathy in the hospital for school staff embracing outpatient programs. Sibylle Escalona, TRI by LJF, New York, Nov. 7, 1983, on her 1943 experience.

48. "Speech KAM made at Southard School Seminar," Jan. 1938, 3–4, Inst. Archives, M, "hard [to] get along with children." Hazelle Bruce, TRI by LJF, Topeka, Jan. 13, 1985, on Karl finding the children in pajamas and on the infrequency of his visits. Children's staff regularly underscored Karl's rare visits and his difficulty relating to the children: Edward Greenwood, PI by LJF, Topeka, Sept. 12, 1985; Dorothy Fuller, TRI by LJF, Topeka, Feb. 29, 1984; J. Cotter Hirschberg, TRI by LJF, Topeka, June 1, 1983. KAM to Grace Menninger, Aug. 19, 1938, KAM Papers, M, on Southard children visiting his farm. Karl on "depressing, futile work," *Minneapolis Tribune*, Sept. 5, 1950.

49. KAM to Ella W. Brown, Feb. 17, 1945, KAM Papers, M, "oldest problem child." KAM, "Interview with Dr. Edwin Levy," June 16, 1960, KAM Papers, M, "invalid in my childhood." Winslow, *Story*, 124, on friends and neighbors entertaining the two younger Menninger brothers but not Karl. FVM, "Baby Book," July 21, 1930, 253, KAM Papers, M.

50. Karl's apprehension over Southard children being rooted in his own personal sense of mental-emotional "inadequacy" is emphasized in Lucy Freeman, TRI by LJF, New York, Nov. 8, 1983; Arthur Mandlebaum, TRI by LJF, Topeka, May 25, 1984, and suggested in JLM, PI by LJF, Topeka, Sept. 13, 1986. See also KAM to Grace Menninger, May 4, 1940, KAM to Julia Menninger, Jan. 19, 1940, both in KAM Papers, M.

CHAPTER FIVE: *Karl Menninger and the Émigrés*

1. WCM to CFM, John Stone, KAM, et al., Sept. 11, 1933, H.S. 19, M, on the visit to Vienna. WCM to CWM, Feb. 26, 1935, WCM Papers (private), on American psychiatry as "more advanced." See also WCM to "Dear Folks," Aug. 22, 1933, WCM Papers (private).

2. KAM, "Conversations in Freud's Garden," n.d. (1962), KAM Papers, M, is the most detailed account of the visit to Freud and of what Alexander said to Freud. "Impressions and Reflections on the International Congress for Psychoanalysis in Lucern, Aug., 1934," Oct. 6, 1934, H.S. 20, M, represents Karl's only contemporary account of that visit. KAM, "Footprints," Nov. 30, 1958, 22, KAM Papers, M, underscores Freud's anger then with Alexander. Paul Roazen, *Freud and His Followers* (New York, 1971, 1976), 509–10, on Alexander having left Europe without Freud's approval. KAM, PI by LJF, Topeka, Nov. 16, 1984, recalling the 1934 visit to Freud and noting that he had not known, until decades later, that Alexander had told Freud about his narcissism. KAM, PI by LJF, Topeka, Mar. 12, 1986, on the background to the 1934 visit and on his hurt over Alexander's talking an hour with Freud while keeping him in the garden and then limiting his discussion with Freud.

3. "Impressions and Reflections . . . Aug., 1934," on how Freud was "not disposed to advise . . . utterly impersonal." See also "Conversations in Freud's Garden," n.d. (1962).

4. KAM to Sigmund Freud, Dec. 12, 1936 (copy), KAM Papers, M.

5. KAM, "Sigmund Freud, 1856–1939," *BMC* 13 (Sept. 1941): 141, on sending a cable to Freud. KAM, "Sigmund Freud," *The Nation* (Oct. 7, 1939), 374. KAM to Franz Alexander, Feb. 23, 1940, KAM Papers, M.

6. For general information on the psychoanalytic immigration, see, e.g., Nathan G. Hale, "From Berggasse XIX to Central Park West: The Americanization of Psychoanalysis, 1919–1940," *JHBS* 14 (Oct. 1978): 305; H. Stuart Hughes, *The Sea Change: The Migration of Social Thought, 1930–1965* (New York, 1975), 33; Jacques M. Quen and Eric T. Carlson, eds., *American Psychoanalysis: Origins and Development* (New York, 1978), 136. KAM to Clifford Allen, July 20, 1940, KAM Papers, M, on the émigré analysts coming to work for him in Topeka. KAM to Bettina Warburg, Apr. 23, 1941, KAM Papers, M, claiming nineteen émigrés had worked in his organization by this time (likely an exaggeration).

7. For discussions about the émigrés as a "problem" constituency, see, e.g., CFM to KAM, Nov. 18, 1939, Historical Notebook, 1–2, M; KAM to John Stone, Apr. 26, 1939, and John Stone to KAM, Apr. 27, 1939, both in Stone Papers, M. For Karl's determination to keep the émigrés and recruit more despite their conduct, see, e.g., KAM to Charles Tidd, Oct. 9, 1939, and KAM to Ernest Jones, Aug. 19, 1943, both in KAM Papers, M, and KAM to Bernard Kamm, Nov. 16, 1939, TIP Papers, M.

8. WCM to CFM and FVM, July 26, 1933, WCM Papers (private), on the book burnings. WCM to CWM, July 21, 1933, WCM Papers (private), "Jewish scientists." WCM to CFM and FVM, July 19, 1933, H.S. 19, M, "The Germans seem."

9. For Jacob's background, see "Curriculum Vita—Dr. Gertrude Jacob," H.S. 22, M; Leo Stone, TRI by LJF, New York City, Nov. 7, 1983. For data on Reichenberg, see "Who's Who: Members and Ex-Members of the Staff of the Menninger Clinic, 1925–1943," Inst. Archives, M, and KAM, "Confidential Bulletin to Staff and Residents," June 4, 1936, H.S. 24, M.

10. Bernard Kamm, TRI by LJF, Chicago, Feb. 4, 1984.

11. Martin Grotjahn, TRI by LJF, Los Angeles, Dec. 27, 1983; Bernard Kamm, TRI by LJF, Feb. 4, 1984; KAM, PI by LJF, Topeka, Nov. 16, 1984. KAM to U.S. Dept. of Justice, Alien Registration Div., Feb. 26, 1942, TIP Papers, M.

12. Martin Grotjahn, TRI by LJF, Los Angeles, Dec. 27, 1983; Bernard Kamm, TRI by LJF, Chicago, Feb. 4, 1984; JLM, TRI by LJF, Topeka, Sept. 12, 1985.

13. Martin Grotjahn, TRI by LJF, Los Angeles, Dec. 27, 1983, on Knight recommending him and Kamm, and on noting that the Menningers "saved our lives." "Business [Committee] Minutes," Sept. 25, 1936, Inst. Archives, M, on getting money to the émigrés. Bernard Kamm, TRI by LJF, Chicago, Feb. 4, 1984, and *Topeka Daily Capital*, Sept. 26, 1936, on his arrival in New York. KAM, PI by LJF, Topeka, Sept. 14, 1985, on how neither he nor the émigrés (nor the Menninger staff) spoke much about political developments in Europe for the first several weeks.

14. Edoardo Weiss in *Newsletter of the Menninger School of Psychiatric Nursing* 3 (May 1, 1939):1; *The Chart*, Mar. 23, 1939, H.S. 34, M; and Franz Alexander to KAM, Aug. 24, 1939, TIP Papers, M. Elizabeth Geleerd in *TPR* 1 (Nov. 1–15, 1940): 40–1. Rapaport and Moellenhoff in "Who's Who, 1925–1943," M. KAM, PI by LJF, Topeka, Sept. 12, 1985, on Moellenhoff. Ernst Lewy in *TPR* 5 (Sept. 15, 1944): 4, and Ernst Lewy, TRI by LJF, Los Angeles, May 10, 1984.

15. KAM to CFM, Apr. 26, 1939, KAM Papers, M. John Stone to KAM, June 16, 1939, Stone Papers, M. See also KAM to Stone, June 21, 1939, Stone Papers, M, and KAM to Anna Freud, Jan. 10, 1940, KAM Papers, M.

16. The 1943 recruitment policy shift is explained and justified by John Stone in Executive Committee Meeting, July 8, 1943, Mildred Law Papers, M.

17. Frederick Hacker, TRI by LJF, Los Angeles, Jan. 3, 1984, on his background and on Rapaport as a recruiter. For data on the other émigré recruits of this period, see "Who's Who, 1925–1943," M; *TPR* 4 (Jan.–Feb. 1943): 6, and *TPR* 4 (May–June 1943): 30; Sibylle Escalona, TRI by LJF, New York, Nov. 7, 1983; KAM, "Staff Bulletin 9," Mar. 3, 1943, H.S. 44, M.

18. Douglass W. Orr to LJF, Jan. 26, 1984 (letter).

19. Bernard Kamm, TRI by LJF, Chicago, Feb. 4, 1984; Martin Grotjahn, TRI by LJF, Los Angeles, Dec. 27, 1983; Douglass W. Orr to LJF, Dec. 23, 1983 (letter); Ernst Lewy, TRI by LJF, Los Angeles, May 10, 1984.

20. Ernst Lewy, TRI by LJF, Los Angeles, May 12, 1984, on himself, Grotjahn, Kamm, and Moellenhoff regarding Topeka as a cow town. Martin Grotjahn, TRI by LJF, Los Angeles, Dec. 27, 1983, on Topeka as "nothing culturally." Harlan Crank, PI by LJF, Austin, Nov. 22, 1985, on émigré difficulty hiring servicemen and professionals. Martin Grotjahn, TRI by LJF, Los Angeles, Dec. 27, 1983, "Our butter was better."

21. The difficulties of émigré wives and pressures they made for money or a move from Topeka is noted in Ernst Lewy, TRI by LJF, Los Angeles, May 10, 1984; Martin Grotjahn, TRI by LJF, Los Angeles, Dec. 27, 1983; CWM, PI by LJF, Topeka, Jan. 7, 1983; Harlan Crank, PI by LJF, Austin, Nov. 22, 1985; JLM, TRI by LJF, Topeka, Jan. 7, 1983.

22. KAM to Ernest Jones, Aug. 19, 1943, KAM Papers, M. See also KAM to Ernst Simmel, July 25, 1938, KAM Papers, M, and KAM to John Stone, June 14, 1939, Stone Papers, M.

23. Bernard Kamm, TRI by LJF, Chicago, Feb. 4, 1984.

24. John Stone to KAM, Mar. 10, Mar. 15, June 16, 1939, Stone Papers, M. Ernst Lewy, TRI by LJF, Los Angeles, May 10, 1984.

25. This émigré perspective is covered thoroughly in Martin Grotjahn, TRI by LJF, Los Angeles, Dec. 27, 1983; Harlan Crank, PI by LJF, Austin, Nov. 22, 1985; John Stone to KAM, Apr. 28, 1939, Stone Papers, M. It is noteworthy that émigré estimates of their fair market value were excessive. Some analysts barely made a living in California and New York.

26. KAM to John Stone and WCM, Mar. 23, 1939, Stone Papers, M; KAM to Ruth Brunswick, Feb. 17, 1945, KAM Papers, M; Harlan Crank, PI by LJF, Austin, Nov. 22, 1985. See also John Stone to KAM, May 3, 1939, Stone Papers, M, and JLM to KAM, Apr. 30, 1939, KAM Papers, M.

27. Etalka Grotjahn, TRI by LJF, Los Angeles, Dec. 12, 1983. CWM, PI by LJF, Topeka, Sept. 12, 1985, confirming Grotjahn's account.

28. Ernst Simmel to Franz Alexander, June 15, 1933, KAM Papers, M. See also KAM to Ernst Simmel, Nov. 29, 1938, KAM Papers, M.

29. KAM to Ernest Jones, Aug. 19, 1943, KAM Papers, M.

30. KAM to John Stone, Apr. 26, 1939, KAM Papers, M; KAM to CFM, Apr. 26, 1939, Historical Notebook, 1, M. See also John Stone to KAM, Apr. 28, 1939, Stone Papers, M.

31. KAM to Frankwood E. Williams, Dec. 16, 1935, Frankwood Williams Papers, M, "us Christian boys." KAM to Billy Rose, May 29, 1944, KAM Papers, M, "married to a Jewish physician." KAM, PI by LJF, Topeka, May 18, 1985, and JLM to KAM, Jan.

29, 1939, KAM Papers, M, reveal both Karl's and Jeanetta Lyle's sense of Jewish bonding during the California lay analysis controversy. KAM to Lionel Blitzsten, Feb. 4, 1937, KAM Papers, M. KAM to Ralph Fellows, June 14, 1940, KAM Papers, M, "one Jew at each appointment date."

32. "Some Statements for the Counsel and Guidance of the Trustees and Medical Council . . . in Future Years," Aug. 6, 1952, 9, Inst. Archives, M, "essentially Christian and Protestant." This document was drafted largely by Karl but was also attributed to Will and Charles.

33. For criticism of the émigrés as therapists, see, e.g., CFM to KAM, n.d. (1939), KAM Papers, M; John Stone to KAM, Jan. 7, 1938, KAM Papers, M, and Apr. 27, 1939, Stone Papers, M; Harlan Crank, PI by LJF, Austin, Nov. 22, 1985; Edward Greenwood, TRI by LJF, Topeka, Nov. 10, 1982. Ernst Lewy, TRI by LJF, Los Angeles, May 10, 1984, recalling Will's response to émigrés in his hospital. For émigré criticism of the hospital's guide to the order sheet and physician case conferences, see Martin Grotjahn, TRI by LJF, Los Angeles, Dec. 27, 1983; Ernst Lewy, TRI by LJF, Los Angeles, May 10, 1984; Bernard Kamm, TRI by LJF, Chicago, Feb. 4, 1984. Émigré attacks on the Menningers and their staff for failing to grasp the deeper meanings of Freudian psychoanalysis are found in Lewy, TRI, May 10, 1984; Kamm, TRI, Feb. 4, 1984; Grotjahn, TRI, Dec. 27, 1983.

34. The controversy over Weiss's use of Jungian techniques is reported in KAM, PI by LJF, Topeka, Sept. 14, 1985; Educational Committee Notes of Topeka Psychoanalytic Society, June 16, 1940, TIP Papers, M (including Karl's criticism of his colleagues). See also Martin Grotjahn, "Recollecting Some Analysts I Knew," *Bulletin, Southern California Psychoanalytic Institute,* 50 (Oct. 1977): 6. KAM to Franz Alexander, Aug. 22, 1939, TIP Papers, M, for Karl's fascination but scorn for Weiss's Jungian "spiritualism and mysticism." Yet in KAM to Bettina Warburg, Apr. 23, 1941, KAM Papers, M, he castigated Weiss for failure to contribute "to our teaching program."

35. KAM, *Man Against Himself* (New York, 1938, 1966), 413, "ultimate conqueror" and "prolonging the game." KAM, *Love Against Hate* (New York, 1942), 6, "the logical inference." *Man Against Himself,* 5, "constructive and destructive tendencies." Most of *Love Against Hate* and particularly Part VI ("Reconstruction") in *Man Against Himself,* on hobbies and other ways of encouraging eros. *Love Against Hate,* 5, "encourage love" and 188, "make it possible for us to live and to love."

36. *Man Against Himself,* 41, for oral stage origins of the death instinct turning outward and inward. *Love Against Hate,* 295–6, defending Freud's focus on sexuality against criticisms. *Love Against Hate,* 130, "better to love than to sublimate." More undeveloped expressions of the value of sublimation are found in *Man Against Himself,* esp. 26, 372–3, 385.

37. *Love Against Hate,* 282–3, "In order to achieve."

38. *Love Against Hate,* 190–1, "Freud's skepticism," and "disregarded the fact" that religion was "no illusion" but "a very real defense." *Ibid.,* 193, "Essentially, both are trying." See also Sonya Michel, "American Conscience and the Unconscience: Psychoanalysis and the Rise of Personal Religion, 1906–1963," *Psychoanalysis & Contemporary Thought* 73 (1984): 414–16, for discussion of Karl's reconciliation of religion and psychoanalysis in *Love Against Hate.*

39. *Man Against Himself,* 6, "sort of equilibrium." The theoretical underpinnings of this volume are best grasped by close attention to Part I ("Destruction"), IV ("Focal Suicide"), and VI ("Reconstruction").

40. *Man Against Himself,* 7.

41. Frederick Hacker, TRI by LJF, Los Angeles, Jan. 3, 1984. See also KAM, TRI by Hacker, Topeka, Apr. 18, 1971, M.

42. Russell Jacoby, *The Repression of Psychoanalysis: Otto Fenichel and the Political Freudians* (New York, 1983), is the most comprehensive account of Fenichel and his European circle. *Ibid.,* 119, on Fenichel's 1938 stop in Topeka and Karl's perception of him. KAM to Otto Fenichel, Nov. 6, 1942, KAM Papers, M, sending *Love Against Hate.* See also Fenichel to KAM, Mar. 10, 1943, Sept. 20, 1945, KAM Papers, M.

43. KAM, PI by LJF, Topeka, Nov. 16, 1984, Sept. 12, 1985, on his rapport with Lewy. Lewy confirmed that growing rapport and Karl's mood when he announced his departure in Lewy, TRI by LJF, Los Angeles, May 10, 12, 1984. See also "Ernst Lewy: A Sketch," *TPR* 5 (Sept. 15, 1944): 4.

44. The formation of Karl's psychoanalytic study seminar is noted in KAM to Ralph Fellows, Feb. 29, 1932, H.S. 18, M; KAM to Margaret Ribble, Aug. 30, 1932, KAM Papers, M. For data on the formation and early years of the Psychoanalytic Study Group of Topeka, see Robert P. Knight, "Topeka Psychoanalytic Society" (Jan. 1939), H.S. 34, M; KAM to Sigmund Freud, Dec. 12, 1939, and KAM to Ernst Simmel, June 18, 1936, both in KAM Papers, M.

45. For the formal changes of 1938 in the Topeka Study Group, see "By-Laws of the Psychoanalytic Study Group of Topeka," 1938, H.S. 30, M; Robert Knight to Edward Glover, Jan. 17, 1939, H.S. 34, M. Formal recognition in 1942 as the Topeka Institute of Psychoanalysis is covered in KAM, "Recollections," *BMC* 27 (May 1963): 143.

46. Robert Knight to Charles W. Tidd, Dec. 5, 1939, TIP Papers, M, "unofficial protectorate." John A.P. Millet, "Psychoanalysis in the United States," in Franz Alexander et al., eds., *Psychoanalytic Pioneers* (New York, 1966), 558, cogently discusses the elder-statesman status of émigré analysts in other American psychoanalytic societies. Martin Grotjahn, TRI by LJF, Los Angeles, Dec. 27, 1983, and Bernard Kamm, TRI by LJF, Chicago, Feb. 4, 1984, on émigré determination to resist Karl-Knight domination.

47. Peter Gay, *Freud: A Life for Our Time* (New York, 1988), 490–500, for full coverage of Freud on lay analysis. Hendrik M. Ruitenbeek, *Freud and America* (New York, 1966), 95, quotes Freud's 1938 defense of lay analysis. Jacoby, *Repression,* 119, discusses that defense cogently.

48. Robert Jay Lifton, *Thought Reform and the Psychology of Totalism: A Study of "Brainwashing" in China* (New York, 1961), 448, 450, quoting and elaborating Alexander. For the posture of American physicians who were psychoanalytic pioneers on the issue of lay analysis, see Reubin Fine, *A History of Psychoanalysis* (New York, 1979), 96. Karl's posture on the 1938 APA rule change is elaborated in Frederick Hacker, TRI by LJF, Los Angeles, Jan. 3, 1984.

49. The role of Karl and Knight in putting down the California "rebellion" is discussed in KAM to Charles W. Tidd, Jan. 10, 1940, KAM Papers, M; KAM to Franz Alexander, Dec. 7, 1939, TIP Papers, M; Bernard Kamm to Robert Knight, Nov. 14, 1939, TIP Papers, M; Samuel Eisenstein, "The Birth of Our Institute," *Bulletin of the Southern California Psychoanalytic Institute and Society,* 42 (Apr. 1975): 1, 3.

50. Robert Knight to KAM, Dec. 30, 1940, TIP Papers, M, on the need to put down the émigré rebellion. WCM, "Psychiatry and the Army," *BMC* 8 (May 1944): 91–2, demanding "a medical and psychiatric foundation" to practice psychoanalysis. KAM

to Albert A. Wiggam, Apr. 10, 1942, Inst. Archives, M, "competent individuals." KAM to Bernard Kamm, Nov. 16, 1939, TIP Papers, M, "a certain sympathy." KAM to Ernst Simmel, Apr. 12, 1940, TIP Papers, M, "decided gain," "the risk of having psychoanalysis condemned as illegal." KAM to Franz Alexander, Dec. 7, 1939, TIP Papers, M, "front of Americanism." KAM to Bernard Kamm, Nov. 16, 1939, "adjust himself." See also KAM to Ernst Simmel, Charles Tidd, May Romm, and Joe Haenel, Dec. 18, 1941, TIP Papers, M.

51. Karl's recruitment and encouragement of émigré lay analysts in the course of the 1940s is noted in Rudolf Ekstein, TRI by LJF, Los Angeles, Dec. 24, 1983; and Frederick Hacker, TRI by LJF, Los Angeles, Jan. 3, 1984. KAM to Bettina Warburg, Sept. 10, 1942, KAM Papers, M, asks this APA official for "no laymen, please," in sending him referrals. The changes in Topeka society policy on lay analysis are cited in Minutes of Business Meeting of Topeka Psychoanalytic Society, May 27, 1950, WCM Papers, M, and Lewis L. Robbins to Active Members of Topeka Psychoanalytic Society, March 21, 1951, Inst. Archives, M. KAM to Norman Reider, July 2, 1953, KAM Papers, M, "exceptions."

52. KAM to Erik Erikson, July 19, 1945, KAM Papers, M.

53. KAM, "In Memoriam: Leo Bartemeier, M.D. (1895–1982)," *BMC* 47 (Jan. 1983): 72, and KAM, TRI by LJF, Topeka, Mar. 14, 1986, on the details of the commission visit to the ETO. D. Bernard Foster, TRI by LJF, Topeka, Mar. 13, 1985, on Karl's risky front line visits. Robert H. Abzug, *Inside the Vicious Heart: Americans and the Liberation of Nazi Concentration Camps* (New York, 1985), 45–59, describes Buchenwald immediately after liberation and how other Americans responded to it.

54. For Karl's memories of what he saw at Buchenwald, see KAM, TRI by LJF, Topeka, Mar. 14, 1986, Nov. 8, 1987; KAM, *The Vital Balance: The Life Process in Mental Health and Illness* (New York, 1963), 377, 391–2; KAM, *BMC* 47 (Jan. 1983): 72. His comments on the Buchenwald prisoner-doctor are reported in KAM, *Sparks* (New York, 1973), 87, and *Vital Balance*, 392.

55. *TPR* 6 (June 1, 1945): 10, "truly terrible and depressing place." KAM to JLM, CFM, et al., May 3, 1945, WCM Papers, M.

56. KAM, TRI by LJF, Topeka, Mar. 14, 1986, goes more deeply into the significance of the Jewish guard than any of his written accounts. KAM, "Freud and Psychology," *A Psychiatrist's World: Selected Papers of Karl Menninger, M.D.*, Bernard H. Hall, ed. (New York, 1959), II, 855, "the sterner, sadder tradition of Europe." In WCM to CWM, n.d. (late 1945), WCM Papers (private), Will, too, evidenced difficulty with wartime atrocity: "Just circled over Hiroshima & my oh my what devastation" represented his total response.

57. For migration patterns of postwar Topeka émigrés, see *Topeka State Journal*, Mar. 24, 1950 (Kaiser); *Topeka Daily Capital*, Jan. 4, 1949 (Jokl), Aug. 1, 1968 (Fabian), Mar. 25, 1947 (Gross). "Normalization" of the postwar psychoanalytic profession is discussed in Robert Knight, "The Present Status of Organized Psychoanalysis in the United States," *JAPA* I (1953): 218–19. Irwin Rosen, TRI by LJF, Topeka, July 27, 1983, on émigré attitudes toward new research projects. Philip Holzman to Otto Fleischmann, Feb. 6, 1958, Murphy Papers, M, on almost memorizing Freudian text in TIP courses. Gerald Aronson, TRI by LJF, Los Angeles, Dec. 26, 1983, and Maimon Leavitt, TRI by LJF, Los Angeles, Dec. 25, 1983.

58. Robert Holt, "Notes on discussion with Dr. Karl on selection of psychoanalysts, Apr. 13, 1953," Apr. 16, 1953, Holt Papers, AHAP. See also KAM, PI by LJF, Topeka,

Mar. 15, 1986, where he elaborates further on this developing disenchantment with postwar psychoanalysis; and Robert R. Holt, TRI by LJF, New York, Dec. 28, 1985.

59. In "The Topeka Mystique," American Psychoanalytic Association, Puerto Rico, 1981, transcript, 62, Wallerstein refers to training analysts generally but is obviously referring to the majority of the training analysts—the émigrés. For some measure of the large demand for training analyses and the paucity of staff who could conduct them, see "Minutes of Annual Meeting of Board of Trustees and Governors," Oct. 13–14, 1956, MT; Lewis Robbins to Members of Medical Council, Mar. 24, 1951, Inst. Archives, M. WCM, "Medical Council Meeting of Feb. 16," Feb. 27, 1951, 2–3, WCM Papers, M, recognizing the centrality of the émigré training analysts to the organization.

60. George Klein to Sibylle Escalona, Mar. 16, 1951, George Klein Papers, AHAP. See also Klein to Herbert Schlesinger and Philip Holzman, Mar. 26, 1951, Klein Papers, AHAP.

61. The principal background for the strike of March 1951 is Irving Sheffel, PI by LJF, Topeka, July 26, 1984, Jan. 10, Sept. 13, 1985. Sheffel also gave me copies of confidential Menninger personnel files, which indicated that most émigré training analysts earned about $10,000 on March 1, 1951. By April 1, they had all reached at least $14,000. See also Irving Sheffel to D. Lauder, n.d. (memo), Inst. Archives, M; Rudolf Ekstein to LJF, Sept. 9, 1984 (letter). Lewis Robbins to Members of the Medical Council, Mar. 24, 1951, Inst. Archives, M, makes it obvious that the "strike" took place in March. WCM Diary, Mar. 23, 1951, on Ekstein's role.

62. Irving Sheffel, PI by LJF, Topeka, July 26, 1984, Jan. 10, Sept. 13, 1985; Sheffel to LJF, Jan. 17, 1985 (letter).

63. *Ibid.* See also Karl's list of striking émigrés, misfiled in TMF Medical Council, 1949–1950, Inst. Archives, M, and Sibylle Escalona to George S. Klein, Apr. 9, 1951, Klein Papers, AHAP.

64. Will's warming to postwar émigrés as noted in WCM Diary, Feb. 21, Mar. 23, June 2, 1951. WCM, "Medical Council Meeting of Feb. 16," Feb. 27, 1951.

65. Sheffel, PI by LJF, Topeka, July 26, 1984, on Karl's shout, the day of the strike, to have the émigrés return to Europe.

CHAPTER SIX: *The Cobweb Effect*

1. *Topeka Capital-Journal,* Mar. 10, 1983 (Z. B. Greene, "Gibson's Encore," covering his Topeka activities).

2. William Gibson, *The Cobweb* (New York, 1954), 359, "giant cobweb." *Ibid.,* 247, on nonprofit foundation plans. *Ibid.,* 71, 89, on apprehensions of turning power over to the trustees.

3. KAM to Ruth Brunswick, Apr. 7, 1945, KAM Papers, M, "the conversion." "Statement of Dr. Karl Menninger to Group of 40 Selected Employees," Feb. 17, 1941, KAM Papers, M, "terrific obstacles." KAM, PI by LJF, Topeka, Sept. 12, 1985, on seeing Finkelstein and Brunswick initially as the links between nonprofit status and the divorce, but later seeing deeper links.

4. EAMJr., TRI by LJF, Lillington, N.C., Aug. 17, 1985, details Pearl's role and his own entry into the Menninger home. See also Josephine Boam, TRI by LJF, Topeka, Sept. 12, 1985; and Pearl Boam, TRI by CWM, Topeka, Sept. 25, 1968, M.

5. EAMJr., TRI by LJF, Lillington, Aug. 18, 1985, on Pearl's role with the three family groups and the screen house. See also FVM, *Days of My Life* (New York, 1939), 304–5.

6. FVM to KAM, n.d. (Jan. 1932), KAM Papers, M, and CWM, PI by LJF, Topeka, Mar. 9, 1985, on Flo sensing Karl's marriage was in trouble. Bouts with anorexia are described in an undated KAM memorandum to the Menninger Museum (KAM Papers, M). Grace's background and domesticity in marriage is noted in Julia Gottesman, TRI by LJF, Los Angeles, Jan. 3, 1984; EAMJr., TRI by LJF, Lillington, Aug. 17, 1985. Grace's sense of Karl's insecurity is evident in KAM analysis notes, 1930–32, for Oct. 28, 1930, Feb. 13, 1931, KAM Papers, M. KAM to Karen Horney, Aug. 14, 1933, KAM Papers, M.

7. CFM to KAM, Jan. 22, 1932, unfiled, M, on Beryl Johnson's position. Very explicit data on the liaisons between the Johnsons and the Menningers is revealed in KAM analysis notes, 1930–32, Oct. 29–Nov. 11, 1930, plus Grace Menninger to Lillian Johnson, Nov. 11, 1930, Grace Menninger to KAM, June 23, 1935, "substitutes for Lillian," all in KAM Papers, M. CWM, PI by LJF, Topeka, July 30, 1984, Mar. 9, 1985, on hearing Lillian boast of helping on *The Human Mind.*

8. Jeanetta Lyle's background in misc. notes, Dec. 1940, H.S. 40, M. Julia Gottesman, TRI by LJF, Los Angeles, Jan. 3, 1984, and JLM, TRI by LJF, Topeka, Jan. 7, 1983, on her personality and early rapport with Karl. JLM to KAM, Feb. 2, 1939, KAM Papers, M, "As to your being married." Grace Menninger to KAM, n.d. (1938), KAM Papers, M, "aware of the affair." KAM to Grace Menninger, May 4, 1940, KAM Papers, M, blaming Alexander. EAMJr., TRI by LJF, Lillington, Aug. 18, 1985, on family distress with the divorce. KAM, TRI by LJF, Topeka, Mar. 14, 1986, on choosing between Grace and Jeanetta. Norman Reider, TRI by LJF, San Francisco, Dec. 28, 1983, on high-staff reactions.

9. David M. Levy to KAM, Sept. 18, 1936, H.S. 25, M. Earnings and deficits at Menninger in KAM to Thomas Parran, Apr. 15, 1938, H.S. 31, M; "The Menninger Clinic: Analysis of Financial Statements and Recommendations," 1936, 5, Inst. Archives, M; "Meeting of the Menninger Sanitarium Business Department," n.d. (Jan. 1937), H.S. 26. KAM to L. A. Halbert, Dec., 13, 1934, KAM Papers, M, on charging high fees. KAM to William Alanson White, Nov. 6, 1932, W. A. White Papers, NA. KAM, "1935 Annual Report to Directors," 3–4, H.S. 22, and Lucille Cairns, "A History of the Menninger Clinic" (unpub. Ph.D. diss., Washington University of St. Louis, 1946), 110–11, on the free clinic. KAM to WCM, CFM, John Stone, and Robert Knight, Apr. 12, 1940, H.S. 39, M, "in our actual work."

10. CWM, PI by LJF, Topeka, July 30, 1984, on Topeka reaction to Karl, his marriage, and his affairs. *Topeka Daily Capital,* June 26, 1938, on Karl complaining of spending $1,000 and getting $20. KAM to John Stone, Jan. 13, 1940, Stone Papers, M, "suffer considerably in Topeka"; see also KAM to Stone, Jan. 15, 1940, Stone Papers, M. Stone to KAM, Mar. 10, 1937, H.S. 26, M, on aborting the Santa Barbara move. KAM, PI by LJF, Topeka, Sept. 14, 1985, on the Santa Barbara move.

11. Brunswick's life is covered in considerable detail in Paul Roazen, *Freud and His Followers* (New York, 1971), part IX, chs. 1, 2. Karl wrote a revealing obituary of her in the *New York Times,* Jan. 26, 1946.

12. KAM to CFM, Apr. 26, 1939, KAM Papers, M, "Topeka is my home," and KAM to CFM, Apr. 10, 1940, Historical Notebook, M, "problems which began many years ago."

13. KAM to CFM, Apr. 3, 1940, KAM Papers, M, reassuring the father of his eventual return. KAM to CFM, Apr. 26, 1939, Historical Notebook, M, "the less I tell her." CFM to KAM, n.d. (Apr. 1940), Historical Notebook, M, on the duress experienced due to the son's absence and on his parents' continued support. The same letter points obliquely to Charles's consideration of divorcing his wife; he may have feared visiting Karl in New York out of worry that this topic might come up. CWM, PI by LJF, Topeka, Mar. 5, 1983, recalls Charles vaguely considering divorcing Flo.

14. KAM to Grace Menninger, n.d. (1938), KAM Papers, M. Grace Menninger to KAM, n.d. (1938), KAM Papers, M. Walker Winslow, *The Menninger Story* (Garden City, N.Y., 1956), 255, perceptively noted that Karl's dependence on his mother was at the core of his divorce decision.

15. KAM to Lawson G. Lowrey, June 21, 1927, KAM Papers, M. "I don't think." KAM to Grace Menninger, n.d. (1938), and May 4, 1940, both in KAM Papers, M. Karl recalled these feelings in KAM, PI by LJF, Topeka, Mar. 7, 1983, TRI by LJF, Topeka, Mar. 14, 1986.

16. Josephine Boam, TRI by LJF, Topeka, Feb. 27, 1984; PI, Topeka, Sept. 12, 1985, on Flo calling Karl back to Topeka. FVM to KAM, May 24, 1939, KAM Papers, M, "My world is getting black." FVM to KAM, n.d. (May 1939), KAM Papers, "Menninger name into nothingness." FVM to KAM, Jan. 11, Mar. 24, 1939, Mar. 30, 1940, KAM Papers, M.

17. KAM to FVM, Apr. 7, 1940, KAM Papers, M. Winslow, *Story,* 254, for a penetrating analysis of this moment in Karl's life.

18. WCM to KAM, n.d. (Mar. 1940), KAM Papers, M, supporting Karl. WCM Diary, May 28, 1940, on Karl staying in his home. KAM to Ruth Brunswick, Dec. 31, 1940, KAM Papers, M, on his son in college. KAM, PI by LJF, Topeka, May 21, 1985, on his daughters' problems. FVM Diaries, 1940–41, Jan. 20, 1941, Family Room, M, blaming herself for Karl's decision to divorce.

19. JLM, TRI by LJF, Topeka, June 23, Nov. 11, 1987, on her trip to New York. Roy Lubove, *The Professional Altruist: The Emergence of Social Work as a Career, 1880–1930* (Cambridge, Mass., 1965), 215–16, on Tamblyn and Jones.

20. WCM, "History of the Menninger Foundation," May 5, 1941, H.S. 41, M, and JLM, PI by LJF, Topeka, Mar. 16, Sept. 12, 1985; TRI, June 23, Nov. 11, 1987, on the Tamblyn visit and partners' discussion of his proposal. George O. Tamblyn, "Statement to the Menninger Clinic and Sanitarium," Sept. 29, 1936, H.S. 25, M—his proposal. John Stone to C. C. Burlingame, Oct. 25, 1937, Inst. Archives, M, on becoming like a state hospital. WCM, "History," on his and Karl's postures. Winslow, *Story,* 225, on Charles's posture.

21. Good general background on the origins of these foundations is provided in Barry D. Karl and Stanley N. Katz, "Foundations and Ruling Class Elites," *Daedalus* 116 (Winter 1987): 1–40; Thomas Parrish, "The Foundation: A Special American Institution," in *The Future of Foundations,* Fritz Heimann, ed. (Englewood Cliffs, N.J., 1973), esp. 15. *The Rockefeller Archive Center Newsletter* (Summer 1986), 2, quotes Mrs. Harkness on establishing the Commonwealth Fund.

22. Gerald N. Grob, "Reform or Cooptation: The Creation of the Modern American Medical School," *Reviews in American History* 15 (March 1987): 112, on donations by nine foundations to medical research. Grob, *Mental Institutions and American Society, 1875–1940* (Princeton, 1983), 137–8, on Phipps. Lawrence S. Kubie, *The Riggs Story* (New York, 1960), 126, on Riggs's beginnings as a nonprofit foundation.

23. For tax law changes of the 1930s that encouraged donor foundations, see Robert H. Bremner, *American Philanthropy* (Chicago, 1960), 158–60. Bremner, *Philanthropy*, 157, 195–6, covers the emergence of these foundations and their donation patterns. Raymond B. Fosdick, *The Story of the Rockefeller Foundation* (New York, 1952), 129, on the Medical Sciences Division. Theodore M. Brown, "Alan Gregg and the Rockefeller Foundation's Support of Franz Alexander's Psychosomatic Research," *BHM* 61 (Summer 1987): 158–82, on Chicago Institute support.

24. Resentment over the physician's profits and calls for state assistance during the 1930s is discussed fully in John Burnham, "American Medicine's Golden Age: What Happened to It?" *Science* 215 (Mar. 19, 1982): 1474–8. Thomas N. Bonner, *The Kansas Doctor: A Century of Pioneers* (Lawrence, 1959), 230–2, for the Kansas situation then.

25. WCM, "History of the Foundation, Sept. 9, 1941," 2, Inst. Archives, M, on the proposed nonprofit Southard Corporation. Laura Knickerbocker to KAM, Jan. 30, 1939, H.S. 34, M, on talk of donor money for Southard as early as 1934. JLM, TRI by LJF, Topeka, Jan. 7, 1983, and PI by LJF, Topeka, May 21, 1984, Mar. 16, 1985, Mar. 15, 1986, recalling her early thinking in formulating the Southard nonprofit proposal.

26. "Minutes of Meeting of Bd. of Directors of Menninger School Corporation," July 10, 1936, on the initial rejection of Lyle's conversion proposal. Acceptance and implementation is detailed in "Report of the First Twelve Months of Operations in the Southard School [Corporation]," Aug. 4, 1938, Inst. Records, M; and KAM to Gary C. Myers, Jan. 3, 1938, KAM Papers, M. The Rockefeller grant in "Meeting of Bd. of Directors of the Menninger School Corporation," Aug. 22, 1939, Inst. Records, M. WCM, "History of the Foundation," 2, 9, on the Southard trustees, the Rockefeller grant, and the donation campaign. John Stone to Martin F. Heidgen, Oct. 1, 1937, Inst. Archives, M.

27. John Stone to JLM, Apr. 30, 1938, and "Promotion Activities of 1938," 5 (both in H.S. 31), on John Price Jones. KAM to Ernst Simmel, July 25, 1938, KAM Papers, M. See also KAM to Gary C. Myers, Jan. 3, 1938, KAM Papers, M.

28. WCM, "History of the Menninger Foundation," 2–3, concerning Karl meeting with Finkelstein in New York. KAM to WCM, CFM, John Stone, and Robert Knight, Apr. 12, 1940, H.S. 39, M, on a meeting with Gregg (quoted); KAM to Muriel Shapiro, Apr. 9, 1958, KAM Papers, M, on a 1938 meeting with Gregg and a prior meeting with Finkelstein. KAM to Mildred Law and John Stone, Jan. 5, 1939, Stone Papers, M, on a Gregg visit to Topeka.

29. KAM to John Stone, Jan. 13, 1940, KAM Papers, M. Helen Clapesattle, *The Doctors Mayo* (2nd ed., Minneapolis, 1941), 323, on the beginnings in 1915 of the Mayo Foundation.

30. John Stone, "Interview with Harry Harwick, Feb. 15, 1940," 1–4, Inst. Archives, M, details Harwick's advice on Menninger becoming a nonprofit foundation. Clapesattle, *Mayo*, 590–3, on the 1915–19 Mayo transition from a separate foundation to one controlling all components of the organization.

31. "Agreement, Nov. 30, 1938," H.S. 33, M, on the new ownership arrangements.

32. John Stone to Harry Harwick, Apr. 12, 1940, Inst. Archives, M; JLM, PI by LJF, Topeka, Mar. 15, 1986.

33. WCM, "Kansas State Medical Society Meeting, Wichita, Kansas—May 14, 15, 1940," H.S. 39, M, on Will's meeting with Harwick. JLM, PI by LJF, Topeka, Mar. 1, 1984, Mar. 15, 1986, on Will being persuaded on Harwick's first step. WCM to Irving

Harris, May 6, 1952, RWM Papers, Tower Bldg., M, recalling the pledge of his former patient.

34. KAM to WCM, CFM, John Stone, Robert Knight, Apr. 12, 1940, H.S. 39, M, "People are not interested" and "perfectly logical." "Exec. Comm. Meeting, June 25, 1940," Law Papers, M, recommending foundation status. KAM, PI by LJF, Topeka, May 25, 1984, on consulting Finkelstein and Brunswick. Winslow, *Story,* 255–6, on Foundation creation in 1941.

35. FVM, *Days of My Life: Memories of a Kansas Mother and Teacher* (New York, 1939), vii–ix.

36. KAM to FVM, CFM, and Pearl Boam, Aug. 21, 1939, KAM Papers, M, on covering the period to Will's birth. FVM to KAM, Sept. 23, 1939, FVM Papers, Family Room, M. KAM to EAM, Oct. 28, 1939, FVM Papers, on the chapters Edwin and Karl revised. FVM to KAM, Nov. 13, 1939, FVM Papers, on avoiding Edwin's divorce.

37. KAM to EAM, Oct. 28, 1939, FVM Papers, M, on Karl taking charge of the publication effort and finances. FVM to "Dear Folks," Jan. 28, 1940, FVM Papers, on being diverted by Karl's book notices. EAMJr., TRI by LJF, Lillington, Aug. 18, 1985, on his father's and Karl's rationalization for the book's poor sales.

38. KAM to CFM, Jan. 1, 1940, Historical Notebook, M. KAM, "Mss. on History of Menninger Clinic" (1940), H.S. 8, M, on the history he envisioned. Verne Horne, "History of Museum and Archives," Aug. 1982, 1, unfiled, M.

39. Alice Dangerfield to LJF, Apr. 9, 1986 (letter), recounts in great detail working with Charles on the history and his minimal enthusiasm. See also Dangerfield to WCM, Dec. 9, 1942, H.S. 43, M.

40. KAM to Smith Ely Jelliffe, Dec. 4, 1941, KAM Papers, M. "Statement of Dr. Karl Menninger to Group of 40 Selected Employees," Feb. 17, 1941, KAM Papers, M, and a recollection of that meeting in Peggy Ralston Shelton, TRI by Irving Sheffel, Topeka, Jan. 15, 1983. KAM to John Whitehorn, Feb. 24, 1942, KAM Papers, M.

41. KAM to Grace Menninger, Jan. 4, 1940, KAM Papers, M, on Hamilton pressing for a $100,000 settlement. KAM to Maurice Finkelstein, Nov. 1, 1942, KAM Papers, M, on off-color jokes. See also KAM to Mary O'Neil Hawkins, Feb. 24, 1944, and Hawkins to KAM, May 25, 1944, both in the Hawkins Papers, Brill Library, NYPsa.

42. KAM to Ruth Brunswick, July 1, 1940, on the money demands of Grace's attorney; Dec. 31, 1940, "suffering womanhood" and "beautiful relationship"; Apr. 18, 1941, "nasty cracks"; Oct. 28, 1942, on the effect of the analysis and the divorce on relations with his children; Aug. 23, 1941, "jittery and ambivalent"; all in KAM Papers, M.

43. Josephine Boam, TRI by LJF, Topeka, Sept. 12, 1985, on divorce news in the newspapers on Martha's birthday. Olga Weiss, TRI by Verne Horne, Topeka, n.d., M, on staff cutting out newspaper notices of the divorce. CWM, PI by LJF, Topeka, July 30, 1984, on physicians' wives fearing their husbands might run off with secretaries. Harlan Crank, PI by LJF, Austin, Nov. 22, 1985, on Topeka physician ostracism. G. L. Harrington, Jr., TRI by LJF, Los Angeles, May 11, 1984, on depriving Karl of office in the APA.

44. Information on Karl's immediate family after the divorce in RGM, PI by LJF, Topeka, Feb. 27, 1984; EAMJr., TRI by LJF, Lillington, Aug. 18, 1985; Josephine Boam, TRI by LJF, Topeka, Sept. 12, 1985; KAM to Ruth Brunswick, Sept. 19, Nov. 19, 1942, KAM Papers, M; KAM to Martha Menninger, Mar. 13, 1942, KAM Papers, M; KAM, "Comments on *The Menninger Story,*" June 12, 1980, KAM Papers, M.

45. KAM to CWM, Aug. 5, 1970, WCM Papers (private), on Will revering Grace. WCM Diary, Dec. 31, 1941, on the remarriage bringing Karl happiness. CWM, PI by LJF, Topeka, Sept. 10, 1985, on her ambivalence. KAM to WCM, July 28, 1944, WCM Papers (private), "affection" and "loyalty." For postures of all members of the wider Menninger family, see Josephine Boam, TRI by LJF, Topeka, Sept. 12, 1985, and EAMJr., TRI by LJF, Lillington, Aug. 17, 18, 1985. Basil Cole, TRI by LJF, Topeka, May 31, 1983, on Ben Boam's "blackmail" file. CFM to KAM, n.d. (Apr. 1940), KAM Papers, M, on EAMJr.

46. FVM to WCM, Apr. 2, 1944, WCM Papers (private), "can't get them." See also Josephine Boam, TRI by LJF, Topeka, Sept. 12, 1985, and EAMJr., TRI by LJF, Lillington, Aug. 17, 1985.

47. Virginia Eicholtz, TRI by LJF, Topeka, Jan. 9, 1985, for the perception of a neighbor who often visited Flo after the divorce. FVM, "Mother's Day, 1944," May 1944, "nothing definite." FVM to KAM, Mar. 13, 1940, FVM Papers, M, "filling the days." KAM, TI by Harold Maine, Topeka, Aug. 20, 1952, 14, M, on the day before Flo died.

48. KAM, "Diaries—Appointment Books (1933–63)," Feb. 9, 1945, KAM Papers, M; *TPR* 13 (Oct. 15, 1952): i; Loraine Nuzman to Olga Weiss, Mar. 1, 1945, WCM Papers, M; KAM to Ella W. Brown, Feb. 17, 1945, KAM Papers, M.

49. Winslow, *Story,* 280–1, on Charles's response to the death. Phillip B. Menninger Diary, Feb. 9, 1940, Phillip Menninger Papers, Family Room, M, on Will's response. KAM to Ruth Mack Brunswick, Feb. 17, 1945, KAM Papers, M. See also KAM, "Days of Her Life," *TPR* 6 (Feb. 16, 1945): 12. Josephine Boam, TRI by LJF, Topeka, Sept. 12, 1985, on the drinking and smoking after the funeral. FVM, *Days,* 52–3, on her father's funeral.

50. Winslow, *Story,* 255–6.

51. "Executive Committee Meeting," July 21, 1943, Law Papers, M, for a report by Merle Hoover of substantial wartime profits. "Board of Trustees Meeting," Oct. 12, 1943, S-73, Inst. Archives, M, for Karl's report.

52. John Stone, "Mental Illness is a National Problem," Sept. 7, 1944, H.S. 47, M.

53. WCM to KAM, John Stone, et al., July 23, 1944, WCM Papers (private).

54. KAM to Smith Ely Jelliffe, Oct. 27, 1944, KAM Papers, M; KAM to Ruth Brunswick, Sept. 11, 1944, unfiled, M; KAM to WCM, July 28, 1944, WCM Papers (private); KAM, "Report of the President" to trustees annual meeting, Oct. 24, 1944, 13, Inst. Archives, M., "We should be training."

55. KAM, WCM, John Stone, "To the Menninger Foundation, Oct. 27, 1944," H.S. 48, M, deed of assets. KAM, "Report of the President," Oct. 24, 1944, Inst. Archives, M, "renouncing all ownership" and "most convenient." Robert Knight, "Report of the Secretary for 1945–46," n.d., 1, Inst. Archives, M, and John Stone to Mildred Law, June 5, 1946, Law Papers, M, on the dates legal absorption occurred.

56. "Menninger Foundation Board of Trustees & Executive Committee Minutes," I (1941–45), 101, 103, 107, 120–1, MT, on transfer of sanitarium stock to the foundation. KAM to Harold Maine, July 7, 1954, KAM Papers, M, "every penny."

57. For Karl working to circumscribe the new board of trustees, see Norman Reider, TRI by LJF, San Francisco, Dec. 28, 1983; "Trustees Meeting," Oct. 7, 1947, 1–2, Inst. Archives, M. Robert Knight to KAM, Sept. 20, 1945, RPK Papers (private), "to remain as the 'boss.' "

58. KAM to Ruth Brunswick, Feb. 17, 1945, and KAM to Jill Brunswick, Apr. 7,

1945, both in KAM Papers, M; KAM, "Days of Her Life," *TPR* 6 (Feb. 16, 1945): 12.

59. CWM, PI by LJF, Topeka, July 30, 1984, on the Jeanetta-Karl relationship and how it influenced her. KAM, *Love Against Hate* (New York, 1942), viii, "collaborating author." WCM Diary, Dec. 31, 1951, on Catharine's new role.

60. EAMJr., TRI by LJF, Lillington, Aug. 17, 1985, on the marriages of Karl's children. General data on the adoption of Rosemary in "Baby," n.d., plus Mary Hawkins to KAM and JLM, Apr. 7, 1948, JLM to Hawkins, Apr. 14, 1948, all in Brill Library, NYPsa. KAM to B. Jelliffe, Jan. 11, 1949, KAM Papers, M.

61. Bernard H. Hall, ed., *A Psychiatrist for a Troubled World: Selected Papers of William C. Menninger* (New York, 1967), I, xvi–xvii, on Will's army career. Lester Roach, PI by LJF, Topeka, Mar. 9, 1983, on Will's job offers (like Pittsburgh) and on leaving the army. WCM Diary, Sept. 22, 1945, on a particularly attractive job offer.

62. KAM, "A Psychiatrist Replies," *Christian Century*, Aug. 23, 1944, boasting of Will in the army. CWM, PI by LJF, Topeka, Sept. 10, 1985, on her letters to Karl during the war demanding that Will be treated differently.

63. KAM to WCM, June 22, 1943, July 28, 1944, both in WCM Papers (private).

64. WCM to FVM, CFM, and Pearl Boam, Dec. 19, 1944, KAM Papers, M; Loraine Nuzman to WCM, Mar. 5, 1946, WCM Papers, M.

65. WCM Diary, Apr. 22, Dec. 8, 1949; Aug. 23, 1951, Sept. 9, 1953; CWM, PI by LJF, Topeka, July 30, 1984, Mar. 9, 1985. Julia Gottesman, TRI by LJF, Los Angeles, Jan. 3, 1984.

66. WCM to KAM, John Stone, et al., July 23, 1944, WCM Papers (private). WCM to Dayton J. Edwards, Jan. 5, 1948, WCM Papers, M. For Karl's pressure on his son, see KAM to RGM, Nov. 21, 1947, and KAM to Douglas Bond, Nov. 21, 1947, both in Family Room, M.

67. For the early 1940s Charles-Pearl relation, see Josephine Boam, TRI by LJF, Topeka, Sept. 12, 1985; EAMJr., TRI by LJF, Lillington, Aug. 17, 1985. For the two traveling together, see FVM Diaries, June 30, 1948, FVM Papers, M; CFM to KAM and JLM, Dec. 13, 1945, H.S. 51, M.

68. Leo Bartemeier, TRI by Verne Horne, Topeka, Sept. 23, 1975, M; Virginia Eicholtz, TRI by LJF, Topeka, Jan. 9, 1985; Winslow, *Story,* 306.

69. Josephine Boam, TRI by LJF, Topeka, Feb. 27, 1984, Sept. 12, 1985; EAMJr., TRI by LJF, Lillington, Aug. 17, 1985; Winslow, *Story,* 307.

70. Josephine Boam, TRI by LJF, Topeka, Sept. 12, 1985; JLM, PI by LJF, Topeka, Mar. 15, 1986; CWM, PI by LJF, Topeka, Mar. 14, 1986.

71. CWM to "Dear Folks" (Mr. & Mrs. Roy Wright), June 20, 1948 (copy in possession of Josephine Boam); Josephine Boam, TRI by LJF, Topeka, Feb. 27, 1984, Sept. 12, 1985; WCM Diary, June 15, 1948; CWM, TI by Verne Horne, Topeka, Jan. 17, 1974, M.

72. CWM to "Dear Folks," June 20, 1948; CWM, PI by LJF, Topeka, Mar. 14, 1986.

73. Josephine Boam, TRI by LJF, Topeka, Feb. 27, 1984; CWM, PI by LJF, Topeka, Mar. 14, 1986; WCM Diary, June 11, 1947, May 23, 1953.

CHAPTER SEVEN: *Education and Pluralism*

1. KAM to George A. Elliott, Aug. 1, 1945, KAM Papers, M.

2. Gerald N. Grob, *Mental Illness and American Society, 1875–1940* (Princeton, 1983), 284, on 1930s warnings by the National Committee for Mental Hygiene. Raymond B.

Fosdick, *The Story of the Rockefeller Foundation* (New York, 1952), 130, on Medical Science Division grants. Leland V. Bell, *Treating the Mentally Ill: From Colonial Times to the Present* (New York, 1980), 150–1, and Robert R. Holt and Lester Luborsky, *Personality Patterns of Psychiatrists: A Study of Methods for Selecting Residents* (New York, 1958), I, 8, on World War II producing new patient populations and a need for psychiatric personnel. KAM to Mildred Law and John Stone, Jan. 5, 1939, Stone Papers, M; KAM to Harvey J. Tompkins, Mar. 12, 1948, KAM Papers; and KAM, TRI by Frederick Hacker, Topeka, Apr. 18, 1971, show Karl understanding fully about the new funding sources, patient clientele, and personnel shortages.

3. KAM, TRI by LJF, Topeka, Mar. 15, 1986.

4. KAM to John Stone and Mildred Law, Jan. 5, 1939, KAM Papers, M.

5. Jeanne L. Brand, "The National Mental Health Act of 1946: A Retrospect," *BHM* 39 (May–June 1965): 236–7; Gerald N. Grob, "Psychiatry and Social Activism: The Politics of Specialty in Postwar America," *BHM* 60 (Fall 1986): 478.

6. Wartime neuropsychiatric troop casualties are discussed in Bernard Hall, ed., *A Psychiatrist for a Troubled World: Selected Papers of William C. Menninger, M.D.* (New York, 1967), II, 530. Walter E. Barton, "Advances in Administration in Psychiatry During the Past Fifty Years," in *Hope—Psychiatry's Commitment,* A.W.R. Sipe, ed. (New York, 1970), 251–2. Grob, *BHM* 60, 478. JLM, "To the Members of the Foundation," Jan. 27, 1944, Inst. Archives, M.

7. KAM, PI by LJF, Topeka, Nov. 9, 1982, on the war experience and his continuum concept. Will wrote much on army psychiatric reorganization during the war; see, e.g., "Psychiatric Experience in the War, 1941–1946," *AJP* 103 (Mar. 1947): 577–86; "Psychiatric Problems in the Army," *JAMA* 123 (Nov. 20, 1943): 751–4; the first part of his *Psychiatry in a Troubled World* (New York, 1948).

8. In "A Critique of Psychiatry," *AJP* 101 (Nov. 1944): 287, Alan Gregg notes his rapport with Karl. Brand, *BHM 39,* 231–45, remains the definitive study of the precedents for and the drafting of the 1946 National Mental Health Act.

9. KAM to William A. White, Jan. 23, 1928, Records of St. Elizabeths Hospital, NA, record group 418, reveals Karl's earliest interest in federal cooperation and support. KAM to James C. Magee, Jan. 29, 1941, KAM Papers, M. KAM to John Whitehorn, Feb. 24, 1942, KAM Papers, M, on the three-year residency. KAM to Harry M. Woodring, July 15, 1942, H.S. 43, M, and KAM to Sanford Larkey, Feb. 17, 1943, Inst. Archives, M, urging the army to invest in Menninger training.

10. Executive Committee meeting, Jan. 2, June 9, 1943, Mildred Law Papers, Inst. Archives, M; KAM to John Porter, Jan. 14, 1943, KAM Papers, M; KAM to WCM, June 25, 1943, WCM Papers (private); KAM to Sanford V. Larkey, Mar. 11, 1943, KAM Papers, M. KAM to Jack Sherwood, May 18, 1943, KAM Papers, M. The November proposal of a "school" with foundation support is noted in KAM to Malcolm J. Farrell, Nov. 19, 1943, KAM Papers, M. It was hastily suggested in KAM to Harlan Crank et al., Oct. 27, 1943, WCM Papers (private).

11. KAM, "Report of the President," Oct. 12, 1943, H.S. 45, M, to the foundation trustees. KAM to Leo H. Bartemeier, Oct. 7, 1944, TIP Papers, Inst. Archives, M, on the duty of the APA. *Rochester* (Minn.) *Post Bulletin,* Mar. 9, 1945, for Karl's proclamation on daily discharge rates.

12. WCM Diary, Dec. 1945 ("Major Events of the Year"), on the importance for Karl of the ETO trip. *Topeka State Journal,* Dec. 7, 1945, quotes Karl on treating veterans regardless of their social class.

13. *Topeka State Journal,* Nov. 4, 1946, and Walker Winslow, *The Menninger Story* (New

York, 1956), 284–5, on the VA under Hines and the muckraking exposé of its hospitals. KAM to Albert Deutsch, Jan. 16, 1945, KAM Papers, M, on the Hines VA ignoring his pleas.

14. Bell, *Treating*, 152, 158, and Paul Haun and Z. M. Lebenson, "New Trends in Hospital Design," *AJP* 114 (Feb. 1948): 555, on new VA leadership and its psychiatric commitment. See also KAM, "A Brief Survey of Psychiatric Training in V.A. Hospitals" (1952), 1, Inst. Archives, M; *Topeka State Journal,* Jan. 24, 1946; *Army Times,* Dec. 8, 1945, in H.S. 51, M.

15. KAM to Paul R. Hawley, Sept. 5, 1945, KAM Papers, M, proposing Winter as a training center. For the views of a Washington VA office employee at the time on Karl's initial impact upon Hawley and Bradley, see Irving Sheffel, PI by LJF, Topeka, July 28, 1982. Winslow, *Story,* 286–8 on Hawley's tentative decision to close Winter. Sylvia Marshall, TRI by LJF, Jan. 1, 1984, Woodland Hills, Calif., on Bradley as well as Hawley promoting Marshall's Topeka trip.

16. Maimon Leavitt, TRI by LJF, Los Angeles, Dec. 25, 1983. See "The Topeka Mystique," 21–2 (session transcript), American Psychoanalytic Association, Puerto Rico, 1981, on the Leavitt-Marshall connection.

17. Karl recalled the October 1945 meeting with Marshall in KAM to Arthur Marshall, Mar. 6, 1964, AM Papers (private); KAM, PI by LJF, Topeka, Nov. 19, 1982, May 21, 1984. Marshall's recollection is in "1964 Annual Meeting," Board of Governors, 2–4, AM Papers (private), and "Minutes of 24th Annual Meeting of Bd. of Trustees and Governors," Oct. 3–4, 1964, MT.

18. Gregory G. Yardley, "The Relation of Dr. Karl Menninger to the Inception of Winter General V.A. Hospital" (B.A. paper, Washburn University, 1969), 8, on Marshall's initial meeting with Hawley and Bradley. JLM to Alice Dangerfield, Nov. 20, 1945, KAM Papers, M, on Wadsworth Hospital.

19. KAM to B. C. Moore, July 7, 1948, KAM Papers, M; KAM, PI by LJF, Topeka, Sept. 29, 1983; and "1964 Annual Meeting," 4, on Hawley's accord with Karl.

20. WCM to KAM, Feb. 7, 1944, WCM Papers (private); KAM to Arthur Capper, May 28, 1943, H.S. 45, M; Education Committee Meeting, Sept. 28, 1945, 1, Inst. Archives, M; Thomas Dolgoff, TRI by LJF, Topeka, Jan. 4, 1983; Julius Schrieber, PI by LJF, Bowling Green, Ohio, Apr. 22, 1983; WCM to James W. Duckworth, July 14, 1945, KAM Papers, M, on Will's interest in Winter Hospital and his subtle representation of the foundation. CWM, PI by LJF, Topeka, Nov. 8, 1982, on Will informing Hawley of the Menninger training program. WCM to KAM, Sept. 7, 1945, WCM Papers (private) on VA job offer. Winslow, *Story,* 288, on Will's apprehensions over the extent of the pledge to Winter. See also WCM to KAM, Sept. 7, 1945, WCM Papers (private).

21. Lillabelle Stahl, TRI by Irving Sheffel, Topeka, Feb. 24, 1983, on the sanitarium staff apprehension of the VA accord. KAM to WCM, July 3, 1956, CFM Papers, M, on Rapaport's strong initial opposition to the accord. Robert P. Knight to KAM, Sept. 20, 1945, RPK Papers (private), "fool's Paradise." See also John Stone to WCM, Jan. 9, 1947, KAM Papers, M.

22. KAM to Naomi and Maurice Finkelstein, Dec. 20, 1945, KAM Papers, M, on temporary resignation. Details on the transition from an army to a VA hospital are in John Stone, "The Menninger Institutions Merge Assets into the Menninger Foundation," Jan. 30, 1946, H.S. 52, 3–4, M.

23. Herbert C. Modlin, "Contributions of the Menninger School of Psychiatry to

Psychiatric Education," *BMC* 47 (May 1983): 255, 257; "Topeka Mystique," 31; Lewis Robbins, TRI by LJF, New York, Aug. 23, 1983.

24. Holt and Luborsky, *Personality Patterns,* 19; KAM, PI by LJF, Topeka, Sept. 29, 1983; "J. F. Casey, A Remembrance," June 1972, 1, in Daniel Blain Papers, APA; "Experience with the Psychiatric Residency Program at Winter V.A. Hospital from January 1946 to April 1952," 1, Robert Holt Papers, AHAP.

25. Eric F. Goldman, *The Crucial Decade—and After, 1945–1960* (enl. ed., New York, 1960), 13–14, on postwar public expectations and planning efforts. "Minutes of the Executive Committee," Nov. 28, 1945, 3, MT, "mother of everything."

26. Thomas Bonner, *The Kansas Doctor: A Century of Pioneering* (Lawrence, 1959), 277, on MSP training half of all VA residents in 1946. Quantitative data on MSP residency applications and actual residents in "The Selection of Candidates for Training in Psychiatry: Philosophy and Methods," *BMC* 11 (May 1947): 83; Albert Deutsch, "Vets Bureau Launches New Program for 'Psycho' Cases," *P.M.*, Jan. 22, 1946, H.S. 52, M; KAM to Albert Deutsch, Jan. 25, 1946, H.S. 52, M. "J. F. Casey, A Remembrance," 5–6, notes mistakes in 1946 residency selection and two suicides. Harlan Crank telephone interview by LJF, June 8, 1987, cited three suicides and heard, as Menninger staff physician, that there were more. Lester Luborsky, codirector of the MSP Selection Project, claimed as many as eleven suicides for 1946 (Luborsky, PI by LJF, Philadelphia, Apr. 4, 1987). "Education Committee Meeting," MSP, July 13, 1946, M, 1, on the 1946 suicides. Robert P. Knight, "To Members of the Foundation," May 29, 1946, H.S. 54, M, on MSP proportion of all residents. *Kansas City Star,* May 4, 1947, on MSP share of American psychiatric residents.

27. Holt and Luborsky, *Personality Patterns,* 21, and *Topeka State Journal,* Sept. 12, 1946, on Winter as pilot VA hospital. Richard M. Restak, "Psychiatry in America," *Wilson Quarterly* (Autumn 1983), 110, on new NIMH funding.

28. Edith Beck, "The Development of a Social Work Program at the Winter Veterans Administration," *BMC* 11 (Nov. 1947): 208; "Coordinating Programs for Psychologists, Nurses, Social Workers, and Others," *BMC* 11 (May 1947): 107–8.

29. Albert R. Gilgen, *American Psychology Since World War II: A Profile of the Discipline* (Westport, Conn., 1982), 177, on VA and Public Health Service funding; "School of Clinical Psychology," Aug. 1947, 1–3, Inst. Archives, M; "J. F. Casey, A Remembrance," 8; *Topeka Daily Capital,* June 15, Oct. 22, 1946; Margaret Brenman to Bert Boothe, Apr. 17, 1946, Inst. Archives, M.

30. The Boothe appointment is detailed and analyzed in Sibylle Escalona, TRI by LJF, New York, Nov. 7, 1983; TPR 6 (Oct. 5, 1945): 1; *Topeka Daily Capital,* May 5, 1946; May 24, 1950.

31. For data on Marshall's role, see Sylvia Marshall, TRI by LJF, Woodland Hills, Calif., Jan. 1, 1984; *Topeka State Journal,* Jan. 24, 1946; and esp. Rudolf Ekstein, "Arthur Marshall, M.D.: Happy Rebel with an Established Cause, 1911–1971," AM Papers (private).

32. "J. F. Casey, A Remembrance," 10; *Hospitals* 22 (Aug. 1948), H.S. 66; KAM to R. H. Felix, July 30, 1930, KAM Papers, M.

33. Marshall in "1964 Annual Meeting," AM Papers (private), on the vacated Oklahoma hospital. Winslow, *Story,* 299, on Karl disregarding *Rules and Procedures.* Marshall in *Topeka State Journal,* Jan. 26, 1946, on cutting red tape. See also KAM, PI by LJF, Topeka, Sept. 29, 1983, on the breaches of VA requirements. Harold Maine to Robert Holt, Aug. 24, 1953, Holt Papers, AHAP, on federal officials out to "get" Winter.

34. Thomas Dolgoff, TRI by LJF, Topeka, Jan. 4, 1983. The freeze of 1947 in VA hospitals is noted in KAM to Omar N. Bradley, Mar. 6, 1947, and Bradley to KAM, Mar. 17, 1947, both in H.S. 58, M; KAM to Mary Switzer, Sept. 9, 1947, and KAM to Harvey J. Tompkins, Mar. 12, 1948, both in KAM Papers, M.

35. VA cuts and their impact on Winter are noted in *Kansas City Times,* Mar. 25, 1950; "Notes on Chapter 3," 1, in Holt Papers, AHAP; Martin Mayman, TRI by LJF, Ann Arbor, Apr. 27, 1983. KAM to WCM, June 15, 1954, KAM Papers, M, "mediocrities" and "a lifeless bureaucracy."

36. "Education Committee Meeting, Winter General Hospital," Mar. 23, 1946, 1, Inst. Archives, M, reporting Karl's discussion with Knight and the Education Committee over admitting the black resident. KAM, PI by LJF, Topeka, Sept. 12, 1985, on the Grey Ladies. WCM to Sol Ginsberg, Sept. 7, 1946, WCM Papers, M, and *Washington Post,* Apr. 10, 1946, concerning the eventual admission of the black resident.

37. Richard Kluger, *Simple Justice: The History of Brown v. Board of Education and Black America's Struggle for Equality* (New York, 1976), I, final chapter, "The Menninger Connection," represents a very comprehensive treatment of the Menninger role in the Brown case. See especially 419, 427, on Karl's role in the litigation and "did not wish to involve" remark. See also Joan and Edward Greenwood, TRI by LJF, Topeka, Nov. 10, 1982, and Sydney Smith, PI by LJF, Topeka, June 23, 1987.

38. KAM to WCM, Sept. 30, 1947, Inst. Archives, M, on the MSP nominee. KAM to Mary Switzer, Sept. 9, 1947, KAM Papers, M, "gestapoing," etc. Eli Feldman to KAM, May 14, 1949, and KAM to Eli Feldman, May 18, 1949, both in KAM Papers, M, represent Karl's correspondence with the accused Winter intern. KAM to Mary Switzer, Apr. 29, 1952, MT, on the European doctor. See also KAM and JLM, PI by LJF, Topeka, Sept. 12, 1985, noting that Karl was on good terms with FBI officials investigating Winter doctors while he spoke well of the doctors. Julius Schrieber, PI by LJF, Bowling Green, Ohio, Apr. 22, 1983, on Will (not Karl) offering to be his character witness during the McCarthy period.

39. Holt and Luborsky, *Personality Patterns,* 36, on the marital status and average age of the early MSP residents. "The Students Educational Committee, Winter V.A.," Apr. 13, 1946, 2, in Inst. Archives, M, statement of the fellows. Lester Luborsky, "Selecting Psychiatric Residents: Survey of the Topeka Research," *BMC* 18 (Nov. 1954): 257, also found the fellows impatient and pressed. KAM to Bert E. Boothe, May 6, 1948, Inst. Archives, M, on pressures for psychotherapy for staff. Lester Luborsky, PI by LJF, Philadelphia, Apr. 4, 1987, on resident suicides and on the beginnings of the Selection Project. Harlan Crank, PI by LJF (telephone), June 8, 1987, on heavy and rapid exposure to psychotic patients as contributing to fellows' suicides.

40. Social characteristics of the early residents in Holt and Luborsky, *Personality Patterns,* 38, and Kay S. Hymowitz, ed., *The Spirit Unconsumed: A History of the Topeka Jewish Community* (Topeka, 1979), 63. George Klein to Martin Mayman, Apr. 8, 1953, Klein Papers, AHAP, "Yidlack." Marilyn Barnard, TRI by LJF, Los Angeles, Jan. 2, 1984, "the sinkhole." Lucy Freeman, ed., *Sparks* (New York, 1973), 161, "imported lots of foreigners." Problems of fellows living in Topeka are discussed in Maimon Leavitt, TRI by LJF, Los Angeles, Jan. 2, 1984; William R. Robinson, PI by LJF, Topeka, May 16, 1985; Jerome Katz, TRI by LJF, Topeka, Mar. 10, 1983. Sylvia Marshall, TRI by LJF, Woodland Hills, Calif., Jan. 1, 1984, on lox and bagels.

41. The living situation in the former army barracks is noted in Rosalee T. Lewis, "The First History of the Winter Wives' Club" (unpub. ms., 1954), 6, Inst. Archives, M; Peter Fleming, TRI by Verne Horne, Topeka, Dec. 3, 1974, M; William Rotters-

man, TRI by LJF, Atlanta, Mar. 26, 1983; William Robinson, PI by LJF, Topeka, May 12, May 16, 1985. Gerald Aronson, TRI by LJF, Los Angeles, Dec. 26, 1983, notes how barracks residency forged bonds between psychiatric residents and psychologists.

42. "Winter Wives and the Community Nursery School," n.d., Holt Papers, AHAP; Rosalee T. Lewis, "The First History of the Winter Wives' Club"; KAM to Julia Gottesman, Jan. 9, 1952, KAM Papers, on "Jewish Winter Wives."

43. Kluger, *Simple Justice*, 391; Hymowitz, *Spirit Unconsumed*, 64; Irving Sheffel, PI by LJF, Topeka, July 27, 1984.

44. The exciting and open-ended intellectual milieu at early Winter is recalled by George L. Harrington, TRI by LJF, Los Angeles, Jan. 4, 1984; William R. Robinson, PI by LJF, Topeka, May 12, 1985; Irving and Ruth Kartus, TRI by Irving Sheffel, Leawood, Kans., Apr. 3, 1983; Milton Wexler, TRI by LJF, Los Angeles, Dec. 24, 1983; Peter D. Fleming, "Fond Memories of Topeka in 1946," *Alumni Association Bulletin* 8 (Aug. 1957): 2.

45. Early MSP classroom teaching is recalled in William R. Robinson, PI by LJF, Topeka, May 12, 1985; Maimon Leavitt, TRI by LJF, Los Angeles, Dec. 25, 1983; William B. Spriegel, TRI by LJF, Winnetka, Ill., Feb. 4, 1984; James R. Hodge, TRI by LJF, Akron, Jan. 12, 1984. See also Rudolf Ekstein to Robert Holt and Lester Luborsky, Oct. 21, 1947, Holt Papers, AHAP. The pressure to shift to seminar or conference style is noted in Tom Devine to WCM, Aug. 22, 1949, Inst. Archives, M, and WCM, "Report to Trustees and Governors," Sept. 17, 1951, 2, Inst. Archives, M.

46. "Notes for Chapter 3," 20, in Holt Papers, AHAP; "The Didactic Curriculum," *BMC* 11 (May 1947): 95; "Experience with the Psychiatric Residency Program at Winter V.A. Hospital from January 1946 to April 1952," 5, Holt Papers, AHAP.

47. "Notes for Chapter 3," 3, 22, in Holt Papers, AHAP; Lewis Robbins to Bert E. Boothe, May 12, 1947, Inst. Archives, M; Petition to the MSP, Aug. 15, 1946, Inst. Archives, M, "Minutes of Executive Committee, Division of Psychiatry and Neurology," Jan. 22, 1949, 2, Inst. Archives, M; Modlin, *BMC* 47, 258–9, recalls that it was not until the early 1950s that comprehensive testing of the knowledge that MSP residents assimilated came into being.

48. "Experience with the Psychiatric Residency Program at Winter V.A. Hospital from January 1946 to April 1952," 2–3, in Holt Papers, AHAP; George L. Harrington, TRI by LJF, Los Angeles, Jan. 4, 1984; and "J. F. Casey, A Remembrance," 2, on residents with administrative posts and relative autonomy for residents on the wards. H. C. Modlin to J. F. Casey, Mar. 26, 1948, Inst. Archives, M, on residents "left too much to their own devices" and lack of supervision on the wards producing deficiencies in patient care. See also "Annual Report of M.S.P., July 1, 1949–June 30, 1950," Inst. Archives, M, and Gerald Aronson, TRI by LJF, Los Angeles, Dec. 26, 1983, on efforts to increase supervision. Robert Holt and Lester Luborsky, "Research in the Selection of Psychiatrists: A Second Interim Report," *BMC* 16 (July 1952): 134, on relative independence of proficient student clinicians.

49. William Robinson, TRI by LJF, Topeka, May 16, 1985; Maimon and Peggy Leavitt, TRI by LJF, Los Angeles, Jan. 2, 1984; Lewis, "Winter Wives' Club"; George L. Harrington, TRI by LJF, Los Angeles, Jan. 4, May 11, 1984, on the centrality of Freudian theory to the residents. Peter Fleming, "Fond Memories of Topeka in 1956," *Alumni Association Bulletin*, Apr. 1957, 3, on "with" and "without" rest rooms. MSP Education Committee Meeting, Nov. 29, 1950, 1, WCM Papers, M, on Karl noting the MSP ban on analysis of Winter patients.

50. Marvin A. Klemes, TRI by LJF, Los Angeles, Jan. 4, 1984; John R. Adams and William B. Spriegel, TRI by LJF, Winnetka, Ill., Feb. 4, 1984; "Topeka Mystique," 53.

51. KAM to Kurt Lewin, Apr. 10, 1946, KAM Papers, M, on supply and demand for training analysts. Richard Rich Associates, "Report on the Menninger Foundation," June 1948, 22, Inst. Archives, M, on the situation in 1948. Luborsky and Holt, *Personality Patterns*, 72, 173, on the 36 percent applicant decline in 1949.

52. Harlan Crank, PI by LJF, Austin, Nov. 22, 1985, elaborated the "pimp and whore" characterization, particularly on candidate selections. Luborsky, PI by LJF, Philadelphia, Apr. 4, 1987, on his research on TIP selections; he stressed the politics of personality for the late 1940s and early 1950s.

53. Henry Zukier, "Freud and Development: The Developmental Dimensions of Psychoanalytic Theory," *Social Research* 52 (Spring 1985): 40, for cogent discussion of the interminable nature of orthodox Freudian analysis. See also David Kairys, "The Training Analysis: A Critical Review of the Literature and a Controversial Proposal," *PQ* 33 (Oct. 1964): 489–501. Robert Wallerstein, "Reflections About Psychiatry, Psychoanalysis, and Research at the Menninger Foundation," Aug. 5, 1965, esp. 11, Lester Roach Papers, M, suggesting that Topeka was not immune from the pervasive training analysis problems. Luborsky, PI by LJF, Philadelphia, Apr. 4, 1987, concurs with Wallerstein.

54. John R. Adams, TRI by LJF, Winnetka, Ill., Feb. 4, 1984, recalling discussion with Will early in the 1950s concerning the transient labor pool of low-salaried MSP trainees and junior staff that training analysis helped to facilitate. L. T. Roach to Executive Committee, Mar. 23, 1966, Roach Papers, M, echoed that point. George S. Klein to David Rapaport, Sept. 27, 1949, Klein Papers, AHAP, "all of that delicious poison." There is considerable literature underscoring the tendency of the analysand to propagate the views of his training analyst. See, e.g., Frank J. Sulloway, "Freud as Conquistador," *New Republic*, Aug. 25, 1979, 30, and Rosemary Dinnage, "Psycho-Mom," *New York Review of Books* 33 (May 8, 1986): 18, both quoting the warnings of Edward Glover. Kairys, *PQ* 33, 486, quoting Anna Freud's warning. A great many former Menninger staff close to the training analysis process during the late 1940s and early 1950s underscored its "infantilizing" and "dependency"-building qualities at TIP and the propensity of the MSP student analysand to follow the workplace postures of his analyst. Howard Shevrin, TRI by LJF, Ann Arbor, Sept. 16, 1983, stated this strongly. Lewis Robbins to members of Medical Council, Mar. 24, 1951, Inst. Archives, is more general but perhaps also more persuasive. See also Leonard Duhl, PI by LJF (telephone), Mar. 16, 1987; William R. Robinson, PI by LJF, Topeka, May 12, 1985; George L. Harrington, TRI by LJF, Los Angeles, Jan. 4, 1984. There is also advantage in reading closely Luborsky and Holt, "The Selection of Candidates for Psychoanalytic Training: Implications from Research on the Selection of Psychiatric Residents," *Journal of Clinical Experimental Psychopathology* 18 (June 1957): 166–76. Finally, Lester Luborsky to KAM, July 1, 1952 (memo in possession of Luborsky), concerns excluding analysands from research projects.

55. Robert Jay Lifton, *Thought Reform and the Psychology of Totalism: A Study of "Brainwashing" in China* (New York, 1961), 448–9, reports Alexander's warning in the late 1930s against totalitarian aspects of training analysis. Leonard J. Duhl, PI by LJF (telephone), Mar. 16, 1987, "analyzed out of him." Kathleen Bryan, PI by LJF, Topeka, Sept. 12, 1986, a recollection of Karl's secretary to the effect that he told other staff doctors on the telephone the state of certain analysands on staff. Lester Luborsky,

PI by LJF, Philadelphia, Apr. 4, 1987, on Karl volunteering data on his student analysands to Luborsky's research project and threatening to delay certain training analyses as a mode of social control. Luborsky to KAM, July 1, 1952, indicates that Karl volunteered data.

56. The Saturday morning colloquium is discussed in Prescott Thompson, TRI by LJF, Los Angeles, May 9, 1984; Holt and Luborsky, *Personality Patterns,* 30; William R. Robinson, PI by LJF, Philadelphia, May 12, 1985; John R. Adams, TRI by LJF, Winnetka, Feb. 4, 1984; Victor Bikales, TRI by LJF, Kansas City, Mar. 9, 1985, "steel against a wheel."

57. KAM, *A Manual for Psychiatric Case Study* (New York, 1952), vii–x.

58. August Hoch and George Amsden, "A Guide to the Descriptive Study of Personality," *State Hospital Bulletin* (New York) VI (1913): 344–55.

59. KAM, *Manual,* 68, "counteract . . . the unfortunate specialization." *Ibid.,* 165–6, on the need to accompany diagnostic labels with clear descriptions.

60. KAM, *Manual,* 114–15, "The physician himself"; 161, "to a certain extent an art"; 10, "reverence for the mystery"; xi, "dignity, sympathy, earnestness."

61. KAM to Albert Deutsch, July 19, 1948, KAM Papers, M. KAM to Murray Bowen, July 17, 1985, KAM Papers, M. See also MSP Education Meeting, July 13, 1946, 2, Inst. Archives, M; KAM to Bert Boothe and MSP Executive Committee, Jan. 28, 1948, Inst. Archives, M.

62. James R. Hodge, TRI by LJF, Akron, Jan. 12, 1984; William R. Robinson, PI by LJF, Topeka, May 12, 1985. For similar disavowals by other fellows of the father image but admissions of Karl's strength over them, see, e.g., Gerald Aronson, TRI by LJF, Los Angeles, Dec. 26, 1983; Irving Kartus, TRI by Irving Sheffel, Leawood, Kans., Apr. 3, 1983; Maimon Leavitt, TRI by LJF, Los Angeles, Dec. 25, 1983; George L. Harrington, TRI by LJF, Los Angeles, Jan. 4, 1984.

63. KAM to Robert Holt, Mar. 22, 1948, Holt Papers, AHAP, on wives in the Winter dining room. Milton Wexler, TRI by LJF, Los Angeles, Dec. 24, 1983, on Karl telling residents not to neglect their wives. KAM, PI by LJF, Topeka, Nov. 16, 1984, recalls voicing dissatisfaction over failures to attend temple services. KAM to Julia Gottesman, June 16, 1950, KAM Papers, "enthusiastic Zionists." William R. Robinson, PI by LJF, Topeka, May 16, 1985, on Karl's apprehensions of a town backlash. KAM to Lewis Robbins and Irving Kartus, June 11, 1954, I.K. Papers (private) on collective bargaining.

64. Intellectualization against Karl's barbs, particularly by Jewish fellows, is noted in Maimon and Peggy Leavitt, TRI by LJF, Los Angeles, Jan. 2, 1984; Harlan Crank, PI by LJF, Austin, Nov. 22, 1985; Gerald Aronson, TRI by LJF, Los Angeles, Dec. 26, 1983.

65. Victor W. Bikales, TRI by LJF, Kansas City, Mar. 9, 1985; V. W. Bikales, "Hit Songs of the Freudian Follies," Sept. 13, 1946, H.S. 55, M.

66. V. W. Bikales, "Libretto of the Freudian Follies of 1948" (Topeka, 1948); V. W. Bikales, TRI by LJF, Kansas City, Mar. 9, 1985.

67. "Experience with the Psychiatric Residency Program at Winter V.A. Hospital from January 1946 to April 1952," 4, 7–8, Holt Papers, AHAP; George L. Harrington, TRI by LJF, Los Angeles, Jan. 4, 1984; *Kansas City Star,* Feb. 9, 1949; all on the separate Winter staff and legal separation from Menninger. Will in *TPR* 10 (Aug. 5, 1949): 3. George L. Harrington, TRI by LJF, Los Angeles, Jan. 4, 1984, and James Folsom, PI by LJF, Topeka, June 19, 1987, on Anderson's administrative qualities. WCM Diary,

402 *Notes to pp. 193–6*

Sept. 10, 1957, "he leans over backward." Irving Sheffel, PI by LJF, Topeka, July 27, 1984, on Karl having a security guard.

68. Text of KAM address, meeting of Friends of the Foundation, Hays-Adams House, Washington D.C., Dec. 3, 1950, 4, KAM Papers, M.

69. George L. Harrington, TRI by LJF, Los Angeles, Jan. 4, 1984, on leaving Topeka to grow up. In "Social Work Meeting," June 10, 1959, 2, Inst. Archives, M, Margaret Mead claimed that as late as 1959, departure of fellows from Topeka was still regarded as "an act of personal disloyalty."

70. Dr. M. L. Perry, TI by WCM, Topeka, Sept. 18, 1945, WCM Papers, M. See also JLM to Lucy McLoughlin, Sept. 18, 1945, MT.

71. Holt and Luborsky, *Personality Patterns,* 11; Janet Colaizzi, "Predicting Dangerousness: Psychiatric Ideas in the United States, 1800–1983" (unpub. Ph.D. diss., Ohio State University, 1983), 221.

72. *Lamps on the Prairie: A History of Nursing in Kansas* (reprint, New York, 1984), 91–2, reports a 1939 U.S. Public Health Service study in which Kansas mental health figures are compared to the national average. The deteriorated 1948 state of affairs in Kansas is covered in Morton M. Hunt, "They Go Home Again in Kansas," *American Mercury,* Sept. 1954, 26, 30, and in John McCormally, "The State Hospitals—A Kansas Crisis," *Emporia Gazette,* Oct. 27–Nov. 7, 1948.

73. Perry's modestly progressive attitude and accomplishments at Topeka State are noted in Barbara Hausechild, "History of Topeka State Hospital" (unpub. ms., 1948), M; Bonner, *Kansas Doctor,* 243–4; Carolyn G. Foland, "The Development Office of Public Information at Topeka State Hospital" (unpub. M.A. thesis, Kansas State University, 1969), 20. Topeka State's condition in 1948 in "Psychiatric Treatment at Topeka State Hospital," 1, Holt Papers, AHAP; Harry Levinson, TRI ("History of Topeka State Hospital"), Aug. 30, 1967, and Levinson, TRI ("Topeka State Hospital Revolution"), Feb. 5, 1964, both in M. The post-Perry deterioration is covered in Levinson, "Topeka State Hospital Revolution"; Hunt, *American Mercury,* Sept. 1954, 26–27; *Topeka State Capital,* Mar. 24, 1952; WCM Diary, Sept. 11, 1948.

74. *Kansas City Star,* Oct. 17, 1948, Feb. 9, 1949; Levinson, "Topeka State Hospital Revolution"; *Topeka State Capital,* Mar. 24, 1952. The conservative APA posture is fully delineated in Jack D. Pressman, "Uncertain Promise: Psychosurgery and the Development of Scientific Psychiatry in America, 1935 to 1955" (unpub. Ph.D. diss., University of Pennsylvania, 1986), 739–40.

75. Hunt, *American Mercury,* Sept. 1954, 25–9; *TPR* 24 (Nov. 1964): 4; *Kansas City Star,* Nov. 19, 1950; *Topeka State Capital,* Mar. 24, 1952.

76. KAM, PI by LJF, Topeka, Nov. 14, 1984; Harry Levinson, TRI by LJF, Belmont, Mass., June 24, 1985; William Rottersman, TRI by LJF, Atlanta, Mar. 26, 1983; Hunt, *American Mercury,* Sept. 1954, 28, on Anderson; Levinson, "Topeka State Hospital Revolution."

77. Levinson orientation talk to Topeka State staff, 1953, in H.S. 86, M; William Rottersman to Leonard P. Ristine, Apr. 20, 1951, MSP Papers, M; Levinson, "History of Topeka State Hospital"; Bert Boothe, "The M.S.P. Historical Facts, etc.," n.d., in Holt Papers, AHAP; *TPR* 11 (July 15, 1950): 19; *Topeka State Capital,* Aug. 21, 1949.

78. Integration of Topeka State fellows into Winter MSP programs is noted in *Topeka State Journal,* May 15, 1950; *MQ* 4 (Oct. 1950): 2; *Topeka State Capital,* July 13, 1949. Levinson, "Topeka State Hospital Revolution," on MSP graduates assuming Topeka State positions. Paul Pruyser, PI by LJF, Topeka, July 31, 1984, on the psycho-

analytic orientation of Topeka State section chiefs. KAM to John Anderson, Jan. 4, 1950, and KAM to Kenneth McFarland, June 19, 1950, both in KAM Papers, M, on hiring blacks at Topeka State. Wilfred T. Miller, "Topeka State Hospital History and Perspective" (unpub. ms., 1979), 8–9, notes the hiring of blacks.

79. Holt and Luborsky, "Psychiatric Training at Topeka State Hospital," Holt Papers, AHAP.

80. Hunt, *American Mercury*, Sept. 1954, 29, details staff numbers at Topeka State in Sept. 1954. Harry Levinson, TRI by LJF, Belmont, Mass., June 24, 1985, and Heinz Graumann, TRI by LJF, Topeka, July 31, 1984, on the biological orientation of the Bay-Feldman administration. WCM to Francis Boyer, Mar. 19, 1955, Gardner Murphy Papers, M, on early Thorazine testing at Topeka State.

81. The heavy focus on concrete patient living conditions at Topeka State is reported by William Tarnower, PI by LJF, Topeka, Nov. 11, 1984; Heinz Grauman, TRI by LJF, Topeka, July 31, 1984; and RGM, PI by LJF, Topeka, May 21, 1984. Paul Pruyser, PI by LJF, Topeka, July 31, 1984, links this focus to the general Bay-Feldman treatment philosophy.

82. Wilfred T. Miller to LJF, Sept. 7, 1984 (letter); William Tarnower, PI by LJF, Topeka, Nov. 11, 1984; Paul Pruyser, PI by LJF, Topeka, July 31, 1984.

83. KAM, "Alumni Reunion," *BMC* 35 (Nov. 1971): 399.

84. KAM, "Psychiatry and Psychology," *BMC* 11 (Mar. 1947): 46, "Never before in history." Made for the inauguration of the School of Clinical Psychology, this remark was equally applicable to the MSP connections to Winter and Topeka State. KAM to Harvey J. Tompkins, Feb. 28, 1950, Inst. Archives, M, on the persistent efforts of the Menningers and their staff to perpetuate cooperative relations with federal and state agencies.

85. WCM to Board of Governors and Committee Members, Aug. 15, 1953, 5, Inst. Archives, M. Don Cameron, "The House of Menninger," *Medical Economics*, Jan. 1955, 13. Max Levin, "The Psychiatrist's Mecca," March 1957, Inst. Archives, M.

86. Marvin A. Klemes, TRI by LJF, Los Angeles, Jan. 4, 1984, recalls Will urging MSP fellows "to extend psychiatry." "Talk by Dr. Karl, M.D., General Director . . . at a meeting of Friends of the Foundation at Hay-Adams House," Washington D.C., Dec. 3, 1950, 3, Historical Notebook, M, "more than 80%."

87. Norma Lee Browning, "Can We Heal the Mentally Ill?" *Chicago Sunday Tribune Graphic Magazine* (Apr. 1, 1951), 6, quotes the 15 percent figure for Topeka trainees. *MQ* 4 (Oct. 1950): 22, on the backgrounds of MSP fellows. *The Menninger Foundation Annual Report for July 1953–June 1954* (Topeka, 1954), 4, slightly underestimating the number of MSP alumni in 1954. Murphy in *Kansas City Star*, July 30, 1950. Sibylle Escalona to George S. Klein, Feb. 26, 1951, Klein Papers, AHAP, "more involved."

CHAPTER EIGHT: *The Home Campus*

1. "Minutes, Eighth Annual Meeting of Bd. of Trustees," October 2, 1949, 13, 17, MT. In KAM to Mrs. Ogden Reid, Oct. 31, 1952, KAM Papers, M, he acknowledged that only about 10 percent of the foundation's revenues derived from federal funding (largely the support of MSP programs) and from state appropriations (for Topeka State operations), while 70 percent came "from private patients whom we still have to see."

2. WCM Diary, Dec. 23, 1952, WCM Papers (private), "essence of the Foundation." WCM Diary, Oct. 23, 1946, "sort of hangs on." "Report of the General Secretary to Executive Committee," Oct. 2, 1946, Inst. Archives, M, warning against further expansion. "Minutes, Eighth Annual Meeting of Bd. of Trustees," Oct. 2, 1949, 13, MT, "I think that's very fallacious."

3. *TPR* 7 (Feb. 1, 1946): 3, "first and foremost to the Clinic." WCM Diary, Apr. 22, Dec. 8, 1949, Aug. 23, 1951, Sept. 9, Nov. 30, 1953.

4. *TPR* 26 (Apr. 1965): 11, on full-time-employee figures for 1946 and 1952. *Topeka State Capital,* Oct. 8, 1947, on staff growth the first year of the MSP. "Remarks by the General Secretary to the Professional Staff," Mar. 10, 1949, 1, WCM Papers, M, on figures for fall 1945 to spring 1949. "Minutes of the Eleventh Annual Meeting of the Bd. of Trustees and Governors," Oct. 12–13, 1952, 425, Inst. Archives, M, on the shifting percentages of professional and nonprofessional staff.

5. Admissions, Adult Clinical Services, MMR, on patient increases. *The Menninger Foundation Sixth Annual Report* (Topeka, 1948), 7, and Lucille Cairns, "A History of the Menninger Clinic at Topeka up to the Time of Its Transfer to the Menninger Foundation, 1919–1945," (unpub. Ph.D. diss., Washington University of St. Louis, 1946), 119, on the growth of the *BMC. Newsletter* II (Aug. 1948): 2, on expanding internal training programs.

6. WCM to General Directors, Directors, and Senior Staff: "Problems Confronting Us in Our Organization and Function," June 9, 1947, 1, M; KAM to Marshall Field, July 11, 1949, KAM Papers, M; WCM Diary, June 1947; "The Menninger Foundation Progress Report to the Trustees," Feb. 21, 1949, H.S. 68 (1949), M; "Annual Report of Activities Therapy Department," July 1949–50, Inst. Archives, M; William Pious, "Monthly Report—June 1947, Department of Clinical Services," 1, Inst. Archives, M.

7. *Topeka Daily Capital,* Oct. 9, 1953, on foundation net worth between 1947 and 1953. Lewis Robbins to Medical Council, Mar. 24, 1951, Inst. Archives, M.

8. WCM Diary, Mar. 21–7, 1948, on meeting foundation staff. David Rapaport to Lois and Gardner Murphy, Jan. 22, 1953, Inst. Archives, M, on Will having created four general sections of the organization. Prescott Thompson, TRI by LJF, Los Angeles, May 9, 1984, on Will understanding staff apprehensions over the pace of change.

9. Planning and Coordinating Committee, Aug. 21, 1946, Mildred Law Papers, M, for Will's remarks on not being "entirely democratic" but needing to centralize. Will's views and efforts at centralizing everything in the general secretary's office is noted in WCM, "Report of the General Secretary to the Executive Committee, the Menninger Foundation," Oct. 2, 1946, H.S. 46; WCM to Medical Staff, Aug. 22, 1949, WCM Papers, M.

10. Will's postwar offices and activities are noted in WCM Diary, Nov. 29, Dec. 31, 1947 (summary of 1947). WCM Diary, June 30, 1947, "many things to be done" and not "time enough." See also WCM Diary, Nov. 11–16, 1946, Nov. 3, 1948.

11. The pre-Roach administrative style at the foundation is characterized well in Irving Sheffel, Thomas Dolgoff, Roger Hoffmaster, and Duane Swanson, TRI by LJF, Topeka, May 21, 1985; Lester Roach, PI by LJF, Topeka, Mar. 9, 1983; Basil Cole, TRI by LJF, Topeka, May 31, 1983; and esp. by William Gibson's novel *The Cobweb* (New York, 1954).

12. Biographical data on Roach is found in *Topeka Daily Capital,* Nov. 23, 1948; WCM Diary, Mar. 24, 1949.

13. Lillabelle Stahl, PI by LJF, Topeka, July 31, 1984, on Law's role. Roach, PI by LJF, Topeka, Mar. 9, 1983, on replacing Nuss with Sheffel. Sheffel's background in "Information Memo from the Office of the General Secretary," no. 17, Mar. 11, 1949, H.S. 68, M.

14. Irving Sheffel to LJF, July 21, 1986 (letter), on Swirsky; Thomas Dolgoff, TRI by LJF, Topeka, Jan. 4, 1983; Basil Cole, TRI by LJF, Topeka, May 31, 1983.

15. Irving Sheffel, TRI by LJF, Topeka, May 21, 1985; Basil Cole, TRI by LJF, Topeka, May 31, 1983; Sheffel, Dolgoff, Hoffmaster, and Swanson, TRI by LJF, Topeka, May 21, 1985.

16. L. T. Roach, "Progress Report to Dr. Will," Feb. 10, 1949, Roach Papers, M, ordering clearer division of labor, procedural simplification, job descriptions, and the $150 fee increase and its effects. Sheffel to KAM, Feb. 28, 1949, Inst. Archives, M, on negotiating VA contracts.

17. Irving Sheffel, PI by LJF, Topeka, Jan. 10, 1985, on the Roach administration promoting organization-wide procedural clarity. Director of Department of Adult Psychiatry to Chief-of-Staff and General Secretary (Annual Report of D.A.P.), July 1, 1952–June 30, 1953, 4, Inst. Archives, M, on a "greater smoothness" and a less frantic pace.

18. "Admissions—Clinical Services," 1944–1980, MMR. "Annual Report of the Medical Director," 1945–46 to 1953–54, Inst. Archives, M.

19. "Annual Survey of Psychotherapy—1952," Inst. Archives, M; WCM, "Annual Report of the Clinical Service Department, July 1, 1947 to June 30, 1948," 5, Inst. Archives, M; "Annual Report of the Medical Director," 1945–46 and 1953–54, Inst. Archives, M.

20. Patient employment characteristics in "Annual Survey of Psychotherapy— 1952," and "Annual Report of the Medical Director" 1945–54.

21. *Los Angeles Daily News,* June 17, 1949, and *Chicago Herald-American,* Dec. 7, 1948, on Robert Walker. *Kansas City Times,* Feb. 7, 1950, and *New York Daily News,* Feb. 10, 1950, on Jane Froman. *Topeka State Journal,* June 7, 1951, and *San Francisco Chronicle,* July 29, 1951, on Dan Dailey. Akim Tamiroff in *Topeka State Journal,* Apr. 29, 1950. Gene Tierney, *Self-Portrait* (New York, 1979), 190, 207–16. The party at Romanoff's as reported in *Topeka State Journal,* June 2, 1953.

22. Lester Luborsky, "Clinician's Judgments of Mental Health: A Proposed Scale," *Archives of General Psychiatry* 7 (Dec. 1962): 43, charts the results of the 1952 Survey of Psychotherapy at the Menninger Hospital using the Health-Sickness Rating Scale. Lewis Robbins, "Instructions for Annual Survey of Psychotherapy," Mar. 17, 1952; "Instructions for Health-Sickness Rating Scale," Apr. 1, 1952; and especially "Sample Case Descriptions," 1–14 (all in Inst. Archives, M), reveal specific maladies for 1952 hospital patients. Hospital annual reports and random patient files for 1946–51 yield the same general condition of patients at initial diagnosis as the 1952 survey indicated.

23. Gerald N. Grob, "Psychiatry and Social Activism: The Politics of Specialty in Postwar America," *BHM* 60 (Fall 1986): 498–9, cogently assesses the low state of psychiatric knowledge in the postwar period. John M. Reisman, *A History of Clinical Psychology* (New York, 1976), 341–2, on dominant postwar national treatment modalities.

24. Menninger Hospital annual reports for the 1946–54 interval underscore the continuation of the 1930s treatment program. Nurses' daily reports for the late 1940s and Activities Therapy report books for the late 1940s and early 1950s (both in Inst.

Archives, M), show rather fully how the guide and general treatment procedures operated.

25. "Annual Report of the Clinical Services Department, July 1, 1946 to June 30, 1947," 13. Luborsky, *Archives of General Psychiatry* 7, 43, on Psychotherapy Research Project reported "improvement." "The Menninger Clinic—Analysis of Cases in Treatment as of December 15, 1950," Inst. Archives, M.

26. *The Menninger Foundation Ninth Annual Report* (Topeka, 1951), 14–15, on the changed admissions policy. Luborsky, *Archives of General Psychiatry* 7, 43, on greatest "improvement" through expressive therapy.

27. "C. F. Menninger Hospital Statistics," July 1, 1970–June 30, 1971, Table G (Comparison of Hospital Census, 1946–1971); "Department of Adult Psychiatry Annual Report," July 1, 1952–June 30, 1953, Table 6 (Comparison of Hospital Census, 1945–1953); both documents in Inst. Archives, M.

28. John Stone to WCM, June 21, 1947, WCM Papers, M. WCM Diary, Oct. 23–30, 1946. KAM to Omar N. Bradley, Mar. 6, 1947, AM Papers (private). "The Menninger Foundation Progress Report to the Trustees," Feb. 21, 1949, H.S. 68, M, on foundation salary levels. Harlan Crank to LJF, Nov. 20, 1986 (letter), on how "the staff was very much drained and annoyed by resources being expended at Winter and Topeka State Hospital, largely because of KAM's ambitions and commitments."

29. Lewis Robbins to Members of the Medical Council, Mar. 24, 1951, Inst. Archives, M.

30. Robert Worthington to WCM, Apr. 21, 1949, WCM Papers, M; see also Worthington to LJF, Mar. 4, 1984 (letter). John Stone, "RPK: His Reasons for Leaving," Jan. 4, 1947, MT, "Ideas don't rate so high."

31. Helen Clapsattle, *The Doctors Mayo* (Minneapolis, 1941), 549–59, on the Mayo–University of Minnesota connection. John C. Whitehorn to Lewis H. Weed, Oct. 24, 1945, John C. Whitehorn Papers, APA, on the Phipps Clinic's affiliation with Johns Hopkins. Robert P. Knight to WCM, Nov. 14, 1949, MT, sketches the terms of the Pittsburgh offer plus the pros and cons. WCM to Lucy McLaughlin, n.d., MT, "My interest in Pittsburgh." See also Irving Sheffel, PI by LJF, Topeka, Mar. 9, 1983, and Lewis Wheelock to KAM, Dec. 21, 1965, KAM Papers, M, for background on the Pittsburgh offer. Termination of the University of Kansas affiliation as cited in "Annual Report of M.S.P., 1949–50" (Professional Education, 6), M, and "Review of U.S.P.H.S.-Sponsored Clinical Psychology Training Program at the Menninger Foundation, 1948–1954," n.d. (1954), 1–2, Inst. Archives, M. *Topeka State Capital,* Dec. 26, 1953, on the change in types of joint clinical psychology programs offered.

32. Daniel M. Fox, *Health Policies, Health Politics: The British and American Experience, 1911–1965* (Princeton, 1986).

33. Psychology Staff to WCM, Apr. 27, 1951 (petition), WCM Papers, M. *Topeka Daily Capital,* June 5, 1949, and WCM to Lewis L. Robbins, Apr. 25, 1949, LLR Papers (private) on Worthington's departure. Crank's departure in Harlan Crank, PI by LJF, Austin, Nov. 22, 23, 1985; WCM Diary, Jan. 19, 1950; Lester Roach, TRI by Verne Horne, Topeka, Aug. 23, 1974, M.

34. Lillabelle Stahl, PI by LJF, Topeka, July 11, 1984, and Edward Greenwood, PI by LJF, Topeka, Mar. 11, 1985, both recalling Stone characterizing Karl during this period "like a bull let out to pasture." John Stone to KAM, June 3, 1948, KAM Papers, M, comes close to saying this. John Stone to WCM, Aug. 26, 1947, WCM Papers, M, on the passing of the family organization.

35. The details of the Stone revolt against Karl are reported in KAM to Harold

Maine, July 16, 1954, unfiled, M; KAM, TRI by Verne Horne, Topeka, May 20, 1972, M; KAM, PI by LJF, Topeka, May 21, 1984; Lester Roach, TRI by Verne Horne, Topeka, Aug. 23, 1974, M. WCM to J. R. Stone, Aug. 18, 1948, Stone Papers, M, "I wonder if you fully realize."

36. John Stone to KAM, June 3, 1948, KAM Papers, M, "the support & patience." This letter reveals much about his sense of place in the "family organization." Useful context is also found in Stone to WCM, Aug. 26, 1947, WCM Papers, M, and Lester Roach, TRI by LJF, Topeka, Sept. 14, 1985.

37. The details of Stone's illnesses, New York job offer, and death are provided in KAM to Mary O'Neal Hawkins, Mar. 16, 1949, Hawkins Papers, NYPsa; KAM to Harold Maine, July 16, 1954, unfiled, M, noting Memorial Hospital as "too good a job." KAM to J. F. Brown, June 4, 1948, KAM Papers, M; KAM to Julia and Abraham Gottesman, Jan. 10, 1949, KAM Papers, M; WCM to John W. Appel, June 7, 1948, WCM Papers, M; WCM Diary, June 4, 1948; David Neiswanger to Arthur Hopkins, Jan. 6, 1949, David Neiswanger Papers, M. Edward Greenwood, PI by LJF, Topeka, Mar. 11, 1985, on Margaret Stone blaming the Menningers for the death.

38. "An Opportunity for the Development of Psychiatric Education and Research," 1940, 12, H.S. 38, and Knight's vita, M, detail his position and functions.

39. Lawrence S. Kubie, *The Riggs Story: The Development of the Austen Riggs Center for the Study and Treatment of the Neuroses* (New York, 1960), 66–7, details Riggs's approaches to Knight beginning in September 1946. Harlan Crank, PI by LJF, Austin, Nov. 22, 1985, on Knight having to dispense inadequate staff wages. WCM Diary, Jan. 5–11, 1947, and WCM to Norman Reider, Feb. 7, 1947, WCM Papers, M, on Will assuming chief of staff responsibilities to keep Knight from going to Riggs. WCM Diary, Jan. 27, 1947, on hearing that Knight accepted the Riggs offer. Robert Knight to George S. Klein, May 8, 1962, Klein Papers, AHAP, recalling that the Menningers and Stone pleaded with him not to go to Riggs.

40. For Knight's 1930s Camelot vision of Menninger and his hope that Riggs would be like Menninger had been, see John Stone, "R.P.K.: His Reasons for Leaving," Jan. 4, 1947, MT; Adele Boyd, PI by LJF, Stockbridge, June 30, 1985; Martin Mayman, TRI by LJF, Ann Arbor, Sept. 16, 1983; Lewis Robbins, TRI by LJF, New York, Aug. 23, 1983; Stuart Miller, PI by LJF, Lee, Mass., June 30, 1985, recalling "L.S.M.F.T."

41. John Stone to KAM, Jan. 9, 1947, KAM Papers, M; CWM, PI by LJF, Topeka, Mar. 14, 1986, June 20, 1987; Edward Greenwood, TRI by LJF, Topeka, Nov. 10, 1982; Lewis Robbins, "Karl A. Menninger Notes—March 20, 1979," 3, LLR Papers (private); "The Topeka Mystique," transcript, session of American Psychoanalytic Association, Puerto Rico, 1981, 63–4. Harlan Crank, PI by LJF, Austin, Nov. 22, 1985.

42. KAM to Robert P. Knight, Dec. 15, 1965, RPK Papers (private), on how both knew Will would not let Knight get ahead of him. WCM Diary, Feb. 3–8, 1947, "Bob Knight's decision to leave." See also John R. Stone to WCM, Jan. 9, 1947, KAM Papers, M; Robert P. Knight to KAM, Nov. 10, 1944, RPK Papers (private); KAM, TRI by LJF, Topeka, Mar. 14, 1986.

43. Knight's support for and centrality to MSP student culture is revealed in Martin Mayman, TRI by LJF, Ann Arbor, Apr. 27, 1983; Margaret Brenman Gibson, TRI by LJF, Topeka, May 19, 1984; Irving Kartus, TRI by Irving Sheffel, Apr. 3, 1983. Robert Knight to KAM, Sept. 20, 1945, RPK Papers (private), "this new School project . . ." J.R. Stone to WCM, Jan. 9, 1947, in "Minutes of Medical Council," 1949–50, Inst. Archives, M, quoting Knight dissatisfied with his lectures.

44. WCM Diary, Oct. 23, 1946, "normal living"; and WCM Diary, Nov. 11–16, 1946.

Prescott Thompson, TRI by LJF, Los Angeles, May 9, 1984, recalling Will's open misgivings at staff meeting about organizational growth. See also "Meeting of [Trustees] Scientific Work Committee, Jan. 30, 1948," MT.

45. Will's many letters to Catharine during the war years (WCM Papers) (private) represent the fullest account of how he won the army over to psychiatry. See, e.g., WCM to CWM, Dec. 19, 1942, Dec. 5, 1943, n.d. (Apr. 1944). See also WCM to FVM et al., Feb 13, 1944, WCM Papers (private).

46. Grob, *BHM* 60, 477–501, on the postwar struggle within the American Psychiatric Association and Will's important role in it. The GAP Papers in WCM Papers, M, are also helpful.

47. WCM Diary, Dec. 31, 1947, calculating 95 days away from Topeka that year. Will's year-end diary entries for 1948 and 1949 indicate an increasing number of days away.

48. WCM Diary, Nov. 30, 1947, and "General Statement of the Fund-Raising Experience of the Menninger Foundation," n.d., M, on failed efforts with professional fund-raisers. Lester Roach, TRI by Verne Horne, Topeka, Aug. 23, 1974, M, on how he urged Will to become fund-raiser. "Meeting of Bd. of Trustees, Minutes," Oct. 2, 1949, MT, "I just cannot" and "more likely." See also Lillabelle Stahl to Bernard Hall, June 14, 1966, Hall Papers, M. WCM Diary, entries for 1949 to 1953, reveal his inner struggle over becoming a fund-raiser (see esp. Apr. 22, 1949; Dec. 1951; May 22, 1953, Dec. 1953). On Will becoming fund-raiser to be freer of Karl, see Roach, PI by LJF, Topeka, Mar. 9, 1983; Thomas Dolgoff, TRI by LJF, Topeka, Jan. 4, 1983; RWM, PI by LJF, Topeka, Jan. 5, 1983.

49. WCM Diary, Dec. 1953, "From the original point." See also WCM Diary, Dec. 1951, on how he could now "tell people specifically that I want their help."

50. "Private and Federal Government Support of the Menninger Foundation," Apr. 7, 1966, M, on Will's growing contribution after 1949 to total foundation revenue. See also *TPR* 10 (Apr. 1956): 1; Don Cameron, "The House of Menninger," *Medical Economics*, Jan. 1955, 9; CWM, PI by LJF, Topeka, Mar. 9, Sept. 10, 1985, Mar. 14, 1986. Howard Shevrin, TRI by LJF, Ann Arbor, Sept. 16, 1983, on Will's fund-raising effectiveness and the family basis for Menninger operations.

51. Lewis Robbins, TRI by LJF, New York, Aug. 23, 1983, recalled Will unable to recognize hospital director Irving Kartus. See also WCM Diary, Jan. 24, 1955, fully acknowledging minimal contact with staff. WCM Diary, Dec. 1953, "more satisfaction." WCM to Mrs. Roy Wright, July 27, 1949, WCM Papers (private) "stirring ourselves."

52. WCM to EAM, Feb. 17, 1958 (unfiled), M; "Freudian Follies of 1955," H.S. 97, M.

53. WCM Diary, Feb. 3–8, 1947, on Charles's daily routine at the home campus. Charles's efforts to conciliate his sons are noted in Leo Bartemeier, TI by Lewis Robbins and Melvin Herman, Dec. 10, 1977, LLR Papers (private); CWM, PI by LJF, Topeka, Mar. 5, July 29, 1983; James Pratt, TRI by LJF, Topeka, Jan. 6, 1983; Josephine Boam, TRI by LJF, Topeka, Feb. 27, 1984.

54. *Topeka State Journal,* Dec. 1, 1953, on the funeral service. Mel Herman and Lewis R. Robbins, "Dr. Karl: A Biography of Karl Menninger," n.d., n.p., 353, "I'm sixty." In *TRP* 14, no. 12 (Dec. 15, 1953): 1–2, Karl reproduces Will's memorandum. WCM Diary, Dec. 1953, "there wasn't any senior partner."

55. KAM, "A Psychiatric Fable," *BMC* 14 (July 1950): 129–30.

56. *Ibid.*

57. Data on the MSP resident selection process in "Experience with the Psychiatric Residency Program at Winter V.A. Hospital from January, 1946 to April, 1952," in Holt Papers, AHAP. Harlan Crank, PI by LJF, Austin, Nov. 22, Nov. 23, 1985, and Crank, PI by LJF (telephone), June 8, 1987, for a senior hospital physician of the late 1940s disagreeing with Karl's and Knight's residency selection criteria. Burton J. Bledstein, *The Culture of Professionalism: The Middle Class and the Development of Higher Education in America* (New York, 1976), esp. x.

58. KAM, TRI by LJF, Topeka, Sept. 4, 1988, acknowledging that Dr. Smith very closely resembled his father and that he wrote "Fable" with Charles clearly in mind. KAM, *BMC* 14 (July 1950): 129–30.

59. *BMC* 14 (July 1950): 129–30.

60. *Ibid.*

61. KAM, "What the Girls Told," *Saturday Review of Literature*, Sept. 26, 1953, 21, 30–1. I am drawing upon an enlarged Dec. 1953 version of this essay in Bernard Hall, ed., *A Psychiatrists' World: The Selected Papers of Karl Menninger, M.D.* (New York, 1959), I, 466–76.

62. *Ibid.*, 466–8.

63. *Ibid.*, 469–75.

64. *Ibid.*, 469, 473.

65. *Ibid.*, 468, 473.

66. "Psychiatry Looks at Religion," in *ibid.*, 793–810 (quoted material on 794).

67. Peter Fleming to Irving Kartus, n.d. (1956), IK Papers (private), "out of touch." Donald Leventhal, PI by LJF, Bowling Green, Ohio, Feb. 25, 1983, for the staff psychologist's observations on Karl. Similar observations of Karl at this time are found in Crank, PI by LJF, Austin, Nov. 22, 1985, and, Philip Holzman, PI by LJF, Cambridge, Mass., July 28, 1987.

CHAPTER NINE: *The Rapaport Group*

1. The roles of early clinical psychologists are discussed cogently in John C. Burnham, "The Struggle Between Physicians and Paramedical Personnel in American Psychiatry, 1917–1941," *JHMAS* 29 (Jan. 1974): 104–5, and Robert R. Holt, ed., *Diagnostic Psychological Testing by David Rapaport, Merton M. Gill, and Roy Schafer* (rev. ed., New York, 1968), 5. Gerald N. Grob, ed., *The Inner World of American Psychiatry, 1890–1940: Selected Correspondence* (New Brunswick, N.J., 1985), 260–4, on new World War I roles for psychologists and on psychiatrists who were receptive to clinical psychologists.

2. Changing roles of clinical psychologists during World War II are discussed in James H. Capshew, "Psychology on the March: American Psychologists and World War II" (Ph.D. diss., University of Pennsylvania, 1986), esp. 94–110; Stewart H. Brill and James D. Morgan, "Military Psychologists in World War II," *American Psychologist* 1 (Sept. 1946): esp. 437; Albert R. Gilgen, *American Psychology Since World War II: A Profile of the Discipline* (Westport, Conn., 1982), 173–5. WCM to CWM, March 6, 1944, WCM Papers (private), "psychologists included." See also WCM to CWM, Apr. 4, 1944, WCM Papers (private). Chapter three discusses Karl's management of the Menninger hospital during World War II. His *A Manual for Psychiatric Case Study* (New

York, 1952), 75–6, calls for close cooperation and even an interchange of functions between psychiatrist and psychologist.

3. John M. Reisman, *A History of Clinical Psychology* (New York, 1976), 299–302, on the growth of clinical psychology nationally in the late 1940s. Stella Deigman and Esther Miller, "The Support of Research in Medical and Allied Fields for the Period 1946 Through 1951," *Science* 115 (March 28, 1952): 321–43, on growth in federal funding for mental health research.

4. For John Stone's observations, see his 1947 memorandum quoted in Bernard Mackler and Barbara Thacker, "The Menningers: The Bible Belt and Mental Health Reform" (n.d., n.p., M), 26. See also WCM Diary, Jan. 5–11, 1947.

5. Lester Luborsky, TRI by LJF, Philadelphia, Nov. 6, 1983; Roy Schafer, TRI by LJF, New York, Nov. 7, 1983; David Rapaport to WCM, Oct. 14, 1946, Inst. Archives, M; Margaret Brenman Gibson, TRI by LJF, Topeka, May 19, 1984; Gerald Aronson, TRI by LJF, Los Angeles, Dec. 26, 1983.

6. "Staff Announcements," July 2, 1940, H.S. 40, M; Topeka Psychoanalytic Society c.v. for David Rapaport, M; Robert R. Holt, ed., "Motives and Thought: Psychoanalytic Essays in Memory of David Rapaport," *PI* 18/19 (1976): 9–10; Merton M. Gill, ed., *The Collected Papers of David Rapaport* (New York, London, 1967), 50, 289. David Rapaport to KAM, Jan. 31, 1940, M (vault), a cover letter to the test reports on Karl.

7. *TPR* 5 (July 15, 1944): 6; Holt, "Motives and Thought," 9–11, 14–15; Gill, *Rapaport*, 6–7, 99; Stuart C. Miller, ed., *Clinician and Therapist: Selected Papers of Robert P. Knight* (New York, 1972), xii; Robert Knight to KAM, Oct. 15, 1940, Inst. Archives, M; David Rapaport, "Poetry," *BMC* 6 (May 1942): 88; Donald B. Leventhal, PI by LJF, Bowling Green, Ohio, Feb. 25, 1983.

8. For data on Brown, see Wilfred T. Miller, "J. F. Brown, the KU Professor," *Kansas Psychologist* 13 (Spring 1988): 6; "An Opportunity for the Development of Psychiatric Education and Research," 1940, 12, H.S. 38, M; Norman Reider, TRI by LJF, San Francisco, Dec. 28, 1983; Lewis Robbins, TRI by LJF, New York, Aug. 23, 1983; J. F. Brown, "Report of the Work of the Psychology Department," Oct. 1, 1941, 1–2, Inst. Archives, M. WCM Diary, Mar. 20, 1941, on Rapaport. David Rapaport to Lois and Gardner Murphy, Jan. 22, 1953, Inst. Archives, M, recalling his relationship with Brown. "Staff Bulletin," Oct. 2, 1942, H.S. 43, M, on Brown resigning and Rapaport taking his place.

9. Brenman is noted in Minutes of Executive Committee, Dec. 10, 1941, Mildred Law Papers, M; J. F. Brown, "Report of the Work of the Psychology Department," Oct. 1, 1941, 2, Inst. Archives, M; *TPR* 5 (July 15, 1944): 6–7; David Rapaport to Lois and Gardner Murphy, Jan. 22, 1953, Inst. Archives, M. Psychology staff recruitment strategies and policies are noted in the transcript of a tape-recorded discussion between Lois B. Murphy and Philip S. Holzman, Nov. 2, 1979, 4–5, M; John R. Stone to Harry Harwick, April 21, 1943, Inst. Archives, M. *TPR* 15 (Feb. 15, 1954): 10.

10. Gill's background and the process of integrating him within the group is noted in David Rapaport to Lois and Gardner Murphy, Jan. 22, 1953, M; *TPR* 5 (July 15, 1944): 7; and Merton Gill, TRI by LJF, Chicago, Mar. 30, 1983.

11. David Rapaport and Merton Gill, "Survey of the Status and Problems of Research at the Menninger Clinic," June 3, 1942, Inst. Archives, M, "concentration of research." The formation of the Research Committee is also noted in Lucille Cairns, "A History of the Menninger Clinic at Topeka, Kansas, up to the Time of Its Transfer to the Menninger Foundation, 1919–1945" (Ph.D. diss., Washington University of St.

Louis, 1946), 124; and "First Annual Report of the Research Committee of the Menninger Foundation," May 7, 1943, Inst. Archives, M. The development of a research-centered group through the Research Committee and, in 1946, the Research Department is revealed in Executive Committee Meeting, Mar. 26, 1943, Inst. Archives, M; Sibylle Escalona, TRI by LJF, New York, Nov. 7, 1983; *The Menninger Foundation Fifth Annual Report* (Topeka, 1947), 29.

12. Schafer data is found in *TPR* 4 (Jan.–Feb. 1943): 6, and *TPR* 5 (July 15, 1944): 6; Roy Schafer, TRI by LJF, New York, Nov. 7, 1983; Escalona and Leitch data in David Rapaport to Lois and Gardner Murphy, Jan. 22, 1953, Inst. Archives, M; Sibylle Escalona, TRI by LJF, New York, Nov. 7, 1983.

13. Martin Mayman, TRI by LJF, Ann Arbor, Apr. 27, Sept. 16, 1983. David Rapaport to Lois and Gardner Murphy, Jan. 22, 1953, Inst. Archives, M, on Bergman.

14. Lewis Robbins, TRI by LJF, Aug. 23, 1983, on postwar additions to the group being attracted primarily to Rapaport. For information on Klein, see David Rapaport to George S. Klein, Feb. 16, June 15, 1942, George Klein Papers, AHAP; Merton Gill and Philip Holzman, eds., *Psychology versus Metapsychology* (New York, 1976), 6–7, 13; *TPR* 7 (Apr. 5, 1946): 5. Robert Holt, TRI by LJF, New York, Dec. 28, 1985, on his background. Lester Luborsky, TRI by LJF, Philadelphia, Nov. 6, 1983. Philip Holzman, PI by LJF, Cambridge, Mass., Apr. 25, 1982. Herbert Schlesinger, TRI by LJF, New York, Dec. 27, 1985. Milton Wexler, TRI by LJF, Los Angeles, Dec. 24, 1983, May 9, 1984.

15. David Rapaport to Lois and Gardner Murphy, Jan. 22, 1953, Inst. Archives, M, on the roles of Brenman and Escalona. Gerald Ehrenreich, PI by LJF, Lawrence, Kans. Sept. 11, 1986, on his tie to Brenman. See also Merton Gill, TRI by LJF, Chicago, Mar. 30, 1983.

16. The political postures of the group are noted in Merton Gill, TRI by LJF, Chicago, Mar. 30, 1983; Margaret Brenman Gibson, TRI by LJF, Topeka, May 19, 1984; *TPR* 6 (Sept. 8, 1945): 3; Notes on Employee Group Meeting, Nov. 23, 1945, 2–3, Inst. Archives, M; David Rapaport to KAM, Oct. 2, 1946, Inst. Archives, M; "Minutes of Clinical Service Committee," Feb. 10, 1951, 1, Roach Papers, M. Basil Cole, PI by LJF, Topeka, Sept. 11, 1986, on the food cooperative. Roy Schafer, TRI by LJF, New York, Nov. 7, 1983, on the academic proclivities of the group.

17. Philip Holzman, PI by LJF, Cambridge, Mass., July 28, 1987, on distinctive social subgroups. Merton Gill, TRI by LJF, Mar. 30, 1983, on the effect of Rapaport's leadership. See also Gill, *Rapaport,* 6. David Rapaport to Lois and Gardner Murphy, Jan. 22, 1953, Inst. Archives, M, reflecting on his role in group life.

18. Sibylle Escalona, TRI by LJF, New York, Nov. 7, 1983; Roy Schafer, TRI by LJF, Nov. 7, 1983; Lester Luborsky, TRI by LJF, Philadelphia, Nov. 6, 1983. See also David Rapaport to Lester Luborsky, Jan. 15, 1960, in Luborsky personal papers, and Robert Holt, TRI by LJF, New York, Dec. 28, 1985. George Klein to Sibylle Escalona, Mar. 17, 1953, George Klein Papers, AHAP.

19. Rapaport's formalism and his behavior socially is noted in Holt, "Motives and Thought," 11–12, and Robert Holt, TRI by LJF, Dec. 28, 1985.

20. Holt, "Motives and Thought," 11–12, "little Jew from Budapest." "The Topeka Mystique," the transcript of session of American Psychoanalytic Association, Puerto Rico, 1981, 24, quotes Holzman on Rapaport as venerable in his carriage. "Mossie" to George Klein, n.d. (1946), Klein Papers, AHAP, on Rapaport as a brilliant tyrant. Martin Mayman, TRI by LJF, Ann Arbor, Sept. 16, 1983. Margaret Brenman Gibson,

TRI by LJF, May 19, 1984. Robert Holt, TRI by LJF, Dec. 28, 1985. Merton Gill, TRI by LJF, Mar. 30, 1983. Frederick Hacker, TRI by LJF, Los Angeles, Jan. 3, 1984, and David Rapaport to Lois and Gardner Murphy, Jan. 22, 1953, Inst. Archives, M, on efforts to involve Hacker in the group.

21. Robert P. Knight, "David Rapaport, September 30, 1911–December 14, 1960," paper presented at Western New England Psychoanalytic Society, New Haven, Jan. 7, 1961, 3, Inst. Archives, M, for the Prussian characterization. Roy Schafer, TRI by LJF, Nov. 7, 1983, on Rapaport as a critic of "loose thinking." Holt, "Motives and Thought," 13, on Rapaport on data collection and writing. Rapaport's expectation for minute memory recall is noted in "Topeka Mystique," 25, and Holt, "Motives and Thought," 13. See also Margaret Brenman to A. H. Maslow, Sept. 22, 1942, Maslow Papers, AHAP; and Martin Mayman to David Rapaport, June 19, 1950, Rapaport Papers, LC. The story of the two-inch stack of papers and the pin is noted in *Menninger Perspective* 18 (1987): 10.

22. David Rapaport to Lois and Gardner Murphy, Jan. 22, 1953, Inst. Archives, M, "picked up the ideas of others," "motor of execution," and "contact with everybody." Margaret Brenman in "Austen Riggs Workshop," transcript of American Psychoanalytic Association session, 1982, 61–2, "the creative energy." Robert Holt, TRI by LJF, Dec. 28, 1985; Sibylle Escalona, TRI by LJF, Nov. 7, 1983; Margaret Brenman Gibson, TRI by LJF, May 19, 1984, on Rapaport in oral discourse and in facilitating a group spirit.

23. Astute observations on the cooperativist trend in American psychological research during the 1940s are provided in J. G. Morawski, "Organizing Knowledge and Behavior at Yale's Institute of Human Relations," *ISIS* 77 (June 1986): 225, 241.

24. WCM Diary, Mar. 1, Feb. 17, 1947, on interviews with Rapaport; June 1947 on budget negotiations; Jan. 5–11, 1947, on Rapaport's personal salary demands on his recruitment preferences. WCM Diary, Feb. 17–28, 1947, "stimulating fellow"; Mar. 20, 1941, on the "brilliant" Hungarian. WCM to David Rapaport, June 4, 1948, WCM Papers, M, "we will miss you." For a retrospective view on Rapaport, see WCM to Philip Holzman, Sept. 9, 1963, KAM Papers, M.

25. KAM to Ruth Mack Brunswick, Mar. 6, 1942, KAM Papers, M. KAM to Robert Wohlforth, Jan. 28, 1944, KAM Papers, M. Gill, *Rapaport*, 249–50, on the American Psychiatric Association paper with Rapaport. KAM to Ruth Mack Brunswick, Sept. 19, Nov. 4, Nov. 19, 1942, KAM Papers, M. KAM to Martha Menninger, Nov. 20, 1942, KAM Papers, M, on Julia Menninger learning testing from Rapaport.

26. KAM, PI by LJF, Sept. 12, 1985; "Topeka Mystique," 24.

27. David Rapaport to Lois and Gardner Murphy, Jan. 22, 1953, Inst. Archives, M.

28. KAM to Lawrence Kubie, Apr. 6, 1942, KAM Papers, M; Margaret Brenman Gibson, TRI by LJF, Topeka, May 19, 1984; "Mossie" to George Klein, n.d. (1946), Klein Papers, AHAP; Edward Greenwood, TRI by LJF, Nov. 10, 1982, on the Erikson visit.

29. Edward Greenwood, TRI by LJF, Nov. 10, 1982, on Rapaport's anger when Karl monopolized Erikson's time. KAM to WCM, Sept. 10, 1945, WCM Papers (private), on Karl being upset by Rapaport's seminar exclusion policy. Lester Luborsky, PI by LJF, Philadelphia, Apr. 4, 1987, on Rapaport's diary-like entries on his meetings with Karl. KAM, PI by LJF, Topeka, Sept. 12, Sept. 14, 1985, on his disputes with Rapaport.

30. "Minutes of Executive Committee," Mar. 26, 1941, Inst. Archives, M. *TPR* 5 (May 1, 1944): 1; "Meeting of the Scientific Work Committee [of the Trustees]," (1948), Neiswanger Papers, M.

31. "Minutes of Executive Committee," June 5, 1946, Inst. Archives, M, preventing Rapaport from assigning associates to his operation. "Planning and Coordinating Committee," meeting, May 15, 1946, Law Papers, M, is also relevant to this. David Rapaport to John Stone, Oct. 24, 1944, and Rapaport to WCM, Oct. 14, 1946, both in Inst. Archives, M, fighting for staff and research hours.

32. "Staff Education Meeting," May 28, 1949, 5, and David Rapaport to Lois and Gardner Murphy, Jan. 22, 1953, both in Inst. Archives, M, on making psychological tests standard practice.

33. Education Committee Meeting, July 13, 1946, 3, Inst. Archives, M; KAM to Leslie Farber, Mar. 14, 1942, KAM Papers, M; Lester Luborsky, PI by LJF, Philadelphia, Apr. 4, 1987.

34. Gill, *Rapaport,* 252, on Rapaport embracing Karl's continuum concept in 1947. KAM to Gardner Murphy, Jan. 23, 1953, Murphy Papers, M, "making research our main activity."

35. Gill, *Rapaport,* 235, summarizes the essential elements of the 1946 Rapaport-Schafer paper. David Rapaport and Roy Schafer, "The Psychological Internship Training Program of the Menninger Clinic," *JCP* 10 (July–Aug. 1946): 216–20, makes many of the same points. David Rapaport, Merton Gill, and Roy Schafer, *Diagnostic Psychological Testing* (Chicago, 1946), I, 11, "lifeless numerical-test results" and "living clinical dynamics."

36. The introduction and diverse portions of *Diagnostic Psychological Testing* underscores these points.

37. Sydney Smith, ed., *The Human Mind Revisited* (New York, 1978), 9, on Karl's interest, through Southard, in psychological testing. In "An Analysis of Psychoanalysis," *New York Times Magazine,* May 18, 1947, 50, "specific measurements." Carl Tillman to David Rapaport, Sept. 24, 1940, Inst. Archives, M. Modest opposition to the testing of the group is revealed in "Exec. Comm. Meeting," Apr. 8, 1942, Law Papers, M. *TPR* 6 (May 16, 1945): 5, on the quality of tests administered at Menninger. Rapaport et al., *Diagnostic Psychological Testing,* I, 5, on the full Rapaport test battery.

38. Gill, *Rapaport,* 259–60, insisting that those who test become familiar with clinical and psychological functioning. "Admin. Staff Meeting," Apr. 2, 1949, Inst. Archives, M, on Rapaport's clinical manner.

39. Martin Mayman, "Psychoanalytic Theory in Retrospect and Prospect," *BMC* 40 (May 1976): 200; Mildred Law to WCM, June 14, 1947, WCM Papers, M; KAM to Eli Ginzberg, Feb. 15, 1945, KAM Papers, M; Stephen A. Appelbaum, "Rapaport Revisited: Practice," *BMC* 40 (May 1976): 231.

40. Rapaport as quoted in *The Menninger Foundation Ninth Annual Report* (Topeka, 1951), 43. This observation was made in 1950.

41. Gill, *Rapaport,* 162–3, on psychologists mastering the ways of the psychiatrist. Two Rapaport "model" test reports are carried in Lewis L. Robbins, "File No. 6608," Apr. 11, 1941, and "File No. 6687," Oct. 24, 1941, LLR Papers (private).

42. Rapaport et al., *Diagnostic Psychological Testing,* I, 3–4; Holt, "Motives and Thought," 7; Gill, *Rapaport,* 265; *TPR* 6 (July 6, 1945): 3.

43. Appelbaum, *BMC* 40, 231. Lester Luborsky, TRI by LJF, Nov. 6, 1983; Gill, *Rapaport,* 163.

44. Knight, "David Rapaport," 4, Inst. Archives, M, on the group cultivating a borderland. Gilgen, *American Psychology,* 177, on VA and Public Health Service funding.

45. The "Boulder model" is discussed clearly in David Shakow, "Clinical Psychol-

ogy Seen Some 50 Years Later," *American Psychologist* 33 (Feb. 1978), 153–4; Gilgen, *American Psychology,* 178; David Chiszar and Michael Wertheimer, "The Boulder Model: A History of Psychology at the University of Colorado," *JHBS* 24 (Jan. 1988): 86.

46. David Rapaport to Helen Sargent, Jan. 16, 1957, Rapaport Papers, LC. Gill, *Rapaport,* 17–18, 274; Rapaport, *Diagnostic Testing,* II, 11; Robert Holt to George Klein, June 12, 1961, Klein Papers, AHAP.

47. David Rapaport, "Psychoanalysis as a Psychology," n.d. [mid-1940s], 1–3, Inst. Archives, M, "a practical discipline," "a scientific and rational therapy." In this essay, Rapaport lists the Freud writings he is focusing upon in his metapsychological pursuit. Lester Luborsky, PI by LJF, Philadelphia, April 4, 1987, and Philip Holzman, PI by LJF, Topeka, June 20, 1987, on Rapaport's turn away from clinical work and toward metapsychology.

48. Merton Gill and Philip Holzman, eds., "Psychology versus Metapsychology," *PI,* Monograph 36 (1976). Merton Gill, "Metapsychology Is Irrelevant to Psychoanalysis" and Paul W. Pruyser, "Metapsychology as the Whipping Boy," both in Smith, *Human Mind Revisited,* 349–96, for review of the most salient issues and literature in the crusade against metapsychology. Roy Schafer, *A New Language for Psychoanalysis* (New Haven, 1976), is perhaps the most thoroughly reasoned manuscript within that crusade. Martin Mayman, "Psychoanalytic Theory in Retrospect and Prospect," *BMC* 40 (May 1976): 204–7, attacking Rapaport's abstract metapsychology. Robert Holt, TRI by LJF, Dec. 28, 1985, "increasingly pointed questions."

49. Denials that the crusade against metapsychology originated in Topeka are found in Milton Wexler, TRI by LJF, Dec. 24, 1983; Roy Schafer, TRI by LJF, Nov. 7, 1983; Lester Luborsky, TRI by LJF, Nov. 6, 1983; Merton Gill, TRI by LJF, Mar. 30, 1983; Margaret Brenman Gibson, TRI by LJF, May 19, 1984; Robert Holt, TRI by LJF, Dec. 28, 1985; Martin Mayman, TRI by LJF, Apr. 27, 1983; Sibylle Escalona, TRI by LJF, Nov. 7, 1983. John E. Gedo, *Conceptual Issues in Psychoanalysis: Essays in History and Method* (Hillsdale, N.J., 1986), 77, exemplifies a pervasive view that "his disciples" rose up against Rapaport only after he had died in 1960.

50. Appelbaum, *BMC* 40, 229; Roy Schafer, TRI by LJF, Nov. 7, 1983; and Merton Gill, TRI, Mar. 30, 1983, on Gill and Schafer noting differences in preparing *Diagnostic Testing.* Sibylle Escalona, "Some Problems Related to Earliest Phases of Ego Development," n.d., 5, Inst. Archives, M; Sibylle Escalona, "Use of Infant Tests for Predictive Behavior," *BMC* 14 (July 1950): 128. David Rapaport to George Klein, June 15, 1942, Klein Papers, AHAP; George Klein to Jerome S. Bruner, Nov. 2, 1948, Klein Papers, AHAP; *New York Times,* Mar. 29, 1948, on Klein's laboratory.

51. Sibylle Escalona, TRI by LJF, Nov. 7, 1983; Robert Holt, TRI by LJF, Dec. 28, 1985; George Klein, "Conference with D.R. [Rapaport], April 30, 1947," Klein Papers, AHAP. In Robert Holt to LJF, Aug. 27, 1986, he links the thought behind his proposal with Klein (the details of which he does not reveal) to Klein's plans to develop a laboratory.

52. Sibylle Escalona, TRI by LJF, Nov. 7, 1983; Merton Gill, TRI by LJF, Mar. 30, 1983; Roy Schafer, TRI by LJF, Nov. 7, 1983; Martin Mayman, TRI by LJF, Apr. 27, 1983.

53. Martin Mayman, TRI by LJF, Apr. 27, 1983.

54. Gedo, *Conceptual Issues,* 81, cogently observes that as a Kantian, Rapaport became less interested in behaviors (the outcomes of mental processes) and more interested in the nature of mental processes. Philip Holzman, PI by LJF, Topeka, June 20,

1987, and Cambridge, July 28, 1987, and Herbert Schlesinger, TRI by LJF, New York, Dec. 27, 1985, on how they and Klein were less distressed. They noted how in some way they became closer to Rapaport as his research on attention cathexis deepened. Merton Gill, TRI by LJF, Mar. 30, 1983, on Rapaport's growing disinterest in the more explicitly clinical investigations in the group.

55. H. Stuart Hughes, "Social Theory in a New Context," in *The Muses Flee Hitler,* ed. J. C. Jackman and C. M. Borden (Washington, D.C., 1983), 120, on Central European Freudian intellectuals retaining and elaborating theory while dealing with the practical. David Rapaport to Lois and Gardner Murphy, Jan. 22, 1953, Inst. Archives, M, "I came to testing." Rapaport's evolution from clinician to teacher-supervisor-theorist is noted in Merton Gill and George Klein, "The Structuring of Drive and Reality," *IJP* 40, pt. 4 (Oct. 1964): 487; Robert Holt, TRI by LJF, Dec. 28, 1985; Gill, *Rapaport,* 16; Roy Schafer, TRI by LJF, Nov. 7, 1983.

56. Mayman, *BMC* 40, 203–4, sketches Rapaport's drift from clinician to pure theorist. Rapaport is intelligently linked as a pure theorist to Heinz Hartmann and Charles Brenner in Thomas A. Kohut, "Psychohistory as History," *American Historical Review* 91 (Apr. 1986), 344, including n. 14.

57. Gedo, *Conceptual Issues in Psychoanalysis,* chap. 5, "Kant's Way: The Epistemological Challenge of David Rapaport," provides a full discussion of Rapaport's Kantian perspective.

58. Gill, *Rapaport,* 10–11, 75, on Rapaport deploying psychoanalysis to build a general theory of thinking and learning. The point is also underscored in Mayman, *BMC* 40, 202. Gill, *Rapaport,* 302, "the only school."

59. Gill and Klein, *IJP* 40, 485, on Rapaport's tragic view of the human condition. Nathan G. Hale, "From Berggasse XIX to Central Park West: The Americanization of Psychoanalysis, 1919–1940," *JHBS* 14 (Oct. 1978): 307, notes how Freudian drives and restraints could not deal with the concerns of academic psychologists. Focusing entirely upon the American setting, Robert C. Fuller discusses the same point in *Americans and the Unconscious* (New York, 1986), 122–4.

60. Gill, *Rapaport,* 138, for the passage in Rapaport's 1942 paper on the "Concept of Memory" approximating Hartmann. See also *ibid.,* 126. Several of Rapaport's early-1947 publications (*ibid.,* 266, 298) demonstrate that he had read Hartmann's *Ego Psychology* essay in 1946 if not earlier and saw it as his major point of departure. Indeed, he translated it from the German. See also Holt, "Motives and Thought," 4; Gill and Klein, *IJP* 40, 484. For a most perceptive analysis of the place of the Hartmann essay in intellectual history, see H. Stuart Hughes, "Heinz Hartmann and the Conflict Free Sphere," *American Scholar* 44 (Winter 1974–75): 101–9. Merton Gill, TRI by LJF, Mar. 30, 1983, on Rapaport being willing by the late 1940s to elect metapsychology over clinical findings. Gedo, *Conceptual Issues,* 64–81, cogently elaborates on this Rapaport priority.

61. For Rapaport distancing himself from the group, see, e.g., David Rapaport to Mary Switzer, Dec. 6, 1947, KAM Papers, M; John R. Stone to WCM, Mar. 7, 1947, Inst. Archives, M; John R. Stone, "Some Notes on Rapaport's Problem," May 16, 1947, 3, Inst. Archives, M.

62. David Rapaport, Merton Gill, and Margaret Brenman to Alan Gress and Robert S. Morrison, Dec. 8, 1947, KAM Papers, M; "Report on the Activities of the Research Department, July 1, 1947–July 1, 1948," 5, Inst. Archives, M; Robert Morrison to WCM, Dec. 12, 1947, Inst. Archives, M.

63. Lawrence S. Kubie, *The Riggs Story: The Development of the Austen Riggs Center for*

the Study and Treatment of the Neuroses (New York, 1960), 94. Rapaport, Gill, and Brenman to Gregg and Morrison, Dec. 8, 1947, KAM Papers, M; Stuart Miller, PI by LJF, Lee, Mass., June 30, 1985.

64. Kubie, *Riggs Story,* 69, on Schafer departing first for Stockbridge. See also Stuart Miller, PI by LJF, Lee, Mass., June 30, 1985.

65. Karl's treatment of the group is discussed in Roy Schafer, TRI by LJF, Nov. 7, 1983; Merton Gill, TRI by LJF, Mar. 30, 1983. KAM to Mary Switzer, Dec. 3, 1947, KAM Papers, M, on Karl's initial reaction to the exodus. KAM to Gardner Murphy, Jan. 22, 1953, unfiled, M, on his "terrific disappointment" and on how the exodus made research "rather hopeless." The brothers' close friend, journalist Albert Deutsch, warned them after the exodus how "word gets around" that Menninger "is no longer the inspiring, research and treatment center that attracts top notch people" (Deutsch to KAM and WCM, Sept. 8, 1951, Deutsch Papers, APA).

66. David Rapaport to WCM, Oct. 14, 1946, Inst. Archives, M, warning on group discontent. For Rapaport's protests over insufficient research time, see, e.g., Rapaport to John Stone, Jan. 26, 1946, H.S. 52; Rapaport to KAM, Sept. 30, 1946, KAM Papers, M; Rapaport to WCM, Feb. 14, 1947, KAM Papers, M. Margaret Brenman to WCM, July 18, 1947, WCM Papers, M.

67. WCM Diary, Nov. 28, 1947, on how the four brought on their own work load and why it made no sense for them to leave with the Rockefeller grant coming. John Stone to Robert Morrison, Nov. 8, 1947, Inst. Archives, M.

68. David Rapaport to Mary E. Switzer, Dec. 6, 1947, KAM Papers, M. See also Stuart Miller, PI by LJF, June 30, 1985.

69. The points are made, if never fully developed, in Margaret Brenman Gibson, TRI by LJF, May 19, 1984; Merton Gill, TRI by LJF, Mar. 30, 1983; Robert Wallerstein, TRI by LJF, San Francisco, Dec. 29, 1983; Stone, "Some Notes on Rapaport's Problem," 1; Miller, *Papers of Knight,* ix–x; "Austen Riggs Workshop," 50.

70. For Knight's apprehensions over charges of ethical impropriety, see Robert P. Knight to MFSP Fellows, Feb. 10, 1947, WCM Papers, M, and Knight to KAM, Dec. 9, 1947, KAM Papers, M. Schafer's arrangements for analysis with Knight are discussed in KAM to Mary Switzer, Dec. 3, 1947, KAM Papers, M, and Roy Schafer, TRI by LJF, Nov. 7, 1983.

71. The complex dimensions of Knight's analyses of Gill and Brenman are noted in Merton Gill, TRI by LJF, Mar. 30, 1983 (which also discusses the close Gill-Brenman personal relationship); KAM, PI by LJF, Topeka, March 11, 1986; Harlan Crank, PI by LJF, Austin, Nov. 22, 1985; Lewis Robbins, TRI by LJF, New York, Aug. 23, 1983; Margaret Brenman Gibson, TRI by LJF, May 19, 1984; and Brenman, "Austen Riggs Workshop," 69, "incestuous period."

72. Margaret Brenman Gibson, TRI by LJF, May 19, 1984; and Brenman, "Austin Riggs Workshop," 69, 72–3, details her session with Knight. Merton M. Gill to LJF, Apr. 12, Apr. 28, 1988, suspecting Knight intended to invite him and Rapaport as well even before Knight's session with Brenman. Philip Holzman, PI by LJF, Topeka, June 20, 1987, recalls that many Rapaport group members felt Knight was more interested in recruiting Brenman than Rapaport; Holzman himself felt this way.

73. Margaret Brenman Gibson, TRI by LJF, May 19, 1984; "Austin Riggs Workshop," 69–73 ("incestuous training," 69); *Topeka State Journal,* Dec. 13, 1947; Lewis Robbins, TRI by LJF, New York, Aug. 23, 1983 (on Gill initiating divorce proceedings as well as Knight).

74. WCM to KAM, John Stone, and Mildred Law, June 17, 1948, WCM Papers, M, on being "much impressed" with Escalona. See also David Rapaport to Mary E. Switzer, Dec. 6, 1947, KAM Papers; *Topeka State Journal,* Dec. 13, 1947.

75. "Report . . . of the Activities of the Research Department, July 1, 1947–July 1, 1948," 1–4, Inst. Archives, M; Sibylle Escalona, "Minutes of the Meeting of the Medical Council," Jan. 3, 1951, Inst. Archives, M.

76. David Rapaport to Lois and Gardner Murphy, Jan. 22, 1953, Inst. Archives, M, "principle of respect." Escalona's determination for a policy shift toward greater autonomy is indicated in Sibylle Escalona, TRI by LJF, Nov. 7, 1983. See also Lois B. Murphy, TRI by LJF, Topeka, Oct. 1, 1983.

77. Sibylle Escalona, TRI by LJF, Nov. 7, 1983, on Klein noting pressure easing, and greater freedom, after Rapaport departed. See also George S. Klein, "The Menninger Foundation Research on Perception and Personality, 1947–1952: A Review," *BMC* 17 (May 1953): 98. Sibylle Escalona to WCM, June 29, 1949, Inst. Archives, M, encouraging what became the Psychotherapy Research Project. Lolafaye Coyne, TRI by LJF, Topeka, March 11, 1985. Sibylle Escalona to WCM, June 19, 1951, Inst. Archives, M, on projects not directly linked to psychoanalysis. Sibylle Escalona to George Klein, Jan. 31, 1952, Klein Papers, AHAP, "fit into existing patterns."

78. George Klein to David Rapaport, Apr. 15, 1950, Klein Papers, AHAP, on his impending departure from Harvard. Gill and Holzman, "Psychology versus Metapsychology," 7–8, on Klein at Harvard and NYU. George Klein to Robert Holt, Nov. 14, 1950, Klein Papers, AHAP, "taste the flavor of clinical thinking." Sibylle Escalona to George Klein, Nov. 19, 1951, Klein Papers, AHAP, chastising Klein.

79. Gregg's friendship with Karl and Will is indicated in a Gregg file within both the KAM and WCM Papers, M. Gregg's appraisal of Menninger is reported in WCM, "Interview with Dr. Alan Gregg," Oct. 30, 1950, KAM Papers, M; "Minutes of the Meeting of the Medical Council," Nov. 1, 1950, Inst. Archives, M; Sibylle Escalona to George Klein, Nov. 2, 1950, Klein Papers, AHAP.

80. Escalona on the Gregg report in "Minutes of the Meeting of the Medical Council," Jan. 3, 1951, Inst. Archives, M; and Sibylle Escalona to George Klein, Nov. 2, 1950, Klein Papers, AHAP. Sibylle Escalona to KAM, Dec. 27, 1950, KAM Papers, M, tempering Karl's response to Gregg.

81. Hospital physicians' snipes at Research Department personnel are indicated in George Klein to Sibylle Escalona, May 29, 1951, and Klein to Robert Holt, Nov. 13, 1950, both in Klein Papers, AHAP; D. Bernard Foster, TRI by LJF, Topeka, Mar. 15, 1985. Medical Council opposition to Gregg's report is indicated in "Minutes of the Meeting of the Medical Council," Nov. 1, 1950, Inst. Archives, M. KAM to Gardner Murphy, Jan. 22, 1953, unfiled, M, "thirty or forty projects."

82. Sibylle Escalona, TRI by LJF, Nov. 7, 1983, on her perceptions of morale among researchers and of some considering jobs elsewhere. Sibylle Escalona to George Klein, Apr. 9, 1951, Klein Papers, AHAP, "unattached woman" and "need to narrow down." See also George Klein to Sibylle Escalona, May 29, 1951, Klein Papers, AHAP, and WCM Diary, Feb. 11, 1952.

83. Sibylle Escalona to George Klein, Apr. 9, 1951, Klein Papers, AHAP, on informing Will of her intention to leave in 1952. "Annual Report of the Research Department for the Year 1951–52," 1, Inst. Archives, M, on Holt replacing Escalona temporarily. *New York Times,* Apr. 6, 1952, on Escalona leaving and Murphy due to replace her.

CHAPTER TEN: *"In the Hands of the Barons"*

1. The planning of C. F. Menninger Hospital is covered in *Topeka State Journal,* Dec. 12, 1951; *Topeka Daily Capital,* Mar. 29, 1953; *TPR* 16 (Jan. 15, 1955): 4; Lewis Robbins, TRI by LJF, New York, Aug. 24, 1983; Irving Kartus, TRI by Irving Sheffel, Leawood, Kans., Apr. 3, 1983; Mildred Law, TRI by CWM, Topeka, Sept. 29, 1969, M. *The Menninger Foundation Annual Report for July 1953–June 1954* (Topeka, 1954), 2, "bright sunshine and brighter hopes."

2. Irving Sheffel, PI by LJF, Topeka, Nov. 14, 1984, critiques fully how Law's hospital plans failed to reflect future competition. "Psychiatric Hospitals for Referral of Patients," Oct. 1955, Inst. Archives, M, details that competition. See also "Professional Staffing Pattern in Private Psychiatric Hospitals—1967," Inst. Archives, M.

3. George E. Gifford, Jr., ed., *Psychoanalysis, Psychotherapy and the New England Medical Scene, 1894–1944* (New York, 1978), 290, and Lawrence S. Kubie, *The Riggs Story: The Development of the Austen Riggs Center for the Study and Treatment of the Neuroses* (New York, 1960), 123, report on Austen Riggs developments. Ezra Stotland and Arthur L. Kobler, *Life and Death of a Mental Hospital* (Seattle, 1965), 229–30, on the Menninger link to the "Crest Hospital" (Pinel Clinic) in Seattle. Lewis L. Robbins, "Survey of the Hillside Hospital" (unpub. ms., Feb. 1959), LLR Papers (private) on the Menninger link with that facility. S. B. Sutton, *Crossroads in Psychiatry: A History of the McLean Hospital* (Washington, D.C., 1986), 273–4, on Stanton's reforms. "Psychiatric Hospitals for Referral of Patients," Oct. 1955, Inst. Archives, M, reports on the Langley-Porter Clinic and the Institute for Nervous and Mental Diseases.

4. George Klein to Herbert Schlesinger and Philip Holzman, Mar. 26, 1951, Klein Papers, AHAP; WCM to Paul R. Hawley, July 6, 1954, WCM Papers, M; Harry Levinson to Presidential Search Committee, Aug. 9, 1966, 1, Transactions of Presidential Search Comm., M.

5. Walter Bromberg, *Psychiatry Between the Wars, 1918–1945: A Recollection* (Westport, 1982), 165, characterizes the twentieth-century neural sciences in a two-cycle pattern—psychologism alternating with organicity. The advent of the psychotropic drugs in America would seem to represent a return to organicity. Their emergence is discussed in Janet Colaizzi, "Predicting Dangerousness: Psychiatric Ideas in the United States, 1800–1983" (unpub. Ph.D. diss., Ohio State University, 1983), 257; John M. Reisman, *A History of Clinical Psychology* (New York, 1976), 343; William P. Gronfein, "From Madhouse to Main Street: The Changing Place of Mental Illness in Post World War II America" (unpub. Ph.D. diss., SUNY at Stony Brook, 1983), 124–5. *The Menninger Foundation Report of Progress for the Year July 1, 1954–June 30, 1955* (Topeka, 1955), 45–6, on the beginnings of research on Thorazine use.

6. There is a significant if factually imprecise literature on the shift away from state hospitals and the community mental health movement. See, e.g., W. R. Curtis, "The Deinstitutionalization Story," *Public Interest,* Fall 1986, 45–6; Gronfein, "Madhouse to Main Street," 96–8, 138, 187, 222; Andrew T. Scull, *Decarceration: Community Treatment and the Deviant: A Radical View* (Englewood Cliffs, N.J., 1977), 66, 138–9. The most reliable research on the topic is Gerald N. Grob, "The Forging of Mental Health Policy in America: World War II to New Frontier," *JHMAS* 42 (Oct. 1987): 410–46.

7. John R. Neill and Arnold M. Ludwig, "Psychiatry and Psychotherapy: Past and Future," *AJPT* 34 (Jan. 1980): 47, on the general milieu created by the community mental health movement. See also Grob, *JHMAS* 42, 410–46. The impact of that

milieu on Menninger is evidenced in Lois B. Murphy, "Report of the Personnel Policies Committee," June 1, 1966, 6, Inst. Archives, M; Paul Pruyser to Education Council, Feb. 10, 1960, Pruyser Papers, Inst. Archives, M; Irving Sheffel, PI by LJF, Topeka, Jan. 10, 1985.

8. See "Minutes of Twelfth Annual Meeting of Board of Trustees and Governors," Oct. 10–11, 1953, 461, Inst. Archives, M; WCM, "Personally Yours," *MQ* 8 (Winter 1954): 30–2; and *Topeka Daily Capital*, Oct. 12, 1953—all on the 1953 meeting and the Ten Year Plan. Implemented over the next decade, the plan shifted the Menninger budget from 80 percent for the cost of inpatient clinical services and 20 percent for nonclinical endeavors (primarily community programs) to a 60–40 percent mix. This shift is noted in "Executive Committee Minutes of Board of Trustees," Nov. 18, 1967, 5, MT.

9. For the warning that Karl drafted, see KAM, WCM, CFM, "Some Statements for the Counsel and Guidance of the Trustees and Medical Council of the Menninger Clinic and Menninger Foundation in Future Years," Aug. 6, 1952, 3, Inst. Archives, M. See also Lester Luborsky, TRI by LJF, Philadelphia, Nov. 6, 1983, recalling Karl's remarks, and "Minutes of Long Range Planning Committee [of Trustees]," Nov. 19, 1965, 8, KAM Papers, M. WCM to KAM, Oct. 12, 1955, KAM Papers, M.

10. J. Cotter Hirschberg to Presidential Search Committee, Sept. 22, 1966, Transactions of Presidential Search Committee, M, "no longer in the forefront." See also Hirschberg to WCM, Sept. 14, 1953, unprocessed, M. Joseph Satten to KAM, Mar. 16, 1962, Pruyser Papers, Inst. Archives, M. "Summary of Interview with Dr. P. Holzman," Aug. 30, 1966, Transactions of Presidential Search Committee, M, "small private mental hospital."

11. Christine M. Shea, "The Ideology of Mental Health and the Emergence of the Therapeutic Liberal State: The American Mental Hygiene Movement, 1900–1930" (unpub. Ph.D. diss., University of Illinois, 1980), 167–8, on Southard as a pioneer in industrial mental health. The point is underscored in Frederick P. Gay, *The Open Mind: Elmer Ernest Southard, 1876–1920* (Chicago, 1938).

12. *The Menninger Foundation Report of Progress for the Year July 1, 1964–June 30, 1965* (Topeka, 1965), 5, "The pressure of circumstances." "Minutes of Medical Council," June 7, 1950, Inst. Archives, M, on Will creating the Department of Social Applications. "Minutes of Board of Trustees and Governors," Apr. 23, 1960 (Report by Dr. Satten for the Long Range Planning Committee), on the doubling of Menninger programs.

13. The elitist aspect of the new Menninger social programs is discussed in Paul Pruyser, PI by LJF, Topeka, Mar. 11, 1985; RWM, "History," n.d. (1974), 5, from Edward Greenwood.

14. Dale L. Womble, "The Menninger Foundation's Early Experience in Training Marriage Counselors," *FR* 33 (Apr. 1984): 233–6, provides accurate and comprehensive coverage of the Marriage Counseling Service. For Foster's general orientation, see Robert Foster to WCM, KAM, Lewis Robbins, and Edward Greenwood, Apr. 14, 1949, Inst. Archives, M; Foster to Lester Roach, July 31, 1951, WCM Papers, M. For staff debate over the service, see Lewis Robbins, TRI by LJF, New York, Aug. 23, 1983, and Paul Pruyser, PI by LJF, Topeka, Nov. 16, 1983.

15. Thomas W. Klink, "Training in Pastoral Care and Counseling at the Menninger Foundation . . . 1951–1963," n.d. (1963), Klink Papers, M; Paul Pruyser, "A History of Religion and Psychiatry Activities at the Menninger Foundation," n.d., unproc-

essed, M; Pruyser, "Religion and Psychiatry," *MQ* 11 (Sept. 1957): 3; "Religion and Psychiatry at the Menninger Foundation," *MQ* 18 (Winter 1964–65): 10; KAM, PI by LJF, Topeka, Nov. 14, 1984.

16. "Department of Industrial Psychiatry Prospectus: 1955–1956," Inst. Archives, M; "Seminars for Executives," *MQ* 13 (Winter 1959): 10; Lyle M. Spencer, "A Fresh Step Forward," *MQ* 9 (Winter 1955): 1–2; "Meeting Industry's Most Critical Need," *Kansas* (July–Aug. 1960): 4; "Industrial Mental Health," *MQ* 11 (June 1957): 19–20; *TPR*, Mar. 1965, 4; W. Walter Menninger to Philip Menninger, Jan. 9, 1967, Inst. Archives, M.

17. The Law and Psychiatry Division is discussed in *TPR*, Mar. 1965, 7, 9; KAM, PI by LJF, Topeka, Nov. 14, 1984; *The Menninger Foundation Report of Progress for the Year July 1, 1960–June 30, 1961* (Topeka, 1961), 37–8; *The Menninger Foundation Report of Progress for the Year July 1, 1964–June 30, 1965* (Topeka, 1965), 34; W. Walter Menninger to RWM, Jan. 9, 1967, Murphy Papers, M. The Division of School Mental Health is discussed in "Annual Report, Department of Preventive Psychiatry," 1968–69, 2, Inst. Archives, M.

18. "The Retirement and Geriatric Center," *MQ* 16 (Summer 1962): 19–20; William Tarnower, PI by LJF, Topeka, Nov. 11, 1984; Prescott Thompson, TRI by LJF, Los Angeles, May 9, 1984; *The Menninger Foundation Report of Progress for the Year July 1, 1961–June 30, 1962* (Topeka 1962), 39.

19. William H. Robinson, TRI by LJF, Topeka, May 16, 1985.

20. Bergman quoted in Philip Holzman to George Klein, Apr. 17, 1951, Klein Papers, AHAP, "in the hands of the barons!" Paul Bergman to Members of Topeka Psychoanalytic Society, Dec. 17, 1952, 6, Inst. Archives, M.

21. Larry E. Greiner, "Evolution and Revolution as Organizations Grow," *Harvard Business Review—On Management* I (1985): esp. 248.

22. "Minutes of Clinical Council," Feb. 1, 1961, 1, Bernard Hall Papers, M, on the number of councils and "Foundation as a whole." Lester T. Roach to WCM, Feb. 9, 1956, Roach Papers, M, reporting on why Karl was considering abandoning his monthly staff meeting.

23. Harlan Crank, PI by LJF, Austin, Nov. 22, 1985; Robert Holt to George Klein, Nov. 17, 1950, Klein Papers, AHAP. Herbert Modlin, TRI by LJF, Topeka, Mar. 9, 1983. "Summary of Interview with Philip Holzman," Aug. 30, 1966, 1, in Transactions of Presidential Search Committee, M. Philip Holzman to George Klein, Mar. 3, 1967, Klein Papers, AHAP.

24. Lois B. Murphy, "Report of the Personnel Policies Committee," June 1, 1966, 2–3, KAM Papers, M. "Minutes of Executive Committee of Senior Council," Sept. 20, 1963, Inst. Archives, M. "Foundation House Building Committee to Senior Council," Apr. 19, 1965, 1, Pruyser Papers, M. Margaret Mead, "Notes for Bread and Butter Letter," May 27, 1959, Mead Papers, LC; Margaret Mead to Educational Council, Menninger Foundation, Oct. 18, 1963, 13, Inst. Archives, M.

25. Lester T. Roach to WCM, May 4, 1955, Roach Papers, M, on the salaries and salary increases for Menninger's staff; Robbins's and Hirschberg's stand out. Lewis Robbins, "Palace Revolt," Apr. 30, 1979, LLR Papers (private); J. Cotter Hirschberg, TRI by LJF, Topeka, June 1, 1983.

26. For hospital patient census and earnings data, see *The Menninger Foundation Report of Progress for the Year July 1, 1956–June 30, 1957* (Topeka, 1957), 75; "Foundation Staff Meeting Report #6," June 6, 1967, 7, Inst. Archives, M; Irving Sheffel, PI by LJF,

Topeka, Nov. 14, 1984, and Sheffel's detailed ledger for foundation income and expenses, 1953–1970. Hospital leadership perceptions of being drained of staff and paying for other programs, particularly research, are revealed in "Minutes of Meeting of Clinical Services Committee," Jan. 2, 1957, Inst. Archives, M; Peter Fleming to J. Cotter Hirschberg, Nov. 23, 1966, Inst. Archives, M; "Committee on Clinical Work: Preliminary Report," Mar. 19, 1966, 1, Roach Papers, M.

27. The size of hospital growth factor undercutting the guide tradition is noted in Ann Appelbaum to LJF, Nov. 8, 1983 (letter); RGM, PI by LJF, Topeka, Aug. 2, 1984. Lewis Robbins, TRI by LJF, New York, Aug. 23, 1983, on the importance of Will's absences. The difficulty new hospital physicians had with the guide is revealed in "Administrative Conference," Mar. 16, 1949, 1, Inst. Archives, M; "Minutes, Hospital Administrative Meeting," Apr. 7, 1959, Inst. Archives, M; Gerald Aronson, TRI by LJF, Los Angeles, Dec. 26, 1983; Herbert Schlesinger, TRI by LJF, New York, Dec. 21, 1985; "A.T. Unit Leaders Meeting with Dr. Robert Menninger," June 10, 1959, 2, Inst. Archives, M. Sydney Smith, ed., *The Human Mind Revisited* (New York, 1978), 458; and Peter Novotny, PI by LJF, Topeka, Feb. 28, Nov. 11, 1984, on how the guide failed to incorporate ego psychology. Peter Hartocollis, "A Brief History of a Psycho-Analytic Hospital," *Newsletter, American Psychological Association,* June 1975, 6–7, "the hospital aimed at protecting."

28. The need to revise the guide was brought up in "Minutes, Hospital Administrative Meeting," Apr. 7, 1959, Inst. Archives, M; informal meetings to revise the guide are recalled in Ann Appelbaum to LJF, Nov. 8, 1983 (letter), and James Pratt, PI by LJF, Topeka, Sept. 29, 1983.

29. WCM to Lewis Robbins, Apr. 25, 1949, WCM Papers, M, making Robbins hospital director. Robbins's general conduct and goals as hospital director are indicated in Robbins, TRI by LJF, New York, Aug. 23, 1983; Hazel Bruce, PI by LJF, Topeka, Jan. 11, 1985.

30. Lewis L. Robbins to Paul Pruyser, July 15, 1982, LLR Papers (private), "the basic truths." See also "Minutes of Section Chiefs Meeting," June 26, 1952, Inst. Archives, M. A good characterization of Robbins's hospital vision is found in Robert P. Knight to KAM, Jan. 6, 1966, KAM Papers, M. Peter Fleming, TRI by Verne Horne, Topeka, Dec. 24, 1974, M, on doctors protesting against and sometimes even meeting with Robbins. "Minutes of Medical Council," Nov. 14, 1951, Inst. Archives, M, on Robbins delegating authority to team captains.

31. Lewis Robbins, TRI by LJF, New York, Aug. 23, 1983; and Robbins to Paul Pruyser, July 15, 1982, LLR Papers (private).

32. For Kartus's administrative style as director, see Irving Kartus, TRI by Irving Sheffel, Leawood, Kans., Apr. 3, 1983; KAM to WCM, Nov. 7, 1957, KAM Papers, M; KAM to Irving Kartus, June 6, 1957, IK Papers (private); Kartus to Dexter Bullard, Oct. 21, 1957, Mildred Law Papers, M.

33. The Van der Waals background and style is conveyed in *Roundabout,* Apr. 16, 1959, 6; Van der Waals to KAM, Apr. 26, 1961, KAM Papers, M; Activities Therapy Planning Committee, July 8, 1959, 1, Mar. 22, 1961, 2, Inst. Archives, M; "Minutes. Hospital Administrative Meeting," Mar. 13, Mar. 31, Apr. 7, 1959, Inst. Archives, M. ("Stephanie Michaels") "Years óf Change" (unpub. ms., 1975), 135–6, provides an interesting contrast between the character of the hospital under Kartus and Van der Waals from the perspective of a patient.

34. Fleming's *de facto* control of the hospital under Kartus and Van der Waals is

revealed in Bernard Hall, Otto Kernberg, and William Tarnower, TRI on Coughlin Case, Topeka, Sept. 30, 1961, M; Peter Fleming to Irving Kartus, Dec. 5, 1958, Inst. Archives, M; Fleming, TRI by Verne Horne, Topeka, Dec. 24, 1974, M; Pancho Gomez to Bernard Hall, Aug. 6, 1968, RWM Papers, M. See Ruth Bernard to Lewis Robbins in "Annual Report, Fiscal Year 1949–50, Personal Evaluations," Inst. Archives, M, on Fleming's take-charge attitude on joining the hospital staff.

35. Peter Fleming c.v., M; KAM, PI by LJF, Topeka, Nov. 14, 1984.

36. Peter Fleming to J. Cotter Hirschberg, Nov. 12, 1966, Inst. Archives, M, "closer to the clinical workings." Fleming, TRI by Verne Horne, Topeka, Dec. 24, 1974, M, on limiting the power of the Topeka Institute.

37. Hall, Kernberg, Tarnower, TRI on Coughlin Case, Sept. 30, 1961, M, on Fleming's centralization policy and his view that nurses and attendants were to be direct extensions of physicians. Peter Fleming to Herman Van der Waals, Dec. 10, 1959, Inst. Archives, M, on seeking to merge nursing and activities therapy departments. Donald Frey to Social Workers, Adult Services, Feb. 18, 1966, Inst. Archives, M, on Fleming seeking to make the physician and social worker the core of the treatment team.

38. William A. Roberts, TRI by LJF, Topeka, July 31, 1984, on Fleming's use of associates like Schloesser and his running affairs under Van der Waals. Peter Novotny, PI by LJF, Topeka, Nov. 11, 1984, June 2, 1987, on Fleming's manipulations to win over staff. Fleming, TRI by Verne Horne, Topeka, Dec. 24, 1974, M, on Fleming's sensitivity to his doctors. Stephen Appelbaum, TRI by LJF, Prairie Village, Kans., June 24, 1987, on Fleming's *ad hoc* approach to staff. KAM, PI by LJF, Topeka, Nov. 11, 1984, on Fleming's management of Karl in hospital affairs.

39. "Professional Staffing Pattern. 10 Private Psychiatric Hospitals—1967," M, is a chart detailing the number of hospital patients and the number of staff at each professional rank at Menninger and nine of its private competitors.

40. Peter Fleming, TRI by Verne Horne, Topeka, Dec. 24, 1974, M; "Minutes of Meeting of Chief of Sections," Aug. 21, 1952, Inst. Archives, M; Linda Hilles, "Changing Trends in the Application of Psychoanalytic Principle to a Psychiatric Hospital," *BMC* 32 (1968): 203–18; Harvey Schloesser, TRI by LJF, Topeka, June 21, 1987.

41. Otto Kernberg and Ann Appelbaum, "A Crisis in the Adjunctive Therapy Department," Oct. 13, 1971, 1–2, RWM Papers, M; Ann Appelbaum to LJF, Nov. 8, 1983 (letter); Ann Appelbaum, et al., "Dependency versus Autonomy: The Group Conference Method Applied to an Organizational Problem," *BMC* 39 (Jan. 1975): 56.

42. "Eighth Annual Meeting, Board of Trustees," Oct. 2, 1949, 5, MT; "Department of Adult Psychiatry Report to Trustees," Oct. 1949, Exhibit B, 1, Roach Papers, M; Thomas Dolgoff, TRI by LJF, Topeka, Jan. 4, 1983; RGM, PI by LJF, Topeka, Aug. 2, Nov. 15, 1984.

43. Martin Mayman, "Style, Focus, Language and Content of an Ideal Psychological Test Report," *Journal of Projective Techniques* 23 (1959): 456; "Annual Report for 1952–53, Adjunctive Therapy Department," 4, Inst. Archives, M; "Nursing—A.T. Meeting, Dec. 4, 1962, of Activities Planning Committee," 1, Inst. Archives, M.

44. Cautious receptivity to the new drugs is indicated in *TPR* 16 (Jan. 15, 1955): 4; Philip Holzman to DAP Psychological Staff and Thorazine Research Committee, Apr. 2, 1955, Inst. Archives, M; WCM to George Jackson, Feb. 24, 1956, and to Claude Petrus, July 6, 1960, both in WCM Papers, M; C. B. Palmer, "New Laurels for the Menningers," *New York Times Magazine,* Nov. 6, 1955, 44, 47. Concrete changes in hospital policy under Fleming in drugs and general biopsychiatric areas are noted in

Harvey Schloesser, TRI by LJF, Topeka, June 21, 1987; Philip Holzman, PI by LJF, Cambridge, Mass., July 28, 1987; Ursula Zimmerman, TRI by LJF, Topeka, Nov. 13, 1984; William Simpson, "Clinical Research at the Menninger Hospital," Jan. 25, 1966, KAM Papers, M.

45. The therapeutic community concept emerging in postwar England is discussed well in Smith, *Human Mind Revisited,* 458, and Alfredo Namnum, PI by LJF, Topeka, Jan. 3, 1983.

46. National receptivity to the therapeutic community concept is discussed in Sutton, *Crossroads in Psychiatry,* 255; Gifford, *Psychoanalysis, Psychotherapy,* 274–8. The deployment of measures at Menninger consistent with the therapeutic community concept is noted in Hartocollis, *Newsletter. American Psychoanalytic Association,* June 1975, 6–7; Gerald Aronson, TRI by LJF, Los Angeles, Dec. 26, 1983; Audrey Johnson, "Social Work Staff Meeting," Nov. 19, 1958, 1, Inst. Archives, M. ("Stephanie Michaels") "Years of Change," esp. 81–8 on the development of patients' rights traditions. Michaels's view is backed, for example, by Minnie Harlow, "A System of Groups in the Hospital Community Dealing with the Social Functioning of the Patient Population," Feb. 7, 1964, Special Collections, M; Ursula Zimmerman, TRI by LJF, Topeka, Nov. 13, 1984. See also "Stephanie Michaels," PI by LJF, Topeka, June 20, 1987.

47. Staff expressions of greater freedom and more choices are reported in William Simpson, TRI by LJF, Topeka, July 27, 1983; Peter Fleming, TRI by Verne Horne, Topeka, Dec. 18, 1974, M; Prescott Thompson, TRI by LJF, Los Angeles, May 9, 1984, "using our best judgment." ("Michaels") "Years of Change," 111.

48. "Hospital Rates," 1954–1983, from Menninger Office of Vice President for Operations. "The Magic of Menninger," *Medical World News,* Mar. 27, 1964, reports a 25 percent insurance coverage average. Del Gerstenberger to Irving Sheffel, May 20, 1987 (in possession of LJF), suggests the coverage was lower; he recalled only about fifty health insurance claims processed each month in the mid-1960s. Hospital social characteristics in the 1950s and 1960s are reported in Linda Hilles, "Class Differences in the Mental Illness of Young Hospitalized Patients," *BMC* 33 (July 1969): 198–203; Harvey Schloesser to Bernard Hall, Sept. 15, 1965, Bernard Hall Papers, M; Harvey Schloesser, TRI by LJF, Topeka, June 21, 1987; "Stephanie Michaels," PI by LJF, Topeka, June 20, 1987; "Hospital Statistics," July 1, 1961–June 30, 1962," MMR.

49. For "improved"/"unimproved" outcome percentages, see "Hospital Statistics," July 1, 1956–June 30, 1957, July 1, 1957–June 30, 1958, MMR; "Annual Report of the Hospital Division," July 1, 1957–June 30, 1958, M; Hilles, *BMC* 33, 204. "Hospital Statistics," July 1, 1970–June 30, 1971, lists readmission rates from 1946 to 1971. It is significant that "Hospital Statistics," July 1, 1958–June 30, 1959, July 1, 1961–June 30, 1962, July 1, 1965–June 30, 1966, revealed something that had not existed under hospital administrations before Fleming. Statistics on "diagnosis and condition at termination of psychotherapy" were divided in a way that distinguished three separate categories of patients. One category was "Social Adjustment" cases; these involved efforts to help patients get along better with others. Treatment consistently yielded good outcomes—82% "improved" and 18% "unimproved" in 1958–59, 70%/30% in 1961–62, and 71%/29% in 1965–66. "Character Structure" disorders, the second category, involved fundamental developmental flaws in the patient's character makeup. These cases consistently yielded the most unsuccessful outcomes. Although the "improved"/"unimproved" ratio was 61%/39% in 1958–59, it shifted very drastically to 21%/79% in 1961–62 and to a somewhat better 32%/68% in 1965–66.

Percentages for the third category of patients, "Psychiatric Syndrome" maladies like deep depression, psychoses, and narcissistic disorders, were most encouraging. In 1958–59, 12% were "in complete remission" and 77% were "improved," while only 11% were "unchanged or worse." In 1961–62, the break was 8%/74%/18%, whereas it stood at 12%/65%/23% in 1965–66. This suggests that without the increase in patients with character disorders under Fleming, the improvement in the general "improved"/"unimproved" ratio over what it had been in the immediate postwar years might have been even greater.

50. Robert S. Wallerstein, *Forty-Two Lives in Treatment: A Study of Psychoanalysis and Psychotherapy* (New York, 1986), 515. Raw data for this PRP publication is found in Inst. Archives, M.

51. Robert L. Kahn, Max Fink, Nathan Siegel, "Sociopsychological Aspects of Psychiatric Treatment," *Archives of General Psychiatry* 14 (Jan.–June 1966): 20–5; Hilles, *BMC* 33, esp. 204.

52. Charles K. Kanno and Raymond M. Glasscote, *Private Psychiatric Hospitals—A National Survey* (Washington, D.C., 1966). In "Report of the Multidiscipline Planning Committee of the C. F. Menninger Memorial Hospital," Feb. 15, 1967, Inst. Archives, M, esp. 23, staff comparisons to several private hospital rivals are detailed. See also William Robinson, TRI by LJF, Topeka, May 16, 1985, and James Horne, PI by LJF (telephone), Apr. 28, 1987, for examples of Fleming's staff reflecting on their performance with their patients.

53. The immediate 1952 physical plant changes are discussed in "Minutes of Medical Council," Mar. 24, 1952, Inst. Archives, M; *TPR* 13 (Aug. 15, 1952): 16; *TPR* 13 (Nov. 15, 1952): 15–16. A land purchase for the future physical plant is cited in "Meeting of the Board of Trustees and Governors," Mar. 22, 1953, MT; Secretary to Board of Governors in "Annual Report of the Secretary," Sept. 10, 1953, 6, Inst. Archives, M. The details of negotiations to recruit Hirschberg are noted in "Minutes of Medical Council," Feb. 20, 1952, Inst. Archives, M; WCM to Board of Governors in "Annual Report of the General Secretary," Sept. 8, 1952, 6, Inst. Archives, M; J. Cotter Hirschberg, TRI by LJF, Topeka, June 1, 1983; Arthur Mandelbaum, TRI by LJF, Topeka, May 25, 1984.

54. "Board of Trustees' Eighth Annual Meeting," Oct. 2, 1949, 35, Inst. Archives, M; "Annual Meeting of Board of Trustees and Governors," Oct. 20–1, 1951, 15, MT; "Requests for Grant-in-Aid for the Southard School to the National Institute of Mental Health," Jan. 12, 1953, 2, Inst. Archives, M; Lester Roach, TRI by LJF, Topeka, Sept. 14, 1985.

55. For the new perspective of the Menninger brothers toward the Children's Division, see *TPR* 14 (Jan. 1953): 2; "Minutes of Board of Trustees and Governors," Mar. 28, 1954, Oct. 15–16, 1955, Apr. 23, 1960; all in MT.

56. J. Cotter Hirschberg and Keith A. Bryan, "Problems in the Differential Diagnosis of Childhood Schizophrenia," *Neurology and Psychiatry in Childhood* 34 (1956): 460; "Annual Report of the Child Psychiatry Department for 1952–53," 1–2, H.S. 87, M; J. Cotter Hirschberg, "The Basic Functions of a Child Psychiatrist in Any Setting," *Journal of American Academy of Child Psychiatry* 5 (Apr. 1966): 365.

57. *Ibid.*, 365, "less definite clear-cut neuroses." "Annual Report of the Child Psychiatry Department for 1952–53," 15, H.S. 87, M, "modify classical analytic techniques."

58. The Ekstein opposition is indicated in J. Cotter Hirschberg, TRI by LJF, Topeka,

June 1, 1983; Rudolf Ekstein, TRI by LJF, Los Angeles, Dec. 24, 1983; Lois B. Murphy, TRI by LJF, Topeka, Oct. 1, 1983. Unfortunately, it is not treated in Dorothea Oberlauter's rather eulogistic *Rudolf Ekstein—Leben und Werk* (Salzburg, 1985). WCM Diary, May 29, 1953, "split."

59. Rudolf Ekstein, Judith Wallerstein, Arthur Mandelbaum, "Counter-Transference in the Residential Treatment of Children: Treatment Failure in a Child with Symbiotic Psychosis" (unpub. ms., 1957), 23, Otto Fleishman Papers, M; J. Cotter Hirschberg, "A Long-Range Plan for Child Psychiatry," Sept. 30, 1951, 2–3, Inst. Archives, M.

60. KAM to WCM, Apr. 10, 1957, KAM Papers, M, on the short work week of Hirschberg's staff and his refusal to send any staff to the adult hospital. "Annual Report of General Secretary, from WCM to all Members of Board of Governors," Sept. 8, 1952, 6, Inst. Archives, M, "the broad spread in age groups." Arthur Mandelbaum, TRI by LJF, Topeka, May 25, 1984, comments on this policy. Lester Roach to WCM, Feb. 9, Mar. 23, 1956, Apr. 19, 1957, Roach Papers, M, attacking Hirschberg. Hirschberg to Jane Froman, Jan. 27, 1954, unprocessed, M, and Mandelbaum, "The Menninger Foundation Department of Child Psychiatry," 1956, 10, unprocessed, M, on the comfortable atmosphere of the division.

61. "Training Program in Child Psychiatry. Child Psychiatric Service of the Menninger Clinic," Nov. 1, 1956, 5, unprocessed, M, "special problems." For Roach's criticism of Hirschberg, see Lester T. Roach to WCM, Feb. 9, Mar. 23, 1956, Apr. 19, 1957, Roach Papers, M. WCM Diary, July 12, 1956, explains his disenchantment with Hirschberg. KAM, PI by LJF, Topeka, May 25, 1984; and KAM to WCM, Sept. 30, 1955, Apr. 10, 1957, KAM Papers, M, on his opposition to Hirschberg.

62. Arthur Mandelbaum, TRI by LJF, Topeka, May 25, 1984; Mandelbaum, "Department of Child Psychiatry," 35; "Annual Report of the Child Psychiatry Department for 1952–53," 9, H.S. 87, M; Dorothy Fuller et al., "Some Research Implications in the Evaluation of a Borderline Psychotic Child," *BMC* 18 (Mar. 1954): 73, "helping the parents"; J. Cotter Hirschberg and Manuel Escudero, "The Impact of an Emotionally Disturbed Child on His Family," Oct. 1955, 2, Special Collections, M.

63. The beginnings of the scholarship program are covered in J. Cotter Hirschberg to David Rapaport, Feb. 1, 1955, David Rapaport Papers, LC; WCM to Board of Governors, Feb. 22, 1955, MT; Lester Roach to David Neiswanger, May 12, 1955, MT; J. Cotter Hirschberg to Clay Judson, June 1, 1955, MT; *The Menninger Foundation Report of Progress for the Year July 1, 1955–June 30, 1956* (Topeka, 1956), 64; *Topeka State Journal,* Oct. 15, 1955. Mandelbaum, "Department of Child Psychiatry," 5–6, explains how the scholarship program lowered per capita cost. Basil Cole, PI by LJF, Topeka, Sept. 11, 1986, on Children's Division royalty donations and the Seeley contribution.

64. The potential for adolescent patients is noted in "Minutes of the Clinical Council," Oct. 6, 1965, 2, Bernard Hall Papers, M. See also Charlton R. Price, " 'House Research' on Organizational Change in a Residential Treatment Center," 1962, 1–2, Special Collections, M. Robert Switzer, TRI by LJF, Trevose, Pa., Nov. 4, 1983, on Will exploring fund-raising in child psychiatry, on the Good Samaritan donation, and on Hill-Burton funds. See also WCM Diary, Dec. 31, 1956, Oct. 16, 1958.

65. Robert Switzer, TRI by LJF, Trevose, Pa., Nov. 4, 1983. Switzer, TRI by Southard School Journalism Class, n.d. (1986).

66. KAM, PI by LJF, Topeka, Nov. 11, 1984; Lester Roach, PI by LJF, Topeka, Mar. 9, 1983; Arthur Mandelbaum, TRI by LJF, Topeka, May 25, 1984; Robert Switzer, TRI

by LJF, Trevose, Pa., Nov. 4, 1983; WCM Diary, May 8, 1957, "wants to be an administrator."

67. Switzer, TRI by LJF, Trevose, Pa., Nov. 4, 1983; Price, " 'House Research,' " 3; Basil Cole, PI by LJF, Topeka, Sept. 11, 1986.

68. Tarlton Morrow to Robert Switzer, Nov. 2, 1966, "does not necessarily mean disloyalty"; William B. Easson to Drs. Switzer, Hirschberg, Morrow, Mar. 23, 1965; Charlton Price, "Children's Service Research, April 1961–July 1962"; William Easson to Robert Switzer, June 29, 1967; all in Switzer Papers, M. Betty Bowling, TRI by LJF, Topeka, Sept. 13, 1986, on Switzer's naval captain image and mannerisms.

69. Arthur Mandelbaum, TRI by LJF, Topeka, May 25, 1984; Roger Hoffmaster, PI by LJF, Topeka, Mar. 15, 1985; Robert Switzer to Bernard Hall, July 16, 1965, Switzer Papers, M; "Minutes of the Executive Committee of Senior Council," Dec. 28, 1964, 1, Pruyser Papers, M; "Staff Memo #26" (by RWM), Sept. 19, 1966, 1, Roach Papers, M.

70. Robert Switzer, TRI by LJF, Trevose, Pa., Nov. 4, 1983. Basil Cole, PI by LJF, Topeka, Sept. 11, 1986.

71. Robert Switzer and Arthur Mandelbaum, "Selection of Patients for Child Psychiatric Inpatient Care," 1959, 1, 5, Inst. Archives, M; Paul Toussieng to Thomas W. Klink, Aug. 16, 1960, Klink Papers, M; "Evaluation Book Conference," Apr. 28, May 5, 1960, Inst. Archives, M.

72. Robert Switzer, TRI by LJF, Trevose, Pa., Nov. 4, 1983; Betty Bowling, TRI by LJF, Topeka, Sept. 13, 1986; Price, " 'House Research,' " 2–4.

73. Murphy's general background is revealed in his article "Notes for a Parapsychological Autobiography," *Journal of Parapsychology* 21 (Sept. 1957): esp. 165–6; Gardner Murphy to KAM, Mar. 13, 1959, Murphy Papers, M; Lois B. Murphy to "Dear Friends," Apr. 22, 1979, Murphy Papers, AHAP; Ledford J. Bischof, *Interpreting Personality Theories* (New York, 1964), 511–12. See Gardner Murphy, "Types of Word-Association in Dementia Praecox, Manic Depressives, and Normal Persons," *AJP* 2 (1923): 539–71, for his continuum observations on Manhattan State Hospital patients.

74. Murphy's contact at CCNY with future members of the Menninger Research Departments is revealed in George Klein, "The Menninger Foundation Research on Perception and Personality, 1947–1952: A Review," *BMC* 17 (May 1953): 93–4; Lois B. Murphy–Philip Holzman, tape-recorded discussion, n.p., Nov. 2, 1979, 1,2, M; Roy Schafer, *The Clinical Application of Psychological Tests* (New York, 1948), 9; Martin Mayman, TRI by LJF, Ann Arbor, Apr. 27, 1983; Rudolf Ekstein to Lois Murphy, Apr. 16, 1979, Murphy Papers, AHAP. The Murphy-Rapaport connection is indicated in Gardner Murphy to David Rapaport, Jan. 23, 1958, Inst. Archives, M, and Murphy-Holzman, Nov. 2, 1979, 4.

75. Bischof, *Interpreting Personality,* 511–12; WCM Diary, Dec. 10, 1951; Lois B. Murphy–Philip Holzman, tape-recorded discussion, n.p., Nov. 2, 1979, 6–7, M; Philip Holzman to George Klein, Nov. 2, 1951, Klein Papers, AHAP.

76. Lois B. Murphy–Philip Holzman, tape-recorded discussion, n.p., Nov. 2, 1979, 2, 7, M; George Klein to Sibylle Escalona, May 29, July 28, 1951, Klein Papers, AHAP; Sibylle Escalona, TRI by LJF, New York, Nov. 7, 1983; Philip Holzman to George Klein, Oct. 18, 1951, Klein Papers, AHAP.

77. Gardner Murphy to David Rapaport, July 10, 1959, Rapaport Papers, LC, "much about psychoanalytic theory." Gardner Murphy to George Klein, Dec. 13, 1957, Murphy Papers, AHAP, "secularism, or provincialism." Gardner Murphy, "Psychoanalysis

as a Unified Theory," in *The Freudian Paradigm,* Md. Mujeeb-ur-Rahman, ed. (Chicago, 1977), 361–2, Freud's conceptions, "socioculturally stained." *Ibid.,* 357, "different structural composition of groups."

78. Lois Murphy, TRI by LJF, Topeka, Sept. 27, 1983; Gardner Murphy, "There Is More Beyond," in *The Psychologists,* T. S. Krawiec, ed. (New York, 1974), II, 336; Gardner Murphy to WCM, Dec. 31, 1951, Murphy Papers, AHAP; George Klein to Margaret Brenman, July 6, 1951, Klein Papers, AHAP; Lois B. Murphy–Philip Holzman, tape-recorded discussion, n.p., Nov. 2, 1979, 2, 40, M; Lois B. Murphy to Sibylle Escalona, n.d. (Feb. 1952), Klein Papers, AHAP.

79. WCM Diary, June 4, 1955, Dec. 21, 1956; Lester T. Roach to WCM, Mar. 2, 1955, Sept. 25, 1958, Roach Papers, M; Sibylle Escalona to Gardner Murphy, Jan. 11, 1952, Inst. Archives, M.

80. Lois Murphy, TRI by LJF, Topeka, Sept. 27, 1983; Lois Murphy to Lewis Robbins, Apr. 15, 1983, LLR Papers (private); Robert Wallerstein, TRI by LJF, San Francisco, Dec. 29, 1984; KAM to WCM, Oct. 4, 1951, KAM Papers, M; KAM to Gardner Murphy, Jan. 22, 1953, KAM Papers, M; Sibylle Escalona to George Klein, May 11, 1953, Klein Papers, AHAP.

81. Robert Wallerstein to LJF (letter), Jan. 19, 1984; Gardner Murphy to Sibylle Escalona, May 12, 1953, Inst. Archives, M. WCM, "Personally Yours," *MQ* 8 (Winter 1954): 31; WCM Diary, Jan. 4, 1954; Robert Wallerstein, TRI by LJF, San Francisco, Dec. 29, 1984.

82. "Meeting of Trustees and Governors," Mar. 22, 1953, MT, quoting Murphy on the "feather in our cap." Bergman's early investigations are noted in David Rapaport, "Psychotherapy Research Project," Jan. 6, 1948, 1–2, Inst. Archives, M. Activities of Bergman's committee are noted in "Second Draft of the Project 'Evaluation of the Results of Psychoanalytic Therapy,' " June 16, 1949, 1, Inst. Archives, M; Wallerstein, *Forty-Two Lives,* 5; Robert Wallerstein to LJF, Jan. 19, 1984 (letter); Lester Luborsky, TRI by LJF, Philadelphia, Feb. 6, 1984; Gerald Aronson, TRI by LJF, Los Angeles, Dec. 26, 1983.

83. Robert Wallerstein, TRI by LJF, San Francisco, Dec. 29, 1984; Robert Wallerstein to LJF, Jan. 19, 1984.

84. Lester Luborsky, TRI by LJF, Philadelphia, Feb. 6, 1984; Robert Wallerstein to Laurence Wyatt, Apr. 27, 1963, unprocessed, M; John M. Shlien, ed., *Research in Psychotherapy* (Washington, D.C., 1968), III, 584.

85. Wallerstein, *Forty-Two Lives,* 13; *TPR* 27 (July–Aug. 1967): 10; Robert Wallerstein, "Psychotherapy Research: One Paradigm," in *Communication and Social Interaction,* Peter F. Ostwald, ed. (New York, 1977), 190–1, 200–1; Shlien, *Research,* III, 588; Otto Kernberg et al., "Psychotherapy and Psychoanalysis: Final Report of the Menninger Foundation's Psychotherapy Research Project," *BMC* 36 (Jan.–Mar. 1972): vii, 90.

86. Wallerstein, "Psychotherapy Research," 197–201; Kernberg et al., *BMC* 36, 41,55, 150–1, 177–8, 190; Lolafaye Coyne, TRI by LJF, Topeka, Mar. 11, 1985.

87. Murphy's interactionist perspective is characterized well in Bischof, *Interpreting Personality,* 513, 554–7. See also Gardner Murphy, "The Current Impact of Freud upon Psychology," Aug. 30, 1956, 2, Murphy Papers, AHAP. Gardner Murphy and Robert Wallerstein, "A Policy Question Regarding Long-Range Research Planning," n.d. (June 1955), 19, unprocessed, M, "We should be building."

88. *The Menninger Foundation Report of Progress for the Year July 1, 1963–June 30, 1964*

(Topeka, 1964), 40, on Rennick; . . . *for the Year July 1, 1965–June 30, 1966,* 19, 24, on Kovach and Green; . . . *for the Year July 1, 1956–June 30, 1957,* 49–50, on the thyroid project. Murphy and Wallerstein, "A Policy Question," 12–14, and Gardner Murphy to Lester Roach, Sept. 24, 1963, unprocessed, M, on Murphy's desire to move into genetics and psychopharmacology.

89. *The Menninger Foundation Report of Progress for the Year July 1, 1965–June 30, 1966* (Topeka, 1966), 22; James B. Taylor, "Active Intervention in Low-Income Families," Apr. 1966, 12, Roach Papers, M; RWM to Trustees and Governors, Aug. 29, 1967, Murphy Papers, M.

90. Gardner and Lois Murphy, TI by T. S. Krawiec, n.d. (circa 1975), 21, Murphy Papers, AHAP, "nurturing research." Gardner Murphy, "Annual Meeting [of Trustees] Presentation," 1954, 2, Murphy Papers, AHAP, "the utmost pains." Murphy, *Journal of Parapsychology* 21, 174, on the midwife role. Lois Murphy–Philip Holzman, TI, Nov. 2, 1979, 7–9, M, on Gardner Murphy's facilitator role. Robert Wallerstein to Lois Murphy, Mar. 30, 1984, Inst. Archives, M, "every single sprout." Charles M. Solley, "Gardner Murphy: As a Research Director," Feb. 13, 1984, Inst. Archives, M, comparing Murphy to Whitman.

91. Gardner Murphy, "Annual Meeting [of Trustees] Presentation," 1954, 2, Murphy Papers, AHAP, on helping "all research personnel . . . in coordinating research thinking." Richard S. Siegal to Gardner Murphy, Feb. 9, 1967, Inst. Archives, M.

92. Research Department growth and internal communication is discussed in W. Walter Menninger to Philip Menninger, Jan. 16, 1967, Inst. Archives, M; WCM, "Staff Memo #6," Sept. 17, 1965, KAM Papers, M; Leonard Horwitz to Roy Whitman, Mar. 15, 1967, RWM Papers, M. Robert Wallerstein to Lois Murphy, Mar. 16, 1984, Inst. Archives, M, "loose conglomeration." See also Charles M. Solley to Lois Murphy, n.d. (1984), Inst. Archives, M, on this "conglomeration" perception.

93. Roger Hoffmaster to Gardner Murphy and Lester Roach, Dec. 1, 1966, Roach Papers, M, on $830,000 from federal grants. The department's funding picture is also revealed in Riley Gardner, TRI by LJF, Topeka, Jan. 11, 1985; Gardner Murphy, "Some Aims of the Research Department of the Menninger Foundation," Dec. 13, 1966, 9, Inst. Archives, M; Paul Pruyser, PI by LJF, Topeka, July 31, 1984.

94. "Minutes of the Twelfth Annual Meeting of the Board of Trustees and Governors," Oct. 10–11, 1953, 467, Inst. Archives, M, regarding Murphy membership on the executive committee. "Campus Planning and Capital Expansion Committee of the Board of Governors," Oct. 12, 1956, 9, Inst. Archives, M, on the new building for research. Roger Hoffmaster, PI by LJF, Topeka, Mar. 15, 1985, on department autonomy through federal grants.

95. Gardner Murphy to KAM, Oct. 16, 1957, KAM Papers, M, exemplifies the unsuccessful quest for university affiliation. Robert Wallerstein to KAM, Jan. 10, 1962, Bernard Hall Papers, M, on the proposed new hospital wing. The struggle over release time for hospital staff to join Research Department projects is exemplified in WCM, "Conference with Drs. Gardner Murphy and Cotter Hirschberg," Jan. 8, 1953, KAM Papers, M; Lois Murphy–Philip Holzman, Nov. 2, 1979, 9, M.

96. Lois Murphy to Lewis Robbins, Apr. 15, 1983, LLR Papers (private), on Gardner Murphy expecting the same autonomy he had at CCNY. Gardner Murphy to Robert Holt, July 10, [1953], Murphy Papers, AHAP, "fragmentation of my time." Murphy's explorations of academic jobs are indicated in Gardner Murphy to Robert M. Allen, May 20, 1958, Murphy Papers, M; Gardner Murphy to George S. Klein, Sept. 29, 1958,

Murphy Papers, AHAP; Gardner Murphy to Robert Holt, May 11, 1959, Murphy Papers, AHAP.

97. Lois Murphy to Lewis Robbins, Apr. 15, 1983, LLR Papers (private); WCM, "Staff Memo #6," Sept. 17, 1965, KAM Papers, M; Robert Wallerstein to RWM and Lester Roach, May 11, 1966, Roach Papers, M; Leonard Horwitz, TRI by LJF, Topeka, Nov. 14, 1984; Lois Murphy, TRI by LJF, Topeka, Sept. 27, 1983; Roger D. Hoffmaster, PI by LJF, Topeka, Mar. 15, 1985.

98. Samuel P. Hays, *The Response to Industrialism, 1885–1914* (Chicago, 1957); Hays, "The Politics of Reform in Municipal Government in the Progressive Era," *Pacific Northwest Quarterly* 55 (1964): 157–69; Robert H. Wiebe, *The Search for Order, 1877–1920* (New York, 1967), esp. ch. 5; Gerald N. Grob, *Mental Illness and American Society, 1875–1940* (Princeton, 1983), esp. ch. 9.

99. Anna Freud, "Observations," *BMC* 27 (May 1963): 148–9; Lewis Robbins to Members of the Medical Council, Mar. 24, 1951, Inst. Archives, M. Interestingly, the "Freudian Follies of 1958" (Audio Room, M) opened with a skit in which children of TIP training analysts registered unrivaled power over the children of other staff.

100. "Minutes of Education Council Meeting," Mar. 6, 1961, Pruyser Papers, M, 1–2, "mysterious, aristocratic." WCM, "Medical Council Meeting of Feb. 16," Feb. 27, 1951, Inst. Archives, M, 2–3, on senior analysts demanding deference. WCM Diary, Oct. 15, 1949, on TIP analysts, notably Jan Frank, "taking me to pieces." Paul Bergman to Members of Topeka Psychoanalytic Society, Dec. 17, 1952, Murphy Papers, M, "scientific discussions" and "tended to . . . retreat." The smug, orthodox, nearly anti-intellectual tone of senior analysts is underscored in Philip Holzman to Otto Fleishmann, Feb. 6, 1958, Murphy Papers, M; Robert Wallerstein to Lewis Robbins, Oct. 28, 1964, LLR Papers (private); Lewis Robbins, TRI by LJF, New York, Aug. 23, 1983; Maimon Leavitt, TRI by LJF, Los Angeles, Dec. 25, 1983.

101. Paul W. Pruyser, PI by LJF, Topeka, July 31, 1984; Harvey L. Schloesser, TRI by LJF, Topeka, June 21, 1987 (Schloesser learned reasons for his exclusion from TIP training analyst Hugh Galbraith).

102. Lewis Robbins to members of the Medical Council, Mar. 24, 1951, Inst. Archives, M, "the wife of one." Paul Bergman to members of the Topeka Psychoanalytic Society (an essay on psychoanalysis), Dec. 17, 1952, 6, Inst. Archives, M, "candidates in servitude." Irwin Rosen, TRI by LJF, Topeka, July 27, 1983, on Ekstein's analysands. James Folsom, PI by LJF, Topeka, June 19, 1987, on the Fleishmann-Anderson relationship. Paul Pruyser, PI by LJF, Topeka, July 31, 1984, on Ramzy's analysis of Robert Menninger and its relevance to the Karl-Ramzy relationship; see also Ishak Ramzy, PI by LJF, Topeka, Mar. 15, 1985.

103. KAM to Ralph Greenson and Ernst Lewy, Oct. 18, 1952 (draft), KAM Papers, M, "old womanish gossip." The point is underscored in Harvey Schloesser, TRI by LJF, Topeka, June 21, 1987. Lester Luborsky to KAM, July 1, 1952, Luborsky Papers (private), pleading with Karl not to volunteer data. See also Luborsky, PI by LJF, Philadelphia, Apr. 4, 1987. A great many interviewees (preferring not to be identified, for obvious reasons) discussed instances where Karl breached analytic confidentiality. I am indebted to Peter Novotny (PI, Topeka, Sept. 12, 1986) for sharing his considerable research on national standards of confidentiality during the 1950s and 1960s.

104. Robert Wallerstein in "The Topeka Mystique," TI of American Psychoanalytic Association session, Puerto Rico, 1981, 62. Augmentation of the power of the senior training analyst by other foundation positions is discussed at length in Stephen Appel-

baum, TRI by LJF, Prairie Village, Kans., June 24, 1987, and Harvey Schloesser, TRI by LJF, Topeka, June 21, 1987.

105. Philip Holzman, PI by LJF, Cambridge, Mass., July 28, 1987, details the incident. Holzman's story was identical to that of Sydney R. Smith, PI by LJF, Topeka, June 22, 1987. KAM to RWM, May 27, 1968, KAM Papers, M, notes the incident and names the analysand. Nothing in the Menninger archives on the research director search calls into question any part of Holzman's account. See, e.g., RWM to Gardner Murphy, Nov. 14, 1967, Murphy Papers, M; Paul Thetford to RWM, May 9, 1967, Roach Papers, M; RWM, PI by LJF, Topeka, June 23, 1987; Philip Holzman to George Klein, July 13, 1967, Klein Papers, AHAP.

106. "Minutes of Annual Meeting of Board of Trustees," Oct. 13, 1957, MT, announcing Will as president. Lester Roach, PI by LJF, Topeka, Mar. 9, 1983, "I ran the place."

107. Lester Roach, TRI by Verne Horne, Topeka, Sept. 6, 1974, M; Roach, PI by LJF, Topeka, Mar. 9, 1983.

108. WCM Diary, July 12, 1955, "very good session with Karl." See also WCM Diary, Apr. 26, 1962, for a similar observation. Irving Sheffel, PI by LJF, Topeka, Mar. 13, 1986, on he and Roach meeting with the brothers. The commitment of Roach and Sheffel to the family is revealed most fully in Roach, TRI by LJF, Topeka, May 26, 1983; Lewis Robbins, TRI by LJF, New York, Aug. 23, 1983; Martin Mayman, TRI by LJF, Ann Arbor, Apr. 27, 1983; RWM, PI by LJF, Topeka, Sept. 12, 1985.

109. Lester Roach to WCM, Mar. 2, 1955, Roach Papers, M, supporting Murphy's request. Roach discussed his approach to Fleming, Switzer, and "barons" generally in Roach, PI by LJF, Topeka, Mar. 9, 1983 and in Roach, TRI by LJF, Topeka, May 26, 1983. See also Irving Sheffel, PI by LJF, Topeka, Mar. 13, 1986; Roach to WCM, Feb. 3, 1951, WCM Papers, M.

110. Irving Kartus, TRI by Irving Sheffel, Leawood, Kans., Apr. 3, 1983; Martin Mayman, TRI by LJF, Ann Arbor, Apr. 27, 1983.

111. Albert Deutsch to KAM, Mar. 30, 1957, Deutsch Papers, APA. RWM, PI by LJF, Topeka, Mar. 11, 1986, "a roving, restless spotlight." KAM to Harold Maine, Nov. 25, 1953, Maine Papers, M, "my life consists."

112. KAM to Members of Senior Council, June 20, 1963, Hall Papers, M, on how Karl was not at the hospital even two hours a day. Irving Sheffel, TRI by Lewis Robbins, Topeka, July 10, 1979, LLR Papers (private); KAM to Irving Kartus, Aug. 22, 1957, IK Papers (private); Lewis Robbins, TRI by LJF, New York, Aug. 24, 1983.

113. Hazel Bruce, PI by LJF, Topeka, Jan. 11, 1985, on Robbins's instructions concerning interruptions. KAM to WCM, Nov. 11, 1957, KAM Papers, M, and KAM to Lester Roach, et al., Mar. 6, 1962, KAM Papers, M, on Karl replacing Kartus and Van der Waals. Karl's impact on Fleming is revealed in Peter Fleming to Irving Kartus, n.d. (1956), Jan. 28, 1958, IK Papers (private); KAM, PI by LJF, Topeka, Nov. 11, 1984; Harvey Schloesser, TRI by LJF, Topeka, June 21, 1987.

114. See, e.g., William A. Roberts, TRI by LJF, Topeka, July 31, 1984; Lewis L. Robbins, TRI by LJF, New York, Aug. 23, 1983.

115. KAM to WCM, June 17, 1957, Nov. 10, 1964, KAM Papers, M; Robert Switzer, TRI by LJF, Trevose, Pa., Nov. 4, 1983; Paul W. Toussieng to Robert Switzer, n.d. (Nov. 1964), Dec. 8, 1964, Switzer Papers, M.

116. Lois Murphy, TRI by LJF, Topeka, Sept. 27, 1983; Wallerstein, "Topeka Mystique," 60; Peter Novotny, PI by LJF, Topeka, Nov. 11, 1984, on the PRP issue.

117. Karl's visit to Mayo is discussed in Irving Sheffel to LJF, Jan. 13, 21, 25, 1988, Feb. 15, 1988 (letters); William Rottersman, TRI by LJF, Atlanta, May 26, 1983. Prescott Thompson to LJF, Feb. 17, 1988 (letter). All three accompanied Karl there. See transcript of Karl's "Twentieth Century" interview, Sept. 15, 1961, 13, WCM Papers, M, for his exchange with Cronkite.

118. Seward Hiltner to KAM, "Some Reflections on the School of Psychiatry," Dec. 6, 1957, Hiltner Papers, PTS. Pressure by Will and Karl on their sons to train in psychiatry and return is evident in WCM Diary, July 9, 1953, Dec. 1953; WCM to KAM, John Stone, et al., July 23, 1944, WCM Papers (private); KAM and WCM, "Some Statements for the Counsel and Guidance of the Trustees and Medical Council . . . in Future Years," July 24, Aug. 6, 1952, KAM Papers, M; KAM to RGM, Nov. 3, 1947, Family Papers, M.

119. Karl's efforts to get Robert admitted to medical school are evident in KAM to George Whipple, May, 12, 1947; KAM to Elliot Cutler, June 23, 1947; KAM to RGM, Nov. 3, 1947; KAM to Douglas Bond, Nov. 21, 1947; RGM to KAM, n.d. (Jan. 1948); all in Family Room, M. Robert's acceptance for a TIP training analysis is discussed in KAM to RWM, June 9, 1961, KAM Papers, M; RGM, PI by LJF, Topeka, Mar. 12, 1985. Robert's rapid advancement at Menninger is covered in RGM, PI by LJF, Topeka, Mar. 12, 1985; "Minutes of the Personnel Committee of the Senior Council," Dec. 1, 1964, Inst. Archives, M.

120. KAM, PI by LJF, Topeka, Jan. 9, Mar. 16, 1985, on his apprehensions about Robert. WCM to KAM, Nov. 11, 1957, KAM Papers, M, "Bob is such a level headed . . . fellow." For staff complaints over Robert's laxness, see, e.g., Richard Benson, PI by LJF, Topeka, Mar. 14, 1985; James Horne, PI by LJF, Topeka, Sept. 3, 4, 1988.

121. RGM, PI by LJF, Topeka, Mar. 12, 1985; "A.T.—Nursing Meeting, Jan. 10, 1962, Activities Planning Committee," 7, Inst. Archives, M, "when he only thinks." James Horne, PI by LJF, Topeka, Sept. 4, 1988, and Ishak Ramzy, PI by LJF, Topeka, Mar. 13, 1985, on Robert's strategic position.

122. Julia Gottesman, TRI by LJF, Los Angeles, Jan. 3, 1984, Julia Gottesman to KAM and JLM, Oct. 9, 1966, KAM Papers, M; Philip B. Menninger, PI by LJF, Topeka, Jan. 14, 1985; Philip B. Menninger to Edwin A. Menninger, Dec. 21, 1962, Family Room, M; WCM Diary, July 11, 1953, June 9, 1956 (on Philip).

123. RWM, PI by LJF, Topeka, Mar. 11, 1986; KAM to RWM, June 9, 1961, KAM Papers, M; KAM, PI by LJF, Topeka, Mar. 11, 1985; CWM to RWM, Dec. 4, 1960, RWM Papers, Tower Bldg.; WCM to RWM, Nov. 11, 1960, RWM Papers, Tower Bldg., "this place is ours."

124. Irwin Rosen, TRI by LJF, Topeka, July 27, 1983, and KAM, PI by LJF, Topeka, Mar. 11, 1985, on senior staff fears of being displaced. The quality of Roy's clinical work in the hospital and the outpatient division are discussed in Bernard Hall, TRI by LJF, New York, Aug. 25, 1983 (noting, too, how Will urged him to cover for Roy); Sydney Smith, PI by LJF, Topeka, June 23, 1987; James Horne, PI by LJF, Topeka, Sept. 12, 1986. KAM to WCM, Sept. 18, 1963, KAM Papers, M, and WCM to KAM, Oct. 26, 1965, RWM Papers, M, both making clear the brothers' intention (as early as 1963) to move Roy to direct Preventive Psychiatry. KAM to RWM, June 9, 1961, KAM Papers, M, on the pending TIP decision over his candidacy, but also noting that "sentimentally everyone would like to see you follow along the lines of your father and uncle."

125. W. Walter Menninger, PI by LJF, Topeka, Jan. 10, 1985, on his background

and his feelings toward his father and the foundation. WCM to KAM, Sept. 26, 1963, KAM Papers, M, "I am so pleased," and on not being able to continue his current pace for long.

126. W. Walter Menninger, PI by LJF, Topeka, Jan. 10, 1985, on Fleming's warning to him and on his feelings during analysis. *TPR,* Feb. 17, 1984, 1, 6, covers Walter's professional career rather comprehensively.

CHAPTER ELEVEN: *The Palace Revolt*

1. General foundation-wide ignorance of events of the week in April is indicated in Lewis Wheelock to KAM, Jan. 3, 1967, KAM Papers, M; Lewis Robbins, "Karl A. Menninger Notes, Feb. 15, 1980," LLR Papers (private); Peter Fleming, TRI by Verne Horne, Topeka, Jan. 7, 1975, M; Irving Sheffel, Duane Swanson, Roger Hoffmaster, and Thomas Dolgoff, TRI by LJF, Topeka, May 21, 1985. Individual testimony of personal ignorance of the week is revealed in Donald Leventhal, PI by LJF, Bowling Green, Feb. 25, 1983; Ray E. Bullard to Lewis Robbins, May 18, 1977, LLR Papers (private). Vernon Muller, PI by LJF, London, July 2, 1986, on the ignorance of post-1965 staff.

2. Irving Sheffel–Thomas Dolgoff tape-recorded discussion of the events of April 1965, Topeka, May 11, 1965 (in possession of Sheffel; hereafter "Sheffel-Dolgoff, May 11, 1965"). Irving Sheffel, TRI by Lewis Robbins, Topeka, July 10, 1979, LLR Papers (private); Lester Roach, TRI by Verne Horne, Topeka, Sept. 6, 1974, M; Lester Roach, PI by LJF, Sept. 14, 1985; WCM Diary, Apr. 22, 1965.

3. Sheffel-Dolgoff, May 11, 1965. WCM Diary, Apr. 22, 1965, paraphrasing Roach's "took over the running" remark.

4. Sheffel-Dolgoff, May 11, 1965; WCM Diary, Apr. 22, 1965.

5. Sheffel-Dolgoff, May 11, 1965, on Will summoning the group of senior staff. See also WCM Diary, Apr. 22, 1965; Lewis Robbins, "Brief Notes re Principles Involved in Palace Revolt," n.d., LLR Papers (private); JLM to Julia Gottesman, May 6, 1965, KAM Papers, M.

6. The April 22 meeting is discussed in Sheffel-Dolgoff, May 11, 1965; Sheffel, TRI by Robbins, Topeka, July 10, 1979, LLR Papers (private); "Draft Discussion in Departmental Head Meeting," n.d. (1965), 5, Switzer Papers, M; Sheffel, PI by LJF, Topeka, July 27, 1984; Peter Fleming, TRI by Verne Horne, Jan. 7, 1975, M. WCM Diary, Apr. 22, 1965, "a shift in our functional alignment." RWM, "Notes," May 1, 1965, RWM Papers, Tower Bldg., M, on "the revolution which father has, in effect, engineered."

7. Sheffel-Dolgoff, May 11, 1965; WCM Diary, Apr. 23, 1965; and Robert Switzer, TRI by LJF, Trevose, Pa., Nov. 4, 1983, on the events of the meeting. Peter Fleming, TRI by Lewis Robbins, San Jose, July 7, 1979, LLR Papers (private), on the sense of Oedipal revolt.

8. Sheffel-Dolgoff, May 11, 1965; Sheffel, PI by LJF, Topeka, July 27, 1984; Sept. 10, 1986; WCM Diary, Apr. 23, 1965.

9. Sheffel-Dolgoff, May 11, 1965; WCM Diary, Apr. 24, 1965; Sheffel, TRI by Lewis Robbins, Topeka, July 10, 1979, LLR Papers (private); Sheffel, PI by LJF, Topeka, July 27, 1984, Sept. 10, 1986; RWM, "Notes," 1–2; CWM, telephone interview by LJF, Aug. 14, 1985; CWM, PI by LJF, Topeka, Nov. 7, 1987; KAM, TRI by LJF, Topeka, Sept. 10, 1986.

10. Sheffel-Dolgoff, May 11, 1965. WCM Diary, Apr. 24, 1965, "what a difficult time."

11. *Ibid.*

12. Sheffel-Dolgoff, May 11, 1965; RWM, "Notes," 2; Sheffel, TRI by Lewis Robbins, Topeka, July 10, 1979; Sheffel, PI by LJF, Topeka, July 27, 1984; WCM Diary, Apr. 25, 1965.

13. Sheffel-Dolgoff, May 11, 1965; Sheffel, TRI by Lewis Robbins, Topeka, July 10, 1979. Between 1955 and 1958, a new VA hospital (Colmery-O'Neil) was completed on the old Winter grounds.

14. *Ibid.*

15. *Ibid.*

16. Sheffel-Dolgoff, May 11, 1965; RWM, "Notes," 3; Peter Fleming, TRI by Lewis Robbins, San Jose, July 7, 1979.

17. "President's Report to Annual Meeting of Board of Trustees," Oct. 1, 1965, 3–4, Inst. Archives, M.

18. WCM Diary, Nov. 3, 1960, "this business of two heads." Meetings between the brothers are discussed in Lester Roach, TRI by Peter Fleming and Bernard Hall, Topeka, n.d. (May 1966), Roach Papers (private); Sheffel, TRI by Lewis Robbins, Topeka, July 10, 1979, LLR Papers (private); Thomas Dolgoff, TRI by LJF, Topeka, Jan. 4, 1983; Edward Greenwood, TRI by LJF, Topeka, Nov. 10, 1982. WCM Diary, Mar. 9, 1965, "gets so intent." WCM Diary, Feb. 28, 1955, "spend very little time together." See also WCM Diary, Jan. 23, 1955.

19. Bernard Hall, ed., *A Psychiatrist for a Troubled World: Selected Papers of William C. Menninger, M.D.* (New York, 1967), II, 770, "vision and guidance"; "Minutes of Long-Range Planning Committee of Board of Trustees," Nov. 19, 1965, 4, KAM Papers, M, for Karl noting how he and Will balance each other.

20. KAM, *The Vital Balance: The Life Process in Mental Health and Illness* (New York, 1963), 3–4.

21. *Ibid.*, esp. 85.

22. Cogent analysis of the general history of the continuum concept is provided in Gerald N. Grob, "The Forging of Mental Health Policy in America: World War II to New Frontier," *JHMAS* 42 (Oct. 1987): esp. 413, 428. Bertalanffy is used at various points in *The Vital Balance*, with his relevance particularly evident on 114. Like Bertalanffy, Karl maintained that an organism loses and regains general systemic equilibrium among its parts and between its parts and its external environment.

23. KAM, "Statement of the Reorganization Committee," Nov. 19, 1965, MT.

24. Close stop-and-go review of the film reel of Cronkite's interview with foundation audio-video specialist Tally Fisher, May 22, 1985, made it obvious that the brothers were not sitting together.

25. WCM Diary, Nov. 23, 1959, Nov. 28, 1960. Irving Sheffel, TI by CWM, n.d. (c. 1980), WCM Papers (private), quoting Will, "You know." CWM, PI by LJF, Topeka, Mar. 19, 1985, on Will's condition after the department went to Karl. See also KAM, "Discussion with Dr. Will. Subject: Social Psychiatry," Mar. 23, 1964, KAM Papers, M; Roach, TRI by Verne Horne, Topeka, Sept. 6, 1974, M.

26. RWM, "Notes," Mar. 10, 1965, 3, RWM Papers, Tower Bldg., M, and RWM, PI by LJF, Los Angeles, May 11, 1984, on Will's depression and his inability to talk to Karl. KAM to WCM, Feb. 22, 1965, KAM Papers (unsent), M, "clam up and stare me away" and "a passive war" contributing to "your bronchitis."

27. WCM Diary, Aug. 2, 1959; Lester Roach to David Neiswanger, Dec. 22, 1949, Neiswanger Papers, M; "Minutes of Board of Trustees Executive Committee," Aug. 10, 1955, July 16, 1959, Jan. 30, 1960; *TPR* 19 (July 1959): 1–2; WCM Diary, June 3, 1955, on Karl's plan for the land.

28. *TPR* 19 (July 1959): 1; Lester Roach, TRI by Verne Horne, Topeka, Sept. 6, 1974, M; Emlin North, PI by LJF, Topeka, July 26, 1983; Lois B. Murphy, "Report of the Personnel Policies Committee (of P.S.O.)," June 1, 1966, 2, Inst. Archives, M. Margaret Mead, "Institutional Expression of Ideas" in Sydney Smith, ed., *The Human Mind Revisited* (New York, 1978), 481.

29. KAM to KAM, Jan. 11, 1965, KAM Papers, M, a note to himself on the importance of purchasing western lands. KAM in *The Menninger Foundation Report of Progress for the Year July 1, 1964–June 30, 1965* (Topeka, 1965), 10–11, "We *can* afford it"; "West Campus Land Purchases," Feb. 2, 1965, KAM Papers, M; "Minutes, Senior Council," Jan. 21, 1964, Feb. 23, 1965, Inst. Archives, M; "Minutes, Annual Meeting of Board of Trustees and Governors," Oct. 6–7, 1962, MT; "Executive Committee Minutes, Board of Trustees," Jan. 30, Apr. 25, 1962, MT; KAM, PI by LJF, Topeka, Mar. 13, 1985, Sept. 12, 1986.

30. KAM to WCM, Feb. 22, 1965, KAM Papers, M. (unsent), "we ought to be buying." WCM Diary, July 31, 1962, "want to spend the money" and "hard to get money." Opposition by Will, Roach, Fleming, Sheffel, the trustees, and others to further land purchases is also indicated in Sheffel-Dolgoff, May 11, 1965; WCM Diary, Mar. 29, 1962, Feb. 3, Feb. 9, 1965; Peter Fleming, TRI by Lewis Robbins, July 7, 1979, LLR Papers (private); Irving Sheffel, TRI by Lewis Robbins, July 10, 1979, LLR Papers (private). KAM to Professional Council, Administrative Council, Board of Trustees Executive Committee, Feb. 3, 1965, KAM Papers, M, "our younger men." In my discussion with Karl on Sept. 12, 1986, as we drove over the land he was not able to purchase, he remarked that hospital treatment was secondary to his proposed uses for the land, despite the opinion of the "sons of bitches" who opposed him.

31. Philip Holzman, PI by LJF, Cambridge, Mass., Apr. 25, 1982.

32. The Coordinating Council is discussed and characterized in "Meeting of Trustees Executive Committee," Feb. 17, 1961, 1, MT, and KAM, "Discussion with Sheffel and Roach," Sept. 4, 1961, KAM Papers, M. KAM to Trustees, n.d. (Feb./Mar. 1963), KAM Papers, M, "prepare them for leadership." For other data on the development and fate of the Senior Council, see KAM, "Senior Council Charter," Feb. 13, 1963, KAM Papers, M; "Minutes of the Senior Council," Nov. 26, 1963, June 23, 1964, Inst. Archives, M; KAM to Robert Knight, Jan. 26, 1965, KAM Papers, M; "Draft for Discussion in Department Head Meeting," n.d. (1965), 3–4, Switzer Papers, M.

33. Apprehensions by senior staff over the Menninger sons is noted in Irwin Rosen, TRI by LJF, Topeka, July 27, 1983; Howard Shevrin, TRI by LJF, Ann Arbor, Sept. 16, 1983. WCM to KAM, Nov. 11, 1957, KAM Papers, M, on Robert Menninger as director of the adult hospital. WCM to KAM, Oct. 26, 1965, RWM Papers, M, on plans as early as 1963 for Roy to be director of the Department of Preventive Psychiatry.

34. Sheffel-Dolgoff, May 11, 1965.

35. Sheffel-Dolgoff, May 11, 1965. "President's Report, Annual Meeting of Board of Trustees," Oct. 1, 1965, 4, KAM Papers, M, on decentralization promoting a greater staff participation. See also WCM to Marion E. Kenworthy, May 7, 1965, KAM Papers, M; "Suggestions for Improving the Foundation Operation," May 6, 1965, 2, RWM Papers, Tower Bldg, M.

36. Support by powerful department heads for Will's decentralization plans is indicated in "Minutes of Senior Council," Sept. 29, 1965, Pruyser Papers, M; Bernard Hall to B. Goldberg, Oct. 26, 1965, Hall Papers, M. KAM to WCM, Feb. 22, 1966, KAM Papers, M, "departmental laissez faireism." "Summary of Discussion, Board of Trustees Meeting," Oct. 2–3, 1965, 6–7, MT, "the Foundation as a whole." KAM, "Report of the Chairman of the Board of Trustees," Oct. 1, 1965, 3–4, KAM Papers, M, offering three proposals for future reorganization.

37. Leonard Horwitz, TRI by LJF, Topeka, Aug. 1, 1984, on the initial purpose of the PSO and its subsequent transformation.

38. "The Professional Staff Organization of the Menninger Foundation," n.d. (1965), 1, Inst. Archives, M, for the May 14 proclamation. Lois B. Murphy to John Sutherland, Feb. 22, 1966, Gardner Murphy Papers, M, "blossoming of talents." P.S.O. Committee structure, membership, eligibility, and officer voting is noted in "Report of the Membership Committee of the P.S.O.," May 11, May 23, 1966, Inst. Archives, M, and "Minutes of Board of Trustees," Apr. 15–16, 1966, 4–5, Roach Papers, M. At the trustees meeting, Shevrin noted "rejuvenation."

39. "A Report by the Committee of the Staff Organization to Be Submitted for Discussion September 22, 1965," n.d., KAM Papers, M, "administrative leadership given by Doctor Karl and Doctor Will" and "give younger staff the opportunities." Lois Murphy, "Report of the Personnel Policies Committee," n.d. (1965), 7, Roach Papers, M, "infantile dependent role." PSO response to the department heads, to Will on decentralization, and to Karl on centralization is indicated in "The Professional Staff Organization of the Menninger Foundation," n.d. (1965), 2, Roach Papers, M; "Minutes, Trustees Long-Range Planning Committee," Nov. 19, 1965, 3, MT. PSO Study Group to PSO, Jan. 24, 1966, Murphy Papers, M. "Professional Staff Organization of the Menninger Foundation: Articles of Organization. Adopted March 13, 1967," 1, Roach Papers, M, on broad staff participation.

40. Political incapacities of PSO leaders are noted in William Tarnower, PI by LJF, Topeka, Nov. 11, 1984; KAM, PI by LJF, Topeka, Nov. 14, 1984. Tarnower to KAM, Dec. 28, 1965, KAM Papers, M, "feel in some ways like members of the family." WCM, "President's Report," Oct. 1, 1965, 6, Roach Papers, "valuable reservoir." Leonard Horwitz, TRI by LJF, Topeka, Aug. 1, 1984, on PSO leadership being sympathetic to Will. "Minutes, Trustees Annual Meeting," Oct. 1–3, 1965, MT, for Thompson representing the PSO as an academic faculty. Internal divisions within the PSO are noted in William Tarnower, PI by LJF, Topeka, Nov. 11, 1984; Howard Shevrin, TRI by Verne Horne, Topeka, May 25, 1973, M.

41. Gardner Murphy to Robert Wallerstein, Aug. 18, 1966, Murphy Papers, M.

42. Howard Shevrin, TRI by Lewis Robbins, Ann Arbor, Apr. 9, 1979, LLR Papers (private), on the trustees' understanding that the PSO represented a new voice. Study Group to PSO, Jan. 24, 1966, 2–3, Inst. Archives, M, "identify ourselves."

43. Martin Mayman, TRI by LJF, Ann Arbor, Apr. 27, 1983; Martin Mayman, TRI by Lewis Robbins, Ann Arbor, Apr. 11, 1979, LLR Papers (private); WCM Diary, Sept. 14, 1965, "won't stay hitched." Sheffel-Dolgoff, May 11, 1965, on the May 8 meeting with Holzman, Schlesinger, and Pruyser. See also WCM Diary, May 10, 14, 24, 1965; KAM, PI by LJF, Topeka, Sept. 29, 1983.

44. KAM memorandum, n.d. (Fall 1965), KAM Papers, M, "vested rights" and "effective and responsible administrator." KAM, "Report of the Chairman of the Board of Trustees," Oct. 1, 1965, 3, KAM Papers, M, "I will continue"; KAM, "State-

ment to the Reorganization Committee," Nov. 19, 1965, KAM Papers, M, calling for Vivian to replace Roach. Karl's all-or-nothing posture on his partnership with Will in "Minutes, Trustees' Long Range Planning Committee," Nov. 19, 1965, 4, KAM Papers, M.

45. Details of Karl's contractual negotiations with the foundation are covered in KAM to WCM, May 22, 1965, KAM Papers, M; Willard King, TRI by Lewis Robbins, Topeka, May 13, 1979, LLR Papers (private); Robert Anderson, PI by LJF, Topeka, Mar. 11, 1986; CWM, PI by LJF, Topeka, Mar. 9, 1985. "Contract for Professional Services," Oct. 7, 1966, KAM Papers, M, represents the final document. KAM memorandum, n.d. (1965), KAM Papers, M, "permit the use of my name."

46. Grace Menninger to KAM, Sept. 12, 1966, KAM Papers, M, on how Will never admitted error to him. Karl's meetings with Will urging him to reunite are noted in RWM, "Notes," June 18, 1965, 2, RWM Papers, Tower Bldg., M; KAM to WCM, Feb. 22, 1966, LLR Papers (private); KAM memorandum, June 27, 1966, KAM Papers, M, "corruption." Private meetings between the brothers and the two oldest sons are reported in Herbert J. Schlesinger, "dictation during 'palace revolution,' " June 17, 1965, Schlesinger Papers (private); RWM, "Notes," June 18, 1965, 2; WCM Diary, May 24, 1965.

47. The Fabian-Holzman-Mayman group and its advice is discussed in Martin Mayman, TRI by LJF, Ann Arbor, Apr. 27, 1983; Frederick J. Hacker to KAM, Nov. 16, 1965, KAM Papers, M. The Jeanetta-Hacker-Wheelock group's advice is in Frederick Hacker to Ernst Ticho, Nov. 17, 1965, KAM Papers, M; Hacker to KAM, Nov. 16, 1965, KAM Papers, M; Lewis Wheelock to Julia Gottesman, Mar. 3, 1966, KAM Papers, M; Wheelock to Presidential Search Committee, Sept. 8, 1966, M, "creative genius" and "institutional suicide." Additional data on these two advisory groups is found in WCM Diary, Oct. 7, 1965; KAM, PI by LJF, Topeka, Sept. 9, 1986.

48. W. Clement Stone, TRI by LJF, Lake Forest, Ill., Jan. 18, 1988; WCM to KAM, Roach, Sheffel, and Klink, Jan. 30, 1964, KAM Papers, M, "eccentric" and "asinine books"; CWM, PI by LJF, Topeka, Nov. 7, 1987.

49. For Karl's thinking about moving to Chicago, see KAM, "The Development of a Comprehensive Community Mental Health Center in Chicago, Illinois," Oct. 21, 1965 (2nd draft), KAM Papers, M; KAM to WCM, Feb. 22, 1966, KAM Papers, M; KAM, PI by LJF, Topeka, Sept. 9, 1986. See also Lewis Wheelock, TI by Verne Horne, Topeka, Mar. 18, 1970, KAM Papers, M; and W. Clement Stone, TRI by LJF, Lake Forest, Ill., Jan. 18, 1988.

50. WCM to Irving Sheffel, Feb. 14, 1966, unprocessed, M; WCM to WCM (memo), June 10, 1966, WCM Papers, M.

51. W. Clement Stone contract with Menninger Foundation, Aug. 31, 1966, KAM Papers, M. Lewis F. Wheelock to Robert B. Hulsen, Aug. 18, 1966, KAM Papers, M, delineating Karl's contract with Stone-Brandel. Melvin Herman, "Notes from Interview with Leo Bartemeier," Dec. 10, 1977, 5, LLR Papers (private), on Karl's life style in Chicago.

52. Harold Visotsky, TI by Lewis Robbins and Melvin Herman, Chicago, June 19, 1980, LLR Papers (private), on the financial uncertainties of the Stone-Brandel Center and its bleak prospects in the late 1960s. W. Clement Stone, TRI by LJF, Lake Forest, Ill., Jan. 18, 1988, on the collapse of his center.

53. Erik H. Erikson, *Childhood and Society* (New York, 1963), 268–74.

54. The post–April 1965 conduct and apprehensions of the rebels are described in

Martin Mayman, TRI by LJF, Ann Arbor, Apr. 27, 1983; KAM to May Switzer, Jan.
12, 1967, KAM Papers, M; Irving Sheffel, PI by LJF, Topeka, July 27, 1984; KAM to
KAM, July 8, 1965, KAM Papers, M.

55. KAM to KAM, Apr. 19, 1966, KAM Papers, M, "Dr. Fleming need feel insecure."
See also Peter Fleming, TRI by Lewis Robbins, San Jose, July 7, 1979, LLR Papers
(private); Fleming, TRI by Verne Horne, Jan. 7, 1975, M. KAM, TRI by LJF, Topeka,
Mar. 14, 1986, recalling his analysis of Fleming and how it related to Fleming's
conduct in the mid-1960s.

56. Fleming's emotions and his cancer episode are discussed in WCM Diary, Nov.
3, 1965; WCM to Thomas Dolgoff, Nov. 3, 1965, WCM Papers, M; Fleming, TRI by
Verne Horne, Jan. 7, 1975, M. Bernard Hall to All Staff, Apr. 30, 1968, RWM Papers,
M, on Fleming's ouster.

57. Martin Mayman, TRI by LJF, Ann Arbor, Apr. 27, 1983, on Hall having been
one of Karl's favorites. Hall's heavy drinking and fear of the consequences of revolting
against the father in Bernard Hall, TRI by LJF, New York, Aug. 25, 1983; Paul Pruyser,
TRI by Lewis Robbins, Topeka, July 10, 1979, LLR Papers (private). Julia Gottesman
to JLM and KAM, Oct. 18, 1965, KAM Papers, M, on Hall noting "Karl spoke to me."
WCM to Bernard Hall, Jan. 3, 1966, WCM Papers, M, on Julia calling Hall "a power
grabber." Rumors on Hall's public exhibits of homosexuality are discussed in KAM,
PI by LJF, Nov. 11, 1984; Philip Holzman, PI by LJF, Cambridge, Mass., Apr. 25, 1982.
For evidence of Hall's homosexual advances with patients, see RGM telephone memorandum, Aug. 21, 1970; RGM to RWM, Aug. 28, 1970; Dean Collins to RWM, Oct.
9, 1970; RWM to Bernard Hall, Oct. 7, 1970; all in RWM Papers, M.

58. Paul Pruyser, TRI by Lewis Robbins, Topeka, July 10, 1979, LLR Papers (pri-
vate); Lewis Robbins, "Paul Pruyser," Oct. 23, 1980, LLR Papers (private); Julia
Gottesman, TRI by LJF, Los Angeles, Jan. 3, 1984; Bernard Hall, TRI by LJF, New
York, Aug. 25, 1983; Martin Mayman, TRI by LJF, Ann Arbor, Apr. 27, 1983; Lewis
Robbins, TRI by LJF, New York, Aug. 23–24, 1983; Paul Pruyser to KAM, Jan. 10,
1972, KAM Papers, M, "appraise the last ten years."

59. Robert Switzer, TRI by LJF, Trevose, Pa., Nov. 4, 1983; KAM, PI by LJF,
Topeka, Nov. 11, 1984; RWM to Robert Switzer, June 30, 1971, RWM Papers, M;
RWM, "Staff Memo #134," Feb. 8, 1973, RWM Papers, M.

60. Schlesinger's role in the revolt is characterized in Peter Fleming, TRI by Verne
Horne, Topeka, Jan. 7, 1975, M; Bernard Hall, TRI by LJF, New York, Aug. 25, 1983;
Herbert Schlesinger, "dictation during 'palace revolution,'" June 17, 1965, Schles-
inger Papers (private).

61. See, e.g., George S. Klein to David Rapaport, Mar. 22, 1949, Klein Papers,
AHAP, on Schlesinger's "indecision, doubt, procrastination, and anxiety" since his
analysis with Ekstein. Herbert Schlesinger, TRI by LJF, New York, Dec. 27, 1985, on
his possession of key documents concerning the revolt, his review of them, and his
refusal to share them or say much about their contents. Herbert Schlesinger to KAM,
July 12, 1973, KAM Papers, M, "insights and points of view."

62. Will's health and general condition before the revolt is revealed in WCM to
EAM, Dec. 27, 1963, Jan. 27, 1964, and WCM to RWM, Jan. 30, 1964, all in WCM
Papers (private); KAM to WCM, Feb. 22, 1965, KAM Papers, M; RWM, PI by LJF,
Topeka, Jan. 5, 1982. "Are You Always Worrying," *Time* 52 (Oct. 25, 1948): 70, on
his two packs of Chesterfields daily. Will's physical condition between late April 1965
and December 1965 in WCM to Robert P. Knight, Oct. 11, 1965, WCM Papers, M;

WCM Diary, May 5, Oct. 25, Dec. 23, 1965. His emotions and feelings toward Karl during these months are indicated in RWM, "Notes," May 1, 1965, 1, RWM Papers, Tower Bldg., M; "Confidential Memo by WCM for WCM," Nov. 19, 1965, RWM Papers, Tower Bldg., M; WCM to Leo Bartemeier, July 20, 1965, WCM Papers, M. WCM Diary, Sept. 16, 1965, "There is something new every day."

63. WCM Diary, Dec. 23, 1965, and a memorandum "Dictated by L. F. Wheelock," Dec. 27, 1965, KAM Papers, M, on the discovery of the cancer. Will's subsequent treatment regimen at Mayo is covered in WCM to Bernard Hall, Feb. 21, 1966, unprocessed, M; RWM to Prescott Thompson and Walter Menninger, Jan. 10, 1966, WCM Papers, M.

64. Julia Gottesman to KAM and JLM, Oct. 9, 1966, KAM Papers, M; Julia Gottesman, TRI by LJF, Los Angeles, Jan. 3, 1984.

65. Harry Levinson, "Conflicts That Plague Family Businesses," *Harvard Business Review*, Mar.–Apr. 1971, 95, notes younger brother guilt for turning against older brothers in family businesses. Levinson to LJF, June 19, 1985 (letter), claims that his article was based on observing the Menningers when he worked with Will at the foundation. In Levinson, TRI by LJF, Belmont, Mass., June 24, 1985, the guilt hypothesis is explicated fully as the principal "cause" of Will's death.

66. *Topeka Daily Capital*, Sept. 10, 1966, and *Wellington* (Kans.) *News*, Sept. 10, 1966, on the funeral service. White's column, *Emporia Gazette*, Sept. 11, 1966.

67. Obituary notices and letters of condolence are found within *In Memoriam for Doctor Will* (Topeka, 1966).

68. *Ibid.*, 4–5. Irving Sheffel, PI by LJF, Topeka, July 27, 1984, recalling having heard Karl reprimand Will in the months before his death.

69. CWM, PI by LJF, Topeka, July 30, 1984, on how Roy's appointment as interim chair violated Will's long understanding with Karl. See also Bernard Hall, TRI by LJF, New York, Aug. 25, 1983; Irving Sheffel, TRI by Lewis Robbins, Topeka, July 10, 1979, LLR Papers (private).

70. "Minutes of Senior Council, Department Heads, and Representatives of the Professional Staff Organization," Dec. 26, 1965, 1–2, Pruyser Papers, M; "Dictated by L. F. Wheelock," Dec. 27, 1965, 1, 3, KAM Papers, M; Howard Shevrin, TRI by Verne Horne, Topeka, May 25, 1973, M.

71. WCM to RWM, Jan. 4, 1966, WCM Papers (private), "I don't want." RWM, "Staff Memo #16," June 7, 1966, 1, Roach Papers, M, on special advisory committee.

72. Roy's rapport with the members of Will's old alliance is indicated in Paul Pruyser to WCM, Feb. 22, 1966, WCM Papers, M; Robert Switzer to Irving Sheffel, Aug. 4, 1966, in Transactions of Presidential Search Committee, M; Irving Sheffel, Thomas Dolgoff, Roger Hoffmaster, and Duane Swanson, TRI by LJF, Topeka, May 21, 1985. "Minutes of Executive Board of P.S.O.," Mar. 23, 1966, 1, Roach Papers, "involving the staff." Lester Roach to WCM, Feb. 10, 1966, WCM Papers, M, reporting Roy's statement to the directors that the PSO must be circumscribed. RWM, "Notes," May 26, 1966, 1, RWM Papers, Tower Bldg., M, "the sins of our fathers."

73. R. Charles Clevenger to all Employees, Oct. 10, 1966, KAM Papers, M.

74. Irving Sheffel to LJF, Oct. 2, 1986 (letter), speculating that Will and two trustees (Clevenger and Willard King) decided the numerical composition of the Search Committee to assure that the trustees controlled the search process. The committee was charged with constructing a list of candidates, soliciting staff opinion, and offering a recommendation to the board of trustees. Although the full board could reject the

committee's recommendations, this was unlikely because a majority on the committee were trustees.

75. Roy's feeling on becoming permanent president are discussed in RWM, PI by LJF, Topeka, Sept. 12, 1985; W. Walter Menninger, PI by LJF, Topeka, Jan. 8, Jan. 10, 1985; CWM, PI by LJF, Topeka, July 30, 1984; Peter Fleming, TRI by Verne Horne, Topeka, Jan. 7, 1975, M; Howard Shevrin, TRI by Lewis Robbins, Ann Arbor, Apr. 19, 1979, LLR Papers (private). Lester Roach, PI by LJF, Topeka, Sept. 14, 1985, on Roy's wife encouraging him to seek the presidency.

76. Bernard Hall, TRI by LJF, New York, Aug. 25, 1983, on Will's decision to support Roy's candidacy. WCM to Charles Clevenger, June 13, 1966, KAM Papers, M, "President ought to be a physician," and "staunch friends." WCM to Irving Sheffel, July 11, 1966, KAM Papers, M, "playing quarterback." See also Irving Sheffel, PI by LJF, Topeka, July 27, 1984.

77. Overwhelming trustee support for a Menninger as president is indicated in Robert B. Hulsen to RGM, Sept. 8, 1966, KAM Papers, M; Thomas W. Klink, "My Understanding of the Meeting of the Search Committee," Aug. 20, 1966, Klink Papers, M; Lester Roach, TRI by LJF, May 26, 1983; J. Cotter Hirschberg, TRI by LJF, Topeka, June 1, 1983. "Minutes of Presidential Search Committee," Aug. 20, 1966, Klink Papers, M, on the results of the trustees' poll.

78. For the rebels' support for Roy, see Search Committee TI of Peter Fleming (Aug. 30, 1966) and Bernard Hall (Sept. 1, 1966), Transactions of Presidential Search Committee, M; "Minutes of Search Committee," Aug. 13, 1966, 2, Transactions of Presidential Search Committee, M; Robert Switzer, TRI by LJF, Trevose, Pa., Nov. 4, 1983.

79. The Ticho-Kernberg support for Roy is reported in Howard Shevrin, TRI by LJF, Ann Arbor, Sept. 16, 1983; Search Committee TI of Otto Kernberg (Aug. 31, 1966), Ernst Ticho (Sept. 7, 1966), Gertrude Ticho (Sept. 8, 1966), Transactions of Presidential Search Committee, M. Wallerstein's opposition to Roy in "Minutes, Search Committee," July 23, 1966, Klink Papers, M. Roach's position on Roy in Search Committee TI of L. T. Roach (Sept. 13, 1966), Transactions of Presidential Search Committee, M, containing the remark "he's too democratic"; Lewis F. Wheelock to KAM, Sept. 26, 1966, KAM Papers, M.

80. For Karl's initial opposition to Roy's candidacy, see RWM, "Notes," May 23, 1966, RWM Papers, Tower Bldg., M; RGM, PI by LJF, Topeka, Aug. 2, 1984. Karl was urged to support Robert in Lewis Wheelock to KAM, Aug. 16, 1966, Jan. 3, 1967, KAM Papers, M. Julia Gottesman to R. Charles Clevenger, Aug. 31, 1966, KAM Papers, is also supportive of Robert's candidacy. The less than serious nature of Robert's candidacy is discussed in Sheffel-Dolgoff, May 11, 1965; Robert Switzer, TRI by LJF, Trevose, Pa., Nov. 4, 1983; KAM, PI by LJF, Topeka, Jan. 9, 1985. RWM, "Notes," May 26, 1966, RWM Papers, Tower Bldg., M, on Robert approaching him about becoming chief of staff. RGM to R. Charles Clevenger, Aug. 18, 1966, KAM Papers, M, on the foundation remaining in "the family."

81. Lewis Wheelock, "KAM vs. TMF," Mar. 29, 1967, KAM Papers, M, outlines Karl's effort to secure an interim presidency for McCain. *Menninger Perspective* 18 (1987): 28, on McCain's background. Karl's positions in late 1966 and early 1967 are noted in KAM to May Switzer, Jan. 12, 1967, KAM Papers, M; Peter Fleming, TRI by Verne Horne, Topeka, Jan. 7, 1975, M.

82. The apolitical aspect of PSO opposition to Roy is evident from Prescott Thomp-

son, TRI by LJF, Los Angeles, May 9, 1984; Irving Sheffel, PI by LJF, Topeka, July 27, 1984. Prescott Thompson to RWM, Nov. 2, 1966, Inst. Archives, M, on the PSO executive board finally going on record against Roy's candidacy. See also Search Committee TI of Edward Greenwood (Oct. 1, 1966), Michalina Fabian (Sept. 27, 1966), Carrol Elmore (Sept. 1, 1966), William Tarnower (Sept. 2, 1966), Prescott Thompson (Sept. 9, 1966), all in Transactions of Presidental Search Committee, M.

83. KAM to Lewis Wheelock, Sept. 26, 1966, and Wheelock to KAM, Sept. 26, 1966, KAM Papers, M, on Roach's willingness to halt Roy's candidacy. See also Lester Roach, PI by LJF, Topeka, Sept. 14, 1985.

84. The proposal for a Sutherland candidacy is best outlined in Howard Shevrin, TRI by Lewis Robbins, Ann Arbor, Apr. 9, 1979, LLR Papers (private), and Shevrin, TRI by LJF, Ann Arbor, Sept. 16, 1983. Support for the candidacy among senior members of the Research Department is evident in Gardner Murphy to Lester Roach, Apr. 26, 1966, Roach Papers, M; Gardner Murphy to William H. Cousins, Jr., Feb. 20, 1967, Murphy Papers, M; Robert Wallerstein to Arthur Mandelbaum, July 27, 1966, Klink Papers, M. Wallerstein in "Minutes of Search Committee for President," July 23, 1966, Klink Papers, M; Wallerstein, TRI by LJF, San Francisco, Dec. 29, 1984; Search Committee TI of Philip Holzman (Aug. 30, 1966), Transactions of Presidential Search Committee, M.

85. Willard King, TRI by Lewis Robbins, Topeka, May 13, 1979, LLR Papers (private), on the Sutherland candidacy. Willard King, TI by CWM, Jan. 3, 1983, WCM Papers (private), recalling Will telling him Roy needed seasoning, and later on his favoring the Rome candidacy but being persuaded by Mag to back Roy. John D. Sutherland, TRI by Verne Horne, Topeka, Mar. 31, 1978, M, on his rejection of candidacy; see also Irving Sheffel, PI by LJF, Topeka, July 27, 1984.

86. William M. Cousins, Jr., to President of Search Committee, Mar. 31, 1967, Transactions of Presidential Search Committee, M, listing the five final candidates. "Minutes of Board of Trustees," Apr. 29, 1967, KAM Papers, M, on King reporting Roy as the committee nominee and on trustee acceptance of the nomination. Debate and voting in the Search Committee is reported in Irving Sheffel, TRI by Lewis Robbins, Topeka, July 10, 1979, LLR Papers (private); Sheffel, PI by LJF, Topeka, July 27, 1984, Sept. 10, 1986; Ishak Ramzy, PI by LJF, Topeka, Mar. 15, 1985; Lester Roach, PI by LJF, Topeka, Sept. 14, 1985. Howard Shevrin, TRI by LJF, Ann Arbor, Sept. 16, 1983, on Catharine pressuring the trustees.

CHAPTER TWELVE: *Roy Menninger's Presidency*

1. "Minutes of Board of Trustees," Apr. 29, 1967, KAM Papers, M, for Karl introducing Roy to the board. CWM, PI by LJF, Topeka, July 30, 1984, Nov. 7, 1987, and Robert Hulsen to KAM, May 8, 1967, KAM Papers, M, reporting Karl's introductory mannerisms and tone. RWM, "Notes," May 26, 1966, 2, RWM Papers, Tower Bldg., "knights and barons from the countryside" (an idea Roy continued to voice over the next several years). RWM, PI by LJF, Topeka, Sept. 12, 1985, on "countryside" solicitations and his great pains to be cordial.

2. Roy's early proclivity toward consultants (unlike Karl and Will) is underscored in Irving Sheffel, Thomas Dolgoff, Roger Hoffmaster, and Duane Swanson, TRI by LJF, Topeka, May 21, 1985; RWM in "Foundation Forum with Margaret Mead," 1974

(tape), M; W. Walter Menninger, PI by LJF, Topeka, Jan. 10, 1985. RWM to LJF, June 1, 1988 (letter), on being a firstborn son of a thirdborn father and his "difficult . . . task."

3. RWM, "Staff Memo #41," 1, Sept. 8, 1967, Roach Papers, M; Brakeley, John Price Jones, Inc., "The Menninger Foundation: A Study of Developmental Potential and Courses of Action," Aug. 1972, 36–7, Special Collections, M.

4. The 1967–72 foundation-wide financial crisis is characterized in Brakeley, John Price Jones, Inc., "The Menninger Foundation," 46, 60, 66; RWM, "A Heritage of Excellence, a Future of Promise," *Menninger Perspective* 18, nos. 3 and 4 (1987): 5; C. Marvin Curtis to Rockefeller Brothers Fund, Apr. 13, 1967, Rockefeller Brothers Fund Papers, Box 58, RFA; Irving Sheffel, PI by LJF, Topeka, Jan. 8, 1985; W. Walter Menninger, PI by LJF, Topeka, Jan. 8, 1985; Philip B. Menninger, PI by LJF, Topeka, Jan. 14, 1985; RWM, PI by LJF, Topeka, Mar. 11, 1986.

5. Seward Hiltner to RWM, Oct. 8, 1968, Hiltner Papers, PTS; John Sutherland, TRI by Verne Horne, Mar. 31, 1978, M.

6. RWM, "Foundation Staff Meeting Report #1," Dec. 6, 1966, 2, "we have expanded" and RWM, "Foundation Staff Meeting Report #13," Sept. 10, 1968, 2, "to replace our charismatic leadership," both in RWM Papers, Tower Bldg.; *TPR* 27, nos. 5 and 6 (May–June 1967): 6, "It is not a one-man organization." RWM, PI by LJF, Topeka, Sept. 12, 1985, on establishing group relations conferences. See also RWM, "The Impact of a Group Relations Conference on the Menninger Foundation," for American Group Psychotherapy Association, New York, Feb. 12, 1972, RWM Papers, Tower Bldg. RWM, PI by LJF, Nov. 13, 1987 (telephone), "psychologically handicapped" and "dependency culture." RWM, *Menninger Perspective* 18, nos. 3 and 4 (1987): 6, reiterates the "dependency culture" appraisal of staff in 1967. RWM to Mrs. George Dallas, June 15, 1968, KAM Papers, M, "de-emphasize the family."

7. RWM to Mrs. George Dallas, June 25, 1968, KAM Papers, M, "I could not go along with a shift."

8. The assignment of Walter Menninger to Topeka State is discussed in W. Walter Menninger, PI by LJF, Topeka, Jan. 10, 1985; Frances Rothman, "The Menningers: Memoirs & Memos," *The Week Ahead,* June 25, 1971. RGM, PI by LJF, Topeka, Mar. 12, 1985, on his role under Roy. RWM to Dan Pop, Mar. 4, 1968, RWM Papers, Tower Bldg., "a real job." RGM to Roy, Walter, and Philip Menninger, Mar. 16, 1967, Inst. Archives, M, on his exclusion from contact with large donors.

9. Karl's efforts to advise Roy and Roy's response patterns are typified in KAM to RWM, Feb. 15, 1968, and RWM to KAM, Dec. 2, 1967, Apr. 25, 1968, all in KAM Papers, M. For Roy's relief at having Karl away in Chicago, see RWM, PI by LJF, Nov. 13, 1987 (telephone). RWM, "Foundation Staff Meeting Report #19," Nov. 19, 1969, 8, KAM Papers, M, announcing Karl's "retirement."

10. Karl's marked copy of "Foundation Staff Meeting Report #19," KAM Papers, M. See KAM to Lewis Wheelock, July 3, 1973, KAM Papers, M, for Karl's sense of powerlessness despite "my arrogant nephew's blundering."

11. WCM Diary, Dec. 31, 1963, suggests Roy's marriage had been troubled for some time. Various aspects of the separation, divorce, and remarriage are noted in Seward Hiltner to KAM, Oct. 18, 1971, Hiltner Papers, PTS (linking it to Karl's divorce); Harvey Schloesser, TRI by LJF, Topeka, June 21, 1987. RWM to IDC members, Sept. 13, 1971, Inst. Archives, M, "the business of the organization . . ."

12. William Tarnower, PI by LJF, Topeka, Nov. 11, 1984, on Roy initially acknowl-

edging the principle of consulting regularly with the PSO. RWM to Robert Hulsen, Nov. 7, 1968, KAM Papers, M, "preempting my responsibility." Leonard Horwitz, TRI by LJF, Topeka, Aug. 1, 1984, on his confrontation with Roach in 1968.

13. Leonard Horwitz to PSO Executive Committee, Apr. 14, 1969, Inst. Archives, M; Howard Shevrin, TRI by Lewis Robbins, Ann Arbor, Apr. 9, 1979, LLR Papers (private); Howard Shevrin, TRI by Verne Horne, n.d. (May 1973), M; Horwitz, TRI by LJF, Aug. 1, 1984.

14. Sheffel, Dolgoff, Hoffmaster, and Swanson, TRI by LJF, Topeka, May 21, 1985, clarifies fully the transition in administrative structures and personnel early in Roy's presidency. "Foundation Staff Meeting Report #13," Sept. 10, 1968, 1, RWM Papers, Tower Bldg., announces Hoffmaster on the west campus and Swanson on the east campus; see also RWM, "Staff Memo #63," Sept. 4, 1968, RWM Papers, M. Useful, too, in understanding the administrative history of the period are Lester Roach, PI by LJF, Topeka, Sept. 14, 1985; Duane Swanson, PI by LJF, Topeka, May 17, 1985; Roger Hoffmaster, PI by LJF, Topeka, Mar. 15, 1985; RWM, "Notes for Foundation Staff Meeting," Feb. 13, 1968, RWM Papers, Tower Bldg.; Irving Sheffel to RWM, Jan. 29, 1971, RWM Papers, M.

15. RWM to KAM, Feb. 28, 1968, KAM Papers, M, "difficulties." Bernard Hall to "All Staff" (memo), Apr. 30, 1968, RWM Papers, M, announcing Fleming was to be "senior consultant." RWM to RWM (memo), May 16, 1967, RWM Papers, Tower Bldg., on Fleming and on Hall's inadequacies in the Outpatient Department. Robert Switzer, TRI by LJF, Trevose, Pa., Nov. 4, 1983, and esp. Robert Switzer, PI by LJF, Nov. 14, 1983 (telephone), on reasons for his departure. RWM to Robert Switzer, July 10, 1969, RWM Papers, M, accusing him of circumventing the presidency. RWM to Robert Switzer, June 30, 1971, RWM Papers, M, "a set of isolated baronies." RWM, "Staff Memo #134," Feb. 8, 1973, RWM Papers, M, replacing Switzer. *Alumni Newsletter* 34, no. 3 (July 1987): 7, and KAM to RWM, Feb. 24, 1978 (unsent), KAM Papers, M, on Pruyser.

16. "Foundation Staff Meeting Report #13," Sept. 10, 1968, 4, RWM Papers, Tower Bldg., "With our beginning." RWM to Dan Pop, Feb. 7, 1968, RWM Papers, M.

17. Decentralization policy and the establishment of the general councils are noted in RWM, PI by LJF, Topeka, Sept. 12, 1985; Marjorie Smith, "Problems of and Prospects for East Campus–West Campus Relations at the Menninger Foundation," 1972, 4–8, Inst. Archives, M.

18. RWM, "Foundation Staff Meeting Report #17," Feb. 11, 1969, 4, 11; RWM, PI by LJF, Topeka, Sept. 12, 1985; Marjorie Smith "Problems," 8; "Summary of IDC Meeting," May 23, 1972, Inst. Archives, M.

19. RWM, "Foundation Staff Meeting Report #17," Feb. 11, 1969, 1, "Our present structure." "Staff Meeting Report #19," Nov. 11, 1969, 6–7, "private negotiations." "Executive Committee Minutes of Trustees," Nov. 18, 1967, 5, MT, "unrelatedness." Donald Colson to Members of Clinical Cabinet, Sept. 23, 1968, Inst. Archives, M; Vernon Muller, PI by LJF, London, July 2, 1986. Recruitment of group therapy consultants in Ann Appelbaum et al., "Dependency versus Autonomy: The Group Conference Method Applied to an Organizational Problem," *BMC* 39, no. 1 (Jan. 1975): 57.

20. In the IDC Minutes, Nov. 21, 1972, Apr. 13, 1973, Inst. Archives, M, Roy is advised to centralize owing to budgetary problems. "IDC Retreat," May 2, 1971, Inst.

Archives, M, "like feudal barons." IDC Minutes, Nov. 7, 1972, Roy giving up hopes on the IDC; Jan. 23, 1973, Roy creating the CMC. See also Roy in IDC Minutes, July 6, 1973, Inst. Archives, M.

21. Daniel M. Fox, *Health Policies, Health Politics: The British and American Experience, 1911–1965* (Princeton, 1986), coined the term "hierarchical regionalism" and skillfully elaborated its meaning.

22. RWM to Seward Hiltner, Oct. 13, 1966, Hiltner Papers, PTS, "so swamped by the responsibilities." Roy's suggestion of a possible move to Kansas City as recalled by Sydney Smith, PI by LJF, Topeka, June 23, 1987. The fullest study of the development of the Menninger-Antioch program is Stephen Lerner and Thomas R. Haugsby, "Advanced Work and Study in the Mental Health Field for the Undergraduate," unpub. ms., 1979. Howard Shevrin, PI by LJF, Oct. 26, 1987 (telephone), on his role in creating the Antioch program. Search Committee TI of Otto Kernberg, Aug. 31, 1966, Transactions of Presidential Search Committee, M, " 'magic mountain' atmosphere."

23. Irving Sheffel, PI by LJF, Topeka, Sept. 10, 1986, and Howard Shevrin, TRI by Lewis Robbins, Ann Arbor, Apr. 9, 1979, LLR Papers (private), on TIP factional politics in the 1960s, with Kernberg-Ticho faction dominant. Search Committee TI of Otto Kernberg, Aug. 31, 1966, of Ernst Ticho, Sept. 7, 1966, of Gertrude Ticho, Sept. 8, 1966, all in Transactions of Presidential Search Committee, M. RWM, PI by LJF, Topeka, Sept. 12, 1985, on Ernst Ticho expecting to be named as his senior vice-president and desirous of controlling Roy.

24. Gertrude Ticho to RWM, June 30, 1970, RWM Papers, M, was returned to her with Roy's notation "I am delighted (and relieved)" over her reelection. RWM, "Notes on Conversation with Philip Holzman," n.d., RWM Papers, M, and "Staff Memo #89," June 26, 1969, RWM Papers, M, announcing James Taylor as Research Department director. RWM to Otto Kernberg, June 26, 1969, RWM Papers, M, appointing Kernberg hospital director with "great satisfaction." Roy's general rapport in this period with the Tichos and Kernberg is discussed in RWM, PI by LJF, Topeka, Sept. 12, 1985; Roger Hoffmaster, PI by LJF, Mar. 15, 1985; Duane Swanson, PI by LJF, Topeka, Sept. 10, 1985.

25. Roy in "Minutes of Trustee Executive Committee," Nov. 18, 1967, 6, MT; "Report of Site Visit to Topeka Institute for Psychoanalysis," 1969, 29, unprocessed, M; Harry Levinson, TRI by LJF, Belmont, Mass., June 24, 1985; Lewis Robbins, "Palace Revolt," Apr. 3, 1979, 6, LLR Papers (private); RWM to Ernst Ticho, Nov. 11, 1970, RWM Papers, M; RWM, PI by LJF, Topeka, June 23, 1987.

26. RWM, PI by LJF, Topeka, Sept. 12, 1985; Paul Pruyser, PI by LJF, Topeka, July 31, 1984; and Duane Swanson, PI by LJF, Topeka, May 17, 1985, Sept. 10, 1986, on disputes between the three émigrés and Roy over TIP and psychoanalysis generally. RWM to Ernst Ticho, Nov. 11, 1970, RWM Papers, M, rebuking him for failure to encourage group therapy approaches. When Ernst Ticho left Menninger in 1973, he had added group, family, and marital therapy to Psychotherapy Services (*TPR*, Oct. 5, 1973, 1).

27. Irving Sheffel, PI by LJF, Topeka, Sept. 10, 1986; Peter Novotny, PI by LJF, Topeka, Sept. 10, 1986, Sept. 6, 1988; RWM, PI by LJF, Topeka, June 23, 1987; *TPR*, Oct. 5, 1973, 1.

28. Dan Pop to RWM, Feb. 7, 1968, RWM Papers, M, exemplifies the memorandum filled with bureaucratic phrases. "The Menninger Foundation Proposed Operating

Budget. Fiscal Year Beginning July 1, 1973," June 25, 1973, 2, M, "The basic question" (written by the foundation treasurer).

29. RWM, PI by LJF, Topeka, Sept. 12, 1985, June 23, 1987, underscoring his group orientation to the presidency. RWM to LJF, June 1, 1988 (letter), on his Swarthmore background. An untitled chart Roy drew with his advisers in 1970 (in Duane Swanson Private Papers) correlated personal events with staff unrest, aesthetics, etc.

30. Stephen Appelbaum, TRI by LJF, Prairie Village, Kans., June 24, 1987; Sydney Smith, PI by LJF, Topeka, June 23, 1987; Irving Sheffel, PI by LJF, Topeka, June 22, 1987; Peter Novotny, PI by LJF, Topeka, June 21, 1987.

31. *Ibid.*

32. Systematic data comparing staffing ratios in specific private psychiatric hospitals is difficult to find. The National Association of Private Psychiatric Hospitals has not compiled it. General statistical data for 149 unidentified private facilities is provided in Charles K. Kanno and Raymond M. Glasscote, *A National Survey: Private Psychiatric Hospitals* (Washington, D.C., 1966). However, Menninger compared its own staffing numbers with its nine major "new psychiatry" private competitors in a way that permits precise comparative ratios to be formulated. This was done in a major in-house document, "Professional Staffing Pattern in 10 Private Psychiatric Hospitals— 1967," Inst. Archives, M. Although I have found no similar in-house Menninger document for 1975, information that high Menninger officials released to the *New York Times*, Nov. 13, 1975, indicated that this comparative data continued to be collected and that the results for that year were much like 1967. The Menninger Foundation Proposed Operating Budgets, Fiscal Years 1967–68 to 1973–74, M, show hospital projected expenses and income compared to other foundation operations. Actual rather than projected hospital expenses and income in this foundation-wide context, where it is compared to other foundation programs and operations, is found in an extensive ledger that Irving Sheffel maintained beginning in 1952.

33. "C. F. Menninger Hospital Statistics," an annual in-house publication in MMR, provides the data cited here for the 1964–65 to 1973–74 period. For more difficult to treat illnesses, it indicates that in 1964–65 only half of the patients with "psychotic disorders" had "improved" on release; by 1973–74 it was closer to two thirds. Slightly less than 60 percent of "personality disorder" cases concluded with "improvement" in 1964–65, compared to somewhat over 75 percent in 1973–74. "C. F. Menninger Hospital Statistics" also reveals that readmission statistics generally turned downward during Roy's early administration; a range of 22–31 percent for 1960–65 had declined to a 15–32 percent range (often approximating 22 percent) between 1966 and 1974. Another useful source for outcomes is "Adult Psychotherapy and Chargeable Casework," July 1, 1971–June 30, 1972, MMR.

34. "Department Directors Retreat," June 15, 1967, 21–22, MT; "The Menninger Foundation: A Study of Development Potential and Courses of Action" (by Brakeley, John Price Jones, Inc., 1972), 26, Inst. Archives, M; RWM, PI by LJF, Topeka, Sept. 6, 1988.

35. RWM, "Mission Statement: The Menninger Foundation," draft, Mar. 1988, RWM Papers, Tower Bldg.

36. Bev Menninger, "The Woman Behind the Man," *Menninger Perspective* 13, no. 2 (1982): 13; *Update,* Oct. 1984, 2–3; Mimi Barber, PI by LJF, Topeka, Sept. 5, 1988.

37. *Menninger Perspective* 19, no. 3 (1988): 30, citing awards it has received. "Report of the President," *TPR,* Nov. 8, 1985, cites the extensive marketing and public rela-

tions activities. Menninger is acknowledged as America's finest in *Family Circle,* Oct. 20, 1987, 133; *Good Housekeeping,* Nov. 1984, 141–4; *Town & Country,* Mar. 1987, as cited in *Alumni Newsletter* 35 (July 1988): 1. John Sutherland, TRI by Verne Horne, Mar. 31, 1978, M.

38. "Chart 3. Operating Expense & Income," 1972, M, and *TPR,* May 20, 1983, 2, on the shift from roughly one third (perhaps as high as 40 percent) to 6 percent. Del Gerstenberger to Irving Sheffel, May 20, 1987 (memo in possession of LJF), on adult inpatient health insurance receipts by percentage for the fiscal years 1973 to 1986. In *TPR,* July 1, 1983, 1, 5, Roy underscored problems with insurance carriers and other serious problems for the foundation budget. *TPR,* May 22, 1987, "A Letter from the President," on the uses of Rains's bequest.

39. New programs are cited in *Menninger Perspective* 18, nos. 3 and 4 (1987): 9; RWM, *The Menninger Foundation: Toward a Caring Society* (New York, 1985), 19–20; *Update,* Dec. 1986, 6. *Topeka Capital-Journal,* May 25, 1984, on Roy's plans for new campuses to "seek outpatients." The campuses are discussed in *TPR,* Aug. 22, 1986, 1, 3; *Update,* Dec. 1986, 4; *Menninger Perspective* 19, no. 4 (1988): 29.

40. RWM, "Ground Breaking Ceremony for West Campus," May 1, 1980 (tape), M. RWM, PI by LJF, Topeka, Sept. 6, 1988, underscoring the importance he saw in the move.

41. *Menninger Perspective* 18, nos. 3 and 4 (1987): 7, on the ill repair of the east campus. *Kansas City Star,* Nov. 1, 1979, and *Parsons Sun,* Oct. 29, 1979, on the fundraising tour and the costs of the move. The construction plans are detailed in Esther Kuntz, "Menninger Foundation Plans New 166-bed Adult Psychiatric Hospital," *Modern Health Care,* Oct. 1979, 52–3.

42. RWM, "A Heritage of Excellence, a Future of Promise," *Menninger Perspective* 18, nos. 3 and 4 (1987): 7–8, underscoring reduced patient suicides and kindred ills. *Ibid.,* 29, on the interest rates of revenue bonds (initially 10 percent but reduced to 6.75 percent under 1987 refinancing).

43. *Ibid.,* 8, "the end." *Menninger Perspective* 13, no. 2 (1982): 17–19, on the "Campaign for Brains & Bricks." Many veteran staff characterized Roy's modification of Will's "Brains before Bricks" slogan as signaling "Bricks before Brains," but none permitted me to cite them by name. I was on leave at Menninger just before the move in the fall of 1981 and heard many such interpretations of the slogan—how it allegedly underscored a vacuous quality in the presidency. In RWM, PI by LJF, Topeka, Sept. 6, 1988, Roy admitted that he was aware of this characterization of him and tried to counter it by proclaiming that buildings were only the "envelopes" in which treatment operated.

44. *TPR,* Mar. 23, 1987, 1, 5, for Roy's explanation to staff of the meaning of the restructuring. See also *Menninger Perspective* 19, no. 1 (1988): 24. Irving Sheffel, PI by LJF, Topeka, Sept. 6, 1988, on pressure among lawyer trustees for the legal change and on accounting problems it created plus staff complaints over changing stationery.

45. *TPR,* Feb. 17, 1984, 1, 6; *TPR,* Sept. 7, 1984, 1–2; *Update,* Oct. 1984, 2–3, on Walter's return and promotions. KAM, PI by LJF, Topeka, Feb. 28, 1984, "family inheritance." CWM, PI by LJF, Topeka, July 29, 1983, on the long-standing hostility between Roy and Walter being much like the Karl-Will conflict. RWM, PI by LJF, Los Angeles, May 11, 1984, and Topeka, June 6, 1988, on pressures to bring Walter back and promote him, and on fears of a replication of 1965.

46. KAM to RWM, Feb. 24, 1978, unprocessed, M; Verne Horne, PI by LJF, Nov.

23, 1988 (telephone); KAM at "Ground Breaking Ceremony for West Campus," May 1, 1980 (tape), M; KAM, "Project—Get this Family Together," Sept. 14, 1982, KAM Papers, M.

47. KAM, TRI by LJF, Topeka, Sept. 4, 1988; W. Walter Menninger, PI by LJF, Topeka, Jan. 8, Jan. 10, 1985; Laura Fisher, PI by LJF, Topeka, Sept. 4, 1988.

48. *Lawrence* (Kans.) *Journal-World,* July 16, 1988; KAM to Thoralf M. Sandt, Aug. 11, 1988, KAM Papers, M; *Arkansas City Traveler,* July 16, 1988.

49. KAM, TRI by LJF, Topeka, Sept. 4, Sept. 5, 1988.

50. KAM, TRI by LJF, Topeka, Sept. 4, 1988.

51. KAM, TRI by LJF, Topeka, Sept. 4, Sept. 5, 1988.

52. *Ibid.*

53. Shirley A. Sloan to LJF, Sept. 27, Oct. 20, 1988 (letters), detailing the evolution of Karl's connection with The Villages. KAM, TRI by LJF, Topeka, Sept. 4, Sept. 5, 1988; *Topeka Capital-Journal,* July 23, 1988; and *Wichita Eagle-Beacon,* July 23, 1988, all describe The Villages' birthday celebration.

54. KAM, TRI by LJF, Topeka, Sept. 4, Sept. 5, 1988, plus KAM to Lawrence Wagner, Sept. 8, 1988, KAM Papers, M. Karl and I discussed preliminary drafts of his letter to Wagner on Sept. 4 and 5.

A Bibliographical Note

This study is built primarily from unpublished materials in the Menninger Archives. It is supplemented by unpublished data from other archival centers and by oral histories. The length and specificity of the endnotes will guide the reader through these materials. Yet publications, especially secondary works, require brief comment.

Although this is the first full-length study of the Menningers and their workplace, Walker Winslow's *The Menninger Story* (Garden City, 1956) remains mandatory reading on the family. Winslow can be supplemented with Flo Menninger's very informative *Days of My Life: Memories of a Kansas Mother and Teacher* (N.Y., 1939). It is regrettable that Karl—the central figure within the family—lacks a sensitive, scholarly biography. James E. Carney, "Karl A. Menninger's Psychoanalytic Odyssey, 1920–1950" (unpub. M.A. thesis, Bowling Green State University, 1986), and Paul W. Pruyser, "Religio Medici: Karl A. Menninger, Calvinism, and the Presbyterian Church," *Journal of Presbyterian History* 59 (Spring 1981): 59–72, represent probing essays on the man. But Howard J. Faulkner and Virginia D. Pruitt, eds., *The Selected Correspondence of Karl A. Menninger, 1919–1945* (New Haven, 1988), is not terribly helpful. Essays to introduce parts of the volume are uninformed, there is no index, and important letters underscoring Karl's complexity are omitted. Bernard H. Hall provides a greater service; he fully reproduces many of Karl's major essays in *A Psychiatrist's World: The Selected Papers of Karl Menninger, M.D.* (2 vols., N.Y., 1959). Hall makes the same contribution for Will—*A Psychiatrist for a Troubled World: The Selected Papers of William C. Menninger, M.D.* (2 vols., N.Y., 1967)—though a comprehensive biography of the younger brother would be a welcome addition to scholarship.

Lucille Cairns's "A History of the Menninger Clinic at Topeka, Kansas, up to the Time of Its Transfer to the Menninger Foundation, 1919–1945" (unpub. Ph.D. diss., Washington University of Saint Louis, 1946), is the only prior investigation of Menninger organizational history. Written by one of the first Menninger social workers, it provides data on formal workplace policies and procedures. Jean Lange, "A Community Image Study of the Menninger Foundation" (unpub. M.S. thesis, Kansas State University, 1973), traces the gradual decline of hostility to the Menninger campus from the local citizenry. Although Margaret Mead leaves us several perceptive essays on Menninger, based on periodic visits, her most comprehensive and reflective is "Institutional Expressions of Ideas: The Menninger Foundation and Its Associated Institutions, 1943–77," in Sydney Smith, ed., *The Human Mind Revisited: Essays in Honor of Karl A. Menninger* (N.Y., 1978), 473–92. Two sensitive novels based, in part, on the Menninger campus are also worth reading—William Gibson's *The Cobweb* (N.Y., 1954) and Carol Ascher's *The Flood* (Freedom, Calif., 1987).

If historians of specific twentieth-century American psychiatric hospitals tend to lack the rich and extensive data that I have, some account for their research quite well. Gerald N. Grob's *The State and the Mentally Ill: A History of Worcester State Hospital in Massachusetts, 1830–1920* (Chapel Hill, 1966), heads the list. A remarkable volume, it analyzes simultaneously the internal dynamics of a mental hospital and related psychiatric issues at local, state, and national levels. A great deal of data and some cogent analysis can be garnered from William L. Russell, *The New York Hospital: A History of the Psychiatric Service* (N.Y., 1945). Less critical hospital histories abound, though there is some value in perusing L. Vernon Briggs, *History of the Psychopathic Hospital, Boston, Massachusetts* (Boston, 1922); Lawrence S. Kubie, *The Riggs Story: The Development of the Austen Riggs Center for the Study and Treatment of the Neuroses* (N.Y., 1960); Bliss Forbush, *The Sheppard and Enoch Pratt Hospital 1853–1970* (Philadelphia, 1971); Francis J. Braceland, *The Institute of Living: The Hartford Retreat 1822–1972* (Hartford, 1972); and S. B. Sutton, *Crossroads in Psychiatry: A History of the McLean Hospital* (Washington, D.C., 1986). Three classic sociological studies of mental hospitals merit close reading—Alfred H. Stanton and Morris S. Schwartz, *The Mental Hospital* (N.Y., 1954); Erving Goffman, *Asylums* (N.Y., 1961); and Ezra Stotland and Arthur L. Kobler, *Life and Death of a Mental Hospital* (Seattle, 1965). Finally, all students of hospitals—psychiatric and other—should be familiar with Charles E. Rosenberg's rich new volume, *The Care of Strangers: The Rise of America's Hospital System* (N.Y., 1987). Though the hospitals examined happen to be in Kansas, one can still profit from Thomas N. Bonner's *The Kansas Doctor: A Century of Pioneering* (Lawrence, 1959).

There is substantial scholarship on the American mental health professions in the twentieth century. Gerald N. Grob, *Mental Illness and American Society, 1875–1940* (Princeton, 1983), provides a strong interpretive overview. David J. Rothman, *Conscience and Convenience: The Asylum and Its Alternatives in Progressive America* (Boston, 1980), offers an interesting and more critical view of those professions. David E. Tanner's "Symbols of Conduct: Psychiatry and American Culture, 1900–1935" (unpub. Ph.D. diss., University of Texas, 1981), is a thoughtful analysis of Adolf Meyer, William Alanson White, and other contributors to the "American School" of psychiatry. S. P. Fullinwider, *Technicians of the Finite: The Rise and Decline of the Schizophrenic in American Thought, 1840–1960* (Westport, 1982), treats the same psychiatric theorists; it also houses an innovative analysis of William James's perspective on psychiatry and mental illness. Child psychiatry is scarcely treated in these general studies. Consequently, one must turn to Helen L. Witmer's classic *Psychiatric Clinics for Children* (N.Y., 1940), which can be matched with Kathleen W. Jones's well-constructed "As the Twig Is Bent: American Psychiatry and the Troublesome Child, 1890–1940" (unpub. Ph.D. diss., Rutgers University, 1988), and Hamilton Cravens's important "Child Saving in the Age of Professionalism, 1915–1930," in *American Childhood: A Research Guide and Historical Handbook* (Westport, 1985), 415–88. Olga M. Church, "The Noble Reform: The Emergence of Psychiatric Nursing in the United States, 1882–1963" (unpub. Ph.D. diss., University of Illinois Medical Center, 1982), represents a helpful general source on that profession. I found it complemented by the WPA Writers Program volume *Lamps on the Prairie: A History of Nursing in Kansas* (N.Y., 1942). Even with abundant writing on the history of American psychology, it is helpful to consult Donald S. Napoli, *Architects of Adjustment: The History of the Psychological Profession in the United States* (London, Port Washington, 1981), and James H. Capshew's "Psychology on the March: American Psychologists and World War II" (unpub. Ph.D. diss., University of Pennsylvania, 1986). For a preview of Gerald Grob's forthcoming book on postwar psychiatric policy and the mental health professions, see "The Forging of Mental Health Policy in America: World War II to New Frontier," *Journal of the History of Medicine and Allied Sciences* 42 (Oct. 1987): 410–46. Broad wartime and postwar trends are also analyzed cogently in Jack D. Pressman, "Uncertain Promise: Psychosurgery and the Development of Scientific Psychiatry in America, 1935 to 1955" (unpub. Ph.D. diss., University of Pennsylvania, 1986).

Owing to Menninger's heavy psychoanalytic traditions, it is necessary to consult the extensive literature on the history of psychoanalysis. Peter Gay's *Freud: A Life for Our Time* (1988) covers a great deal of the

European background and offers a comprehensive bibliography. But it is also important to consult Paul Roazen's *Freud and His Followers* (1975). A full scholarly study is needed on the European psychoanalytic immigration to America. Although Russell Jacoby's *The Repression of Psychoanalysis: Otto Fenichel and the Political Freudians* (N.Y., 1983) offers a lively discussion of some of the psychoanalytic émigrés, it is polemical. John C. Burnham, "Psychoanalysis and American Medicine, 1894–1918: Medicine, Science, and Culture," *Psychological Issues* 5, no. 4, monograph 20 (1967), and Nathan G. Hale, *Freud and the Americans* (N.Y., 1971), remain the best studies of the early decades of psychoanalysis in America. However, Robert C. Fuller, *Americans and the Unconscious* (N.Y., 1986), and Jacques M. Quen and Eric T. Carlson, eds., *American Psychoanalysis: Origins and Development* (N.Y., 1978), are well worth consulting. With the psychoanalytic profession falling upon hard times in recent years, several exciting books have been published on the meaning and utility of psychoanalytic traditions. Among the most interesting are Janet Malcolm, *Psychoanalysis: The Impossible Profession* (N.Y., 1981); Adolf Grünbaum, *The Foundations of Psychoanalysis: A Philosophical Critique* (Berkeley, 1984); Sherry Turkle, *Psychoanalytic Politics: Freud's French Revolution* (N.Y., 1978); Morris N. Eagle, *Recent Developments in Psychoanalysis: A Critical Evaluation* (N.Y., 1984), and John E. Gedo, *Conceptual Issues in Psychoanalysis* (Hillsdale, N.J., 1986).

In large measure, *Menninger* studies the overlaps between family culture and workplace culture. Unlike Christopher Lasch in his provocative *Haven in a Heartless World: The Family Besieged* (N.Y., 1977), I do not argue that the family became subordinated to the workplace. My findings are more congruent with Tamara K. Hareven's exciting case study, *Family Time and Industrial Time: The Relationship Between the Family and Work in a New England Industrial Community* (N.Y., Cambridge, 1982), which shows how family habits can sometimes dominate workplace procedures. Sophisticated theoretical literature on the reciprocal relationship between family and workplace is difficult to find. If Harry Levinson, "Conflicts That Plague Family Businesses," *Harvard Business Review*, Mar.–Apr. 1971, 90–8, moves in the right direction, it is skeletal. The growing body of writing on family systems theory is useful, particularly the material of former Menninger resident Murray Bowen; see, e.g., Bowen's *Family Therapy in Clinical Practice* (N.Y., London, 1978). Bowen and his followers are among the few family therapists who have thought seriously about theoretical dimensions of family-workplace overlaps.

Index

Chidester, Leona, 99
child psychiatry, 91, 93–4
Children's Division (Menninger),
  298
  new campus, 278, 282
  postwar expansion, 278–9
  scholarship program, 281–2
Christ's Hospital (Topeka), 8, 48,
  49, 62, 83
City College of New York, 204,
  228, 229
Clay Center (Kans.), 6
Clevenger, R. Charles, 328–9, 334
Cobb, O. J., 93
Cobb, Sam E., 49
Cobweb, The (Gibson), 139, 142
Coffman, Stella, 96–8
Cole, Basil E., 204, 305
Commonwealth Fund, 92, 102, 148,
  170
community mental health
  movement, 259–60
Congress of Industrial
  Organizations, xii
continuum, concept of, 124–5, 169,
  235, 284, 310–11
Cook County Juvenile Court, 92
Coordinating Council (Menninger),
  266, 314
Copp, Owen, 40
Cornell Medical School, 53
Coulson, Jackson, 22
Coulson, Jane, 22
Coyne, Lolafayne, 251
Craig House, 38, 39, 73
Crank, H. Harlan, 84, 211, 267
Crank, Lou Davie, *see* Davie, Lou
Cronkite, Walter, xi, 299, 311
Cult of the Lady, 11
Crumbine, Samuel, 3, 42

Dailey, Dan, 206
Danforth Foundation, 263

Dangerfield, Alice, 154
Davie, Lou, 83
Days of My Life (F. Menninger)
  preparation of, 153–4
  sales and reception of, 154–5
"deinstitutionalization," 259, 282
Delancey, Frank, 24
Department Directors Committee
  (Menninger), 327–8
Deri, Francis, 128
Descartes, René, 244
Deutsch, Albert, 171, 190, 298, 416
  n.65
Dewey, John, 98
Diagnostic Psychological Testing
  (Rapaport), 240–1
Diderot, Denis, xv
Dix, Dorothea L., 46–62
Dolgoff, Thomas, 179, 204, 338
Duckworth, James, 174
Duke, James B., 148

East Lodge, 50, 55
*Ego Psychology and the Problem of
  Adaptation* (Hartmann), 245
Ehrenreich, Gerald A., 230
Eicholtz, Virginia, 358 n.42
Ekstein, Rudolf, 134, 280, 325
electroshock therapy, 89, 207
Elliott, George A., 167
Ellis, Havelock, 220
Emerson, Louisville, 29
emigration, psychoanalytic (to
  Topeka), 111–15
émigrés (at Menninger), 111–15
  compare Topeka to European
    cities, 115–16
  criticize hospital therapy
    program, 119
  discomfort in Topeka, 115
  disenchantment with them, 120
  English proficiency of, 113
  financial squabbles, 116–19

A Note About the Author

Lawrence J. Friedman is Professor of History and American Studies at Bowling Green State University in Ohio, where he also directs the History graduate program. His previous books include *Gregarious Saints: Self and Community in American Abolitionism* (1982), *Inventors of the Promised Land* (1975), and *The White Savage: Racial Fantasies in the Postbellum South* (1970). Professor Friedman is a three-time recipient of fellowships from the National Endowment for the Humanities.

A Note on the Type

This book was set in a type face called Baskerville. The face itself
is a facsimile reproduction of types cast from molds made for
John Baskerville (1706–1775) from his designs. Baskerville's
original face was one of the forerunners of the type style known
to printers as "modern face"—a "modern" of the period A.D.
1800.

Composed By ComCom
Division of The Haddon Craftsmen, Inc.,
Allentown, Pennsylvania

Printed and bound by Fairfield Graphics,
Fairfield, Pennsylvania

Designed by Valarie Jean Astor